FREEDOM OF EXPRESSION
AND
THE CHARTER

EDITED BY

DAVID SCHNEIDERMAN

Executive Director, Centre for Constitutional Studies

Thomson Professional Publishing Canada
a division of Thomson Canada Limited

Canadian Cataloguing in Publication Data

Main entry under title:

Freedom of expression and the Charter

Includes index.
ISBN 0-459-35711-5

1. Freedom of speech — Canada — Congresses.
2. Censorship — Canada — Congresses. 3. Freedom
of information — Canada — Congresses. 4. Canada.
Canadian Charter of Rights and Freedoms —
Congresses. I. Schneiderman, David, 1958-   .

| KE4418.F74 1991 | 342.71'0853 | C91-094389-3 |
| KF4770.F74 1991 | 76/99 | |

© 1991 Thomson Professional Publishing Canada
a division of Thomson Canada Limited,
except A. Alan Borovoy

A Carswell Publication

ISBN 0 459 35711 5

ACKNOWLEDGEMENTS

The papers collected here were presented at the Centre for Constitutional Studies' Third National Conference on the Constitution entitled "Freedom of Expression and Democratic Institutions" held on April 19-21, 1990 in Edmonton, Alberta. There are many institutions and persons to thank for the conference's success. In particular, the generous financial assistance of the Alberta Law Foundation to the conference and to the ongoing operation of the Centre is gratefully acknowledged. In addition, the Secretary of State for Canada, Alberta Federal and Intergovernmental Affairs, Alberta Multiculturalism, the office of the University of Alberta – Vice President (Academic) and the University of Alberta Conference Funds Committee, all contributed financially to the conference. The 80 or so registrants to the conference deserve our gratitude as well. The conference committee was composed of Bruce P. Elman, Chair of the Centre Board, Ronald Hamowy, A. Anne McLellan and June Ross. The excellence of the program was due, in large part, to the guidance and participation of Bruce Elman. The conference was run efficiently and smoothly due to the tireless efforts of Christine Urquhart, Executive Assistant to the Centre.

In addition to the authors, a number of others deserve thanks for making presentations at the conference. They are Paul Bender, Neil Brooks, Stevie Cameron, Justice Peter Cory, Réal Forest and Alan Hunter. Our rapporteurs for the closing session, André Lajoie and Robert Sharpe, deserve thanks for their perseverance in attending, and insightful commentary of, the conference presentations.

Others deserve mention for their part in the publication process. In addition to the authors themselves, who handled all of my demands, requests and pleas with extreme goodwill, Glenn Solomon deserves a large measure of thanks for assisting in the editorial enterprise, applying his talents with his usual enthusiasm and humour. Craig Jordheim of Carswell helped shepherd the project through to completion, always fully supportive of the enterprise. Thanks are due as well to Jane Austin and Gerry Bazinet of Carswell's Calgary office. Christine Urquhart again proved why she is so invaluable to the Centre's activites, having put the manuscript into publishable form.

TABLE OF CONTENTS

TABLE OF CASES

Introduction

FREEDOM OF EXPRESSION AND THE *CHARTER*: BEING LARGE AND LIBERAL

David Schneiderman[1]

"Freedom is a very good horse to ride, but to ride somewhere."

Matthew Arnold[2]

I

In the summer and fall of 1983, the province of British Columbia experienced enormous social unrest as a result of the Social Credit government's "restraint" budget. The budget was accompanied by 26 proposed Bills which taken together seriously undermined trade union practices, collective bargaining and social welfare rights. In response, the "Operation Solidarity" movement called for a province-wide general strike; the first to be on the picket line would be provincial government employees on lawful strike.[3] Among the sites of peaceful picketing would be courthouses across the province, including the busy Vancouver Provincial and Supreme Court buildings. On the morning of the first day of the strike, the province's Chief Justice, Alan McEachern, issued an *ex parte* injunction — on his own motion — restraining picketing "at the entrances . . . or within the precincts" of the courts.[4] That order was subsequently upheld by the Chief Justice, the British Columbia Court of Appeal and the Supreme Court of Canada.

The Supreme Court affirmed the ban on picketing primarily because the exercise of the constitutionally guaranteed right of freedom of expression could not be condoned at the expense of "massive interference with the legal and constitutional rights of the citizens of British

---

1   I am grateful to Annalise Acorn, Bruce Elman, Anne McLellan, and Glenn Solomon for their helpful comments and criticisms.
2   Matthew Arnold, *Friendship's Garland* (1903), at 141 as quoted by Raymond Williams, *Culture and Society 1780-1950* (London: Chatto & Windus, 1967), at 117.
3   The story is told in Bryan D. Palmer, *Solidarity: The Rise and Fall of an Opposition in British Columbia* (Vancouver: New Star Books, 1987).
4   See *B.C.G.E.U. v. B.C. (A.G.)*, [1988] 2 S.C.R. 214 at 222.

Columbia."[5] The court came to this conclusion despite the affidavit evidence sworn by a designate of the Canadian Bar Association that "Persons appearing to have business inside the [Vancouver Provincial] Court House entered and left the building at will and at no time appeared to be impeded in any way by the picketers."[6]

In the result, the court displaced and relegated the *Charter*'s guarantee of freedom of expression to a constitutionally inferior position *vis-à-vis* other constitutional rights.[7] More strikingly, the court invoked the *Charter* to dislocate otherwise lawful picketing.[8] If the infringement of freedom of expression which took place in this case could be so easily justified, what impact might the *Charter*'s guarantee of freedom of expression have on Canadian law? Is there reason to be optimistic about the consequences of the constitutionalization of freedom of expresssion?

Critics assert that there is no reason for such optimism; the *Charter*'s guarantees, such as freedom of expression, constitutionally enshrine a particular value system, that of liberal individualism.[9] *Charter* rights and freedoms are seen as being hostile to the collectivist aims of the modern welfare state and effectively may stifle any further encroachments into, or any transformation of, the currently prevailing rcgime of private property. If this critique is correct, then it would appear that the *Charter*'s guarantees are not as indeterminate as some have claimed,[10]

---

5   *Ibid.*, at 233.

6   *Ibid.*, at 221.

7   The Supreme Court of Canada recognized that picketing was a constitutionally protected form of expression in *R.W.D.S.U., Loc. 580 v. Dolphin Delivery Ltd.*, [1986] 2 S.C.R. 573 [B.C.]. On the relationship between picketing in a labour dispute and other forms of collective labour action, such as the right to strike and the right to engage in collective bargaining, see Peter Gall, "*Dolphin Delivery* and the Process of Constitutional Decision-making — Some Lessons to be Learned" in this volume.

8   This is significant because, unlike the *Charter*'s impact in the field of labour relations generally, the effect of the decision was not simply benign but dislocative. On the generally benign effects of the *Charter* in labour law, see Paul C. Weiler, "The Charter at Work: Reflections on the Constitutionalizing of Labour and Employment Law" (1990), 40 U.T.L.J. 117.

9   Allan C. Hutchinson and Andrew Petter, "Private Rights/ Public Wrongs: The Liberal Lie of the Charter" (1988), 38 U.T.L.J. 278.

10   See Allan C. Hutchinson and Patrick J. Monahan, "Law, Politics, and the Critical Legal Scholars: The Unfolding Drama of American Legal Thought" (1984), 36 Stan. L.Rev. 199 at 206. See also Joel C. Bakan, "Constitutional Arguments: Interpretation and Legitimacy in Canadian Constitutional Thought" (1989), 27 O.H.L.J. 123 at 185. Hutchinson and Monahan do acknowledge that "actual judicial decisions are heavily conditioned by a pervasive ideology" at 201.

for the *Charter*, ultimately, favours one of many possible ways of understanding the world.[11]

Charter optimists agree that the *Charter* enshrines a particular way of viewing the world — one so particular that it permits courts to derive in practice the "one right answer" to constitutional cases. These writers are encouraged by the potential effects that the *Charter* can have on reforming Canadian law to the advantage of the cause of social justice.[12]

The aim of this introduction is to show how each of the authors in this volume contributes to an understanding of the tradition of freedom of expression as enshrined in the *Charter*. I hope to elucidate some of the common and recurring themes that arise in the papers, but leave primarily to each author the task of convincing the reader of the justness of the author's position. It is also my aim to place the papers within the larger debate over the legitimacy of *Charter* review. The variety of rationales which are alleged to underlie the guarantee of freedom of expression will be reviewed briefly. These are particularly important in view of the competing values which often collide with free expression claims.[13] Some of those competing values — privacy, equality and the regulation of commerce — will then be discussed in light of the papers collected here. By reviewing the authors' analyses and the Supreme Court's jurisprudence in these areas, the reader may then be better equipped to assess the arguments marshalled in these papers. The variety, overlap and conflict amongst them can then be seen as a manifestation of the indeterminacy which pervades *Charter* review. But the ambit of indeterminacy is only so wide. *Charter* interpretation is guided, in large measure, by our existing liberal institutions and free-market culture. Similarly, the *Charter*'s guarantee of free expression derives its meaning from our practices — it gives expression to a particular way of life.

---

11 Mark Tushnet, *Red, White, and Blue: A Critical Analysis of Constitutional Law* (Cambridge, Mass.: Harvard University Press, 1988), at 305.

12 See, *e.g.*, David M. Beatty, *Talking Heads and the Supremes: The Canadian Production of Constitutional Review* (Toronto: Carswell, 1990), and David M. Beatty, *Putting the Charter to Work: Designing a Constitutional Labour Code* (Kingston & Montreal: McGill-Queen's University Press, 1987), at 5: "the disadvantaged and relatively powerless workers should be able to put the Charter to work in the cause of enhancing the social justice of the legal environment in which they are employed."

13 According to Dickson C.J.C. in *R. v. Keegstra*, [1991] 2 W.W.R. 1 at 26 (S.C.C.) [Alta.], "the values promoted by the freedom help not only to define the ambit of s. 2(b), but also come to the forefront when discussing how competing interests might co-exist with the freedom under s. 1 of the Charter." The competing values discussed below are not meant to be exclusive of each other or exhaustive. They overlap and interconnect: the values of privacy and commerce, for example.

II. COMPETING RATIONALES: THE CONSEQUENCE OF BEING LARGE

Liberal legalism is signified by the infusion of liberal values, such as freedom of expression, into the legal system.[14] This infusion can take the form of constitutional enactments, such as the value system enshrined in the *Charter*. As those values are broadly worded statements of general intent, courts have required that, in order to be able to invoke their protection, claimants be able to ground their claims in one of the rationales for the constitutionally guaranteed freedom. In s. 2(b) jurisprudence, this has meant satisfying any one of a number of traditonal rationales for free speech. Most of them are invoked by the authors in this collection.

The rationale derived from self-government views the Constitution as embodying procedural guarantees which enable persons, both individually and collectively, to choose intelligently those representatives who will govern them.[15] It also enables the people, as David Kretzmer argues in his paper,[16] to "have every chance not only of exposing the government to their views, but of communicating views to each other." The guarantee of freedom of expression often is characterized from this rationale, as Rodney Smolla suggests in his contribution, as "the most powerful restraint mankind has yet devised on tyranny."[17] The democratic rationale is an important component of any theory of free expression, but it can only explain some of the forms of expression worthy of constitutional protection. Aesthetic and artistic expression, for example, would be difficult to justify protecting under this rationale.

The rationale argued from individual autonomy views the Constitution as guaranteeing space for people to pursue their own notion of the good life, and the freedom of expression provides the vehicle for spreading one's good news about which form that life should take.[18] The corollary of this notion is that persons should be entitled to receive information that may be important to their own self-realization. As

---

14 Judith N. Shklar in *Legalism* (Cambridge, Mass.: Harvard University Press, 1964), at 1 describes legalism as an ideology which "holds moral conduct to be a matter of rule following."

15 This rationale is most often associated with Alexander Meiklejohn. See his *Political Freedom: The Constitutional Powers of the People* (New York: Oxford University Press, 1965).

16 David Kretzmer, "Allocating Police Resources to Protect Demonstrations: The Israeli Approach," in this volume.

17 Rodney A. Smolla, "Balancing Freedom of Expression and Protection of Reputation Under Canada's *Charter of Rights and Freedoms*," in this volume.

18 See Ronald Rotunda, "Commercial Speech and the Platonic Ideal: Libre Expression et Libre Entreprise," in this volume.

Lorraine Weinrib describes the rationale in her contribution, the "constitutional guarantee of free speech reflects the understanding that language and other forms of meaningful expression actualize the capacity for human self-realization."[19] This rationale probably protects too much expression[20] and collapses into an argument for liberty generally and not expression particularly.[21]

The rationale derived from the pursuit of truth, an inheritance from J.S. Mill,[22] views the guarantee of freedom of expression as creating the optimum environment within which the truth is more likely to emerge than not.[23] This is the "marketplace of ideas" that has been so seriously discredited in the modern age. The course of history has established that faith in the human capacity to discern between truth and falsity may be misplaced.[24]

None of these rationales, then, either individually or collectively, is sufficiently tailored to protect the kind and variety of forms of expression which may be deserving of constitutional protection.[25] This is why the rationale articulated by Frederick Schauer — the rationale derived from "governmental incompetence" — is immediately attractive.[26] This rationale sees governments as inherently incapable of acting in the field of expression without drawing faulty lines or failing to account for the subtleties of human interaction. It is a negative justification which sees governments as foes rather than as friends. It recognizes

---

19 See Lorraine E. Weinrib, "Does Money Talk? Commercial Expression in the Canadian Constitutional Context," in this volume.

20 See the text associated with notes 95 to 114, *infra*. Admittedly, Edwin Baker's, and Lorraine Weinrib's self-realization approach would stop short of protecting purely economic speech. See Baker's "Scope of the First Amendment Freedom of Speech" (1978), 25 U.C.L.A. L.Rev. 964, and Lorraine Weinrib, *ibid.*

21 This point is made in Frederick Schauer, *Free Speech: A Philosophical Enquiry* (Cambridge: Cambridge University Press, 1982), at 65.

22 Mill's utilitarian argument is grounded "on the permanent interests of a man as a progressive being." See his "On Liberty," in J.S. Mill, *Utilitarianism, Liberty & Representative Government* (London & Toronto: J.M. Dent & Sons, 1910), at 74. But see the comments at note 24, *infra.*

23 See Harold Levy, "Press-umed Innocent," and Peter Desbarats, "Free Speech, the Press and the Administration of Justice," both in this volume.

24 As Edwin Baker notes, "emotional or 'irrational' appeals have great impact; 'subconscious' repressions, phobias, or desires influence people's assimilation of messages . . . these psychological insights, extensively relied upon in practice by advertisers and propagandists, eviscerate the faith in the ability of the marketplace of ideas to lead to the 'best' truths or understandings": *supra*, note 20 at 976-77.

25 See Dale Gibson, case comment on *Irwin Toy Ltd. v. Qué. (A.G.)* (1990), 69 Can. Bar Rev. 339 at 343-45.

26 Schauer, *supra*, note 21 at 80 *ff.*

that governments are "particularly bad at censorship, [and] that they are less capable of regulating speech than they are of regulating other forms of conduct."[27]

What should concern one most about the rationale from governmental incompetence is its suspicion of democratic politics. Regulation is considered inherently suspect, notwithstanding its motivation.[28] It artificializes all government action without acknowledging any "background understanding" of that which society values as important.[29] This approach has significant implications for legislative moves in the direction of a progressive, or even liberal-welfare, legislative agenda. Any regulation of speech, no matter its public virtue, is inherently suspect, no matter what the subject-matter — whether it involves regulation of telephone books in the home or commercial signs on the highway.

The rationale also accords with the evolving Supreme Court of Canada jurisprudence of freedom of expression. That jurisprudence suggests that any legislative moves in the direction of regulating expression will attract constitutional scrutiny.[30] The court has ruled that s. 2(b) be given "a large and liberal interpretation" and "a broad and inclusive approach."[31] The *Charter* guarantee will protect all forms of expression "irrespective of the meaning or message sought to be conveyed."[32] Such legislative limitations on the freedom can be "saved," however, as reasonable limits under s. 1. The court's approach is one of *defining* matters *out* of the guarantee of freedom of expresssion through the vehicle of s. 1, rather than *defining* matters *in* at the s. 2(b) interpretive stage.[33]

27 *Ibid.*, at 81.
28 Owen Fiss, for example, argues that when "the state acts to enhance the quality of public debate, we should recognize its actions as consistent with the first amendment," in "Free Speech and Social Structure" (1986), 71 Iowa L. Rev. 1405 at 1416. This is essentially the position advanced by the majority in *Keegstra, supra,* note 13 at 56 ("one must be careful not to accept blindly that the suppression of expression must always and unremittingly detract from values central to freedom of expression").
29 See Charles Taylor, "What's Wrong With Negative Liberty," in Taylor, *Philosophy and the Human Sciences: Philosophical Papers 2* (Cambridge: Cambridge University Press, 1985), at 218.
30 The two-step approach to s. 2(b) jurisprudence does little to act as a brake on this course. The two-step approach considers, first, whether the activity at issue is expressive so as to fall within s. 2(b) and, second, whether the purpose or effect of the legislation is to regulate expression: see *Irwin Toy Ltd. v. Qué. (A.G.)* (1989), 58 D.L.R. (4th) 577 at 605-13 (S.C.C.), and *Keegstra, supra,* note 13 at 29.
31 *Irwin Toy, ibid.,* at 607.
32 *Per* Lamer J. (as he then was) in *Ref. re Criminal Code, ss. 193 & 195.1(1)(c),* [1990] 1 S.C.R. 1123 at 1181. This was adopted by the majority judgment of Dickson C.J.C. in *R. v. Keegstra, supra,* note 13 at 29.
33 See Frederick Schauer, "Categories and the First Amendment: A Play in Three

It is not clear, nor apparently consistent with an argument that relies in part on the rationale derived from self-government, why the judiciary are particularly able to determine the scope of permissible legislative action in the field of expression. Indeed, the ground of debate may have moved beyond the capacity of the judiciary to govern (which is not conceded), to one of whether private power (the marketplace) or public power (our legislative assemblies) are the preferable institutions for deciding what expression may be permissible.[34] In any event, it is apparent that the traditional rationales are not doing the job we might wish them to do. If, at the end of the day, we are dissatisfied with the results they offer, we might move away from the application of abstract rationales to more pragmatic understandings of who benefits according to what outcome; a move away from the purposive and towards the purposeful.[35]

III. COMPETING VALUES: THE TRAGEDY OF BEING LIBERAL

Any theory of society that fails to take account of the variety of human experience is doomed to fail. As Judith Shklar has written, "[p]luralism ... is a social actuality that no contemporary political theory can ignore without losing its relevance."[36] This is simply to recognize that, due to contemporary social arrangements, people have differing social experiences and priorities.[37] Those experiences and priorities can also conflict when we speak about them or prefer one over another in our legal regimes. There are, John Dewey wrote, "a multitude of conflicts not between individuals and society but between groups and other groups, between some individuals and other individuals."[38] The disagreement amongst the contributors can be seen as a reflection of these conflicts, with their resolution advocated along different lines.

Acts" (1981), Vand. L. Rev. 265 at 279-80.

34 On this debate, see Frederick Schauer, "Who Decides?" in Judith Lichtenberg (ed.), *Democracy and the Mass Media* (Cambridge: Cambridge University Press, 1990), at 202, and Frank Michleman, "Conceptions of Democracy in American Constitutional Argument: The Case of Pornography Regulation" (1989), 56 Tenn. L. Rev. 291.

35 This is somewhat along the lines of the approach advocated by Daniel Farber and Phillip Frickey in "Practical Reason and the First Amendment" (1987), 34 U.C.L.A. L. Rev. 1615.

36 Judith N. Shklar, *supra*, note 14 at 5.

37 Pierre J. Schlag, "An Attack on Categorical Approaches to Freedom of Speech" (1983), 30 U.C.L.A. L. Rev. 671.

38 John Dewey and James H. Tufts, *Ethics*, revised ed. (New York: Henry Holt and Company, 1932), at 359.

This is what has been coined the "tragedy" that accompanies human freedom: how to choose between important social values that compete for priority.[39]

This tragedy is not exclusively the terrain of traditional liberal theory.[40] The socialist "prophetic" pragmatism of Cornel West, for example, "tempers its utopian impulse with a profound sense of the tragic character of life and history."[41] Roberto Unger criticizes this "tragic liberalism" for its inability to recognize the transformability of the social settings "which give these values their detailed meaning."[42] But even he is forced to acknowledge the inevitable clash which accompanies competing values. In his romantic vision of the community, Unger grants "immunity rights," which "protect the individual against oppression by concentrations of public or private power." By conceding such immunity rights, Unger makes some amount of "tension" between the scope of that immunity and the necessity for government intervention "unavoidable."[43]

How do claims to freedom of expression stack up against competing values in the balancing process called for under s. 1? The following discussion lays out some of those competing values and how the authors and the court engage in that balancing process.

A. The Value of Privacy

Liberal society's catalogue of shared beliefs and fundamental understandings are few; its notion of public solidarity is premised on a cynical conception of what is possible. According to Michael Sandel, liberalism "fails to take seriously our commonality."[44] Liberal politics is

---

39 Sidney Hook, *Pragmatism and the Tragic Sense of Life* (New York: Basic Books, 1974), c. 1.

40 Nor is there complete consensus among writers in the liberal tradition that tragedy is inherent to the human condition. Nancy Fraser criticizes Richard Rorty for naively understating fundamental social antagonisms: "Rorty homogenizes social space, assuming tendentiously that there are no deep social cleavages capable of generating conflicting solidarities and opposing 'we's'." See Nancy Fraser, *Unruly Practices: Power, Discourse and Gender in Contemporary Social Theory* (Minneapolis: University of Minnesota Press, 1989), at 104.

41 Cornel West, *The American Evasion of Philosophy: A Genealogy of Pragmatism* (Madison: The University of Wisconsin Press, 1989), at 228.

42 See his *Social Theory : Its Situation and Task* (Cambridge: Cambridge University Press, 1987), at 37.

43 See his *False Necessity: Anti-Necessitarian Social Theory in the Service of Radical Democracy* (Cambridge: Cambridge University Press, 1987), at 524-26. This is also acknowledged in Ellen Meiksins Wood, *The Retreat From Class: A New "True" Socialism* (London: Verso, 1986), at 154-56.

44 Michael Sandel, *Liberalism and the Limits of Justice* (Cambridge University Press, 1982), at 174.

limited because its vision of human solidarity is limited — there are only so many reasons that justify public intervention in the life of a community.[45] The rights and freedoms assembled under the *Charter*, therefore, can be seen as embodying a limited number of shared fundamental values, many of which are designed to prevent majoritarian intrusions on those values through the vehicle of government.

This is not necessarily an unhealthy paranoia. The 20th century has seen political movements which embrace the totality of human affairs as "shared values" and make that commonality the full-time business of the state. The failed attempts at total regulation in the name of absolute freedom can be found in the totalitarianism of both fascism and communism.[46]

By contrast, shared values in a liberal legal regime emerge generally by voluntary association among individuals: they are not the territory of government regulation. Rather, these values are to be claimed and pursued in the "private" arena. An important facet of the liberal legal regime, therefore, is this public/private distinction.[47] The guarantee of freedom of expression can be seen as an integral component within this framework.[48]

Thus, the *Charter* often is portrayed as a document which reinforces relationships of power: a document that enshrines human rights as property rights.[49] Centres of private power are entitled to invoke the *Charter* to insulate them from the regulatory schemes which usurp private space for public goals, such as in the context of using mall property for expressive activity. These privacy arguments fail to recognize the public role that the state plays in recognizing and, thereby, enhancing the role of public property. As Allan Hutchinson and Andrew Petter have written, "the relevant issue is not whether the state ought to 'intervene'; the state is already there."[50] Moe Litman, in his paper

---

45 Stephen Macedo, *Liberal Virtues: Citizenship, Virtue, and Community in Liberal Constitutionalism* (Oxford: Clarendon Press, 1990), at 264.

46 The liberal reply to Sandel, according to Richard Rorty, is "that even if the typical character types of liberal democracies *are* bland, calculating, petty, and unheroic, the prevalence of such people may be a reasonable price to pay for political freedom." See Richard Rorty, *Objectivity, Relativism, and Truth: Philosophical Papers Volume 1* (Cambridge: Cambridge University Press, 1991), at 190. See also J.-F. Lyotard, *infra*, note 113.

47 See Ronald Rotunda, *supra*, note 18. Also see the dissenting judgment of La Forest J. in *Edmonton Journal v. Alta. (A.G.)* (1990), 64 D.L.R. (4th) 577 at 600 *ff.* (S.C.C.), and Richard Rorty, *Contingency, Irony and Solidarity* (Cambridge: Cambridge University Press, 1989), c. 4.

48 As might be considered the requirement of a division between church and state.

49 See Mary Ellen Turpel, "Aboriginal Peoples and the Canadian *Charter*: Interpretive Monopolies, Cultural Differences" (1989-90), Canadian Human Rights Yearbook 3 at 15.

50 *Supra*, note 9 at 285.

exploring how the *Charter* may inform the common law,[51] pursues the logic of this approach in the context of the mall owner seeking to prohibit certain public uses of mall property. By tracing the historical development of property rights, Litman shows how the common law concept of private property has been subject to qualifications in the interests of the public good. By analogy, the mall owner's seemingly absolute right to exclude expressive activities, such as boycotts, picketing and labour organizing, can be qualified in order to provide a positive right of access to the unpropertied interests of labour and others. On the other hand, Peter Gall argues in his contribution[52] that the *Charter* has no useful role to play in the field of labour relations, and should leave to labour and management the responsibility of defining the permissible limits of labour expression. This approach necessarily loads the dice in favour of those with control and ownership of property, in effect, a *laissez-faire* approach to *Charter* interpretation.

The rhetoric of privacy, in addition, predominates the debate over the regulation, by use of defamation laws, of the media's ability to publish remarks about the conduct of public officials. Libel laws have been viewed traditionally as carving out an exception to freedom of expression in an attempt to secure a zone free from public intrusion.[53] Lewis Klar, in his contribution,[54] explores the development of the defamation action and the defences available at common law, all of which favour the public figure at the expense of the public "right to know." Coupled with the litigious nature of Canadian politicians and public figures,[55] the laws are unjustifiably restrictive of freedom of expression. Richard Dearden, in his contribution,[56] pursues this line of inquiry in the context of the case of *Coates v. The Citizen*,[57] where the court found the law of defamation not to infringe the *Charter* freedom of expression. Dearden explores how the *Charter* may yet disrupt the terrain by having a twofold effect on defamation law: first, it may inform the common law of defamation and thereby unravel some of its unjustifiable restrictions and presumptions and, second, it may do the same to Canada's statutory regimes of defamation insofar as it unduly

---

51 M.M. Litman, "Freedom of Speech and Private Property: The Case of the Mall Owner," in this volume.
52 Peter Gall, "*Dolphin Delivery* and the Process of Constitutional Decision-making — Some Lessons to be Learned," in this volume.
53 Thomas Emerson, *The System of Freedom of Expression* (New York: Vintage Books, 1970), at 517.
54 Lewis Klar, " 'If You Don't Have Anything Good to Say About Someone . . .'," in this volume.
55 See "Libel Power" 10:15 (December 13-19, 1990), NOW 10.
56 Richard G. Dearden, "Constitutional Protection for Defamatory Words Published About the Conduct of Public Officials," in this volume.
57 (1988), 85 N.S.R. (2d) 146 (T.D.).

restricts media discussion of public officials. So far, the courts have proven unreceptive to such *Charter* arguments notwithstanding persuasive evidence tendered by the media evidencing the present law's "chilling effect."[58]

It must be borne in mind that *New York Times v. Sullivan*[59]-type libel rules also have the effect of freeing up private power — that of the owners of the media of communication. David Lepofsky, in his paper,[60] highlights some of the rhetoric surrounding claims by the media for greater press freedom and skeptically inquires into the role the media claims it plays as "surrogate" for the public eye. He intimates that if the press wants to claim such a role for itself, it might submit itself to the same standards of accountability demanded of government institutions.[61] Jean Jacques Blais, in his contribution,[62] considers whether tolerance of the present concentration of media ownership in Canada is in the public interest. He suggests that there might be a positive role for government to play in diffusing ownership to ensure a more vigorous exercise of freedom of expression amongst the mass media.

Notions of privacy are invoked by other defenders of government regulation. For example, privacy can be invoked as a shield to protect the identity of those who submit themselves to the jurisdiction of the legal process, or are otherwise swept up in proceedings as informants, deponents or complainants. These are some of the "status concerns" discussed by Stan Cohen in his contribution.[63] Strong advocates of media access to court proceedings, such as Harold Levy and Peter Desbarats in their contributions,[64] argue that access is *prima facie* a component of a free society and a check on the authoritarian tendencies of government power. While access is presumptively necessary, others wonder whether too much access is too much of a good idea. Concerns are suggested by David Lepofsky in his contribution about how an instrument like the *Charter* can be used to undo a number of very

---

58   Richards J. characterized this evidence as "opinion, hearsay, speculation and editorial comment." See *Coates, ibid.*, at 150-51 and Dearden, *supra*, note 56 at text associated with notes 31-35.
59   376 U.S. 254 (1964). The background to the case is discussed by Rodney Smolla, *supra*, note 17.
60   See M. David Lepofsky, "Open Justice 1990: The Constitutional Right to Attend and Report on Court Proceedings in Canada," in this volume.
61   See also William W. Van Alstyne, *Interpretations of the First Amendment* (Durham, N.C.: Duke University Press, 1984), at 65.
62   Jean Jacques Blais, "Freedom of Expression and Public Administration," in this volume.
63   Stanley A. Cohen, "Free Press vs. Fair Trial: A Law Reform Perspective," in this volume.
64   See Harold J. Levy, "Press-umed Innocent" and Peter Desbarats, "Freedom of Expression and the Administration of Justice," both in this volume.

sensitive procedural frameworks, such as the protection of the identities of complainants in sexual assault cases.[65]

The Supreme Court of Canada in *Canadian Newspapers Co.* accepted the value of privacy as one of the main reasons for upholding such a law, "since fear of publication is one of the factors that influences the reporting of sexual crimes."[66] The same value, however, was not sufficiently important to save the limited reporting of matrimonial proceedings permitted by the Alberta *Judicature Act*.[67] Here, potential infringements of privacy rights which, it was argued, encouraged access to court by those seeking relief in matrimonial matters, proved of minimal importance compared to the wholesale prior restraint of media reports. At stake in this case, however, was hardly the type of sensitive procedural framework described by David Lepofsky.[68]

B. The Value of Equality

In addition to the value of privacy, the value of equality is also seen as conflicting with the value of freedom of expression.[69] The conflict

---

65 But see Jamie Cameron, "Comment: The Constitutional Domestication of our Courts — Openness and Publicity in Judicial Proceedings Under the Charter," in Anisman and Linden (eds.), *The Media, The Courts and the Charter* (Toronto: Carswell, 1986), 331 at 342.

66 *Canadian Newspapers Co. v. Can. (A.G.)*, [1988] 2 S.C.R. 122 at 132 [Ont.].

67 *Edmonton Journal, supra*, note 47. See the discussion in David Lepofsky, *supra*, note 60.

68 See Lepofsky, *ibid.*, in text associated with notes 263 to 317.

69 Although I do not wish to enter into an extensive discussion here, some liberal theorists attempt to avoid the conflict between liberty and equality by constructing a social picture which subsumes liberty into the notion of equality. John Rawls, for example, constructs a regime of rights selected by persons in the "original position" operating behind the veil of ignorance, so that liberties such as freedom of expression, association and religion are justified as part of the regime of equality which each player in the original position would demand. In this way, such constitutional rights are beyond reproach and part of the package of rights associated with equality. See John Rawls, "The Basic Liberties and their Priority," in Sterling M. McMurrin (ed.), *Liberty, Equality, and Law: Selected Tanner Lectures on Moral Philosophy* (Salt Lake City: University of Utah Press, 1987). Similarly, Ronald Dworkin attempts to muffle the conflict by making any "morally important liberties," such as that of the freedom of expression, an essential component of a regime of equality of concern and respect. He can then write that, "[a]ny genuine contest between liberty and equality is a contest liberty must lose." See Ronald Dworkin, "What is Equality? Part 3: The Place of Liberty" (1987), Iowa L.Rev. 1 at 7. By transforming liberty into an issue of equality, Dworkin can then justify affirmative action programs, but, interestingly, not the regulation of pornography. See "Do We Have a Right to Pornography?" and "Reverse Discrimination" in Dworkin, *Taking Rights Seriously* (Cambridge, Mass.: Harvard University Press, 1977).

arises sharply in the papers collected here on such issues as the regulation of obscenity and hate propaganda. The equality argument empha-
sizes that obscene and hateful expression is anathema to democractic
society inhabited by women and minorities, who have traditionally
been the subject of discrimination, physical abuse and venomous verbal
attack. These groups are the subordinates in society's power structure
and speech that vilifies them, by portraying them as willing accomplices
to all matters sexual (in the case of women) and conspirators and traitors
(in the case of certain minorities), contributes to an atmosphere which
condones violence, discrimination and humiliation. Obscene and
hateful expression thus is seen as the practice of sexual and racial
discrimination.

The notion of pornography/hatred as discrimination is asserted in
the contributions by Kathleen Mahoney,[70] John McLaren[71] and Irwin
Cotler.[72] They argue that obscene and hateful expression, in light of our
commitment to a society based on equality, a commitment which is
given constitutional recognition in s. 15 of the *Charter*, are not entitled
to constitutional protection under s. 2(b) of the *Charter*. The argument is
an attractive one, for at least two reasons. First, it speaks in language
which is understood by liberalism: discrimination and violence are evils
to be combatted via legal means.[73] Second, liberal society's catalogue of
shared values is thin. That society has committed itself to a regime of
equality, even if only in the formal sense, suggests that any form of
expression which undermines that commitment might well deserve
ejection from the catalogue of protected expression. After all, if we agree
on so little, we might as well act on the things we can agree on.

On the other hand, argue Thelma McCormack[74] and Alan Borovoy,[75] we cannot expect to have a society of equality without liberty.
They reply that stifling such expression is self-defeating; it ensures the
continued dominance of the status quo. A society that condones the

---

This reasoning has been turned against Dworkin in Rae Langton, "Whose
Right? Ronald Dworkin, Women, and Pornographers" (1990), 19 Phil. & Pub.
Affairs 311.

70 Kathleen Mahoney, "Canaries in a Coal Mine: Canadian Judges and the
Reconstruction of Obscenity Law," in this volume.

71 John P.S. McLaren, " 'Now You See It, Now You Don't': The Historical
Record and the Elusive Task of Defining the Obscene," in this volume.

72 Irwin Cotler, "Racist Incitement: Giving Free Speech a Bad Name," in this
volume.

73 Beverly Brown, "Debating Pronography" (1990), 1 Law & Critique 131 at 136 *ff.*
The drawback for advocates of regulation is that evidence of "harm" which is
recognizable to the liberal tradition must be tendered.

74 Thelma McCormack, "Must We Censor Pornography? Civil Liberties and
Feminist Jurisprudence," in this volume.

75 A. Alan Borovoy, "How Not To Fight Racial Hatred," in this volume.

overbroad censorship of politically charged expression is not likely to create conditions which will permit any radical, or even mildly transformative, change. McCormack claims that the messages contained in pornography are often ambiguous and argues that such expression should be tolerated only so that other, different voices may also emerge. Their reply is underscored by the critique of indeterminacy. Borovoy's concern is that language is too imprecise a tool to catch the expression we dislike, while avoiding the capture of the expression we would be loath to interrupt.

There may be no satisfactory way of accommodating the theorists on both sides of the conflict over the legal regulation of pornography and hate propaganda, but there may be extra-legal ways out. John McLaren, in his contribution to this volume,[76] shows us that too often the legal regulation of expression was simply the vehicle for pursuing conservative, rather than transformative, moral ends. Similarly, Cyril Levitt's account in this volume[77] of the effectiveness of the Weimar Republic's hate laws indicates how little such laws aid in doing battle with systemic and deeply-entrenched hatred. Theirs are cautionary tales about using the law in order to silence others and, in the end, being silenced yourself. Perhaps one way of resolving this impasse is to recognize that the law, particularly because of its indeterminacy and susceptibility to being hijacked by what McLaren calls "moral vigilantes," is not the only or appropiate response.[78]

Devising such a strategy requires an acknowledgment that, in many ways, both sides to the debate are correct. As author Jane Rule has written, "one of the basic failures in recent debates . . . about pornography and censorship is some women's inability to see that censorship won't work and some men's inability to see that pornography is as important an issue as, and separate from, freedom of expression."[79] By side-stepping the avenue of legal regulation, and advancing along the avenue of coalition building, men and women can join together in the fight against the debasement and degradation of women and minorities.[80]

It might be alleged that this type of action evidences a failure to take

---

76 *Supra*, note 71.
77 Cyril Levitt, "Racial Incitement and the Law: The Case of the Weimar Republic," in this volume.
78 Carol Smart, *Feminism and the Power of Law* (London: Routledge, 1989), c. 6.
79 "Censorship," in Jane Rule, *A Hot-Eyed Moderate* (Tallahassee, Florida: The Naiad Press Inc., 1985), at 125.
80 Frank Michelman argues that the non-legislative route is subject to the same vigilantism. The virtue of majoritarian politics is that it ensures that the majority designs the appropriate mechanism of response. See his "Conceptions of Democracy," *supra*, note 34 at 311-12.

seriously the complaints of the victims of that expression. But a collective response need not only take the form of legal rules. Such an approach valorizes the "power of law" and underestimates the power of collective action.[81]

Why should this strategy differ from that advocated by those who seek to place limits on expenses associated with electoral campaigns? Desmond Morton, in his essay,[82] argues in favour of imposing spending limits in electoral campaigns as a means of equalizing the electoral expression of those with large corporate and private support and those without. By limiting excess expenditures and third party campaign speech, the law could enable alternative voices to be heard, particularly those which otherwise would be drowned out in the cacophony of talking money.

The equality argument articulated with respect to spending limits is not apparently dissimilar from that made by Catharine MacKinnon regarding the legal regulation of pornography.[83] Prohibitions, such as those contained in the Indianapolis and Minneapolis Ordinances, permit the previously silenced voices of victims of pornography to emerge. The arguments, however, may differ significantly. Unlike the target of obscenity laws, the target of electoral expense laws is precise dollar amounts; it is not representations, symbols or ideas.[84]

The Supreme Court of Canada recently resolved the issue of the constitutionality of laws prohibiting the promotion of hatred and their relationship to equality[85] in the trilogy of decisions in *Keegstra*,[86] *Andrews*[87] and *Taylor*.[88] All the members of the court agreed that racist incitement was a constitutionally protected form of expression. As a result, all agreed that the promotion of hatred laws infringed s. 2(b) of

---

81 Carol Smart, *supra*, note 78 and Nancy Fraser, *supra*, note 40 at 110, note 24.
82 Desmond Morton, "Should Elections Be Fair or Just Free?" in this volume.
83 See "Francis Biddle's Sister: Pornography, Civil Rights, and Speech," in Catharine A. MacKinnon, *Feminism Unmodified: Discourses on Life and Law* (Cambridge, Mass.: Harvard University Press, 1987), 163 at 195: "The situation of women suggests that the urgent issue of our freedom of speech is not primarily the avoidance of state intervention as such, but getting affirmative access to speech for those to whom it has been denied."
84 While the Minneapolis Ordinance refers to specific representations, it also would catch, among other things, women "presented in postures of sexual submission." See Margaret Baldwin, "The Sexuality of Inequality: The Minneapolis Pornography Ordinance" (1984), 2 Law & Inequality 629 at 649.
85 As David Lepofsky, *supra*, note 60, reports at text associated with notes 68-70, the Supreme Court of Canada did not even refer to the equality argument made by the Women's Legal Education and Action Fund in the context of the s. 2(b) case of *Can. Newspapers Co., supra*, note 66.
86 *Supra*, note 13.
87 *R. v. Andrews* (1991), 117 N.R. 284 (S.C.C.) [Ont.].
88 *Taylor v. Can. (Human Rights Comm.)* (1990), 75 D.L.R. (4th) 577 (S.C.C.).

the *Charter*. The majority, however, found the laws in question to be reasonable limits of the freedom and, thereby, upheld the legislations in all four cases. McLachlin J., writing for the minority, found the laws in question to be too vague and overbroad to satisfy the proportionality component of the s. 1 test. For the majority, the values of equality, multiculturalism and dignity of the individual were objectives sufficiently important so as to justify the infringements of freedom of expression that such laws necessitated. They came to this conclusion despite their earlier pronouncement in *Irwin Toy*, which described the purpose of s. 2(b) as the means to protect from legal regulation expression "however unpopular, distasteful or contrary to the mainstream."[89]

The decision in *Keegstra*, however, should not be seen as a striking out of a bold new Canadian tradition. It is firmly within it, as evidenced by the Cohen Report,[90] the *Equality Now* Report[91] and the Law Reform Commission of Canada working paper on hate propaganda.[92] It also has strong links to the jurisprudence developed under the *European Convention for the Protection of Human Rights and Fundamental Freedoms*.[93] Some commentators, however, are of the view that the Supreme Court's record under the *Charter* is both bold and innovative, a collection of jurisprudence which is original both in its formulation and conclusion.[94]

---

89   *Irwin Toy, supra*, note 30 at 606. This *dictum* in *Irwin Toy* is consistent with the broad interpretation given s. 2(b) in the hate propaganda trilogy. The inconsistency with the hate trilogy appears to arise from the fact that the characterization of freedom of expression in *Irwin Toy* might have been more appropriately a s. 1 consideration in the hate cases, which may have then led to a different result.

90   Canada, *Report of the Special Committee on Hate Propaganda in Canada* (Ottawa: Queen's Printer, 1966).

91   Canada, House of Commons, *Report of the Special Committee on Visible Minorities in Canadian Society* (Ottawa: Queen's Printer, 1984).

92   Canada, Law Reform Commssion of Canada, *Hate Propaganda* (Working Paper 50) (Ottawa: L.R.C., 1986).

93   See *Glimmerveen v. Netherlands* (1979), 4 E.H.R.R. 260, and the cases discussed in *Keegstra, supra*, note 13 at 47-48.

94   See David Beatty, *Talking Heads, supra*, note 12 at 4 ("a group of nine judges, struggling from first principles, without the use of prior cases to assist them, trying to make sense of and ascribe some meaning to a written, constitutional bill of rights"), and Michael J. Tilleard, "Commercial Expression Comes of Age: The Path to Constitutional Recognition Under the Canadian Charter of Rights" (1990), 28 Alta. L.Rev. 604 at 621 (commenting on *Ford* and *Irwin Toy*, they reflect a "trend to approach *Charter* issues such as freedom of expression from an independent, uniquely Canadian, standpoint, where American jursiprudential influences play little, or no part at all, in the judgment handed down").

C. The Value of Commerce

The early and formative decisions on freedom of expression were about whether the *Charter*'s guarantee of freedom of expression extended to speech regarding commercial transactions. The Supreme Court eschewed, at least in these early decisions, categorical definitions which would preclude most forms of expression from *Charter* scrutiny.[95] As a result, the court, in the *Ford* case,[96] could protect the commercial expression of non-francophone business establishments in Quebec who were prohibited from using any language other than French on their outdoor commercial signs. In that case the use of language was so intimately connected to expression that the court readily applied the Quebec *Charter*[97] protection of such expression. The court, at the same time and without any immediate necessity for doing so, acknowledged that commercial expression "plays a significant role in enabling individuals to make informed economic choices, an important aspect of individual self-fulfillment and personal autonomy."[98] This had the effect of opening up a wide variety of regulatory schemes to *Charter* review which, by many accounts, lie far beyond the "core" values which freedom of expression was designed to protect.

Irwin Toy,[99] for example, concerned television advertising aimed at children under 12 years of age in the Province of Quebec; *Rocket*[100] concerned professional disciplinary regulations regarding advertising by dentists. The former law was found by the full panel of the court to offend s. 2(b) of the *Charter*, but was saved as a reasonable limit under s. 1 by a majority of three to two. In the latter case, the disciplinary code was struck down by a unanimous court.[101] Each of these decisions can be seen as favouring the interpretation of freedom of expression under the *Charter* as advocated by Ronald Rotunda in his paper.[102] He argues that laws "which restrict free speech in order to dampen people's consumptive choices" about lawful products are generally unconstitutional. Rotunda sees such laws as reflecting an objectionable paternalism that is

---

95 Except for physical violence. See *Irwin Toy, supra*, note 30 at 607. But even threats of violence were acknowledged to be granted *Charter* protection in *Keegstra, supra*, note 13 at 31-32.

96 *Ford v. Qué. (P.G.)* (1988), 54 D.L.R. (4th) 577 (S.C.C.).

97 *Charter of Human Rights and Freedoms*, R.S.Q. 1977, c. C-12, s. 3.

98 *Supra*, note 96 at 604.

99 *Supra*, note 30.

100 *Rocket v. Royal College of Dental Surgeons* (1990), 71 D.L.R. (4th) 68 (S.C.C.).

101 But see *Lapointe c. Comité de Discipline de l'Ordre des denturologistes (Qué.)*, [1990] R.J.Q. 2315 (C.S.), which upheld certain disciplinary provisions prohibiting professional advertising.

102 *Supra*, note 18.

fundamentally undemocratic. In *Irwin Toy*, the Supreme Court of Canada essentially adopted this free market model of constitutional interpretation by granting *Charter* protection to commercial advertising directed at children. In *Rocket*, the court went even further and characterized the court's decision in *Ford* as acknowledging "advertising's intrinsic value as expression."[103]

In these cases the court simply has recognized that the discourse of economic exchange predominates Canadian society. Intimate decisions regarding lawful market transactions remain *prima facie* out of state control. The ability to make decisions based on the free market thereby becomes part of the panoply of *Charter* rights. Lorraine Weinrib, in her essay,[104] criticizes the courts for buying into the doctrine of commercial expression beyond that necessary to satisfy the demands of the rationale from autonomy. She sees the court's move in the direction advocated by Rotunda as being the result of an overly simplistic adoption of American constitutional constructs.

Much expression has an economic motive, and often (some would say always) political and economic expression are closely connected.[105] Economic expression often has a cultural aspect, as it did in the *Ford* case.[106] This is strikingly apparent when one takes account of the small commercial enterpises, some of them long-standing neighbourhood establishments, which were forced by Quebec's language laws to remove signs of being part of a non-francophone cultural heritage. Commercial signs were, in this way, cultural artifacts worthy of protection.[107]

It is too often difficult to distinguish between expression that is purely "economic" and that which has other aspects. An example of this phenomenon is the "California Raisins," the singing raisins used as a promotional device by the California Raisin Growers Association in the late 1980s. At what stage did "The Raisins" cease to be a vehicle for promoting dried fruit, to become animated entertainment, and then to become a recording group led by the legendary rock drummer Buddy Miles? The court's decisions indicate that it, too, finds these forms of expression difficult to distinguish in form and in value. As a result, forms of expression that are predominately economic, whether they be

---

103 *Supra*, note 100 at 74.
104 *Supra*, note 19.
105 Steven Shiffrin, "The First Amendment and Economic Regulation: Away From a General Theory of the First Amendment" (1983), 78 Northwest. Univ. L.Rev. 1212.
106 *Supra*, note 96.
107 Marshall McLuhan, *Understanding Media: The Extensions of Man* (New York: New American Library, 1964), at ix ("Each new technology . . . turns its predecessor into an art form").

letters of recommendation of employment,[108] professional advertising by dentists,[109] or solicitation by prostitutes,[110] are granted constitutional protection. Well-educated adults have argued that the regulation of the colour of margarine is an infringement of freedom of expression.[111] Sometimes there are real slippery slopes.

Zygmunt Bauman has written that freedom has moved into its consumer phase:[112] "the concern with acquisition of the goods and services attainable only through the market has taken the place once occupied by the 'work ethic'." The court simply has recognized this central role that commercial transactions play in the everyday life of the late 20th century Canadian citizen. The court has also recognized that the *Charter* attains its meaning within a modern capitalist economy, where most everything and everyone obtain their value through open exchange on the free market.[113] The court has done no more than to treat expression as a commodity like any other.[114]

IV. CONCLUSION

We have good reason, given the foregoing, to be skeptical about the prospects of *Charter* review under s. 2(b). *Charter* interpreters have little choice but to protect too much expression, much of which deserves to remain solely in the regulatory domain of our legislative assemblies. But does that necessarily mean that we cannot expect any good to come out of freedom of expression claims under the *Charter*?[115] While that is a

---

108 *Slaight Communications Inc. v. Davidson*, [1989] 1 S.C.R. 1038.

109 *Rocket, supra*, note 100.

110 *Prostitution Reference, supra*, note 32.

111 *Inst. of Edible Oil Foocs v. Ont.* (1987), 63 O.R. (2d) 436, affirmed 64 D.L.R. (4th) 480, leave to appeal to S.C.C. refused 41 O.A.C. 267n.

112 Zygmunt Bauman, *Freedom* (Milton Keynes: Open University Press, 1988), at 74-75.

113 J.-F. Lyotard characterizes capitalism as totalitarian, not in the political sense, but in "terms of language since it calls for the complete hegemony of [a] type of economic discourse" which provides that "every object and every action is acceptable (or permitted) if it can enter into economic exchange." See his "Notes on Legitimation," in Reiner Schürmann, *The Public Realm* (Albany: State University of New York Press, 1989), 167 at 179.

114 I am paraphrasing Mark V. Tushnet, "Corporations and Free Speech," in David Kairys (ed.), *The Politics of Law: A Progressive Critique* (New York: Pantheon Books, 1982), at 254. It is for these reasons that Roger Shiner, recalling the generation of United States Supreme Court "substantive due process" jurisprudence associated with *Lochner v. N.Y.*, 198 U.S. 45 (1905), has characterized the court's turn in this direction as one towards *Irwin*-ism. See Roger Shiner, "Freedom of Commercial Expression," at 29 (unpublished).

115 See A. Wayne McKay, "Freedom of Expression: Is It All Just Talk?" (1989), 68 Can. Bar Rev. 713 at 722.

large (and liberal) question which cannot be addressed fully here, to date there are a handful of encouraging legal victories which are positive outcomes from the point of view of democracy and the disadvantaged. In Nova Scotia, the *Charter* was successfully invoked by the news media to gain access to the public galleries of the Nova Scotia House of Assembly for television broadcasting purposes.[116] In Edmonton and Toronto, the *Charter* was used by anti free-trade activists to successfully challenge municipal by-laws which prohibited the affixing of posters on public utility poles: an effective means of political organizing for the less affluent.[117] The *Charter* was successfully invoked by an animal welfare rights group to gain access to the ice floes off Newfoundland in order to publicize the annual seal hunt.[118] Recently, the Supreme Court of Canada, in *Committee for the Commonwealth of Canada v. Canada*,[119] held that airport officials infringed the committee members' freedom of expression by prohibiting their political activities on the premises of Montreal's Dorval Airport.

Yet, the principle of free expression needs still to be advanced by creating greater access to scarce media resources[120] and to abundant public forums. Even traditional forums for political expression, such as the area around the House of Commons, have been cordoned off from peaceful protest. In March 1990, the Commons' secretive board of internal economy, in a move designed to silence Greg Kealey, who had been heckling members of the government daily for two years, banned all protestors within 50 metres of the entrances to Parliament. Mr. Kealey and another protestor, Jesuit priest Tony Van Hee who had been conducting a silent vigil against abortion for 140 straight days, subsequently spent four days in jail for their defiance.[121] All of this occurred only eight years after the entrenchment of the *Charter*.

Much of the hard work to preserve a realm of freedom of expression in Canada was done earlier this century, particularly during the course of the struggle for collective labour rights[122] and religious minority

116 *N.B. Broadcasting Co. v. Donahoe* (1990), 71 D.L.R. (4th) 23, affirmed N.S.C.A., Doc. S.H. 68444/89, 21st March 1991 (not yet reported).
117 See *Re Forget* (1991), 74 D.L.R. (4th) 547 (Alta. Q.B.), and *Metro. Toronto v. Quickfall*, Ont. Prov. Ct., May 1990 (not yet reported). But see *Ramsden v. Peterborough (City)*, Ont. Prov. Ct., 28th February 1989 (not yet reported).
118 *Int. Fund for Animal Welfare Inc. v. Can.*, [1989] 1 F.C. 335 (C.A.).
119 (1991), 77 D.L.R. (4th) 385 (S.C.C.).
120 See an example of literature produced by striking Molson workers which could not gain wide dissemination due to restrictions set by the mass media in Alan C. Hutchinson, "Money Talk: Against Constitutionalizing (Commercial) Speech" (1990), 17 Can. Bus. L.J. 1 at 33.
121 See Stevie Cameron, "Hill club gives self disturbing powers" (June 18, 1990), The Globe and Mail at A5.
122 See Desmond Morton with Terry Copp, *Working People* (Ottawa: Deneau & Greenberg, 1980).

rights.[123] The proclamation of the *Charter* in 1982 has permitted other forces to commandeer that liberty. This is not a new phenomenon. John Dewey wrote in 1935 that: "Humanly speaking, the crisis in liberalism was a product of particular historical events. Soon after liberal tenets were formulated as eternal truths, it became an instrument of vested interests in opposition to further social change, a ritual of lip service."[124] Similarly, the *Charter*'s concepts of "liberty," "equality" and "expression" are being co-opted by business and other powerful elites.[125] A healthy skepticism suggests that we be cautious about recovering the liberal tradition found in the *Charter* to the use of more progressive causes. But the power of words remains as effective today as they have in the past. Just as they can change the course of history,[126] perhaps we can harness them to the more modest aim of mediating social change.[127]

---

123 See Walter Surma Tarnopolsky, *The Canadian Bill of Rights*, 2nd ed. (Toronto: McClelland & Stewart, 1975), c. II.

124 From his *Liberalism and Social Action* reprinted in J. Ratner, *Intelligence in the Modern World: John Dewey's Philosophy* (New York: The Modern Library, 1939), at 451.

125 See J.M. Balkin, "Some Realism About Pluralism: Legal Realist Approaches to the First Amendment" (1990), Duke L.J. 375 at 393.

126 On this, see Vaclav Havel, "Words on Words" (1990), 36 N.Y. Rev. Books 5.

127 See Dewey, *supra*, note 124 at 451.

PART I

FREE PRESS vs. FAIR TRIAL: FREEDOM OF EXPRESSION AND PROCEEDINGS IN THE COURTS

Although there is a long-standing tradition of holding court proceedings in the open, the advent of the *Charter* has been accompanied by a proliferation of freedom of expression claims against the administration of Canadian justice. As a result, Canadian courts have been called upon to redefine the rules of openness, balancing the benefits of open justice, such as the right to a fair trial, with concerns regarding the privacy of litigants and witnesses and the maintenance of effective law enforcement. The authors in this part discuss the degree of openness which the *Charter* demands.

David Lepofsky reviews the important open justice litigation and the resulting jurisprudence arising from the claims which media outlets and others have made against the justice system from 1984 to mid-1990. He finds that Canadian courts have ventured substantially beyond the common law demands of open justice and have fashioned a more sensible approach than the one which previously prevailed, while remaining distinct from the course plotted by American courts. He closes his analysis with a critical review of the rhetoric which has tended to predominate the debate about open justice.

Harold Levy defends the media's role as the surrogate for the public eye in the court room. By focusing on the judicial performance in a number of specific closed court incidents, he attempts to show that there can be no fair trial without a free press. In each of the instances he cites, injustice would have ensued had the press not intervened. Levy examines the harm that could result from closed court proceedings and critically examines some proposals for further secrecy.

Stanley Cohen focuses on the Law Reform Commission of Canada's proposals on public and media access to the courts. He discusses the difficulty of accommodating all of the demands on the system while maintaining an adversarial process, and reviews the limitations which have been placed on open justice by the judiciary. Cohen reviews some of the major proposals by the commission regarding reform of the law, none of which has received any legislative expression to date.

OPEN JUSTICE 1990: THE CONSTITUTIONAL RIGHT TO ATTEND AND REPORT ON COURT PROCEEDINGS IN CANADA

M. David Lepofsky*

---

*   The author is counsel with the Constitutional Law and Policy Division, Ontario Ministry of the Attorney General. This article is written in the author's personal capacity and does not purport to represent the views of Ontario's Attorney General or his Ministry. As it is appropriate for me to indicate to the reader on which of the cases cited in this article I served as counsel or as co-counsel, those cases are noted at their initial citation by an asterisk (*).

I. INTRODUCTION

A. General

In the nine years since the *Charter*'s enactment, no subject has secured as much judicial attention under the *Charter*'s free expression guarantee as the question of the public's right to attend court proceedings, and to report on these proceedings to others. *Charter* s. 2(b) provides, as a part of the supreme law of Canada,[1] that "Everyone has the ... freedom of ... expression including freedom of the press and other media of communication."[2] Under the rubric of this and other *Charter* provisions, representatives of the organized media, accused persons, victims' rights groups, police and prosecutors have been embroiled in an unprecedented debate in the judicial forum over the meaning of Canada's concept of open justice. Paralleling the litigation

---

1   *Constitution Act, 1982*, being Schcd. B of the *Canada Act 1982*, 1982 (Eng.), c. 11, s. 52(1).
2   *Canadian Charter of Rights and Freedoms*, s. 2(b), Pt. I of the *Constitution Act, 1982*, provides, in its entirety, as follows:
       "2. Everyone has the following fundamental freedoms:
       "(b) freedom of thought, belief, opinion and expression, including freedom of the press and other media of communication."

over this topic are fresh examinations of it by Parliament, and by the Law Reform Commission of Canada.[3] This intense public and legal scrutiny focuses on the branch of Canada's governing institutions which has the greatest power to control reports, discussions and criticism of its activities, namely, the judiciary.

Several years ago, my book entitled *Open Justice — The Constitutional Right to Attend and Speak About Criminal Proceedings in Canada* explored the state of Canadian and U.S. law in this area up to early 1984.[4] Six years have passed since the research for that book was completed. A volume of new judicial decisions has accumulated in the interim. The time has thus come to update this book. The purpose of this article is, therefore, to examine the constitutional developments in the open justice field from early 1984 to mid-1990.

This article is divided into four parts. This first part introduces the subject, and brings the reader up to date on Canada's legal approach to open justice as of the completion of my book on this subject. It begins with a review of the core conclusions which were identified in *Open Justice*. It then summarizes the three phases which have occurred in the evolution of Canada's approach to open justice, in a general overview. Thereafter, the core purposes which are served by Canada's new constitutional regime of open justice are surveyed.

In part II, the contents of the various *Charter* provisions are reviewed as they apply to the affirmative rights of the press and public in relation to the openness of our justice system. This part surveys the various constitutional claims of rights which have been advanced under the *Charter*, and which, if valid, would require governmental justifications to be adduced under *Charter* s. 1.

Part III explores the scope of the state's power to limit the public's right to attend and report on court proceedings, under the s. 1 "reasonable limits" clause. This part reviews the content of the s. 1 test, canvasses the governmental policy objectives which can be advanced to justify limits on open justice, and then explores the validity of specific attempts to limit open justice.

Finally, part IV provides an overview of the current state of Canada's constitutional system of open justice. A comparison is offered between the treatment of open justice under the Canadian and American constitutions. This is followed by concluding reflections on some of

---

3   See Law Reform Commission of Canada, *Public and Media Access to the Criminal Process*, Working Paper 56 (Ottawa: Law Reform Commission of Canada, 1987).

4   See M.D. Lepofsky, *Open Justice - The Constitutional Right to Attend and Speak about Criminal Proceedings* (Toronto: Butterworths, 1985); hereinafter cited as Lepofsky, *Open Justice*.

the rhetorical claims which are advanced in debates over open justice issues, both in court and in legislative and policy discussions.

B. Evolution of Canada's Approach to Open Justice

As long as society has had an organized system for the administration of justice through courts, it has been confronted by the open justice question. This question asks: to what extent are members of the public, including the media, permitted to attend court proceedings as observers, and to report to others what they have seen transpiring there? At this question's core is the controversy over how well the concepts of justice and openness can live together. If court proceedings are closed, or subject to publication bans, can justice be administered? Does closed justice become secret injustice? On the other hand, where courts are open to public attendance and media reporting, can justice be achieved? Can open court at times amount to open injustice?

As documented in *Open Justice*,[5] several fundamental values vie for vindication when one explores open justice's core content. These include freedom of expression and press, the public's so-called "right to know" about the events occurring in court, the accused's interest in having a fair trial, the court participants' interest in their personal privacy and their reputation, the maintenance of the authority of courts, and the public's interest in winning the war on crime and in ensuring that justice is properly administered. In fashioning a society's system of open justice, the most efficacious way to reconcile and further these often competing goals is neither easy nor obvious. When addressing open justice issues, it is tempting for a court to reflexively fasten upon those values in this list which have the most intuitive appeal, or the seemingly greatest urgency on the immediate case's facts. Yet, the complexity of the open justice question is so profound that this "ad hocracy" leads only to contradictory results and incoherent jurisprudence.

The evolution of Canada's treatment of the open justice question, including its effort at reconciling these diverse fundamental values, is divided into three phases. The first phase occurred during the period of the several decades leading up to April 1982 — the pre-*Charter* era. During this period, the public's entitlement to attend and report on court proceedings was entirely governed by regular statute law and common law. There existed no constitutional right to attend and report on court proceedings before the *Charter*.[6] In one case,[7] an appellate court

---

5   See Lepofsky, *Open Justice, ibid.*, at 11-12.
6   Before the *Charter*, the Supreme Court had flirted with the idea of an "implied" constitutional right of freedom of expression, especially in the political arena.

had construed the free press clause of the statutory *Canadian Bill of Rights* as giving the media a right to attend court. However, the *Canadian Bill of Rights* was generally treated as simply statutory, and not constitutional in character.[8]

Under the pre-*Charter* regime of statute and common law, there prevailed a strong legal presumption that criminal proceedings were to be held in the presence of the public.[9] However, there were a number of substantial restrictions imposed both by statute and common law on public attendance and on media publications about criminal proceedings.[10] Of these, the most invasive were the common law offences of *sub judice* contempt of court, and of scandalizing the court. The *sub judice* contempt rule banned any pre-trial publications which might have a reasonable tendency to prejudice a fair trial, or to interfere with the administration of justice in an upcoming case.[11] The crime of contempt of court by scandalizing the court prohibited publications or public statements which were critical of the courts, of a judge, or of a judicial decision, if such statements had the reasonable tendency to bring the administration of justice into disrepute.[12]

The definition of these offences was very vague, and so, imposed a substantial chill on publications about court proceedings. The truth of the published statement was a defence in the case of neither offence. In both cases, a statement could give rise to a conviction if it simply had a reasonable tendency to adversely affect the justice system. An accused was not exculpated by proof that their statement ultimately did not, in fact, have any prejudicial effect.[13]

In imposing restrictions on access to and reports about a court proceeding during the pre-*Charter* era, it was unnecessary for either Parliament or the courts to be satisfied that these restrictions were in fact needed in a particular case to protect the right to a fair trial or the proper administration of justice. In the contempt of court context, courts paid free speech only minimal lip service in fashioning and applying legal

---

(See, *e.g.*, the *Alberta Press* case, *Ref. re Alta. Legislation*, [1938] S.C.R. 100, affirmed (*sub nom. A.G. Alta v. A.G. Can.*) [1939] A.C. 117 (P.C.).) However, this case law was downplayed in the 1970s (see, *e.g., A.G. Can. v. Montreal*, [1978] 2 S.C.R. 770). It was never construed so as to include a constitutional right to attend and report on court proceedings.

7   *F.P. Publications (Western) Ltd. v. Conner Prov. J.* (1980), 51 C.C.C. (2d) 110 (Man. C.A.).

8   See W.S. Tarnopolsky, *The Canadian Bill of Rights*, 2nd ed. (Toronto: McClelland and Stewart, 1975).

9   See Lepofsky, *Open Justice, supra*, note 4 at 23 *ff.*

10   *Ibid.*, at 32 *ff.*

11   *Ibid.*, at 55 *ff.*

12   *Ibid.*, at 93 *ff.*

13   *Ibid.*, at 56.

principles in the case law.[14] Legislative provisions generally imposed non-publication requirements mandatorily, or automatically at the request of a party. There was generally no statutory requirement for a court to consider whether a case's specific circumstances necessitated the imposition of restrictions on freedom of expression during this first phase in the evolution of Canada's approach to open justice.[15]

At the same time as the law imposed extensive restrictions on access to, and reports about, judicial proceedings in the pre-*Charter* era, particularly in the name of securing an accused's right to a fair trial, the pre-*Charter* law did not serve effectively to protect an accused whose fair trial was in fact prejudiced by media publicity. Under the then prevailing case law, it was exceedingly difficult, if not impossible, to have a conviction reversed on the ground that a fair trial was prejudiced by publicity.[16] Hence, in the pre-*Charter* era, the law insufficiently protected both freedom of expression and the right to a fair trial. This was so despite claims that both of these interests were fundamental to Canadian justice.[17]

The second phase in the evolution of Canada's treatment of open justice occurred during the first year or two after the *Charter*'s enactment. During this period, Canada's Constitution provided a firm foundation for extensive judicial review of the pre-*Charter* restrictions on attendance at court and reporting on court proceedings.[18] However, with few exceptions, Canadian trial and appellate courts approached the *Charter* with great hesitancy and serious reluctance. Lower courts appeared to be awaiting some signal from the Supreme Court of Canada on whether the *Charter* was to be judicially enforced with greater vigour than the moribund statutory *Canadian Bill of Rights*.[19] Accordingly, during this second phase, Canadian courts often were unwilling to employ the *Charter* to reconsider the propriety of existing restrictions on open justice.[20] For the public and the media, the second phase did not result in any dramatic change from the pre-*Charter* era.

The third phase of the evolution of Canada's approach to open justice began at the time that the Supreme Court of Canada started handing down *Charter* rulings, and continues to the present. Beginning

---

14 *Ibid.*, at 57 *ff.*
15 *Ibid.*, at 56.
16 *Ibid.*, at 19-20.
17 See, *e.g., ibid.*, at 49 *ff.*, and *R. v. B. (C.R.)* (1982), 30 C.R. (3d) 80 (Ont. H.C.), *per* Smith J.
18 Lepofsky, *ibid.*, c. 5.
19 See, *e.g., R. v. Potma* (1982), 136 D.L.R. (3d) 69 (Ont. H.C.), *per* Eberle J.
20 See Lepofksy, *Open Justice, supra*, note 4 at 219 *ff.* The greatest exception to this trend in the *Charter*'s initial two years was in the Ontario Court of Appeal's decision in *Re Southam Inc. and R. (No. 1)* (1983), 3 C.C.C. (3d) 515, discussed further, *infra*.

with its first *Charter* decision,[21] the Supreme Court made it clear through an early line of rulings that the *Charter* was to be taken very seriously, that its rights were to be interpreted in a liberal fashion, and that governmental power to place limits on these rights pursuant to the *Charter*'s "reasonable limits" clause was to be construed narrowly.[22] Canadian courts began to recognize more forcefully that open justice is now a constitutional requirement and that the power to restrict public attendance at court and media reporting on legal proceedings is to be tolerated only in the narrowest range of circumstances. During this third phase, the Supreme Court of Canada has been in the lead in fashioning a new, more principled and potent approach to open justice. Lower Canadian courts have often lagged behind the Supreme Court somewhat, with a mixed performance. In some instances, lower courts have taken a less principled and liberal approach to open justice, and so, have appeared to be stalled in the second era of the evolution of open justice. In fashioning a new and uniquely Canadian conception of open justice, those Canadian courts which have proceeded beyond this second phase have gone on to reconsider the balance to be struck among the fundamental values at stake in this area. As described further in the balance of this essay, our courts in many instances have plotted a course which is a distinct distance from both the pre-*Charter* Canadian position on open justice, and which at the same time is different from the current U.S. constitutional approach to open justice.

C. Goals Served by Open Justice

In enunciating general principles for interpreting the *Charter*, the Supreme Court of Canada has ruled that the rights and freedoms set out in it must be given a purposive construction. By this, a court determines the content of a *Charter* right by first ascertaining the purposes which that right is intended to achieve, and by then fashioning a construction of the right which most effectively advances those purposes.[23] This exercise is carried out with an eye to the *Charter*'s overall goals. These goals include the unremitting protection of basic human rights, and the securing of a free and democratic society for Canada which is based on a fundamental commitment to freedom, equality and social justice.[24]

---

21 See *L.S.U.C. v. Skapinker*, [1984] 1 S.C.R. 357 [Ont.].
22 See *Hunter, Dir. of Investigation & Research, Combines Investigation Branch v. Southam Inc.*, [1984] 2 S.C.R. 145 [Alta.]; *R. v. Big M Drug Mart Ltd.*, [1985] 1 S.C.R. 295 [Alta.]; *R. v. Oakes*, [1986] 1 S.C.R. 103 [Ont.].
23 See *Hunter v. Southam, ibid.*, at 156 *ff.*
24 *Ibid.* See also *R. v. Big M Drug Mart, supra*, note 22 at 336 *ff.*; *R. v. Oakes, supra*, note 22.

To identify the purposes served by the *Charter*'s commitment to open justice, it is first necessary to review the purposes which are served in general by the *Charter*'s guarantee of freedom of expression. Then, it is appropriate to examine the purposes which Canadian courts recognized in the pre-*Charter* era for the traditional commitment to open courts. Finally, it is necessary to turn to the specific purposes for freedom of expression in relation to the justice system which have been judicially recognized under the *Charter*.

The Supreme Court has acknowledged, at least to some extent, a number of objectives which are served in general by the *Charter*'s guarantee of freedom of expression. These include the securing of democratic self-government, achieving good or intelligent government, fostering participation in political and social decision-making, providing a balance between stability and change in society, facilitating the search for truth and knowledge through a marketplace of ideas, promoting social pluralism and diversity, safeguarding individual autonomy and self-development, and providing the necessary underpinning for other rights and freedoms in society.[25] These objectives overlap. Some have secured greater judicial attention than others.

Before the *Charter*, Canadian courts had recognized a number of values which are served by the openness of courts to public attendance. Openness of the courts serves to promote the effective administration of justice, to prevent abuse of the individual by judges, prosecutors or police, to ensure public scrutiny of the courts, to foster public confidence in the administration of justice, to foster the giving of honest testimony, and to ensure that justice is not only done, but is seen to be done.[26] However, in identifying these functions, Canadian courts in the pre-*Charter* era did not generally link them to the fundamental value of freedom of expression. Indeed, with rare exception,[27] freedom of expression and press received little or no mention in judicial discussions of the functions served by open justice.[28]

In light of this background, what have Canadian courts said about the values served by freedom of expression in relation to open justice under the *Charter*? In *Edmonton Journal v. Alta. (A.G.)*,[29] the Supreme

---

25 See *R.W.D.S.U., Loc. 580 v. Dolphin Delivery Ltd.*, [1986] 2 S.C.R. 573 [B.C.]; *Ford v. Qué. (P.G.)*, [1988] 2 S.C.R. 712; *Irwin Toy Ltd. v. Qué. (A.G.)*, [1989] 1 S.C.R. 927. See generally, M.D. Lepofsky, "Towards a Purposive Approach to Freedom of Expression and its Limitation," in F.E. McArdle (ed.), *The Cambridge Lectures 1989* (Montreal: Les Éditions Yvon Blais, 1990).

26 See *Lepofsky, Open Justice, supra*, note 4 at 47. See also *MacIntyre v. N.S. (A.G.)*, [1982] 1 S.C.R. 175 at 183, *per* Dickson J. (as he then was).

27 See *R. v. Quesnel* (1979), 51 C.C.C. (2d) 270 (Ont. C.A.).

28 See Lepofsky, *Open Justice, supra*, note 4 at 47 *ff*.

29 *(1989), 64 D.L.R. (4th) 577 (S.C.C.).

Court of Canada reiterated the fundamental values served by public access to courts, as enunciated in the pre-*Charter* case law.[30] It went further by explicitly linking the importance of public access to the court room to the important functions served by the freedom to report to others on events observed there.[31] The court did not specifically link the specific requirement of the open court room to the actual content of the *Charter*'s guarantee of freedom of expression. However, it acknowledged a direct nexus between the goals served by the requirement of openness on the one hand, and the purposes served by free communication about courts on the other.

The Supreme Court has enujciated additional goals served by freedom of expression in relation to the open courts, beyond those recognized in the pre-*Charter* access jurisprudence. It recognized that free expression about courts promotes the rule of law. Communications about court also foster the levelling of constructive criticism of court behaviour.[33]

In a concurring opinion, Wilson J. suggested in *Edmonton Journal* that, by promoting the integrity of the trial process, the openness of courts fosters confidence in the justice system on the part of the public and on the part of the litigants who submit themselves to that process.[34] She opined that the benefits of openness are not restricted to criminal trials. In matrimonial proceedings, judges can disclose their own attitudes towards interpersonal relationships. Freedom of expression enables the public to learn about these attitudes, and to respond negatively to them if they are out of touch with current community values.[35] This will contribute to the improved functioning of the courts.[36]

Wilson J. also held in *Edmonton Journal* that publicity about courts generally serves to educate the public on the operation of courts.[37] At the same time, it can contribute positively to the catharsis that litigants can experience during a trial, because they are afforded a public opportunity to seek rectification of injustices from which they have suffered in silence until then.[38]

In sum, the Supreme Court has maintained a critical jurisprudential link with the past, by reaffirming under the *Charter* the traditional rationalia for open justice. At the same time, it has broken with the past, by linking those rationalia not only to the tradition of open court, but

30   *Ibid.*, at 607-608, *per* Cory J.
31   *Ibid.*, at 610.
33   *Ibid.*, at 611.
34   *Ibid.*, at 587, *per* Wilson J., concurring in part.
35   *Ibid.*, at 587-88.
36   *Ibid.*
37   *Ibid.*, at 588.
38   *Ibid.*, at 588-89.

with the constitutional guarantee of freedom of expression as well. It has also supplemented these traditional rationalia with new societal and individual purposes served by freedom of expression in relation to the courts.

In charting this new ground, the Supreme Court has laid an ample jurisprudential foundation for the evolution of important new constitutional protections for open justice. This could be enhanced if the court were to further elaborate on the values served by freedom of expression and open justice. There is room for the judicial recognition of additional values intrinsic to the constitutional concept of open justice. For example, publicity of court proceedings does not simply provide a vehicle for catharsis for parties to a court case; it also provides an avenue for community catharsis. Thus, in the case of a notorious and shocking crime, the publicized conviction and sentencing of the offender provides society with an outlet for the strong emotions which can build up in the wake of the initial news of the crime. As well, in the *Charter* era, when more and more important public policy questions are litigated in court, freedom of expression in relation to the open justice system provides the disadvantaged in society with the opportunity to secure needed public attention for their plight during their court proceedings. This links the openness of the courts to the goal of fostering social reform.

Bearing in mind both this historical perspective on the Canadian approach to open justice and the purposes served by open justice, attention can now turn to the contents of the specific rights which the *Charter* guarantees in relation to open justice.

II. CONTENT OF THE CHARTER'S GUARANTEES IN RELATION TO OPEN JUSTICE AS OF 1990

A. Introduction

This part surveys the content of those *Charter* rights which address the openness of Canada's justice system. The purpose of this discussion is to enumerate the core content of the public's constitutional rights concerning open justice which the *Charter* guarantees, subject to the government's mandate under *Charter* s. 1 to place reasonable limits on them. A number of claims have been advanced under *Charter* ss. 2(b), 7, 11(d) and 15 in this area. Some have been judicially accepted, while others have been rejected. The net result is that the *Charter* enshrines a potent guarantee of open justice, principally comprising a right to attend judicial proceedings, and to disseminate reports to others about the events occurring in court.

B. Right of Public to Attend Court Proceedings under *Charter* Section 2(b)

Within about a year of the *Charter*'s proclamation, Canadian courts began to recognize that the *Charter*'s free expression guarantee in s. 2(b) includes a constitutionalization of the common law tradition of holding court in public.[39] While there was initially some division in provincial superior courts about this view,[40] the Ontario Court of Appeal ultimately rendered a strong ruling, affirming that the public, including the media, have a s. 2(b) right to attend court proceedings.[41] In *Re Southam Inc. and R. (No. 1)*,[42] the Ontario Court of Appeal held that the right to attend juvenile delinquency proceedings is an integral and implicit part of the *Charter*'s free expression guarantee.

Although the media brought this *Charter* challenge, the court described the media's right to attend as forming part of the general rights of all individuals. The court declined to frame it as a special right of the media deriving from s. 2(b)'s free press clause. The reporters' right to attend is no greater than that of the public generally.[43] Of course, the s. 2(b) right of public access to court is open to restrictions, if justifiable under the s. 1 reasonable limits clause. This ruling is frequently cited with approval[44] and has in effect become Canada's leading authority on the point.

Standing in marked contrast to the trend of lower court open justice jurisprudence is *A. v. B., Southam Inc. and C.*[45] There, the Quebec Court of Appeal upheld the validity of a Quebec Superior Court's order, denying public access to a civil action court file, and banning publication of the identities of the parties to that proceeding. This order per-

---

39 *Re Southam Inc. and R. (No. 1), supra*, note 20.
40 Compare *Re Can. Newspapers Co. and R.* (1983), 6 C.C.C. (3d) 488 (B.C.S.C.), recognizing a s. 2(b) right of public access to court proceedings, with *Edmonton Journal v. A.G. Alta.* (1983), 4 C.C.C. (3d) 59 (Q.B.), where the Alberta Court of Queen's Bench rejected such an approach.
41 *Re Southam Inc. and R. (No. 1), supra*, note 20.
42 *Ibid.*
43 *Ibid.* See also *R. v. R.(T.) (No. 1)* (1984), 7 D.L.R. (4th) 205 at 208-209 (Alta. Q.B.).
44 See, *e.g., R. v. Thomson Newspapers Ltd.**, 11 W.C.B. 436 (Ont. H.C.) (December 8, 1983), *per* Anderson J.; *Can. Newspapers Co. v. Can. (A.G.)*, 49 O.R. (2d) 557, reversed *[1988] 2 S.C.R. 122; *Squires v. R.* *(1986), 50 C.R. (3d) 320 (Prov.Ct.), affirmed *69 C.R. (3d) 337 (Dist.Ct.), leave to appeal to Ont. C.A. granted 25th October 1990 (not yet reported); *Southam Inc. v. R.* (1984), 48 O.R. (2d) 678, affirmed 53 O.R. (2d) 663 (C.A.); *Southam Inc. v. Coulter* (1990), 75 O.R. (2d) 1 (C.A.).
45 Que. C.A., Nos. 500-09-001495-894, 500-05-006042-897, 20th August 1990 (not yet reported).

tained to a university student's civil action against certain defendants for committing a gang sexual assault against her.

The Court of Appeal held that the sealing and non-publication orders do not infringe s. 2(b) rights for two reasons, each of which is seriously flawed. First, it held that s. 2(b) is sufficiently respected where the Quebec Civil Code provides that court proceedings are generally open to the public, except in cases where the court exercises discretion to exclude the public or to ban certain reporting.[46] No s. 2(b) infringement occurs when this discretionary power is actually exercised to exclude the public or to ban reports of some aspect of the case. In other words, so long as the law generally requires justice to be administered in the open, there is no s. 2(b) infringement in a particular case where public access or publication is prohibited. There is, thus, no need to advance a s. 1 justification, even if public access or publications are banned in a case whose circumstances do not require such restrictions. This reasoning is defective. From the *Charter* plaintiff's perspective, one's rights are no less infringed in a particular case, simply because there may be other cases where no infringement has occurred.

Second, the Quebec Court of Appeal held that the *Charter* does not even apply at all to orders excluding the public from a case, sealing the court record, or banning reports of specified information about the case.[47] The court relied on the Supreme Court of Canada decision in *Retail, Wholesale and Department Store Workers Union, Local 580 v. Dolphin Delivery Ltd.*[49] which had held that the *Charter* does not apply to purely private litigation. Because the impugned restrictions on disclosure and publication were made in the context of a private lawsuit, the Quebec court held that the *Charter* could not invalidate these orders.

In so holding, the Quebec court grossly over-extended the reach of *Dolphin Delivery*.[50] That case does not immunize from *Charter* scrutiny all court orders made during private litigation. Here, the court order was made pursuant to a legislative provision. To the extent that the legislative provision purports to authorize the making of an order which infringes *Charter* rights, it must be tested under the *Charter*. If not justified under s. 1, the authorizing statute is unconstitutional to the extent that it mandates unconstitutional orders.[51]

---

46 *Ibid.*, at 14 *ff.*, *per* Monet J.A.
47 *Ibid.*, at 11 *ff.*
49 *Supra*, note 25.
50 It is strongly arguable that *Dolphin Delivery*, *ibid.*, was wrongly decided. On its face, it purports to place judicial conduct above the Constitution, in the context of private common law, a context where courts have been subject to the least democratic mandating of their actions. Its reasoning is itself contradictory. It is reasonable to expect that, in the future, the Supreme Court will either reverse *Dolphin Delivery* or substantially narrow its reach.
51 See s. 52 of the *Constitution Act, 1982*, *supra*, note 1.

The Supreme Court of Canada has not yet pronounced on the question of whether s. 2(b) confers on the press and public a constitutional right to attend court proceedings. In pre-*Charter* jurisprudence, the Supreme Court has emphasized the fundamental importance of the common law's open court requirement.[52] In *Edmonton Journal v. Alberta (A.G.)*,[53] the Supreme Court proclaimed with vigour the importance of open court, and of the *Charter*'s guarantee in s. 2(b) of a right to report to others on court proceedings. However, the leap from a common law requirement of open court to a supreme constitutional requirement of such does not necessarily and automatically follow from the Supreme Court's treatment of freedom of expression to date.

The Supreme Court has elaborated on freedom of expression as encompassing the right to communicate through speech, picketing, or other activity which is intended to convey meaning.[54] At a minimum, an exercise of freedom of expression must include some activity which constitutes "expression." "Expression" is defined by the Supreme Court as action, apart from violence, which is intended to convey meaning to others.[55] Because public attendance at a court proceeding is not itself speech, or activity which itself conveys meaning, a person's attendance at court could not fall within the Supreme Court's current definition of s. 2(b).

The Ontario Court of Appeal's determination that s. 2(b) includes a constitutional right to attend court proceedings was reached before the Supreme Court had pronounced on the meaning of s. 2(b). Hence, it includes no attempt to link attendance at court with the Supreme Court's approach to s. 2(b). The Supreme Court would now have to articulate a new and expanded test for identifying the content of s. 2(b) before that provision could be seen as incorporating a public constitutional right of access to court proceedings.

If there is a constitutional right to attend judicial proceedings under *Charter* s. 2(b), what is the scope of this right? The constitutional open court principle applies not only to youth court proceedings, but to a wide range of judicial proceedings as well. These include, for example, civil child protection cases[56] and proceedings before a justice of the peace,

---

52   See *MacIntyre v. N.S. (A.G.)*, *supra*, note 26.
53   *Supra*, note 29.
54   See *Ford v. Qué. (P.G.)*, *supra*, note 25; *Irwin Toy Ltd. v. Que. (A.G.)*, *supra*, note 25; *Dolphin Delivery*, *supra*, note 25.
55   See *Irwin Toy*, *ibid.*
56   See also *M.(Y.) v. Children's Aid Soc.* (1989), 65 D.L.R. (4th) 427 (N.S. Co.Ct.), which took this *Charter* ruling into account in deciding to admit a reporter to closed child protection proceedings, pursuant to a statutory discretion to permit media access to an otherwise closed child protection trial.

where the justice considers whether to issue process against a person concerning whom an information has been laid.[57]

Would a constitutional right to attend court include within it a right to inspect court documents which form part of the record of a judicial proceeding? This issue has not been decided authoritatively in the constitutional realm. It has been held as a matter of common law that the public's right to attend judicial proceedings includes the right to inspect documents which form part of the public record.[58] At common law, this right of inspection applies to documents pertaining to all stages of the judicial process, including both the pre-trial and trial phases.[59] It is subject only to the authority of the court to exclude public inspection, in order to secure a social objective of superordinate importance, pursuant to the court's inherent jurisdiction over its records.[60] This common law right does not, however, include a right of a reporter to demand that a court official search through a large number of informations or other court documents, to determine who was charged with a particular offence, in circumstances where the reporter does not know the accused's name.[61]

It is reasonable to expect that those courts which construe s. 2(b) as including a constitutional right to attend court will also find a right of inspection within that *Charter* provision. This is so since the constitutional right to attend court is strongly rooted in the common law right of public access. As well, *Charter* court access decisions often cite with approval the Supreme Court's common law public access ruling.[62]

---

57 See *Can. Newspapers Co. v. R.* (1987), 38 C.C.C. (3d) 187 at 191 (Ont. H.C.), applying *Re Southam Inc. and R. (No. 1), supra*, note 20, to proceedings under s. 455.3 of the *Criminal Code*. See also *Southam Inc. v. Coulter, supra*, note 44.
58 See *MacIntyre v. N.S. (A.G.), supra*, note 26.
59 *Ibid.*
60 *Ibid.*
61 In *London Free Press Printing Co. v. Ont. (A.G.)* (1988), 66 O.R. (2d) 693 (H.C.), a reporter learned at a police press conference that a large number of persons had been charged with certain sexual offences, but was not able to obtain the accuseds' names from the police. He asked court officials to search through all informations on court record for a specified period of time, to locate the names of the accused. For reasons of cost and staff time, court officials refused. Holding that the case did not appear to raise any *Charter* issues, the Supreme Court of Ontario dismissed an application for an order requiring the officials to do the reporter's search. It held that the reporter's right of access at common law was sufficiently respected where the court officials had offered to produce the desired charging information, only if the reporter provided the officials with the accuseds' names, so as to make the search practicable.
62 See, *e.g., Re Southam Inc. and R. (No. 1), supra*, note 20, citing *MacIntyre, supra*, note 26, with approval.

C. Right to Report on Facts of Court Proceedings

It would have seemed obvious from the *Charter*'s inception that a core component of s. 2(b)'s free expression guarantee is an entitlement to publish, broadcast or otherwise disseminate accurate reports of factual information about events occurring in open court. This would have seemed especially self-evident where the disseminated information was lawfully obtained through one's attendance at an open court proceeding. However, in the *Charter*'s earliest years, this proposition was not free from doubt. During the first two years of the *Charter* era (that is, during the second phase of the evolution of Canada's approach to open justice), some courts contemplated that s. 2(b) was not absolute. They contended in some cases that s. 2(b) contained internal limitations which could go so far as to permit restrictions on media reporting on courts in some situations.[63]

However, it is now beyond dispute that s. 2(b) is infringed where a law restricts the publication of factual information about a court proceeding, whether that restriction is permanent or only temporary. In *Edmonton Journal v. Alta. (A.G.)*,[64] the Supreme Court of Canada found that a provision of Alberta's *Judicature Act*[65] infringed *Charter* s. 2(b) where it imposed sweeping, permanent restrictions on the publication of information about a matrimonial case, either before or after the proceeding. The offending provision also banned virtually all pre-hearing publications about a civil case, except for the scant information that one would find in a writ of summons. Similarly, the Supreme Court held in *Canadian Newspapers Co. v. Can. (A.G.)*[66] that a court order, under s. 442(3) (now s. 486(3)) of the *Criminal Code*, which permanently bans publication of the identity of a sexual assault complainant, violates s. 2(b) rights.

In both of these Supreme Court cases, the parties before the court conceded that the impugned legislation infringed s. 2(b),[67] with one exception. In *Canadian Newspapers*,[68] the Women's Legal Education and Action Fund (LEAF) intervened in the appeal on its behalf and on behalf of a coalition of sexual assault victims' counselling organizations,

---

63 See, *e.g., R. v. Banville* (1983), 3 C.C.C. (3d) 312 (N.B.Q.B.), *per* Harper Prov. J.; *Re Global Communications and A.G. Can.* (1984), 10 C.C.C. (3d) 97 (Ont. C.A.).

64 *Supra*, note 29.

65 R.S.A. 1980, c. J-1, s. 30.

66 *[1988] 2 S.C.R. 122.

67 The fact that parties before the court concede that a law infringes *Charter* s. 2(b) does not remove from the court its important obligation to assess for itself whether there has been a *prima facie* infringement of that right. Constitutional findings cannot be made simply through the consent of parties before the court.

68 *Supra*, note 66.

to defend the legislated protection which s. 442(3) of the *Criminal Code* provides to sexual assault victims. LEAF argued, among other things, that a judicial ban on media identification of a sexual assault complainant did not infringe s. 2(b). They contended that s. 2(b) should be internally constrained by *Charter* s. 15's guarantee of equality to women. The effect of publishing sexual assault complainants' names would be to deter reporting of sexual crimes against women, and to let more male offenders go unpunished, LEAF submitted. Because s. 442(3) of the *Criminal Code* promotes the equality of women, and especially women's access to justice, s. 2(b) should not be construed as subverting such an egalitarian initiative.

The Supreme Court implicitly rejected LEAF's argument in *Canadian Newspapers*,[69] since it found that s. 442(3) of the *Criminal Code* infringed *Charter* s. 2(b). The judgment itself makes no reference to the LEAF argument, and sets out its s. 2(b) finding in only a brief passage.[70] It seems especially ironic that the Supreme Court did not squarely address LEAF's s. 2(b) argument in *Canadian Newspapers*, since, in its later decision in *Edmonton Journal v. Alberta (A.G.)*,[71] the court went on at great length about the purposes, rationale and importance of publications about court proceedings, in a case where, unlike *Canadian Newspapers*, no party disputed that the impugned restrictions on such publications breached s. 2(b).

When the Supreme Court decisions in *Canadian Newspapers*[72] and *Edmonton Journal*[73] are taken together, it is clear that *Charter* s. 2(b) is breached whenever a party is restrained from publishing factual information about a case, whether the infringement takes the form of an automatic statutory ban on publication or is comprised of an individual judicial order banning publication. For s. 2(b) purposes, the difference between judicial prior restraints on publication and statutory subsequent punishments of publication appears to have little or no significance. There is, of course, still room for such to have relevance under s. 1, though this has received little or no judicial consideration to date in the highest court.

Standing in marked contrast to this compelling Supreme Court jurisprudence are two lower court decisions on the scope of s. 2(b), as it relates to the freedom to publish information about a court proceeding. In the Manitoba Court of Appeal decision in *Manitoba (A.G.) v. Groupe Quebecor Inc.*,[74] a media establishment's conviction for *sub judice* con-

---

69   *Ibid.*
70   *Ibid.*, at 129.
71   *Supra*, note 29.
72   *Supra*, note 66.
73   *Supra*, note 29.
74   (1987), 45 D.L.R. (4th) 80.

tempt of court was upheld as constitutional. Upon the arrest of two murder suspects, the police department called a press conference, during which the police described the arrestees' criminal records. A media outlet was charged with the common law crime of contempt out of the face of the court for publishing this information. This offence prohibits publication of matters before trial which may tend to prejudice a fair trial. The media outlet was convicted, despite the fact that the trial was still a long way off, and despite the absence of any intent to interfere with a fair trial.[75]

The Manitoba Court of Appeal rejected the media's claim that the contempt conviction infringed the constitutional right to freedom of the press under *Charter* s. 2(b). Relying on pre-*Charter* jurisprudence, the court held that the *Charter*'s free expression provision only includes a guarantee of freedom of speech circumscribed by law.[76] This implies that *any* legal restrictions on publications by the media are consistent with *Charter* s. 2(b). This conclusion flies in the face of the *Charter*'s supremacy over all ordinary legislation.[77]

The Manitoba court ruled that s. 2(b)'s guarantee of "freedom" is not absolute, and contains internal limits which can be imposed without a need to resort to *Charter* s. 1.[78] These limits include restrictions imposed to protect the rights of others, the court held. The *sub judice* contempt offence was found not to infringe s. 2(b) because it is aimed at protecting the accused's fair trial rights.[79]

The court did not consider whether the impugned publication had in fact prejudiced the accused's fair trial. Because the police's press conference statements were published well in advance of the trial, it may have turned out that a jury could be selected, or indeed that one was selected, which was unaware of the media's reports of the accused's criminal records. In that event, the contempt conviction could not be sustained as a measure needed to protect the accused's right to a fair trial.

The Manitoba court took the unprecedented view that:[80]

> The right of the accused persons to a fair trial cannot be debated publicly before the verdict is rendered without prejudice to the very interest that the right is intended to protect. The freedom of the press

---

75 *Ibid.*, at 91. Because the Court of Appeal did not offer any reasons specifically focusing on this argument, future attempts in lower courts at similar lines of argument might be reconsidered on their merits.

76 *Ibid.*, at 94, *per* Twaddle J.A.

77 See *Constitution Act, 1982*, s. 52(1), and *Hunter v. Southam, supra,* note 22.

78 *Supra,* note 74 at 95 *ff.*, *per* Twaddle J.A.

79 *Ibid.*, at 97.

80 *Ibid.*

may even be enhanced by the requirement that the press delay the publication of information as to the antecedents of an accused person until the relevance of the information to a matter of public concern is known.

This suggests that most public discussion of any criminal case, prior to verdict, threatens the fairness of a criminal trial. Such a view is simply not borne out by a vast societal experience with media reporting on criminal cases. Moreover, the Manitoba court's suggestion that the freedom of the press is enhanced, rather than threatened, by prosecutions for the pre-trial reporting of accurate information about a case of public interest, does not withstand scrutiny if regard is had to the core purposes which freedom of expression serves in a democracy. The substantial suppression of pre-trial reporting on a criminal case of public importance or interest denies the public the opportunity to know about, discuss and debate the operations of its criminal justice system in an informed way at a time when such discussions achieve the greatest immediacy.

The *Groupe Quebecor* decision suffers from highly problematic reasoning, and appears to be wrongly decided.[81] Its result directly contradicts the Supreme Court's subsequent, and more authoritative, approach to s. 2(b) in the *Canadian Newspapers* and *Edmonton Journal* cases.[82] On the basis of those decisions, the better view is that the *sub*

---

81   It is ironic that in this case, the media was criminally punished, at the behest of the provincial Attorney General, for reporting information handed out by the police at a press conference. It would have been far more just, and more consonant with the *Charter*'s values, to have prevented this problem from arising by stopping the police from giving out such prejudicial information to the media at a press conference in the first place. Indeed, it might be seen as an abuse of process for one arm of the government, the police, to call a press conference for the avowed purpose of delivering information to the media for publication, and then for another arm of the government, the Attorney General, to prosecute the media for doing that for which the press conference was called.

In an odd, contrasting situation, see *London Free Press Printing Co. v. Ont. (A.G.), supra,* note 61, where another police force called a press conference after a mass arrest, but properly declined to divulge the name of the accused persons to the media. When a reporter asked court officials to review all charges in the court files, issued at the material time, to discover the names of the accused, the court officials refused, due to obvious practical constraints. The Supreme Court of Ontario declined to order the court officials to undertake this research project for the reporter. Yet, the court commented that if the reporter wanted the accuseds' names, he could get this information from the police. Yet, the court declined to consider that the police had acted in a commendable fashion by declining to give out this information, and that such restraint on the part of the police could avert many of the fair trial concerns which have been advanced to justify sweeping publication bans in the past.

82   *Supra,* notes 66 and 29, respectively.

judice contempt rule violates *Charter* s. 2(b), and that convictions under that rule can only be sustained under *Charter* s. 1 on facts where punishment of a media outlet is necessary to avert actual prejudice to a fair trial. This more appropriate approach to the application of s. 2(b) to the *sub judice* offence is found in the Newfoundland Supreme Court's decision in *R. v. Robinson-Blackmore Printing & Publishing Co.*[83] That case held that the *sub judice* contempt rule violates *Charter* s. 2(b) and must be justified under s. 1. While the court there claimed that s. 2(b) may contain some internal limits (which is questionable in this context in light of the Supreme Court's approach to publication bans relating to court proceedings), that decision held that where limits on expression are based on the competing rights of others, they are to be addressed under s. 1, and not under s. 2(b).[84]

In another problematic decision, the Nova Scotia Supreme Court held that the media's *Charter* s. 2(b) rights were not *prima facie* infringed by a non-publication order, during an accused's retrial on influence-peddling charges. In *R. v. Barrow*,[85] the accused was convicted at his first trial. On appeal, a new trial was ordered. A publication ban prohibited reporting of information respecting the outcome of the original trial, the sentence imposed at the first trial, the person who brought the appeal, and the appeal's disposition. The ban extended until the jury's retirement for deliberations at the second trial.

The court held that it had an inherent power to ban these publications to protect the accused's fair trial rights, even absent a legislative mandate to do so.[86] It concluded that this order did not infringe s. 2(b) rights, because it is aimed at protecting the accused's right to a fair trial. It did not explain why this consideration should be considered under s. 2(b), and not exclusively under s. 1. In light of the Supreme Court's *Canadian Newspapers* and *Edmonton Journal* rulings, this part of the *Barrow* case is no longer good law.

Despite these aberrational holdings, the vast majority of lower courts have followed the Supreme Court's lead. They have generally held that non-publication orders regarding reports about court cases *prima facie* infringe *Charter* s. 2(b), and must be justified under s. 1.[87]

---

83 (1989), 47 C.C.C. (3d) 366 (Nfld. T.D.).

84 *Ibid.*, at 374. As is discussed later in this essay, the Newfoundland court's approach to s. 1 was problematic, although its approach to s. 2(b) was not. See the text associated with notes 360-367, *infra*.

85 (1989), 48 C.C.C. (3d) 308 (N.S.T.D.).

86 In Lepofsky, *Open Justice, supra*, note 4 at 32, I argue that courts do not have any inherent power to ban publications about a case, and that such bans can only be judicially ordered if clearly authorized by legislation.

87 See, *e.g., Southam Inc. v. R., supra*, note 44; *Can. Newspapers Co. v. Can. (A.G.)* (1986), 31 D.L.R. (4th) 601 (Man. Q.B.); *Toronto Sun Publishing Corp. v. A.G. Alta.*, [1985] 6 W.W.R. 36 (Alta. C.A.).

D. Right to Criticize Courts

In addition to factual reporting on court proceedings, *Charter* s. 2(b) guarantees a constitutional right to criticize courts and judicial behaviour. Before the *Charter*, the common law substantially restricted criticism of courts. The common law crime of contempt of court included a ban on scandalization of the courts.[88] It has been a crime, punishable by fine and/or imprisonment, to make any critical statement which has a reasonable tendency to bring the administration of justice into disrepute.[89] The fact that the criticism was truthful, or that the statement did not in fact bring the administration of justice into disrepute was not a defence. If a court was satisfied that a statement had a *reasonable tendency* to bring the administration of justice into disrepute, a conviction could be sustained.[90] The contempt test was vague and discretionary. Its effect was to curtail most public criticism of courts, deserved or otherwise.

The scandalization offence's constitutionality was tested before the Ontario Court of Appeal in *R. v. Kopyto*.[91] The Supreme Court of Ontario had convicted a Toronto lawyer for contempt because of his critical comments made to the press after losing a civil Small Claims Court case. Kopyto's client had unsuccessfully sued a police officer. Kopyto was quoted as saying:[92]

> This decision is a mockery of justice. It stinks to high hell. It says it is okay to break the law and you are immune so long as someone above you said to do it. Mr. Dowson [Kopyto's client, the unsuccessful plaintiff in the civil case] and I have lost faith in the judicial system to render justice. We are wondering what is the point of appealing and continuing this charade of the courts in this country, which are warped in favour of protecting the police. The courts and the RCMP are sticking so close together that you would think they are put together with krazy glue.

Kopyto argued that the scandalization offence denied his freedom of expression. The Ontario Court of Appeal overturned his contempt conviction, in a decision which has the practical effect of repealing the scandalization offence.[93] A majority of the Court of Appeal held that s.

---

88 See generally, Lepofsky, *Open Justice, supra*, note 4 at 93 *ff.*
89 *Ibid.*
90 *Ibid.*
91 (1987), 24 O.A.C. 81.
92 *Ibid.*, at 86.
93 Compare *Garrison v. Louisiana*, 379 U.S. 64 (1964), holding that the U.S. First Amendment provides constitutional protection for criticism of judges by a district attorney, except where critical comments are proven to be made with knowledge of their falsity or reckless disregard as to their truth. There, a district

2(b) extends constitutional protection to criticism of the courts.[94] The only possible exception to this protection might be deliberately false criticism, that is, criticism of courts which involves factual allegations which the speaker knows to be untrue.[95]

As a general principle, the Supreme Court has recognized that certain kinds of expression can fall closer to s. 2(b)'s core than others.[96] For example, political speech can be more closely linked to s. 2(b)'s purposes than purely commercial speech.[97] In this context, public criticism of courts and judges, even if caustic and incisive, lies at the core of s. 2(b). It constitutes political speech targeted at an important governing institution, and concerns a matter of deep public interest.[98] It can be the forcefulness or acidity of criticism which spurs on needed social reform.[99]

Unhampered criticism of courts has always been important to Canadian society, even if its importance had not been fully judicially recognized before the *Charter*. It is increasingly essential during the *Charter* era. Since 1982, Canadian courts frequently have deliberated on critical and often controversial policy issues, such as abortion, minority language rights and gender equality. Judicial decisions in these cases must be open to intense scrutiny and criticism, in light of their profound impact on Canadian society.

Alongside the question of whether criticisms of courts may be expressed is the related question of how these criticisms may be expressed. The Supreme Court has recognized that s. 2(b) includes protection for the utterance of words, and for the engaging in physical conduct, which is intended to convey meaning.[100] This is subject to one crucial

---

attorney had accused local state judges of being lazy and inefficient, and of hampering his efforts at law enforcement. This is perhaps the converse of the *Kopyto* comments.

94 The court divided on the extent to which such criticism could be permissibly punished in accordance with *Charter* s. 1. This is discussed further in the text associated with notes 368-388, *infra*.

95 See also *R. v. Zundel* (1987), 35 D.L.R. (4th) 338 (Ont. C.A.); *New York Times v. Sullivan*, 376 U.S. 254 (1964); *Garrison v. Louisiana, supra*, note 93.

96 See, *e.g., Ref. re Criminal Code, ss. 193 & 195.1(1)(c)* (1990), 77 C.R. (3d) 1 (S.C.C.) [Man.], hereinafter the "*Prostitution Reference*"; see also *R. v. Skinner* (1990), 77 C.R. (3d) 84 (S.C.C.) [N.S.]; *R. v. Stagnitta* (1990), 74 Alta. L.R. (2d) 193 (S.C.C.).

97 See, *e.g., Rocket v. Royal College of Dental Surgeons*, [1990] 2 S.C.R. 232 at 241 *ff*. [Ont.].

98 *Kopyto, supra*, note 91 at 93, *per* Cory J.A. (as he then was). In *Edmonton Journal v. Alta. (A.G.), supra*, note 29 at 588 *ff*., when Wilson J. described the core functions of open justice and free speech in relation to courts, she acknowledged the importance of criticism of courts as a means towards reform and improvement of the law and of the justice system.

99 *Kopyto, ibid.*, at 91, *per* Cory J.A.

100 *Irwin Toy, supra*, note 25.

exception. *Charter* s. 2(b) does not protect violent activity, even when it is intended to convey meaning.[101]

The undertaking of marches or demonstrations can fall within *Charter* s. 2(b) when this activity is intended to communicate a message.[102] Thus, the *Charter prima facie* constitutionally protects critical speeches about courts and, as well, demonstrations aimed at criticizing a court, judge or judicial decision.

E. Right to Televise Judicial Proceedings

In addition to their interest in attending court proceedings, the media, and especially the television media, have expressed an interest in using photographic equipment to film court proceedings for broadcast or publication. The media's desire is to enhance news reports on court proceedings with pictures, and in the case of television, with sound and pictures. In those American states where filming in court is liberally allowed, court room footage virtually is always edited into brief clips from a day's proceedings, which are used as part of a television story about the case. It is extremely rare that a case is entirely televised "gavel-to-gavel," because of both the high cost of doing so, and the scarcity of available air time.[103]

In several cases, the media has argued that *Charter* s. 2(b) confers on them a constitutional right to televise either full court proceedings or evidence received in court. They have achieved mixed results under s. 2(b). Yet, they have had essentially no practical success under *Charter* s. 1.

In the earliest such case, the C.B.C. and The Globe and Mail sought a trial judge's permission to photocopy or film some documentary evidence, tendered at a highly publicized anti-combines trial. In *R. v. Thomson Newspapers*,[104] a Supreme Court of Ontario Judge refused to permit filming of the documents. He had made copies of exhibits available to reporters for their perusal during portions of the trial. The media moved before the trial judge for an order permitting them to film or photocopy this documentary evidence, pursuant to *Charter* s. 2(b).

The court dismissed this *Charter* application, finding that s. 2(b) did not confer on the media a constitutional right to film documentary

---

101 *Ibid.*, at 970. See also *R. v. Keegstra*, [1991] 2 W.W.R. 1 (S.C.C.), *per* Dickson C.J.C.

102 *Dolphin Delivery, supra*, note 25.

103 Some Canadian royal commissions have admitted television cameras to their proceedings. These have produced similar news clip reports and, in some cases, gavel-to-gavel broadcasts on cable TV community channels.

104 *Thomson Newspapers, supra*, note 44.

evidence. The court held that s. 2(b), liberally construed, conferred on the media a constitutional right to personally attend the proceedings, and to report to others what has gone on during the trial. It granted to them nothing more than this. In particular, the court stated:

> Dealing specifically with the motion brought on behalf of the C.B.C., when the essence of the relief sought is analyzed, what is contended for, under the banner of freedom of expression and access to the court, is in truth an attempt to require the court to make available to a reporter certain evidence in a certain way . . . There is, in my respectful view, no obligation on the part of the court to make evidence available in that way.

In a subsequent case, a C.B.C. television reporter challenged the validity of restrictions on using cameras in the court room, or in court house corridors, found in s. 67 of Ontario's *Judicature Act*.[105] In *Squires*

---

105 S. 67 of the *Judicature Act*, R.S.O. 1980, c. 223, now superseded by the largely comparable s. 146 of the *Courts of Justice Act*, S.O. 1984, c. 11, provides as follows:

> "67.(1) In this section,
> (a) "judge" means the person presiding at a judicial proceeding;
> (b) "judicial proceeding" means a proceeding of a court of record;
> (c) "precincts of the building" means the space enclosed by the walls of the building.
>
> (2) Subject to subsection (3), no person shall,
> (a) take or attempt to take any photograph, motion picture or other record capable of producing visual representations by electronic means or otherwise,
>   (i) at a judicial proceeding, or
>   (ii) of any person entering or leaving the room in which the judicial proceeding is to be or has been convened, or
>   (iii) of any person in the precincts of the building in which the judicial proceeding is to be or has been convened where there is reasonable ground for believing that such person is there for the purpose of attending or leaving the proceeding; or
> (b) publish, broadcast, reproduce or otherwise disseminate any photograph, motion picture or record taken or made in contravention of clause (a).
>
> (3) Subsection (2) does not apply to any photograph, motion picture or record taken or made upon authorization of the judge,
> (a) where required for the presentation of evidence or the making of a record or for any other purpose of the judicial proceeding;
> (b) in connection with any investive, ceremonial, naturalization or similar proceedings; or
> (c) with the consent of the parties and witnesses, for such educational or instructional purposes as may be approved by the judge.
>
> (4) Every person who is in contravention of this section is guilty of an offence . . ."

v. R.,[106] a reporter was charged with filming a victim/witness at a preliminary inquiry into murder conspiracy charges,[107] who was leaving the court room and entering the court house corridor by means of his wheelchair. The reporter moved to quash the charges on the ground that s. 67 violated her s. 2(b) rights. A five-week evidentiary hearing ensued on the constitutional question. Numerous witnesses testified on the asserted benefits and harms of television filming in the court room and court house corridors, including lawyers, judges and victims assistance experts from U.S. jurisdictions which permit the extensive use of cameras in the court room.

The trial judge held that s. 2(b) does not confer on the press a constitutional right to film in court rooms or court house corridors. The court relied, *inter alia*, on the Supreme Court of Ontario's approach to freedom of expression in *Thomson Newspapers*.[108] He concluded that s. 2(b) guarantees the media a right to attend court proceedings, and to report on what occurs. However, it does not include a right to televise the proceedings, nor does it impose on the state a constitutional duty to take steps to accommodate the use of cameras in court house facilities. As is discussed further, *infra*, he also held that even if cameras in the court were enshrined in s. 2(b), the *Judicature Act*'s restrictions would be saved under *Charter* s. 1.[109]

After the reporter was convicted of filming in a court house corridor, she appealed to the Ontario District Court, relying on her constitutional claim.[110] Unlike the trial judge, the District Court concluded that *Charter* s. 2(b) confers on reporters a *prima facie* constitutional right to film in court rooms and court house corridors. The Crown had argued that s. 2(b) provides constitutional protection for the dissemination of information, but not for the gathering of news. The Crown also argued that the public's s. 2(b) rights were fully respected if the public is permitted to attend court proceedings, and to report to others about the case in as full detail as is desired. The reporter argued that s. 2(b) provides special constitutional rights for journalists. This, she argued, includes constitutional protection for news gathering, including a constitutional right to gather information by video camera. The District Court held that s. 2(b) extends constitutional protection for news gather-

---

106 *Supra*, note 44.
107 The preliminary hearing itself dealt with a highly newsworthy case. Certain persons were charged with a terrorist-style attempt to murder a Turkish diplomat in Ottawa. The witness being filmed was the victim of the murder attempt.
108 *R. v. Thomson Newspapers Ltd., supra*, note 44.
109 *Squires v. R., supra*, note 44 (Prov.Ct.), and see the text associated with notes 242-261, *infra*.
110 *Squires, supra*, note 44 (Dist.Ct.).

ing. In accepting the reporter's position, the District Court attempted to distinguish the *Thomson Newspapers* case.

Despite this s. 2(b) finding, the District Court upheld the constitutionality of the reporter's conviction. It found that s. 1 saved the impugned provision of the *Judicature Act*, for reasons similar to the trial judge's, with one exception. The District Court opined that it was unnecessary for the *Judicature Act* to restrict filming in court to situations where the film was to be used for educational or instructional purposes.[111]

The media sought an opportunity in Quebec to broadcast a videotape which had been admitted into evidence in a well-publicized criminal case. In *Re R. and Lortie*,[112] a gunman entered the Quebec National Assembly and went on a shooting rampage. Portions of these events were captured on videotape by the legislative building's camera system. This videotape was entered into evidence at Lortie's trial. Certain media establishments had obtained a copy of the tape. Others asked the Quebec Court of Appeal for access to it, relying on s. 2(b).

A majority of the Quebec Court of Appeal held that s. 2(b) gave the media no constitutional right to receive this video evidence. L'Heureux-Dubé J.A., dissenting, opined that s. 2(b) entitled the media to have access to the film in question. She saw this as bound up with the right of access to court.

In the U.S., the media has repeatedly claimed that they have a constitutional right to use cameras in the court room, pursuant to the free speech and press clauses of the First Amendment to the U.S. Constitution. These efforts have met repeatedly with failure. The First Amendment has been construed to confer a sweeping right on press and public to attend court proceedings[113] and a virtually absolute right to report on them.[114]

However, American courts have held that the First Amendment confers no right to film in court for the purpose of televising court proceedings[115] or to copy audio exhibits for broadcast.[116] The U.S.

---

111 *Ibid.*, at 356-58. The trial judge had concluded that the "educational or instructional purposes" clause did not preclude the media from filming in court for news gathering purposes. See *Squires v. R., supra*, note 44 at 369 (Prov.Ct.).
112 (1985), 21 C.C.C. (3d) 436 (Que. C.A.).
113 See *Richmond Newspapers v. Virginia*, 281 S.E. 2d 915 (1981); see generally, Lepofsky, *Open Justice, supra*, note 4 at 128 *ff.*
114 See *Nebraska Press Assn. v. Stuart*, 427 U.S. 539 (1976); see generally, Lepofsky, *Open Justice, ibid.*, at 153 *ff.*
115 See, *e.g., U.S. v. Hastings*, 695 F. 2d 1278 (11th Circ., 1983).
116 *Nixon v. Warner Communications Inc.*, 98 S. Ct. 1306 (1978). Here the media was unsuccessful in its attempt to secure copies of the famous Nixon Watergate tapes, in order to broadcast their contents to the public.

Supreme Court has held that it is open to states to experiment with television in the court room, so long as the accused's due process rights are respected.[117] However, the state and federal courts are under no constitutional duty to admit television cameras to their proceedings. Indeed, there is no violation of the First Amendment where a court rule bans cameras from the court room, even where all the parties to the proceeding consent to being televised.[118]

F. Right to Require Witnesses to Identify Themselves

The media, attending a coroner's inquest, have no constitutional right under s. 2(b) to require a coroner to compel witnesses to identify themselves during their testimony. In *Canadian Newspapers Co. v. Isaac*,[119] a coroner permitted a witness to testify without identifying himself. The witness was a "street person," who testified on what it is like to be homeless. In exchange for the witness agreeing to testify, it had been arranged in advance that he would not be required to give his name in testimony.

A media establishment objected to this arrangement. It wanted the coroner to compel the witness to give his name. The coroner refused. The news outlet sought judicial review of this refusal.

The Divisional Court of the Supreme Court of Ontario dismissed the media's application. While questioning the coroner's jurisdiction to make the arrangement in question,[120] the court held that *Charter* s. 2(b) does not give the media any right to intervene in the manner in which an inquest is conducted.[121] The media's status at such a proceeding is that of observer.

While this ruling only involved a coroner's inquest, it applies with equal force to the media's role at court proceedings as well. The media's function at such proceedings is as a conduit for information to flow to the public, to ensure that the justice system is truly open. If there is some impropriety with the way that the proceeding is conducted, the public

---

117 See *Chandler v. Florida*, 101 S. Ct. 802 (1981), reversing *Estes v. Texas*, 381 U.S. 532 (1965). As of the *Chandler* decision, the U.S. Supreme Court was not prepared to hold that any televising of a criminal trial, over the accused's objection, was an automatic denial of due process, absent proof of actual prejudice. It took the position that the question of whether televising court proceedings is disruptive to the trial process was still a debated and controversial matter in the U.S. as of 1981.

118 See *U.S. v. Hastings, supra*, note 115; *Westmoreland v. C.B.S.*, 752 F. 2d 16 (2nd Circ., 1984).

119 (1988), 63 O.R. (2d) 698 (Div.Ct.).

120 *Ibid.*, at 701-704.

121 *Ibid.*, at 704-705.

can bring pressure to bear on the government to reform the process or to correct the specific injustice. The media's function is to communicate the fact of such an impropriety or injustice to the public. It is not for itself to call upon the courts through legal process to correct the alleged deficiency.

G. Public's Right to Attend Administrative Tribunals

The bulk of *Charter* open justice litigation concerns the right to attend and report on courts. Yet, the media has also attempted to expand open justice beyond courts, to administrative tribunals as well. To date, these efforts have yielded mixed results.

Each jurisdiction has a plethora of regulatory agencies which make innumerable decisions on the rights, obligations, privileges, benefits and burdens of the citizenry. These include, for example, decisions regarding one's entitlement to welfare, to union certification, to human rights protection, to business licences, and so on. These decisions can be as important to the individual as any made by a court. Indeed, much of the business which legislatures have now assigned to administrative agencies can be, and previously was, within the courts' traditional mandate.

Because administrative agencies and tribunals are not part of the formal court system, they are not required at common law to conduct their business in public. The common law provides only that those administrative tribunals which are judicial or quasi-judicial in character have an inherent discretion to conduct their hearings in public, if they so desire.[122] Unless their governing legislation specifically stipulates whether their hearings are to be public or private, such tribunals have the discretion to conduct their proceedings in public, or in private, as they see fit. The rules of natural justice impose common law procedural obligations on judicial and quasi-judicial regulatory agencies over and above those imposed by statute.[123] Natural justice does *not* require tribunals to hold their proceedings in public.[124] A court would not judicially review a tribunal's decision to hold its hearings in private unless it was established that there had been an error of law or abuse of discretion in deciding to go *in camera.*[125]

There has been some legislative reform in this area. The most

---

122 *Re Yuz and Laski* (1986), 32 D.L.R. (4th) 452, affirming 48 O.R. (2d) 161 (C.A.).
123 *Ridge v. Baldwin*, [1964] A.C. 40 (H.L.).
124 *Supra*, note 122; see also, generally, S.A. De Smith and J.M. Evans, De Smith's *Judicial Review of Administrative Action*, 4th ed. (London: Stevens & Sons, 1980).
125 *Supra*, note 122.

comprehensive initiative is Ontario's *Statutory Powers Procedure Act*,[126] which provides a procedural code for all provincial tribunals that are required by law to hold a hearing before exercising a statutory power of decision. Section 9 of that Act provides the following for such agencies:[127]

> 9.(1) A hearing shall be open to the public except where the tribunal is of the opinion that,
>
> (a) matters involving public security may be disclosed; or
> (b) intimate financial or personal matters or other matters may be disclosed at the hearing of such a nature, having regard to the circumstances, that the desirability of avoiding disclosure thereof in the interests of any person affected or in the public interest outweighs the desirability of adhering to the principle that hearings be open to the public,
>
> in which case the tribunal may hold the hearing concerning any such matters *in camera.*

For s. 2(b) to require that administrative tribunals be publicly accessible, it is necessary to extend the *Southam (No. 1)*[128] openness holding beyond the court room setting, and to apply it to administrative tribunals. In support of such a position, it can be argued that tribunals which exercise judicial or quasi-judicial functions should be bound by all of the trappings of the judicial process. This includes an openness requirement. Openness would provide the same benefits for tribunals as it does for courts. It would promote fair and accurate decision-making. It would deter witnesses from giving false testimony. It would help avoid the abuse of official power. It would foster public confidence in the administration of regulatory justice.

In opposition to an extension of *Southam (No. 1)* to regulatory tribunals, it can be argued that *Southam*'s constitutionalization of the open court requirement is tied inextricably to the powerful, long-standing tradition of open court. In contrast, there is no comparable tradition for administrative tribunals which s. 2(b) could constitutionalize. As well, a core focus of modern administrative law has been to avoid an excessive judicialization of the regulatory state, in order to leave the legislature free to fashion new, alternative modes for promoting public policy, outside the framework of the traditional judicial paradigm.

Initial media invocations of the *Charter* to gain access to administrative hearings were unsuccessful. In *Edmonton Journal v. Can.*

---

126 R.S.O. 1980, c. 484.
127 Except for those agencies whose enabling statute provides explicitly that it operates notwithstanding the *Statutory Powers Procedure Act.*
128 *Supra*, note 20.

(A.G.),[129] the media challenged an Alberta provision governing fatality inquiries, which did not require them to be open to the public. McDonald J. rejected the media claim, with the subsequent approval of the Alberta Court of Appeal,[130] holding:[131]

> The decision of the Ontario Court of Appeal in *Re Southam Inc. and The Queen (No. 1)* should not be read as authority for a broad proposition that the "freedom of the press" protected by s. 2(b) encompasses a general "right of access" to information generated in the process of government beyond the judicial process.

Similarly, the Federal Court Trial Division rejected a claim that s. 2(b) guarantees the media a right to attend proceedings of the Canadian Human Rights Commission.[132]

More recently, the media has met with greater success. In *Southam Inc. v. Can. (Minister of Employment and Immigration)*, the Federal Court of Appeal concluded that an immigration tribunal, which exercises judicial or quasi-judicial powers, is constitutionally required by s. 2(b) to admit the public to its proceedings.[133] The Federal Court applied the traditional administrative law test for distinguishing between administrative and judicial functions, as a means for deciding whether the tribunal must comply with a judicial-style openness requirement. This is odd because, as indicated above, common law natural justice doctrine, which creates this judicial/administrative categorization of regulatory agencies, has never required regulatory tribunals to be open to the public, even if they are judicial or quasi-judicial in character.

An Ontario administrative tribunal made history by itself concluding that *Charter* s. 2(b) requires its proceedings to be held in public. It admitted the public to its hearing, despite provincial legislation requiring its proceedings to be *in camera*. In *Canadian Newspapers Co. v. College of Physicians and Surgeons of Ontario*,[134] The Globe and Mail and the London Free Press wanted to cover a hearing of the Discipline Committee of the College of Physicians and Surgeons of Ontario, into

---

129 (1983), 5 D.L.R. (4th) 240, affirmed 13 D.L.R. (4th) 479, leave to appeal to S.C.C. refused 13 D.L.R. (4th) 480 [Alta.].
130 *Ibid.*
131 *Ibid.*, at 246.
132 See *McKenzie v. Can. Human Rights Comm.* (1985), 16 C.L.L.C. 16,144 (Fed. T.D.). See also *Southam Inc. c. Lafrance*, [1990] R.J.Q. 219 (C.S.), where the media was denied access to a disciplinary proceeding of a lawyer who was later to face criminal proceedings on the basis that the public disclosure of the proceedings in the former could amount to a contribution to evidence for the prosecution in the latter.
133 [1987] 3 F.C. 329 (C.A.).
134 Ont. Div.Ct., No. 948-89, 30th October 1989 (not yet reported).

allegations that certain physicians were guilty of professional misconduct or incompetence. The case arose out of the widely reported death of a boy in a Toronto hospital, from internal disorders which hospital staff had allegedly misdiagnosed as purely psychosomatic. Prior to the Discipline Committee hearing, these events had been the subject of a coroner's inquest and a proceeding before Ontario's Health Disciplines Board,[135] each of which was conducted in public and attracted press coverage.

Section 12(4) of Ontario's *Health Disciplines Act*[136] required the College's Discipline Committee proceedings to be held *in camera*, except if the accused physician requested a public hearing. Even in the face of such a request, the committee may still proceed *in camera* if it considers that the circumstances of the case so warrant. The press first attacked s. 12(4) by an application to Ontario's Divisional Court for judicial review.[137] The court dismissed the application on jurisdictional grounds, finding that the media should first challenge the legislation before the Discipline Committee. This is because of an Ontario Court of Appeal decision,[138] holding that an administrative tribunal can have the right and duty to consider constitutional challenges to legislation governing the tribunal.

When the media renewed its *Charter* challenge before the Discipline Committee, the committee concluded that s. 12(4) of the *Health Disciplines Act* was unconstitutional,[139] and admitted the public to its proceedings. While the committee's decision is not binding on courts or other tribunals, this result demonstrates that the *Charter* can be used effectively to secure a practical result in the open justice field, without securing either a court judgment or legislative reform.[140]

A contrary result was reached by a board of inquiry, appointed under the *Royal Canadian Mounted Police Act*[141] to inquire into the propriety of certain R.C.M.P. activities. In *Re Application by Southam Inc.*,[142] the media was unsuccessful in persuading the administrative

---

135 See *Re Yuz and Laski, supra,* note 122.

136 R.S.O. 1980, c. 196.

137 *Supra,* note 134.

138 See *Cuddy Chicks Ltd. v. Ont.* (L.R.B.) (1989), 62 D.L.R. (4th) 125 (Ont. C.A.).

139 *College of Physicians & Surgeons of Ont. v. Weinstein, Discipline Ctee. of C. of P. & S. of Ont.,* *5th December 1989 (not yet reported). The oral decision of the committee was rendered after one day of legal argument by the parties on the constitutional question.

140 Compare *Daily Gazette Co. v. West Virginia Bd. of Medicine,* 352 S.E. 2d 66 (1986), where the Supreme Court of Appeals of West Virginia held that the U.S. First Amendment guarantees a constitutional right of the public to attend medical discipline proceedings.

141 R.S.C. 1985, c. R-10.

142 R.C.M.P. Bd. of Inquiry, 30th April 1990 (not yet reported).

board to allow public attendance at its proceedings. The board accepted that the rationale in *Re Southam (No. 1)* should be extended to administrative tribunals discharging judicial or quasi-judicial functions. However, it concluded that its purely investigative and reporting functions were neither judicial nor quasi-judicial in character.

As well, Ontario's Lieutenant Governor's Board of Review, constituted under the *Criminal Code*, has rejected a media claim that *Charter* s. 2(b) gives the public a right to attend hearings of that board. The tribunal annually reviews the detention of accused persons who have been found not guilty of criminal charges on account of insanity, and recommends to the province's Lieutenant Governor whether the detention should be continued, modified or terminated. The final decision on the detainee's case is made by the Lieutenant Governor, though ordinarily this decision conforms with the board's recommendation. The board traditionally proceeds *in camera*.

In *Re Finlayson*,[143] a reporter had sought access to a review hearing, arising out of a highly publicized offence. Relying heavily on McDonald J.'s decision in *Edmonton Journal v. Can. (A.G.)*, the board ruled that the open court requirement does not extend to its proceedings. Having received extensive evidence suggesting that openness would interfere with patient-doctor relations, and would deter disclosure of needed information to the board, the board summarily concluded that even if there were an openness requirement, its displacement was justified under *Charter* s. 1.

In summary, the law is in a state of conflict on whether the *Charter* confers a constitutional right to attend administrative tribunal proceedings. It is clear that some, and perhaps most, tribunals have jurisdiction to decide at first instance whether the media or public have a constitutional right to attend their proceedings. It is unclear whether such a right in fact is conferred by s. 2(b).

H. Right to Publish under *Charter* Section 11(d)

The preceding discussion considers whether the free expression and press guarantees in *Charter* s. 2(b) create a constitutional requirement of open justice. To what extent does *Charter* s. 11(d) impose a requirement of open justice as well? Section 11(d) provides in material part:

11. Any person charged with an offence has the right . . .

(d) to be presumed innocent until proven guilty according to law in

---

143 Ont. Lieut. Gov. Bd. of Review, Callon J., chairperson, 23rd October 1990 (not yet reported).

a fair and public hearing by an independent and impartial tribunal.

This provision empowers an accused at a criminal or other penal proceeding to object if the public is excluded from all or part of the hearing. However, it provides no assistance to the media or public if the accused does not object to the exclusion of the public.

There are two reasons why s. 11(d)'s public hearing requirement does not assist the press or public, unless it is invoked by the accused. First, s. 11's opening words clarify that this provision only provides rights to the accused, and not to the media. Hence, the Supreme Court of Canada expressed doubt in the *Canadian Newspapers* case that the media could itself invoke s. 11(d).[144] Second, in *Canadian Newspapers*, the Supreme Court held that s. 11(d)'s "public hearing" requirement is satisfied when the public is admitted to the court room. It is not infringed when a judge, at a public hearing, orders the media not to publish certain information revealed in open court, such as a sexual assault complainant's identity.[145]

A different spin on s. 11(d) was attempted in an effort to indirectly create a right to publish pursuant to s. 11(d). The preceding discussion pertained to s. 11(d)'s "public hearing" clause. It has also been contended that s. 11(d)'s "fair hearing" requirement can give rise to a right to publish information about a court proceeding. While *Charter* s. 7 was not invoked in their support, it too provides to an accused person a right to a fair trial.

The media has argued[146] that the accused's right to a fair trial requires a case to be open to publicity, because publicity of the case can cause members of the public, who have evidence which bears on the case, to come forward and offer testimony. If media reporting is restricted, these witnesses might not come forward because they are unaware of the case. In *Canadian Newspapers Co. v. Can. (A.G.)*,[147] the media advanced this argument in support of a challenge to the *Criminal Code* restriction on reporting of sexual assault complainants' identities. It was argued that if the complainant's name could be published in a case where that complainant had previously made false allegations of sexual assault, the publicity could lead persons who had previously been falsely accused by that complainant to come forward with exculpatory testimony.[148]

While not specifically holding that such restrictions infringe s.

---

144 See *Can. Newspapers Co. v. Can. (A.G.)*, *supra*, note 66 at 134.
145 *Ibid.*
146 See *Can. Newspapers Co. v. Can. (A.G.)*, *supra*, note 44.
147 *Ibid.*
148 *Ibid.*, at 577.

11(d)'s fair hearing requirement, the Ontario Court of Appeal expressed the view that such publications could contribute to an accused's fair trial.[149] On appeal, the Supreme Court of Canada decided not to address this argument, since the accused had not raised it in that case.[150] The Supreme Court left open the possibility that this argument could be reconsidered in a future case,[151] that is, in a case where the facts warranted it and the accused raised the s. 11(d) claim.

This "fair trial" argument suffers from several defects, and is without merit. The accused's right to a fair trial includes the right to an unbiased adjudicator, the right to know the case against oneself, the right to confront one's accusors, and the right to tender evidence in one's defence.[152] It does not include the right to have the state, the media, or any other body facilitate the accused's search for exculpatory evidence. Once a charge is laid, the police are under no constitutional duty under *Charter* s. 11(d) to find evidence which exculpates the accused. It is for the accused to locate and present exculpatory evidence. The accused's right to a fair trial should not be confused with the accused's desire to win an acquittal.

Moreover, publicity of a case is not necessarily and automatically linked to the securing of exculpatory evidence. If a case is subject to media publicity, the coverage could well lead witnesses to come forward with *incriminating* evidence, rather than exculpating testimony. There is no way to establish (except by pure speculation) that the reportage of a case will in fact generate exculpatory evidence. Whether or not this happens depends on a myriad of uncontrollable and unpredictable factors, such as whether the media chooses to cover the case, what the media chooses to include in its coverage, whether potential witnesses actually read or see the reportage, and whether this coverage causes them to come forward when they otherwise would not have done so. It also would depend on whether their evidence affects the case's outcome, by supporting an acquittal on facts which otherwise would have led to a conviction. This is a very improbable eventuality in most cases. Hence, it is not possible to link media coverage with an accused's fair trial rights, even if it were assumed that this right included an entitlement to media-assisted recruitment of exculpating witnesses.

It is undeniable that one potential advantage served by media coverage of a court proceeding is that, in some instances, it may lead witnesses to come forward with evidence which is helpful to the case of

149 *Ibid.*, at 582.
150 *Ibid.*, at 134-35 (S.C.C.).
151 *Ibid.*, at 134.
152 See generally, D.C. McDonald, *Legal Rights in the Canadian Charter of Rights and Freedoms*, 2nd ed. (Toronto: Carswell, 1989), c. 16, and W.S. Tarnopolsky, *supra*, note 8 at 259-74.

one party or another. In the rare instance when this chain of events might occur, this can be a helpful contribution to the administration of justice. However, it ought not to be transformed into a constitutional entitlement as part of the accused's right to a fair trial.

I. *Charter* Section 15 and Equal Treatment of Different Media

At times, one branch of the media can be heard to complain that they are victimized by discrimination, if they feel that they are not treated as advantageously as other branches of the media. However, the media cannot use *Charter* s. 15's guarantee of equality rights to challenge the differential treatment of different media under legislation. Section 15(1) provides as follows:

> 15.(1) Every individual is equal before and under the law and has the right to the equal protection and equal benefit of the law without discrimination and, in particular, without discrimination based on race, national or ethnic origin, colour, religion, sex, age or mental or physical disability.

Section 15 does not explicitly ban discrimination or differential treatment between the print media on the one hand, and the broadcast media on the other. While s. 15 addresses some forms of discrimination, in addition to those grounds specifically enumerated in it, the list of unenumerated grounds of discrimination is finite. Section 15 only prohibits legislative discrimination based on the enumerated grounds, and such additional grounds as are analogous to the enumerated grounds. A ground of discrimination is analogous to the enumerated grounds if it involves discrimination based on an intimate human or personal characteristic, which is associated with a discrete and insular minority that has historically suffered from social or political disadvantage and disempowerment.[153]

Under this approach, it could not be persuasively contended that legislative differentiation between the print and electronic media can be impugned under s. 15. Neither media is a discrete and insular minority in Canada which has suffered from chronic social and political disadvantage and disempowerment. To the contrary, the media are in a position of enhanced power in Canadian society, because of their unique access to the public, their powerful capacity to influence public opinion, and their concentration of wealth. There is nothing remotely analogous

---

153 *Andrews v. Law Soc. of B.C.*, *[1989] 1 S.C.R. 143; *R. v. Turpin*, [1989] 1 S.C.R. 1296 [Ont.].

between discrimination because of sex or race on the one hand, and differential legal treatment of newspapers and television, on the other.

Three judges of a seven-judge panel of the Supreme Court of Canada have ruled that s. 15 is unavailable to redress different treatment of different branches of the media. In *Edmonton Journal v. Alberta (A.G.)*,[154] a newspaper attacked provincial legislation which substantially limited reports on civil and matrimonial proceedings. In addition to s. 2(b), the newspaper argued that the legislation violated its s. 15 rights, by:

(a) placing restrictions on the print media, but not the electronic media; and

(b) banning such reporting by media in Alberta, when such reporting remained lawful in other provinces.

A four-judge majority of the Supreme Court struck down the law under s. 2(b), and thus found it unnecessary to comment on the s. 15 claim.[155] The three other presiding justices found part of the statute sustainable under s. 2(b). It was thus necessary for them to address the s. 15 contention. La Forest J., for the three, doubted that the corporate media appellant could invoke s. 15, since that provision only gives constitutional rights to human beings, and not to corporations such as the Edmonton Journal. He also opined that the impugned distinctions between branches of the media were not addressable under s. 15, since they are not analogous to the enumerated grounds.[156]

J. *Charter* Section 15 and Differential Protection of Complainants and Accused from Media Identification

Charter s. 15's equality rights guarantee does not enable accused persons to protest the fact that a court has banned media publication of the complainant's identity, but has not banned publication of the accused's identity. In *R. v. D.(G.)*,[157] a clergyman was accused of sexual assault. The trial court banned publication of the identities of both the accused and the complainant, purportedly under s. 442(3) of the *Criminal Code*. That provision only purports to authorize such bans to protect the complainant. In a proceeding brought in the Supreme Court of Ontario to challenge the non-publication order, the accused Minister[158]

---

154 *Supra*, note 29.
155 *Ibid.* The majority was made up of Cory J., with Dickson C.J.C. and Lamer J. (as he then was), concurring, with separate concurring reasons by Wilson J.
156 *Ibid.*, at 604-605, *per* La Forest J.
157 (1988), 39 C.C.C. (3d) 369 (Ont. H.C.).
158 Who, by this time, had been acquitted of the charges.

argued that it would violate his rights under *Charter* s. 15 for the court to protect the anonymity of the complainant, but not that of the accused.

The Supreme Court of Ontario rejected this s. 15 claim. It held that differential treatment of accused persons and complainants under *Criminal Code* s. 442(3) is not discriminatory, because the impugned law's purpose is to protect complainants alone, and not to protect accused persons. In light of the Supreme Court of Canada's subsequent enunciation of s. 15 doctrine, this kind of circular reasoning is now unnecessary to dismiss this s. 15 attack on *Criminal Code* s. 442(3). Now, it can be persuasively argued that different treatment of accused persons and complainants is not addressed by *Charter* s. 15, since it involves no discrimination based on the grounds enumerated in s. 15, nor on any grounds analogous thereto.[159] Such is not discrimination based on an intimate personal characteristic, nor is it targeted at a traditionally disadvantaged, discrete and insular minority.

K. Reporters' Privilege Against Testifying in Court

As the foregoing amply reveals, Canada's mainstream media is at the forefront of *Charter* open justice litigation. Taken together, the media establishments which litigate *Charter* open justice claims have contended that the *Charter* requires (subject to s. 1) that:

(a) court proceedings must be open to public attendance;[160]
(b) court proceedings must be open to unfettered media reporting of all facts attested to in court;[161]
(c) the media must be free to report on the identity of all those caught up in the court process, including, among others, sexual assault victims,[162] accused adults,[163] and accused young offenders;[164]
(d) witnesses must be required to testify to their names in open hearings, so the media can report them if it wishes;[165]
(e) the media must be free to photograph and broadcast the testimony and conduct in court of witnesses and other court participants, even over their objection;[166]

---

159 See *Andrews v. Law Soc. of B.C., supra,* note 153.
160 *Re Southam Inc. and R. (No. 1), supra,* note 20.
161 See, *e.g., Re Global Communications and A.G. Can., supra,* note 63; *Edmonton Journal v. Alta. (A.G.), supra,* note 29.
162 *Can. Newspapers, supra,* note 66.
163 *Re R. and Several Unnamed Persons* (1983), 44 O.R. (2d) 81 (H.C.).
164 *Southam Inc. v. R., supra,* note 44.
165 *Can. Newspapers Co. v. Isaac, supra,* note 119.
166 *Squires v. R., supra,* note 44.

(f) the media must be free to photocopy or film for broadcast exhibits at a trial, including videotape evidence;[167]

(g) the media must be free to film witnesses and others in courthouse corridors, even over their objection;[168] and,

(h) the press and public must be free to attend administrative tribunal proceedings.[169]

In striking contrast to the media's efforts at maximizing the exposure to publicity of people caught up in the justice system, the media has attempted to use the *Charter* to *minimize* its own potential for exposure in the justice system. This effort is clearest in media attempts to argue that *Charter* s. 2(b) gives reporters a constitutional privilege against being compelled to disclose in testimony the identity of their confidential news sources. Typically, the media demands that such a privilege be qualified, and not absolute. They argue that a reporter should not be required to divulge a confidential news source's identity except where this evidence is relevant to the proceeding in question, where it is important to the case, and where it is unobtainable through alternative avenues.

The rationale for demanding this privilege is as follows: news reporters depend heavily on their sources to get stories. Some of these sources require assurances of confidentiality before they are prepared to give newsworthy information to a reporter. For example, the media contends that confidential sources are especially critical when they are well placed government employees who leak stories of official corruption or scandal to the press. The media argues that, absent a confidential news source privilege in law, such news sources will dry up. This would impair the media's ability to effectively report the news to the public. Scandal, corruption and other important stories would go undetected and, hence, unreported. The *Charter*'s free press clause should protect news gathering activities, they contend.

In its Journalistic Policy Manual,[170] the C.B.C. enunciates its policy that where a reporter is compelled by a court to divulge the identity of a confidential source, the C.B.C. will attempt to persuade the court to hear such evidence *in camera*. While the C.B.C. ordinarily contends that open justice is of fundamental importance, it takes the position that

---

167 *R. v. Thomson Newspapers Ltd., supra,* note 44; *Re R. and Lortie, supra,* note 112.

168 *Squires v. R., supra,* note 44.

169 See, *e.g., Southam Inc. v. Can. (Min. of Employment & Immigration), supra,* note 133.

170 Canadian Broadcasting Corporation, *The Journalistic Policy* (Montreal: C.B.C. Enterprises, 1988), at 39.

open justice should be countermanded in the interest of furthering its news gathering activities.

In opposition to media claims for a confidential news source privilege, it can be argued that *Charter* s. 2(b) does not create a constitutional right of assured access to newsworthy information. Put simply, s. 2(b) is not a constitutional freedom of information statute. As well, s. 2(b) does not give reporters any special rights which ordinary members of the public do not similarly enjoy. Members of the public who have knowledge which is relevant to a legal proceeding are ordinarily susceptible to be ordered by subpoena to divulge this knowledge in court. The fact that the person having such knowledge is a reporter ought not to give them some special exemption from this ordinary duty of citizenship.

It can also be contended that, despite media claims to the contrary, confidential news sources do not play so critical a role in the news process, and that the claimed qualified privilege is unnecessary to ensure effective news reporting. At present, confidential news sources have been willing to give stories to reporters at a time when Canadian law does not provide them with any assurance of confidentiality. Moreover, the qualified privilege which reporters ordinarily seek would not give sources the assurance of confidentiality which is claimed to be needed in order to motivate them to give news stories to reporters. Because the asserted privilege is qualified, and not absolute, reporters could be compelled to name their sources in some cases, despite the privilege, and despite reporters' promises of secrecy to their informants.

To date, the media has been unsuccessful in its effort to establish a *Charter* s. 2(b) news source privilege.[171] In *Moysa v. Alberta (Labour Relations Board)*,[172] a reporter refused to testify before a provincial labour board on her sources for a news story. The board ordered her to testify. She sought judicial review of this order. The Alberta Court of Queen's Bench dismissed her application. It found that s. 2(b) confers no journalistic testimonial privilege.[173] The court rejected the suggestion

---

171 The U.S. case law on point is rather confused. The U.S. Supreme Court considered whether the First Amendment confers a constitutional confidential source privilege in *Branzburg v. Hayes*, 408 U.S. 665 (1972). While the court dismissed the privilege claim, it split badly on the question whether any such privilege ever exists and, if so, on what terms. Lower U.S. courts have divided in their interpretations of *Branzburg*. Some claim that the First Amendment creates a privilege, while others take the opposite view. Compare *State v. St. Peter*, 315 A. 2d 254 (Vt. S.C., 1974); *Zelenka v. State*, 266 N.W. 2d 279 (Wisc. S.C., 1978); and *Wilkins v. Kalla*, 459 N.Y.S. 2d 985 (S.C., 1983), with *In Re Farber*, 394 A. 2d 330, *cert.* denied 99 S. Ct. 598 (1978).

172 (1986), 28 D.L.R. (4th) 140 (Alta. Q.B.), affirmed, *infra*, notes 175, 176.

173 *Ibid.*, at 150.

that reporters have constitutional rights under s. 2(b) which are superior to those of the public.[174]

The Alberta Court of Appeal affirmed this finding.[175] On a further appeal, the Supreme Court of Canada set down the constitutional question of whether *Charter* s. 2(b) creates a reporters confidential news source privilege.[176] However, after oral argument, the court essentially declined to rule on the claim's merits.

The Supreme Court held that the reporter had failed to tender evidence showing that a requirement to name her sources would have the effect of impairing the media's access to news.[177] As well, the record did not establish that her sources were, in fact, confidential.[178] Accordingly, the appeal was dismissed. The court declined to rule on the media's substantive claim that s. 2(b) guarantees to it a constitutional right of access to the news. Thus, the highest authority on whether s. 2(b) creates a confidential news source privilege is the Alberta Court of Appeal's decision in *Moysa*, rejecting such a claim.[179]

L. Summary

As a result of the plethora of *Charter* claims, there are some aspects of the law which are clear, and some which are not. It is well settled that s. 2(b) gives a constitutional right to report on the facts of court cases and to criticize the conduct of judges. As far as provincial appeal courts are concerned, s. 2(b) also gives a right to attend court. Whether this right would be affirmed by the Supreme Court, and whether it should be extended to administrative tribunals, are both unclear. Lower courts are divided on whether s. 2(b) includes a *prima facie* right to televise legal proceedings over the objection of trial participants. However, it is clear

---

174 *Ibid.*, at 148 *ff.*
175 *Moysa v. Alta. (L.R.B.)* (1987), 43 D.L.R. (4th) 159.
176 *(1989), 60 D.L.R. (4th) 1 (S.C.C.).
177 *Ibid.*, at 5 *ff.*
178 *Ibid.*
179 In *The Citizen v. Coates* (1986), 29 D.L.R. (4th) 523 (N.S.C.A.), a similar issue was raised. However, the decision did not categorically rule on this question. Similarly, a constitutional source privilege was asserted in the wake of *Moysa* by a C.B.C. reporter and two other media establishments in *Colter J. v. McAuliffe*, Ont. Div.Ct., No. 300/89 (not yet reported). There, the parties developed an extensive evidentiary record on the question of the asserted need for a confidential news source privilege, in a case where a reporter was to be asked to disclose the identity of confidential sources in testimony before a Royal Commission. The application was adjourned *sine die* in the summer of 1989, pending further proceedings before the Royal Commission, without the court ruling on the merits of the *Charter* claim.

that s. 15 will not assist the media in advancing claims concerning open justice, and that when a reporter goes from covering a case, to being called as a witness in a case, the *Charter* provides him or her with no immunity from the duty to testify.

III. LIMITS ON OPEN JUSTICE UNDER *CHARTER* SECTION 1

A. General

With a liberal interpretation of s. 2(b) yielding the results described above, s. 1 of the *Charter* plays a critical role in most open justice adjudication. *Charter* s. 1 provides that:

> 1. *The Canadian Charter of Rights and Freedoms* guarantees the rights and freedoms set out in it subject only to such reasonable limits prescribed by law as can be demonstrably justified in a free and democratic society.

In this part, the impact of s. 1 on the constitutional requirement of open justice is examined. The test for applying s. 1 is described. An analysis follows of the fundamental social objectives which can justify limits on open justice. Finally, a review is presented of some of the key results of s. 1's application in open justice litigation.

B. Section 1 Test

The Supreme Court of Canada has had ample opportunity to enunciate a test which breathes life into *Charter* s. 1's vague and open-textured language.[180] In a series of cases,[181] a s. 1 test has first been outlined, and then fleshed out. Under this test, the Crown has the burden of proof to demonstrate that a limit on *Charter* rights meets s. 1's strictures.[182] The test requires that a limitation on constitutional rights

---

180 In *Open Justice, supra*, note 4 at 184 *ff.*, I proposed an approach to s. 1 at a time when the Supreme Court of Canada had not yet addressed this question. While the Supreme Court's s. 1 test uses somewhat different terminology, its test is substantially the same as the one I proposed in 1985. As such, the s. 1 analysis offered in *Open Justice* remains applicable to the present day, despite the passage of time.

181 See *R. v. Big M Drug Mart, supra*, note 22; *R. v. Oakes, supra*, note 22; *R. v. Edwards Books and Art*, [1986] 2 S.C.R. 713 [Ont.]; *Can. Newspapers Co. v. Can. (A.G.), supra*, note 66; *Andrews v. Law Soc. of B.C., supra*, note 153; *Irwin Toy Ltd. v. Que. (A.G.), supra*, note 25; *Edmonton Journal v. Alta. (A.G.), supra*, note 29.

182 *Hunter, Dir. of Investigation & Research, Combines Investigation Branch v. Southam Inc., supra*, note 22.

must:[183]
(a) be clearly prescribed by law, either by a statute, a regulation, or by the common law;
(b) be aimed at securing a social or governmental objective which is of sufficient importance to warrant an infringement of the *Charter* right in question. The measure must be aimed at objectives which are of pressing and substantial importance in a free and democratic society, and must not involve objectives which are discordant with the *Charter*'s values;
(c) be rationally related to the law's objectives, in the sense that the measure tends to promote achievement of the stated objectives;
(d) be the least restrictive alternative open to government to achieve its objectives. To meet this requirement, the measure must impair the *Charter* right as little as is necessary to ensure effective achievement of the measure's important goals. Another option will not constitute a less restrictive alternative unless it both imposes a lesser burden on *Charter* rights and is equally effective at promoting the government's goals; and,
(e) be proportional to its goals.

In applying this test, a court must take into account the severity of a *Charter* infringement. Where the infringement is more severe, the justification which s. 1 demands is greater.[184] The severity of an infringement of a *Charter* right is not measured solely in a quantitative sense. One should consider how much the infringement impairs the purposes which the *Charter* right is designed to achieve.

C. Social Goals Which Justify Limits on Open Justice

What social objectives are sufficiently important to warrant restrictions on constitutional rights concerning open justice? Objectives which Canadian courts have scrutinized are considered here. While analyzed separately, these objectives can, at times, overlap. Thus, they can be invoked collectively to defend the same impugned law. Of course, the simple recognition of a law's social objective as sufficiently important under s. 1 is only the s. 1 test's first stage. To survive s. 1 scrutiny, an impugned law or other government action must also meet the rational connection, least impairment, and proportionality requirements.

A first objective which can justify limits on access to and publicity about court proceedings is the right to a fair trial.[185] A party to a legal

---

183 See the cases cited at note 181, *supra.*
184 *Prostitution Reference, supra,* note 96.
185 See *Global Communications* and *R. v. Banville,* both *supra,* note 63; *Squires v. R., supra,* note 44.

proceeding has the right to have the court decide all factual and legal issues through a fair and impartial examination of the evidentiary record, and applicable law, free from any outside influence. If the case's outcome is influenced by media publicity, a fair trial is denied. The goal of securing a fair trial can justify limits on freedom of expression, whether the case is criminal[186] or civil.[187]

Second, the twin goals of promoting the proper administration of justice and of winning the war on crime, are sufficiently pressing and substantial to warrant restrictions on open justice. The proper administration of justice includes the Crown's right to a fair trial free from prejudicial publicity.[188] The goal of winning the war on crime includes, *inter alia*, the effectiveness of search warrants as a surprise-based tool for investigating crime.[189] It also includes the fostering of crime victims to come forward to report their victimization and to testify.[190]

A third social objective which can justify restrictions on freedom of expression in relation to the court process is the promotion of access of individuals to justice. In the open justice context, the term "access to courts" ordinarily refers to the physical access of reporters and other members of the public to the court room, that is, the right to personally attend and watch court proceedings. The somewhat similar phrase "access to justice" has a different and important meaning. In contrast, access to justice refers to the right of members of the public, who have a legal grievance, to bring their problem to court in order to invoke the legal machinery of the state to seek justice. "Access" in this context means meaningful access.

The right of access to justice is infringed if persons with legal problems are prevented or deterred from invoking the court process, whether the impediment is physical or psychological. A physical barrier can take the form of a picket or demonstration outside a court house, which blocks one's ability to physically get into the court. Such expressive activity can be restricted, in the interest of promoting access to the courts.[191] For a physically disabled person, a physical barrier to access to justice can take the form of an inaccessible entrance to the court house, for example, where the only access to the building is up a flight of stairs.

A psychological impediment to access to justice exists where a person becomes unwilling to utilize the court process to redress legal wrongs, because of a fear that by proceeding in court they could be

---

186 See, *e.g., Global Communications, ibid.*
187 See *Edmonton Journal v. Alta. (A.G.), supra*, note 29.
188 See *Squires v. R., supra*, note 44.
189 See, by analogy, the pre-*Charter* case of *MacIntyre v. N.S. (A.G.), supra*, note 26.
190 See *Can. Newspapers Co. v. Can. (A.G.), supra*, note 66; *Squires, supra*, note 44.
191 See *B.C.G.E.U. v. B.C. (A.G.),* [1988] 2 S.C.R. 214.

exposed to unwanted media publicity. This concern lies at the core of *Canadian Newspapers Co. v. Can. (A.G.),*[192] where the Supreme Court of Canada upheld a *Criminal Code* provision requiring a judge to ban publication of a sexual assault complainant's name, if she so requests. Although the court did not explicitly utilize the term "access to justice," a core consideration in its ruling is the importance of having non-publication orders available so that victims will be encouraged to report their victimization. The Supreme Court later explicitly affirmed the importance under s. 1 of "access to justice" as a rationale for limiting open justice in *Edmonton Journal v. Alberta (A.G.).*[193]

A fourth objective which can justify limits on s. 2(b) rights concerning open justice is the protection of individual privacy. A core objective of the *Charter* is the protection of the dignity and worth of the human person.[194] A central attribute of individual dignity and worth is a person's privacy.

Historically, Canadian law provided minimal explicit protection for individual privacy as such. At most, certain common law protections afforded a measure of privacy protection under the rubric of property and defamation law.[195] In recent years, Canada has increasingly recognized the importance of individual privacy, through royal commission reports,[196] through Law Reform Commission recommendations,[197] and through the enactment of legislation which provides protection for privacy.[198]

Before the Supreme Court was called upon to address privacy-based restrictions on open justice under the *Charter*, it had already recognized that the interest of individuals in their personal privacy had

---

192 *Supra*, note 66.

193 *Supra*, note 29 at 614, *per* Cory J., and at 601-602, *per* La Forest J., dissenting in part. The Supreme Court divided on the question whether the impugned Alberta provision was too wide-sweeping to meet s. 1's proportionality requirement. However, there was consensus among the justices that the goal of fostering access to justice was sufficiently important to justify some restrictions on s. 2(b) rights.

194 *Ibid.*, at 60 *ff.*, *per* La Forest J., concurring in part; *Ref. re S. 94(2) of Motor Vehicle Act (B.C.),* [1985] 2 S.C.R. 486; *R. v. Morgentaler,* [1988] 1 S.C.R. 30 at 161 *ff.*, *per* Wilson J.

195 See, *e.g., Krouse v. Chrysler Can. Ltd.* (1974), 40 D.L.R. (3d) 15 (Ont. C.A.).

196 See Ontario, *Report of the Commission of Inquiry into the Confidentiality of Health Information* (Ontario: Queen's Printer, 1980) (Commissioner: Krever J.); Ontario, *Report of the Commission on Freedom of Information and Individual Privacy* (Ontario: Queen's Printer, 1980) (Chairman: D.C. Williams).

197 See Ontario Law Reform Commission, *Report on Powers of Entry* (Toronto: Ministry of the Attorney General, 1983).

198 See, *e.g.: Privacy Act,* R.S.C. 1985, c. P-21; *Freedom of Information and Protection of Privacy Act,* S.O. 1987, c. 25; *Privacy Act,* S.B.C. 1968, c. 39; *Privacy Act,* S.M. 1970, c. 74; *Privacy Act,* S.S. 1974, c. 80.

achieved a new and fundamental constitutional dimension because of the *Charter*'s enactment. It had ruled that the purpose of the *Charter* s. 8 right of security against unreasonable search and seizure is the respect for the individual's reasonable expectation of privacy.[199] Similarly, one of the rationales for *Charter* s. 11(c)'s protection against an accused's being compelled to testify against himself or herself in a penal proceeding is the respect for privacy.[200]

In the first judicial recognition of the justifiability of privacy-based restrictions on publicity concerning courts under the *Charter*, the Ontario Provincial Offences Court ruled that a court participant's interest in privacy is sufficiently important to justify restrictions on televising court proceedings.[201] Thereafter, in *Canadian Newspapers Co. v. Can. (A.G.)*,[202] the Supreme Court of Canada gave tacit recognition to the privacy interests of sexual assault complainants, who are prepared to lay charges and testify, but who wish to prevent the media from reporting their names. However, the Supreme Court did not employ the term "privacy" in this decision.

This development culminated with the Supreme Court's *Edmonton Journal v. Alberta (A.G.)*[203] decision. There, the court ruled specifically that the protection of privacy can provide a s. 1 justification for restricting publications about an open court proceeding. The court split on the question of whether the impugned law was too broad to meet this objective. However, it was united on the question whether, as a matter of principle, privacy is a sufficiently important objective to justify limits on s. 2(b) open justice rights.[204]

These privacy findings are noteworthy for several reasons. First, it remains for the courts to expound what is encompassed within this privacy concept. Before the *Charter*, the Supreme Court had held at common law that an individual's sensibilities was not a sufficient cause for holding *in camera* proceedings.[205] Because of the s. 1 recognition of privacy's importance, this pre-*Charter* ruling may not be cited as grounds for automatically subjecting all court participants to unfettered publicity, regardless of its impact on them personally. In fashioning a judicial definition of privacy, it is critical to respect that an invasion of one's privacy necessarily is injurious to one's sensibilities.

Second, whatever may be that concept's farthest reaches, it clearly

---

199 *Hunter, Dir. of Investigation & Research Combines Investigation Branch v. Southam Inc., supra*, note 22.
200 *R. v. Amway Corp.* (1989), 56 D.L.R. (4th) 309 (S.C.C.).
201 See *Squires v. R., supra*, note 44.
202 *Supra*, note 44.
203 *Supra*, note 29 at 614, *per* Cory J. and at 601-602, *per* La Forest J.
204 *Ibid.*, at 602, *per* La Forest J.; at 618, *per* Cory J.; at 589 *ff.*, *per* Wilson J.
205 *MacIntyre v. N.S. (A.G.), supra*, note 26.

enjoys far greater sophistication and subtlety than as a simple antithesis of public information. This is because the Supreme Court has sanctioned a situation where a court proceeding is held in public, and yet certain information disclosed there may not be further publicized by the media. A measure of privacy can thus co-exist alongside a public hearing.

Third, the recognition of privacy as a ground for restricting press coverage of a court proceeding flies in the face of the media's conventional wisdom. To many, if not most, journalists, persons caught up in open court proceedings are generally considered "fair game" for media reporting. Privacy has no part to play in the process. The *Charter*'s recognition of privacy's pressing importance may require journalists to rethink this conventional wisdom.

A fourth societal objective which can support restrictions on constitutional open justice rights is the protection of the best interests of children. Children involved in juvenile delinquency[206] or young offender[207] proceedings, may be protected through law from the harmful effects of public access to, or publicity about, the court proceedings in which they are involved.

A fifth policy objective appears to be the only one which the Supreme Court has rejected in relation to open justice. This is the goal of protecting public morals. In *Edmonton Journal v. Alberta (A.G.)*,[208] Alberta attempted to justify under s. 1 a sweeping ban on most publications concerning matrimonial proceedings in that province, by arguing (among other things) that such restrictions are needed to protect public morals.

The court rejected this claim, largely because it doubted that the impugned law would in fact serve to protect public morals.[209] Yet, the decision's overall tenor suggests that in the latter part of the 20th century, the defensibility of the state's role as protector of the morals of adult persons through the suppression of free speech is questionable, at least insofar as media reporting on court proceedings is concerned.

The foregoing only reviews those social objectives for restricting constitutional rights regarding open justice which have received authoritative judicial consideration to date. It is open to open justice litigants to advance additional societal goals for limiting such rights. In so doing, they can attempt to show that such additional objectives are analogous or are of comparable importance to those objectives which have been judicially approved to date.

---

206 See *Re Southam Inc. and R. (No. 1), supra*, note 20.
207 See *Southam Inc. v. R., supra*, note 44.
208 *Supra*, note 29.
209 *Ibid.*, at 613, *per* Cory J.

What specific restrictions on open justice are permissible under s. 1 in order to protect the pressing objectives of fair trial, effective administration of justice, winning the war on crime, protecting individual privacy, access to justice and the protection of young persons? It is to this question that attention now turns for the balance of this part. The defensibility of efforts to protect these interests are here considered when pursued at the expense of the public attending court, the televising of court proceedings, the media's dissemination of factual reports about court proceedings, and finally, the criticism of courts.

D. Specific Limits on Public Access to Court Proceedings

What limits may constitutionally be imposed on public attendance at criminal proceedings? Attention first turns to proceedings against adult persons. This is followed by proceedings against children and youths.

The *Criminal Code* provides, in s. 486(1), for a presumptive statutory requirement that criminal proceedings against adults be held in public. Restrictions on this requirement which are prescribed by that provision must now meet the strictures of s. 1. This would generally be tested on a case-by-case basis, since the *Charter*'s openness requirement is reflected on the face of the statutory provision.

The only categorical challenge which could now be levelled at s. 486(1) of the *Criminal Code* concerns the statutory power to exclude the public from a criminal proceeding in order to protect public morals. As noted in the preceding section, the Supreme Court has cast substantial doubt on the appropriateness of the protection of public morals as a reason under s. 1 for limiting open justice. The public needs no protection from sexually explicit or otherwise aberrant situations which can arise in criminal proceedings. Accordingly, the power to exclude the public from court proceedings on public morals grounds ought to be struck down as unconstitutional.

There is a narrow range of adult criminal proceedings which is not covered by s. 486(1) of the *Criminal Code*. This includes *ex parte* proceedings under s. 507 of the *Criminal Code* before a justice of the peace, where the justice decides whether to issue process against a person for an alleged breach of the criminal law, after information alleging a crime is laid before the justice. Such pre-charging proceedings are traditionally held *in camera*.

In *Southam Inc. v. Coulter*,[210] a journalist challenged the validity of the public's exclusion from this pre-charging proceeding, in a widely

---

210 *Bindman v. A.G. Canada, supra*, note 44.

reported case where a private citizen had laid fraud and other charges against senior officials of the Federal Government. The Ontario Court of Appeal held that neither the common law openness rule nor the public access guarantee in *Criminal Code* s. 486(1) applied to such proceedings.[211] It ruled that *Charter* s. 2(b) *prima facie* guarantees the public a right to attend these proceedings.[212] However, the public's automatic exclusion from all such proceedings was found to be justified under *Charter* s. 1 regardless of the individual circumstances of each case.[213]

The Court of Appeal viewed public exclusion from pre-charging hearings as less invasive of open justice than exclusion from proceedings occurring after charges are instituted.[214] *In camera* proceedings at a pre-charging hearing protects the rights of the innocent from having their reputation besmirched by publicity, including the untested hearsay allegations which can be levelled during such hearings.[215] Where a pre-charging hearing results in the institution of charges, the conduct of pre-charging proceedings *in camera* protects the accused from prejudicial pre-trial publicity which could threaten his or her right to a fair trial.[216] Similarly, *in camera* proceedings protect the privacy interests of persons against whom charges have been *demanded*.[217]

Because the person against whom criminality is alleged is not present at the *ex parte* pre-charging hearing, openness of these proceedings would threaten the due administration of justice. Publicity of these proceedings could forewarn the potential accused that process has issued against him or her. This could enable the accused to flee the jurisdiction to evade service.[218]

Based on the foregoing, the Court of Appeal held that public exclusion from pre-charging proceedings furthers the compelling goals of fair trial, the administration of justice, individual privacy and protection of the innocent,[219] all of which are objectives that the Supreme Court has sanctioned.[220] The Court of Appeal held under s. 1 that the public's automatic exclusion from all pre-charging proceedings impairs s. 2(b) rights as little as possible, having regard to the nature of these proceedings. The accused cannot request a non-publication order at the pre-

---

211 *Ibid.*, at 9 *ff.*, *per* Krever J.A.
212 *Ibid.*, at 18 *ff.*
213 *Ibid.*, at 25 *ff.*
214 *Ibid.*, at 26 *ff.*
215 *Ibid.*, at 27.
216 *Ibid.*
217 *Ibid.*
218 *Ibid.*
219 *Ibid.*
220 *Ibid.*, at 12, citing with approval *Edmonton Journal v. Alta. (A.G.)*, *supra*, note 29, and *MacIntyre v. N.S. (A.G.)*, *supra*, note 26.

charging hearing, because he or she is not present at this *ex parte* proceeding. Moreover, there is no statutory authority to make such an order. A judicial discretion over public attendance, exercised on a case-by-case basis, is unworkable, because there is no information before the justice on which a discretion could be exercised intelligently. For example, a justice could not predict in advance whether public attendance at the hearing could tip off the accused, and lead the accused to flee the jurisdiction.

To what extent can the *Charter*'s open court requirement be overridden during appeals to court from administrative tribunals, which involve sensitive personal information? The British Columbia Court of Appeal has held that *Charter* s. 1 can be invoked to justify a court order, sealing a physician's discipline hearing record during an appeal from the tribunal to court. In *Re Hirt and College of Physicians and Surgeons of B.C.*,[221] a physician, accused of having sexual relations with several patients, appealed his discipline to court. The court was asked to seal the appeal record, and to use pseudonyms for the patients involved, so that intimate personal information about the complainant and other patients would not be publicly disclosed and published.[222]

The B.C. court assumed that this order violated *Charter* s. 2(b), by reference to the *Southam (No. 1)* holding that s. 2(b) includes a constitutional open court requirement.[223] It held that the requested order imposes, at most, only a minor burden on freedom of expression, and was necessary to protect the rights and confidentiality of innocent persons.[224] As well, the court held that such measures are needed to foster the filing of complaints against doctors by patients.[225]

The question of what limits may be placed on the constitutional right to attend court proceedings has been litigated predominantly in the area of proceedings against children and youth. Shortly after the *Charter*'s enactment, the Ontario Court of Appeal struck down a provision of

---

221 *Hirt v. College of Physicians & Surgeons (B.C.)* (1985), 17 D.L.R. (4th) 472 (B.C.C.A.).

222 Compare *Orpin v. College of Physicians & Surgeons (Ont.)* (1988), 25 C.P.C. (2d) 19 (Ont. Div.Ct.), *per* Campbell J., where the Divisional Court of Ontario refused a doctor's request to ban publication of his name pending a comparable appeal. However, the court did ban media identification of the complainant. The court did not undertake any *Charter* review of these orders.

223 *Re Hirt, supra*, note 221 at 480.

224 *Ibid.*, at 483.

225 *Ibid.*, at 484. It is noteworthy that the court went on to hold that the judge, hearing the appeal, could, if he or she felt it appropriate, ban publication of the identities of the patients involved in the proceedings. There was no discussion in the case of the constitutionality of such an order, nor of the legal authority, if any, that the court would have to make such an order.

the *Juvenile Delinquents Act*[226] which required all juvenile delinquency proceedings to be conducted *in camera* regardless of the circumstances.[227] The court accepted that exclusion of the public could be justified in situations where such was needed to protect a child's best interests.[228] However, a blanket ban on public attendance at all juvenile delinquency proceedings was excessive, in light of the Crown's concession that there could be some cases where the ban on public attendance is unnecessary.

The *Young Offenders Act*[229] was subsequently proclaimed to replace the *Juvenile Delinquents Act*. The new statute provides that youth court proceedings will be conducted in public, except where the court is satisfied that the public's presence would be injurious to a young person involved in the proceeding as an accused, a witness or a victim.[230] The Supreme Court of Ontario[231] and the Ontario Court of Appeal[232] both upheld the validity of this discretionary power to exclude the public. It was adjudged to be a reasonable means for balancing the public's right to attend such proceedings under s. 2(b) against the protection of the best interests of children.[233]

A Nova Scotia County Court implicitly applied the constitutional right to attend court when it decided to admit a reporter to an otherwise *in camera* child protection proceeding. In *M.(Y.) v. Children's Aid Society*,[234] a court had a statutory discretion to admit a member of the public to an otherwise *in camera* child protection proceeding. The statute presumed that the hearing would be *in camera*. It placed the burden on the person seeking to attend to prove that such should be allowed.[235]

On the case's specific facts, the court decided to admit a reporter to the closed hearing, on condition that in his reports on the case, he must

---

226 R.S.C. 1970, c. J-3, s. 12.
227 *Re Southam (No. 1), supra*, note 20.
228 *Ibid.*, at 536.
229 R.S.C. 1985, c. Y-1.
230 S. 38(1) [am. 1986, c. 32, s. 29] of the *Young Offenders Act* provides as follows:
     "38.(1) Subject to this section, no person shall publish by any means any report

                                    . . .

     "in which the name of the young person, a child or a young person who is a
     victim of the offence or a child or a young person who appeared as a witness
     in connection with the offence, or in which any information serving to
     identify such young person or child, is disclosed."
231 *Southam Inc. v. R., supra*, note 44.
232 *Ibid.*
233 *Ibid.*
234 *Supra*, note 56.
235 *Ibid.*, at 431.

not identify the parties or certain other persons.[236] While the court did not purport to hold the applicable statute unconstitutional, its reasons for admitting the reporter refer specifically to the *Charter* right of access to courts.[237] The court appears to have approached the case on the assumption that the reporter should be admitted, where the court has no reason to exclude him. This effectively reverses the onus of proof established in the governing legislation.

From these cases, it can be gleaned that a statute, dealing with public attendance at court, is more likely to survive s. 1 scrutiny if it includes at least an initial presumption that court proceedings will be open to the public, and if it includes a discretion to allow for closure in demonstrably justified situations. However, this is not an absolute necessity under s. 1. It is possible for a law to survive *Charter* scrutiny if it bans public attendance in an entire category of cases, and leaves a judge no discretion to override this general practice.

E. Specific Limits on Filming in Court

If one assumed that s. 2(b) of the *Charter* gives the media a constitutional right to televise court proceedings,[238] what limits may be imposed on this activity consonant with s. 1? In *Squires v. R.*, the Ontario Provincial Offences Court[239] and Ontario District Court[240] considered this question. Each considered whether such filming can be restricted to situations where the parties and witnesses in a proceeding consent to be filmed, and where the judge approves of the filming for educational or instructional purposes.[241]

In *Squires*, a C.B.C. television reporter was charged with filming a witness while in an Ottawa court house corridor, contrary to a provincial statute. She challenged the validity of the law under which she was charged, arguing that *Charter* s. 2(b) creates a constitutional right to film in court rooms and in court house corridors. The trial court heard some 27 witnesses, most of whom were experts, who testified about the alleged benefits and harms of cameras in the court room and in the court house.

Both courts affirmed the validity of the party and witness consent

---

236 *Ibid.*, at 431 *ff.*

237 *Ibid.*

238 In the text associated with note 104 *ff., supra*, the divided jurisprudence is reviewed on the question of whether s. 2(b) confers a constitutional right to film in court.

239 *Supra*, note 44, *per* Vanek Prov. J. (Prov.Ct.).

240 *Ibid., per* Mercier D.C.J. (Dist.Ct.).

241 These are the conditions for filming in court imposed by s. 67 of the Ontario *Judicature Act*, since replaced by similar restrictions in s. 146 of the Ontario *Courts of Justice Act*.

requirement under *Charter* s. 1.[242] They agreed that the purposes of the impugned restrictions on filming in court are to protect the accused's right to a fair trial, the proper administration of justice, the dignity and decorum of the court room and court house, and the rights, dignity and privacy of all participants in the court process, including victims of crime.[243] They each found these goals to be sufficiently important to justify limits on television cameras in the court room and in court house corridors.[244]

Reviewing the competing testimony about the effects of television in U.S. court rooms from American judges, lawyers, victims assistance experts, social scientists and a televised trial witness, both courts held that television in the court room poses a real and substantial threat to the fairness of trials.[245] They can intimidate witnesses, distract jurors, and influence the conduct of lawyers and judges.[246] They can deter crime victims and other witnesses from reporting offences to the authorities, or from being willing to testify in court.[247] They can inflict a psychological injury or stress on crime victims, and cause an invasion of privacy of court participants.[248] These adverse effects are caused by cameras, as distinct from the impact of simply having the court room open to public attendance and conventional media reporting.[249]

The trial judge held, with the District Court's affirmation,[250] that Squires had not established that cameras in the court room would have a significant impact on public knowledge about the courts, or on judicial accountability. No such benefits had been documented in the U.S. as a

---

242 *Squires v. R., supra*, note 44.
243 *Ibid.*
244 *Ibid.*
245 *Ibid.*
246 *Ibid.*, at 355-56 (Prov.Ct.); at 353-54 (Dist.Ct.).
247 *Ibid.*
248 *Ibid.*, at 367 (Prov.Ct.); at 355-56 (Dist.Ct.).
249 *Ibid.* The trial and appeal courts also considered whether cameras in the court room would have a social value, over and above the societal benefits of having the court room open to public attendance and conventional media reporting. Squires argued that filming in court would educate the public about the workings of the justice system, improve the public's understanding of and confidence in the courts, and provide an accurate and neutral portrayal of cases, in contradistinction to the subjective conventional reports provided by journalists. The Crown disputed these claims, arguing that the camera is selective in how it portrays an event, and that the image on the television screen is heavily influenced by the editing and contextualization of court room footage that is broadcast in a news story. Such footage would ordinarily take the form of a 15- to 30-second court room clip, excerpted from an entire day's testimony. This, the Crown argued, would not be educational or informative for the public, over and above the advantages of conventional media coverage.
250 *Ibid.*, at 362-65 (Prov.Ct.); at 359 (Dist.Ct.).

result of the widespread use of cameras in court rooms there.[251] He rejected the reporter's claim that filming in court gives the home television viewer the same experience as if they attend court in person.[252] He found the media's claims regarding the benefits of filming in court to be inconclusive.[253]

Having found the benefits of filming in court to be unproven, and the harms which they pose to the justice system to be serious, both courts concluded that it is justifiable under s. 1 to limit the use of cameras in court to those situations where the parties and witnesses consent to being filmed.[254] On appeal, the District Court suggested that it would be appropriate to add to the legislation a requirement that filming in court not be permitted unless jurors also consent to their use.[255] Squires had opposed this consent requirement, arguing that it poses a substantial barrier to the media, since parties and witnesses usually do not consent to being filmed.

At trial, the Provincial Offences Court ruled that s. 1 permits the restriction of filming in court to circumstances where the presiding judge approves of it for educational or instructional purposes.[256] He held that this proviso does not preclude the use of cameras in the court room for news gathering in appropriate situations.[257] In contrast, the District Court, on appeal, felt that there might be some circumstances where news gathering is not permissible under the "educational or instructional" purposes proviso. Accordingly, the District Court stated that it would declare this proviso to be severable, and unconstitutional, as an unnecessary restriction on filming in court.[258]

The trial judge also held that the photography of parties and witnesses in court house corridors provides minimal benefits to reporters, and would be nothing more than a convenience or expediency for journalists, as contrasted with filming these persons just outside the court house building.[259] It is justifiable to ban such photography, because when filming in court house corridors has been permitted in the United States, it results in "wolfpack journalism," where reporters mob

---

251 *Ibid.*
252 *Ibid.*
253 *Ibid.*
254 *Ibid.*, at 368-69 (Prov.Ct.).
255 *Ibid.*, at 359 (Dist.Ct.).
256 *Ibid.*, at 369 (Prov.Ct.).
257 *Ibid.*
258 *Ibid.*, at 358 (Dist.Ct.). It should be noted that because the District Court had decided to affirm Squires' conviction for filming in a court house corridor, it was unnecessary for the court to decide on the permissible scope of limits on filming in court rooms. Hence, this ruling can be treated as *obiter dicta*.
259 *Ibid.*, at 366 (Prov.Ct.).

and harass witnesses and parties in an effort to obtain a photo opportunity.[260] The District Court affirmed these findings.[261]

F. Specific Limits on Dissemination of Factual Information About a Case by Publication Bans

1. General

As discussed in the previous part, strong Supreme Court authority
provides that legal restrictions on the media's reporting of facts pertaining to a judicial proceeding violate s. 2(b).[262] What is the scope under
Charter s. 1 for limiting media reporting through judicial bans on the
publication of some or all facts relating to a court case? Much case law
has developed in this area between 1984 and 1990. In this section, the
Supreme Court's pronouncements on publication bans are considered
first. This is followed by an examination of lower court decisions regarding statutory non-publication orders. Finally, lower court cases are
considered which deal with non-statutory restrictions on publications
about court proceedings, including those imposed pursuant to the so-
called inherent power of the court, and pursuant to the common law *sub
judice* contempt offence.

2. Supreme Court Jurisprudence on Publication Bans

In *Canadian Newspapers Co. v. Can. (A.G.),*[263] its first *Charter* open
justice ruling, the Supreme Court of Canada upheld the constitutionality of a statute authorizing the mandatory banning of a sexual
assault complainant's name, at her request. *Criminal Code* s. 442(3)[264]
provides that a judge must ban the media from publishing a sexual
assault complainant's identity, or information which would tend to
identify her, if the complainant or prosecutor requests this order. The
provision also empowers a judge to ban the publication of this information on his or her own motion if this appears appropriate, even if the
complainant or prosecutor do not request this order.

In *Canadian Newspapers*, the media accepted that, in appropriate
cases, a s. 442(3) ban could be justifiable under *Charter* s. 1.[265] However,

---

260 *Ibid.*
261 *Ibid.*, at 355-56 (Dist.Ct.).
262 As discussed in the text associated with note 64 *ff., supra.*
263 *Supra*, note 66.
264 Now s. 486(3) of the *Criminal Code*, R.S.C. 1985, c. C-46.
265 *Supra*, note 66 at 129.

it argued that s. 442(3) is overbroad, because it automatically bans media reports of the complainant's name in *every* case.[266] The Ontario Court of Appeal had accepted this contention.[267] It struck out the words of s. 442(3) which made such orders mandatory whenever requested by the complainant. The appellate court left in force only the portion of s. 442(3) which allowed for publication bans when they were deemed appropriate in a judge's discretion.[268]

The Court of Appeal expressed the concern that there may be cases where the complainant's sexual assault allegations are false. Where such is the case, publication of the complainant's identity might lead others, against whom the same complainant had levelled false allegations previously, to come forward and give exculpatory testimony.[269] The mandatory aspect of s. 442(3) thus appeared to the court to be excessive.[270]

In a landmark judgment elaborating on the s. 1 test, the Supreme Court of Canada reversed the Court of Appeal decision. It upheld the entirety of s. 442(3), including its requirement that the non-publication order be made automatically whenever a complainant requests it.[271]

Section 442(3)'s undisputed purpose was held to be the fostering of complaints by victims of sexual assault.[272] The Supreme Court accepted that this objective is sufficiently compelling to override freedom of expression.[273] This is because of the seriousness of the crime of sexual assault, the substantial extent to which this offence now goes unreported, and the fact that one reason for this underreporting is the victim's fear of having others find out about her victimization.[274]

The media did not dispute the social importance of governmental efforts at promoting this objective. They also did not dispute that, in general, s. 442(3) orders tend to promote the fostering of complaints by sexual assault victims.[275] They only objected to s. 442(3)'s means for furthering this goal.[276]

The core dispute before the Supreme Court was whether bans on media reports of sexual assault victims' names must be mandatory, or whether their issuance should be left to a judge's discretion. The media argued that a discretionary power impairs freedom of expression less than s. 442(3)'s mandatory requirement. They thus claimed that the

---

266 *Supra*, note 44, *per* Howland C.J.O. (C.A.).
267 *Ibid.*, at 576, 581.
268 *Ibid.*, at 581-82.
269 *Supra*, note 66.
270 *Ibid.*, at 130.
271 *Ibid.*
272 *Ibid.*, at 130.
273 *Ibid.*
274 *Ibid.*, at 131-32.
275 *Ibid.*, at 132.
276 *Ibid.*, at 130.

discretionary option must be preferred under *Charter* s. 1.[277] The Crown responded that s. 442(3)'s mandatory feature is justified, because it is necessary to assure sexual assault victims that their names definitely will not be published by the media, if they wish such anonymity.[278]

The Crown argued that the critical time for ascertaining which legislative option is preferable is at the point immediately after the offence is committed, that is, when the victim decides whether to report the crime to the authorities. If the victim has a legal assurance that she can keep her name out of the press, she will be more likely to report the crime, the Crown argued. If the court had a discretion to ban such publications, rather than a mandatory duty to do so on the complainant's request, victims, who are deciding whether to report their victimization, would have no certainty that they could keep their names out of the news. They would therefore be more reluctant to report the offence. Thus, the discretionary option would be less effective at fostering sexual assault victims to report their victimization.

The Supreme Court accepted the Crown's contention. It held that the media's discretionary option does not meet s. 1's "least restrictive alternative" requirement, because it does not provide sexual assault victims with the certainty they require to be encouraged to report their victimization.[279] The court rejected the Court of Appeal's concern about the hypothetical situation where publication of the complainant's identity might induce witnesses to come forward with exculpatory evidence.[280] The Supreme Court criticized the appellate court's review of the brief evidentiary record tendered at trial.[281] The Women's Legal Education and Action Fund, an intervenor in the Supreme Court, had criticized the Court of Appeal's emphasis on the false sexual assault complainant. The Court of Appeal's concern was seen as a throw-back to earlier times, when the procedural, substantive and evidentiary doctrines applying to sexual assault were preoccupied with a stereotype of the sexual assault complainant as typically being a malicious falsifier of rape charges.

In *Canadian Newspapers*, the Supreme Court established a clear guide for the application of the "least restrictive alternative" branch of the s. 1 test. A law, infringing a *Charter* right, will not be invalidated under s. 1 simply because another law could have been drafted which would impose a lesser burden on *Charter* rights. The court will prefer an alternative to the impugned law only if the alternative is both less burdensome on *Charter* rights, and is at least as effective at promoting

---

277 *Ibid.*, at 132.
278 *Ibid.*, at 131-32.
279 *Ibid.*, at 132-33.
280 *Ibid.*, at 130-31.
281 *Ibid.*

the government's goals as is the impugned law. In *Canadian Newspapers*, the discretionary option was not preferred over the mandatory option incorporated in *Criminal Code* s. 442(3) because the discretionary option, while less burdensome on freedom of expression, is nevertheless less effective at advancing s. 442(3)'s goals than a discretionary banning power.

The Supreme Court also rejected the media's argument that s. 442(3) is not proportional to its objectives, because its ban on publishing identifying information is allegedly too vague. The media claimed that a reporter could not know what information would tend to identify the complainant. The provision could chill the publishing of perfectly lawful information.[282]

The Supreme Court gave this argument short shrift. It believed that media establishments have the capacity to make fair judgments of what information can be published and what cannot.[283] This holding is especially important, since many statutory non-publication provisions employ a similar requirement.[284]

In its second *Charter* open justice pronouncement, the Supreme Court struck down a sweeping provincial limitation on media reports concerning matrimonial and other civil cases. In *Edmonton Journal v. Alberta (A.G.)*,[285] the Supreme Court declared unconstitutional s. 30 of the Alberta *Judicature Act*.[286] That provision banned, in perpetuity, all publications regarding any matrimonial proceeding in Alberta, except the names, addresses and occupations of the parties and witnesses, a concise statement of the charges, defences and counter-charges in support of which evidence is given, submissions and rulings on points of

---

282 *Ibid.*, at 133.

283 *Ibid.*, at 134.

284 In *Re Southam and R.* (1987), 37 C.C.C. (3d) 139 (Ont. H.C.), the Supreme Court of Ontario quashed a non-publication order, purportedly made by a lower court judge pursuant to s. 442(3) of the *Criminal Code*, where the order banned publication of the accused's name. In that case, there was nothing before the court to suggest that media identification of the accused would have the effect of identifying the victims to the public. The court held that a court could ban publication of an accused's identity in a sexual assault case where the victim is related to the accused, or where the accused stands *in loco parentis* to the victim, such that identification of the accused would lead the public to identify the victim. However, in this case, there was no such relationship between the accused and the victim. While this case appears to turn on a construction of s. 442(3), rather than on a ruling on its constitutionality as applied here, the court noted at the end of the decision that the order had interfered with *Charter* s. 2(b) rights, the judge having improperly exercised his discretion in issuing the order.

285 *Supra*, note 29.

286 R.S.A. 1980, c. J-1.

law in the case, the jury charge, and the court's decision and judicial observations thereon.[287]

The Alberta provision also banned the pre-trial or pre-settlement publication of any statement in pleadings, discoveries, or affidavits in any civil proceedings in Alberta, except the names and addresses of the parties and their solicitors, and a concise statement of the claims and defences involved in the case.[288] The Alberta Legislature took the unprecedented step of including in the provision an actual example of the kinds of descriptions of a case which are permissible. Section 30(2) gives as an example: where "the claim is for the price of goods sold or delivered," or "the claim is for damages for personal injuries caused by the negligent operation of an automobile."

The section exempted from the ban any publication required for the legal proceeding[289] and any *bona fide* law report, or medical or legal journal.[290] Hence, the impugned provision treats the proscribed information as safe for release to doctors and lawyers, but to no one else, even if the parties to the proceedings involved take no objection to the proscribed publications. The non-publication requirement goes into effect automatically in all cases. A judge need not be asked to make a specific non-publication order, and has no statutory power to lift the non-publication requirement in cases where it is unnecessary.

The Supreme Court unanimously held that the impugned law contravenes the freedom of expression guaranteed in *Charter* s. 2(b).[291] It divided on whether the law was saved by s. 1.[292] The majority held that it was not salvageable.

Speaking for the majority, Cory J. noted that the Attorney General for Alberta defended these provisions as being necessary to protect public morals, litigants' access to justice, the privacy of litigants, and, in the case of the pre-trial ban on reports of civil proceedings, the litigants' right to a fair trial.[293] The majority rejected these s. 1 defences.[294] It held that in the modern day, public morals would not be threatened by media reports of family cases.[295]

While access to justice was seen as an important social goal, the

---

287 *Ibid.*, s. 30(1).
288 *Ibid.*, s. 30(2).
289 *Ibid.*, s. 30(3)(i), (ii).
290 *Ibid.*, s. 30(3)(iii).
291 *Edmonton Journal, supra,* note 29 at 612, *per* Cory J.; at 589, *per* Wilson J.; at 594, 598, *per* La Forest J.; but note that this was conceded anyhow, at 594.
292 *Ibid.*, at 612 *ff., per* Cory J.; at 593, *per* Wilson J.; at 604, *per* La Forest J.
293 *Ibid.*, at 613 *ff., per* Cory J.
294 *Ibid.*
295 *Ibid.*, at 613, *per* Cory J.

court was not satisfied that media reporting of the proscribed information would deter litigants from bringing family claims to court.[296] In contrast to *Canadian Newspapers*, the court had no evidentiary record before it showing a rational connection between the impugned publication ban and the willingness of matrimonial litigants to institute court proceedings.[297] To the contrary, official statistics show divorce litigation to be on the increase, even in provinces which have no comparable publication ban.[298]

The court agreed that the protection of litigants' privacy is a sufficiently important goal to justify limits on freedom of expression.[299] However, it found the impugned law to be excessively broad, thereby failing to meet s. 1's "least impairment" and "proportionality" branches.[300] Litigants' privacy interests could be protected effectively by *in camera* proceedings or narrower publication bans where needed. For example, litigants' privacy could remain intact if publications were allowed dealing with the substance of a case, including matters of public interest and importance, so long as the media withholds litigants' names and identifying information.[301]

In general, the majority took the position that restraints on the reporting of court proceedings can only meet the s. 1 test if they are minimal in character. Here, in sharp contrast to the publication ban on sexual assault complainants' names upheld in *Canadian Newspapers*, the restrictions are vast. They unnecessarily preclude reporting on issues of great importance to the public.[302]

Condemning as "repressive" the sweeping pre-trial ban on virtually all reports of civil proceedings under s. 30(2) of the *Judicature Act*, the majority opined that some restrictions on pre-trial media reporting of civil proceedings can be justified under s. 1 to protect civil litigants' fair trial and privacy rights.[303] However, the impugned provision is too broad to meet s. 1's "least impairment" requirement. It bans media coverage of important matters, such as litigation against government agencies in the constitutional and administrative law fields.[304] Wilson J.

---

296 *Ibid.*, at 613-14, *per* Cory J.
297 *Ibid.*
298 *Ibid.*, at 613-14.
299 *Ibid.*, at 614, *per* Cory J.; at 589 *ff.*, *per* Wilson J.; at 600, *per* La Forest J., dissenting in part on other grounds.
300 *Ibid.*, at 615-16, *per* Cory J.; at 593, *per* Wilson J.; La Forest J. felt that the s. 1 requirements had been met and that the law should be upheld.
301 *Ibid.*, at 615, *per* Cory J.
302 *Ibid.*, at 615-16, *per* Cory J.
303 *Ibid.*, at 615-18, *per* Cory J.
304 *Ibid.*, at 612, *per* Cory J.

filed a separate opinion concurring with the majority decision, and adding some detail to its general conclusions.[305]

La Forest J.[306] filed an opinion concurring in part and dissenting in part. He agreed that the impugned provision violates *Charter* s. 2(b), and that its restrictions on pre-trial reporting of civil matters in s. 30(2) of the *Judicature Act* cannot withstand s. 1 scrutiny. However, he opined that the permanent ban on detailed reporting of matrimonial proceedings is immunized from challenge by s. 1.[307]

As a matter of statutory construction, La Forest J. held that this provision did not ban the publication of as much information as the majority had suggested.[308] In relation to the social value served by publication of the details of matrimonial disputes which are prohibited by s. 30(1), he found it[309]

> ... difficult to take seriously the contention that the general public would learn very much about what their rights are or how their problems might be dealt with in court by permitting the revelation by the media of specific details of particular cases dealing with marital questions.

He viewed the burden on freedom of expression imposed by the impugned law as being minimal.[310] He found that this restriction was proportional and rationally related to the important goals of protecting individual privacy and access to justice.[311]

In his core disagreement with the majority, La Forest J. felt that the provision infringes freedom of expression as little as possible to achieve its goals. It only applies to a narrow range of cases which ordinarily involve personal and intimate disclosures, and is subject to a range of exemptions.[312] A discretionary judicial power to ban publication of information regarding matrimonial cases would be less effective, he found, based on a British Royal Commission report regarding matrimonial law.[313]

In striking down the Alberta law in its entirety, the Supreme Court of Canada took an approach to remedies different from the Alberta Court of Appeal in the same case.[314] The Court of Appeal held that the

---

305 *Ibid.*, at 581 *ff.*, *per* Wilson J.
306 L'Heureux-Dubé and Sopinka JJ., concurring.
307 *Ibid.*, at 604.
308 *Ibid.*, at 595 *ff.*
309 *Ibid.*, at 599, *per* La Forest J.
310 *Ibid.*, at 600, *per* La Forest J.
311 *Ibid.*, at 603-604, *per* La Forest J.
312 *Ibid.*, at 595-96, *per* La Forest J.
313 *Ibid.*, at 597, *per* La Forest J.
314 See *Edmonton Journal v. Alta. (A.G.)* (1987), 41 D.L.R. (4th) 502 (Alta. C.A.).

impugned provision could violate freedom of expression, and that there were at least some situations in which its publication restraints are unnecessary.[315] However, it felt that the law could be left in force, because a court could relieve a party from its application under the *Charter* in those fact situations where it could not constitutionally be applied.[316]

In contrast, the Supreme Court found the statute to be so significantly overbroad that total invalidation of it was the appropriate remedy in the circumstances. This leaves open the possibility that some non-publication provisions might be left in force, despite the fact that they may not be constitutionally applicable in some fact situations, so long as their overbreadth is not substantial. In such cases, any overbreadth in the law could be addressed by the grant of constitutional exemptions from the law in individual cases. The Supreme Court did not explicitly address this question in *Edmonton Journal*, and hence it remains open for future consideration.

Taken together, the two Supreme Court *Charter* open justice rulings provide strong authority for an approach to open justice claims which places a substantial burden on the Crown to justify publication restraints. Its approach generally accords with that proposed in *Open Justice*.[317] As the following discussion shows, this approach is frequently not reflected in the open justice rulings of lower courts across Canada, decided both before and after these Supreme Court judgments were handed down.

3. Lower Court Rulings on Statutory Publication Bans

A large portion of *Charter* open justice litigation has dealt with proceedings involving children as parties, as victims, or otherwise as witnesses. This is no more apparent than in the litigation over statutory restrictions on media reporting of court proceedings in lower courts.

In *Southam Inc. v. R.*, the Supreme Court of Ontario,[318] with the affirmation of the Ontario Court of Appeal,[319] upheld s. 38(1) of the *Young Offenders Act*[320] as a reasonable limit on freedom of expression under s. 1 of the *Charter*. Section 38(1) permanently and automatically bans the media publication of the names of young persons involved in Youth Court proceedings, whether as an accused or as a witness. The

---

315 *Ibid.*, at 518.
316 *Ibid.*, at 518-19.
317 Lepofksy, *supra*, note 4 at 194-95.
318 *Supra*, note 44.
319 *Ibid.*
320 R.S.C. 1985, c. Y-1.

provision also bans publication of information which would tend to identify these persons. At the time that the provision was challenged in court, it did not provide any exceptions. Thus, such publications were banned even if the young person consented to being named by the media.[321]

The Supreme Court of Ontario received the extensive testimony of experts in child psychology about the harms which the proscribed publications can cause for young persons involved in the juvenile justice system. The court found that these publications can harm young persons by interfering with their rehabilitation.[322] While there may be some cases where the prohibited publications might not pose this threat, the evidence suggested that it would not necessarily be possible for the court to identify those cases.[323]

The Supreme Court of Ontario held that the goal of fostering the rehabilitation of young persons charged with offences is a sufficiently important objective under s. 1. It considered that the impugned provision only infringes free expression minimally. While there may be cases where the ban is unnecessary, the court found that the means employed by the legislation are nevertheless reasonable.

Affirming this ruling, the Ontario Court of Appeal held that a law need not be perfectly designed to be sustained under *Charter* s. 1.[324] The Alberta Court of Queen's Bench reached a comparable result when it upheld, under s. 1, the validity of s. 12(3) of the *Juvenile Delinquents Act* in *R. v. R. (T.)*.[325] There are two differences between Ontario's *Southam Inc. v. R.* case and Alberta's *R. (T.)* case. First, the Alberta case did not appear to involve an extensive evidentiary record to support its s. 1 conclusions, in contrast to *Southam Inc. v. R.* Second, *Southam Inc. v. R.* involved a challenge to a *Young Offenders Act* provision which bans the publication of information about the accused young person in every case. In contrast, the *R. (T.)* case dealt with the predecessor provision in the *Juvenile Delinquents Act*, which empowered a court to provide special leave to permit publication of such information.

The Manitoba Court of Queen's Bench struck down s. 443.2(1) of the *Criminal Code* in one of the many open justice decisions bearing the name *Canadian Newspapers Co. v. Canada (A.G.)*.[326] The impugned provision provided that:

---

321 The impugned provision was later amended to allow for publication of the identity of a young person, contrary to this provision's general ban, in circumstances where the disclosure of information would not be contrary to the best interests of the person being identified; see, *supra*, note 230, s. 29(1.4).

322 *Re Southam Inc. and R. (No. 1)* (1982), 70 C.C.C. (2d) 257 (Ont. H.C.).

323 *Ibid.*, at 263.

324 *Southam Inc. v. R., supra*, note 44 (C.A.).

325 *Supra*, note 43.

326 *Supra*, note 87. Now s. 487.2(1) of the *Criminal Code*, R.S.C. 1985, c. C-46.

Where a search warrant is issued under section 443 or 443.1 or a search is made under such a warrant, every one who publishes in any newspaper or broadcasts any information with respect to

(a) the location of the place searched or to be searched, or
(b) the identity of any person who is or appears to occupy or be in possession or control of that place or who is suspected of being involved in any offence in relation to which the warrant was issued,

without the consent of every person referred to in paragraph (b) is, unless a charge has been laid in respect of any offence in relation to which the warrant was issued, guilty of an offence . . .

The court held that this provision infringed s. 2(b), and was not saved under s. 1 of the *Charter.*

In the court's view, the ban on the publication of information relating to a search warrant is aimed at the twin goals of protecting the privacy of innocent persons who are the targets of search warrants, and of promoting the effectiveness of police investigations through the suppression of publications which might tip off an investigation's target. These were held to be sufficiently important objectives to warrant overriding the freedom of expression.[327] No reasoning was provided for this outcome of the balancing of these competing objectives.[328] The court concluded that the impugned provision does not impair s. 2(b) rights as little as possible, in order to achieve these goals. This is because its sweeping wording bans the publication of more information than is necessary to further its goals.[329] This decision stands as one of the few lower court decisions on the validity of non-publication orders in which this s. 1 "least impairment" test is effectively implemented.

4. Lower Court Rulings on Non-statutory Publication Bans

Within the rubric of s. 1 of the *Charter*, to what extent may courts suppress media publications or public statements about court proceedings, in circumstances where no statute explicitly clothes judges with the power to do so? To address this question, attention first turns to the validity of non-publication orders purportedly made pursuant to the court's inherent power. Then, attention turns to the constitutionality of the common law crime of *sub judice* contempt of court.

In several cases, courts have claimed to have the inherent power to ban publications about a case before them, even where there is no statutory power to do so. In *Open Justice*, an argument is presented to

---

327 *Ibid.,* at 605-606.
328 *Ibid.*
329 *Ibid.,* at 605-607.

the effect that no such inherent power does or should exist.[330] Put simply, it is not for courts to invent of their own volition as profound a power as the authority to silence some aspect of media reporting about a court proceeding, absent a clear mandate from a democratically elected legislature. This is especially compelling in the *Charter* era, since the power to ban publications necessarily infringes s. 2(b) rights. That non-elected judges can grant themselves the power to suppress media coverage of their actions is inherently suspect in light of the Supreme Court's enunciation of the fundamental importance to a free and democratic society of judicial proceedings being subject to media coverage.[331]

In *Toronto Sun Publishing Corp. v. A.G. Alberta*,[332] the Alberta Court of Appeal upheld the constitutionality of a trial judge's apparently permanent ban on publication of information disclosed during a *voir dire* conducted during a blackmail trial. Section 576.1 of the *Criminal Code* provides for a ban on publication of information disclosed at a *voir dire*. However, it explicitly limits the force of such orders, by providing that they only apply up until the time that the jury retires to deliberate. Here, the trial judge purported to make the ban continue until *after* the jury deliberated and rendered a verdict. Most peculiar is the fact that before commencing its deliberations, the jury had been instructed by the trial judge to render a guilty verdict, because of the information disclosed to the judge at the *voir dire*. Hence, there was no need for an s. 576.1 non-publication order to protect the jury from prejudicial publicity against the accused.

The Alberta Court of Appeal ruled that the trial judge had jurisdiction to issue non-publication orders even where there is no legislative foundation for such an order.[333] According to the court, a banning order was justified under *Charter* s. 1 to protect the identities of the blackmail victims involved in the case, since this would help foster blackmail victims to report their victimization to the authorities in the future.[334] The appellate court varied the trial judge's order, based on this reasoning. It affirmed an ongoing ban on the publication of information disclosed at the *voir dire* which would tend to reveal the identities of the victims or others involved with the accused. Other information could be published.

What is anomalous about this decision was the court's admitted lack of an evidentiary foundation for its *Charter* ruling. There appeared to be no evidence about the need to protect the identities of blackmail

---

330 Lepofsky, *supra*, note 4 at 76 *ff.*
331 See *Edmonton Journal v. Alta. (A.G.)*, *supra*, note 29 at 607-10, *per* Cory J.
332 *Supra*, note 87.
333 *Ibid.*, at 38.
334 The court relied heavily on *Hirt v. College of Physicians & Surgeons (B.C.)*, *supra*, note 221.

victims. There was also no evidence of what information was disclosed during the *voir dire*, since the record of the trial proceedings had already been destroyed. Thus, there may have been no new information to disclose, and no harm caused by any disclosure. On such a thin foundation, it is difficult to see how a permanent non-publication order, outside the trial judge's statutory mandate, could be demonstrably justified in a free and democratic society.

In *R. v. MacArthur*,[335] the Supreme Court of Ontario issued a ban on the publication of the identities of certain witnesses who were to testify at a murder trial, absent statutory authorization for this ban. Being prison inmates, these witnesses were to testify about statements made to them by the accused while in custody. They feared for their lives if their fellow inmates discovered their intention to testify for the Crown in a murder prosecution. The Crown feared that if their identities could be disclosed, other prison inmates would be deterred from providing the Crown with testimony in future cases, to the detriment of the administration of justice.

The court adverted to the possibility that *Criminal Code* s. 442(1)[336] might authorize this ban.[337] However, this could not be correct. That provision only gives the court power to exclude the public from a court proceeding. It provides no authority to ban publications regarding an open court proceeding.

The court acknowledged that it must take the *Charter* into account in deciding whether to issue the ban. It concluded that the ban is constitutionally permissible as a means to protect the lives of witnesses and the proper administration of justice.[338] The court differentiated between a witness' fear of embarrassment, on the one hand, and a fear of being killed, on the other.[339] The latter appeared to be the situation on this case's facts. The court undertook no rigorous s. 1 analysis. It did not, for example, consider whether the prisoner/witnesses could be adequately protected by being relocated to other detention facilities.

In *R. v. Barrow*,[340] the Nova Scotia Supreme Court ruled that it is constitutional to ban the publication of the disposition of an accused's previous trial in an influence peddling case where a new trial was ordered. The ban was sought for the period up until the jury retired to deliberate. After ruling that such an order does not infringe *Charter* s.

---

335 *R. v. McArthur* (1984), 13 C.C.C. (3d) 152 (Ont. H.C.).
336 Now s. 486(1), R.S.C. 1985, c. C-46.
337 *Supra*, note 335 at 155.
338 *Ibid.*, at 155-56.
339 *Ibid.*, at 155.
340 *R. v. Barrow, supra*, note 85.

2(b), the court held in the alternative that the order is saved under s. 1 in any event in the interest of protecting the accused's right to a fair trial.[341]

This conclusion is flawed, because it involved no consideration of whether the accused's fair trial rights could be protected effectively by alternative measures which do not so severely burden the freedom of the press. The court acknowledged that another option for protecting the accused's fair trial rights was to sequester the jury during the trial.[342] The accused conceded that if the non-publication order was not issued, he would request sequestration.[343] The Supreme Court's s. 1 test required the court to inquire whether the proposed non-publication order impaired freedom of expression as little as necessary in order to protect fair trial rights. On these facts, it did not meet this least impairment requirement. Hence, the court should have found the order unconstitutional.[344]

In contrast to the foregoing cases, the Supreme Court of Ontario has held that at least some courts do not have jurisdiction to ban the publication of reports about a court proceeding unless legislatively mandated to do so. In *R. v. D.(G.)*,[345] the court ruled that a provincial court, being a statutory court, had no jurisdiction to ban the publication of the identity of a clergyman who was charged with sexual assault. This was so even though it had jurisdiction under the *Criminal Code* to ban the publication of the sexual assault complainant's identity.

The Ontario Court ruled that a ban on the reporting of the accused's name violates *Charter* s. 2(b).[346] The protection of the accused from the embarrassment caused by media reporting of being charged with sexual assault was not a matter of superordinate importance warranting an infringement of freedom of expression.[347] In the court's view, the public has an interest in knowing who is charged with offences, in order to have confidence in the fair and equal application of the law in the courts of the land.[348]

---

341 *Ibid.*, at 315.
342 *Ibid.*
343 *Ibid.*
344 Compare *R. v. Brackenbury*, Ont. Prov.Ct. (Crim.Div.), Langer Prov.J., 22nd December 1987 (unreported). There, a Provincial Court Judge refused to ban the media from publishing potentially incriminating evidence disclosed at a criminal trial *voir dire*. It held that such a publication ban was sought by the accused to protect his reputation, and not to protect his fair trial rights. The accused was in no different position than any accused person, whose reputation may be tarnished by publicity of evidence disclosed at the criminal trial. It held that neither exclusion of the public nor a non-publication order of such evidence would be authorized by *Criminal Code* s. 442(1) in such circumstances.
345 *Supra*, note 157.
346 *Ibid.*, at 375.
347 *Ibid.*
348 *Ibid.*, at 374.

The court's ultimate disposition in this case was extraordinary. On the basis of the foregoing reasons, the court had overwhelming grounds to quash the unconstitutional non-publication order. However, it chose not to do so. The court noted that it had a remedial discretion over whether to quash the impugned order.[349] It expressed strong sympathy for the accused minister, who had since been acquitted, and who had suffered a loss of employment and public obloquy because of his sexual assault trial. Because of this, the court exercised its discretion to decline to quash the non-publication order.[350]

In the result, a non-publication order which had no legislative foundation, and which violated the supreme law of Canada, was allowed to remain in force. This was so on account of a simple exercise of judicial discretion — a discretionary judgment based on the sympathy generated by the accused's personal plight. It was erroneous for the court to proceed to exercise a discretion which the Constitution of Canada forbids by any form of government action.[351]

The Ontario Court of Appeal has also limited the extent to which a superior court's inherent power can be used to ban media publications, absent a statutory mandate therefor. In *R. v. Unnamed Person*,[352] the Ontario Court of Appeal quashed a lower court's order, which had perpetually banned the publication of the identity of an accused. After issuance of the banning order, the accused had pleaded guilty to infanticide. The appellate court concluded that a superior court's inherent power can only be used to ban media reports about a court proceeding

---

349 *Ibid.*, at 375.

350 *Ibid.*, at 375 *ff*.

351 Compare *Southam Inc. v. R.* (1987), 37 C.C.C. (3d) 139, where the Supreme Court of Ontario quashed a provincial court's order banning the publication of the name of a schoolteacher charged with sexual assault. The Supreme Court held that this order could not be made under *Criminal Code* s. 442(3), where, as here, there was no evidence tendered to show that publication of the name of the accused would lead to the identification of the complainant. While this ruling was based on non-*Charter* grounds, the court noted that because freedom of the press is of great importance, restrictions on it should only be imposed in extraordinary circumstances.

See also *Orpin v. College of Physicians & Surgeons (Ont.)* (1988), 25 C.P.C. (2d) 19 (Div.Ct.), *per* Campbell J., where a doctor appealed to court from a disciplinary finding that he had committed professional misconduct by engaging in certain sexual activity with a patient. The Divisional Court banned publication of the complainant's identity, without specific statutory mandate to do so, but refused to ban publication of the doctor's identity. Although the court did not address itself to the *Charter*'s impact on such bans, it noted that there is no presumption in law that a doctor has a right to keep his identity from being published, until all avenues of appeal are exhausted, when the College of Physicians and Surgeons has found him guilty of unprofessional behaviour.

352 *Re R. and Unnamed Person* (1985), 22 C.C.C. (3d) 284 (Ont. C.A.).

where such is needed to ensure that justice is effectively administered either by that court or, where needed, by a lower court.[353] This power could not be deployed to ban an accused's identity where, as was the case there, it was aimed at protecting the accused from embarrassment or other hardships.[354]

While this is not a *Charter* ruling *per se*, it can influence the outcome of future *Charter* challenges to non-publication orders which were made based on a court's inherent power. If the only permissible basis for the exercise of this inherent power to ban media reports is the protection of the court process itself, other rationalia cannot be credibly advanced under s. 1 to defend non-publication orders purportedly issued pursuant to the inherent power. One cannot advance one rationale for a non-publication order to bring it within the inherent power, and then advance another rationale for the same order to found a s. 1 defence.

As an interesting variation on this theme, is it possible for a judge to issue a non-publication order, absent a statutory mandate therefor, if the order's purpose is to effectively enforce the court's order excluding witnesses from the court room? A Supreme Court of Ontario Judge has declined to make a publication ban on trial testimony, as part of an order excluding witnesses from the court room prior to their testimony. In *R. v. Robinson (No. 1)*,[355] the court, hearing murder charges, made the usual order excluding witnesses. The defence asked that the court ban the publication of evidence at trial to enforce this order. There is no statutory mandate for any such order.

Without resorting to the *Charter*, the court declined to issue the requested non-publication order. Recognizing that the courts are to be open to the public, the court noted that the practical way in which witness exclusion orders are enforced is through the assistance of counsel. As officers of the court, lawyers are routinely expected to advise upcoming witnesses not to read or watch media coverage of a case when a witness exclusion order is in effect.[356]

This case provides a good example of effective s. 1 reasoning being implicitly employed, albeit without a *Charter* argument having been advanced. The court was satisfied that there were adequate means available to ensure the effectiveness of the witness exclusion order, short of an impairment of free speech. Hence, the non-publication order was refused. Had the order been made, it would have been unconstitutional, as it would fail to meet the s. 1 test.

---

353 *Ibid.*, at 288.
354 *Ibid.*, at 287.
355 Ont. H.C., Reid J., 24th October 1983 (unreported).
356 *Ibid.*

With the law in a state of flux, and confusion on both the availability and the constitutionality of non-statutory non-publication orders where they are based on a court's inherent power, it is of assistance to turn to an area of common law which was more evolved before the *Charter*. To what extent does s. 1 sustain the traditional common law *sub judice* contempt offence? This offence bans pre-trial publication of information which tends to threaten the administration of justice.[357]

As is discussed earlier, despite some conflicting authority on the point, the better view is that the *sub judice* offence infringes *Charter* s. 2(b), and must be justified under s. 1. In *Open Justice*,[358] I contended that this offence must be substantially narrowed to meet s. 1's requirements. It should only be available constitutionally to convict a media outlet for reporting about a court case where it is proven that the coverage in fact had irreparably prejudiced a fair trial. Where a fair trial can be preserved by other procedural means, such as jury sequestration, careful jury selection, venue changes and adjournments, a publication should not be the target of a contempt prosecution.[359]

The Newfoundland Supreme Court reached a contrary conclusion in *R. v. Robinson-Blackmore Printing & Publishing Co.*[360] The court there held that the *sub judice* offence is a reasonable limit on freedom of expression which is saved by s. 1 of the *Charter*. The court sustained the constitutionality of a media outlet's prosecution for the pre-trial publication of facts pertaining to a homicide case, including the fact that the accused had AIDS, and that he had purportedly attempted to spread it to others while in jail.[361] Dismissing a media motion to strike the proceeding on *Charter* grounds, the court held that the contempt power is a rational means to promote the pressing objective of protecting an accused's fundamental right to a fair trial.[362]

There are three difficulties with the court's s. 1 reasoning. First, in deciding whether the *sub judice* contempt offence is the least restrictive

---

357 For a recent application of the offence, albeit absent a *Charter* argument, see *Que. (A.G.) v. Publications Photo-Police Inc.*, 54 C.C.C. (3d) 576, reversing 42 C.C.C. (3d) 220 (S.C.C.). There, a newspaper was cited for contempt for breaching a non-publication order, and it was held, in the end that s. 442(3) of the *Criminal Code* preserved the court's inherent jurisdiction to punish for contempt, whether by way of summary procedure or by indictment.

358 *Lepofsky, supra*, note 4 at 55 *ff.*

359 In support of this view, one can reason by analogy to the Ontario Court of Appeal's powerful ruling in *R. v. Kopyto, supra*, note 91, discussed at length, *infra*, to the effect that the contempt offence of scandalizing the court is either entirely unconstitutional or, at least, is drastically narrowed because of the *Charter*.

360 *Supra*, note 83.

361 *Ibid.*, at 369.

362 *Ibid.*, at 375-76.

option for protecting the administration of justice, the court only considered the alternative of striking down the entire contempt law, and leaving the media free to publish anything they wished about a pending case. This option obviously threatens a fair trial considerably more than the alternative of retaining the pre-existing contempt law. The court did *not* consider whether the contempt offence would be less restrictive of freedom of speech, and yet as effective at promoting a fair trial, if it were left in effect, but was construed more narrowly, as is proposed in *Open Justice*. Had the court considered this option, it should have concluded that the existing definition of the *sub judice* offence is too broad, and impairs *Charter* rights more than is necessary to ensure a fair trial.

The second flaw with the Newfoundland court's decision is that it in effect revamped the definition of *sub judice* contempt, without acknowledging that it was doing so. In what appears to be a back door effort at narrowing the offence, the court held that this offence only prohibits those publications which pose a serious risk to the administration of justice.[363] Yet, the offence's traditional definition provides that it prohibits any publication which merely has the reasonable tendency to interfere with the administration of justice.[364] If the contempt offence is to be read down pursuant to the *Charter*, it is more appropriate for the court to acknowledge that that is what it is doing. Moreover, even this implicit diminution of the *sub judice* offence, while positive in its direction, still is insufficient to meet s. 1's requirements. It fails to require a court to consider whether a fair trial could be protected by means short of a s. 2(b) infringement.

The third flaw with the Newfoundland court's s. 1 reasoning is that the court failed to find that the common law definition of the *sub judice* rule is so vague that it does not meet the s. 1 requirement that a limit on *Charter* rights be clearly prescribed by law.[365] The *ad hoc* definition of *sub judice* contempt fails to provide publishers with reasonable guidance as to what may be published and what may not.[366] The court did not undertake any vagueness analysis under s. 1. It did consider whether this offence is unconstitutionally vague under *Charter* s. 7's fundamental justice requirement. However, it erroneously concluded that the contempt offence is defined with sufficient clarity to comply with the s. 7 requirement of fundamental justice[367] — a result which is hard to square with the accumulated, abstruse contempt jurisprudence which has developed over this century.

---

363 *Ibid.*, at 373.
364 Lepofsky, *Open Justice, supra*, note 4 at 56.
365 See *Ont. Film & Video Appreciation Soc. v. Ont. Bd. of Censors* (1984), 5 D.L.R. (4th) 766 (Ont. C.A.), and *Prostitution Reference, supra*, note 96.
366 See Lepofsky, *Open Justice, supra*, note 4 at 63 and 245 *ff.*
367 *R. v. Robinson-Blackmore Printing, supra*, note 83.

G. Specific Limits on Criticism of Courts and Judges

With judicial recognition of new constitutional protection for the right to criticize judges and courts having been enunciated in *R. v. Kopyto*,[368] the question follows as to what legal restrictions may permissibly be imposed on this *Charter* right consonant with s. 1. The most authoritative and thoroughgoing pronouncements on this issue are found in the Ontario Court of Appeal's *Kopyto* decision, where the court reversed a lawyer's contempt conviction for criticizing a court, on the grounds that it could not be sustained under *Charter* s. 1. At the level of legal doctrine, the court divided on the scope of justifiable limits on such expression by way of prosecution for the common law crime of contempt of court by scandalizing the court. However, the decision's practical effect, regardless of these divisions, is to render the constitutional right to criticize judges and courts virtually unfettered, by making criminal prosecutions for such criticisms practically impossible in all but the most extreme and unimaginable of cases.

In *Kopyto*, Cory J.A. (as he then was) held that the contempt offence's goal, protecting the integrity of the administration of justice, is sufficiently important to warrant some limits on freedom of expression. However, he concluded that the traditional offence of scandalizing the court was not carefully designed to achieve this goal. He also opined that it does not impair freedom of expression as little as possible.[369]

In the view of Cory J.A., a contempt conviction could not be sustained under the *Charter* unless there is actual proof that the accused's critical statement did in fact bring the administration of justice into contempt or disrepute.[370] The evidence must disclose a serious risk or clear and present danger of prejudice to the administration of justice.[371] It would also be necessary to prove *mens rea* on the accused's part, namely that he or she intended to bring the administration of justice into disrepute, or was reckless as to whether disrepute would follow from his or her statements.[372]

Cory J.A. cited with approval U.S. First Amendment authority which had noted that criticism of courts can contribute to their improvement, while the legal suppression of criticism of courts can itself bring the administration of justice into disrepute.[373] He found that the existing contempt offence is not saved by *Charter* s. 1, but that it could be modified by the courts or legislature to bring it into conformity with the

---

368 *Supra*, note 91.
369 *Ibid.*, at 102.
370 *Ibid.*
371 *Ibid.*, at 97.
372 *Ibid.*, at 101.
373 *Ibid.*, at 94 *ff.*

Charter.[374] In practice, the modifications which Cory J.A. would require in accordance with the foregoing principles would render it virtually impossible to convict an accused for scandalizing the court.

Houlden J.A., concurring, rejected a claim that the contempt offence is too vague to meet s. 1's requirements. He viewed the offence as being defined with reasonable clarity.[375] This finding is, however, contradicted by the experience with this offence prior to the *Charter*, which is fraught with inconsistencies and uncertainties.[376]

Houlden J.A. concurred that the contempt offence is excessively broad. However, rather than redefining the offence, he preferred simply to declare it unconstitutional.[377] He felt that Canadian courts could withstand any criticism of cases which have been decided, no matter how outrageous the criticism may be.[378] The public is not so gullible, he opined, that it needs to be shielded from such comments.[379]

Goodman J.A., concurring, held that it was sufficient in disposing of the *Kopyto* appeal simply to reverse the appellant's conviction on constitutional grounds.[380] He thought it unnecessary to consider whether any constitutional room is left for scandalization prosecutions in the future.[381] However, he went on to hold that such prosecutions would not meet s. 1's proportionality requirement even where the Crown proves that an accused's criticism in fact brought the courts into disrepute. Almost any intemperate criticism of courts will impugn the courts' reputation in the minds of at least some, he noted.[382]

Goodman J.A. further muddied the contempt offence by holding that a statement, critical of courts, could only amount to a contempt where the utterance would "bring the administration of justice into disrepute in the eyes of a reasonable man, dispassionate, and fully apprized of the circumstances of the case."[383] He also would require proof that the utterance would constitute a "clear, significant and imminent or present danger to the fair and effective administration of justice."[384] This could include statements of fact, made with knowledge of their falsity or with reckless disregard as to their probable falsity.[385] It could also include statements of opinion which are not sincerely held, so

---

374 *Ibid.*, at 102 *ff.*
375 *Ibid.*, at 110.
376 See Lepofsky, *Open Justice, supra*, note 4 at 57.
377 *Supra*, note 91 at 113.
378 *Ibid.*
379 *Ibid.*
380 *Ibid.*, at 117.
381 *Ibid.*
382 *Ibid.*, at 116 *ff.*
383 *Ibid.*, at 118.
384 *Ibid.*
385 *Ibid.*

long as these statements have the harmful effects referred to above.[386] The intemperance of the language used will not be dispositive of these injuries, he opined.[387]

Whichever of these approaches to the scandalization offence is applied in the future,[388] it is doubtful that the Crown could discharge the supremely heavy burden of proof proposed by the various members of the Court of Appeal panel. It is likely that the scandalization offence will now fall into complete disuse, while public criticism of judicial behaviour will intensify, shielded by the *Charter*'s protection.

The foregoing considers what limits may be placed on the content of statements which criticize courts, consistent with *Charter* s. 1. Associated with this is the issue of what limits does s. 1 tolerate on the means by which criticism of the courts is expressed. This issue arises because, as is established earlier in this paper, s. 2(b)'s protection for criticism of courts includes both the right to speak critically, and the right to engage in critical demonstrations, short of violence.

Until now, the Supreme Court of Canada has recognized only one basis for limiting demonstrations aimed at courts. In *B.C.G.E.U. v. B.C. (A.G.)*[389] the court rejected a union's *Charter* challenge to an injunction against a labour picket outside a B.C. court house. The Supreme Court held under *Charter* s. 1 that the injunction was a justifiable restriction on the guarantee of freedom of expression,[390] needed to ensure that members of the public could have physical access to the courts.

IV. OVERVIEW

A. General

The final part of this article provides a reflective overview of Canada's current approach to the constitutional open justice requirement. It begins with a comparison of the current Canadian and U.S. constitutional approaches in this field. This is followed by reflections on some of the rhetoric which can find its way into juridical and policy debates about open justice.

---

386 *Ibid.*

387 *Ibid.*, at 118-19.

388 Dubin J.A., with Brooke J.A. concurring, found that the utterances in this case did not constitute a contempt. Hence he would have allowed the appeal and quashed the conviction without needing to resort to the *Charter*. He suggested that the scandalization offence would not infringe freedom of expression, in any event. In this regard, he is in the minority, clearly outweighed by the opinions of the rest of the panel.

389 *Supra*, note 191.

390 One could supplement the picketers' claim by adding entitlements to freedom of peaceful assembly under s. 2(c) and freedom of association under s. 2(d).

B. Comparing the Canadian and American Constitutional Approaches to Open Justice

Before the *Charter*'s enactment, Canadians enjoyed a far more restricted right to attend and to speak about criminal court proceedings than did Americans.[391] Any rights which Canadians possessed in this regard were based on statute or common law alone, whereas the American open justice requirement was supplemented and substantially expanded by strong constitutional imperatives.

With nine years of *Charter* experience, it is evident that Canadians now enjoy substantially increased rights to attend or hear about court proceedings. However, although expanded, these rights are still not as far-reaching as are the equivalent entitlements under the U.S. Constitution. In this comparison of the current American and Canadian constitutional approaches to open justice, the similarities of treatment in each country are highlighted, followed by the differences in their approaches.

Perhaps the most striking similarity in the approaches of the two countries is discerned at a level of some generality. The courts of both Canada and the United States have now recognized that members of the public have a fundamental constitutional right to attend court proceedings,[392] to report to others about events occurring in court,[393] and to criticize courts.[394] The constitutions of both countries allow for limitations on these rights only in those compelling situations where the government can affirmatively establish that such restrictions are needed to achieve compelling social objectives which cannot be attained short of such intrusions into the principle of open justice.[395] The power of governments to impose limits on open justice is implicit in the text of the U.S. Constitution, while it is express in s. 1 of Canada's *Charter*. However, the standard of justification in both countries is high.

While both countries have extended forceful constitutional protection to the right to attend, report on and criticize courts, each country has declined to recognize a constitutional right to televise judicial proceedings without the consent of court participants.[396] As a practical

---

391 See Lepofsky, *Open Justice, supra*, note 4 at 23 *ff.*, 103 *ff.*
392 Compare *Re Southam Inc. and R. (No. 1), supra*, note 20 with *Richmond Newspapers v. Virginia, supra*, note 113.
393 Compare *Edmonton Journal v. Alta. (A.G.), supra*, note 29 with *Nebraska Press Assn. v. Stuart, supra*, note 114.
394 Compare *Kopyto, supra*, note 91 with *Bridges v. California*, 314 U.S. 252 (1941), and *Craig v. Harney*, 331 U.S. 367 (1947).
395 Compare *Re Southam Inc. and R. (No. 1), supra*, note 20 and *Edmonton Journal v. Alta. (A.G.), supra*, note 29 with *Richmond Newspapers v. Virginia, supra*, note 113 and *Nebraska Press Assn. v. Stuart, supra*, note 114.
396 Compare the Canadian authorities in the text associated with note 103 *ff.*, *supra*, and in the text associated with note 237 *ff.*, *supra*, with the American authorities listed in, *supra*, note 117.

matter, however, one finds television cameras being permitted more frequently in the state courts of a number of American states as a matter of court policy and practice. In contrast, cameras in the court room are a rarity in Canadian courts.

In tandem with these similarities are several important differences between the Canadian and U.S. constitutional approaches. For the doctrinal reasons explained in the following paragraphs, one still finds at the greatest level of generality that Americans enjoy broader rights of access to and speech about court proceedings than do Canadians. This is because the constitutional test for justifying limits on open justice is harder for government to meet both as a matter of practice and principle in the U.S.

Under s. 1 of the *Charter*, a social objective can justify limits on open justice if it is "sufficiently important" or "pressing and substantial." In contrast, a limit on access to or reports about court proceedings in the U.S. is constitutionally required to be targeted at a "compelling state interest." Canadian courts have yet to define whether these standards are different. However, Canada's judiciary has been more willing to deem an objective to be "sufficiently important" under the *Charter* than the U.S. Supreme Court has been to find a law's objective to be tied to a "compelling state interest."[397] These terms are fungible to some extent. Thus, comparisons are more useful if based on actual examples than if they are based on a mere juxtaposition of constitutional terminology.

Canadian and U.S. courts differ on the possibility of a blanket justification being established for a category of speech restrictions. In the U.S., it is a virtually absolute necessity that the need for such restrictions be demonstrated by specific factual findings in each individual case where the restriction is to be applied. The First Amendment generally does not tolerate a statute which imposes blanket limits on attendance at, or speech about, court proceedings.[398] A court must have a discretion over the application of that law, whose exercise must be closely tied to factual findings as to the necessity for its application. In contrast, Canadian courts have been willing to uphold a law imposing

---

397 Compare Canadian judicial decisions holding that reducing the public nuisance of street soliciting by prostitutes (*Prostitution Reference, supra,* note 96) and protecting the dairy industry from competition from margarine producers (*Inst. of Edible Oil Foods v. Ont.* *(1987), 63 O.R. (2d) 436, affirmed 64 D.L.R. (4th) 380, leave to appeal to S.C.C. refused 41 O.A.C. 267n) with American judicial decisions (L. Tribe, *American Constitutional Law,* 2nd ed. (Mineola, N.Y.: The Foundation Press, 1988), c. 12).

398 See, *e.g., Nebraska Press Assn. v. Stuart, supra,* note 114; *Globe Newspaper Co. v. Sup. Ct. of Norfolk Co.,* 102 S.Ct. 2613 (1982).

blanket restrictions[399] or restrictions which are automatically imposed at the request of a party or witness where the categorical need for such a blanket rule is established under *Charter* s. 1.[400]

Canadian and U.S. courts take substantially different approaches to the validity of prior restraints on publications about court proceedings. It is a common theme in the jurisprudence of both countries that the more serious an infringement of freedom of expression, the greater the burden of justification on the government.[401] In this context, American courts have recognized for several decades that a "prior restraint" on expression is the most invasive infringement of free speech.[402] Prior restraints thus require more stringent justifications than other speech restrictions.[403]

Prior restraints are those restrictions imposed on speech or publications in advance of their dissemination, which are instituted by a judge or other public official.[404] They include injunctions and non-publication orders by judges, or censorship decisions by film censor boards. They differ from a "subsequent punishment" of speech, because under a prior restraint, the restriction on expression is imposed pursuant to the decision of a specific public official, and not simply pursuant to a blanket statutory provision. The official imposing such restrictions is ordinarily not democratically accountable. Moreover, once imposed, a prior restraint freezes expression for the time being, since a party is bound to comply with it, despite its potential conflict with the First Amendment, until a court rules the restriction unconstitutional.[405]

Under U.S. jurisprudence, it is virtually impossible to defend the constitutionality of a prior restraint on publications pertaining to court proceedings, such as a pre-trial judicial ban on the publication of preliminary hearing evidence or other pre-trial proceedings.[406] In contrast, Canadian courts generally have not recognized the concept of a prior restraint on expression, or the increased severity of its burden on free

---

399 See, *e.g., Southam Inc. v. R., supra*, note 44 (C.A.), upholding a blanket automatic ban on publication of the identity of young persons involved in Youth Court proceedings.

400 See, *e.g., Can. Newspapers Co., supra*, note 66; *Global Communications, supra*, note 63; *Southam Inc. v. Coulter, supra*, note 44.

401 See *Prostitution Reference, supra*, note 96; compare *U.S. v. O'Brien*, 391 U.S. 367 (1968).

402 See *Near v. Minnesota*, 283 U.S. 697 (1931); *New York Times Co. v. U.S.*, 403 U.S. 713 (1971) (the Pentagon papers case); *Nebraska Press Assn. v. Stuart, supra*, note 114.

403 *Ibid.*

404 *Ibid.* See also Lepofsky, *Open Justice, supra*, note 4 at 64 *ff.*, 261 *ff.*, 289 *ff.*

405 See Lepofsky, *ibid.*, at 153 *ff.*

406 *Nebraska Press Assn. v. Stuart, supra*, note 114.

speech. To date, Canadian courts have not treated prior restraints on expression about judicial proceedings as being harder to justify under s. 1 of the *Charter* than other forms of restrictions on speech.

Indeed, both the Ontario Court of Appeal[407] and the Supreme Court of Canada[408] have upheld the validity of judicially imposed prior restraints on publications about courts. They have done so without acknowledging that these involved prior restraints. They also did not consider whether such prior restraints are more severe invasions of s. 2(b) rights.

As an interesting counterpoint to the foregoing, Canadian courts, dealing with s. 1 open justice issues, as in other areas, have tended more and more to receive sworn testimony, including voluminous expert evidence, on the s. 1 claim's factual underpinnings. These proceedings can stretch into days of *Charter* evidence.[409] In contrast, the leading U.S. cases in this area tended to be decided on the basis of a trial record pertaining mainly to the adjudicative facts giving rise to the constitutional claim, and perhaps some unsworn materials relied on through the "Brandeis brief."[410]

When applying their different tests for justifying limits on open justice, Canadian and American courts have adopted different positions on the values which can warrant a limit on access to or publicity about court proceedings. The jurisprudence in each country has recognized that the protection of an accused's right to a fair trial is a goal of sufficient significance to warrant some restrictions on open justice.[411] Yet, Canadian courts have gone further. Canada's judiciary has recognized that these restrictions can also be justified if aimed at protecting the privacy of court participants, or at promoting access to the justice system for members of the public.[412] None of these values are recognized in First Amendment jurisprudence as acceptable reasons for imposing limits on open justice.

The different constitutional positions in Canada and the U.S. come into sharpest focus when one examines the actual outcomes in a small selection of analogous cases. In Canada, it is constitutionally permissible for courts to automatically ban publication of the identity of sexual

---

407 See *Re Global Communications and A.G. Can., supra*, note 63.

408 *Can. Newspapers, supra*, note 66.

409 See, *e.g., Squires v. R., supra*, note 44; *Can. Newspapers, supra*, note 66; *Southam Inc. v. R., supra*, note 44.

410 See, *e.g., Nebraska Press Assn. v. Stuart, supra*, note 114; *Nixon v. Warner Communications Inc., supra*, note 116; *Richmond Newspapers v. Virginia, supra*, note 113.

411 Compare *Nebraska Press Assn. v. Stuart, supra*, note 114 with *Global Communications, supra*, note 63.

412 See *Edmonton Journal, supra*, note 29.

assault complainants at the complainant's request.[413] However, in the U.S., the press has a sweeping constitutional right to publish the name of a sexual assault victim, once this information is disclosed in an open court record or proceeding.[414] In Canada, a judge, presiding at a bail hearing, must ban the publication of evidence tendered and arguments made at the inquiry, if such is requested by the accused.[415] Yet, non-publication orders of open pre-trial court proceedings are virtually always unconstitutional in the United States, except in the extremely rare case where the accused can show that such publications will in fact prejudice a fair trial, and that absolutely no alternative means are available to effectively ensure a fair trial.[416]

C. Rethinking Rhetoric About Open Justice

While the first eight years of open justice litigation under the *Charter* has produced for Canadians a more open and accessible justice system, there remains considerable room for further discussion and debate in this area, in both the legislative and judicial arenas. In undertaking these, it is important to be aware of misconceptions that can make their way into the dialogue and rhetoric of open justice discussions. This section considers a few of these.

A first key misconception which finds its way into the dialogue about open justice pertains to the media's role in attending at court proceedings, and reporting on them. Media advocates often describe the media as the agent for the public, which represents the public at court proceedings. In this way, the journalist is explicitly or implicitly cast in a special role, *vis-à-vis* the public, and can be heard or perceived to claim entitlement to special or superior rights as a consequence.

There are several difficulties with a conception of the media as the public's "agent." The relationship between the press on the one hand, and the public on the other, lacks the key ingredients of agency. A principal ordinarily selects their agent, instructs them, and has the power to terminate their agency, if the principal so desires. However, the public has neither chosen the media as an institution, nor individual journalists, to serve as its agents. The public does not instruct reporters on their conduct when attending at court. Moreover, the public has no authority to discharge reporters whose performance is unsatisfactory to the public. Indeed, the media would ordinarily claim that the freedom of the press assures them a status of independence from the public, and that

---

413 *Can. Newspapers, supra,* note 66.
414 See *Cox Broadcasting Co. v. Cohn,* 420 U.S. 469 (1974).
415 *Global Communications, supra,* note 63.
416 *Nebraska Press Assn. v. Stuart, supra,* note 114.

this liberty prevents the public from discharging a reporter from his or her job, on the grounds that the public was not satisfied with the reporter's coverage.

On closer scrutiny, this "agent of the public" rhetoric appears implicitly (and unquestionably unintentionally) to characterize the media as itself a kind of quasi-governmental agency. Such rhetoric can, in effect, depict the media as the public's watchdog on courts and other governmental agencies, on the public's behalf, and as the public's representative. However, this conception is problematic. It could turn democracy on its head. The public's representative is not the media. It is the government, which the public has elected, and which is constitutionally accountable to the public through the checks and balances of democracy. Indeed, unlike the government, the media lacks any constitutional mechanisms for democratic accountability to the public, with perhaps the single, indirect and, at best, tenuous, exception of the Crown-owned C.B.C.

The danger in infusing such rhetoric into the open justice debate is that it tends to lead some towards a belief that reporters should enjoy special rights under s. 2(b) of the *Charter*, in excess of those enjoyed by all members of the public, by virtue of their special role as agents for the public. The anti-egalitarian notion that some in society should enjoy special and superior constitutional rights, especially in the field of democratic rights and fundamental freedoms is, however, contrary to the fundamental tenets of democracy.

Additionally, a conception of reporters as a special group with superior constitutional rights is also fraught with practical difficulties. Although some may refer colloquially to journalists as professionals, and to journalism as a profession, (thereby making seemingly distinctive the class of persons who would enjoy such special constitutional rights), it is not feasible to characterize reporters as a profession. Journalism lacks the core indicia of a profession. Anyone can immediately become a reporter, since there are no educational, training, apprenticeship or licensing requirements for admission to the practice of journalism. There are no standards which one must meet in order to become a reporter. There is no compulsory self-governing regulatory body for journalists. Perhaps most compelling, there is no generally accepted code of professional conduct for journalists, which is binding on all who practice in this field.

It does not follow from the foregoing that the media do not have an important role to play in the constitutional system of open justice, or that the importance of this role should be ignored or downplayed in formulating legal doctrine under the *Charter*. Indeed, because of the physical limitation of space in court rooms, and because of the impracticality for most to attend court proceedings, the public must necessarily depend on the media's attendance at these proceedings, and on their reports thereon, if the public is to learn about the daily workings of the justice system.

However, it is important that the media's function and status in this connection not be exaggerated or inflated in the terms that some media rhetoric can at times suggest. The Supreme Court has correctly noted that the media's practical role in attending court proceedings is as the public's surrogate.[417] As a surrogate, the media ought not, and need not, to enjoy any special status or rights greater than those enjoyed by the public. The media should not be characterized as the public's agent, nor should they be explicitly or implicitly cast in a quasi-governmental representative role. Rather than characterizing reporters as a professional group with superior rights, they should be viewed as lay persons whose important job it is to retail information to other laypersons.

A second rhetorical claim requiring critical scrutiny is the media's frequent assertion that in undertaking its news gathering activity, it purports to act on the public's so-called "right to know." While the Supreme Court has adverted on one occasion to this "right to know,"[418] it is doubtful that this "right" has any serious juridical status. Journalists typically use the rhetoric of a "public right to know" as a way of justifying their demands to have access to information which they consider newsworthy. However, when a reporter on the trail of a story tells a potential news source that the "public has a right to know" about a desired piece of information, it is likely more correct to state that in the reporter's judgment, the public has a *desire* to know, or perhaps that the reporter has a desire to find out and tell.

Generally speaking, the public does not have a legal right to compel a potential source of news to pass on newsworthy information. It has been judicially recognized that s. 2(b) guarantees both the right to disseminate information and the right to receive it. Section 2(b) gives rights to both speakers and listeners.[419] However, properly understood, this holding only pertains to the right of willing speakers to transmit information to willing listeners, and, in turn, for willing listeners to receive information from a willing speaker. It should not be inflated or overextended, so as to give a listening audience, such as the public, a right to compel access to information from a person or organization who does not wish the information released. *Charter* s. 2(b) is not a constitutional freedom of information Act.

Even if the "public" had a "right to know" of some kind, it is doubtful that a reporter can enforce this right on the public's behalf. As

---

417 See *Edmonton Journal, supra,* note 29 at 610, *per* Cory J.
418 *Ibid.*
419 *Ibid.*

discussed above, the media are not appointed by the public as their agent, and have no authority to purport to exercise the public's rights. The danger of using this "right to know" rhetoric in dealing with s. 2(b) is that it can lead one to transform a claim of public interest into an assertedly higher claim of public right or, indeed, of supreme constitutional right.

Another rhetorical assertion meriting examination holds that in the open justice context, the media acts pursuant to a "duty" to inform the public about Canada's justice system and keeps judges accountable to the public. In fact, media coverage of legal proceedings frequently does not effectively inform the public about the justice system.

With the rare exception of some documentary coverage, the vast preponderance of media coverage of courts is for the purpose of reporting news. News is conventionally understood by the media itself, and by the public which consumes the news, to be reportage of the most immediate, important and interesting events occurring in society. A matter becomes newsworthy because it is unusual, or because it has an immediate impact on the general public.

Most court cases are not perceived as being the least bit newsworthy by reporters. The run-of-the-mill motor vehicle damage claim, drunk driving prosecution, pre-trial interlocutory motion or divorce hearing attracts no news attention whatsoever, because these proceedings do not appear to be unusual or interesting to the public, in reporters' judgment. A review of the ordinary content of news reports on court proceedings discloses that court cases only secure news coverage if they involve extreme violence, such as murder or sexual offences, if they involve novel issues having general public impact, such as challenges to the constitutionality of abortion laws, if they involve well-known public figures, such as a drug possession charge against a provincial premier, or if they involve bizarre facts.

Of those cases which secure any media attention at all, it is extremely rare that a court proceeding will receive media coverage throughout the entirety of the case. It is more common that a reporter will attend only part of the proceedings, and that he or she will only report on those events during the case that appear to be the most interesting or unusual from the audience's perceived perspective. This coverage is constrained by several important factors. These include the reporter's sense of the case's news value, the extent of the reporter's familiarity with the workings of the legal process, the availability of the media outlet's resources including the availability of staff reporters for ongoing coverage of the case, the imminence of deadlines for getting the story ready for print or broadcast, the limitations of space in the newspaper or broadcast, and the media outlet's expectations regarding their competitors' treatment of the case.

Consequently, the image of the justice system which the public receives is not a representative or comprehensive account of the court process in action. It is not a journalistic attempt to maintain an independent watch on the behaviour of judges on behalf of the public. Instead, it is a limited depiction of the most extraordinary or unusual events in the justice system. This picture does not reflect the usual operations of the system of justice. It does not purport to capture even a minuscule proportion of the business transacted in court.

This is not due to any intention or desire on the media's part to distort the image of justice. It is a simple, and perhaps inescapable, product of the traditional test for newsworthiness which reporters apply, and of the forces which prevail in the business of operating a media establishment. It is not due to legal restrictions on open justice, since the majority of fully open legal proceedings secures no media attention whatsoever.

As a result of these forces, any function which the media serves in reporting on court proceedings is limited. At most, the media informs the public about the most unusual aspects of the system, and not about its mainstream operations. Similarly, the media can only serve to keep judges accountable to the public in those rare and unusual cases which reporters choose to cover. In the vast majority of court proceedings, the media's check on judicial conduct is non-existent, even though proceedings are generally open to attendance and eligible for reporting. Indeed, important cases, with important issues at stake, can go uncovered and unreported now, even though such proceedings are open to the public, simply because no media establishment attends.

From this, two observations follow. The first is that it is not appropriate to fashion open justice rules or principles on the premise that the media effectively informs the public about the overall court system or that it effectively and comprehensively ensures judicial accountability. This is not to denigrate the media's important role in covering courts. The media serves in practice as the lifeline of an open justice system, since it is largely from the media that the public have any hope of knowing what goes on in courts, once their doors are open to public attendance. However, this lifeline must be understood as a limited one, an imperfect one, and one whose effectiveness and objectives should not be exaggerated.

A second observation is that while the news media can properly be criticized from time to time as taking a selective and even a sensationalistic approach to the reporting of legal proceedings, and that the media should be receptive to robust criticism when its court coverage yields a distorted picture of the courts, criticism of the press must not be translated into antipathy against the freedom of the press. One need neither love, nor even approve of, the conduct of reporters to endorse a strong, expansive guarantee of the *Charter*'s free expression and press guarantee. It is both too easy and too dangerous to advocate the imposition of strong legal restrictions on media coverage of courts because of criticisms of how the media have covered courts in the past. This action would threaten many of the core purposes for guaranteeing freedom of expression and press — purposes which are critical to the maintenance of a free and democratic society. A principled and purposive approach to open justice can be achieved when legal doctrine in this field is founded on a realistic, sensitive understanding of how the media works, and how the justice system works, in an increasingly complex legal system.

PRESS-UMED INNOCENT

Harold J. Levy

Defining a debate in terms of "free press vs. fair trial" is risky. It suggests that there is a necessary opposition between the two values. It obscures the fact that a free press, in the sense of a press that has full access to judicial proceedings, is essential for fair trials, in the sense that public accountability is necessary if justice is to be done.

My central thesis is that openness is not merely an attribute of justice. It is much more than that. It is the very life-blood of our justice system. Put another way, I do not believe that there can be justice without openness. I am concerned about tendencies to curtail openness and the right of the press to report on a variety of judicial proceedings in order to accommodate a myriad of interests ranging from national security to the privacy of crime victims.

The reason, of course, is that the court room is a forum in which the powers of the state are directed against the individual. If that power is not made subject to public scrutiny, there is an enormous opportunity for abuse. Besides, secrecy is hardly the way to maintain public confidence in important public institutions. True, when court room doors are closed, we are often told not to worry. The judge will ensure that the process is pure. With respect to the nation's judiciary, that is hardly good enough. The public believes, rightly or wrongly, that judges are political hacks who got their job through patronage, and therefore tend to favour the government and its agents. Even where the judge is of the highest cut — like René Marin, recently appointed to conduct an inquiry into allegations that the Royal Canadian Mounted Police (RCMP) set out to entrap Senator Michel Cogger — if the proceedings are conducted behind closed doors and the force is cleared of any impropriety, suspicion is bound to be the order of the day.

In my view, it is not enough for justice to depend on the reputation of the judge conducting closed proceedings. Judges must earn their respect by performing their role openly, in plain public view, and by publicly demonstrating their fairness and independence from the government.

It is time to examine much more closely some of the arguments that are habitually trotted out by the state's agents in order to secure closed hearings.

In the Cogger case, for example, commission lawyers wanted the public, and therefore the press, barred from all hearings in order to protect RCMP investigative techniques. They argued that opening the inquiry to the public could provide the criminal element with valuable insights into the force's investigative techniques and the way that it deals with confidential sources.[1] Well, let us stop for a moment and ask what valuable insights the public might possibly gain from this experience. Have we already forgotten the insights gained from the 1980 MacDonald Commission report, which revealed RCMP techniques such as barn-burning, abduction, and the disruption of legitimate political groups in the 1970s?[2]

In response to the old chestnut that secrecy is necessary to protect the identity of confidential informants, it is worth heeding the advice of the Federal Law Reform Commission that it is possible to have both openness and protection by limiting secrecy to the narrow end of protecting identities and descriptive information that would reveal them. Otherwise, a full hearing in public should be held.[3]

It was also argued that secrecy is essential to protect innocent persons whose names may come up at the inquiry. This is advanced as a social value of superior importance that justifies overriding freedom of the press. Without minimizing the interest of innocent persons, surely at a time when public confidence in a federal police force already under other clouds of suspicion is seriously threatened, the freedom of the press must prevail. The press must then report proceedings carefully to ensure that innocent persons are not harmed unnecessarily.

Some might be tempted to accuse me of being a cynic for such a distrust of proceedings and judicial acts conducted behind closed doors, and for my reluctance to warmly embrace those who say "trust me." There are examples that demonstrate how our justice system can work when no one is looking — or is allowed to look.

In 1980, Globe and Mail reporter Peter Moon received information that he would find some interesting action in a court room at Toronto's District Court House. However, when he got there, he found that the court room door was closed tight. There was not even a case-list posted outside the door. After Moon knocked loud enough, a court official opened the door and told him that he could not enter, because the judge had made an order excluding the public. Moon was persistent. He then

---

1   "RCMP probe to be closed, head rules" (May 1, 1990), The Globe and Mail, at A5.

2   Canada, Commission of Inquiry Concerning Certain Activities of the Royal Canadian Mounted Police, *Freedom and Security Under the Law*, vols. 1 & 2 (Ottawa: Supply and Services Canada, 1981) (Commissioner: Justice D.C. McDonald).

3   Law Reform Commission of Canada, *Public and Media Access to the Criminal Process* (Working Paper 56) (Ottawa: Law Reform Commission of Canada, 1987), and see Stanley A. Cohen, "Free Press vs. Fair Trial — A Law Reform Perspective," in this volume.

asked for a copy of the indictment, and was told that the indictment could not be produced — it too was secret. Moon then entered the court room, and asked the judge for an adjournment so that he could bring legal counsel to challenge the secret hearing. Ultimately, this proved unnecessary. The orders were rescinded and Moon learned what this was all about. It was not a towering matter of national security. It was not an explosive drug case involving members of the Medellin drug cartel. Nor was it a civil matter involving trade secrets. Moon learned that the accused before the court was a chauffeur who had driven the Chief Justice of Ontario and other justices to and from work. The accused stood charged with illegal possession of wire-tap equipment. The judge explained that the accused had sought the order to save the justices from embarrassment. However, confronted by Moon, he reversed himself and ruled that the exclusion powers granted under s. 442 of the *Criminal Code*[4] could not be used merely to avoid embarrassment. My question is, what would have happened if Peter Moon had not had the temerity and know-how to force his way into the court room and challenge the secret proceedings? Although nothing untoward may have been taking place, the possibility remains that anything can happen behind closed doors — even when a judge is inside — and the public will be left, blissfully ignorant, in the dark.[5]

Publicity is not only required to prevent and expose perfidy and abuse of power, it is also required as a safeguard against error, incompetence, laziness or plain indifference in judicial proceedings. In Sarnia, Ontario, shortly after the *Young Offenders Act*[6] was proclaimed in 1984,[7] a judge sentenced two teenage girls charged with separate offenses to substantial closed custody terms, on the same day. No one in that court room, including the defence lawyer, or the Crown prosecutor, realized that the judge had absolutely no power to imprison the girls for the offenses committed. Fortunately, there was a reporter in that court room. A knowledgeable lawyer read her report, realized that a terrible mistake had been made, and brought it to the attention of the Crown. Without that intervention, the girls would have spent many more months serving the illegal jail terms. In fairness, the media cannot just sit back and criticize closed hearings. It must do its fair share of informing the public about what is happening in the nation's courts — at all levels — by devoting more resources to the task.

I am often surprised by the extent to which the public, and the courts, are willing to trust the word of police officers about their inves-

4   R.S.C. 1970, c. C-34, s. 442.
5   "Judge Opens Trial to Public After Reporter Protests" (November 5, 1980), The Globe and Mail, at 1.
6   S.C. 1980-81-82-83, c. 110.
7   R.S.C. 1985, c. Y-1.

tigations, without requiring them to submit their work to public scrutiny. In particular, I am referring to the *Criminal Code* provisions that require the affidavit used by an officer to obtain a wire-tap authorization to remain sealed, unless it can be demonstrated that the order was fraudulently obtained. That, of course, poses a catch-22. It is impossible to demonstrate fraud unless one is able to get inside the sealed packet and examine the sworn affidavit. The best way to discover the abuse made possible by this process is to examine a case in which the packet was ultimately opened, and to test the assertions made in the affidavit using the tool of cross-examination in the court room. Take, for example, the case of five men charged in Hamilton, Ontario with plotting a campaign of terror in India. One of these was Talwinder Singh Parmar, head of a Sikh fundamentalist sect. Here is the analysis I prepared for an Insight article that appeared in The Toronto Star.[8]

> Bowen, the respondent, swears under oath in the affidavit that Parmar is the leader of a Sikh terrorist group which has claimed responsibility for more than 40 assassinations, creating the impression that Parmar was a Carlos-like leader of a notorious international terrorist group such as Direct Action or the Red Brigade. In fact, the evidence showed that Parmar was the high priest of the Babbar Khalsa, a legitimate Sikh fundamentalist religious sect.

> Bowen swears that Parmar escaped from India in 1981 and came to Canada as a fugitive from justice in order to avoid numerous criminal charges — including six counts of murder. In fact, Parmar had been a permanent Canadian resident since 1970 and is a Canadian citizen. The six murders had occurred two months after he had left India.

> Bowen does not disclose in his affidavit that Parmar had been arrested in West Germany in 1983 on an Interpol extradition warrant for the Indian crimes. After being held in custody for a year he was exonerated. His passport showed that he was thousands of miles away from the place where the crimes were committed.

> The affidavit incorrectly states that Parmar was "presently" facing a charge of possessing explosives in Duncan, B.C. In fact, three days before the affidavit was sworn, Parmar was exonerated after the British Columbia prosecutor told the court that the evidence contemplated at the time of the charges had not materialized. Bowen testified he was not aware that Parmar had been freed. His discharge had been widely reported in newspapers across Canada and on the CBC and CTV national news.

> Several pages of the affidavit summarize the Duncan evidence so as to leave the impression that Parmar is connected to a dynamite explosion outside Duncan. (That was the evidence that did not materialize in B.C.). The affidavit fails to disclose that the noise heard was actually

---

8 "Shoddy police 'evidence' used for wiretap order" (April 19, 1987), The Toronto Star, at B1.

the sound of a gun, and that several searches by an explosives expert and a trained dog had failed to disclose any evidence of an explosion or explosives which could be connected with Parmar.

The affidavit referred to existing wiretaps in B.C. which were said to have disclosed unspecified illegal activities. In fact, the officer did not provide [Judge] McRae with available transcripts of these conversations which would have showed him that not a single illegal activity was suggested. If anything, the undisclosed transcripts demonstrated Parmar's priestly activities, and his benevolence toward people in his homeland who had been abused by the police.

Bowen's affidavit refers to surveillance which shows Parmar travelling to Ontario and meeting several individuals, in a manner which suggests that these meetings were conspiratorial. It does not disclose that he was the sect's priest and that the surveillance showed him attending to his priestly functions by visiting various temples throughout southern Ontario. Had these facts been disclosed, like so many others, the affidavit would have taken on a totally different complexion.

After reading this analysis, one can well understand why the Supreme Court Justice granted the *ex parte* application. After all, the judge is in no position to challenge the assertions in the affidavit, and therefore must rely on trust and the oath. Police officers, therefore, have great latitude to play loose with the contents of the affidavits, particularly if they can be confident that they will remain sealed and never see the light of day. Looking at it another way, if leave had not been granted to open the packet in this case, the defence counsel never would have been able to mount a constitutional challenge to the serious charges that their clients faced, and their clients may have been convicted wrongly of the crimes. Surely, as the Canadian courts are beginning to realize, there should be no objection to ordering the packets to be opened at trial, subject to the protection of informants to the degree necessary, as the wire-taps have already been concluded, and the investigative procedure is no longer at risk.

In 1980, a mother lodged complaints with the Ontario College of Physicians and Surgeons, after her son died of a heart attack while in hospital. The doctors had concluded that the boy suffered from psychological problems and had ordered him to clean up his own vomit. After the complaint was dismissed in a closed hearing, the mother finally succeeded in obtaining a court order requiring a public hearing by the Ontario Health Discipline Board into the manner in which the complaint had been investigated. It is instructive to examine how the secret complaint committee hearing held up in the light of open scrutiny. As I pointed out in an Insight article in The Toronto Star:[9]

---

9   "She beat the medical profession's secrecy" (December 8, 1987), The Globe and Mail, at A23.

It seems that the committee decided not to obtain a transcript of the inquest into his death. Instead, it placed the burden on his mother to provide them with any portions of this immensely important document — which she did not have — and which she might consider relevant.

Although two experienced pediatricians were appointed by the college to make a separate inquiry into the death, their reports and related material were not placed before the complaints committee.

The committee did not obtain any opinions or assessments from independent, qualified experts to help evaluate the conduct of the physicians who were the subjects of the complaints.

Crucial doctor's orders for January 30, 1980, described by the Health Disciplines Board as "a significant date in Steven Yus's treatment", were missing from the hospital's records. The board noted that, "There may not be anything that the committee could reasonably do to replace that information, but the college record is devoid of any attempts to do so".

Other supposedly missing information was, in fact, available.

A key x-ray film was not viewed by the committee even though it "was obviously located and was available".

In addition to these glaring acts and omissions, the board questioned the lack of critical analysis exercised by the complaints committee when dealing with specific complaints. Its 30-page decision criticizes failures to analyze facts, explain conclusions, investigate inconsistencies and pursue serious errors in order to determine whether they are "mere misadventure" or "professional misconduct".

Perhaps this explains why the doctors fought for five years in the courts to avoid a public review.

In essence, if the *Charter*[10] protection of free expression is to be meaningful, requests to close courts, or ban publication, must be submitted to the closest examination and probing, and granted only in the narrowest terms. This requires both members of the media and the legal profession to remain closely on guard against abuses.

In 1989, I was horrified to discover a recommendation in the report by the Security Intelligence Review Committee to Parliament (SIRC) — the public watchdog over Canada's security service — that judges be empowered, where national security is involved, to remove not only the accused person from the court room, but also the defence counsel and the jury.[11] If Parliament adopted that recommendation, the only persons permitted to remain in the court room while national security

---

10 *Canadian Charter of Rights and Freedoms*, Pt. I of the *Constitution Act, 1982*, being Sched. B of the *Canada Act 1982*, 1982 (Eng.), c. 11.

11 Security Intelligence Review Committee, *Annual Report 1988-89* (Ottawa: Supply and Services Canada, 1989), at 67-68.

evidence is given would be the judge, the police and the prosecutor. This recommendation, which played havoc with the most sacred principles of criminal law, was justified in the name of protecting national security. Fortunately, after an angry editorial appeared in The Toronto Star,[12] SIRC Chairman, Ron Atkey, withdrew the recommendation when he appeared before the parliamentary committee considering his report, after acknowledging that it was "excessive and unfair to accused persons."[13]

I also take issue with two other recommendations to restrict the publication of court proceedings.

First, in 1989, Metro Toronto Police Chief, William McCormack, announced that as of January 1, 1991, the day that provincial privacy legislation became applicable to municipalities,[14] the force would no longer be able to release to the media either the names of persons charged with crimes or crime victims. In doing so, McCormack was clearly relying on a worst-scenario interpretation of the privacy legislation. As The Toronto Star pointed out in an editorial, this interpretation would prevent the media from reporting the truth about crime in the community. As the editorial says, in part:[15]

> In other words, this new law could be a new lever for police to restrict the timely flow of information to Metro residents about crime in their community, perhaps to make the city seem safer than it really is.
>
> If this interpretation is right, media outlets could be hindered in their daily job of putting a human face on crime: If a mugging victim's identity is a police secret, how can photographers convey the impact of crime on people?
>
> The failure, too, to name people who are charged with criminal offences can lead to groundless suspicion, speculation and harm to others. If one lawyer is charged with embezzlement of clients' funds but his identity is kept secret, every lawyer is unfairly branded as an accused thief.
>
> Will people care as much if crimes are committed against nameless, faceless people in unspecified neighbourhoods? How will Crime Stoppers solicit public help in solving a burglary or a rape if it can't say where the crime happened?
>
> When the community knows less about crime because the police choose to say less, people will be less able to judge how well the police do their job. If the new law gives them an excuse to curb the flow of

---

12 "A Threat to Justice" (October 30, 1989), The Toronto Star.

13 Canada, House of Commons, *Minutes of Proceedings and Evidence of the Special Committee on the Review of the CSIS Act and the Security Offences Act* (November 23, 1989), at 4:7.

14 *Freedom of Information and Protection of Privacy Act*, S.O. 1987, c. 25, s. 2(1)"institution", (3).

15 "When Crime Is Secret" (March 12, 1990), The Toronto Star, at A16.

information to the public, the vital principle of accountability will be undermined.

There are times when individuals could be hurt by the careless release of their identities. For example, the *Criminal Code* already prohibits publication of the names of sexual assault victims or youthful victims of crime; young offenders also are shielded, so that their chances for rehabilitation aren't damaged.

In a parliamentary democracy like Canada with its Charter of Rights, a balance must be struck between the public's right to know and the protection of privacy. It can hardly be in the public interest if the police use a law to tip the scales for their own purposes.

Second, a dissenting view in the Law Reform Commission working paper on media access to the criminal process recommends that judges should be able to prohibit publication in exceptional circumstances, at the request of an accused person, victim or witness. This power could be exercised "where identification would result in substantial and extraordinary harm to the applicant or others, and the public interest in the applicant's identity is minimal."[16] The dangers inherent in this proposal were set out in a Toronto Star editorial which pointed out, in part, that:[17]

This sentiment may be humane, but it is also naive. The publication bans will likely be obtained by persons who are wealthy enough to retain high-powered lawyers.

And it is dangerous, as no matter how clear the criteria are made for imposition of the bans, judges are bound to apply them differently in different places, and pockets of secrecy in our courts would soon become the order of the day. Surely we must be able to find out who in the community has been subjected to prosecution so that all citizens will be protected from the invisible and potentially arbitrary exercise of power by the state.

Arguing the other side in the same working paper, other commissioners say that a publication ban should only be considered where reporting the name of the accused would, by association, identify the complainant, the victim or a young person in sexual offenses. They maintain that the public has a genuine interest in knowing the identity of an accused person as it may put the community at ease, and speculation about others who were not charged, or even draw forward witnesses whose evidence may assist the accused. They are right.

In sum, with the advent of the *Charter*, there is a recognition of the primacy of the values of openness and accountability in our justice system. Bans and restrictions that may have been imposed routinely

16 *Supra*, note 3 at 55.
17 "For Open Court" (June 5, 1987), The Toronto Star, at A18.

must be strictly justified and narrowly confined. Openness is not the enemy of the fair trial; it is the prerequisite that makes it possible. We must be wary of intrusions which, though well-intended, can undermine its protective effect.

FREE PRESS vs. FAIR TRIAL: A LAW REFORM PERSPECTIVE

*Stanley A. Cohen**

I. INTRODUCTION

This paper will focus on the Law Reform Commission's Working Paper 56 on *Public and Media Access to the Criminal Process.* While the commission had articulated a philosophy — one developed over many years — expressing its commitment to the task of furthering respect for, and bolstering fundamental values in all aspects of, the criminal process,[1] its efforts in the area of media coverage of the criminal process nevertheless had to overcome some unique challenges.

In large measure, this was because its work elsewhere on criminal

---

*   The author wishes to acknowledge his reliance in the preparation of this article on Allen Linden's consideration of these issues in "Limitations on Media Coverage of Legal Proceedings: A Critique and Some Proposals for Reform," in Anisman and Linden (eds.), *The Media, The Courts and The Charter* (Toronto: Carswell, 1986), at 301.

1   See, *e.g.*, Report 3, *Our Criminal Law* (Ottawa: Law Reform Commission of Canada, 1976), and Report 32, *Our Criminal Procedure* (Ottawa: Law Reform Commission of Canada, 1988).

procedure has generally required it to confront a classic dichotomy in approaches to legislative policy-making, namely, the need to advance the public interest in effective law enforcement while at the same time protecting and enhancing respect for individual rights (a task which is also in the public's interest). These competing impulses find expression in any criminal justice system, but in systems characterized as "adversarial" this contest is (theoretically, at least) perhaps more often resolved in favour of due process values and against crime control values. Thus, most policy questions affecting the adversary system that we at the commission confronted over the years were articulated in terms of the interests of the state, the police and prosecutor on the one hand, and those of the accused on the other.

II. MAJOR PROPOSALS OF THE LAW REFORM COMMISSION'S WORKING PAPER

On reflection, it is perhaps not surprising, although it was something of a revelation to us at the time, to discover that the role of the press is not easily accommodated in this bipolar universe. Third party interests premised on fundamental values such as freedom of the press in some manner oppose, or at least are in a state of tension with, the interests that are characteristically, or traditionally, at play in the adversary system.[2]

The public's fascination with law and the courts as we see it today contrasts strongly with the situation which existed not so many years ago where complaints were voiced that too little attention was being devoted to legal issues. Greater coverage of the criminal process has led to heightened public awareness, but this shift has itself generated significant concerns that the rapid, widespread dissemination of views can have serious, possibly deleterious, effects on the privacy rights of individuals who are somehow caught up in the court process — whether they be accused persons (whom we "presume" to be innocent), innocent third parties, or equally innocent victims or complainants — and in the criminal justice system generally.

As its work on public and media access to the criminal process progressed, the commission came to a deeper appreciation of the fact that the ability of the public to have access to its criminal courts and proceedings, both directly and through the media, is simply one facet of the concept of an open government. The importance of openness to a

---

2   It should be noted that there is no constitutional provision that expressly guarantees the right of the public to attend legal proceedings. However, at the same time it should also be recognized that limitations on access may constitute an infringement on freedom of the press or the right to a public trial.

society founded on democratic principles can scarcely be overstated. The criminal process is, after all, capable of being used as an instrument of tyranny. Openness in the process ensures the responsible exercise of the drastic, but necessary, powers of the state. Ultimately, the commission was led to conclude that, in general, neither the criminal process nor the public benefits from excessive restrictions on access to criminal proceedings or overbroad constraints on the publication of the facts and results of such proceedings.

Since 1982, the *Charter*[3] has required the courts to assess the importance of openness of judicial proceedings and measure it against the weight of other competing interests. Free press and public trial guarantees stand alongside other fundamentals warranting fairness to persons accused of crime. Many cases have since been litigated challenging the reasonableness of various limitations imposed on the public and the press by the *Criminal Code* and other statutes. This has been a useful process, but it is hardly a sufficient one. Re-evaluation of the limitations on publicity and access to the courts should not be left simply to case-by-case challenges under the *Charter*. In this *Charter* era a formal and fundamental review of the basic principle of openness of judicial proceedings, and of the exceptions to it, is required. The soundness of the basic principle of openness must be reaffirmed. Deviations from this principle must also be examined for their continued necessity and validity and, further, it must be determined whether or not the interests of those involved in judicial proceedings are being given due attention. This is essentially what has been attempted in Working Paper 56 on *Public and Media Access to the Criminal Process*.

Working Paper 56 surveys and catalogues the numerous limitations contained in the present law affecting the freedom of the public and the media to attend criminal proceedings, examine court documents, and communicate what has been learned to others. The composite picture that emerges is one of vague, and often excessively restrictive, laws.

The Working Paper specifically identifies some 20 statutory provisions that curtail, in some way, the public's access to the criminal process. These selected illustrations do not exhaustively cover all of the restrictions in the present criminal law. Among the most prominent are:

(1) the provisions, now discredited, prohibiting the publication of the location of a search or the identity of occupants and suspects where a search with warrant is carried out;[4]

---

3   *Canadian Charter of Rights and Freedoms*, Pt. I of the *Constitution Act, 1982*, being Sched. B of the *Canada Act 1982*, 1982 (Eng.), c. 11.
4   *Criminal Code*, R.S.C. 1985, c. C-46, s. 487.2.

(2) restrictions on the evidence that is received at bail hearings[5] and preliminary inquiries;[6]

(3) exclusion of the public from a preliminary inquiry;[7]

(4) exclusion of the public from any proceeding in the interest of public morals;[8]

(5) prohibitions on publishing the identity of a complainant in a sexual offence;[9]

(6) exclusion of the public from a *voir dire* into the admissibility of a complainant's sexual history[10] and publication bans in relation to those proceedings;[11] and,

(7) the exclusion of the public from the trial of young persons,[12] as well as press prohibitions concerning the identity of young accused persons, victims or witnesses.[13]

Other restrictions exist at common law.

Of course, the fact that these restrictions exist sheds little light on the intrinsic worth of any of them. All have a history and presumably all were enacted for a purpose that made some sense having regard to the time and circumstances of their enactment. However, like many sections in the present *Code*, there is little linkage to be discovered amongst these seemingly related, but widely scattered, provisions. Amendments have been engrafted on the basic structure of the *Code* with little regard paid to organization, structure and, perhaps most importantly, thematical coherence. Little evidence exists in our *Code* (at least in this area) of congruence and philosophical unity. The absence of guiding principle is apparent and constitutes a particularly telling defect in the law. Where principles guide reform, the warranted expectation is generated that consistency, uniformity and rationality will characterize the result.

The present restrictions that exist in our law fall into essentially three descriptive categories, which may be identified in terms of the concerns that they address: (1) status concerns, (2) procedural justice concerns, and (3) public interest concerns.[14]

---

5   *Ibid.*, s. 517.

6   *Ibid.*, ss. 539, 542.

7   *Ibid.*, s. 537.

8   *Ibid.*, s. 486(1).

9   *Ibid.*, s. 486(3).

10 *Ibid.*, s. 276(3).

11 *Ibid.*, s. 276(4).

12 *Young Offenders Act*, R.S.C. 1985, c. Y-1, s. 39(1).

13 *Ibid.*, s. 38(1).

14 See Linden, "Limitations on Media Coverage of Legal Proceedings: A Critique and Some Proposals for Reform," *supra*, note * at 306-11, where these concerns are described in terms of individual, due process and societal interests.

Status concerns receive attention and result in restrictions under our law in instances where it is believed that certain vulnerable persons or classes of persons require protection. Thus, we have rules designed to protect certain victims and complainants,[15] shelter mentally disabled persons who have been called on to give evidence in legal proceedings,[16] as well as rules which safeguard young persons who are involved in judicial proceedings whether as accused persons or witnesses.[17]

Procedural justice characteristically entails a concern to ensure the fairness and integrity of the judicial process, and thus secure the rights of the litigants. Of course, *all* litigants have a right to expect fair and untainted procedures, but in the criminal adversary process, where the state with all of its vast resources is one of the parties to the litigation and the liberty of the subject rests in the balance, procedural justice focuses primarily on the individual.

This concern to ensure basic, fundamental justice to accused persons goes beyond the confines of the ordinary law and finds generous expression in the *Charter*'s legal rights provisions.[18] In the context of free press versus fair trial, this has resulted in a variety of measures (including the common law of contempt of court)[19] that are designed to insulate the judicial process from outside influences and prevent the contamination of the ultimate trial. An accused is entitled to have his or her case determined solely on the basis of evidence received and heard at the trial itself. To curb the public discussion of evidence that may have been received or discussed at either the preliminary inquiry or in the course of a bail hearing, provisions in the *Code* allow publication bans to be imposed at these early stages of the process. The *Code* also provides a prohibition on the publication of any admission or confession of an accused, since any publication of such a statement before its admissibility has been determined at trial would be highly prejudicial.

Such public interest restrictions as exist in our present law are characteristically expressed in vague and general terms such as the "protection of public morals," the "safeguarding of national security," or the furtherance of some especially important law enforcement interest (such as the "preservation of secrecy pertaining to the techniques of law enforcement investigation"). These restrictions, while typically framed in the broadest and most open-ended manner imaginable, also include some particular, more limited and precise examples (such as "the need to protect the identity of informers").

---

15 As in s. 276(3), (4) — *voir dire* on past sexual history, and identity.
16 *Scott v. Scott*, [1913] A.C. 417 (H.L.).
17 *Young Offenders Act*, ss. 38(1), 39(1) — exclusionary orders and publication bans.
18 Those legal rights are found in ss. 7-14.
19 See *B.C.G.E.U. v. B.C. (A.G.)*, [1988] 2 S.C.R. 214, for an interesting discussion.

The Working Paper contains some 23 specific recommendations designed to improve the present system. These proposals have been hailed by at least some in the media as progressive, overdue steps which, if implemented, would go some distance towards removing the veil of mystery from the criminal process. The Working Paper was released on June 4, 1987. Regrettably, no legislative action has occurred in the three years since its publication.

At this point, a brief description of the commission's major proposals is in order.

A. A Presumption of Openness Should Govern the Criminal Process

All criminal proceedings should be conducted in public, the public should be allowed to examine all court documents, and all communication about the criminal process should be permitted, subject only to narrow exceptions which protect other substantial social values, such as effective law enforcement and the right to a fair trial.

B. A National Experiment with Electronic Media Coverage of Court Proceedings Should Be Conducted

A national experiment should be conducted to examine what effect, if any, the presence of the electronic media (that is, television cameras) would have on participants in the criminal process, such as witnesses, lawyers, judges and jurors. As an interim measure, the commission recommends that electronic media coverage be permitted in criminal appeals, since no fact-finding takes place there. Also, the commission suggests that the use of audio recorders should be allowed in all criminal proceedings as a means of ensuring accuracy in the transmission of statements made in open court, but not for broadcast purposes.

Frankly, I find the resistance that we have encountered to our limited suggestion to permit cameras in the court room baffling. To my mind there is a certain inevitability to cameras finding a proper place in the visitors gallery, just as there has been an inevitable progression towards their finding a quiet, non-intrusive corner in Parliament and in certain public inquiries.

My impression is that, at least in part, we have been witnessing a kind of Luddite resistance to the advance of technology. Those who oppose change because they fear the Americanization of what they believe are kinder, gentler, more decorous courts with an emphasis on politesse and formality cling to a vision of court room demeanour that, if it in fact exists, is within the power of the judiciary to maintain —

cameras or no cameras. Cameras, in this regard, may well even turn out to be the instrument that will serve to restore the modern, harried, urban community's sense of itself. Certainly they provide the medium for best realizing the community's wish to know what is transpiring in its midst. While there may be some risk, as there is with all media, in pandering to salacious, prurient interests, there is also the promise that technology, properly employed, will serve to reinforce respect for law and foster democratic values. The commission is, however, prepared to be proven wrong on this — but, if so, it should be by Canadian data generated in a Canadian environment. It is our impression that critics of this essentially modest proposal are jumping to the kind of conclusions that the experiment itself is designed to investigate.

C. No Exclusion Orders or Publication Bans Based on "Public Morals" Should Exist

At present, the public may be excluded from criminal courts, and the media prohibited from publishing "indecent matters" arising in criminal proceedings, in order to protect "public morals."

Although such exclusionary powers based on public morals as exist appear to have been used infrequently and with restraint, the ambit of these restrictions is arguably greater than is tolerable in a free and democratic society. In the commission's view, the discretion to grant protection in the area that is loosely described as public morals should be more structured; especially since there is a real difficulty in defining which public morals, if any, need this type of judicial protection in contemporary Canadian society. After all, the administration of justice is a matter of public record. While in another era it might have been thought that the Canadian public was well served by those seeking to shield it from such sordid realities of human nature as from time to time surface in a criminal trial, protective sentiments of this nature are now viewed as distinctly anachronistic.

D. Automatic Publication Bans Should Be Abolished

No publication bans should apply automatically on the request of one party. A number of these bans presently exist in the *Criminal Code*.[20]

Courts should always have a discretion to refuse an application for a publication ban where there is no demonstrable need for it.

---

20   See, *e.g.*, *Criminal Code*, R.S.C. 1985, c. C-46, ss. 517, 539.

E. Some Discretionary Publication Bans and Exclusion Orders Should Be Allowed in Carefully Limited Circumstances

Members of the public should be excluded from courts only when necessary to obtain the evidence of a young person, maintain order, prevent disclosure of sealed documents, or when a court is determining whether to admit evidence of a complainant's sexual history.

If the public is excluded from a criminal proceeding, certain measures should be taken by courts to keep the public informed. The presiding judge should state generally what transpired behind closed doors. The public should be allowed access to transcripts of certain closed proceedings. Courts should have the discretion to allow researchers to attend closed proceedings on appropriate terms and conditions.

The commission also proposes that the identities of victims of sexual crimes, confidential informants and, in some cases, other witnesses whose safety may be in danger, be protected. A court should have the power to lift these bans where necessary to ensure a fair trial.

F. Search Warrant Documents Should Be Accessible to the Public After Search Has Been Conducted

The present *Criminal Code* restrictions on publication of the location of a search and the identities of all the occupants and suspects without their consent should be repealed.[21] If replaced, it should be with a limited court power to obscure information from warrant documents or to deny public access temporarily.

III. CONCLUSION

That, then, is something of the background to the commission's efforts to reshape the law in an area that is of current interest to this assembly.

The commission views the enactment of its proposals for the reform of laws relating to public and media access to the criminal process as just one small part of a much larger enterprise. It has placed many sound, workable proposals before the powers that be. Despite what some critics might say, they are not academic abstractions. There is a general acceptance among knowledgeable people that a material im-

---

21 *Supra*, note 6.

provement in the criminal justice system is possible, and there is some momentum to have reforms enacted.

Properly conceived, the reform of our laws of media coverage is an important element in a comprehensive criminal law reform exercise. These proposals do not represent the only solutions to the problems posed, but they do represent a significant repository of considered advice. In the meantime, the old laws and practices continue to hold sway — at least until the courts pronounce them to be constitutionally inadequate (as indeed they have, for example, with respect to challenges involving *Criminal Code* restrictions respecting publicity of searches conducted under the authority of a warrant).[22]

It is not that new laws will be perfect or immune to constitutional challenge and even protracted litigation, but the hope is that new criminal laws fashioned in a conscientious law reform endeavour — one that is sensitive to fundamental values — will prove more resistant to constitutional rebuke than those constructed in other times with other considerations in mind.

---

22 See *Can. Newspapers Co. v. Can. (A.G.)* (1986), 29 C.C.C. (3d) 109 (Ont. H.C.), and *Can. Newspapers Co. v. Can. (A.G.)* (1986), 28 C.C.C. (3d) 379 (Man. Q.B.).

PART II

OBSCENITY: THE SCOPE OF LIBERTY AND EQUALITY

The debate over the censorship of pornography pervades the entire political spectrum. Conservative moralists are seen as objecting to the proliferation of all material of a sexual nature; liberals and social democrats are seen as being indifferent to the proliferation of, and the harms caused by, pornography; and feminists are seen as being concerned solely with the resulting harms to women, while being indifferent to the discussion and exploration of sexuality. The authors in this chapter attempt to place the current debate over the censorship of pornography within a historical, constitutional and sociological context.

John McLaren traces the history of the regulation of sexual imagery and finds several recurring themes. In particular, he surveys the social and legal confusion about what is obscene and pornographic and the resulting disorder in the enforcement of censorship laws. The breadth of this history is surveyed, with a view towards suggesting contemporary reform of the law. McLaren warns us to be aware of the degree of degrading material which is actually in circulation, and the susceptibility of the law to being high-jacked by small, but vocal, groups of moral vigilantes. McLaren posits that by prosecuting those who produce and distribute highly offensive material, we will begin to shift our social attitudes away from favouring, or being indifferent to, degradation and violence and towards favouring equality.

Kathleen Mahoney reviews the record of the Canadian judiciary in the enforcement of the *Criminal Code* prohibitions against the possession, production and proliferation of obscene material. She provides a searching critique of the traditional way in which judges have interpreted the *Criminal Code* prohibitions, and the perceived failure of the judiciary to recognize and characterize the harms of pornography. In particular, she denounces the application of the community standards test for masking the real harm of pornography and, in some instances, making judges the unwitting allies of pornography producers. Mahoney ties the criminal liability analysis to a constitutional one, discussing how the *Charter*'s freedom of expression guarantee must be read in conjunction with the *Charter*'s equality rights. By this interpretation, it is asserted that pornography should fall outside the ambit of constitutionally guaranteed free expression.

Thelma McCormack addresses the role that freedom of expression plays in the achievement of gender equality. She traces that relationship in the context of the cultural history of the 20th century: from changing class structures and the sexual revolution of the '60s through to the present neo-conservative environment. McCormack argues that a feminist construction of freedom of expression is contingent on a distinction between text and deed and a tolerant social democracy in which women have greater access to the media of communication. She argues that freedom of expression and equality cannot be separated, for freedom of expression is a necessary, though not sufficient, condition for the equality of women.

"NOW YOU SEE IT, NOW YOU DON'T": THE HISTORICAL RECORD AND THE ELUSIVE TASK OF DEFINING THE OBSCENE

*John P.S. McLaren**

I. INTRODUCTION

It is a trite observation that it is difficult to define, with anything close to precision, what is "obscene" or "pornographic" for legal purposes. Definitions which have been devised by the framers of the criminal law in the past, whether judges or legislative drafters, have tended to be either too inclusive or too exclusive. In either case, the result has been judicial vacillation, and thus uncertainty, as to the true scope of the law. As experience with the broadly framed *Hicklin*[1] "corrupting impact" test showed, an expansive definition may, in time, fall out of sync with changing social and moral views and become in-

---

* My thanks are due to my research assistant, Burt Harris, for his assistance with background research and to my colleague, Jamie Cassels, for his helpful comments on an earlier draft.
1   *R. v. Hicklin* (1868), L.R. 3 Q.B. 360.

creasingly anachronistic. In this instance, as time went by, the courts found the test difficult to work with, and the temptation developed among some judges to interpret it more restrictively. By the same token, s. 159(8) [now s. 163(8)] of the *Criminal Code* with its emphasis on "undue exploitation," a provision designed to attack a limited range of publications, was interpreted by judges with a more liberal mindset than its sponsor, and became the accepted general definition for obscenity in the criminal law, effectively replacing the *Hicklin* test.[2] The use of the so-called "community standards" test as the agent of this transformative process has added even greater imprecision to the *Code* provision, because it can be manipulated to satisfy such a wide range of philosophic views on what is obscene. Having said that, it is important to add that recent attempts to reform Canadian criminal law to accommodate more precise and detailed definitions of "obscenity" or "pornography" have floundered, demonstrating that the task of translating what the law is supposed to catch into more elaborate verbal formulations is not an easy one.[3]

The difficulty of definition is, in large part, a reflection of widely differing conceptions of what is obscene or pornographic and of the social and legal significance of the production and use of such material. The result of this lack of social consensus has been, and still is, a diverse babble of discourses about obscenity and pornography and what, if anything, should be done about them as a matter of law.

The main object of this article is to consider the historical record with a view to exposing the various discourses surrounding obscenity and pornography, the extent to which some of these have affected the evolution of the law and resistance to its use and what historical analysis may have to suggest in terms of contemporary legal strategies in dealing with obscene or pornographic material.

II. OBSCENITY IN HISTORY

A. The Ancient and Mediaeval Worlds: Erotica as Art, Obscenity as Comedy and Satire

Obscenity in terms of the use of sexual representation or allusion as a form of social statement is as old as humankind's ability to translate thoughts, emotions and fantasies about sex, sexuality and gender relations into media of communication. Obscenity, as well as "erotica" (the

---

2   W. Charles, "Obscene Literature and the Legal Process in Canada" (1966), 44 Can. Bar Rev. 243.

3   J. McLaren, "New Puritans: 0 Free Speech United: 0 — The Great Canadian Pornography Shoot-Off" (1988), 9 Journ. of Media Law & Practice 128.

portrayal of sexual love) which was seen as having artistic merit in and of itself, were well known in the ancient world (in both Greece and Rome). However, then, as in the succeeding millennium, obscenity was used and was widely recognized as being used for comic relief and satire, a form of social catharsis or critique. As a consequence, there was little, if any, pressure to censor it. Works such as Aristophanes' *Lysistrata*, the *Carmen 16* of Catullus, and Geoffrey Chaucer's *The Miller's Tale*, seem to have been accepted in the comic or satirical spirit in which they were written.

Although obscenity did not, in general terms, generate the strong sense of social and moral anxiety which we associate with the post-Renaissance and post-Reformation periods, it was certainly recognized by the great Greek philosophers that "art" had what Walter Kendrick describes as "irrational power."[4] They disagreed, however, on the consequences of experiencing that power.[5]

> Plato makes art out to be something like poison, slowly accumulating in the system and strangling it. In the Aristotelian view art is homeopathic medicine to be taken as needed and put back on the shelf.

While Aristotle considered that art had a transitory, cathartic, and generally therapeutic quality, the Platonic view was that "for susceptible minds, representations of certain sorts had irresistible power, metaphoric or not," which was often evil in its effects.[6] This latter belief in the suggestive and negative quality of art is one which is central to the fears about representations of sex and sexuality which have translated into arguments for their legal suppression over the centuries.

With the spread of Christianity and, in particular, its Pauline tradition, the portrayal of images which might engender lustful feelings, as well as the physical expression of those feelings, was labelled as sinful. Among the church fathers, Origen described immoral books as "cups offering for drink the poisons of Babylon" and St. Augustine as "toads coming up out of the mouth of the beast."[7] Because of the church's interest in suppressing "sins of the flesh," in the dual system of religious

---

4   W. Kendrick, *The Secret Museum: Pornography in Modern Culture* (New York: Viking Press, 1987), at 40.

5   *Ibid.*

6   *Ibid.*, at 38. N. St. John Stevas in his book, *Obscenity and the Law* (London: Secker & Warburg, 1956), notes that, in 378 B.C., Plato was advocating the expurgation of Homer's *Odyssey* to make it more suitable for young readers. Moreover, in *The Republic* (London: Everyman, 1935), at 67, he has Socrates advising the "omission of passages such as those describing the lust of Zeus for Hera since they were not 'conducive to self restraint.' "

7   R. Thiesen, *A Moral Evaluation of the American Law Regarding Literary Obscenity* (Rome: Catholic Book Agency, 1957), at 55.

and secular justice which evolved in England from the 12th century, instances of obscenity which attracted official attention fell within ecclesiastical jurisdiction and were subject to the penances set by church courts and authority.[8] The classification of the sin seems to have been venial rather than mortal. Quantitatively there was relatively little action, except perhaps during periods of acute social tension. By and large, sexual representations were excused as genuinely artistic or as the product of comedy or satire. Exceptions would be made where material was blasphemous or defamatory of the community as well as obscene.[9] Challenges to the sanctity of the church and its doctrine, and stirring up the community, were seen as much more serious than "sexual indulgence." The corrupting effects of obscene literature were to excite more official disapprobation with the invention of the printing press.[10] Even then, seditious and blasphemous works attracted far greater attention. The Roman Catholic church, impelled by both the wide circulation and durability of the printed word and the Protestant Reformation, developed an index of banned books (*Index Librorum Prohibitorum*), first published in 1559. The list indicates that heresy was the major focus of concern. However, the *Index* did refer specifically to the treatment of "lascivious or obscene matters."[11] In tune with the reverence accorded to the classical sages, even those of the pre-Christian era, an exception was included for "the ancient writings of the pagans . . . because of their elegance and style."

B. The Post-Reformation Era, 1530-1780: Obscenity and Secular Morality

With the Reformation and the spread of puritan religion to parts of Europe, including England, the representation of sexuality or sexual activity assumed a moral and social significance that was qualitatively different from that of previous ages.[12] Reconstructed and labelled with the evocative term "vice" were a series of sexual and recreational pursuits which were seen as leading the faithful from the path of virtue and implanting irresponsible and immoral notions in their minds. Because of the high level of illiteracy, it was the visual and aural representations of sex and sexuality, especially plays, which initially

---

8   St. John Stevas, *supra*, note 6 at 12-13.
9   *Ibid.*, at 12-13.
10   *Ibid.*, at 5-6.
11   Thiesen, *supra*, note 7 at 58.
12   D. Underdown, *Revel, Riot and Rebellion: Popular Politics and Culture in England, 1603-1660* (Oxford: O.U.P., 1987), at 9-43.

came in for the bitterest attack.[13] There was also an important shift in jurisdiction over sins of the flesh from ecclesiastical to secular courts.[14] As a consequence, the focus of moral concern shifted perceptibly from the need for individual repentance to a developing concern with the corruption of community values.

In England, although the puritan view of vice held temporary sway in the formal statement of the law during the period of Commonwealth, 1640-1660, its impact was felt more at the level of law enforcement, and then only episodically, in particular during periods of political and social unrest and religious revival.[15] For most of the period from 1550 to 1850, the official position of those in government seems to have been "hands off" obscene publications. Until 1700, the concern of the representatives of the state with publications was with the opportunities they provided for the dissemination of seditious and, to a lesser extent, blasphemous copy. The main role of the law was to establish and maintain a regulatory monopoly over printing to minimize the chances that dangerous material of this type would find a publishing outlet.[16] Obscenity did attract the attention of the authorities in one case during the Restoration period, that involving the notorious rake and poet, Sir Charles Sidley. Although Sidley's offence was obscene and indecent conduct, its legal treatment was to prove suggestive in terms of the emergence of a common law offence covering obscene publications. In Sidley's trial for breaching the peace by exposing and relieving himself in public, as well as blaspheming, the Court of King's Bench, for the first time, asserted jurisdiction over such a case by virtue of its self-styled position as "custodian of the morals of all the king's subjects"; this despite the accused's historically correct argument that his offence should be tried by an ecclesiastical court.[17] With this decision, there now existed a precedent for the exercise of power by the common law courts over obscene behaviour, however manifested.

---

13 *Ibid.*, at 50-53.
14 This was particularly true in England during and after the period of Commonwealth (1640-1660) when both prerogative and special courts were abolished or had their powers curtailed, and some of their business was absorbed by the common law courts. See G. Robertson, *Obscenity: An Account of Censorship Laws and their Enforcement in England and Wales* (London: Weidenfeld and Nicolson, 1979), at 21.
15 For the outburst of puritan zeal in the late 15th and early 16th centuries, see Underdown, *supra*, note 12 at 9-43, and for a repetition approximately a century later in the form of the Societies for the Reformation of Manners, see E. Bristow, *Vice and Vigilance: Purity Movements in Britain since 1700* (Dublin: Gill & MacMillan Ltd., 1977), at 11-31.
16 Robertson, *supra*, note 14 at 17-19.
17 *R. v. Sidley* (1663), 1 Sid. 168, 82 E.R. 1036 (K.B.).

It was not until the early decades of the 18th century that the common law relating to obscene publications began to receive some definition. First, the courts, after denying its existence in *Read's* case,[18] recognized a common law crime of obscene libel in the celebrated prosecution of the shady book publisher and pornographer, Edmund Curl, in 1727 for publishing an erotic book, *Venus in the Cloister*, or *The Nun in her Smock*.[19] In so doing, it accepted the legal position of the Attorney General that *Sidley* was authority for judicial legislation against any conduct which "tends to corrupt the morals of the King's subjects." Secondly, in 1737, the theatre which had continued to incur the wrath of puritan moralists with its biting sexual satire and to create anxiety in governmental circles with its political attacks and irreverence, was made subject to a licensing regime under Lord Chamberlain, who was given the power of prior censorship of any play to be performed on the British stage.[20]

Despite the judicial creation of a common law offence of obscene libel, ostensibly designed to prevent His Majesty's liege subjects from having their heads filled with corrupting material, there seems to have been little impulse on the part of officialdom to use it to deal with plain obscenity for the remainder of the 18th century. Widespread illiteracy, a generally tolerant attitude towards sexual licence in literature, and concern about interference with the rights of educated users of the obscene or pornographic, meant that it was typically only if an individual was otherwise a thorn in the flesh of authority that the law would be invoked to suppress this type of material or its use. Thus, while the publication of John Cleland's *Fanny Hill* in 1748 (long considered to be a pornographic classic) excited belated, and then only passing, concern of the establishment, the discovery of an obscene parody, *Essay on Woman*, in the possession of John Wilkes, the radical populist politician, in 1763 was the cause of outrage in the House of Lords and attempts to silence him by law.[21] The political messages in human communica-

---

18 *R. v. Read* (1708), 11 Mod. Rep. 142, 88 E.R. 953 (K.B.). Read was tried for publishing *The Fifteen Plagues of Maidenhead*, poetry suggesting that chastity was another form of malnutrition.

19 *R. v. Curl* (1727), 2 Strange 788, 93 E.R. 849 (K.B.). Curl had a great capacity for attracting attention to himself by his boasting and complete lack of political tact: see H. Montgomery Hyde, *A History of Pornography* (London: Heinemann, 1964), at 156-62; Robertson, *supra*, note 14 at 22-23.

20 Kendrick, *supra*, note 4 at 100. The legislation granting the power was *An Act to explain and amend so much of an Act of the twelfth year of the Reign of Queen Anne as relates to the common players of Interludes*, 1737 (10 Geo. II, c. 28), ss. 3-4. St. John Stevas indicates (*supra*, note 6 at 21) that it was Henry Fielding's attacks on the Prime Minister, Robert Walpole, in two productions in 1736 which was the effective spur to this statute.

21 Hyde, *supra*, note 19 at 163-64; Kendrick, *supra*, note 4 at 97-99.

tion were still more feared than the moral — the cry of the orator more unsettling than the pen of the author. Obscenity among the lower classes would have been, in most instances, oral rather than written, and so largely hidden from official scrutiny. It was the pliability of mobs at the behest of dangerous demagogues which put the wind up the authorities, rather than their recreational pursuits.

C. The Age of Vigilance, Fear and Vigilantes, 1780-1920: The Invention of Pornography

Walter Kendrick has argued plausibly that focusing on sexual representations for their own sake, as opposed to using them to make more general cultural or social statements, is a relatively modern phenomenon.[22] He notes, in particular, that "pornography" did not enter the English language until the mid-19th century, and then was given the medical meaning of "a description of prostitutes or of prostitution, as a matter of public hygiene." It was conspicuously absent from Dr. Johnson's *Dictionary* of 1755. Although work which we would now label as pornographic because it is designed to arouse the reader or observer sexually, for example the 16th century *Postures* of Pietro Aretino and the Restoration poetry of Sidley's companion John Wilmot, Lord Rochester, existed earlier, these emanations had limited circulation among "the high born," and were largely forgotten until the dawning of the "pornographic age."[23] "Pornography," suggests Kendrick, entered social discourse not as a term of moral criticism, but as the construction of scholars analyzing and seeking to make sense of the many erotic and obscene representations and artifacts found at the site of Pompeii from the early 18th century, and of continental and English public health physicians who, from the early 19th century, sought to describe and warn against prostitution and the diseases associated with it.[24] Although the audiences for which both sets of experts wrote were small, educated and exclusively male, the detachment of the representation of sex and sexuality from comedy and satire, and its reconstruction as a matter of independent and supposedly detached analysis and critique, gave the study of pornography a life of its own. As literacy spread and increasing numbers of the population sought diversion in the written word, and as works of art became more accessible during the course of the 19th century, the fear emerged both within the political establishment and the expanding middle class that the preserve of the scholar and medical expert would become the domain of the public-at-large, of

---

22 Kendrick, *supra*, note 4 at 1-2.
23 *Ibid.*, at 54-66.
24 *Ibid.*, at 1-32.

women and children as well as of men, of the working classes as well as of their intellectual and moral betters.

From the latter decades of the 18th century there was a new outburst of moral concern associated with the emergence of evangelical renewal in the Church of England led by William Wilberforce and the Clapham Sect. The evangelicals had obscene literature, songs and "art" on their reform agenda.[25] Central to the thinking of this robust form of Christianity was that the faithful had an obligation to lead both those who had fallen morally or were at moral risk to virtue. As a middle class movement, it saw vice and its temptations as endemic among the lower orders, but rejoiced in the optimistic view that with the application of energy and resolve convinced Christians could, by a combination of the teaching of religious precept, training for service, and personal example, reform the lives of their unfortunate charges. This breed of zealous reformer was concerned to see that support for moral renewal existed in the law. Following a 1787 proclamation of George III against vice at the behest of the evangelicals, which urged the suppression of "all loose and licentious prints, books, and publications, dispensing poison to the minds of the young and unwary, and to punish the publishers and the vendors thereof,"[26] Wilberforce founded what became, in 1802, the Society for the Suppression of Vice. This organization, which was for good reason not willing to entrust enforcement to the ramshackle law enforcement agencies of the state, instituted its own prosecutions of those publishing and selling obscene material. Between 1802 and 1857 the Society launched 159 prosecutions, all but five of which were successful.[27] The majority seem to have been against small-time publishers and booksellers specializing in what would now be described as pornography, centered in Holywell Street in London. The apparent profitability of the trade, and the ability of its agents to bounce back after successful prosecution, meant that this onslaught by the Society had little or no perceptible effect in restraining the pornography business.[28] According to Bristow, the Society seems to have had greater success with street balladeers specializing in indecent lyrics. It was able, by a combination of prosecution and harassment, to clear most of these from the streets by 1820.[29]

---

25 Bristow, *supra*, note 15 at 37-44.
26 Bristow, *ibid.*, at 38, notes that the document was described as a "Proclamation for the Encouragement of Piety and Virtue, and for the Preventing and Punishing of Vice, Profaneness and Immorality."
27 Hyde, *supra*, note 19 at 167.
28 Robertson, *supra*, note 14 at 26.
29 Bristow, *supra*, note 15 at 44. The result was that the erotic and obscene was driven indoors into taverns and "free and easies," the forerunners of the 19th century music hall.

The Vice Society's central concern was that the absorption of obscene material led inexorably to descent into a vicious round of immorality and debauchery on the part of those who used it and, worse still, to the commission of sexual offences, especially among the working classes. The opening up of educational opportunities to a wider segment of the population, and the growth in literacy, added to the anxiety. So did the knowledge that middle class women not only had access to educational opportunities, but greater leisure. As Walter Kendrick has observed, the concern "that monkey see, monkey do," with its supporting rhetoric of "poisonous" influence implicit in the Platonic view of the dangers of art and in the common law courts' espousal of an ill-defined morals jurisdiction, was in the process of becoming a well-established element in socio-legal discourse.[30] The Society for the Suppression of Vice was not hesitant to expose the source of this new danger to the moral fibre of the nation, "continental pollution." The prosecution of materials originating on the continent, or continental pedlars of obscenity, was living proof of the external nature of the threat to English values in this material.[31]

The Vice Society was not without its critics. In particular, it was upbraided for its targeting of the vices of the poor and its indifference to individual rights.[32] Dr. Lushington, speaking in the House of Commons in 1821, described the Society as "a set of cowardly, pusillanimous hypocrites, who prosecuted the poor and helpless, but left the great and noble unmolested."[33] For this member it was imperative that the initiative for obscenity prosecutions be shifted to the Attorney General.[34] In a debate two years later, the proceedings by the Society were described as vexatious by Sir Francis Burdett,[35] while Joseph Hume condemned the activities of such organizations as "little better than conspiracies against the liberty of the subject."[36] All of this was so much water off a duck's back to the zealots running the Society who had no intention of abandoning their mission. They were assisted in their resolve to prosecute by the Law Officers of the Crown who, as Colin Manchester

---

30 Kendrick, *supra*, note 4 at 67-68.
31 Robertson, *supra*, note 14 at 27. Bristow, *supra*, note 15 at 42-43 notes that the prosecution at the Society's behest of an Italian pedlar selling obscene pictures produced on the continent to the denizens of a girl's boarding school was to be openly and vigorously applauded by the Lord Chief Justice, Lord Ellenborough.
32 Colin Manchester, "Obscenity Law Enforcement in the Nineteenth Century" (1981), 2 Journal of Legal History 44 at 47-48.
33 U.K., H.C., *Parliamentary Debates*, N.S., vol. 5 (July 3, 1821), at 1491.
34 *Ibid.*, at 1485.
35 U.K., H.C., *Parliamentary Debates*, N.S., vol. 8 (March 26, 1823), at 729.
36 *Ibid.*, at 709.

observes, "seemed by no means anxious to take over this mantle."[37] The evangelical "smut hounds" happily continued to fill the resulting vacuum.

Walter Houghton has exposed the essentially contradictory character of Victorian thought — on the one hand, its overbrimming confidence and idealism, on the other, its deep anxiety over the pace of change and fear about the less pleasant social and moral impacts of that change.[38] In matters of sex and sexuality these two sides of the Victorian mind complemented and fed off each other. To middle class Victorians the family was the central institution of society — the moral core which provided peace from the busy, and often rapacious, world outside and the companionship necessary for positive human relationships.[39] The idealized family was one dependent upon a gender-based division of labour in which the husband and father went out into the public domain to the challenges of professional or business life to earn the material wealth to support himself and his family, and the mother assumed the physical care and moral management of the household and family. This differentiation of responsibilities was justified, increasingly, in terms of the superior moral sensibilities and pure qualities of women.[40] This idealized view of womanhood was one which manifested itself in a significant amount of sentimentality and in what has been described as the "cult of domesticity," in which virtuous females were placed on pedestals and treated as part angel, part idiot. In the forefront of this process of characterization were members of the clergy, ever ready to remind women of their high moral duties to God, state and family, and physicians concerned to see that women were subject to their direction in carrying out their vital functions of reproduction and child rearing. The reconstitution of the family, and the role of the woman within it, became the basis of both the middle class' definition of itself and a critique of the working classes. In both instances, fear of the breakdown of the moral order was strong. In terms of its own moral welfare, the concern of middle class Victorians was to ensure the protection of the family and especially its female members, wives and daughters, from sexual assault and moral corruption. Their natural naivety, it was supposed, made them especially susceptible to those who would exploit

---

37   Manchester, *supra*, note 32 at 48.
38   W. Houghton, *The Victorian Frame of Mind, 1830-1870* (New Haven: Yale Univ. Press, 1957).
39   *Ibid.*, at 341-48. As John Gillis points out in *For Better, For Worse: British Marriages 1600 to the Present* (Oxford: Oxford University Press, 1985), at 241-42, this new sense of "conformity" in views on the family was a product of the evolution of industrial capitalism and the division of labour which it produced.
40   *Ibid.*, at 348-53.

them and pervert their minds. In one of the grand generalizations associated with Victorian middle class social ideology, the working classes were considered to be morally flawed and thus particularly prone to developing vicious habits.[41] Working class vice was dangerous because it caused physical and mental suffering, stood in the way of a reliable, disciplined source of labour and, if unchecked, might well contribute to general disaffection and disorder. It was thus detrimental to the general welfare of society. Furthermore, because vice was contagious, there was no guarantee that the weaker members of respectable society, women and children, would be able to resist it.

It was this complex of sensibilities and fears which led to a growing campaign to suppress the obscene literature, song and art. As literacy and more democratic approaches towards education developed, so there was a redefinition and expansion of what was dangerous ("poisonous") in books, song, pictures, sculpture and dramatic performances. Walter Kendrick has observed, the test of what was unacceptable was whether the material or performance in question would, in the words of Dickens' Mr. Podsnap, "call a blush into the cheek of a young person."[42] Given the gender-based nature of the concern with the power of artistic words and representations, it was not at all surprising that the "young person" in question was female.

The pressure for censorship manifests itself in a variety of ways. The classics, which increasingly came under scrutiny as the search was made for passages unfit for the eyes or ears of children and women, became the expurgator's obsession. The model was established with the publishing by Dr. Thomas Bowdler of his *Family Shakespeare* in 1807.[43] Among novelists and some poets the growing fears expressed about fiction's capacity for exciting sexual passions, and in turn immoral acts, was significant enough to induce forms of self-censorship. Leading English novelists of the 19th century, such as William Thackeray, George Eliot, Matthew Arnold, Charlotte Bronte, and Anthony Trollope, spoke out against the realistic portrayal of sexual licence in literature and some went as far as to suggest that English fiction, in contrast to its continental counterpart, was family oriented.[44] Moreover, as Thomas Boyle has pointed out, when the English novel turned sensationalist, as it did in the 1860s in the hands of Dickens, Wilkie Collins,

---

41 F. Mort, *Dangerous Sexualities: Medico-Moral Politics in England Since 1830* (London: Routledge & Kegan Paul, 1987), at 11-61.

42 Kendrick, *supra*, note 4 at 49, 51 and 67-94. The reference is to that paragon of English rectitude, the ultimate chauvinist, Mr. Podsnap, and his hypersensitive daughter from *Our Mutual Friend* (London: Oxford Univ. Press, 1952), at 127-43.

43 *Ibid.*, at 51-53.

44 Houghton, *supra*, note 38 at 356-61.

Mary Braddon and others, it was the object of considerable criticism, both literary and moral, as having transgressed the bounds of acceptable story-telling.[45] Particular concern was voiced about the suggestiveness of the detailed treatment of the lives of ostensibly respectable female characters who, like Braddon's Lady Audley, broke all the rules of conventional behaviour associated with virtuous women. Ironically, at the same time that this national penchant for moral self-flagellation was occurring in respect of literature and art, British families were being treated to the most graphic descriptions of real life crime and immorality at their breakfast tables in the columns of their newspapers.[46] Obscenity and pornography were apparently more dangerous in the form of fiction than of fact!

Until the last quarter of the 19th century, the focus of the law in Britain seems to have remained on material associated with the back street pornographer, the pedlars of obscene pictures and objects and the sellers and performers of indecent ballads. The fundamental concern was that these forms of communications were dangerous in their effects on the working classes. It was a belated realization of, and shock concerning, the ready availability of "low life" publications that led the Lord Chief Justice of England, Lord Campbell, to press for legislation which would complement the common law and give the police the power to seize obscene material. As noted above, the prosecutions by the Vice Society had not had a noticeable adverse effect on the trade. One reason was that, in most cases, although an accused was convicted, that person or his associates could retain the offending publication and continue or start up the business again with little difficulty. Pornographers often had the resources to outlast, and thus outwit, private prosecutors. It was material of this type, in the form of a story of seduction in a "penny weekly" put out by a notorious pornographer, William Strange, which the Vice Society had pursued that brought such publications to the attention of the Chief Justice:[47]

> After reading this account [the seduction story], Lord Campbell expressed his "astonishment and horror", particularly at the low price at which it was sold, declared it to be a "disgrace to the country" and proclaimed that it was "high time that an example should be made".

The *Obscene Publications Act*[48] was introduced and passed in 1857.

---

45 T. Boyle, *Black Swine in the Sewers of Hampstead: Beneath the Surface of Victorian Sensationalism* (New York: Viking Press, 1989), at 119-200.

46 *Ibid.*, at 11-38.

47 C. Manchester, "Lord Campbell's Act: England's First Obscenity Statute" (1988), 9 Journ. of Legal History 221 at 226.

48 1857 (20 & 21 Vict., c. 83).

Its passage was only secured after vigorous debate and the acceptance of amendments designed to salve the concern of those (including Lord Chancellor Cranworth and Lords Brougham and Lyndhurst) who feared that it represented an unnecessary intrusion into the private domain, put classical literature at risk, and constituted a dangerous extension of police powers. The purpose of the Act was not substantive (nowhere was the term "obscene" defined). Its object was to provide a pro-active procedure by which obscene literature could be destroyed. There was to be no trial in the strict sense. Material considered to be obscene by the police or a citizen could be seized on a magistrate's warrant and, if it was shown to his satisfaction at a show cause hearing that publication would be "a misdemeanour proper to be prosecuted," he could order its destruction.[49] Despite Lord Lyndhurst's pessimistic warning that subsequent judicial interpretation over which the draftsman would have no control might well subvert his intention, Lord Campbell assured his critics that it would not be applied to works of art and literature but "exclusively to works written for the single purpose of corrupting the morals of youth and of a nature calculated to shock the common feelings of decency in a well regulated mind." Furthermore, he expressed confidence that this procedure would put an end to the insidious trade on Holywell Street.[50] He was to be proven wrong on both counts!

During the first half of the 19th century moral concerns similar to those in Britain emerged in North America as an expanding middle class became the repository of economic power and the arbiter of social policy and moral values. The notion that immorality, even among the "lower orders," was not inevitable or natural took firm root, especially in the minds of religious evangelicals, most notably the Methodists, and of political utilitarians and businessmen committed to creating a society which conduced to the maximization of both social happiness and economic opportunity. The initial impulse of these forces of moral reform was to create fear of the dire effects to the individual, the family, and ultimately the community, associated with involvement in vice and to attack its agents in the pulpit, the columns of a vigorous religious press, and in the counsels of municipal government. The lack of a long-standing artistic and literary tradition in Canada meant that there was little in the way of domestic visual art or books. What there was bore all the marks of the country's moralistic heritage.[51] The circulation of pictures and literature of dubious quality from foreign sources was

49 *Ibid.*, s. 1.
50 Robertson, *supra*, note 14 at 29.
51 D. Staines (ed.), *The Canadian Imagination: Dimension of a Literary Culture* (London: Harvard Univ. Press, 1977), at 9. Staines observes: "[i]f the early [Canadian] writings did attempt the important task of defining the landscape, they also refrained from confronting life."

almost certainly limited to a small educated elite who would have been beyond the reach of the law. It was the theatre to which a larger cross-section of the community had access which seems to have been the earliest target of evangelical fervour. The stage was suspect both because of the character of those who acted upon it, and because drama was thought to have a corrupting effect on the minds of women, especially poor women (always ripe, it was thought, to be lured into prostitution). The *Canada Christian Advocate* described the theatre in 1849 as:[52]

> Satan's synagogue. It is the constant resort of the most corrupt portions of society — the pick-pocket — the blackleg — the prostitute and the profane are there ... It is known that the morals of thousands have been ruined both for time and eternity by attending these haunts of vice.

Mary Shortt has observed that rhetoric of this sort was effective in persuading many women, especially those who considered themselves respectable, not to patronize the theatre.[53]

For most of the 19th century, the law relating to obscenity in Canada seems to have been confined to vagrancy provisions copied from English legislation of 1824. That Act had provided that "every Person willfully exposing to view in any Street, Road, Highway or public Place, any obscene Print, Picture or other indecent Exhibition" was to be "deemed a rogue or vagabond" and was subject to a jail term of not more than three months.[54] In tune with vagrancy law more generally, the object of this provision seems to have been a mixed one of protecting public morals and preventing public disorder. It reflected the socially conservative view that all that one could realistically do about vice among the "lower orders" was to control and contain it. As English common law had been received into the British North American colonies, presumably it was open to the authorities to prosecute for obscene libel as the existence of that offence was established before any of the relevant reception dates. Thus far there is no evidence that it was. After 1850, almost certainly reflecting reform concerns about the spread of vice, local authorities were granted the power to enact anti-obscenity by-laws under the restructured system of municipal government.[55] As problems associated with "obscene" productions, art and literature

---

52 Quoted from M. Shortt, "Victorian Temptations" (1988), 68(6) The Beaver 4 at 5.

53 *Ibid.*, at 6.

54 *Act for the Punishment of idle and disorderly persons and Rogues and Vagabonds, in that part of Great Britain called England,* 1824 (5 Geo. 4, c. 83), s. 4.

55 See C. Backhouse, "Involuntary Motherhood: Abortion, Birth Control and the Law in Nineteenth Century Canada" (1983), 3 Windsor Y.B. Access Just. 61 at 117, n. 160.

were seen as local in their context and impacts, it was apparently considered appropriate that the solution should be fashioned in local communities.

Colin Manchester has noted that the enactment of the *Obscene Publications Act*[56] in 1857, although it had a short-term positive impact in slowing down the trade, was destined to make an insignificant dent in it in the long run.[57] Pornographers, as seems to be their wont, adjusted to the new situation and began using the mails to advertise and distribute their wares. Indeed, a number found it profitable and safer to locate on the continent and mail materials from there. Bristow, for his part, has pointed out that technological invention, especially of the stereoscope and photograph, provided new outlets for the purveyors of obscene material (the age of "What the Butler Saw" had arrived!).[58] While the Vice Society continued to be active, directing their attention to photographs and prints, the pace of police activity slowed down, perhaps because of the new realities of supply, distribution and technology. This was true even in the case of known domestic sellers of written pornography. The result was that the trade was again alive and well on Holywell Street by 1868.[59]

Although there was in England a recognizable offence of criminal obscene libel by this time, as well as an ostensibly effective process for destroying obscene material, there was still no legal definition of what the term "obscene" meant. The judges and juries, one supposes, "knew it when they saw it." Walter Kendrick has suggested that one has to look to France for the first extensive analysis of the legal meaning of obscenity in art and literature. In 1857, Gustave Flaubert's *Madame Bovary* was prosecuted for "outrages to public morality and religion" in the stultifying atmosphere of Napoleon III's Second Empire.[60] The cases for the state and the defence were, Kendrick argues, to set the pattern for all subsequent obscenity litigation, with the former concentrating exclusively on the supposedly moral impact of the impugned material (that is, its effect on the imaginary "young person") which might be only limited passages of a much larger work, and the latter responding by emphasizing the intention of the artist or author, which could only be divined by looking at the work as a whole. As Kendrick wryly notes, "[i]t is provocative to see, before the word 'pornography' was even in use, that the lines of argument had already been laid down, the unanswerable question posed."[61]

---

56 *Supra*, note 48.
57 Manchester, *supra*, note 32 at 51-53.
58 Bristow, *supra*, note 15 at 47-48.
59 Manchester, *supra*, note 47 at 232-33.
60 Kendrick, *supra*, note 4 at 106.
61 *Ibid.*, at 115.

When the English courts came to address the issue of the meaning of obscenity, it was the prosecution's view in the *Bovary* trial which prevailed. In 1868, a propagandist tract, *The Confessional Unmasked; Shewing the Depravity of the Romanish Priesthood, the Iniquity of the Confessional and the Questions Put to Females in Confession*, put out by a group of religious zealots, the Protestant Electoral Union, which contained passages on sexual practices purportedly taken from Roman Catholic ecclesiastical literature was ordered destroyed under the procedures established by the 1857 legislation. On appeal to the Court of Queen's Bench, Chief Justice Cockburn, while finding that the subjective purpose of the accused in whose house the tracts had been found was "to expose the errors and practices of the Roman Catholic Church in the matter of confession," branded it obscene because its tendency was objectively "to deprave and corrupt those whose minds are open to such immoral influences, and into whose hands a publication of this sort may fall."[62] The Chief Justice put it beyond doubt that adverse moral impact was the test of the "obscene" because of its corrupting quality. The work here "would," he said, "suggest to the minds of the young of either sex, or even to persons of more advanced years, thoughts of an impure and libidinous character."[63] The evidence satisfied him that it was distributed in such a way that it was available to all classes, young and old, whose minds, "hitherto pure," would be "exposed to the danger of contamination and pollution from the impurity it contains."[64] It was also clear from his judgment that it was perfectly correct for a court to concentrate on select passages, as opposed to the work as a whole, in reaching its decision on its quality. Like Lord Campbell before him, Chief Justice Cockburn could not believe that anything he had said could be used to attack established works of literature, even though they might contain "immodest," even "immoral," passages.[65] This, despite the fact that the objectifying of the obscene in the decision and its application to segments of a larger work contained no internal limits which would exclude serious literature. Presumably, one could trust the good judgment of those prosecuting and trying obscenity cases!

The genie was, in fact, out of the bottle. Geoffrey Robertson has pungently observed:[66]

Armed at last with a definition of obscenity, Victorian prosecutors proceeded to destroy many examples of fine literature and scientific speculation. The sting of the new definition was in its tail: depravity

---

62   *R. v. Hicklin, supra*, note 1 at 370-71.
63   *Ibid.*, at 372.
64   *Ibid.*
65   *Ibid.*, at 371.
66   Robertson, *supra*, note 14 at 30.

and corruption were to be judged, not by a book's effects on its most likely readership, but upon those susceptible persons — children, psychopaths, women, the working class — whose minds were assumed to be open to immoral literature, and into whose hands any publication might one day conceivably fall.

After ultimately failing in an 1877 prosecution of *The Fruits of Philosophy — An Essay on the Population Problem*, a publication advocating birth control which had been republished by Annie Besant and Charles Bradlaugh to challenge the obscenity laws, because of a flaw in the indictment,[67] the state, egged on by a new group of moral zealots, the National Vigilance Association (N.V.A.), was able to chalk up a series of victories against works of literary, and even scientific, merit. The first victims were a series of realistic novels by French writers, including Emile Zola, Gustave Flaubert, Alphonse Daudet, Guy de Maupassant and Theophile Gautier published by the respectable, but hapless, publisher and bookseller Henry Vizetelly. These were marked for destruction in 1888 during a particularly strong outburst of moral anxiety about the supposedly poisonous effects of French literature on English readers.[68] Vizetelly was effectively hounded by the prosecutors in successive trials until, beaten and humiliated, he withdrew from publishing entirely.[69] In the decades which followed, valuable scientific works such as Havelock Ellis' study of homosexuality, *Sexual Inversion*, and various works of Freud, and serious novels, including D.H Lawrence's *The Rainbow*, James Joyce's *Ulysses* and Radclyffe Hall's *The Well of Loneliness* (a sensitive treatment of lesbianism) were partially or totally suppressed by actual or threatened prosecution all because of their allegedly corrosive qualities.[70] This notwithstanding a chorus, increasing in number and volume, of artists, writers, scientists, philosophers and politicians opposed to censorship in general and its use in specific instances to attack works of genuine artistic, literary or scientific interest and value. Meanwhile, the back street pornographers peddled their wares with relative impunity. It was apparently much easier to muzzle the respectable publishers than their seedy counterparts.

As Robertson has pointed out, "[t]he Victorian *cordon sanitaire* was rounded off" by vagrancy, post office and customs legislation "which collectively prohibited the display, posting or importation of 'indecent' material" and the *Law of Libel Amendment Act*[71] of 1888 "which rendered newspapers liable to prosecution if they quoted . . .

---

67   *The Times* (June 19, 1877).
68   Robertson, *supra*, note 14 at 31; Manchester, *supra*, note 32 at 55-56.
69   Robertson, *ibid.*, at 31-32.
70   *Ibid.*, at 34-40.
71   (51 & 52 Vict., c. 64).

obscene passages which had been read in open court."[72] In 1889 the *Indecent Advertisements Act*[73] was added at the behest of the N.V.A. to outlaw ads and handbills "relating to complaints or infirmities arising from sexual intercourse."[74] This direct legal censorship was buttressed by administrative and quasi-administrative regulation exercised by public boards and committees, such as the London County Council Theatre and Music Halls Committee which, full of moral ardour, sought to ban "indecent" acts and songs,[75] and local library committees which often took it upon themselves to decide what the public should and should not be allowed to read.[76]

In Canada, after confederation in 1867, there was little movement in giving substance to concerns about obscenity in the criminal law. The vagrancy laws, including that related to obscene or indecent displays, were consolidated in 1869 in a Dominion statute,[77] but no attempt was made to introduce in legislative form the offence of obscene libel, although there were, from time to time, calls for Parliament to emulate English law and its special seizure procedure. Both the *Postal Service Act*[78] and the *Customs Act*[79] included provisions proscribing the use of the mails for the transmission and importation of obscene or immoral material. One suspects that it was here, and especially by the operation of the customs schedule, that any effective censorship and control of obscene material was exercised in Canada prior to the enactment of the *Criminal Code* in 1892. As in England, the mimetic qualities associated with the reading and viewing of immoral, and even immodest, material were stressed in the religious, secular and even literary press. "Immorality," wrote a pundit in the Week (a literary journal) on October 8, 1885,[80]

> . . . should never be allowed to prosper for more than a short time, and then its downfall should be greatly emphasized . . . It should never be described in luxurious surroundings . . . the immoral in fiction should never be taken as a matter of course and acquiesced in as a mere foible that all at some time must give way to.

The hostility observed in Britain towards the French "naturalist"

72 *Supra*, note 14 at 32.
73 (52 & 53 Vict., c. 18).
74 Bristow, *supra*, note 15 at 204 and *ibid.*, s. 4.
75 *Ibid.*, at 209-15.
76 A. Thompson, *Censorship in Public Libraries in the United Kingdom during the Twentieth Century* (Essex: Bowker, 1975), at 1-10.
77 *Act respecting Vagrants*, S.C. 1869, c. 28, s. 1.
78 S.C. 1875, c. 7, s. 72.
79 S.C. 1879, c. 15, Sched. D.
80 A.G. Bailey, *Culture and Nationality* (Toronto: McClelland & Stewart, 1972), at 73, quoting from C.D. English, "The Immoral in Fiction" (October 8, 1885), Week.

authors was emulated in Canada. Library boards, suggests A.G. Bailey, were still "apt to be of the opinion that all foreign literature emanates from the devil."[81] Literary critics, while less crass, found that the French literature of Zola and his "school" were calculated "to trouble the mind" rather than "to strengthen the moral fibre."[82]

Although there is evidence of pressure, especially from local communities, for federal obscenity legislation before 1892,[83] it was not until the *Criminal Code* of 1892 that the criminal law of Canada finally sought to emulate English legislation on obscene publications. The opportunity was used to give greater specificity to what was meant by obscenity than in the common law offence. Under the general heading "Offences against Morality," s. 179 made it an indictable offence "without lawful justification or excuse" to sell or expose for sale obscene material "tending to corrupt morals"; to exhibit "any disgusting object or . . . indecent show"; or to offer for sale, advertise or publish an advertisement or have for sale "any medicine, drug or article intended or represented as a means of preventing conception or causing an abortion."[84] A public good defence was included ("public good" being designated as a question of law).[85] The framers of the *Code* also transferred to it a provision formerly in postal services legislation making it an indictable offence to mail obscene material.[86] These provisions were in addition to the pre-existing vagrancy offence of setting up an indecent exhibition in a public place. Subsequent amendments extended responsibility in the case of obscene material to producers, distributors,[87] those in possession for sale or distribution and those assisting in production, sale or distribution.[88] Added to the list of products which it was illegal to sell or advertise were products "for restoring sexual virility or curing venereal disease or diseases of the generative organs."[89] In 1903 the *Code* was amended to proscribe the presentation of, or involvement in as an actor or otherwise, "any immoral, indecent or obscene play, opera, concert, acrobatic, variety or vaudeville performance."[90] By the same amendment, it also became an offence to appear in "any indecent costume." In most instances, these amendments seem to have been accepted without demur. However, occasionally a member spoke out against the dangers

---

81 *Ibid.*, at 72.
82 C. Bissell, "Literary Taste in Central Canada During the Late Nineteenth Century" (1950), 31 Can. Hist. Rev. 237 at 246.
83 Backhouse, *supra*, note 55 at 117-19, n. 160.
84 S.C. 1892, c. 29, s. 179(1).
85 *Ibid.*, s. 179(2).
86 *Ibid.*, s. 180.
87 *Act further to amend the Criminal Code*, S.C. 1900, c. 46, s. 3.
88 *Act to amend the Criminal Code*, S.C. 1909, c. 9, s. 2 (Sched.).
89 *Act to amend the Criminal Code*, S.C. 1913, c. 13, s. 8.
90 *Act to amend the Criminal Code*, S.C. 1903, s. 2.

of parliamentarians playing into the hands of new puritans. In discussing the 1903 amendments relating to theatrical performances, Sir Charles Hibbert Tupper made exactly that point:[91]

> We know that there is a large class of the community who think that all modern novels and all modern plays are, to use the language of this Bill, indecent and immoral. For myself, I do not hesitate to say that I think these persons hold very extreme views. Merely because there are events in a play or in a book that are such as would not be taught in a Sunday school but which are meant to illustrate the condition of society through the ages, is not a sufficient reason for suppressing them. . . .
>
> We do not want to drive out of the country the best talent who are now producing modern plays that might come under the category mentioned in this clause, in the minds of some people.

Even Sir Charles, at the end of the day, convinced himself that there was some material which was beyond the pale, and agreed that, while "indecent" and "immoral" were vague descriptors open to liberal interpretation by puritans, "obscene" was a much stronger term with an accepted and more limited meaning which adequately captured the type of performances which the law should be aimed at.

The *Code* of 1892 did not include a seizure provision similar to that in the English *Obscene Publications Act* of 1857. This may account for the unexceptional nature of the reported cases on obscenity in Canada until relatively recent times. Unlike the infamous literary trials in England of the late 19th and early 20th century, their Canadian counterparts are singularly unexciting. Prosecutions were taken against an obscene song performed with indecent gestures in Quebec,[92] the sale of a medicine for stimulating or renewing menstrual flow by a Toronto proprietary medicine manufacturer,[93] a series of religious rantings in a pamphlet penned in Windsor, Ontario,[94] the pedlar of obscene books, pictures and photographs up from Buffalo,[95] a New Brunswick satirical newspaper entitled "Free Speech,"[96] a movie of a prize fight in Montreal,[97] a religious bulletin put out by a Toronto minister to expose the "obscene" shows put on at a Toronto theatre[98] and a private letter in Saskatchewan.[99]

---

91 Canada, House of Commons, *Debates*, 317 (March 23, 1903).
92 *R. v. Jourdan* (1900), 8 C.C.C. 337 (Montreal Recorder's Ct.).
93 *R. v. Karn* (1903), 5 O.L.R. 704 (C.A.).
94 *R. v. Beaver* (1905), 9 O.L.R. 418 (C.A.).
95 *R. v. Graf* (1909), 19 O.L.R. 238 (H.C.).
96 *R. v. MacDougall* (1909), 15 C.C.C. 466 (N.B.C.A.).
97 *R. v. L'Heureux* (1910), 17 R.L.N.S. 32 (Que.).
98 *R. v. St. Clair* (1913), 28 O.L.R. 271 (C.A.).
99 *R. v. Goyer* (1917), 9 Sask. L.R. 399 (S.C.).

Despite their drab quality, the reported obscenity cases in Canada closely tracked the reasoning of the English courts. The *Hicklin* test was readily accepted by Canadian judges and accorded the same objective quality that had been given to it by its author, Chief Justice Cockburn. This was true notwithstanding the existence of rather different motives on the part of some accused. Thus, in *R. v. Beaver*,[100] although in the words of Justice Osler the printed matter (a pamphlet put out by a religious zealot) "is suggestive, rather of the disconnected ravings of a lunatic, than of anything tending to corrupt morals," there were "one or two punning allusions" which could be said to have warranted the trial judge finding the publication obscene.[101] Even the laudatory motive of exposing "filth" was not to be allowed to undercut an assumption of corruptive power, as a leading social purity activist was to find to his cost in *R. v. St. Clair*.[102] The accused, a Toronto minister, concerned about an obscene play being presented at the Star Theatre and the apparent lack of vigour in enforcing the law by the city's police department, printed up 1,000 copies of a "special bulletin" after seeing a performance from which he recorded "obscene passages." The publication was then circulated to clergy colleagues. A majority of the Ontario Court of Appeal, applying the *Hicklin* test, agreed with the trial judge that the publication was objectively obscene and that the evidence led for the accused that exposure of the production was necessary in the circumstances did not meet the requirements of the "public good" defence. The court was not satisfied that the problem identified by the Reverend St. Clair could not have been dealt with successfully through normal channels.

The jurisprudence also demonstrates the same concern among Canadian judges about the suggestive and indelible effects of obscene material that we have seen with their English counterparts. In the process of convicting Martin Graf of Buffalo for selling obscene books, pictures and photographs, Justice Riddell took the opportunity to decry the modest nature of the penalty prescribed for the offence.[103]

[O]nly two years' imprisonment can be inflicted for this heinous offence. One who administers physical poison so as to inflict upon another grievous bodily harm is liable to 14 years' imprisonment; one who administers mental and moral poison, and thereby inflicts grievous harm upon the mind and soul, even if this is not possibly, indeed probably, accompanied by bodily harm as well, is let off with two years — rather a reversal of the injunction not to fear them that kill the body and after that have no more that they can do.

---

100 *Supra*, note 94.
101 *Ibid.*, at 422.
102 *Supra*, note 98.
103 *Supra*, note 95 at 248.

One can also find evidence of a belief among the judiciary that the relaxed standards of sexual morality in continental Europe, especially France, were responsible for the decline in Canadian morals. Even the Recorder of Montreal, A.E. Poirier, warned Montrealers against imitating Paris and New York. Of French influence, he remarked:[104]

> The artists who come to us from France may depend upon the sympathies of our population, but for the love of art, for the glory of their country, for the honor of the institutions where they have been trained, let them avoid what may tend to corrupt the youth of our country.
>
> Let us borrow what is good from the cities of the old continent, but let us not pervert our noble youth with ideas of art and freedom opposed to the beautiful and good, and productive of all sorts of evil.

The reported cases on obscenity in Canada between 1892 and 1920 do not give a complete picture of legal initiatives against obscenity. The records of various social purity groups of the period suggest that moral vigilantism was strong, especially after 1900, and that moral reformers were able to pressure the authorities into action against those dealing in "obscene material," even that contained in serious literature. The social purity movement which had support in the mainline Protestant evangelical churches, the Methodist and the Presbyterian, and women's groups, such as the National Council of Women and the Women's Christian Temperance Union, reflected increasing unease in middle class Canadian society associated with the adverse moral and social effects of urbanization, industrialization, the weakening of family bonds in the wake of greater labour mobility and opportunity and increased immigration, particularly by communities lacking a white, Anglo-Saxon, Protestant frame of reference.[105] This group of reformers was of the optimistic view that it was possible with the application of moral commitment, physical and mental energy and the practical force of the law to reverse the slide into immorality and to build a community of Christian virtue in Canada. On their lengthy agenda was the suppression of obscenity.

Largely, it seems, at the urgings of the Board of Moral and Social Reform of the Presbyterian Church of Canada and the Moral Reform Council of Canada (a cooperative venture of the Presbyterians and

---

104 *Supra*, note 92 at 339-40.

105 J. McLaren, " 'White Slavers':The Reform of Canada's Prostitution Laws and Patterns of Enforcement, 1900-1920" (1987), 8 Crim. Justice History 53. For an excellent history of the religious inspirations to this movement, see B. Fraser, *The Social Uplifters: Presbyterian Progressives and the Social Gospel in Canada 1875-1915* (Waterloo: Sir Wilfred Laurier Univ. Press, 1988).

Methodists established in 1907), the authorities in Toronto moved against two booksellers in 1910 who were charged with, and convicted of, having obscene matter for sale.[106] The impugned works included Sir Richard Burton's *Arabian Nights* (unexpurgated version), Honore de Balzac's *Droll Stories*, a series of works by Guy de Maupassant and recent sensationalist novels by Elinor Glyn and Hubert Wales. Through a process of lobbying the Department of Customs, the reformers seem to have been successful too in having all of these works included on the schedule of prohibited books administered by customs officers.[107]

The reformers were also successful in embarrassing the authorities, even the Dominion government, on the issue of obscenity. Such was the case in 1910 when the Minister of Justice, Thomas Aylesworth, in response to a plea for clemency from their counsel, advised the Governor General to reduce the prison sentences of, and release, two Toronto booksellers, Skill and King, who had pleaded guilty to a charge of selling obscene books. Aylesworth had persuaded himself that the men's "crime" was dealing in serious literature. The outrage of the social purists, who were aware that the two booksellers both advertised and sold other, more salacious items, was felt both inside and outside Parliament.[108] By way of rubbing salt into the wound, it was pointed out by the reformers that the United States Postal Censor, Anthony Comstock (a regular super-prude), had reported that circulars from the two booksellers had fallen into his hands. Although Aylesworth did not step down, it is clear from Hansard that he went through a harrowing experience at the hands of his detractors.

As in England, moral censors in Canada were active at a less formal level. This was especially true of the National Council of Women which, in 1906, established a Committee upon Objectionable Printed Matter. As its convenor, Minnie Gardiner, noted:[109]

What is the work of this Committee? is a question asked us. We make

---

106 United Church Archives, *Minutes, Executive,* Board of Moral and Social Reform, Presbyterian Church of Canada (January 28, 1909); N.A.C., *Minutes,* Moral and Reform Council of Canada A.G.M. (September 26, 1911), at 17.

107 M. Ernst and W. Seagle, *To the Pure . . . A Study of Obscenity and the Censor* (New York: Viking Press, 1928). In App. III at 297 *et seq.* the authors include a "List of Publications Prohibited to Be Imported into Canada," prepared under the *Customs Act* of 1907. The list is dated March 1, 1914 and includes the works mentioned in the text of this article.

108 Canada, House of Commons, *Debates,* 7068-70 (April 14, 1910); 7183-7187 (April 15, 1910); 7517-18 (April 20, 1910); 8344-52 (April 28, 1910). See also N.A.C., *Minutes,* Moral and Social Reform Council of Canada A.G.M., 20-25 (September 23, 1910), and "The Release of Skill and King, Immoral Book Vendors," Report of the Executive of the Moral and Social Reform Council of Canada (United Church Archives: 1910).

109 N.C.W., *Handbook* (1906), at 53-54.

answer that we are trying to begin the work of eradicating from this grand Canada of ours all books, papers, prints, advertisements and publications of any kind that are obscene or objectionable. Verily, a tremendous undertaking! But who would hesitate to plant an acorn because it is not an oak? And if we faithfully keep hold of the little threads to this end God will in his good time weave them into the strong net.

As the annual handbooks of the N.C.W. reveal, both the national organization and the local chapters were vigorous in the pursuit of indecent and immoral materials.[110] Pressure was brought to bear on the Postmaster General to suppress "objectionable newspaper matter" and magazines containing "immoral advertisements" and to monitor carefully suggestive postcards; libraries in local communities were the objects of surveillance and complaints lodged against the circulation of offensive items (French books in particular were closely scrutinized); campaigns were launched against objectionable posters, slot machines dispensing lewd postcards, immoral theatre and vaudeville productions, and Saturday supplements of daily newspapers (especially the comic strips which they contained). The new form of media, the movies, while seen as a potential force for good in the right hands, were decried if they transgressed the narrow bounds of propriety. Monitoring of films was instituted by chapters in several cities and towns. The formal censorship of both films and postcards, as well as the municipal regulation of visual representations, was strongly advocated.

In the absence of further primary research it is difficult to determine with any degree of certainty the effects of these formal and informal initiatives against obscenity in Canada prior to 1920. Actual and threatened vigilantism at a local level undoubtedly had a constraining impact, in an era when moral reputation in the community was an important factor in doing business. The customs authorities, working with set lists of proscribed publications, probably kept some material out, especially that in bulk packages. Cooperation by the postal authorities with the redoubtable Mr. Comstock in the United States may well have had a dampening effect on the use of the mails to distribute obscene material. Both the customs and postal services undoubtedly had lists compiled by them, and supplemented by vigilance groups, of those known to receive and distribute obscene material. None of this would have been enough to thwart those who sought access to pornographic material, who wanted it badly enough and had the resources to acquire it covertly. As far as the direct sale and distribution of pornography was concerned, law enforcement was as vigorous or as lackadaisical as the police thought it should be. As in the case of other morals offences, for example those

110 N.C.W., *Handbooks* (1906-1919).

related to prostitution, the absence of a regular pattern of prosecutions suggests that most police forces would only move aggressively against the purveyors of smut when the public heat got too intense. For the most part, obscenity was low on their list of priorities, and either tolerated or dealt with by informal censorship.[111]

D. Fading Moral Agendas and New Anxieties: Obscenity Law in Canada, 1920-1990

After 1920 there is a complete absence of reported cases of obscenity in Canada until the mid-1940s. One might speculate that, with the fading of the politics of "moral uplift," especially in the wake of the repeal of prohibition legislation in the 1920s, moral vigilantism decreased in volume and effectiveness, leaving the control of the law entirely to the police.[112] Given the cyclical character of concern about dangerous publications, it was only a matter of time before a new outbreak of anxiety occurred. As proof that Mr. Podsnap's "young person" was not yet dead, although she had undergone a sex change, a campaign developed in the late 1940s against a new form of publication which was thought to have a significant capacity to corrupt the minds and influence the actions of children — crime comics.[113]

The emergence of the comic book in the late 1930s in the United States had led to increasing concern in that country about the criminogenic effects of the crime and horror stories which formed a major segment of that genre of publication. A key champion of suppression was Dr. Frederick Wertham, a psychiatrist, who claimed through the media during the 1940s that there was irrefutable proof of the suggestive and corrupting effect of these representations of criminal activity on children, as evidenced by his own clinical work and reported court cases. Wertham's message was not lost on Canadians, increasingly anxious about the adverse impact of what was seen as an odious form of American culture on youthful virtue in Canada. The leading campaigner was a young Tory British Columbian M.P. from Kamloops, E. Davie Fulton, who, apparently in response to fears voiced by the British Columbia Parent Teacher Association, made it his mission to include within the

---

111 For an interesting insight into police attitudes during this period, see *R. v. St. Clair, supra*, note 98 at 291-300, per Maclaren J.A., dissenting.

112 On the fading of the politics of moral uplift, see J.H. Thompson, *Canada 1922-1939: Decades of Discord* (Toronto: McClelland & Stewart, 1985), at 58-75.

113 J. Dickin McGinnis, "Bogeymen and the Law: Crime Comics and Pornography" (1988), 20 Ottawa L. Rev. 3-23. On the international concern about these publications, see A. Brannigan, "Moral Panics and Juvenile Delinquents in Britain and America" (1988), 9 Criminal Justice History 181.

obscenity section of the *Criminal Code* a provision outlawing crime comics. Despite doubts voiced by the Liberal Minister of Justice Ilsley about its efficacy in view of the lack of any perceptible harm associated with the use of such material, Fulton's proposals drew support from all sides of the House of Commons. When the Liberal government did introduce a draft subsection for the *Code* in language similar to that of the *Hicklin* test, it was, at Fulton's behest, substantially amended so that it would be the quality of the material, rather than its supposed impact on the reader, which would constitute the core of the offence. The crime comics provision came into force in 1950.[114] For the purposes of the offence, "crime comic" was defined in terms of character and content as a publication comprising "matter depicting pictorially (a) the commission of crimes, real or fictitious, or (b) events connected with the commission of crimes, real or fictitious, whether occurring before or after the commission of the crime." Although there was little in the way of prosecutorial activity using the new provision,[115] the fact that the legislation was perceived as having widespread support among the public seems to have persuaded crime comic producers that a system of self-censorship was desirable. Although concern about obscenity was a minor part of this campaign, the model of a criminal law provision on objectionable publications in which the quality of the material, rather than its anticipated effects, was the central issue was to prove suggestive in the context of Canadian obscenity. Mr. Fulton's agenda was not yet complete!

By 1959, E. Davie Fulton was Canadian Minister of Justice. That year he introduced into the House of Commons the first statutory definition of obscenity in Canada:[116]

> [A]ny publication a dominant characteristic of which is the undue exploitation of sex, or of sex and any one or more of the following subjects, namely, crime, horror, cruelty and violence.

Contrary to subsequent commentary on this provision, which has tended to see its purpose as a move away from the conservative morality enshrined in the *Hicklin* test, it is clear, as Professor Charles has established in his analysis of the parliamentary debates on the new provision, that Mr. Fulton was seeking to toughen up the law. This, he felt, was necessary to proceed more effectively against the pulp pocket books and "girlie" magazines which had begun to appear on Canadian news-stands

---

114 *Criminal Code*, S.C. 1953-54, c. 51, s. 150(7)(b).
115 Dickin McGinnis, *supra*, note 113 at 4, indicates that there were only four reported cases in which the new provision was invoked. She could only find reference to three unreported cases dealing with it.
116 *Act to amend the Criminal Code*, S.C. 1959, c. 41, s. 11.

in the 1950s.[117] The Minister of Justice, who expressed frustration at the difficulty in securing convictions under the existing common law test, viewed the new definition as providing a clear, no-nonsense basis for moving against this material, a process which would be assisted by the introduction of a seizure provision based on the British legislation of 1857.[118] Mr. Fulton's statements in debate make it clear that the revised subsection was not designed to replace the *Hicklin* test, which he fully expected would be the gauge against which serious literature and art would continue to be judged. The ghosts of Lord Campbell and Chief Justice Cockburn must have chuckled at this confident prediction!

There is no doubt that the new definition and the seizure provision inspired greater activity on the part of both police and prosecutors. However, the obscenity provision was interpreted by the Supreme Court of Canada, not without some dithering, as replacing the *Hicklin* test in relation to all allegedly obscene publications.[119] Ironically, the occasion for this decision was the exploits of Lady Chatterley and her lover, hardly the sort of publication which the Minister of Justice had supposed would be the object of attention of the reformed law. In subsequent decisions, courts, including the Canadian Supreme Court, were to interpret the words "undue exploitation" in a more liberal spirit, even in the context of material which Mr. Fulton had supposed would have been an easy target for conviction under the revised definition. A developing openness in Canadian social discourse concerning sex and sexuality, together with a greater sensitivity to freedom of speech and expression as basic legal values, were reflected to some degree in changing judicial opinions. The new concern to strike a balance between the avoidance of undue censorship and the felt need to strike at socially reprehensible material was embodied in the "community standard" test. The test received its classic articulation in the dissenting opinion of Freedman J.A. in *R. v. Dominion News & Gifts (1962) Ltd.* (adopted on appeal by the Supreme Court). The standards, he said:[120]

> ... are not set by those of lowest taste or interest. Nor are they set exclusively by those of rigid, austere, conservative, or puritan taste and habit of mind. Something approaching a general average of community thinking and feeling has to be discovered.

Here, in contrast to the high morality of the *Hicklin* test and the

---

117 Charles, *supra*, note 2 at 253-60.
118 *Supra*, note 116, s. 12.
119 *Brodie v. R.*, [1962] S.C.R. 681.
120 2 C.C.C. 103 (Man. C.A.), Freedman J.A., dissenting, affirmed [1964] S.C.R. 251. In this case the Supreme Court, relying on Freedman J.A.'s formulation, agreed that two publications described as being of the "girlie variety," *Dude* and *Escapade*, were not obscene.

suppositions of Mr. Fulton about the clear meaning of the obscenity definition in the *Criminal Code*, was a more open-ended statement which provided a basis for excluding work having "serious artistic value," and even pornography which lacked artistic quality but was not excessively offensive.

Although the "community standards" test was developed in the spirit of liberal rights ideology and used to qualify the traditional assumptions of a common conservative morality, it was by its very character open to interpretation and potentially sensitive to changing communitarian notions of acceptable and unacceptable representations of sexual conduct. It was this tensile quality of the standard which allowed some courts in the early to mid-1980s to incorporate a new and different basis for attacking obscenity. During the 1970s and early 1980s, a feminist critique of pornography had developed which sought to attack such material not as morally corrupting or unduly sexually explicit, but as a manifestation and celebration of misogyny which, it was suggested, was linked with violence to particular women and hurtful and threatening to women in general. The result of this work by feminist writers was a campaign to press for a rewriting of Canadian obscenity law to reflect the concerns of women about the production and circulation of this material with its harmful propensities. This attempt to recharacterize obscenity struck a responsive chord with some judges.

In a series of trial decisions, and in a concurring opinion in the British Columbia Court of Appeal, during the early to mid-1980s, a distinction was drawn between material portraying violent, degrading or dehumanizing sexual activity (mostly directed against women) on the one hand and that which, while explicit, lacked those elements and was apparently consensual, on the other.[121] In several of the trial decisions expert testimony was heard, including the evidence of a feminist politician and of a behavioural psychologist, which influenced the courts in their findings.[122] As the decisions in several of these cases show, it was possible under this reformulation of the test to rule as not obscene material which was pornographic in the sense that it contained representations of obsessive sexuality, presumably designed to arouse the viewer or user. The suggested basis for distinguishing obscene and non-obscene material was applauded by many feminists as representing a step in the right direction in reformulating the law.

The most explicit and sensitive acceptance of the feminist critique

---

121 See *R. v. Doug Rankine* (1983), 9 C.C.C. (3d) 53 (Ont. Co. Ct.); *R. v. Ramsingh* (1984), 14 C.C.C. (3d) 230 (Man. Q.B.); *R. v. Wagner* (1985), 36 Alta. L.R. (2d) 301 (Q.B.); *R. v. Red Hot Video* (1985), 18 C.C.C. (3d) 1 (B.C.C.A.).

122 See *Rankine* and *Wagner, ibid.*

of pornography was that of Justice Anderson of the B.C. Appeal Court in
R. v. Red Hot Video:[123]

> If true equality between male and female persons is to be achieved it
> would be quite wrong in my opinion to ignore the threat to equality
> resulting from the exposure to male audiences of the violent and
> degrading material described above. As I have said, such material has a
> tendency to make men more tolerant of violence to women and creates
> a social climate encouraging men to act in a callous and discriminatory
> way towards women.

The justice concluded that the materials in the case before him were
obscene. "[T]hey constitute," he said, "a threat of real and substantial
harm in the community" because "[t]hey approve the domination of
women by men as an acceptable social philosophy."[124] The judgment
was clearly influenced by both feminist scholarship and the equality
provisions of s. 15 of the *Charter of Rights and Freedoms*.[125] It contemplates the replacement of an obscenity test influenced, on the one hand,
by outdated precepts of conservative morality and, on the other, by
liberal notions of individual autonomy, for one which postulates a social
definition of harm reflecting both the experience and struggle of women
and the political and social commitment of the Canadian state to gender
equality. Moreover, it assumes that true equality of women is only
achievable if the law assists in creating conditions in which it can be
enjoyed.[126]

That the opinion of Justice Anderson is not the last word on
obscenity, even from his own court, is evident in two more recent
decisions of the Manitoba and British Columbia Courts of Appeal. Both
represent a swing in judicial sentiment towards the pre-feminist "community standards" test. The Manitoba court, in *R. v. Video World*,[127]
concluded that the only legitimate focus in obscene publications cases is
whether or not the material involves "undue exploitation," which depends upon the degree of sexual explicitness involved. In *R. v. Pereira-
Vasquez*[128] the British Columbia Court of Appeal put it more bluntly by
suggesting that the role of the court is to consider the "plain language" of

---

123 *Supra*, note 121 at 23.
124 *Ibid.*, at 24.
125 *Canadian Charter of Rights and Freedoms*, Pt. I of the *Constitution Act, 1982*,
being Sched. B of the *Canada Act 1982*, 1982 (Eng.), c. 11.
126 For a favourable commentary on Justice Anderson's position, see S. Noonan,
"Gender Neutrality and Pornography," in L. Bell (ed.), *Good Girls/ Bad Girls*
(Toronto: Women's Press, 1987), 42 at 44-45.
127 (1986), 22 C.C.C. (3d) 331 (Man. C.A.).
128 (1988), 43 C.C.C. (3d) 82 (B.C.C.A.).

s. 159(8) [now s. 163(8)], and the full jurisprudence applying to it, distinguishing only between material with some pretension to artistic quality and "dirt for dirt's sake."[129] The court added that earlier decisions had confused a feminist "tributary" of concern with violent and degrading pornography which had been erected as the basis of an exclusive definition of obscenity, with the "mainstream" of national opinion, which in fact reflects a broader range of concerns about this type of material and thus warrants a more inclusive definition.[130]

Where this leaves us, in the absence of a definitive decision by the Supreme Court of Canada on the test for determining what is "obscene" under the *Criminal Code*, is difficult to determine, particularly as that court has given somewhat mixed messages in dealing with the issue. In *Towne Cinema Theatres Ltd. v. R.*, several of the judges used language suggesting a degree of sympathy with the feminist critique of pornography.[131] However, the court's summary rejection of the appeal from Manitoba in *Video World*[132] could be read as a continuing commitment to the older interpretation of the "community standards" test. For the moment, it is left to trial judges and provincial courts of appeal to navigate the imprecision of meaning and changing social attitudes as best they may.[133] The only observation which can be made with any

---

129 *Ibid.*, at 85-100. The immediate source of the terminology seems to have been a reference by Freedman C.J. to "skin-flicks" which he characterized as "dirt for dirt's sake" in contrast to the film *Last Tango in Paris*, which he found not obscene, in *R. v. Odeon Morton Theatres Ltd.* (1974), 16 C.C.C. (2d) 185 at 194 (Man. C.A.).

130 *Ibid.*, at 99. For a convincing feminist critique of this decision, see S. Noonan, "Pereira-Vasquez: Obscenity — For the Sake of Dirt" (1988), 64 C.R. (3d) 277.

131 (1985), 18 D.L.R. (4th) 1 at 10-11 (S.C.C.), *per* Dickson C.J.C.; *per* Wilson J. at 25. For a helpful analysis of this case from a feminist perspective and the difficulties with it on the issue of what is "obscene," see B. Baines, "Annotation" (1985), 45 C.R. (3d) 3.

132 *R. v. Video World Ltd.* (1986), 35 C.C.C. (3d) 191 (S.C.C.). See also *Germain v. R.* (1985), 21 C.C.C. (3d) 289 (S.C.C.), in which the court upheld a conviction from Quebec for the sale of obscene articles, described as sex stimulators.

133 In a recent trial decision from Manitoba, *R. v. Butler* (1989), 50 C.C.C. (3d) 97, reversed 60 C.C.C. (3d) 219 (Man. C.A.), Wright J. sought to circumvent decisions such as *Video World* and *Pereira-Vasquez*, which he accepted cut off the *Rankine* tributary, by appeal to s. 1 of the *Charter*. He drew a distinction between representations involving violence or cruelty intermingled with sexual activity, depicting lack of consent to sexual contact or otherwise dehumanizing individuals in a sexual context which, he felt, could justifiably be proscribed under s. 1, and sexually explicit material reflecting consensual activity by adults, which could not. Within this latter category he included depictions of masturbation, group sex, and homosexual or heterosexual activity, including incestuous relations. Although this might be thought to involve a return to a feminist-inspired analysis, Professor Dyzenhaus has argued convincingly ("Should Community Standards Determine Obscenity?" (1990), 72 C.R. (3d)

confidence is that the view of most contemporary Canadian judges seems, at least for the moment, to be that the law should not be invoked to attack works of genuine artistic merit, and of scientific or educational value.[134]

III. LESSONS FROM THE HISTORY OF OBSCENITY LAW

An analysis of the historical record relating to the law of obscenity exposes a series of recurring and worrying themes. Contrary to the ahistorical assumptions upon which most of those who favour reform of the law in this area and most of our legislators typically proceed, the problem of obscenity and pornography, which seems so overwhelming and difficult to accommodate within our social and legal structures and ideology, is not a new one. As part of a broader dialectic in western culture, it goes back as far as the time of Plato and Aristotle. As an issue which was seen as warranting legal responses, its much more modest history stretches back to the changes in theology and their moral and social resonances which followed in the wake of the Reformation of the 16th century. Indeed, the story of the modern legal treatment of obscenity and pornography is very much one of a shift from the dictates of religious authority and doctrine and their power over an individual's Christian conscience, to those of secular morality and justice over a community in which individualism in both the political and economic sphere has been increasingly cherished. Although, as we have seen, there have been changes in social attitudes towards obscenity and in the technology of obscene and pornographic images during the period since 1600, there are recurrent messages in the record of law reform and enforcement which we would do well to consider. At the very least, they urge caution in the use of the law to suppress this type of material.

A strong and enduring theme in the development of the law of obscenity has been the assumption of its corrupting and poisonous

---

49) that the impulses here were libertarian rather than feminist, representing a failure to grasp the unequal and exploitative social context in which these representations should be viewed.

134 On cases dealing with scientific and educational material, see *University of Manitoba v. Deputy Minister of Revenue (Customs & Excise)* (1983), 24 Man. R. (2d) 198 (Co.Ct.) (sexually explicit material for presentation to medical students not found obscene as it was designed for legitimate educational purpose); *Serup v. School District No. 57* (1989), 57 D.L.R. (4th) 261 (B.C.C.A.) (court refusing to grant interim injunction to plaintiff to allow her to "review" sex education material lodged in library of local high school where her son was a pupil but reversing summary dismissal of claim for injunction to prevent alleged infringement of *Charter* right).

effect. In moral imagery, which borrows from medical discourse, the absorption of obscene material is described as having the same insidious and debilitating effects as the most deadly physical poisons. The result is not the death of the body, but what may be worse, of the moral consciousness. Death by real poison takes effect naturally and is normally swift. The corruption of the moral senses, which necessarily involves a mimetic process, may take much longer and, as the recipient continues to live and act, may have an extensive adverse effect on others as his conduct progressively reflects pornography's corrosive effects. But the poisonous impact of obscenity may be much quicker, even instantaneous, with those whose moral constitutions are naturally weaker. This is particularly true of children and youth. In the case of young people, the message of "monkey see, monkey do" has been the most dominant and insistent.

For much of the period surveyed, the metaphor of poison and its corrosive qualities used to describe the impact of obscenity was based on the supposition that immorality was normally a state transmitted by a person's social heritage or environment, but which could also be learned (or "caught") by those to whom it did not come naturally. The proof of the former was the congruence of social and economic irresponsibility and immorality among the lower orders or working classes. The latter was shown by the examples of respectable individuals, even from the very best of families, who were led astray into lives of vice, often in their youth. Given the combination of optimism and pessimism which marked the thought of the Anglo-Saxon world in the 19th century and well into the present one, and the infancy of both scientific and social scientific knowledge during the period, this is perhaps not surprising. As Houghton has noted, while we tend to dismiss the Victorians as super-prudes, they did genuinely feel deep anxiety about what was happening to their society, and had cause for concern based on the outward signs of moral and social malaise which they observed.[135]

The "monkey see, monkey do" fear is as real today as it was in previous generations. For those of a highly moralistic persuasion (now significantly reduced in numbers, but still active), most material which is in any way sexually explicit is inherently dangerous because of its suggestiveness and capacity to pervert. There are still, from time to time, outbursts of moral indignation, often at a local level and directed at or through school and library boards, which have led to campaigns for the proscription of realistic art, films and literature. It is not, however, moralistic arguments that are as significant in this context today as those rooted in psychology and supposedly supported by social scientific data. It is claimed that research by behaviourists, who have observed the

---

135 Houghton, *supra*, note 38 at 353-72.

misogynistic effects on male populations subjected to large doses of pornographic materials, supports a direct link between pornography and violence against, and the mistreatment of, women. The view is that pornography, far from being cathartic and therapeutic as sometimes argued by its supporters, is in fact highly suggestive and corrupting.[136] The argument represents a strong element in feminist rationales for changes in the obscenity laws. While it is not my purpose to discredit this research, there are at least substantial doubts raised by other scholars as to the validity of these findings, which necessarily reflect laboratory conditions.[137] Moreover, concerns have been voiced at the readiness of reformers to appropriate the product of the research without recognizing the complex of influences, good as well as bad, to which the human mind is subject, and to deflect attention from both the other stimuli operating in individual cases of gender violence and more general cultural propensities to misogyny.

The second point arising from this analysis has been the tendency of moral reformers, and some lawyers and judges, in the past to view obscenity and pornography as indicative of some external menace, typically associated with the machinations of foreign entrepreneurs. The implication seems to have been that somehow, without the intrusion of these sinister alien interests, British and Canadian society would have been more virtuous by nature and inclination. Apart from the inconsistency of this view with another entertained by moral purists in the past, that vice was associated with the internal menace posed by the domestic lower orders, it proceeded on the failure of middle class reformers to recognize the association of immorality with the human condition in general and the particular social institutions and structures of their own community. To have done so, of course, would have shown them that they and their kind were a significant part of the problem. While we, in our day, are somewhat less prone to seeking foreign scapegoats for the supposed moral decline of our society, there is still a capacity to externalize the problem in terms of identifying it with powerful economic interests located outside the country, especially the United States. The result is, as it was in earlier times, a propensity to gloss over the indigenous cultural conditioning of Canadians, particularly men, which makes the use of this material enjoyable and compelling.

The third major finding which emerges from the historical record is

---

136 For a leading example of this research, see N. Malamuth and E. Donnerstein, *Pornography and Sexual Aggression* (New York: Academic Press, 1984).

137 H. McKay and D. Dolff, *The Impact of Pornography: An Analysis of Research and Summary of Findings* (Ottawa: Dept. of Justice, 1984). This research review was done at the request of the Special Committee on Pornography and Prostitution (the Fraser Committee).

the difficulty, both social and linguistic, in describing exactly what should be the scope or embrace of the law of obscenity — the publications or representations that have the poisonous, corrupting or mimetic effect. That was perhaps easier to describe when, as we have seen during the Victorian era, a vast range of written and visual material was considered suspect, including everything from pornographic classics and "penny dreadfuls" through to mainline plays, novels and poetry. Even at that, there were some in authority, including most of the judges, who, because of the cultural predilections of themselves and their class, were not willing to treat much classical and contemporary serious literature and art as the legitimate domain of the criminal law of obscenity. Their difficulty was that, in order to give the impression of rationality to the statement of the law, they appealed to objective formulations which, in the hands of the less worldly (people would now happily be labelled as the worst sort of Philistines), were used to attack the material which they, the judges, wanted to insulate from legal challenge.

The challenge of identifying what to label obscene or pornographic for purposes of law is not only problematic in periods of intense moral concern. It can be just as frustrating to some at times when a shift to a more tolerant approach to sexual representations within the community is evident. During these periods, those responsible for the design of broad definitions of obscenity in the law, which they anticipated would cast a wide net, have found to their distress that subsequent interpretation has undermined that confident prediction. This was a lesson learned by E. Davie Fulton in providing what he supposed was an additional "objective" definition of obscenity for the purpose of catching a new genre of pornographic material in his 1959 reforms. In this instance, judges, who were influenced to some extent by a more liberal notion of freedom of expression than the former Minister of Justice, gave their own objective interpretation to the test of obscenity in s. 159(8), one which sought to strike a balance between moral concern over the apparent increase in the overt marketing of pornographic publications and a philosophical commitment to freedom of expression as a basic value of a liberal democratic society.

That new philosophical and ideological tensions can replace older ones, even in relation to a common, subsisting definition, is illustrated by the more recent clash in judicial opinion between those who have been affected to one degree or another by feminist discourse over the character of pornography and those who seem content to hold to a more conservative, moralistic view. The arguments which have swirled around the federal government's two abortive proposals for revision of the obscenity sections of the *Criminal Code*[138] show, in bold relief, that if there ever was a time when one could point to widely shared moral notions of what should attract proscription by the law as obscene or pornographic, we have lost any pretence to consensus.[139] At least most Victorians believed that there was a significant core of shared moral values and that, judged by those values, very clearly there were materials beyond the pale of tolerance and therefore warranting the attention of the law. By contrast, the discourses involved in the contemporary debate on pornography range from the extreme moralistic to the extreme libertarian, with a significant middle, reflecting a mix of more traditional moral concerns, liberal pragmatism, and the sociological and cultural critique of feminists. On two occasions the federal government has failed dismally to accommodate the "right" and "centre" by its proposed package of reforms to obscenity law, leaving it to the courts to "soldier on" with the existing *Code* provision.

A fourth feature of the historical record, as it illuminates the difficulty of deciding what is obscene, is the apparent lack of knowledge of both those who press for reform and, in many instances, those who formulate and administer the law of obscenity with respect to the material which is in circulation. The prospect of investigating what may constitute pornography is not a particularly edifying one. As the story of Lord Campbell shows, it is often only when one stumbles on particular types of pornography that revelation sometimes occurs. Historically, it was the covert representations in the form of expensive private publications, or the widely available "dirt for dirt's sake," which tended to elude the gaze of the authorities. The former was the preserve of "gentlemen"; the latter was not material to which the cultured and sophisticated descended.

This inability to visualize what is out there is a problem to this day. While we have a general sense that there is a lot of prurient material available, there is often little appreciation of its range and qualities. As I have argued elsewhere, the current debate on pornography involves assumptions about the character of sexually explicit material that betray considerable ignorance of its character and range.[140] The conservative moralists assume that almost everything that involves a representation of sex and sexuality is bad, without appreciating the sensitive and understanding way in which these issues are dealt with in a variety of media. For some libertarians, most of what passes for pornography is erotic art or, at worst, the fantasizing represented by "girlie magazines"

---

138 Bill C-114, *An Act to Amend the Criminal Code and the Customs Tariff*, 1st Sess., 33rd Parl., 1984-86; Bill C-54, *An Act to Amend the Criminal Code and other Acts in consequence thereof*, 2nd Sess., 33rd Parl., 1986-87.
139 McLaren, *supra*, note 3 at 128.
140 *Ibid.*, at 133-34.

or "stag movies" of their earlier days. There is scant recognition of the more violent and degrading genres which have become increasingly evident in recent decades. In the case of those seeking to chart a middle course, including many feminists, sexually explicit representations are neatly divided into the nasty "pornographic," which does violence to or degrades women, and nice "erotica," which shows healthy, consensual love-making. The reality is that there is a huge grey area dealing with images of obsessive sexuality which is portrayed as consensual, which does not fit neatly into either category. This middle category is, of course, the type of pornography which the courts continue to grapple with and flip-flop on.

A vigilante mentality is the fifth phenomenon which has historically attended attempts to suppress the obscene and pornographic. The record demonstrates that it was in most instances not the state, but private citizens who were the most vigorous and enthusiastic agents of suppression and censorship. Indeed, it was during the periods of anti-pornography crusades that the greatest dents were made in the "problem." While that may be a comforting thought in the abstract, the reality of obscenity law enforcement in the past was that a significant price was paid in terms of mindless literary and artistic censorship.

Vigilantism was inevitable prior to the 1830s because of the basic indifference of the law officers of the Crown towards this form of conduct and the lack of a competent police presence in Britain and Canada. However, the tradition did not die out with an increase in state-initiated prosecutions and the advent of professional police forces. The prosecutorial authorities continued to be dubious about trampling on individual rights. For their part, the police felt that they had much more important law enforcement items on their agenda than pursuing pornographers. The latter, as we have seen, had a capacity for recovery, for finding new modes of production and distribution, and utilizing new technologies. Moreover, the police seem to have subscribed to the socially conservative view that it was impossible to suppress vice. The best that one could hope for was to contain it by the episodic application of the law, and informal modes of harassment. One supposes that, if they had doubts about pursuing sexual aberration in the flesh, there cannot have been much enthusiasm in pursuing it in fictional form. This lack of resolve on the part of the official guardians of the law was noted by moral crusaders who organized to fill the vacuum. In Britain, they were assisted by the seizure provisions which meant they could either proceed independently, as they did through the efforts of the Vice Society and the National Vigilance Association, or shame the police into action. In Canada, which did not have a seizure provision until 1959, the reformers had to rely more on lobbying, moral suasion and shaming. As the saga of the Reverend St. Clair demonstrates, there were occasionally legal dangers associated with this approach. The greatest success seems to have been achieved in this country with law enforcement officers, especially customs officials, who had a more well-defined and circumscribed role in pursuing smut, and who tended to be guided by the rule book. A greater identity of mission is evident between these agents of the state and the moral reformers.

Apart from the dangers associated with the excessive zeal of moral vigilantes in pursuing what they considered to be obscene, the historical record suggests that vigilantism waxed and waned as social conditions and priorities changed, with the result that the enforcement of the law had a cyclical quality to it. The credibility of legal proscription and penalty tended to suffer as a result.

All in all, moral vigilantes have given obscenity law a bad name. Indeed, if one is looking for reasons for the strong and consistent resistance to censorship among liberal theorists, perhaps the most influential is the record of asinine harassment of good literature, art and genuine satire by the "law."

Vigilantism is not merely an historical phenomenon. There is ample evidence in North America in recent decades that a new generation of moral prudes is at work seeking to dictate to school and library boards, museums and theatres, what is good for the rest of us. Even feminists who find no joy in the widespread use and dissemination of pornographic images have suffered the indignity of having their descriptions of the realities of sexual and gender relations consigned to the moralists' "index."[141] For the reasons which have been identified in the historical analysis, police ideology and motives towards pornography have not changed significantly since the 19th century, despite the highly publicized special squads and details which some forces have established. Moreover, when the police are moved to act, there is a tendency to move against individuals and organizations which they despise and see as being outside the mainstream of normal society, most notably gays and lesbians.

Given these realities in criminal law enforcement methods and patterns, contemporary Canadian society, too, may expect continued vigilante pressure.

IV. CONCLUSION

With the rather dismal record of legal evolution outlined in this article, and the obvious resonances between the traditional and modern problems of enforcement in the area, the prognosis for effective invoca-

---

141 Leading Canadian novelists, such as Margaret Laurence and Alice Munro, have found themselves under attack from the fundamentalist right for their frank portrayals of sexuality.

tion of the existing law or its amendment is not encouraging. The pervasiveness of liberalism in our society, as well as its pluralistic character, not to mention the pace of technological change in providing more sophisticated and clandestine vehicles for the dissemination of obscenity and pornography, means that a policy of suppression of this material is doomed to failure. The best to be hoped for in that context is the occasional making of an example and the episodic harassment of local distributors. Furthermore, the moral, educative value ascribed to the law in the past, whatever social impact it may have had then, is now largely non-existent, even at a merely symbolic level.

It is clear, therefore, that if the criminal law is to continue to be invoked to deal with obscene and pornographic material, it is difficult to justify its role on purely, or even primarily, moralistic grounds. The question is whether there is any alternative rationale for its use which would achieve enough support to amount to a consensus in Canadian society and would attract more effective enforcement efforts. To achieve consensus and to increase the chances of more vigorous enforcement, the definition of obscenity or pornography chosen would have to be both narrower and more reflective of contemporary political and social values than the existing one. Shifting the spotlight to representations which, it may fairly be said, are openly subversive of social tolerance towards, and understanding of, others in the community might be the place to start. There exists a wide degree of social consensus in this country that material which expressly or even implicitly preaches or condones the sexual exploitation of children, or legitimates sexual violence against or the sexual degradation of women within the larger community, should be subject to proscription and criminal sanction. Legal arguments in support of this position are greatly assisted by the recognition of equality in a substantive sense as a basic value of the Canadian community. In light of the *Charter of Rights and Freedoms* it is difficult to claim that freedom of expression can be considered any longer in a vacuum. It should be balanced against the basic constitutional value of equality articulated in s. 15, the presence of which reflects strong political and social concern for the welfare of disadvantaged and marginalized groups in our society, and of the need to protect them from discrimination.

Given the history of obscenity law and the difficulties in defining clearly what should be proscribed, the challenge of where to draw the line between the tolerable and intolerable will remain. The linking of pornography, as a form of legitimation of gender and sex power and discrimination, with the exploitation of children and violence and dehumanizing conduct against women, in contexts in which the desire to play to prurient tastes and misogynistic feelings is clear, is probably the closest Canadian society can hope to get to a workable modern definition of the obscene for the purposes of applying the sanctions of the criminal law.[142]

In the line of cases from *Rankine* to *Red Hot Video*, judges with some sensitivity to the feminist analysis and critique of the exploitative and unequal context of gender relations which is justified and reinforced by pornography began to move in the direction suggested. Those decisions indicate that some, perhaps a lot, of pornographic material which is obsessive and tasteless will be beyond the law's reach. The fact that that material is the most pervasive and popular suggests that the steps which we need to take to counteract it lie not so much in the law but in other and continuing strategies of education and socialization. If the historical record tells us anything, it is that the law has been of minimal value in changing cultural biases in the matter of gender relations. Traditionally, it has all too often reinforced them.[143]

Whether the police would act more vigorously in the pursuit of material comprehended by a redefined statement of what is obscene or pornographic is difficult to determine. There is at least a chance that, with a narrower designation, they would find it easier, and perhaps more palatable, to move against those producing and distributing the highly offensive type of material proscribed. At least they would know that a significant segment of the population, far outstripping in number the high moralists, were in support of their endeavours. It is also possible that a narrower definition of the obscene or pornographic would provide something of a defence to the pressure from latter-day moral vigilantes for the suppression of sexually explicit material in general. Obviously, no verbal formulation, however precise and limited, provides a complete shield from the activities of moral zealots, whether inside or outside the law. However, the definition contemplated would

---

142 Even with more specific definitions of what is obscene or pornographic for legal purposes, it is important to make sure that zeal to get at the bad stuff does not result in overly inclusive provisions. Both C-114 and C-54, in an understandable concern to outlaw child pornography, used language which was so inclusive that many legitimate and important portrayals of both natural and exploitative sexuality involving children would have been proscribed. See S. Diamond, "Childhood's End: Some Comments on Pornography and the Fraser Committee," in J. Lowman, M. Jackson, T. Palys and S. Gavigan (eds.), *Regulating Sex: An Anthology of Commentaries on the Findings and Recommendations of the Badgley and Fraser Reports* (Burnaby: Simon Fraser Univ., 1986), at 143.

143 This concern had led some feminists to decry the use of the criminal law to deal with pornography. The argument which is made is that to do so deflects attention and energy from the real battle against patriarchy. Moreover, they suggest, using the criminal law plays into the hands of the moral censors who have no commitment whatsoever to the feminist agenda and are prone to using the law to suppress all sexual representations including those created and cherished by women: see V. Burstyn (ed.), *Women Against Censorship* (Vancouver: Douglas & McIntyre, 1985).

effectively rule out proceeding against a wide range of material which offends a relatively small minority but is enjoyed, or at least tolerated, by the majority of Canadians.

Expatiating on contemporary social and legal policy and crystal ball-gazing are not seen as profitable, some would argue not even legitimate, enterprises for historians to engage in. There is indeed much to be said for leaving it to the reader to draw his or her own conclusions from the historical record. This article ends, therefore, where it began, with the observation that the definition of what is "obscene" or "pornographic" for legal purposes is elusive. In the final analysis, perhaps all that can be claimed for this historical account is that it demonstrates that the dialectic formed approximately a millenium and a half ago in the context of the Platonic and Aristotelian view of the effect of art is as central and as vexing an issue in western culture as ever it was.

CANARIES IN A COAL MINE: CANADIAN JUDGES AND THE RECONSTRUCTION OF OBSCENITY LAW

Kathleen Mahoney

I. INTRODUCTION

The obscenity provisions of the *Criminal Code*[1] have yet to be tested constitutionally at the Supreme Court level. The issue of whether they infringe freedom of expression guarantees, or whether the government can justify them as reasonable limits, prescribed by law in a free and democratic society,[2] will depend on how obscenity is defined and how its harms are characterized.

Over the past six years, it has become obvious that courts have been making some major changes in the law of obscenity. Past interpretations and definitions of the law are being, and have been, reconsidered.[3] The

---

1 R.S.C. 1985, c. C-46.
2 The *Canadian Charter of Rights and Freedoms*, Pt. I of the *Constitution Act, 1982*, being Sched. B of the *Canada Act 1982*, 1982 (Eng.), c. 11, s. 1.
3 Borins J. in *R. v. Nicols* (1984), 43 C.R. (3d) 54 at 57 (Ont. Co. Ct.), stated, because of the vagueness of the law in this area, "that the time may have come when the appellate courts may wish to reconsider the interpretation of s. 159(8)."

underlying rationale for the regulation of obscenity has been altered, as well as the scope of material regulated through new definitional approaches. Obscenity is beginning to be viewed as an equality issue as much as it is viewed as an expression issue. Some judges are recognizing that certain forms of obscenity harm women by violating their equality rights. If women, individually and as a group, are perceived as victims of obscenity, then the harm it causes is gender-specific. This departs from the historical perception which characterized obscenity as a moral issue, a victimless crime. Laws controlling it were interpreted as having a moral purpose, to protect society from moral decay.

The development of a new underlying rationale for obscenity law has taken place for a number of reasons, not the least of which is the influence that feminist writers have brought to bear on the issue of pornography.[4] Their characterization of pornography as a form of sex discrimination[5] has been strengthened by equality provisions in the *Canadian Charter of Rights and Freedoms* and the Supreme Court's view that equality is one of the underlying values and principles of a free and democratic society,[6] and that discrimination is to be assessed contextually,[7] taking into account stereotyping, historical disadvantage or vulnerability to political and social prejudice.[8] The linkages between equality interests and pornography are apparent in the many definitions of pornography. A common definition is: sexually explicit verbal or pictorial material, on paper or on film, that presents women as deserving or desiring to be treated as objects of domination or violation.[9]

---

4 Feminists make a distinction between pornography and obscenity. The term "pornography" is reserved for sexually explicit material indicated as harmful to women. "Obscenity" by contrast, legally has meant sexually explicit material disvalued because of its offensiveness to community sensibilities and morals. In this paper, the terms are often used interchangeably, because judges have expanded the legal meaning of obscenity to include pornography.

5 See, *e.g.*, A. Dworkin, *Pornography: Men Possessing Women* (New York: G.P. Putnam & Sons, 1981); C. MacKinnon, *Feminism Unmodified* (Cambridge, Mass.: Harvard University Press, 1987); L. Lederer (ed.), *Take Back the Night: Women Against Pornography* (New York: Morrow, 1980); Colloquium, "Violent Pornography: Degradation of Women Versus Right of Free Speech" (1979), 8 N.Y.U. Rev. L. & Soc. Change 181; C. MacKinnon, "Not a Moral Issue" (1984), 2 Yale L. & Pol'y Rev. 321; K. Mahoney, "Obscenity, Morals and the Law: A Feminist Critique" (1985), 17 Ottawa L.R. at 33.

6 *R. v. Oakes*, [1986] 1 S.C.R. 103 at 136; *R. v. Big M Drug Mart Ltd.*, [1985] 1 S.C.R. 295 at 336, *per* Dickson J. (as he then was).

7 *Andrews v. Law Soc. of B.C.*, [1989] 1 S.C.R. 143; *R. v. Turpin*, [1989] 1 S.C.R. 1296 at 1331.

8 *Turpin, ibid.*, at 1333.

9 See Brest and Vanderberg, "Politics, Feminism and the Constitution: The Anti-Pornography Movement in Minneapolis" (1987), 39 Stan. L. Rev. 607 at 610-11. Many other definitions exist, but all have abuse of power relations in a sexual context as their premise.

A further reason for the changes in the law may be a recognition by the courts that enforcement of sexual morality by way of the criminal law in today's world is a somewhat dubious proposition. The Canadian government has taken the position that the only proper basis for criminal law is to address the threat of serious harm.[10]

The changes occurring in the law are taking place at two levels. The first is at the liability stage, the second, at the stage of constitutional analysis. In this paper, both levels of the analysis are discussed. In the first part of the paper, the legal framework of obscenity is set out and a critique is provided of the traditional way judges have interpreted the definition of obscenity and characterized its harms. New approaches to the definitional and harm issues are commented upon, particularly the pronouncements of the Supreme Court in the landmark *Towne Cinema*[11] case which, although it adopts a discourse on harm consistent with the discrimination argument, leaves some questions up in the air regarding the scope of obscenity law. This has caused problems in some lower courts, but the discrimination analysis has definitely taken hold. In the second part of the paper, the interrelationship between the characterization of harm for the purposes of assessing liability and the constitutional determination of the validity of obscenity provisions is discussed. An argument is made that pornography should fall outside of the ambit of the constitutional protection of free expression or, alternatively, that the obscenity provisions are saved by s. 1 of the *Canadian Charter of Rights and Freedoms*. Emphasis is placed on recent Supreme Court jurisprudence on freedom of expression, most particularly, the case of *Irwin Toy v. Quebec*.[12]

II. THE LEGAL FRAMEWORK

A. Purpose of the Law

The original purpose of obscenity law was to protect public morality. This is clear when one looks at the legislative history of the obscenity provisions in the *Criminal Code*. The first Canadian prohibition of obscenity was enacted in 1892. Section 179 prohibited the public sale, without lawful excuse, of obscene publications "tending to corrupt morals." When this section was repealed in 1949, the words "tending to corrupt morals" were dropped, but the emphasis on morality was perpetuated through the judicial application of the "*Hicklin* test," enunci-

---

10 *The Criminal Law in Canadian Society* (Ottawa: Department of Justice, 1982), at 52-53.
11 *Towne Cinema Theatres Ltd. v. R.* (1985), 45 C.R. (3d) 1 (S.C.C.)[Alta.].
12 *Irwin Toy Ltd. v. Que. (A.G.)*, [1989] 1 S.C.R. 927.

ated by Cockburn C.J. in *R. v. Hicklin*.[13] This rather weak and simplistic test determined what was obscene based on whether the matter charged as obscenity tended to deprave and corrupt those who were likely to be depraved and corrupted by it. The test suppressed obscenity for the sake of the moral purity of its consumers. After much criticism, the test was replaced in 1959 by a legislated definition of obscenity, which remains to this day.[14] The definition reads:

> 159.(8) For the purposes of this Act, any publication a dominant characteristic of which is the undue exploitation of sex, or of sex and any one or more of the following subjects, namely, crime, horror, cruelty and violence, shall be deemed to be obscene.

By broadening the scope of the definition to take into account sex combined with crime, horror, cruelty and violence, Parliament seemed to recognize that harm to society could occur through depictions which showed people being harmed.[15]

Section 163(1)(a) of the *Criminal Code* created the offence. It reads as follows:[16]

> 163.(1) Every one commits an offence who
>
> (a) makes, prints, publishes, distributes, circulates, or has in his possession for the purpose of publication, distribution or circulation any obscene written matter, picture, model, phonograph record or other thing whatever.

Even though the words Parliament chose to define obscenity indicated concern beyond the narrow moral harm to consumers addressed by the *Hicklin* test, the judicial interpretation of the definition continued to emphasize public morality concerns, tempered by a new sensitivity to freedom of speech and expression. No judicial concern was expressed about the exploitation of women in obscene depictions nor its effects on women's lives generally.[17] Perhaps the reason for this was the

---

13 (1868), L.R. 3 Q.B. 360 at 371.
14 In *Brodie v. R.* (1962), 132 C.C.C. 161, the Supreme Court of Canada concluded that the 1959 definition was exhaustive, rendering the *Hicklin* test obsolete. See also *R. v. Dechow* (1978), 76 D.L.R. (3d) 1 (S.C.C.)[Ont.].
15 But see J.P.S. McLaren, "Now You See It, Now You Don't: The Historical Record and the Elusive Task of Defining the Obscene" in this volume. In his historical review, Professor McLaren says that the real intent of the new definition was not to replace the *Hicklin* test, but rather to strengthen it and its emphasis on the quality of the material as it related to moral concerns.
16 *Supra*, note 1.
17 See *Dominion News & Gifts Ltd. v. R.*, [1963] 2 C.C.C. 103, affirmed [1964] S.C.R. 251 [Man.].

relatively mild content of pornography which, until the late 1970s, consisted primarily of female nudity and simulated sex acts. Little public opposition was expressed and the feminist analysis had yet to emerge in mainstream law journals and other media.[18]

B. The Community Standards Test

To determine whether or not material would be found obscene, courts invented the device of the community standards test. Its function was to assess whether or not the exploitation of sex in any material charged was "undue." The test has been refined and developed to require that the community standards be Canadian rather than local, contemporary or current rather than fixed, and measured by a level of objective tolerance for others' tastes.[19] Evidence of community standards is admissible by either the Crown or the defence to assist the trier of fact in arriving at a decision as to the community tolerance, but is not required.[20] Often this evidence takes the form of expert testimony as to the impugned material's literary or social merit.[21] Opinion poll evidence is admissible,[22] as well as evidence of a provincial censor or classification board. Market availability and the character of the audience and its reaction are used by some judges as indicators of community standards,[23] whereas others say the standards must not be set by those of lowest taste or interest, nor should they be set exclusively by those of rigid, austere, conservative or puritan taste.[24] Something approaching a

18   Most of the feminist scholarship on pornography was published during or after 1979: see A. Dworkin, *supra*, note 5; L. Lederer, *supra*, note 5; K. Barry, *Female Sexual Slavery* (Englewood Cliffs, N.J.: Prentice-Hall, 1979); C. MacKinnon, "Not a Moral Issue," *supra*, note 5; K. Lahey, "The Canadian Charter of Rights and Pornography: Toward a Theory of Actual Gender Equality" (1984-1985), 20 New England L. Rev. 649; C. MacKinnon, "Pornography, Civil Rights and Speech" (1985), 20 Harv. C.R. - C.L.L. Rev 1.

19   *R. v. Butler*, 46 C.R.R. 124 at 130, reversed [1991] 1 W.W.R. 97 (Man. C.A.), citing *R. v. Sudbury News Service Ltd.* (1978), 18 O.R. (2d) 428 (C.A.), *Towne Cinema Theatres Ltd. v. R.*, *supra*, note 11 at 17.

20   *Ibid.*

21   *R. v. Odeon Morton Theatres Ltd.* (1974), 16 C.C.C. (2d) 185 (Man. C.A.).

22   *R. v. Prairie Schooner News Ltd.* (1970), 1 C.C.C. (2d) 251 (Man. C.A.).

23   *R. v. Mrdjenovich*, [1988] N.W.T.R. 394 (S.C.). In *Towne Cinema Theatres Ltd. v. R.*, *supra*, note 11, Dickson C.J.C., Lamer J. (as he then was) and Le Dain J. concluded that the audience that might be anticipated to view the impugned material should be a factor in determining what excess of the level of tolerance will result in "undue" exploitation. Beetz, Estey, Wilson and McIntyre JJ. concluded that it is not.

24   *R. v. MacLean* (1982), 1 C.C.C. (3d) 412 (Ont. C.A.); *R. v. Sudbury News Service Ltd.*, *supra*, note 19; *R. v. Odeon Morton Theatres Ltd.*, *supra*, note 21; *R. v. Kleppe* (1977), 35 C.C.C. (2d) 168 at 174 (Ont. Prov.Ct.); *R. v. Campbell* (1974), 17 C.C.C. (2d) 130 at 135 (Ont. Co.Ct.).

"general average" of community thinking and feeling has to be discovered,[25] but the part of the community that does care, one way or the
other about such matters, is to be considered, rather than the standards
of the apathetic.[26] Ultimately, the community standards decision is left
up to the judge to decide, based on his or her experience.[27]

Even with all of these refinements, the community standards test is
seriously deficient. It is criticized for the reasons that it is a difficult test
to prove; it masks the real harm pornography causes; its use discriminates against women; and, in some instances, it makes judges unwitting
allies of pornography producers. These criticisms are discussed below.

1. Problems Proving Community Standards

Justice Wright pinpointed a number of the evidentiary problems
with the community standards test in his decision in *R. v. Butler*.[28] He
said that when there are serious difficulties in even identifying a contemporary Canadian community standard, satisfying a judge beyond a
reasonable doubt as to its existence is almost impossible.[29] Justice
Borins in *R. v. Doug Rankine Co.* voiced similar concerns when he
commented that the legislature cannot credibly expect a trier of fact to
have his finger on the "pornographic pulse" of the nation.[30] Other judges
have pointed out the unreliability and cost of gathering evidence of
community standards, the difficulty of review on appeal, and the problems of monitoring and measuring changing standards inherent in
determining what contemporary Canadian society will tolerate.[31] Some
even question whether a community standard on pornography exists in
a pluralistic society made up of rural and urban populations.[32] In the
end, the community standards test requires the judge to make a moral
judgment on questions of a speculative nature about which she or he has
imperfect knowledge.

---

25 *Dominion News & Gifts Ltd. v. R., supra*, note 17 at 116-17; *R. v. Ariadne
    Developments Ltd.* (1974), 19 C.C.C. (2d) 49 (N.S.C.A.); *R. v. MacMillan Co.*
    (1976), 31 C.C.C. (2d) 286 at 289 (Ont. Co.Ct.).
26 *R. v. Chin* (1983), 9 W.C.B. 249 (Ont. Prov.Ct.).
27 *R. v. Great West News Ltd.*, [1970] 4 C.C.C. 307 at 314 and 315 (Man. C.A.).
28 (1989), 72 C.R. (3d) 18 (Man. Q.B.).
29 *Ibid.*, at 18-19.
30 (1983), 36 C.R. (3d) 154 at 172 (Ont. Co.Ct.).
31 See also M. MacDonald, "Obscenity, Censorship and Freedom of Expression:
    Does the Charter Protect Pornography?" (1985), 43 U. of T. Fac. L. Rev. 130; C.
    MacDougall, "The Community Standards Test of Obscenity" (1984), U. of T.
    Fac. L. Rev. 79.
32 See Borins J.'s comments in *R. v. Nicols, supra*, note 3; T. Tongg, "State v. Kam:
    Do Community Standards on Pornography Exist?" (1987), 9 Univ. of Hawaii
    L. Rev. 727.

2. *Problems of Covering Up Real Harm*

For many years the courts assumed that the harm of obscenity was its undermining effect on society's morals. Nudity, explicitness, excess of candour, prurience and unnaturalness were qualities judges looked for when assessing "harm." In other words, offensiveness or aesthetic considerations were paramount. The community standards test determined how much "sex" or harm to morals the community could tolerate. Notwithstanding the s. 159 definition, which allowed judges to look beyond explicitness for crime, horror, cruelty and violence combined with sex, no judicial attempt was made to assess or analyze the harm the depictions may have caused to women portrayed in them or to women as a class. In fact, the courts assiduously and deliberately avoided identifying any demonstrable harm. For example, Freedman J.A. stated in *R. v. Prairie Schooner News Ltd.*:[33]

> It is not for the Court to determine whether publications of this kind hurt anyone or do any demonstrable harm. Parliament has already made that determination . . . All that remains is for the Court to decide whether, according to contemporary Canadian standards, the present publications are within the definition or without it.

By taking this approach, the courts rendered the effects of pornography — the sexual subordination and the practice of sexual violence and coercion against women — irrelevant to the analysis. By abstracting and generalizing the analysis to "undue exploitation of sex," the judges made women's interests disappear, and successfully distanced themselves from any consideration of gender inequality issues. But the form and content of mass-produced pornography began to change in the late 1970s and early 1980s. Instead of soft focus nudes and suggestive poses, pornographers began exploiting sex in a way which sexualized violence. Brutality, degradation and humiliation of women were presented as socially acceptable, sexually satisfying and entertaining.[34] At the same time, availability of pornography increased exponentially in the print media, the movie theatres, and particularly in the home video market.[35]

---

33 *Supra*, note 22 at 254-55.
34 Malamuth and Spinner, "A Longitudinal Content Analysis of Sexual Violence in the Best-Selling Erotic Magazines" (1980), 16 Journal of Sex Research at 226. Similar results were reported by Dietz and Evans, "Pornographic Imagery and Prevalence of Paraphilia" (1982), 139 Am. J. Psych. 1493, and in Dietz and Sears, "Pornography and Obscenity Sold in 'Adult Bookstores': A Survey of 5132 Books, Magazines, and Films in Four American Cities" (1987-88), 21 U. Mich. J.L. Ref. 7.
35 Canada, *Report of the Special Committee on Pornography and Prostitution*, vol. 1 (Ottawa: Supply and Services Canada, 1985) (Chairman: Paul Fraser), c. 6.

Trying to apply a community standards test in the context of a rapidly expanding market of increasingly violent, but sexual, material proved to be difficult. Judges deciding what was tolerable in the Canadian community on an explicitness standard were required to evaluate depictions showing ejaculation in the faces of women, incest, forced intercourse, sexual mutilation, beatings, bondage and sexual torture practised on women. It soon became clear, at least to some judges, that harm to morality as the underlying rationale for regulation was inadequate to deal with content more related to human rights and the status of women than aesthetic considerations of community morality. While there may be some logic to the vague morality-based test from either a liberal or a moral perspective, it is completely illogical from the perspective of harm to women.

3. *Problems of Inherent Discrimination in the Test*

A further criticism of the community standards test is the inherent discrimination it contains because of systemic inequality between women and men. In a male-dominated society, existing social consensus permits and condones sexism. In Canada, sex stereotypes of women prevail and sex discrimination is embedded in the system.[36] Even though the community standards test is an objective one, its use under these conditions of inequality will operate almost inevitably to the advantage of the dominant group, particularly when what is being tested is tolerance levels for the sexual exploitation of women designed to "entertain" men. This discrimination is most obvious when judges measure the level of community tolerance by referring to audience character and reaction[37] or market availability.[38] Since it is men who overwhelmingly create, finance, distribute and purchase pornography,[39] utilizing the test in this way results in a male-defined standard of tolerance rather than a community one. It is also most unlikely that pornography consumers will be offended by the very product they seek out. The test discriminates against women because not only does it effectively deny their participation in standard-setting on an issue which directly affects them, it perpetuates their subordination by expressing

---

36 *E.g.*, see *Brooks v. Can. Safeway Ltd.*, [1989] 4 W.W.R. 193 (S.C.C.); *Robichaud v. Canada (Treasury) Board*, [1987] 2 S.C.R. 84; *Canadian National Railway Co. v. Can. (Human Rights Comm.)* (1987), 40 D.L.R. (4th) 193 (S.C.C.); *Janzen v. Platy Enterprises Ltd.*, [1989] 1 S.C.R. 1252.

37 *Towne Cinema, supra*, note 23.

38 *R. v. Arena Recreations (Toronto) Ltd.* (1987), 56 C.R. (3d) 118 (Man. Q.B.).

39 Kutchinsky, "Pornography in Denmark — A General Survey of Censorship and Obscenity," in R. Dhaven and C. Davie (eds.), *Censorship and Obscenity* (London: M. Robertson, 1978), at 76.

male supremacy through the use of a legal guise. When judges determine community standards by referring to the standards of pornography users, they effectively reproduce the pornographic point of view of women as submissive and inferior.[40] By legally condoning the idea that males should decide what degree of female exploitation is tolerable, courts effectively silence women and support the sexist *status quo* and its social norms, which regard women as second-class citizens. Yet the male appropriation of obscenity standards through the use of the community standards test has never been recognized as such by the judiciary.[41]

This point is all the more important in light of a recent study of Canadian attitudes towards pornography which indicates that males, particularly self-reported users, are high condoners of pornography, whereas women generally are not.[42]

These findings are consistent with studies of human development which indicate that women and men view ethical and moral issues differently.[43] Where men generally decide moral issues with a view to maximizing individual freedom, women decide the same issues from the moral standpoint of responsibility to others in a social context.[44] The numerous definitions of obscenity that women and women's groups have developed, bear this out.[45] Whatever their specific wording, they define obscenity contextually, in relation to a portrayal of power relations and social harm.

In addition to the discriminatory aspects of the community standards test, it is arguable that the method of its application has trivialized the crime of obscenity. When judges use words such as "skin flick"[46] and "girlie magazine"[47] to describe the sexual exploitation of women, the

40 MacKinnon, *Towards a Feminist Theory of the State* (Cambridge, Mass.: Harvard Univ. Press, 1989), at 197.
41 But see discussion in the text associated with notes 66 to 68.
42 Schell *et al.*, "Development of a Pornography Community Standard: Questionnaire Results from Two Canadian Cities" (1987), 29 Can. Jo. Crim. 133.
43 For example, the concept forms the basis for Freud's psychoanalytic theory: see Freud, "Some Psychical Consequences of the Anatomical Distinction Between the Sexes", in J. Strachey (trans. ed.), *The Standard Edition of the Complete Psychological Works of Sigmund Freud* (London: Hogarth Press, 1953), vol. XIX at 257-58.
44 Gilligan, *In a Different Voice: Psychological Theory and Women's Development* (Cambridge, Mass.: Harvard University Press, 1982). This theme is developed in relation to obscenity law in Mahoney, "Obscenity, Morals and the Law: A Feminist Critique," *supra*, note 5.
45 See K. Mahoney, "Obscenity and Public Policy: Conflicting Values — Conflicting Statutes" (1985-86), 50 Sask. L. Rev. 75 at 81-84, where a number of definitions are listed.
46 *Supra*, note 21 at 194; *R. v. Mercer* (1988), 88 N.B.R. (2d) 140 at 150 (Prov. Ct.).
47 *R. v. Pereira-Vasquez* (1988), 26 B.C.L.R. (2d) 273 at 278 (C.A.); *Dominion News & Gifts Ltd. v. R., supra*, note 17.

void of feminine perspectives in the law is obvious. One judge equated obscenity to a "foul smelling cigar"[48] and judges sometimes describe obscenity humorously or state how "boring" they find the material to be.[49] This use of language downplays the reality of the sexual subordination of women, and tends to remove it from the context within which it exists — in a society where sexual assault, battering, sexual harassment and prostitution of women is commonplace.[50]

It is not surprising that an absence of context led judges to prefer freedom of speech to censorship or regulation in "close call" cases.[51] Judgments show that the meaning of "speech" for women has not been contemplated.[52] Professor Lahey makes the point that the whole relationship between "freedom" and the social role of pornography must be evaluated.[53] Questions arise such as: How does pornography make men "free" and does it "free" women in the same way? Do women have the same freedom of speech that men have? How would regulation of pornography affect that allocation? She wonders how something can be experienced by one person as "freedom" at the same time it is experienced by another as violence, oppression, containment or some other variant of non-freedom.[54] Instead of asking these relational and contextual questions, judges more often adopted a neutral view which assumed

---

48 *R. v. Kleppe, supra*, note 24.
49 *R. v. Wagner* (1986), 50 C.R. (3d) 175, affirming 43 C.R. (3d) 318, leave to appeal to S.C.C. refused 50 C.R. (3d) 175n [Alta.].
50 See Metro Toronto Task Force on Public Violence Against Women and Children, *Final Report* (The Municipality of Metropolitan Toronto, 1984); Special Committee on Pornography and Prostitution, *supra*, note 35; L. Clark and D. Lewis, *The Price of Coercive Sexuality* (Toronto: Women's Press, 1977); Armstrong, "Wife Beating: Let's Stop it Now" (July 1983), Canadian Living 89; Canada, Report of the Committee on Sexual Offences Against Children and Youths, *Sexual Offences Against Children* (Chairman: Robin F. Badgley) (Ottawa: Supply and Services, 1984), at 180-83; MacLeod, *Wife Battering in Canada: The Vicious Circle* (Ottawa: Minister of Supply and Services, 1980).
51 McLaren, *supra*, note 15.
52 For a discussion of inherent sexism in liberal theories of free speech, see A. Dworkin, *Pornography: Men Possessing Women, supra*, note 5; S. Griffin, *Pornography and Silence: Culture's Revolt Against Nature* (New York: Harper & Row, 1981); L. Clark, "Liberalism and Pornography," in D. Copp and S. Wendell (eds.), *Pornography and Censorship* (Buffalo, N.Y.: Prometheus Books, 1983); C. MacKinnon, "Feminism, Marxism, Method and the State: An Agenda for Theory" (1982), 7 Signs 515.
53 K. Lahey, "The Charter and Pornography: Toward a Restricted Theory of Constitutionally Protected Expression," in Weiler and Elliot (eds.), *Litigating the Values of a Nation: The Canadian Charter of Rights and Freedoms* (Toronto: Carswell, 1986), at 265; K. Lahey, "The Canadian Charter of Rights and Pornography: Toward a Theory of Actual Gender Equality," *supra*, note 18.
54 Lahey, "The Canadian Charter of Rights . . . ," *ibid.*, at 661-64.

that men and women have equal access to the market-place of ideas and that maximizing speech for pornography producers and consumers maximizes speech for everyone. This approach ignores the history of gender inequality and exploitation which shows that women's views have been systematically neglected, distorted, undervalued and excluded from the market-place of ideas.[55] It diverts the legal analysis away from the social meaning of what is being done by pornography and forces a defence of it on neutral ground. This, in turn, reduces society's responsibility for the result being reached, and protects freedom of expression as a process without a public context or egalitarian dimension. It does not allow for any consideration as to whether or not "free speech" might have the result of diminishing, eradicating or colliding with the freedoms of others.

4. Complicity Problems

A further problem with the community standards test is its vulnerability to manipulation by pornography producers. It is a well understood fact in the pornography trade that pornography consumers become bored and desensitized to sex depictions unless more unusual, shocking or bizarre content is introduced.[56] To overcome the "desensitization factor" and maintain consumer demand for their product, pornographers developed new mediums for pornography and increased its "hard core" content.[57] The judicial use of "sex blind" criteria of market availability or audience reaction to determine community standards allowed pornography producers to successfully make transitions to lower standards without offending obscenity laws.[58] Pornographers needed only to flood the market with new material for which a demand existed. If the lower standards were sufficiently widespread, they could not be found obscene on a market standard, since its street presence indicated that the community accepted it. Ineffective customs legislation, evidenced by the very small number of prosecutions brought under the legislation[59] in comparison to the size of the pornography industry

---

55 *Ibid.*; see also T. McCormack, "Two(b) or not Two(b): Feminism and Freedom of Expression," in J. Lennox (ed.), *Se Connaître: Politics and Culture in Canada* (North York: York University Press, 1985), cited in Lahey, "The Charter and Pornography . . . ," *supra*, note 53.

56 D. Zillman, "Effects of Prolonged Consumption of Pornography," in D. Zillman and J. Bryant (eds.), *Pornography: Research Advances and Policy Considerations* (Hillsdale, N.J.: Erlbaum, 1989).

57 Malamuth and Spinner, *supra*, note 34; see also Dietz and Evans, *supra*, note 34.

58 *Supra*, note 21 at 198, *per* Monnin J.A., citing the trial judge in the unreported Provincial Court decision.

59 R.S.C. 1970, c. C-40.

and the amount of illegal material in circulation, and a brisk business in smuggling pornography across the border,[60] helped pornographers to lower the standards.

An example of a successful manipulation of the community standards was evident in the decision of *R. v. Arena Recreations (Toronto) Ltd.*[61] Penthouse magazine widely distributed a magazine depicting partially nude Japanese women bound by ropes, masked, and hanging from trees. At this point in the evolution of obscenity law in Canada, bondage was considered to be beyond the pale of Canadian community standards.[62] The Canadian market was nevertheless flooded with the magazine, and when retailers were charged under the obscenity provisions, they successfully argued that it met Canadian community standards because the wide circulation of the material indicated an apparent degree of community acceptance.[63]

In summary, as the central variable in the definition of obscenity, the community standards test as traditionally applied was inherently vague, elusive, discriminatory and incoherent.

C. The Beginning of the Reconstruction

The first indication of a fundamental change in judicial thinking with respect to the underlying rationale of obscenity law started in 1983 when judges first recognized that some pornographic depictions degraded and dehumanized women as a class. This realization started a movement away from viewing obscenity as a threat to the community's sexual morality, and towards seeing it in relation to human dignity and equality. Judge Borins of the Ontario County Court, in *R. v. Doug Rankine Co.*, was the first judge to articulate this view.[64] Instead of using explicitness as the touchstone of "undue exploitation," he turned to the other listed criteria of violence and cruelty in conjunction with sex, saying:[65]

... films which consist substantially or partially of scenes which por-

---

60 *Supra*, note 50 at 1168-69.
61 *Supra*, note 38.
62 See *R. v. Doug Rankine Co., supra*, note 30.
63 *Supra*, note 38 at 123. Note, however, that in *R. v. Metro News* (1986), 53 C.R. (3d) 289, leave to appeal to S.C.C. refused 57 O.R. (2d) 638n [Ont.], the Penthouse photos were found to exceed community standards by a jury of 12 persons. A Provincial Court in Saskatchewan also found them to be obscene, but the judge in *Arena Recreations* was not persuaded that community standards had been exceeded. See, *supra*, note 38 at 130.
64 *Supra*, note 30.
65 *Ibid.*, at 173.

tray violence and cruelty in conjunction with sex, particularly where the performance of indignities degrades and dehumanizes people upon whom they are performed, exceed the level of community tolerance.

By tying the community standards test to violence and cruelty, Judge Borins opened the door to many new considerations. Unlike the explicitness rationale which provided no incentive to probe into the issue of harmful effects, the dignity rationale Judge Borins proposed allowed for judicial reflection on how pornography presents human sexuality and what it says about women. The benefit of this approach is that it allows judges to think about pornography more broadly and contextually, and to stop simply assuming that sexual explicitness represents a special case that justifies more regulation. The advantage of Judge Borins' approach over the explicitness test was not that it necessarily provided better answers, but that it triggered the right questions about what pornography depicts and communicates. Questions such as: Does it reinforce sexual inequality or does it not? Does it sexualize women's subordination? Does it sexualize violence?

Judge Borins broke further new ground in applying the community standards test when he determined that women may have a different level of tolerance for pornography than men. He stated: "I can think of very few women in this country who would tolerate the distribution of motion pictures portraying indignities to other human beings, particularly women, in the name of entertainment."[66] The importance of this comment should not be underestimated. For the first time, in more than 200 years of obscenity law, a judge expressly contemplated obscenity from a women's point of view, from a point of view of subordination to men. He must have recognized that when obscenity is controlled by males, it is from a standpoint of domination.

Even though Judge Borins relied primarily on standards of violence and cruelty, he kept the explicitness standard alive by saying that even absent scenes containing violence and cruelty, certain sexual depictions could still exceed community standards based on the degree of explicitness contained in them. However, since he decided that scenes of group sex, lesbianism, fellatio, cunnilingus and anal sex were tolerable within the contemporary Canadian community standard, it is difficult to imagine what material would offend an explicitness standard. It would have been more consistent with his earlier analysis had Judge Borins held instead that, absent cruelty and violence, material could still be obscene if it degraded and dehumanized the participants in it. In this way, he would have underlined the premise that it is not sex *per se* that obscenity law should be concerned with, but the manner of its portrayal.

---

66 *Ibid.*, at 160.

The Manitoba Court of Appeal, in a later case,[67] took a different view about the degree of tolerable explicitness. It emphasized that the obscenity definition has two parts — one which addresses the undue exploitation of sex, the other, undue exploitation of sex combined with crime, horror, cruelty or violence. Justice Matas said that, while it is correct to say that the Canadian community will not tolerate publications falling within the second part of the definition, that does not mean that the absence of crime, horror, cruelty or violence will preclude a finding of obscenity.[68] The Manitoba court went on to disagree with the degree of explicitness Judge Borins felt that the Canadian community would tolerate. By doing so, the explicitness standard was re-emphasized, with the result that the morality rationale remained important to the determination of obscenity.

The next precedent-setting case was *R. v. Wagner,*[69] where Justice Shannon of the Alberta Court of Queen's Bench analyzed obscenity entirely through a contextualized, victim-centred approach. He said that the manner in which sexual interaction is portrayed must be examined, not just the degree of explicitness. For the first time, a court made a linguistic and factual distinction between erotica and obscenity. Justice Shannon defined erotica as portraying "positive and affectionate human sexual interaction, between consenting individuals participating on the basis of equality."[70] He went on to say that the contemporary Canadian community will tolerate erotica "no matter how explicit it may be."[71]

In Justice Shannon's analysis, explicitness assumes relevance only within a context in which there is violence, lack of consent or inherent inequality between the parties. By contrast, the Manitoba Court of Appeal in *R. v. Video World*[72] did not make this distinction. Erotica and highly explicit depictions were not contextually differentiated from crime, horror, cruelty or violence. By avoiding context, the Manitoba court avoided answering the difficult questions, preferring instead to revert to the moralistic rationale of condemning explicitness *per se.*

In the *Wagner* case, Justice Shannon also took the harm analysis one crucial step further than previous judges, when he specifically identified the harm in obscenity as something different than harm to morals. He said it consisted of "social harm" in the form of viewers' "increased callousness towards women and less receptiveness to their

---

67   *R. v. Video World Ltd.,* [1986] 1 W.W.R. 413 (Man. C.A.).
68   *Ibid.,* at 423, *per* Matas J..
69   *Supra,* note 49 (43 C.R. (3d)).
70   *Ibid.,* at 331.
71   *Ibid.*
72   *Supra,* note 67.

legitimate claims for equality and respect." He linked degradation and dehumanization to equality concerns by explaining that victims in pornography are often verbally abused and portrayed as having animal characteristics. He said that false representations of female sexuality are created which, in turn, reduce women as a group to mere objects of sexual access.[73] By defining obscenity specifically for what it is and what it does, Justice Shannon laid the foundation for the reconstruction of obscenity law both at the liability stage and for the purposes of constitutional evaluation.

The next court to pronounce on the community standards test was the British Columbia Court of Appeal in *R. v. Red Hot Video.*[74] The court used the community standards test to determine undueness, finding that the "degrading vilification of women is unacceptable by any reasonable Canadian community standard."[75] Degrading vilification was held to occur where sexual behaviour is portrayed with one of the "sex-plus" categories of crime, horror, cruelty or violence, or where there is an "unduly exploitative" representation which degrades the participants by "portraying them as having animal characteristics."[76] While the British Columbia Court of Appeal did not comment upon "erotica," Justice Anderson, like Justice Shannon, stressed the equality theme in his characterization of harm. He stated:[77]

> If true equality between male and female persons is to be achieved it would be quite wrong . . . to ignore the threat to equality resulting from the exposure to male audiences of the violent and degrading material . . . such material has a tendency to make men more tolerant of violence to women and creates a social climate encouraging men to act in a callous and discriminatory way towards women.

He concluded that the impugned materials in the case were obscene, reasoning that "they constitute a threat of real and substantial harm to the community" because "they approve [of] the domination of women by men as an acceptable social philosophy."[78] Clearly, the British Columbia Court of Appeal in this case recognized the social commitment of Canada to gender equality as well as the harm to that commitment which pornography engenders. By not at all mentioning the explicitness standard in the judgment, it seemed that the court was replacing the old

---

73 *R. v. Wagner, supra*, note 49 at 331.
74 45 C.R. (3d) 36.
75 *Ibid.*, at 43, *per* Nemetz C.J.B.C.
76 *Ibid.*
77 *Ibid.*, at 59.
78 *Ibid.*, at 61.

morality-based obscenity test with one founded on equality principles, signifying a judicial recognition of the fact that equality cannot be achieved unless the law creates conditions in which it can be enjoyed.[79]

In a subsequent decision of the British Columbia Court of Appeal,[80] however, a differently constituted court adopted the violent and degrading analysis, but once again reintroduced the morality standard by stressing that non-violent, non-degrading "skin flicks" with no redeeming values to offset their explicitness, could also be obscene. Justice Esson resurrected the old "dirt for dirt's sake" test,[81] but then distinguished "dirt" from erotica as defined by Justice Shannon in *Wagner*,[82] tying it to a degrading and dehumanizing standard.[83] He still maintained, however, that, absent violence or degradation, certain forms of "depraved sludge" could still be found obscene.[84] By resurrecting the moralistic and subjective "dirt for dirt's sake" test, Justice Esson unnecessarily confused the already complicated problem of applying the community standards test.

The equality rationale would have been preferable because it is more defensible and consistent with the harm criminal law is designed to address. Where the equality approach encourages inquiry into fundamental questions about women's subordination, sex roles and stereotypes which diminish their value as human beings, the focus on sexual explicitness forecloses these questions without any opportunity for reflection. Moreover, the "dirt for dirt's sake" test implies that artistic merit, plot or any socially redeeming aspects could elevate the purpose to make an otherwise obscene depiction, legal. Given the dubious legitimacy of using the criminal law to regulate morality,[85] it is logical to assume a minimal amount of artistic merit or other redeeming quality would save the exploitation from being undue.[86] On the other hand, where the evil sought to be prevented is harm to women, it is likely that courts would be more careful in assessing artistic merit or plot or other redeeming factors before finding that they outweigh a fundamen-

---

79 See comment by S. Noonan, "Gender Neutrality and Pornography," in L. Bell (ed.), *Good Girls/Bad Girls* (Toronto: Women's Press, 1987), at 42 and 44-45; and J.P.S. McLaren, *supra*, note 15.

80 *R. v. Pereira-Vasquez, supra*, note 47.

81 See S. Noonan's comments, "Pereira-Vasquez: Obscenity — For the Sake of Dirt", 64 C.R. (3d) 277.

82 *Pereira-Vasquez, supra*, note 47 at 288-89.

83 *Ibid.*, at 291.

84 *Ibid.*

85 See, *supra*, note 10.

86 Upon reviewing past cases, Justice Esson in the *Pereira-Vasquez* case, *supra*, note 47, says at 277: "Where there was something to balance, even where the exploitation of sex was graphic and explicit, the balance has often come down in favour of finding the work not to be obscene."

tal substantive value. They would be forced to consider the relative value of art in relation to the value of women within the terms of the definition of obscenity. If pornography regulation is to stand on a rational basis that can withstand constitutional scrutiny, these serious questions must be addressed, not side-stepped.

The emphasis on the explicitness standard in the *Pereira-Vasquez* case may have come about because of the earlier decision of the Supreme Court of Canada in *Towne Cinema Theatres Ltd. v. R.*,[87] the only Supreme Court decision to date which has addressed the community standards test in terms of degradation and dehumanization.

The court attempted to address and clarify some of the problems in the obscenity law, including the definition of obscenity, the use of community standards as a test, and the necessity of adducing evidence of community standards. The decision is a difficult one to assess because of many different judicial splits and the lack of a clear majority on most of the issues it considered. While no clear direction on all of the issues emerged from the decision, the majority clearly established that the community standards test is an objective one and that audience reaction is irrelevant in the determination of undueness. The court reaffirmed that the community standards test is one of tolerance, and that what matters is not what Canadians think as right for themselves, but what they would not abide other Canadians seeing.[88] Justice Wilson dissented on this point, putting the standard at a higher level. She held that the test should measure the level of exploitation the Canadian community, at any given point, is prepared to accept, not merely tolerate. Since she defined undueness as consisting of degrading and dehumanizing treatment of sex, and since the vast majority of pornography focuses on the female sex, this higher standard makes sense. In a society where gender equality rights are entrenched as a constitutional guarantee, any test that assumes degradation and dehumanization of women could be tolerable would obviously violate *Charter* standards.

Dickson C.J.C., however, with Lamer J. (as he then was) and Le Dain J. concurring, took a different approach. They held that the community standards test is only one of three tests of undueness. The "internal necessities" test, which measures artistic and literary merit, may be applied to determine "undueness"; the accepted standards of tolerance in the contemporary Canadian community is a second test; and a third is one of "degradation," which can be applied even where materials fall within tolerance levels of the contemporary Canadian community.

Explaining the third test, Dickson C.J.C. said that certain materials,

---

87 *Supra*, note 11.
88 *Ibid.*, at 17.

even though tolerated by the Canadian community, may still amount to an undue exploitation of sex if they portray persons in a degrading or dehumanizing way.[89] This approach seems to be designed to prevent the unwitting complicity of the judiciary in the downward spiralling of standards.[90] With degradation and dehumanization as one of the tests of undueness, widespread availability of impugned material could not be used as an argument to say that the community standards test is met. Presumably, it would not matter if a large and profitable market in the degradation and dehumanization of women existed, as the courts could still find such material to be obscene. The majority of the court, led by Wilson J. (Beetz, Estey and McIntyre JJ. concurring), strengthened the point by holding that the particular audience to which the material is targeted is irrelevant when assessing undueness. This corrects the problem of the self-selecting "male only" standard.[91] But, while the court resolved some problems in *Towne Cinema*,[92] it created others.

The way the decision is structured, it appears as though the majority of the court intended violence, degradation and dehumanization to serve only as a back-up test for the explicitness standard. As a result, it may be that the contextualized approach would apply only to materials not explicit enough to be found obscene under the community standards test, but which portray women being badly treated. This analysis is problematic for at least three reasons: it does not direct courts to differentiate between highly explicit erotica and other portrayals; it will lead to more inconsistent decisions; and it permits judges to side-step the difficult contextual questions surrounding the issue of highly explicit, violent or degrading pornography. If these portrayals can be found obscene solely on the grounds of explicitness, the issue of women's equality once again disappears. Furthermore, consensual, non-violent, highly explicit sex may be found obscene without any reference to equality issues. Consequently, the answer to what, if anything, is wrong with highly explicit but non-degrading or dehumanizing depictions other than moral concerns, is still up in the air. This analysis encourages the "dirt for dirt's sake" approach, which is not only unhelpful in establishing a rational basis for regulation, it leaves the door open for highly subjective and inconsistent decisions. While the court took a major and welcome step forward by adopting the degradation, dehumanization and objectification discourse, limiting its application to a back-up test to the explicitness standard perpetuates uncertainty in the law.

---

89 *Ibid.*, at 14.
90 See discussion in the text associated with notes 56 to 63.
91 See discussion in the text associated with notes 36 to 50.
92 *Supra*, note 11.

Wilson J.'s dissent in the case avoids these problems. In her judgment the community standards test is the only test of undue exploitation and it, in turn, is tied to the concept of dehumanization. By stating that "[t]here is nothing wrong in the treatment of sex *per se* but there may be something wrong in the manner of its treatment," she built the contextualized approach into both the definition of obscenity and the community standards test. This is a much clearer, simpler, and more principled test which will require courts to look at messages conveyed by pornography prior to an obscenity finding.

On the question of harm, she stated that women are not the only victims of pornography. In her opinion, male viewers too are harmed. She stated that "undue" refers to the treatment of sex which in some fundamental way dehumanizes the persons portrayed and, as a consequence, the viewers themselves. By limiting the type of social harm underlying the criminal prohibition to dehumanization, Wilson J. recognized an essential requirement for principled adjudication. The harm principle cannot operate as a precise and justified barometer of legitimacy when there is a choice of available harms, such as the harm involved in causing crime, corrupting morals, advocating misogyny or damaging the quality of life.[93] When the harm principle is used this way, as it was by the majority, it loses its coherency. Wilson J.'s analysis focuses on fundamental human rights concerns of human dignity and equality, both of which can be evaluated in terms of the values of a free and democratic society which has equality as a constitutional guarantee.

Wilson J.'s characterization of harm sets up a new paradigm for the pornography debate. Most of the literature criticizing obscenity laws has focused on pornography's effect on women. As women are the primary victims of pornography, this emphasis is correct. The degradation that men experience is more modest and less harmful to their role in a society that they dominate. Yet, if we want to think about pornography in terms of how it presents human sexuality, Wilson J.'s approach can make us more aware that the problem is one of the relationship between the sexes. The "flip side" of degradation and dehumanization of women in pornography is the stereotype of males as cruel, inexhaustible sexual predators driven by a ceaseless need for purely physical satisfaction. In this sense, her analysis requires us to think about pornography more broadly and contextually than the directions provided by any other judgments on pornography to date. Her requirement (in dissent, McIntyre J. concurring) that some evidence of community standards, expert or otherwise, must be adduced by the Crown is a good one. If evidence of

---

93   This argument is presented in a different context by A. Young, in "News From the Front — The War on Obscenity and the Death of Doctrinal Purity" (1987), 25 O.H.L.J. 305 at 320.

undueness was a requirement, less subjective decisions by judges on questions of undueness would result and, at the same time, those who are degraded, dehumanized or objectified by pornography would be empowered by the opportunity to describe its effects.[94]

Although the *Towne Cinema* decision significantly changed the law of obscenity, more clarification is needed. The only conclusive points the court made were evidentiary ones — the objectivity of the community standards test and the irrelevance of audience. While the court implied that the objective of obscenity legislation is to protect society from the dehumanization of certain vulnerable groups, the definition of obscenity, the uniqueness of the community standards test and the necessity of adducing evidence of community standards are still ambiguous because they lack a clear majority.[95] The ambiguities will make any future constitutional analysis of the equality interests in obscenity more difficult.

In summary, at the liability stage of analysis, significant steps have been taken by the judiciary towards the reconstruction of obscenity law. Changes have been made to the community standards test, the definition of obscenity and the characterization of its harms. Unfortunately, the gender-neutral morality rationale is still used to define and justify obscenity laws. This has the effect of downgrading the importance of the gender-specific equality issues which define pornography concretely and specifically for what it depicts and communicates. Unless the underlying rationale for the law is clearly stated as being equality-based, obscenity jurisprudence will continue to be inconsistent, unpredictable and unclear, and the law will be vulnerable to constitutional challenges.

III. THE CONSTITUTIONAL ANALYSIS[96]

Freedom of expression has long been recognized as an essential feature of political and personal freedom. It is constitutionally protected

---

94 B. Baines, annotation, *Towne Cinema Theatres Ltd. v. R.* (1985), 45 C.R. (3d) at 6; note also discussion in the text associated with notes 64 to 68.

95 *Supra*, note 11 at 4 and 5.

96 This analysis is adopted from one developed by a subcommittee of the legal committee of the Women's Legal Education and Action Fund for argument in the trilogy of hate propaganda cases, *R. v. Keegstra* (1985), 19 C.C.C. (3d) 254, reversed 60 Alta. L.R. (2d) 1, which was reversed [1991] 2 W.W.R. 1 (S.C.C.); *R. v. Andrews* (1988), 28 O.A.C. 161, affirmed 75 O.R. (2d) 481n (S.C.C.); *Can. (Canadian Human Rights Commission) v. Taylor* (1987), 37 D.L.R. (4th) 577, affirmed 75 D.L.R. (4th) 577 (S.C.C.), argued before the Supreme Court of Canada in December 1989. The committee members were Helena Orton, Catherine MacKinnon, Linda Taylor, Leslie Hardy, Elizabeth Lennon and the author.

by s. 2(b) of the *Canadian Charter of Rights and Freedoms* which reads:[97]

> 2. Everyone has the following fundamental freedoms:
>
> (b) freedom of thought, belief, opinion and expression, including freedom of the press and other media of communication.

In order to determine the constitutionality of obscenity laws, the scope of freedom of expression in the *Canadian Charter of Rights and Freedoms* must be examined. It is argued here that the obscenity laws do not violate the *Charter*, because the type of expression they prohibit is not protected by the *Charter of Rights and Freedoms*. It either does not qualify as expression within the meaning of s. 2(b) or, in the alternative, if pornographic speech is protected by s. 2(b), the obscenity provisions are nevertheless constitutional because they constitute limits that comport with those set out in s. 1 of the *Charter* which reads:[98]

> 1. The *Canadian Charter of Rights and Freedoms* guarantees the rights and freedoms set out in it subject only to such reasonable limits prescribed by law as can be demonstrably justified in a free and democratic society.

The Supreme Court of Canada set out the general approach for determining *Charter* violations by holding that the scope of a right or freedom is determined by examining the purpose of the guarantee in light of the interest it was intended to protect.[99] More particularly, to be examined were the character and larger objects of the *Charter* itself; the language chosen to articulate the specific right or freedom; the historical origin of the concepts enshrined; and, where applicable, the meaning and purpose of other specific rights and freedoms within the text of the *Charter* with which it is associated.[100]

On the latter point, the two provisions in the *Charter* which are brought into play by the question of whether the freedom of expression guarantee protects pornography are the guarantees against the denial of equality on the basis of sex, ss. 15 and 28. They read as follows:[101]

> 15.(1) Every individual is equal before and under the law and has the right to the equal protection and equal benefit of the law without discrimination and, in particular, without discrimination based on

---

97   *Supra*, note 2.
98   *Ibid.*
99   *R. v. Big M Drug Mart Ltd.* (1985), 18 C.C.C. (3d) 385 (S.C.C.)[Alta.].
100 *Ibid.*, at 424.
101 *Supra*, note 2.

race, national or ethnic origin, colour, religion, sex, age or mental or physical disability.

(2) Subsection (1) does not preclude any law, program or activity that has as its object the amelioration of conditions of disadvantaged individuals or groups including those that are disadvantaged because of race, national or ethnic origin, colour, religion, sex, age or mental or physical disability.

28. Notwithstanding anything in this Charter, the rights and freedoms referred to in it are guaranteed equally to male and female persons.

The way courts have defined and classified obscenity indicates that, for purposes of constitutional analysis, the issue will be whether or not women's equality rights, as protected by obscenity laws, are appropriate limits on freedom of expression.

In framing the constitutional issue as one of equality versus freedom of expression, it is argued that obscenity laws which prohibit such depictions protect and promote equality and, as such, should be supported by s. 15 of the *Charter.* If the proposition that pornography, in and of itself, is a "practice" of inequality is accepted, then, for the purposes of constitutional analysis, provisions such as obscenity laws which provide protection from such practices arguably rate special constitutional consideration prior to any consideration under s. 1.

On the freedom of expression side of the analysis, it is clear that the freedom is not absolute. Limits can be placed on the definition of the freedom itself, without going to the reasonable limits balance under s. 1 of the *Charter.*[102] In the pre-*Charter* case, *Fraser v. Public Service Staff Relations Board,*[103] Dickson C.J.C. stated:

All important values must be qualified, and balanced against, other important, and often competing, values. This process of definition, qualification and balancing is as much required with respect to the value of "freedom of speech" as it is for other values. . .

Sometimes these other values supplement, and build on, the value of speech. But in other situations there is a collision. When that happens the value of speech may be cut back if the competing value is a powerful one.

There is no question that equality is a powerful value in Canadian society. The Supreme Court of Canada identified equality as one of the underlying values of a free and democratic society and the ultimate

---

102 *Operation Dismantle Inc. v. R.*, [1985] 1 S.C.R. 441 at 489; *Jones v. R.*, [1986] 2 S.C.R. 284 at 300 [Alta.].
103 [1985] 2 S.C.R. 455 at 463, 467-68.

standard against which the objects of all legislation must be measured.[104]
It has said that s. 15 is the broadest of all guarantees in the *Charter*,
applying to and supporting all other rights guaranteed by the *Charter*.[105]
In *R. v. Big M Drug Mart Ltd.*[106] Dickson C.J.C. stated:[107] "A free society
is one which aims at equality with respect to the enjoyment of fundamental freedoms and I say this without any reliance upon section 15 of
the *Charter*." This suggests that the value of equality is embedded within
s. 2(b) without reliance upon s. 15. When read with s. 15, the conclusion
is inescapable that freedom of expression must be interpreted in a
manner which accommodates equality rights. This is further supported
by s. 28 which requires that all freedoms and rights in the *Charter* are
guaranteed equally to women and men. Pornographic expression which
causes harm to the social status and concrete interests of women negates
and limits their equality rights, which ss. 15 and 28 affirm as fundamental values of Canadian society. Moreover, free speech rights will be
allocated unequally unless the social discrimination caused by pornography is considered in the determination of the scope of s. 2(b)
protection.[108] As Professor Michelman points out, if pornography
causes grave harms to the social status and concrete interests of many
women, then it also creates difficulty for women trying to make themselves credibly and effectively heard in any social or political cause,
including that of protest against pornography itself. In that sense, he
says pornography also silences women.[109]

A similar view was expressed by Quigley J. in *R. v. Keegstra*[110] in the
context of hate propaganda. He stated:

> ... s. 281.2(2) of the *Code* cannot rationally be considered to be an
> infringement which limits "freedom of expression", but on the con-
> trary it is a safeguard which promotes it. The protection afforded by the
> proscription tends to banish the apprehension which might otherwise
> inhibit certain segments of our society from freely expressing them-
> selves upon the whole spectrum of topics, whether social, economic,
> scientific, political, religious or spiritual in nature.

---

104 *R. v. Oakes, supra,* note 6.
105 In *Andrews v. Law Society of British Columbia, supra,* note 7 at 154, the court
stated: "s. 15 is designed to protect those groups who suffer social, political and
legal disadvantage in our society."
106 *Supra,* note 99.
107 *Ibid.,* at 336.
108 See discussion in the text associated with notes 51 to 55.
109 Frank I. Michelman, "Conceptions of Democracy in American Constitutional
Argument: The Case of Pornography Regulation" (1989), 56 Tennessee L. Rev.
291 at 295-96.
110 *Supra,* note 96 at 258, 268. The Supreme Court of Canada held that the section
did infringe s. 2(b) of the *Charter,* but that the infringement was a reasonable
limit under s. 1.

That equality rights are protected and promoted by obscenity laws is implicit in the classifications describing pornography. In a recent District Court judgment, the three classifications of pornography were summarized by Charron J.:[111]

(1) sexually explicit pornography with violence including the overt use of force, the infliction of pain or the threat of force where women are almost always the victims and are frequently portrayed as enjoying abuse;

(2) sexually explicit depictions without violence but dehumanizing or degrading where characters are verbally abused or treated as animals. Examples are where the participants are led on a leash, urinated upon, ejaculated upon, etc. Women are usually the victims of the abuse and are often portrayed as enjoying it. Women are usually depicted as sexually insatiable, and no matter what their training or professional status, their sole purpose and worth is measured by their physical attributes and their ability to satisfy the sexual needs of men;

(3) sexually explicit erotica which portrays positive, affectionate human sexual interaction between consenting individuals participating on a basis of equality.

A clear statement describing the discriminatory effects of pornography is found in the Report on Pornography by the Standing Committee on Justice and Legal Affairs (MacGuigan Report):[112]

The effect of this type of material is to reinforce male-female stereotypes to the detriment of both sexes. It attempts to make degradation, humiliation, victimization, and violence in human relationships appear normal and acceptable. A society which holds that egalitarianism, non-violence, consensualism, and mutuality are basic to any human interaction, whether sexual or other, is clearly justified in controlling and prohibiting any medium of depiction, description or advocacy which violates these principles.

The extent to which harm to women will have to be proved in order to tip the constitutional balance in favour of upholding obscenity laws will have to be determined.

Numerous social science studies and commissions have reported

---

111 *R. v. Fringe Product Inc.* (1990), 53 C.C.C. (3d) 422 at 433 (Ont. Dist.Ct.), but were first set out in *R. v. Wagner, supra*, note 49. Neither court found erotica to be obscene.

112 Standing Committee on Justice and Legal Affairs, *Report on Pornography* (MacGuigan Report) (Ottawa: 1978), at 18:4.

on the specific effects of pornography.[113] While hundreds of studies indicate that pornography reinforces sexual attitudes and behaviour antithetical to equality rights and contributes to the perpetuation of violent and dangerous behaviour, the same causal and methodological problems arise in this kind of research as in research which attempts to positively prove that alcohol causes traffic deaths or smoking causes cancer. The links are suggestive, but none of them are dispositive. Uncertainty as to the nature and extent of the link, however, should not be enough to make obscenity laws unconstitutional. Evidence of potentially serious harm has justified government regulation of the tobacco and alcohol industries, as well as many others where health and safety are concerned. The effects of pornography on women should be of no less concern when so much evidence suggestive of harm exists.[114]

Consequently, social science data will be helpful to courts in establishing the effect of pornography on women's equality rights, but not determinative. As Charron J. correctly pointed out in the *Fringe Products* case, "the question is not one that can be resolved simply by an assessment of the social scientific data," since there is no requirement that courts adopt a narrow criminological perspective of harm. Evidence demonstrating that exposure to pornographic material produces scientifically measurable harm to society, based on a causative link between exposure to such material and the commission of particular crimes, is not necessary to support government regulation.

Charron J.'s broad view of harm is consistent with the Supreme Court's pronouncements in *Towne Cinema*, where it implicitly found that obscenity is harmful when it promotes inequality through depictions which are degrading, dehumanizing and objectifying to the participants in it.[115] Clearly, our Supreme Court disagrees with those who argue that freedom of expression may not be limited absent scientifically proven direct and demonstrable harm.[116] Like Wilson J., Charron J.

---

113 For example, see Metro Toronto Task Force on Public Violence Against Women and Children, *Final Report* (1984), at 74; Diane E.H. Russell, "Pornography and Rape: A Causal Model" (1988), 9 Political Psychology 41; "Pornography and Violence: What Does the New Research Say?" in Lederer (ed.), *Take Back the Night, supra*, note 5 at 218; N. Malamuth and E. Donnerstein (eds.), *Pornography and Sexual Aggression* (Orlando, Fla.: Academic Press 1984); D.L. Mosher and H. Katz, "Pornographic Films, Male Verbal Aggression Against Women, and Guilt," in *Technical Report of the Commission on Obscenity and Pornography*, vol. 8 (Washington, D.C.: U.S. Government Printing Office, 1971); M. McManus (ed.), *Final Report of the Attorney General's Commission on Pornography* (Nashville: Rutledge Hill Press, 1986).
114 *Ibid.*
115 *Supra*, note 11.
116 See, *e.g.*, H.L.A. Hart, *Law, Liberty and Morality* (Stanford: Stanford Univer-

examined pornography in the context of "a society where gender inequality and sexual violence exist as a social problem," ruling that the harm of pornography is a pressing and substantial concern.[117]

A similar but stronger view of the harm of pornography was expressed in the American decision of Easterbrook J. in *American Booksellers Association v. Hudnut*, where he stated:[118]

> [P]ornography affects thoughts. Men who see women depicted as subordinate are more likely to treat them so. Pornography is an aspect of dominance. It does not persuade people so much as change them. It works by socializing, by establishing the expected and the permissible. In this view, pornography is not an idea; pornography is the injury . . .
>
> Depiction of subordination tends to perpetuate subordination. The subordinate status of women in turn leads to affront and lower pay at work, insult and injury at home, battery and rape on the streets.

Easterbrook J. went further than the Supreme Court of Canada when he suggested that pornography is much more than representational material depicting the subordination of women. His words indicate that pornography does not just subordinate women representationally, it does so actually.[119]

As it is overwhelmingly women who are portrayed in pornographic depictions, the proposition that obscenity promotes inequality based on gender is very difficult to dispute.

The contextualized approach to equality adopted by the Supreme Court in the *Andrews* case[120] will be helpful in establishing that pornography promotes disadvantage to women as a group and, as such, is a

---

sity Press, 1963); Canadian Civil Liberties Association, "Pornography and the Law, Submission to the Special Committee on Pornography and Prostitution" (April 6, 1984); C. Beckton, "Obscenity and Censorship Re-Examined Under the Charter of Rights" (1983), 13 Man. L.J. 351; A. Young, *supra*, note 93.

117 *Supra*, note 11 at 33.

118 771 F. 2d 323 at 328-29 (7th Circ., 1985), affirmed 475 U.S. 1001, rehearing denied 475 U.S. 1132 (1986).

119 This view has been put forward by leading feminist theorists such as C. MacKinnon, *supra*, note 5; S. Brownmiller, *Against our Will: Men, Women and Rape* (New York: Simon and Schuster, 1975), at 441-45; A. Dworkin, *supra*, note 5. In spite of this strong conclusion about the injurious nature of pornography, Easterbrook J. and the rest of the Court of Appeal for the Seventh Circuit proceeded to deny that any governmental effort to censor pornography on the grounds of harm to women as a class asserted in the case could possibly withstand a constitutional challenge. For a comprehensive critique of the judgment, see Penellope Seator, "Judicial Indifference to Pornography's Harm: *American Booksellers v. Hudnut*" (1987), 17 Golden Gate University L. Rev. 297.

120 *Supra*, note 7.

practice of discrimination. If courts follow the direction of the Supreme Court in *R. v. Turpin*,[121] the assessment will involve an inquiry into the larger social, political, and legal context of women's experience. When pornography of the violent and cruel or degrading and dehumanizing variety is assessed in the context of stereotyping, historical disadvantage or vulnerability to political and social prejudice, the broader discriminatory effects of pornography will be easier to demonstrate, and freedom of speech in pornography will be seen as a false freedom — one which is based on denying freedom to its victims.[122]

The scope of the freedom of expression guarantee and its interrelationship with equality interests cannot be determined solely on a mutual accommodation approach, however. Since the Supreme Court's decision in *Irwin Toy Ltd. v. Quebec*,[123] further analysis is needed.

A. Content Regulation

In the *Irwin Toy* decision, the Supreme Court of Canada enunciated a test to be used to determine whether any particular activity is protected by s. 2(b) of the *Charter*. At issue was the constitutional validity of provincial consumer protection legislation prohibiting advertising directed at children under 13 years of age. It was argued that the legislation constituted an unwarranted infringement of expression as guaranteed by s. 2(b). In deciding whether or not this form of commercial speech was protected by s. 2(b), Dickson C.J.C. set out a test as follows:[124]

> ... the first step in the analysis is to determine whether the plaintiff's activity falls within the sphere of conduct protected by the guarantee. Activity which (1) does not convey or attempt to convey a meaning, and thus has no *content* of expression or (2) which conveys a meaning but through a violent *form* of expression, is not within the protected sphere of conduct. [emphasis Dickson C.J.C.'s]

The test makes it quite clear that certain forms of expression, such as violence, will fall outside the scope of the protection of s. 2(b). However, it does not exhaustively describe or list all the forms of expression that are not protected. For example, in *Irwin Toy* the court did not have to consider forms of expression that impinge upon or violate other entrenched constitutional rights. It only had to consider

---

121 *R. v. Turpin, supra*, note 7.
122 As recognized by Quigley J. in *R. v. Keegstra, supra*, note 96 at 268.
123 [1989] 1 S.C.R. 927. See also the more recent decision of the court in *Reference Re Criminal Code, ss. 193 & 195.1(1)(c)* (1990), 77 C.R. (3d) 1 (S.C.C.)[Man.].
124 *Irwin Toy, ibid.*, at 978.

commercial speech. The argument could be made that the violation of constitutionally entrenched interests such as equality should be given equal status with "violence" in determining whether constitutional freedom of expression is violated.

If the court decides to use the concept of "form" as distinct from "content" in the same way American courts have used the speech/action distinction, it will be a backward step. In the United States, the speech/action distinction has led to a doctrinal morass which has caused more confusion than clarity in the American law.[125] In their strict adherence to the instrumentalist and consequentialist approach which is based on the assumption that there is a positive correlation between ideological openness and long-term individual liberty, American courts consistently hold the view that restrictions on expression based on message or viewpoint are constitutionally indefensible. Thus, any attempted restriction on pornography, because it promulgates a "view" (albeit one harmful to women) cannot be suppressed.

What the speech/action distinction does not permit is an evaluation of the social meaning of pornography. It requires a defence on neutral ground. This neutrality reduces society's responsibility for the result being reached, and protects freedom of expression as an empty process. No consideration as to whether or not free speech might have the result of denying the freedoms of others is available to the courts.[126]

Unless the Supreme Court means to adopt the rigid and empty speech/action test, *Irwin Toy* cannot mean that everything with a content or meaning absent physical violence is protected expression. If it does, such forms of expression as advocacy of child sexual abuse, bribery, sexual harassment, conspiracy and treason would be protected speech.

Furthermore, words can take on form and become acts — coercive acts, discriminatory acts and criminal acts. Other words can also amount to violent acts. For example, saying "kill" to a trained guard dog — although purely linguistic — is as much an act as throwing a rock through a window or pulling the trigger on a gun.[127] Similarly, telling someone they are fired because of their religious beliefs — although linguistically expressed — is a discriminatory act, as is posting a sign that says "Whites Only."[128] Just because these acts consist of words which convey meaning should not mean that they automatically fall within the protective ambit of s. 2(b). While some pornographic depictions do

---

125 See Michelman, *supra*, note 109.
126 See discussion in L. Bollinger, *The Tolerant Society: Freedom of Speech and Extremist Speech in America* (New York: Oxford University Press, 1986), at 241.
127 C. MacKinnon, *Feminism Unmodified, supra*, note 5 at 156.
128 *Ibid.*

produce immediate physical violence — to the models in them[129] — others do not. Nevertheless, the restrictions on pornographic depictions which amount to acts of discrimination should not violate s. 2(b).[130] If they did, it would make a mockery of the *Charter* and contradict the court's earlier pronouncements on the definition of rights and the purposive analysis that should inform *Charter* interpretation.[131]

Another of the uncertainties about the *Irwin Toy* test is the meaning of the word "violent." Does it mean direct physical violence or does it have a more nuanced meaning? It obviously includes tactics capable of effecting ideological change such as terror, bombings and other violent direct action. Enforcement of inequality, whether by governmental action or by other forms of social control, is not always violent in the usual physical sense, but it is nonetheless effective and coercive. Dehumanization and degradation arguably exist on the soft end of a violence continuum, the other end being physical violence. Violence is often the way inequality is enforced — as it is against women in the form of pornography, sexual harassment, battering and sexual assault. It may only be necessary to represent that violence in pornographic material to exclude and silence women, thereby enforcing their inequality in relation to men. When inequality is imposed through group defamation, as described by the Standing Committee on Justice and Legal Affairs,[132] its effects include reputational harm — not a violent effect, but nonetheless one that is integral to the maintenance of group disadvantage.

In order to rationalize these problems within the *Irwin Toy* test, the "violent form" criteria must be interpreted as a continuum of regulation applicable to s. 2(b) ranging from communication of ideas that amount to acts on the one hand, and violence, including "violent forms" of expression, on the other. This approach is a much more advanced, nuanced and practical one than the American speech/action distinction.

---

129 In *American Booksellers, supra*, note 118, extensive evidence of harm to women participating in the production of pornography was adduced. See also Public Hearings on Ordinance to All Pornography as Discrimination Against Women, Committee on Government Operations, City Council, Minneapolis, Minn. (December 12-13, 1983). The testimony before the hearings also included social science evidence of pornography's harm.

130 These would consist of those depictions described by Anderson J. in *R. v. Red Hot Video, supra*, note 74 where he stated at 59:

"If true equality between male and female persons is to be achieved it would be quite wrong in my opinion to ignore the threat to equality resulting from the exposure to male audiences of the violent and degrading material described above. As I have said, such material has a tendency to make men more tolerant of violence to women and creates a social climate encouraging men to act in a callous and discriminatory way towards women."

131 See *Andrews v. Law Society of British Columbia, supra*, note 7; *R. v. Big M Drug Mart, supra*, note 99.

132 See the text associated with note 101 *et seq.*

It would allow pornography to be analyzed as a form of discrimination. It would not be viewed as the mere expression of an opinion, nor would it always be viewed as physical violence. Rather, it would be seen as a violent form of expression — the violence ranging from immediate subordination to well documented consequent physical conduct. Viewed as an act which furthers the social definition of women as less than fully human, defined as inferior on the basis of their sex, pornography would be seen as a harm in and of itself as has already been recognized by the courts.[133] Therefore, it could be argued that obscenity laws criminalize pornography not because of its content *per se*, but because of its effect on social life.

The next step in the *Irwin Toy* test is to examine the purpose and effect of the impugned legislation. The legislation will infringe s. 2(b) of the *Charter* if its purpose "is to restrict the content of expression by singling out particular meanings that are not to be conveyed"[134] or if its effect is to restrict the plaintiff's free expression. However, if the plaintiff falls into this category, the onus is on the plaintiff to establish that the activity in question is consonant with one or more of the functions of the freedom of expression guarantee.[135]

As a result of judicial interpretation of the obscenity laws, it is clear that the legislative objective of s. 163(1)(a) is to protect society from the dehumanization of certain vulnerable groups and, in turn, the dehumanization of society as a whole. This is certainly implied in the *Towne Cinema* case where the Supreme Court stated that the definition of "undue" must encompass publications harmful to members of society:[136]

> Even if certain sex-related materials were found to be within the standard of tolerance of the community, it would still be necessary to ensure that they were not "undue" in some other sense, for example, in the sense that they portray persons in a degrading manner as objects of violence, cruelty, or other forms of dehumanizing treatment.

In other words, the clear purpose of the section, as interpreted by the Supreme Court, is to promote equality and protect persons from degrading and dehumanizing treatment, not to restrict expression. In

---

133 *E.g., R. v. Wagner, supra*, note 49; *R. v. Doug Rankine Co., supra*, note 30; *R. v. Red Hot Video, supra*, note 74; *R. v. Towne Cinema, supra*, note 11; *R. v. Fringe Products, supra*, note 111.

134 *Supra*, note 12 at 974.

135 *Ibid.*, at 978-79.

136 *Supra*, note 11 at 15. The court in the *Fringe Products* case, *supra*, note 111, examined the purpose of the obscenity legislation and expressly came to the same finding.

this way, obscenity law is aimed at controlling the consequences of particular conduct, not expression as such.

When it comes to the third part of the *Irwin Toy* test, which is assessing the values and functions of the freedom of expression guarantee in light of the impugned expression, it is difficult to see how pornography can satisfy the test.

The principles or values underlying the protection of freedom of expression were summarized in *Irwin Toy* as follows:

(i) seeking and attaining the truth;
(ii) participation in social and political decision-making;
(iii) individual self-fulfilment and human flourishing.

The expression of pornography is antithetical to the reasons expression is protected. Rather than seeking and attaining the truth, pornography inhibits truth-seeking because it intimidates and silences women, preventing them from asserting the truth. It is hardly persuasive to argue that opinions advocating the sexual torture or degradation of women in pornography can contribute to truth-seeking. While it could be argued that pornography may be of value through educating the population about misogyny, it is far from clear that an open confrontation with pornography in the marketplace of ideas leads to a richer belief in the truth. It is more likely that the opposite result occurs. Debasement of women in pornographic magazines, books, movies, films or television, on street corner newsstands, on covers of record albums and in shop windows is an ever-increasing phenomenon. Three surveys indicate that sales of pornographic magazines in Canada increased by 326.7 per cent between 1965 and 1980. This represents an increase of at least 14 times the growth of the Canadian population during the same period.[137] Furthermore, the messages in pornography that women and children are sex objects available to be violated, coerced and subordinated at the will of men is replicated in real life statistics which are also increasing at a very rapid rate. Widespread sexual assault, wife battery, sexual harassment and sexual abuse of children[138] indicate that the competing idea, that women as human beings are equal to men and that children must be treated with dignity and respect, is not emerging from the marketplace

---

137 *Badgley Report, supra*, note 50.
138 See Department of Justice, *Special Committee on Pornography and Prostitution, supra*, note 35; L. Clark and D. Lewis, *supra*, note 50 at 61 which states that incidents of rape increased by 174 per cent between 1961 and 1971 in Canada. In the period 1969-1973, it increased 76 per cent. Armstrong, *supra*, note 50, states that one woman in ten is beaten by her husband or common-law spouse; *Badgley Report, supra*, note 50 at 180-83, states that 50 per cent of women and 30 per cent of men are victims of unwanted sexual acts, incidents occurring before adulthood.

in any significant way. The "value" of pornography as a truth-seeking device in these terms ranges from remote to none. In light of the facts of abuse and subordination of women and children, it makes no sense to suggest that the uninhibited activity of pornographers is important to maintaining a belief that what they have to say is wrong. Rather than serving as a means to discover truth, pornography conceals the truth about women and takes away or chills their speech through a system of sexism.[139]

If one looks at other areas of social life where the primary objective is the pursuit of truth, the untampered "marketplace of ideas" is not the model used. In the criminal justice system, for example, speech is recognized as being important to the goal of learning the truth, but at the same time its potential to undermine the truth is clearly recognized. Parties may present their arguments as they wish, but speech that is "inflammatory," or highly emotive, may be excluded because of its potential prejudicial effects on the judgment of the judge or jury. In other words, it is recognized that certain forms of speech can undermine the truth. In the case of highly emotive hate speech[140] directed against minorities and women, where the speech seeks to subvert the truth-seeking process itself, a forceful argument can be made that the interests of seeking truth work against, rather than in favour of, speech,[141] and the values relied upon to support freedom of speech lose their force.

Pornography is also antithetical to the other values and purposes underlying the freedom of expression guarantee. Rather than encouraging community participation, pornography restricts social and political participation of women by undermining respect for them. If individuals who traffic in and consume pornography are fulfilled, it is at the expense of the rights of others. Human flourishing cannot be said to be encouraged by material which harms people.

In conclusion, the scope of s. 2(b) of the *Charter* should not extend to pornography because it is a violent form of expression, the purpose of the legislation is to provide protection from certain forms of conduct, and the content of pornography is inconsistent with the reasons freedom of speech is protected. As the obscenity provisions protect and promote equality, they deserve special constitutional consideration prior to consideration under s. 1 of the *Charter*.

---

139 MacKinnon, *supra*, note 5 at 205-206.
140 In *R. v. Andrews, supra*, note 96 at 78, Cory J. described hatred as "one of the most extreme emotions known to human kind."
141 *Supra*, note 126 at 57-58.

B. The Section 1 Balance

Alternatively, if the courts find pornography to be protected by s. 2(b), obscenity laws should be upheld under s. 1. The function of s. 1 is to balance tensions between harms. When obscenity laws collide with the freedom of expression guarantee, the tension is between harms that flow from regulating expression by obscenity laws and harms actualized through the promotion of women's inequality in pornography. In deciding on the proper balance, courts must be guided by the values and principles essential to a free and democratic society which include respect for the inherent dignity of the human person, commitment to social justice and equality, accommodation of a wide variety of beliefs, respect for cultural and group identity, and faith in social and political institutions which enhance the participation of individuals and groups in society.[142] The courts have recognized that it is sometimes necessary to limit rights and freedoms in circumstances where their exercise would be contrary to the realization of collective goals of fundamental importance. Pornography is such a case.

In a society where gender inequality and sexual violence exist as social problems,[143] legislation which guards against material which attempts to make degradation, humiliation, victimization and violence in human relationships appear normal and acceptable[144] would be more in line with principles of a free and democratic society than otherwise.

Moreover, in *Irwin Toy*, the court distinguished between situations where the government mediates between different groups with competing interests and those situations where government is the singular antagonist of the individual whose right has been infringed. Pornographers always cast themselves as victims of government oppression, when in reality the products they produce, distribute and sell, show them to be aggressors in a social conflict between groups. It could be said that obscenity laws advance the interests of women, while pornographers advance the interests of the dominant male group by subordinating women. Pornography laws should therefore be viewed as Parliament's reasonable assessment as to where a line should be drawn between competing interests. In prohibiting the undue exploitation of sex interpreted as violent, degrading and dehumanizing depictions, Parliament has struck a reasonable balance and courts should not second-guess that assessment. It follows that the relative burdens of the parties under s. 1 should be assessed in a mediation context. Pornographers should have to justify limiting the equality rights of women,

---

142 *R. v. Oakes, supra*, note 6, *per* Dickson C.J.C.
143 *Supra*, note 111 at 444.
144 See the discussion in the text associated with note 101 *et seq.*

just as the Crown should have to justify limiting freedom of expression in Canada.

Unlike in the United States, state intervention is not seen as inherently evil in Canada. Sometimes it is required to enhance and achieve the desired goals of the *Charter*. As noted by Dickson C.J.C. in *Reference re Public Service Employee Relations Act (Alta.)*,[145] the notion of "rights" imposes a corresponding duty or obligation on another party to ensure the protection of the right. This pronouncement is consistent with the decision in *Edwards Books*,[146] where the Supreme Court wanted to avoid use of the *Charter* by better situated individuals as an instrument to roll back legislation which has as its object the improvement of the condition of less advantaged persons.

In the case of *Slaight Communications*,[147] the Supreme Court addressed the relationships between free expression and equality, recognizing that under s. 1 an equality interest can outweigh a s. 2 right. The court said that it was concerned to avoid constitutionalizing inequality of power in the workplace and between societal actors in general. The court's observation that "constitutionally protecting freedom of expression would be tantamount to condonation of an abuse of an already unequal relationship," should apply equally to pornography.[148]

In summary, when an equality analysis is used to determine what is a reasonable limit prescribed by law in the context of a free and democratic society, courts allow the government to alleviate the harmful effects of discrimination. From an equality perspective, the means chosen by Parliament to alleviate discrimination through obscenity laws are rationally connected to the objectives of protecting society from dehumanization and degradation. The limitations which the obscenity laws place on expression minimally impair the freedom because pornography is contrary to the principles and values which underlie its protection. Any limit on freedom of expression is slight when compared with the deleterious effect pornography has on women and on society as a whole. An equality analysis further recognizes that the legislative action to deter degradation and dehumanization of people, especially women, goes some way to redress the imbalance of power between the sexes.

---

145 [1987] 1 S.C.R. 313 at 361.
146 *R. v. Edwards Books and Art Ltd.*, [1986] 2 S.C.R. 713 at 752 [Ont.].
147 *Slaight Communications Inc. v. Davidson*, [1989] 1 S.C.R. 1038 at 1056.
148 Dickson C.J.C., writing for the majority of the court in *Keegstra, supra*, note 96, accepted LEAF's submission that the promotion of hatred should be understood as a practice of inequality which also violated s. 15 of the *Charter*. The court accepted that an equality analysis was appropriate in deciding whether the hate propaganda law was a reasonable limit on freedom of expression.

C. Conclusion

Canadian judges are in the process of challenging existing thought about the law of obscenity and about the constitutional protection of freedom of expression. The perimeters of the discussion are changing, and previously hidden underlying issues are being exposed. The obscenity issue is being reframed in equality terms and is being defended as such in constitutional litigation. The question of harm is starting to be addressed in a way that recognizes women's experience of inequality and subordination. Even though there is some distance to go in resolving all of the problems inherent in the law of obscenity, no other jurisdiction in the western world has made the progress or demonstrated the vision and commitment to equality that Canadian judges have on this difficult question.

Canaries were, and sometimes still are, used in coal mines to warn miners of harmful and often lethal substances lurking in their midst which are difficult to detect.[149] Although the analogy with judges is not perfect, the title of this paper was chosen to acknowledge the role of some Canadian judges in their efforts to reconstruct obscenity laws. In order to decide, a judge has to judge. She or he must look at the world around them and be willing to take an occasional chance to challenge conventional practices and precedent. The dark and murky world of pornography presents such a challenge. Insofar as pornography is believed to have noxious impacts on the social world men and women inhabit together, it nevertheless presents a dilemma that both recommends it as a target of regulation as well as something to be protected as politically charged expression. The decisions are not comfortable ones to make. They present the choice of either reflecting society's values or rejecting them and constructing a new vision. Equality is an emerging right, especially for women. Establishing it requires reciprocity of respect and parity of regard for physical dignity and personal integrity. Legal interpretation must be guided by these values and goals and must not further entrench social realities to the contrary if the *Charter*'s mandate of sex equality is to be met. It is hoped that Canadian judges will continue in the direction that has been mapped by a few in deciding what is and is not obscene based on an equality analysis. If they do, women's equality will be enhanced, rather than their inequality entrenched.

---

149 P.W. Thrush, *A Dictionary of Mining, Mineral and Related Terms* (Washington, D.C.: U.S. Bureau of Mines, 1968).

MUST WE CENSOR PORNOGRAPHY? CIVIL LIBERTIES AND FEMINIST JURISPRUDENCE

Thelma McCormack

"The scholarly study, which helps lawmakers and judges decide what government may *reasonably* do to regulate the speech and other expression of the nation — this is what God had in mind for them to do when he created political scientists."[1]

Charles S. Hyneman in his
Presidential Address to the
American Political Science Association

I

Freedom of expression, as we understand it in the western democracies, is based on a 17th century concept of a nation-state, an 18th century model of human nature, a 19th century notion of a free market-place in an age of anti-reason, corporate concentration, proliferating public and private bureaucracies, and the decline of the nation-state. Thus, the foundation for s. 2(b) of the *Charter*[2] is weakened at a time when it is being tested more often by neo-conservative law-and-order governments and in new ways by science and culture. In addition to the changing issues, there has been a shift in language as well. We talk less about freedom of expression and more about freedom of communication, less about law and more about legitimation, less about the rights of the speaker and more about the rights of the listener.[3] Whether the emphasis is on speaker or listener, or legitimation or law, the idea of protecting dissident minority opinions or unpopular views or images from arbitrary authority, from the legal coercions of the state, or from

1   Charles S. Hyneman, "Free Speech at What Price?" (1962), LVI, No. 4, American Political Science Review 848.
2   *Canadian Charter of Rights and Freedoms*, Pt. I of the *Constitution Act, 1982*, being Sched. B of the *Canada Act 1982*, 1982 (Eng.), c. 11.
3   Sean MacBride, *Many Voices, One World* (New York: UNESCO, 1980). See also Thelma McCormack, "The MacBride Report in the Context of Liberal and Marxist Ideology: Toward a New Research Agenda," in Walter C. Soderlund and Stuart H. Surlin (eds.), *Media in Latin America and the Caribbean: Domestic and International Perspectives* (Windsor, Ontario: Ontario Cooperative Program in Latin American and Caribbean Studies, 1985).

the "tyranny of the majority," remains one of the cornerstones of any modern democracy. The files of Amnesty International on political prisoners provide all the documentation we need, or could ever want, of the life of a citizen who is silenced by the magistrates in the name of "national security," "moral virtue" or "public safety."

It is inconceivable, then, that freedom of expression would not be entrenched in the *Charter*, despite the concerns of many thoughtful persons that this step challenges the supremacy of Parliament and reflects a further Americanization of Canadian government.[4] And yet, in retrospect, it is not surprising that it happened, considering that at the time we had a Prime Minister from Quebec who had locked horns with Quebec's dictatorial premier, Maurice Duplessis, and who had seen first-hand the harassment of the Jehovah's Witnesses culminating in the *Roncarelli* case.[5] Trudeau could hardly have let the opportunity go by to incorporate into the Constitution a principle that would give Canadians the same rights and protections guaranteed by the *Universal Declaration of Human Rights*,[6] and regarded as fundamental to the free world.

Americans who know the system well and have studied it closely have their own misgivings, because the courts, despite their deference to Jeffersonian principles, have not consistently protected the press or dissident speech.[7] An example is a recent Supreme Court decision to uphold a ruling by the Department of Justice which labelled three National Film Board films on the environment as "foreign propaganda." By some tortured Orwellian logic, the court declared that these labels, far from being pejorative or having any kind of chilling effect, increased the information available to a viewer.[8] Even more cynical are the prosecutions of obscenity under RICO (Racketeer, Influenced and Corrupt Organizations) legislation.[9]

---

4   Clare F. Beckton, "Obscenity and Censorship Re-examined Under the Charter of Rights" (1983), 13 Man. L.J. 350.

5   *Roncarelli v. Duplessis* (1959), 16 D.L.R. (2d) 689 (S.C.C). S. 2(b) of the *Charter* is close to arts. 18 and 19 of the *Universal Declaration of Human Rights* adopted in 1948 by the General Assembly of the United Nations.

6   *Universal Declaration of Human Rights* (General Assembly Resolution 217 (III)), adopted December 10, 1948.

7   David Kairys, "Freedom of Speech," in David Kairys (ed.), *The Politics of Law* (New York: Pantheon, 1982).

8   *Meese v. Keene*, 107 S.Ct. 1862 (1987); Rodney A. Smolla and Stephen A. Smith, "Propaganda, Xenophobia and the First Amendment" (1988), 67 Oregon L.R. 253.

9   Tod R. Eggenberger, "RICO vs. Dealers in Obscene Matter: The First Amendment Battle" (1988), 22:31 Columbia Journal of Law and Social Problems 71-113. A couple in Virginia, Denis and Barbara Pryba, who had previous convictions for obscenity, were prosecuted as racketeers. Denis Pryba was sentenced to three years in jail and fined $75,000. Barbara was given a suspended sentence and fined $200,000. In addition, and of special concern to legal

Social critics, then, have found much to deplore in the class biases, racism and sexism, as well as sexual repression in the reflexes of the courts, in legal history, law school education and the professional culture which generations of judges and lawyers share. Judicial reasoning may be little more than partisan rationalization disguised by abstractions, in which case the only final review may be the judgment of history. Nevertheless, the courts' severest critics have defended the principle of freedom of expression, and have resisted any attempt to devalue or decentre it. However disillusioned we may have become, it will take more than some *outré* deconstructionist scenario to convince us that freedom of expression is merely a narrative, one among competing narratives which has fortuitously enjoyed a privileged position in bourgeois democracies.[10] It is difficult to imagine Salman Rushdie or Jacobo Timmerman or Gabriel Garcia Marquez appreciating this laid-back interpretation. Nor would they find the other extreme any more palatable, the view that denies any distinction between text and deed, between depictions of murder and murder. That, of course, was the view of the Ayatollah Khomeni. It is also the view of Andrea Dworkin, who defines pornography as creating an erection in men. The text and its response are, she says, one and the same:[11]

> The act that obscenity recognizes is erection, and whatever writing produces erection is seen to be obscene — act, not idea — because of what it makes happen. The male sexual response is seen to be involuntary, so there is no experientially explicable division between the material that causes erection and the erection itself.

Catharine MacKinnon holds the same view.[12] Life and art do not imitate each other, she says, "they *are* each other."

It is not that there is no relationship between thought and act, but that it is, within certain limits of our culture and historical consciousness, indeterminate. What the Ayatollah, Dworkin and MacKinnon have in common is their shared assumption of that which is undiscovered. By foreclosing this crucial act of inquiry, they abrogate what makes us human: the ability to think, to inhibit what we know is wrong, to direct our own behaviour, to make moral choices and to reject

---

scholars, they were required to forfeit their business, 11 stores and a warehouse. All of this because of four videotapes and nine magazines.

10 Kate Ellis, "Stories Without Endings: Deconstructive Theory and Political Practice" (1989), 19 Socialist Review 37.

11 Andrea Dworkin, "Against the Male Flood: Censorship, Pornography and Equality" (1985), 8 Harvard Women's L.J. 8.

12 Catharine A. MacKinnon, *Feminism Unmodified* (Cambridge, Mass.: Harvard University Press, 1987), section III.

the range of choices, to learn and to correct. If that quality of mind is a mere and transient liberal fiction, it has offered western civilizations some protection from modern totalitarianism. No one understood the need to maintain the separation of text and deed better than the late Bruno Bettelheim, eminent child psychiatrist, who spoke out against the editing of traditional fairy tales by concerned parents. Bettelheim claimed that the violence of the stories, their giants, witches and terrible tests, contributed to children's social growth and ego strength.[13] The sweetness and light of *Sesame Street* may please parents, but deprive their children of a more robust mental health.

Meanwhile, considering the two limiting cases — the first that makes freedom of expression illusory, the second that merges text with the deed — with less idealism than earlier times, we affirm freedom of expression and its fundamental distinction between text and deed, glossing over some of its flaws because of the terrible political realities of our century.

Hence, the case for exemption from s. 2(b) must be an exceptional one so that we do not frivolously or impulsively, in response to anger, bargain away a freedom that is essential to the polity, to the political process, and to the development of an independent self. The same *caveat* applies to the feminist case. But, in addition, it must show that criminalizing pornography, or any other form of expression, validates women and, as part of a larger program, contributes demonstrably to the achievement of gender equality. Otherwise, the demand for censorship becomes the politics of revenge. Understandable as it may be, given the social history of women, it is still the politics of revenge.

Feminists are not alone in their disenchantment with freedom of expression. Membership in organizations like the American Civil Liberties Union or the Canadian Civil Liberties Association is aging and not being replaced by the best and the brightest. As an ideal, freedom of expression is less persuasive than it was in earlier times. Neither convincing nor visionary, it has become semantically depleted and no longer carries the deeper meanings and rich associations that made it compelling. Its heroic myths have been lost, forgotten if they were ever known, by political scientists who are in the critical theory or political economy tradition where it is dismissed by Marcuse as "repressive tolerance."[14] Others, including many Holocaust survivors, have been embittered by the defense of Nazis. At best, we defend it defensively and selectively. But ask a graduate student in political science to discuss it and he or she will tell you that it is as relevant to modern life as the concept of the "just war" in an age of nuclear warfare.

13 Bruno Bettelheim, *The Uses of Enchantment* (New York: Knopf, 1976).
14 Herbert Marcuse, "Repressive Tolerance" in *A Critique of Pure Tolerance* (Boston: Beacon, 1969).

An example of how strange it has become, or how irrelevant it can be made, is the ongoing study of Canadian attitudes towards civil liberties conducted by Peter Russell and his associates at the University of Toronto and Stanford.[15] Their major concern and hypothesis involves the differentiation between the general public and elites: What are their differences? How consistent are they? But functional elites are elites, and this study owes more to late 19th century anti-democratic theories, to Pareto and equilibrium theory, than it does to Locke or Mill.

Part of the difficulty in understanding why freedom of expression has become a political liability is guilt by association, for the fate of freedom of expression, it seems, is somehow tied to the fate of liberalism. But those who make that association use the term liberalism to cover a wide sweep of European thought since the Reformation: universalism, rationalism, individualism, self-interest, objectivity, utilitarianism, secularism, functionalism, the public/private basis of politics. It has been described as optimistic, pessimistic, determinist, anti-determinist, materialist and idealist, anti-nature and based on nature. Three hundred years covers a lot of intellectual history and a multitude of sins.

Feminist scholars who have come late to this critical demolition of liberalism have benefited from earlier criticism, but have introduced still other objections. Liberalism, in both form and substance, has been instrumental in the oppression of women. Its formalism and Cartesian dichotomies, its preoccupation with individual rights — these are quintessentially male forms of cognition and provide a standard against which women have failed repeatedly, as a group. At the same time, these standards which judge some men and most women as deficient can be used to reconstruct a feminist canon based on subjectivity, gender specificity, conciliatory modes of conflict resolution, and making the personal political.[16] In an effort to validate their own identity, women have had to reject not just the specific claims to superiority of men but the more general intellectual and philosophical frameworks as well.

In the comments that follow, I will look at a series of questions from a feminist perspective on censorship and pornography. Before undertaking this, I should point out that most feminist literature on pornography and censorship starts from an analysis of pornography. Censorship is, or is not, justified depending on how we understand pornography. The approach taken here reverses this and is centred on censorship.

---

15 *E.g.*, P.M. Sniderman, J.F. Fletcher, P.M. Russell and P.E. Titlock, "Political Culture and the Problem of Double Standards: Mass Elite Attitudes Towards Language Rights in the Canadian Charter of Rights and Freedoms" (1989), 22 Can. J. of Pol. Sci. 259.

16 Seyla Benhabib, "On Contemporary Feminist Theory" (Summer 1989), *Dissent*.

However, either way one starts, we still must examine the various relationships between a *patriarchal state*, a *misogynist culture* and a *radical social movement*.[17] Most analyses restrict their focus to only one of these categories.

The contemporary debates on censorship are, more often than not, debates about liberalism, although the term liberalism, as I suggested earlier, is seldom used with any precision. Rather, it is used broadly and with little acknowledgement of its own intellectual history. For those who think of it as a 19th century doctrine, it is the superstructure of capitalism; for others, who know it through 20th century social policies, and encountered it in the aftermath of the Great Depression, it represents social democracy. I am going to suggest that any feminist model of freedom of expression lies in the context of social democracy.

The major argument used by feminists who want to restrict freedom of expression is that freedom of expression — specifically, in the case of pornography — obstructs the achievement of gender equality. Whether or not it does any tangible harm, such as increasing the probability of rape or desensitizing people to rape, remains problematic. But even in the absence of evidence, one can say that women are working against their own best interests when they allow pornography to circulate freely and unchecked by statute. The chances of reaching gender equality are diminished.

I am going to indicate that freedom of expression and equality cannot be separated; they are one. Freedom of expression is a necessary, though not sufficient, condition for the liberation of women; it is essential to the enormously difficult process of finding and maintaining an identity. To diminish freedom of expression restricts women in this process. Inequality undermines freedom of expression, while the ideologies that sustain gender inequality are concepts of gender; whether there are innate gender differences and how these are manifest. One step removed from the presuppositions of sex differences is a set of rationalizations for inequality based on images that devalue women. They may be negative or positive, but the most common are the latter: the perfect wife-mother who feels strong obligations to her family, a woman whose ways of being are more expressive than instrumental and who are handicapped by reproductive functions. Either way, women are less able, according to the myths, to assume responsibility than men because nature or logic has made them dependent. Thus, the 66 cent dollar women earn in the labour force is the result of a dual labour market

17   By misogynist culture I refer to (1) a cluster of images or stereotypes which marginalize women or idealize them (as pure and innocent) or debase them (as impure and too knowing), (2) a group of themes and relationships that emphasize the "natural" or "logical" dependency of women. These can be found in both discursive systems of thought as well as the dramatic.

justified by theories of gender differences and overlaid by evaluative scripts which undermine women's capacities for problem-solving, decision-making and taking charge of their lives. What starts as an imposed dependency becomes "learned helplessness" and a low sense of self-esteem. (The *Sears, Roebuck* case, discussed later, is an example.) In short, however one looks at the problems of gender inequality, there can be no choice between freedom of expression and equality.

But the most difficult and intractable problems around the issue of censorship concern expressions — statements of fact or symbolic representations — that are either non-discursive or based on pseudo-science, and which can only be described as free but hateful expressions of prejudice. The key to dealing with this issue, I suggest, is to distinguish between dissent and prejudice, between freedom and tolerance. Pornography is the prejudice of a patriarchal society and, I believe, it is a mistake to defend it as dissent. If it is to be defended or not, it must be on the basis of tolerance. Like dissent, it tests the limits of the state or society, and like dissent it arises out of social conflict which generates intergroup and class hostilities, but the two should not be confused. My view is that tolerance is a special characteristic of women, not all women and not a property they are born with, but one which is developed as "other."

Finally, I am going to suggest that freedom of expression, both as a means and an end, is the foundation of feminism and does not conflict with other values. The context for it is, however, a social democracy in which women have access to media resources in order to develop their own art, popular culture, science and information. Meanwhile, the resistance to censorship is a conscious political act, although it does not have the same psychological "high" as video-store arson or marches to "take back the night."

In order to understand why we have a crisis about freedom of expression at present, we have to go back in time and briefly examine the role freedom of expression has played in the transformation of our social and cultural life from traditional to modern. The period covered is roughly the first half of the 20th century and prior to the watershed decade of the '60s.

II

Modernism, first cousin of the Enlightenment, dominated this period, and while it included the whole of our social life, its focus was on the issues of science and culture. They more clearly revealed how we understood ourselves and nature. The theatre of the events was the university, where the challenge to freedom of expression was about academic freedom. Whoever controlled the intellectual life of the university, controlled the spirit of the age. Thus, the right to question Biblical versions of the origin of the species and the right to teach Darwinian evolution, the right to read James Joyce or D. H. Lawrence, symbolized a struggle that began at the turn of the century between 19th century religion and 20th century science, between faith and skepticism, between a Victorian cultural elite based on property and a cultural elite based on education.

Starting in the 1920s, modernism won more cases than it lost, and with each of these victories, whether in the court room or class room, the autonomy of modern science free of religious dogma was legitimated and *avant-garde* art acquired aesthetic distinction, no longer denounced by conservative classicists or yahoo critics. Academics, intellectuals and scientists, who constituted a new class, had arrived, and their status was not seriously challenged until the campus protests of the 1960s. When that happened, the banner of the insurgents was "free speech." The student culture of the '60s was a counter-culture which spelled America with a "k" and celebrated "pornopolitics." Its voice was the underground press which purposely provoked authorities and made a statement about the cultural revolution. A cultural revolution, as distinct from an economic or political revolution, was directed against a society whose institutions were built on sexual repression.[18] As one of the slogans of the day put it: where Id goes, Ego follows.

Although the courts played a major role in the process of modernization, they remained themselves suspicious of the arts, and cast a cold eye on imagination, *Eros* and, more generally, the Pleasure Principle. Political and judicial theory had not caught up with the new social sciences and continued to regard emotion of any sort as a threat to the proper exercise of citizenship. In the extreme, censorship of pornography was regarded as a necessary evil, according to one theorist, not because of the indecency pornography represented but because of its hedonism which was antithetical to reason.[19] Democracy, like capitalism, it seems, depends on a clear mind, and a clear mind depends on deferred gratification.

Although the courts never went that far, they frequently cautioned us not to go too far or too fast. Freedom of expression was not absolute,

---

18 For a theoretical statement, see Herbert Marcuse, *Eros and Civilization* (New York: Vintage, 1962). For elaborations of these ideas, see: Jerry Hopkins (ed.), *The Hippie Papers: Notes from the Underground Press* (New York: Signet, 1968); Jon and Charlotte Paul, *Fire! Reports from the underground press* (New York: E.P. Dutton, 1970); Mel Howard and the Reverend Thomas King Façade, *The Underground Reader* (New York: Signet, 1972); Editors of *Ramparts, Conversations with Reality* (New York: Colophon, 1971).

19 Harry M. Clor, *Obscenity and Public Morality* (Chicago: University of Chicago Press, 1969).

they said, implying that the arts could not plead creativity or artistic licence, and artists could not expect to have the same near absolute protection given to less dramatic or discursive belief systems. As Harry Kalven once observed, "It is easier to champion freedom for the thought we hate than for the thought that embarrasses."[20] Art students, then, who place the American flag on the floor of a major Chicago gallery, encouraging visitors to walk on it, will get what the current President of the United States thinks they deserve: a constitutional amendment prohibiting any desecration of the flag. But the overall record between the 1920s and the 1960s was a liberalizing trend, with the courts acknowledging the reality of rapid social change, a multiplicity of cultures, and the secular mentality of urban environments.[21] They went further than expected and overrode the elitist assumptions and defense of the new highbrow art with a concept of "community standards."[22] Henceforth, the "undue exploitation of sex" would be determined by ordinary people who understood better than moral leaders, or any other self-appointed guardians, the fabric of their lives.

The populist connotations of community standards pleased neither civil libertarians nor cultural elites. The former saw it as capitulating to majoritarian views, instead of protecting the unpopular minority opinion; the latter saw it as justifying the very philistine standards and uneducated bad taste they had set out to correct. Moralists were angered by its relativism, while feminists rejected it on the grounds that it perpetuated a sexist culture. For a while it worked, and the public, at least, was satisfied.

Community standards appealed to the public because it endowed people with a cultural sovereignty; their common sense and middlebrow tastes were solicited and given new respect. These tastes reflected, and were molded by, a popular culture which itself expressed the ethos of a new urban upwardly-mobile middle-class. The new strata had more leisure, higher levels of education and more discretionary income than any generation previously. Its lifestyles were hardly bohemian, yet it was a transition as each generation became more sophisticated than its parents, and the levels of tolerance were 180 degrees removed from an earlier rural or small-town generation whose reading was mail-order catalogues and whose culture was often regional, oral, and shaped by

---

20 Harry Kalven, Jr., " 'Uninhibited, Robust and Wide Open' a note on free speech and the Warren Court" in Richard H. Sayler, Barry B. Boyer and Robert E. Gooding Jr. (eds.), *The Warren Court* (New York: Chelsea, 1968).

21 Thelma McCormack, "Censorship and 'Community Standards' in Canada" in B. Singer (ed.), *Communications in Canadian Society* (Don Mills: Addison-Wesley, 1983), at 209.

22 *Ibid.*

folk traditions. Community standards recognized the new class and its culture.

Community standards worked also because the large-scale industries that produced and distributed popular culture censored themselves. Broadcasting and motion pictures drew up voluntary codes that specified in detail what was and was not permissible on the air and on the screen. They regulated the use of profane or scatological language as well as verbal innuendo, the extent of nudity, sexual imagery, and the arrangement of bedroom furniture. The self-censorship that concerned Harriet Taylor Mill and John Stuart Mill was now more institutional than individual, but the effect was the same: a bland public culture with few innocuous differences from which to make a choice, and little serious debate.

The continuity of this mass-produced media culture was underwritten by a business system that depended on advertising, and advertising, in turn, depended on offending as few people as possible. Anyone following the discussions in the United States about the fate of Pantheon Press, the press most beloved by academics and intellectuals, will see an example of corporate economics in the publishing world. But it was not profit alone which made these organizations overly cautious. The internal rigidities of aging bureaucracies, what Michels called the "iron law of oligarchy," made them more opaque. Publicly-owned systems like the Canadian Broadcasting Corporation became increasingly unresponsive and non-controversial. Let me give you an example. A former student of mine who had dropped out of graduate school to become a full-time peace activist, was busy organizing an anti-nuke rally by affixing posters to telephone poles announcing the event. With all the risk-taking instincts of youth, and the self-destructive instincts of a martyr, he chose a telephone pole right outside the Toronto Morgentaler clinic, which the police had under 24-hour surveillance. Inevitably, he was charged and, eventually, the case was dismissed, but my defense would have been that the media does not offer small dissident groups an opportunity to promote their causes as Harriet Taylor Mill and John Stuart Mill thought they should. However, 25 years earlier he would have been hired as a CBC producer and the public system would have given him, and us, a chance to redress the biases of the pro-nuclear media establishment. My point is that organizational censorship is as "chilling" as economic and political.

New technologies, like video, which must compete commercially against the older and bigger industries for a share of the consumer market, are more likely to draw attention to themselves through shock and an arrogant preoccupation with tabooed subjects. And since their market depends, initially at least, on youth, there is an acute awareness of what is sacrosanct, a tuned-in sensitivity to the dark side of growing up, to the collective unconscious of a youth culture with its narcissistic sexual fantasies, phallic imagery and regressive concerns with defecation. Parent groups are driven to distraction by what appears to be a vile aberration, a "seduction of the innocent," and they have found a champion recently in Tipper Gore, who regularly appeals to Congress to save children from delinquency and a life of crime by bringing these new media under control. The phenomenon of entertainment described as "sexploitation" is market driven, but not necessarily the most profitable sector of the industry. In the record business, labels come and go. But its appeals to freedom of expression are no less worthy. A recent Manitoba trial decision involving video suggests that s. 2(b) of the *Charter* protects what may be culpable under the *Criminal Code.*[23]

By mid-century, the older provincial standards were on the defensive. Freud, who had done so much to change our thinking about sexuality, had normalized sexual fantasy as it appeared in our dreams or humour or the arts, and had pathologized the censors.[24] The crusaders against smut, he argued, were people who were themselves deeply attracted to it, and in an effort to deny this shameful desire both to themselves and others, to deal with their own sexual guilt, they engaged actively and publicly in agitation for censorship or similar measures. Studies of sex guilt give some support to this position. Persons who score high on sex guilt are more prone to interpret texts as pornographic than their cohorts who are low on the scale.[25]

Yet, despite the trend towards the emancipation of culture from morality, there were periods of reaction which often corresponded to periods of economic and political crisis. At present, homophobia has become the obsession of Congressmen, like Senator Jesse Helms of North Carolina, who is outraged by public funds, in this case, the National Endowment of the Arts, being used to sponsor a show of homoerotic photographs by the late Robert Mappelthorpe.[26] (Applicants for grants must now sign a statement saying that the funds will not be used for homoerotic art.) Canadians with more experience in the subsidized arts might teach Americans about the arm's length principle,

---

23 *R. v. Butler*, 46 C.R.R. 124, reversed [1991] 1 W.W.R. 97 (Man. C.A.).
24 Thelma McCormack, "Feminism, Censorship and Sadomasochistic Pornography" in Thelma McCormack (ed.), *Studies in Communication*, vol. I (Greenwich: JAI Press, 1980), at 37.
25 C. G. Galbraith and D. L. Mosher, "Associative sexual responses in relation to sexual arousal, guilt and external approval contingencies" (1968), 10 Journal of Personality and Social Psychology at 142.
26 Mark W. McGinnis, "Banning U.S. Aid for 'Obscene' Art is Sure to Stifle Freedom of Expression" (August 9, 1989), *The Chronicle of Higher Education.* See also Arthur C. Danto, "Art and Taxpayers" (August 21/28, 1989), The Nation.

but not about tolerance when we consider how our overzealous customs officers have held up books intended for gay or lesbian retail bookstores.[27]

For women, the new understanding of sexuality, and the sexual revolution that came with modernity, was crucial. On the one hand, it affirmed sexuality and sexual experimentation. Maslow's "peak experience" was meant for both men and women, but especially for groups who remained locked into their own inhibitions or instrumental notions of sexual gratification.[28] Thus, the sexual revolution provided the distinction feminists made between erotica and pornography, between consensual and coercive sexual representations. On the other hand, feminists quickly grasped that the sexual revolution of the 1960s was a heterosexual revolution which took the guilt out of sex but left a system of gender inequality intact. And, like "no-fault divorce," women were often worse off.

That contradiction has been part of the crisis about modernism, and can be found in other contexts as well; perhaps most vividly in science. It is useful here to compare the J. Robert Oppenheimer case of a distinguished scientist being denied security clearance because of what were alleged to be his Communist sympathies with the discovery of what had occurred among scientists in Germany during the Nazi period. Intellectuals were prepared for the Oppenheimer case. It was a tragedy for him, but the terms of reference covered familiar ground. The disclosures and documented evidence of systemic experimentation on Jews by value-free scientists in Germany, however, was of a different order.[29] All that modernism represented in science and culture was held in some way responsible for its own hideous deformations. Critics of modernism, humanists in particular, saw this as the logical outcome of modernism, a confirmation of their dystopic view of science, just as deep ecologists today see it as part of our biocentrism. Others, however, were just stunned and confused. If *Wissenschaft* was, as Max Weber told us, a *Beruf*, a calling, we were not destined, by the rules of scientific inquiry, to become complicit in the Holocaust.

Modernism's failure to deal with major forms of inequality, and unwillingness to hold science accountable to some larger ethical system, created its own backlash: a revival of neo-nationalism and charismatic fundamentalism. It is sometimes hard to know where one starts and the other leaves off, but it is certain that fundamentalism has put back the progress of women. With its repression of sex, denial of gender equality,

---

27 "Sexually Explicit Media and the Charter" 2(4) C. of R. Newsl. 3.
28 Abraham H. Maslow, *Toward a Psychology of Being* (New York: Van Nostrand, 1968).
29 Benno Muller-Hill, *Murderous Science* (New York: Oxford University Press, 1988).

and the rejection of rationality in favour of faith, with its conformity, unquestioning trust in orthodox texts and blind obedience to male leaders, women have been the losers. In parts of the world where fundamentalism has become widely shared, religious law criminalizes a feminist value system and pornography as belonging to the same larger intellectual system; both degrade women.

Closer to home, and in a more modified form, the spirit of moral fundamentalism can be seen in the thinking of the 1986 United States Attorney General's Commission[30] which investigated pornography. There is no need, according to the report, to argue the case or deduce any evidence; it is sufficient to state categorically that pornography is evil.[31]

> [T]here are acts that need be seen not only as causes of immorality but as manifestations of it. Issues of human dignity and human decency, no less real for their lack of scientific measurability, are for many of us central to thinking about the question of harm. And when we think about harm in this way, there are acts that must be condemned not because the evils of the world will thereby be eliminated, but because conscience demands it.

This is the discourse of a Calvinist whose moral indignation befits *Der Stürmer*, but hardly *The Big Chill*, which was removed from the library shelves of a library in North York. Similar rhetorical exaggeration has become more widespread. Gloria Steinem's view that pornography is "hate literature" suggests she knows little about the structure or themes of "hate literature,"[32] for there is nothing in pornography that corresponds to the denials of the Holocaust or the paranoid themes of run-of-the-mill "hate literature."

To summarize, the first half of the 20th century was characterized by the final transformation of our society from traditional to modern, which included the democratization of culture and the sexual revolution. Whether modernism failed or was just an unfinished revolution hardly matters, for its limitations became clear in the crisis which took place within the scientific community and in the universities during the 1960s. Radical students, inspired by the Civil Rights Movement and the anti-war protest, challenged the structure of the universities and the status of its intellectual elites, while, shortly after, insurgent women questioned the mixed blessing of the sexual revolution. At its best, however, and often for reasons of necessity, the period between the end

---

30 Sometimes referred to as the Meese Commission.
31 United States, *Attorney General's Commission on Pornography*, vol. I (Washington, D.C.: Department of Justice, 1986), at 303.
32 G. Steinem, "A Clear and Present Danger" (November 1978), MS at 53-54, 75-78.

of World War I and the 1960s was conducive to social tolerance, artistic creativity, personal growth and open-mindedness. Since the 1960s, we have moved away from the ethos of this period in two directions, towards more radical challenges to authority and to less; the former is reflected in post-modernism; the latter, in a regressive fundamentalism.

I want to turn now to the feminist analysis of censorship which, as I indicated, is part of the modernist ethos, but also part of its criticism.

III

The debate has taken place on two levels, the more conventional civil libertarian discussion and a more complex one. The first goes something like this:

Ego: Censorship is a deterrent.
Alter: No it isn't. Like capital punishment, it only makes you feel good.

Ego: Censorship may not be a deterrent, but it sends a message.
Alter: What message does it send? And to whom?

Ego: Censorship empowers women.
Alter: Censorship empowers functionaries.

Ego: Censorship protects children.
Alter: Censorship overprotects children; censorship doesn't work.

Ego: It does work; you just don't know how to measure it. Censorship destroys a multi-billion dollar industry that exploits women and children.
Alter: Censorship prosecutes small gay newspapers like The Body Politic, displays in a bookstore window, and student-run film festivals, which are economically marginal, to say the least.

That dialogue is repeated endlessly, and rarely persuades anyone.

On another level, the feminist debate on censorship is centred around three key dimensions: the state, culture, and the social movement. More specifically, the feminist debate concentrates on: (1) the *patriarchal* state, (2) *misogynist* culture, and (3) an *insurgent* social movement based on gender threatening the power structure. What should be emphasized, and it cannot be reiterated often enough, is that it is not sufficient to look at pornography without looking at the state and its instruments of social control, nor sufficient to look at the state without looking at the social movement. Together they constitute the parameters of a political-cultural model.

Failure to look at them together generates another zero sum game. For example, women who score high on feminist issues — daycare, pay equity, pro-choice — and who describe themselves as feminists, score high on the traditional measures of civil libertarians. They start from the premise that feminism is a form of dissent which threatens a power structure based on male authority, male privilege, male status. The patriarchal state can tolerate small equity reforms and adjustments advocated by feminists but, as the pressures for social change escalate, what feminists have most to fear is the censorship of themselves. The hostility of the system towards feminism and feminist aspirations is revealed in the battle for the Equal Rights Amendment in the U.S. and the abortion struggle in both our countries. Hence, feminists who have a long-run stake in freedom of expression regard censorship, as they do law in general, as a form of social control that can be used against them. Censorship is part of a system of social control, and censorship of pornography is control on behalf of the institution of the nuclear family that is central to the patriarchal state.

Alternately, a pro-censorship group starts from a concern with a misogynist culture which causes both diffuse and specific harms. To ignore that culture, or tolerate it, is to approve it and, in the extreme, advocate it. The patriarchal state may ultimately attempt to suppress the movement, but the aggrandizing tendencies of the state can be used in the short run to suppress pornography. In any event, the act of working towards that end contributes to the mobilization of women on the basis of self-interest, and ultimately empowerment. In the extreme, the censorship of pornography is seen as defending us against other forms of censorship. Andrea Dworkin has written:[33]

> One reason that stopping pornographers and pornography is not censorship is that pornographers are more like the police in police states than they are like the writers in police states. They are the instruments of terror, not its victims. What police do to the powerless in police states is what pornographers do to women, except that it is entertainment for the masses, not dignified as political.

A third position begins with the victimization of women, which encompasses a whole range of social problems, including physical abuse and incest as a result of men who either have forced women to participate in the making of pornography or who have intimidated them into acting out pornographic fantasies. The extent of this need not concern us here, for all women, abused or not, may feel the humiliations of inequality and share, with the more serious cases, a sense of victimization. But extreme victims in our society are so deeply alienated that they have little to lose. Their politics are the politics of extremism. Rape victims and their families, for example, often favour capital punishment.

---

33 Dworkin, *supra*, note 11 at 13.

Clearly, the three positions — state, culture and victim — lead in three different directions. Each of these positions is to some degree correct, but incomplete by itself. They can be combined by saying that (a) feminism is dissent threatened by censorship, (b) pornography is a male-centred ideology that (c) depoliticizes women and makes the goals of the movement that much harder to achieve. As a set of statements, it is only a starting point for a new type of research. But whether the state, the culture or the victim is emphasized, the error is to view them separately and as static abstractions that are somehow unrelated to each other. The paradigm proposed here regards them as being in an interactive relationship, so that the patriarchal state is more or less patriarchal, the misogynist culture more or less misogynist, and the women's movement more or less militant. By analyzing the various combinations and permutations in different cultures or at different times in our own culture, we have a basis for understanding the interdependency of the three variables and the processes that connect them. The larger system supporting the various patterns found is a modern industrial economy (capitalist, socialist or some form of a mixed economy) while the spaces are filled with that spongy, but vital, substance with its many countervailing pressures that we call the political culture. Elsewhere I have suggested that the political culture itself may be dualistic and gendered, with a male political culture based on power and a female political culture based on status.[34]

IV

It is useful to situate this debate in recent experience. For convenience, I have divided it into two periods marked by Bill C-54. In the first stages of feminist commentary and activism on pornography, pornography was taken literally. Meetings were held with slide shows, and the National Film Board's Studio D film, "Not a Love Story," was intended to provide those not familiar with pornography with a documentary pictorial representation to demonstrate the sado-masochistic male "gaze." The story of "Not a Love Story" was that of a young woman working in the sex trade as a dancer being rescued by an older woman, a mother figure who came very close to being the stereotype of the liberal social worker. Meanwhile, we got a voyeuristic Leopold Bloom trip through the various arcades and photography studios. By dawn there is a conversion.

---

34 Thelma McCormack, "Toward a Non-sexist Perspective on Social and Political Change," in Marcia Millman and Rosabeth Moss Kanter (eds.), *Another Voice: Feminist Perspectives on Social Life and Social Science* (New York: Doubleday Anchor, 1975), at 1.

"Not a Love Story" became almost required viewing in women's studies courses. The students who viewed it were shocked, and often disturbed, for several hours after. If they had any intellectual doubts about censorship, this experience resolved it. Cooler heads, like Margaret Atwood, thought that it was so obvious that exposure to pornography would lead to sexual aggression that no evidence of the causal connection was necessary.[35] But there was, in fact, empirical research which claimed to provide proof of the harm of pornography to the physical security of women. The research was solidly within a positivist tradition of experimental stimulus/response studies that feminists, and others, had criticized for its narrowness and ahistoricity. Moreover, the studies were based on a theory of human nature which made almost the same assumptions about human nature as pornography did, an irony that was either unnoticed or lost. The larger political objective was to find an alternative to the psychoanalytic view that pornography was a harmless diversion that provided a catharsis, a victimless crime. The experimental stimulus/response studies seemed to provide it.

Most social psychology was neither behaviourist nor psycho-analytic, but the case for censorship presented by feminists was based on this forced polarization: either pornography led to acts of sexual assault and was therefore a serious threat to the safety of women or pornography was wish-fulfilment fantasy that, like other escapist dreams, lowered tension. On that slender and uninformed basis, feminists lobbied strenuously, first for the formation of the Fraser Commission on pornography and prostitution, and later for a Bill that would amend s. 159(8) [now s. 163(8)] of the *Criminal Code*, replacing obscenity with pornography.[36]

Bill C-54,[37] introduced in the spring of 1987, was the outcome of the joint efforts of feminists and conservative women's groups for new and tougher legislation. Many Canadian feminists saw pornography in the same way Gloria Steinem did, as a form of hate propaganda. A new Bill was needed, they claimed, to replace the *Criminal Code* provisions that had become too permissive; further, they wanted a Bill that would deal explicitly with pornography as the degradation of women, rather than nudity or what had been described as obscenity. A new amendment to the *Criminal Code* would sweep away the body of precedent that had grown out of the litigation of s. 159(8) of the *Code*. This new provision would not pander to civil libertarians or male standards of aesthetic merit. Some went further and urged legislation that was "preventive,"

---

35 Margaret Atwood, "Atwood on Pornography" (September 1963), Chatelaine.
36 Thelma McCormack, "Censorship of Pornography: Catharsis or Learning?" (1988), American Journal of Orthopsychiatry 58.
37 *An Act to Amend the Criminal Code and Other Acts in Consequence Thereof*, 2nd Sess., 33rd Parl. (1st reading, May 4, 1987).

so that women's groups would not be drawn into a protracted process of case-by-case litigation.[38] When it came to children and adolescents, what was wrong with prior restraint?

Bill C-54, however, was not the Bill feminists had hoped for.[39] It placed erotica and pornography on the same continuum, the difference between them being one of degree, not kind. C-54 should have been a lesson on the dangers of single-issue politics, especially where it involves coalitions with right-wing groups. Bill C-54 also revealed the patriarchal nature of the state, for the Bill was a response not to the pressures of the feminist lobby, but to the complaints of lawyers and judges about the vagueness of the *Criminal Code* and their difficulties in applying criteria of community standards.[40] When the Bill died on the order paper, conservative women's groups were angered, while feminists, except for a few die-hards, were relieved despite the fact that the whole episode did very little to enhance the reputation of the movement.[41]

In the post C-54 period, the pornography question became more academic and less political. The activism of the earlier period, which influenced the research, quickly wound down, while the research changed from the extreme positivism of experimental studies to qualitative text analyses. The thematic treatment of pornography changed, too, from *a priori* assertions that pornography degraded women, to an awareness of the ambiguity of its meaning, its multi-dimensionality, and alternative interpretations. Even earlier, one could compare Andrea Dworkin's analysis of the Marquis de Sade with Si-

---

38 At hearings to amend the *Broadcasting Act*, Mme. Matte, speaking for the Fédération des Femmes du Québec, described the limitations of the *Criminal Code:*

   "[It] is only invoked in extreme cases. In the first place, it is designed to deal with the worst cases. Secondly, it is always enforced after the fact. Thirdly, it makes its judgment on a case-by-case basis ... we support a preventative approach. If the principles of democratic control are incorporated in specific statutes and regulations governing the media we are concerned about, then there will be preventive intervention."

   House of Commons, "Sexually Abusive Broadcasting" First Session of the Thirty-second Parliament (1980), Debates; *Minutes of the Proceedings and Evidence of the Sub-Committee of the Standing Committee on Communications and Culture* (November 28-29, 1983).

39 Bill C-54, *supra*, note 37. See also National Action Committee on the Status of Women, "AGM rejects new porn bill" (1987), 2:5 Feminist Action 7.

40 Speaking at Hart House, University of Toronto, Mr. Neville Avison, one of the drafters of the Bill, considered it a very liberal step and was perplexed by the feminist criticisms of it.

41 A group called Resources Against Pornography thought the Bill was flawed but could be fixed, and that the alternative of not passing the Bill was worse. Alison Kerr, "Fact vs. fiction in the new anti-pornography bill" (February 26, 1988), The Toronto Star.

mone de Beauvoir's.[42] But a new group of feminist scholars, mostly in the humanities and drawing on post-modernist literary criticism, have analyzed pornography as a scenario with layers of meaning or intertextuality.[43] In retrospect, the statement made by Robin Morgan that "pornography is the theory; rape is the practice" is seen as simplistic.[44] Indeed, there now seems to be very little agreement on the meaning of pornography as a genre, or interest in finding an agreed-upon meaning, but there have been some virtuoso analyses of specific works, including parts of the Bible.[45]

The behaviourist research used in stimulus/response studies was also regarded more critically as feminists developed a new social psychology, and a theory of personality, trying to balance gender difference with sameness and unique gender identity with androgyny.[46] The work of Carol Gilligan belongs to the first; Sandra Bemm, to the second. Still others, outside the field of psychology, locate the origin of gender difference in social history. These theories should alter the future research agenda on censorship and pornography, and beyond that to theories of the state and individual behaviour. We are, then, on the threshold of developing a concept of human nature that is unlike the assumptions made in political theory about the state and the motivation of social groups to conform to its laws.

To summarize, if we look at the period following the 1960s, in which the women's movement was emerging, and if we trace the feminist analysis of pornography and censorship, there has been a major shift. Bill C-54 is a convenient marker of the change from a rhetoric reflecting the exigencies of political activism to scholarship, from a dogmatic understanding of pornography as causing harms to a more thematic analysis of pornography as open. The causes of pornography or its effects are of less interest. Behaviourist explanations are bypassed and, in some instances, no theory of causality is used because causality itself is questioned as a mode of explanation. Apart from scholars in the

---

42 Andrea Dworkin, *Pornography: Men possessing Women* (New York: Perigee Books, 1979); Simone de Beauvoir, *The Marquis De Sade* (London: Calder, 1962).

43 Susan Gubar and Joan Hoff (eds.), *For Adult Users Only* (Bloomington and Indianapolis: Indiana University Press, 1989).

44 R. Morgan, "Theory and Practice: Pornography and Rape," in R. Morgan (ed.), *Going too far* (New York: Vintage, 1978).

45 T. Drorah Setel, "Prophets and Pornography: Female Sexual Imagery in Hosea," in Letty M. Russell (ed.), *Feminist Interpretation of the Bible* (Philadelphia: The Westminster Press, 1985), at 86. See also Mary Jo Weaver, "Pornography and the Religious Imagination," in Susan Gubar and Joan Hoff, *supra*, note 43.

46 Thelma McCormack, "The Androgyny Debate," 9 Atlantis at 118.

humanities, feminist social psychologists have been developing a new theory of development and motivation.

V

The new feminist social psychology is a refinement of an older social psychology which emphasized the social nature of the person and the extent to which we become human in and through relationships. Both sociology and social psychology postulated that we live our lives through relationships, and that our intelligence, emotions and imaginations are shaped by our relationships and in primary groups.

The individualism assumed in classical political theory is humanly impossible and, where attempted, unbearable. Erich Fromm accounted for the rise of authoritarian society as an "escape from freedom," a desperate attempt to deal with the emotional burdens of a dehumanizing individualism.[47] Further, the mind/body dualism has been replaced by a concept of human nature as unified. The assumption that we are motivated by self-interest has been superseded by a concept of motivation-seeking and giving support to others, problem-solving, reducing cognitive dissonance and anticipatory planning. Thus, feminists do not have to argue against a concept of individualism; the burden of proof is on those who construct the fiction. Much of the criticism of liberalism found in feminist literature and elsewhere is based on models that have ceased to have any intellectual force.

Strictly speaking, we should talk about two liberalisms: the liberalism of laissez-faire and the liberalism of social democracy, the liberalism of the invisible hand and the liberalism of social planning, the liberalism of Adam Smith and the liberalism of Gunnar Myrdal, the liberalism of Manchester and the liberalism of the anti-Stalinist left. To illustrate the two versions, we can look at some of the recent debate on censorship. Both examples — the first based on an essay by Beverly Brown; the second, on the Fraser Commission — accept the view that the harms of pornography cannot be demonstrated.

What liberalism does, according to Beverly Brown, is to force feminism to " 'overstate' its case in order to have a case liberalism can recognise at all."[48] It first requires that there be palpable proof of harms which are then weighed against the harms done to the community by censorship. The harms which she regards as most serious are unprovable; they are not rape or violence, but the subtle impact on the mind, on

---

47   Erich Fromm, *Escape from Freedom* (New York: Farrar & Rinehart, 1941).
48   Beverly Brown, "A Feminist Interest in Pornography — Some Modest Proposals" (1981), 5/6 M/F at 13.

the consciousness of women who know themselves through the representations of others. With the present law and the present type of legal reasoning, the argument against pornography is deformed, and, in the long run, feminists lose some of their credibility.

The second view was taken recently by the Fraser Commission.[49] Freedom of expression, the commission said, was the dominant issue of the 19th century; equality is the central and mobilizing principle of the 20th. If the two come into conflict, the commission said, if we must choose between s. 15 of the *Charter* and s. 2(b), the former must prevail.[50] In this model, censorship becomes an ally of the powerless and an instrument of policies to achieve equality of opportunity as well as equality of condition.

The assumption that a choice must be made between freedom of expression and equality is based on a distinction between consciousness and material reality, one of the legacies of modernization theory which separates values, and ranks them on some scale. By splitting freedom of expression and equality, a patriarchal state can drive a wedge between women who are pursuing either liberation or equality. From a feminist perspective, the two values are one and indivisible. Feminist equality is not a mechanistic version of fairness or equivalence or a measure of non-discrimination; it is a qualitative dimension of the workplace, political life, and so on, conducive to the formation of new identities no longer crippled by dependency; it is empowerment.

The structural barriers to equality are many and diverse, but are primarily institutional and emerge chiefly in the private economic sector. The façade for all this, the ideological rationale, is a theory of gender differences. An example is the recent *Sears, Roebuck* case[51] in the United States, where Sears was charged by the Equal Employment Opportunity Commission (EEOC) for failing to live up to employment quotas. The company argued (successfully) that women were not attracted to the kind of employment the company offered: outdoor work, highly competitive, commission-based, requiring a willingness to work nights and weekends. Women were not inferior to men, or less worthy, but held different values. The company's policies, Sears claimed, reflected the value system of the society.

---

49 Government of Canada, Report of the Special Committee on Pornography and Prostitution, *Pornography and Prostitution in Canada* (Ottawa: Supply and Services, 1985) (Chairman: Paul Fraser, Q.C.).

50 A similar argument was put forth recently in the U.S. by a Stanford University law professor. Unrestricted freedom of speech which allowed racist remarks would interfere with a university's policy of created equal opportunity, a policy that enjoyed the same constitutional status. See Jon Wiener, "Academic Freedom for Bigots" (February 26, 1990), Nation.

51 *E.E.O.C. v. Sears, Roebuck & Co.*, 628 F. Supp. 1264, affirmed 839 F. 2d 302 (7th Circ., 1988).

On the basis of this, and similar cases, it is evident that inequality and discrimination are sustained by using gender differences where they are inappropriate and denying them where they are appropriate. There is, then, no need, either logically or politically, to limit freedom of expression to achieve equality. Equality without liberation leaves women unempowered; their standard of living may be higher, and the various discrepancies in income or status may be reduced, but they are still unable to transcend the psychological disabilities of dependency and will remain so, without an atmosphere that allows the fullest possible exploration of ideas and imagery.[52] Playing them off against each other results in neither goal, equality or liberation, being achieved.

The Draconian recommendations of the Fraser Report do not follow from its analysis. Its notion that the validity of an idea depends upon its historical correctness or harmony with the *Zeitgeist*, is bizarre. What bears consideration is the proposition that a feminist model of freedom of expression must be based on the assumptions of a modern social democracy. The difference can best be understood by looking at earlier versions of political economy. In the context of laissez-faire economics, women were marginalized. In the context of a consensus model of the state, their struggle was reduced to protest and interest-group politics. Progress was incremental. Women advanced; feminism as a radical social movement did not. But it is in the welfare state characterized by distributive justice, social entitlement and cultural access that feminist values constitute the dominant ethos. The welfare state is not paradise; it has its social costs, and specific policies are not always directed to the best interests of women. Critics argue that the welfare state is no more gender-blind or neutral than the bourgeois state, that it merely humanizes capitalism[53] and by extension patriarchy. Nevertheless, all of the studies we have of women's attitudes on social policy indicate a normative and political framework that is the foundation of the welfare state.[54]

VI

Freedom of expression as a constituent part of a liberal social democracy is congruent with feminist aspirations, feminist theory, and

---

52 Thelma McCormack, "Pornography and Prostitution in Canada: The Fraser Report" (1987), 13 Atlantis. See also, Thelma McCormack, "Deregulating the Economy and Regulating Morality: The Political Economy of Censorship" (1985), 18 Studies in Political Economy at 173.

53 Ralph Miliband, *The State in Capitalist Society* (London: Quartet Books, 1973).

54 Thelma McCormack, "Politics: The Hidden Injuries of Gender" (unpublished manuscript).

feminist modes of reasoning. To acknowledge that is the first step. It does not, however, resolve the question of whether we must defend bigotry, and whether feminists, in particular, must defend a culture which either denies that women exist or continues to cast them in stereotypical roles — sex-object rather than sex partner, consumer rather than producer, domestic and home-bound rather than public and political. The short answer is that we have a constitutional obligation to defend dissent, no obligation to defend prejudice, and in borderline cases we must give the idea or image or expression the benefit of the doubt.

That guideline is based on a distinction between dissent and prejudice. Analytically, the distinction between them is based on the distinction between state and society. Although state and society are joined at the base, they can be studied separately. The relationship between them has been the subject of theory in Marx, Weber and contemporary social theorists who differentiate the authoritarian society from the totalitarian state. The Marxist tradition has emphasized the primacy of the economy with the state acting as "the executive committee of the ruling class." The Weberian tradition has similarly located the dynamic in the social system, with the state adapting to it, and with citizens acting in accordance with their class or status characteristics. The dependency of the state on the society has led to what Wolin describes with a lament "the sublimation of politics."[55]

Setting aside questions of direction, whether one can predict from the social structure to the political or the reverse, it follows from the distinction that prejudice adheres in the domain of society; dissent in the domain of the state. The state, however, is not always autonomous. Carole Pateman has argued that the modern state rests upon a sexual contract.[56] The transformation from status to contract in modern political organization was a transformation, she suggests, from father to male. And she means quite literally that the basis of the modern state is a sexual contract which gives men control over women's bodies; that is, the marriage contract. When feminism challenges the patriarchal state, it is, in effect, challenging the sexual contract. Thus, the interest of the patriarchal state is to protect the contract, and it is the state that would like to eliminate pornography to keep in place a less controversial misogynist culture and a system of stratification. Like the "Code Noir" of the 18th century slave trade, it recognized that excess, too much cruelty and abuse, endangered the institution of slavery.

Pornography is the prejudice of the patriarchal state, a genre which seeks and finds the taboos of the moment and our ambivalence towards

55 Sheldon Wolin, *Politics and Vision* (Boston: Little, Brown, 1960).
56 Carole Pateman, *The Sexual Contract* (Stanford: Stanford University Press, 1988).

them. It is a mocking genre which touches a sensitive nerve in a hetero-
geneous society with its mixed signals, value contradictions and waver-
ing degrees of conformity. Pornography is protest without politics, a
mindless profanity. Its sexual scripts shock us (as they are supposed to),
not by their imagery which is openly available in any medical or abnor-
mal psychology text, but by the attitude towards it, the supreme indifference to any transgression of prevailing sexual norms. Descriptions of
sado-masochism, bestiality or incest are conveyed to us with exactly the
same clinical and detached attitude as a Herman Kahn scenario on
thermal nuclear overkill.[57] To paraphrase Kahn, pornography is "thinking the unthinkable." The urge to censor pornography is the same urge
we have to censor the Kahn scenarios, precisely because they present a
powerful moral dilemma: to avoid them is to be naïve about the world,
to accept them is to be corrupted by them.

Pornography is disturbing for the same reason, and some of it is
more offensive than others (a difference, incidentally, which does not
necessarily or always correspond to such classifications as soft-core or
hard-core). But it does not, as feminism does, challenge the nuclear
family, the gendered division of labour, the androcentricity of our
political life, and our symbolic systems: art, religion, law and language.
It captures the hypocrisy of our claims to sexual fidelity and restraint,
and often, paradoxically, fails to provide an arousal in either men or
women. But in its most perverse form it tests the tolerance of society, not
the freedom of the state.

Whether we choose to defend it or not requires a different framework based on a theory of tolerance. Yet tolerance is not well understood; scholars have given more attention to intolerance, that is, the
study of social bigotry, than they have to tolerance. Is the intolerance
towards pornography the same as intolerance towards minority groups?
It is different in the sense that it is not directed at stigmatized groups, but
at symbolic systems. It is also different in its origin.

In general, social psychologists who have studied social prejudice
have related it to ignorance of the other group (out-group) or a particular
type of authoritarian personality. There is no shortage of data supporting the view that persons who advocate censorship tend to be more
punitive and less educated, more inflexible, and more prone to stereotyping than their counterparts.[58] Political scientists and sociologists

---

57 Herman Kahn, *Thinking About The Unthinkable* (New York: Horizon, 1962).
58 For a recent review of the literature confirming the importance of education,
    see Lawrence Bobo and Frederick C. Licari, "Education and Political Toler-
    ance" (1989), 53 Public Opinion Quarterly at 285; see also John Sullivan,
    Michael Shamir, Patrick Walsh and Nigel S. Roberts, *Political Tolerance in
    Context: Support for Unpopular Minorities in Israel, New Zealand and the
    United States* (Boulder: Westview Press, 1985).

have examined structural factors and have linked tolerance to the urban environment, where the norm of "live and let live" was a necessity as well as a virtue.[59] Pornography, though not peculiar to cities, was more visible in that environment where it was also more acceptable. Here, too, we have evidence that tolerance of what others regard as "obscene" is higher in cities than suburbs or small towns, higher in communities which support competing newspapers and have access to a large volume of cultural resources: movies, plays, concerts, libraries, bookstores, educational institutions and magazines. Quality, apparently, matters less than quantity. But comparative studies — urban, suburban and rural — demonstrate that the best predictor of broad community standards is urbanization.[60] Based on that model, prejudice was interpreted as a form of cultural lag.

What is problematic, then, is why intolerance has not disappeared, why there has been a resurgence of racism and bigotry on American university campuses or in the new affluent France, why law-and-order governments have been able to seize books, close museums, censor films without protest, and why many of those who should be least supportive of these actions turn out to be most.

A new form of intolerance that differs from traditional older forms has developed out of the prototypical anxiety of a modern knowledge-based society, a psychological phenomenon that is the consequence of modernization, not of its absence or delay. It is an endemic fear of manipulation and can be seen in the discourse on censorship. The scenario of the pro-censorship campaign is an assertion that our society is being flooded with materials imported from elsewhere — from California, if you are a Canadian; from Europe if you are a Californian, and from South America if you are either — and over which we have no control. These books, films, photographs and drawings undermine our value system and social organization. Helpless to stop it, we become even more helpless as a result of it.

Fear of manipulation goes back to Machiavelli, to the end of the

---

59 The classic statement of this was by Louis Wirth, "Urbanism as a way of life" (1938), 44 American Sociological Review at 3. For a more recent confirmation see Thomas C. Wilson, "Urbanism and Tolerance: A Test of Some Hypothesis Drawn from Wirth and Stauffer" (1985), 50 American Sociological Review 117.

60 Coke Brown, Joan Anderson, Linda Burggraf and Neal Thompson, "Community Standards, Conservatism, and Judgments of Pornography" (1978), 14 Journal of Sex Research 81; Marc B. Glassman, "Community Standards of Patent Offensiveness: Public Opinion Data and Obscenity Law" (1978), 42 The Public Opinion Quarterly 161; Harrell R. Rodgers, Jr., "Censorship Campaigns in Eighteen Cities" (1974), 2 American Politics Quarterly 371; Edward G. Stephan and Douglas R. McMullin, "Tolerance of Sexual Nonconformity: City Size as a Situational and Early Learning Determinant" (1982), 47 American Sociological Review 411.

Renaissance, when this adviser to the Prince began to study political behaviour empirically rather than from theological tracts. However, the term "Machiavellianism," which refers to manipulative cunning, tells us less about Machiavelli or the Prince than it does about our own deep fears about secular knowledge, and the power it confers on those who can monopolize it.

Fear of manipulation, which lies at the basis of intolerance, is different from the prudery and "moral panic" described by sociologists as a phenomenon of collective behaviour. Our moral panic is to some extent based on the reality of the monopolies of information storage, the secrecy of information, and the transparent disinformation that issues from press conferences, political advertising and propaganda. Fear of manipulation, then, is latent in the personality structures found in all modern knowledge-based societies, but it is intensified by the politics of information and communication. Hence, the old socialist slogan to nationalize the banks should be adapted to our world by nationalizing the data banks, by democratizing information.

Meanwhile, the bourgeois patriarchal state can exploit our fear of manipulation by creating an image of a society cynically being used by powerful outside groups with known criminal connections, and by groups with possible links to prostitution who enrich themselves by shamelessly peddling sexual consumerism to innocent youth and sexual perversions to deviants. An example of myth-making was the 1986 U.S. Attorney General's Commission on Pornography, which was convinced before it began its hearings that there was a connection between pornography and organized crime. But it was unable to find one, a fact, one would think, which might have given them pause. It did not; the matter was resolved by the simple expedient of redefining organized crime. Thus, with some ingenuity and a penchant for disinformation, the state can use our anxiety to extend its own control.

By resisting the temptation to censor pornography, we are turning back a state that deliberately manipulates our anxieties about sexuality and control. It is a political act. Rightly or wrongly — and I think rightly — it is not a form of passive indifference. However, a decision to protect pornography under s. 2(b) is not to confuse prejudice with dissent. To advocate that obscenity be removed from the *Criminal Code* we are again making a statement, not about freedom but about tolerance, not about the state but about society. Hypothetically, if pornography could be censored and that censorship enforced, the democratic state would not be endangered, but the tolerant society would be. And it is the tolerant society through which women find a new post-patriarchal identity.

To summarize, what I have tried to do here is to sketch the main lines of a feminist analysis of freedom of expression as a *Charter* right which applies to pornography. I am, at this juncture, less interested in pornography than censorship. This is in contrast with much feminist writing which is about the nature of pornography and only about censorship as a consequence. The most extreme version of this is the work of Catharine MacKinnon and Andrea Dworkin, for whom pornography is the prototype of all heterosexual experience, a form of oppression that derives from male needs for sexual gratification. Law, and particularly the First Amendment of the United States *Constitution*, is the superstructure of a sexual script in which male sexuality is the prime mover. MacKinnon is critical, for example, of pro-choice abortion legislation because it deals with the *results* of male sexuality, not male sexuality.[61] Other feminists emphasize reproduction as the distinctive experience of women, pregnancy rather than the moment of impregnation. Held, in a recent attempt to reconstruct a theory of the state, suggests a mother-child relationship as the model.[62] And still others (not exclusively, but especially, Marxists) locate gender specificity in social history. My own view is closer to the latter. But my interest, for purposes of discussion here, is in censorship and freedom of expression.

With that as a point of departure, I raised several questions. Why are 20th century scholars so uninspired by freedom of expression, so unwilling to speak of it with the same iconic reverence they show for other rights? Feminists have been asking why *not* shoot the messenger? And what is wrong with the "chilling effect"? I have suggested that freedom of expression has become part of the current criticism of liberalism, an umbrella term which usually refers to a 19th century model of a competitive marketplace, an 18th century model of individualism and rationality, and a 17th century model of the nation-state. Contemporary liberalism has little in common with these ideas. It recognizes that modern communication systems have made the cultural systems transnational; that modern psychology has defined our behaviour as social, a mix of rational and irrational; and that contemporary social planning includes greater control over the communication systems and the full realization of social, racial and gender equity. The new liberalism is social democracy which retains the core of the old liberalism: (1) the distinction between word and deed, thought and action, and (2) the emphasis *cum* Mill on the transformative experience of intellectual diversity, of overcoming the dependency of age or status by reducing and eliminating overprotection.

The second question is whether feminists have more to gain than

---

61 Catharine A. MacKinnon, "Privacy v. Equality: Beyond Roe v. Wade," in *Feminism Unmodified* (Cambridge: Harvard University Press, 1987).

62 Virginia Held, "Non-contractual Society: A Feminist View," in Marsha Hanen and Kai Nielsen (eds.), *Science, Morality and Feminist Theory* (Calgary: University of Calgary Press, 1987), at 111.

lose from s. 2(b), even if this means turning a blind eye to what is anathema to them. Freedom of expression is necessary, I have suggested, to achieve the two major goals of the feminist movement: liberation and equality. Separating them, as the Fraser Commission did and as many second-wave feminists do, is the legacy of a patriarchal post-Cartesian philosophy that dichotomizes mind and body. The new civil liberties argument is, then, not the traditional one, although it expresses the continuing and deep desire to live in a free society and a culture which is pluralistic in the broadest sense of the word.

The third question is whether feminists have any obligation to defend the pornographic text. I have suggested that it could only be defended as a measure of tolerance, not as a measure of freedom; as prejudice, not dissent. Feminists can never lose sight of the radical nature of feminism as an ideology and the extent to which it is vulnerable to measures of censorship. Pornography is a subset of a system of thought and symbolic expression which devalues women, either through idealizing them by sentimentalizing their virtue or by a phallocentric version of their sexuality. But whether or not we defend pornography, with its disinformation, depends on how much value we put on tolerance as a societal practice.

The most difficult thing to achieve in our contemporary society is tolerance, a property that has characterized women as much as altruism, nurturance, an ethic of caring, and a sensitivity to relationships. To be tolerant is to act; it is not to be passive or non-judgmental. Its origin is in empathy, a habit which again is seen as stronger in women than men. But the problem is not to validate women by validating characteristics which may, in certain situations, be a liability, but to try and understand the nature of intolerance; that is, why there is an extraordinary demand for censoring what we know, intellectually, is of little consequence. I have suggested here that the conceptual framework for studying group intolerance in the social sciences is not adequate for dealing with the fear of manipulation.

Finally, I have raised questions about self-censorship at the institutional level. The media do not dare include sexual candour or, more profoundly, erotic desire. Dr. Ruth notwithstanding, there is a hesitancy to antagonize a mass audience. And, because the major communications organizations are also bureaucracies, they become even more conservative. Either way, whether the pressures are endogenous or exogenous, feminism has no voice. Women are not silenced by pornography; they are silenced by a media system which excludes them.[63] Hence, the need arises for new formats where feminists set the agenda,

---

63 Jerome Barron, *Freedom for the Press for Whom? The Right of Access to the Mass Media* (Bloomington: Indiana University Press, 1973).

and where we do not put each other through some Socratic dialogue or require the adversarial skills of a court room. Programs in women's studies in universities are an example of affirmative access, and constitute a test of academic freedom. Universities, in turn, are part of an educational network which includes the Canada Council, publishing, film-making, and prime-time television. The new feminist aesthetics, and the new feminist social sciences, will provide a more general perspective.

With these in place, it will still be an imperfect world. There will still be an anxiety about manipulation, although women will be more secure than in the past; there will still be parents who want their children protected from images of Oedipal destruction. There will still be profane graffiti on walls, there will still be pornography distributed openly or underground, and there will still be some version of the transgressive script that tests our tolerance. If it were not so, some dialectical understanding of society tells me that we would have to invent one.

PART III

RACIST INCITEMENT: FREEDOM OF EXPRESSION AND THE PROMOTION OF HATRED

While there are vigorous debates about the many forms of expression which may be beyond the pale, there is a broad consensus that expression designed to promote hatred against certain identifiable groups is beyond the realm of the acceptable. A debate has ensued, however, over whether the criminal prohibition of the promotion of hatred is the appropriate avenue for channeling public indignation about such expression. In the meanwhile, persons accused of promoting hatred, and in some of its most vile forms, have sought refuge under the *Charter*'s guarantee of freedom of expression. Are laws which prohibit racist incitement an effective form of creating conditions of equality, or are they needlessly overbroad and dangerous to other more legitimate forms of debate?

Cyril Levitt provides a historical context for the current debate over Canada's laws against racist incitement. Pre-Nazi Germany had in place a number of laws designed to prohibit the promotion of hatred against identifiable groups. With reference to original sources, Levitt reviews the use of those laws in the Weimar Republic. While many prosecutions were successful, others were not because of the anti-Semitic leanings of some judges, while yet other prosecutions provided a platform for the advocacy of racial hatred. Levitt concludes that, in the context of a destabilized political and economic climate, the law would prove to be of little effect, while, in a stable democratic society, a narrowly drawn law which prohibits the promotion of hatred could be more effectively implemented. The paradox is that there would be less of a need for such a law in a stable democratic society, but, when such a law is most needed, it would prove to be of little effect.

Alan Borovoy argues against the prohibition of racist expression through the criminal law. The English language is simply not sufficiently precise to enable the legislative sanction of the type of hateful speech that we would like to prohibit, without the risk of simultaneously snaring the type of speech that a democratic society would be loath to prohibit. By surveying the instances where the anti-hate law has been used, or threatened to be used, Borovoy exposes why it is virtually impossible to formulate a sufficiently precise legal prohibition which does not carry unacceptable risks. Borovoy asserts that the solution does not lie in legal prohibition, but in political censure and the strengthening of our human rights codes.

Irwin Cotler presents the counter-argument. For him, the law prohibiting the promotion of racial hatred is narrowly drawn and provides sufficient protection for legitimate speech by means of the statutory defences specified in the *Criminal Code*. Moreover, the promotion of hatred harms its victims and is antithetical to the values that underlie a free and democratic society. Applying a purposive interpretation to the *Charter*'s protection of free expression, with reference to the *Charter*'s expressed value of multiculturalism, Cotler argues that hate propaganda should not be constitutionally protected expression.

RACIAL INCITEMENT AND THE LAW: THE CASE OF THE WEIMAR REPUBLIC

*Cyril Levitt**

I. INTRODUCTION

When jurists in liberal democracies consider the threat of racial incitement to individuals, to groups and to society as a whole, they often conjure up the image of the Weimar Republic, a democratic state which was subverted and overwhelmed by a politically organized racist movement. However, outside a small number of historians of the period, few know the details concerning the failure of Germany's first experiment with democracy. This fact was made clear to me at a conference on "Racial Incitement and the Law in Canada and Israel," hosted by the Faculty of Law at the Hebrew University of Jerusalem in December 1988. A polarization occurred there between those who favoured the use of legislation against racist expression and organizations and those who were concerned that such legal "medicine" would not only be ineffective, but would damage the only real defence a democracy has against racist attacks, namely, a political culture which respects the civil liberties of those expressing unpopular, distressing or obnoxious points of view.

In relation to several issues raised by one of the Israeli jurists, I

*   The author would like to thank the following individuals who read various drafts of this paper and who offered significant suggestions which strengthened the final copy: Alan Borovoy, Howard Brotz, Irwin Cotler, Bruce Elman, Louis Greenspan, Michael Marrus, David Schneiderman, William Shaffir and Harold Troper.

pointed out that there had been a vigorous prosecution of racist expression in the Weimar Republic, but that, all too often, the defendants were allowed to use the court room as a forum for the dissemination of their ideas. Charges against Julius Streicher in Nuremberg, Joseph Goebbels in Berlin, and against the editors of the Nazi newspaper, *Voelkischer Beobachter*, in Munich were turned by skilful Nazi attorneys, such as Hans Frank and Roland Freisler, into trials of Jewish rituals, Jewish religious texts, Jewish leaders and the "Jew-Republic" — as the Weimar state was cynically called by the nationalist right. At the time, I could not provide the details of these trials, the nature of the legislation or the role that they played in the decline and fall of the republic, but I was encouraged to pursue these matters by many of the participants.

I no longer believe, as I once did, that a thorough knowledge of the Weimar experience will provide us with ready or easy answers to the problem of the use and abuse of the law in matters concerning racist expression in our present context. Nevertheless, I feel that an understanding of the attitudes and actions of the justice system *vis-à-vis* the racist assault upon the first German republic will enhance our sensitivity to the issues we are facing today.

In the introduction to his book on Spinoza, Leo Strauss maintains that it was the weakness of the Weimar democracy, its unwillingness or inability to wield the sword of justice in its self-defence, which was to blame for the calamity which resulted.[1] One often hears spokesmen for organizations of Holocaust survivors exhorting us to pass tough laws against hate groups, to prosecute them without mercy because the failure to legislate and the failure to prosecute these fringe groups in the Weimar Republic had such tragic consequences. Indeed, a large number of people have been convinced that Hitler began with a handful of marginal characters in 1920 and, by means of his evil talent for mesmerizing large crowds, was able to lead his party to power a scant 13 years later. He was able to do this, so common wisdom would have it, because no one tried hard enough to stop him. Anti-hate laws, if they existed at all, were either too weak or not enforced by the authorities. So when our civil libertarians point to the pathetic purveyors of hate in our society and suggest that laws against them either will not be effective or are too dangerous for a democratic society to enact, many people respond: "Hitler and his gang were also pathetic purveyors of hate in 1920, and look what happened as a result of the inaction of a democracy."

There are two fundamental difficulties with this position. The first, which I will call the error of mistaken historical equivalence, concerns the lack of understanding of the specifics of the Weimar situation and

---

1   L. Strauss, *Spinoza's Critique of Religion* (Schocken: New York, 1965), at 1-3.

how they differ from those of the contemporary Western democracies. I will not address myself to this matter, for it would require a detailed review of the historical course of the Weimar Republic, a project for which I am ill-equipped to act as a guide and which, in any event, is beyond the scope of this paper. The second error arises from a lack of knowledge concerning the nature of anti-hate laws, the ways in which they were used by individuals, groups, the police and state prosecutors, how they were interpreted by the courts, the conduct and outcome of trials, and their effectiveness in the struggle against racist expression. It is to these matters which I now turn.

By and large, the struggle against racist anti-Semitism was not considered a high priority by the democratic, republican political parties, the trade unions, churches and other mass organizations in Germany until the fateful election on September 14, 1930, which saw the Nazi Party increase its parliamentary representation from 12 to 107 deputies. The only major exception to this was the organization which represented the majority of Germany's Jews — *Der Central-Verein deutscher Staatsbuerger juedischen Glaubens* (C.V.) — the Central Association of German Citizens of the Jewish Faith.[2] The C.V. was founded in 1893, partly in response to the outbreak of a new wave of anti-Semitism which included electoral gains for anti-Semitic parties and losses for liberal parties and partly as a result of the impetus provided by the founding of a non-denominational group, *Der Verein zur Abwehr des Antisemitismus* (The Association for Combatting Anti-Semitism).[3] By 1891, the C.V. had built a powerful organization, which carried on a defensive struggle on several fronts. This struggle included the mass production of quality anti-anti-Semitic leaflets, pamphlets, posters, bro-

2   See Marjorie Lamberti, *Jewish Activism in Imperial Germany: The Struggle for Civil Equality* (New Haven and London: Yale University Press, 1978); Alfred Hirschberg, "Ludwig Hollaender," in VII *Leo Baeck Yearbook* (London: Secker & Warburg, 1962), at 39-74; Peter Pulzer, "Why was there a Jewish Question in Imperial Germany?," in XXV *Leo Baeck Yearbook* (London: Secker & Warburg, 1980), at 133; Hans Reichmann, "Der drohende Sturm," in Hans Tramer (ed.), *In Zwei Welten: Siegfried Moses zum fuenfundsiebzigsten Geburtstag* (Tel-Aviv: Verlag Bitaon, 1962), at 556; Eva G. Reichmann, *Groesse und Verhaengnis deutsch-juedischer Existenz: Zeugnisse einer tragischen Begegnung* (Heidelberg: Verlag Lambert Schneider, 1974); Jehuda Reinharz, *Fatherland or Promised Land: The Dilemma of the German Jews, 1893-1914* (Ann Arbor: University of Michigan Press, 1975); Ismar Schorsch, *Jewish Reactions to German Anti-Semitism, 1870-1914* (New York: Columbia University Press, 1972).

3   See Barbara Suchy, "Der Verein zur Abwehr des Antisemitismus (I) — From Its Beginnings to the First World War," in XXVIII *Leo Baeck Yearbook* (London: Secker & Warburg, 1983), at 205; B. Suchy, "Der Verein zur Abwehr des Antisemitismus (II) — From the First World War to its Dissolution in 1933," in XXX *Leo Baeck Yearbook* (London: Secker & Warburg, 1985), at 67.

chures and books; the organization of anti-racist rallies, educational forums, panel discussions, and informational public meetings; the maintenance of friendly channels of communication with members of the government, members of political parties, law enforcement agencies and the judiciary; the provision of resource and informational materials to trade unions, political parties, churches and republican organizations concerning anti-Semitism; the publishing of a weekly and a monthly newspaper, and an intellectual journal; and the operation of a publishing house as a source of literature which extolled the virtues of tolerance, justice and the dignity of the individual. In addition to all this, the C.V. kept a watchful eye on anti-Semitic expression, acting as a surrogate watchdog for the republic, documenting, chronicling and publicizing the activities of anti-Semites throughout the country. Beyond this, the C.V. actively sought the prosecution of anti-Semites under the Constitution and laws of the republic, and was active in the law reform movement to close the loopholes in existing legislation.[4]

I wish to concentrate exclusively on this *Rechtschutz*, or legal protection activity, of the C.V., having acknowledged that the scope of the general efforts of the organization was considerably wider than the legal sphere. On the practical side, the C.V. maintained 21 regional offices and had 555 local branches having their headquarters in Berlin, and these offices provided legal assistance to the local communities in dealing with anti-Semitic provocations. This legal aid consisted in the provision of free legal advice and counselling to individuals and groups. The C.V. also provided the lawyers and support staff necessary to take over prosecutions from private individuals and groups who had initially pressed charges, the expert personnel to maintain liaison between Jews

---

4   The most comprehensive work on the defensive struggle of the Central Verein is Arnold Paucker's *Der Juedische Abwehrkampf gegen Antisemitismus und Nationalsozialismus in den letzten Jahren der Weimarer Republik* (Hamburg, 1968); the most comprehensive work on strictly legal defense is Udo Beer's doctoral dissertation published as: *Die Juden, das Recht und die Republik,* Rechtshistorische Reihe 50 (Frankfurt-am-Main, Bern, New York: Peter Lang, 1986). There is a sizeable literature on the general crisis of law in the Weimar Republic which is related to the Jewish question. See Heinrich Hannover and Elisabeth Hannover-Drueck, *Politische Justiz 1918-1933* (Frankfurt-am-Main: Fischer Buecherei, 1966); Gotthard Jasper, "Justiz und Politik in der Weimarer Republik," *Vierteljahrshefte fuer Zeitgeschichte* (1982), 30 Jg., Heft 2, 1982, 167; Klaus Petersen, *Literatur und Justiz in der Weimarer Republik* (Stuttgart: J.B. Metzlersche Verlagsbuchhandlung, 1988); Theo Rasehorn, *Justizkritik in der Weimarer Republik: das Beispiel der Zeitschrift "Die Justiz"* (Frankfurt-am-Main, New York: Campus Verlag, 1985), at 157. Werner Neussel seems to be one of the lone voices defending the record of the Weimar administration of justice. See his *Die Spruchtaetigkeit der Strafsenate des Reichsgerichts in politischen Strafsachen in der Zeit der Weimarer Republik, Inaugural-Dissertation,* Universitaet Marburg, 1971.

and the police and judiciary, and the means to carry appeals to higher courts when justice was not served at the local or provincial level. Even though the C.V. was not formally involved in every prosecution of anti-Semitic expression in the Weimar Republic, its newspaper, the C.V. Zeitung, carried frequent detailed reports of anti-Semitic incidents, arrests, prosecutions, verdicts and sentences. From time to time, the C.V. would publish, through its publishing house, the Philo Verlag, special booklets concerning its legal protection activities and assessments of the efficacy of the law as a weapon in the ongoing struggle against racist expression. I base what follows mainly upon a study of these primary sources.

In 1924, the Philo Verlag published a pamphlet by Ludwig Foerder, the C.V. Legal Secretary in Breslau (today the city of Wrozlaw in southwestern Poland), in which a review of those laws pressed into the judicial struggle against anti-Semitism was undertaken and an assessment of the results of prosecutions conducted under those laws was made. Entitled *Antisemitismus und Justiz* (Anti-Semitism and the Administration of Justice), it appears to have been modelled after a similar review, *Antisemitismus und Strafrechtspflege* (Anti-Semitism and the Administration of Criminal Law), published in 1894 and written by the Legal Counsel of the oldest Berlin Chamber of Commerce, Dr. Max Apt, under the pseudonym Dr. of Law, Maximilian Parmod. It would be instructive to list the laws cited by Foerder and then to illustrate the applications of them by means of examples drawn from actual court cases described in the literature.

The following are the laws under which most of the legal actions against anti-Semitism were prosecuted in the Weimar Republic:

1. Incitement to class struggle (*Criminal Code*, para. 130):

   > (130.) Whoever publicly incites different classes of the population to violent actions against one another in a way which jeopardizes the public peace, will be punished with a fine of 600 marks or with a prison term of up to two years.

2. Religious insult (*Criminal Code*, para. 166):

   > (166.) Whoever blasphemes God in that he causes annoyance in public by expressions of abuse, or whoever publicly insults one of the Christian Churches or another existing religious society with the rights of corporation in the Federal jurisdiction or its institutions or customs, likewise whoever commits insulting mischief in a church or in another specific place which is specified for religious gatherings, will be punished with a prison term of up to three years.

3. Insult (*Criminal Code*, paras. 185-87, 189, 190, 192-196):

(186.) Whoever asserts or spreads a fact in relation to another person which serves to make the other contemptible or demeaned in the public view, will, if this fact is not demonstrably true, be punished with a fine or with arrest or with prison up to one year, and, if this insult is done publicly or through the spread of literature, pictures or representations, with a fine or prison up to two years.

(187.) Whoever against his better knowledge asserts or spreads a fact in relation to another person which makes him contemptible in the public view or which serves to threaten his credit will be punished with prison up to two years on account of defamatory insult, or if the defamation is done publicly or through spreading of literature, pictures or representations, with prison for not under one month. If extenuating circumstances are present, the penalty can be reduced to one day in prison or a fine.

(189.) Whoever insults the memory of a deceased individual in that he asserts or spreads an untrue fact, which would have served to make the deceased contemptible or demeaned in the public view in his lifetime, will be punished with prison up to six months. If extenuating circumstances are present, this can be reduced to a fine.

Prosecution occurs only upon request of the parents, the children or the spouse of the deceased.

(193.) Rebukeful judgments of scientific, artistic or occupational performance, as well as utterances which are made for the execution or defence of rights or for the protection of legitimate interests, as well as reproaches and reprimands of superiors against their subordinates, employment reports or judgments on the part of a civil servant and similar cases are only punishable, when the presence of an insult arises from the form of the expression or from the circumstances under which it occurred.

II. THE ADMINISTRATION OF JUSTICE AND THE CRISIS OF LAW

During the years of the Weimar Republic, opinion was bitterly divided on the question of the impartiality of the justice system. Spokesmen for the SPD and the left-liberal DDP time and again referred to a "crisis of trust" in the administration of law and to a general "crisis of law" in Germany. Within the legal establishment, these charges were forcefully levelled by supporters of the Alliance of Republican Judges — the *Republikanischer Richterbund* (RR) — who suspected a large number of their fellow judges of monarchical tendencies and of interpreting the law in a way which was not consonant with the intent of the framers of the Weimar Constitution. Representatives of the right-liberal

Deutsche Volkspartei (DVP), of the Catholic *Zentrum* and of the nationalist *Deutschnationale Volkspartei* (DNVP), generally rejected this
charge as a fabrication of the liberals and the left. The mainstream
judges association — the *Deutscher Richterverein* — also rejected the
charges, and viewed the attempt to "politicize" the dispensation of
justice by the Alliance of Republican Judges as a move to secure comfortable positions for themselves within the justice system.

A large plurality, if not majority, of the leadership of the C.V. were
supporters of the DDP, and thus shared the views of the liberal-left
regarding the "crisis of law" in the Weimar Republic. But for the
leadership of the C.V., the crisis was both general and specific to the
Jewish community. A good illustration of this can be seen in the activities of Erich Eyck, a noted lawyer who was a member of the C.V. and
active in the RR and the DDP. In 1926 he published a pamphlet entitled
The Crisis of the German Administration of Law in which he dealt with a
wide variety of issues concerning social and political prejudices manifested in the judicial process in general. Then, in his 1927 keynote
speech, "The Attitude of the Administration of Law toward Jews and
Jewry," to a conference of over 400 lawyers convened in Berlin by the
C.V., a speech which was ultimately published by the Philo Verlag, he
outlined the specific grievances of the Jewish community *vis-à-vis* the
justice system. It is clear from this example, and many others that could
be cited, that the perception of a *specifically* Jewish problem did not
exist for the leaders of the C.V. As Zwi Bacharach has pointed out:[5]

> The Jews as staunch Republican Germans often assessed racist anti-
> Semitism as being more of a threat to the Republican order (in which
> they were rooted) than as a threat to their very existence . . .

> Now when Jews set out to protest against the racist doctrine, they did so

---

5   Walter Zwi Bacharach, "Jews in Confrontation with Racist Antisemitism,
     1879-1933," in **XXV** *Leo Baeck Yearbook* (London: Secker & Warburg, 1980),
     at 210. Many historians of Weimar Jewry have testified to the intertwining of
     Jewish interests with those of general German ones. The leaders of the C.V.
     claimed time and again that they were carrying on their fight against anti-
     Semitism not only for the protection of Jewish interests, but for the well-being
     of the German Fatherland. But this well-being depended upon a democratic
     Germany which upheld liberal values. This tied the Jews firmly to the Re-
     publican camp. Peter Pulzer made the following observation in this regard:

     > "What Jews did appreciate was that anti-semitism was also anti-liberal and
     > anti-democratic. The assault on the Jews was also, perhaps primarily, an
     > assault on the Republic. It was therefore more important to defend the
     > Republic than to identify specific enemies."

     Peter Pulzer, "The Beginning of the End," in Arnold Paucker, with Sylvia
     Gilchrist and Barbara Suchy, *The Jews in Nazi Germany: 1933-1945*
     (Tuebingen: J.C.B. Mohr (Paul Siebeck), 1986), at 23.

not first of all as Jews to whom injury had been done — for "it is not merely a Jewish matter that concerns us here, but also a German matter" — they reacted to racism as Germans by presenting opposition thereto in the character of enlightened Germans.

On the other hand, Jewish jurists who were more conservative politically, such as Max Hachenburg, editor of the Deutsche Juristenzeitung, actually *denied* the existence of a general "crisis of law" and, thus, of a Jewish variant of the same.

Post-war scholarly assessments have, generally, upheld the position of the Weimar liberal-left. An attempt by Neussel[6] to defend the conservative view has been independently refuted by Jasper,[7] Rasehorn[8] and Schulz.[9] In 1975, Donald Niewyk attempted to assess the treatment of the Jews in the Weimar courts by means of a quantitative analysis of court decisions. He estimates that, of the 321 cases he studied in which anti-Semites were prosecuted by the courts, only about 7 per cent provide reasonable grounds for criticizing the decisions as favouring the anti-Semitic defendants. These, he argues, are isolated occurrences and were understood to be so by jurists of the Central-Verein themselves. He concludes that:[10]

> Given the virulence of racist propaganda against the Jews, the right-wing sympathies of many judges who were holdovers from Imperial Germany, and the brutality of Nazi activities in the last years of the Republic, German courts achieved an uneven but generally positive record of sheltering Jews from their detractors.

Recently, this view has been championed by Udo Beer. In a study based on his doctoral dissertation, Beer concluded:[11]

> In light of the relevant facts, then it is plain that at least in the field of legal defence the Jews were far more widely recognized as equal citizens with equal rights than has so far been accepted. Indeed, during the life of the Weimar Republic the collective and individual rights of the Jews were effectively protected and enforced by the State and the Jewish organizations.

---

6   Werner Neusel, *supra*, note 4.
7   Gotthard Jasper, *supra*, note 4.
8   Theo Rasehorn, *supra*, note 4.
9   Birger Schulz, *Der Republikanischer Richterbund* (1921-1933) (Frankfurt-am-Main, Bern: Rechtshistorische Reihe 21, Peter Lang Verlag, 1982), 119 at 124-25.
10 Donald L. Niewyk, "Jews and the Courts in Weimar Germany" (1975), XXXVII *Jewish Social Studies* at 113.
11 Udo Beer, "The Protection of Jewish Civil Rights in the Weimar Republic — Jewish Self-Defence through Legal Action," in XXXIII Leo Baeck Yearbook (London: Secker & Warburg, 1988), at 176.

What strikes the reader of the C.V. Zeitung and the various publications of the Philo Verlag as odd, in light of what Niewyk and Beer are suggesting, is the clear sense which one gathers from these documents that the leaders of the Central Verein, by and large, felt that something was clearly wrong with the administration of justice in the Weimar Republic. Erich Eyck, whom Niewyk cites as one of the C.V. figures who *rejected* the notion of a general crisis of law, wrote in advance of the quantitative approach adopted by Niewyk and supported by Beer:[12]

> It has often been said, that these [judicial] errors which have been pointed out, and which are not denied, are not sufficient to establish a general complaint against the administration of justice. For one, they represented only a *limited number* of the total sum of cases prosecuted by our state attorneys and our judges. Furthermore, they primarily concern cases of a *political* bent, and thus have a particularity which is not a determining factor for the whole of the administration of law. In relation to the first point the objection can be raised that above all the total number of cases which gives us concern, of which I can, of course, only discuss a small part, is, nevertheless much too considerable to be overlooked; but above all, it is self-evident, that *one* apparent error can destroy more confidence in the administration of justice than a thousand good and healthy judgments can re-build.

III. THE CASES

It is true, as Niewyk and Beer argue, that the overwhelming majority of cases which went to trial were adjudicated fairly, according to the wording of the law. Nevertheless, there were sufficient numbers of clearly biased verdicts to cause serious alarm in democratic circles, in general, and in the Jewish community, in particular. The examples which follow have been selected because either they are representative of those cases in which the rulings were not in accord with the law, in which case they present the bias of the court against Jews, or those which point out the weakness of legislation from the point of view of the protection of Jewish interests. These cases are extremely important, despite their atypical character, because racists were emboldened and encouraged by them and the Jewish organizations were guided in their actions by them. The mere perception of a crisis of trust in the law would have created an atmosphere of suspicion, uncertainty and, perhaps, fear. We can imagine what the effect of only half a dozen clearly anti-Jewish

---

12 Erich Eyck, *Die Krisis der deutschen Rechtspflege* (Berlin: Verlag fuer Kulturpolitik, 1926), at 30. For a more extensive treatment of the works of Niewyk and Beer, see Cyril Levitt, "The Prosecution of Anti-Semites by the Courts in the Weimar Republic: Was Justice Served?," in Arnold Paucker (ed.), XXXV *Leo Baeck Institute Year Book* (London: Secker & Warburg, 1990) (in press).

rulings in the Canadian judicial system would have on popular opinion, to say nothing of the effect on the Jewish community, despite the thousands of cases adjudicated fairly at the same time.

The crisis of law concerning the Jews was founded on the following considerations: (1) the unequal treatment of Jews from time to time by the justice system; (2) the occasional acceptance by the courts of unreasonable arguments advanced by anti-Semites and/or the rejection of reasonable arguments made by Jewish plaintiffs; (3) the narrow interpretations of the law in some cases involving Jews; (4) the free reign accorded to prominent anti-Semites in some court proceedings in haranguing and badgering their accusers; and (5) the occasional direct anti-Semitic remark made by a court clerk, state attorney or judge during a trial. The following examples are based on reports in the C.V. Zeitung or other publications of the Central Verein.

A. Incitement

In its issue of October 8, 1926, under the heading "Is there actually equal protection of all citizens," the C.V. Zeitung described the case involving two articles, "Der Blutbund" and "Synagoguenjude Schlesinger," which appeared in Der Stuermer. The first article contained a cartoon depicting caricatures of Jewish males sucking the blood out of a naked "Aryan" woman. The sketch was fitted with a descriptive commentary. The local C.V. group in Nuremberg laid a criminal complaint against this incitement under para. 130 of the *Criminal Code* (incitement to class hatred) and demanded the confiscation of the newspaper. The judge ruled as follows:[13]

> The incitement which the plaintiff sees in the two articles "The Blood Bond" and "Synagogue-Jew Schlesinger" must, in order to satisfy the condition [*Tatbestand*] of paragraph 130 of the *Criminal Code*, be an incitement not only to hate or to contempt or to political opposition, but rather an incitement to violent actions. An incitement whose aim is violent actions cannot, however, be inferred from the content of the contested issue [of Der Stuermer]. Even if one were to assume this [to be the case], the further factual legal requirement would be absent, that is, that this incitement be objectively likely to threaten the public peace, namely by *calling forth the danger of the outbreak of violent activities against Jewry*. That the author or the publisher reckoned with such an effect is even less demonstrable.

The author of the report in the C.V. Zeitung lamented that the judge would only have ruled against Der Stuermer if Jews had been beaten to a

---

13 C.V.Z. (Oktober 8, 1926), V Jg. Nr. 41 S. 535. Throughout this paper, the translations from the German are my own.

bloody pulp on the streets of Nuremberg. Foerder had already dealt with this issue in his 1924 pamphlet when he wrote:[14]

> The Supreme Court, moreover, decided in Volume 34, page 268 that the instigation of violent acts against Jews fulfills this requirement when a corresponding fear in the Jews is *subjectively* called forth; it doesn't matter if the invitation is *objectively* likely to cause violent acts to occur. This decision is frequently ignored. Even if it [the Supreme Court interpretation] didn't exist, we should think that the public singing of the song with the refrain: "kill the Jews" is sufficiently suitable to disrupt the public peace ... In a recent case transacted before the police court in Breslau an injunction signed by two experienced state attorneys (head of the political department and department director) is found which suggests [*besagt*] that through the public singing of this refrain "*the public order and security is not threatened or disturbed to any great extent!*" The same position, by the way ... was taken by the Berlin state attorney V. Clausewitz, in that he ordered the suspension of a criminal prosecution against a doctor, who called out on Unter den Linden [a main street in Berlin] "kill the Jews." He took this position on the grounds that it wasn't established that this expression endangered the public peace.

There was a great variation in interpretation of the incitement law among the German courts, although the tendency seems to have been to accept a broader view with the passage of time. In the case of *voelkisch* agitator Berengar Elsner von Gronow, before a court of assessors in Goettingen in January 1927, a broad interpretation of para. 130 by the court led to a conviction. Gronow placed a picture of a ritual murder scene in the window of a *voelkisch* bookstore beside that of the murder of Saint Rudolph along with a note telling parents to beware of this "Kulturschande" — this "cultural defilement." The state attorney, who was about to retire, refused to prosecute, arguing that the juxtaposition of the pictures "did not go beyond the limits of the conflict of opinion protected under the laws" and that the implicit critique was of an old Israelite custom which had no impact upon the Jewish community of the present. Nevertheless, the case was taken up by the new state attorney, who prosecuted vigorously and got a conviction which brought with it a jail term of three weeks or a fine of 300 marks and the removal of the offensive picture. This verdict produced a favourable reaction in the C.V. Zeitung:[15]

> The decision is significant: it exposes the disseminators of this kind of shameful picture as political agitators and takes from them the aura of "enlighteners of the people", with which they so gladly surround themselves.

---

14 Ludwig Foerder, *Antisemitismus und Justiz* (Berlin: Philo Verlag, 1924), at 7.
15 C.V.Z. (January 27, 1927), VII Jg. Nr. 4 S. 40.

It, rightly, does not cling formalistically to an interpretation which sees the condition [*Tatbestand*] of paragraph 130 of the *Criminal Code* (the so-called incitement to class hatred) as given, when violent acts are provoked *expressis verbis*; rather it renews the view expressed long ago by the Supreme Court that the concept of 'incitement' doesn't require a direct provocation but rather the *indirect* influence suffices, e.g. through illustrations without a text.

One legal trick which anti-Semites used to get around the provisions of this law (it was also used to escape the clutches of the law against religious libel, as we shall see) was the claim that the incitement was directed at the Jewish *race*, not at the stirring up of class hatred. Foerder, for example, cites the case involving a student club at a high school in Silesia whose members ambled through the town of Frankenstein singing a song with the refrain:

Grease the guillotine with Jew-fat, Blood must flow, Jew-blood!

Charges could not be laid in this connection under para. 130, according to a state attorney who was also a member of a *voelkisch* organization, since:

According to the recent position advocated by the courts Germans and Jews within the German Reich do not constitute different classes, but different races. Even if one wants to see an incitement in the criticized refrain, only the race antagonisms could be seen to be intensified, but not a provocation to class struggle.

In fact, as Foerder points out, the Supreme Court expressly ruled that Jews are afforded protection under para. 130.[16] He adds that the failure of this law to extend its protection beyond the narrow definition of social class essentially would lead to an open season on minorities living on German soil. The authorities would stand helpless before the incitement to murder members of the Rumanian or Polish populations living within the borders of the Reich.

Finally, what the law meant by "threatening the public peace" was unclear. Did it refer to the *objective* disruption of the peace and order, or would the mere *subjective* feeling of a threat to peace and security suffice for the law to be broken? Once again, there were differing interpretations by the courts.

In order to put teeth into the law and to clarify its provisions, the C.V. supported a revision of the law with the following wording:

Whoever publicly incites to a criminal action or to violent activities

---

16   This ruling is found in vol. 34 at 270. See Foerder, *supra*, note 14 at 8.

against a person or things, will be punished with two years imprisonment or a fine.

Writing in the C.V. Zeitung in 1926, Dr. J. Picard of Cologne assessed the proposed revision as follows:[17]

> ... first, the concept of class is absent here ... Moreover, in place of the word "incitement" [*anreizen*] stands the verb "provoke" [*auffordern*], about which the official reason says that "it refers to every expression which according to the intention of the perpetrator is supposed to have the effect of inspiring in the other the decision to take violent actions." — The ambiguous nature of the disruption of the public peace is entirely missing from here. And above all the stipulation punishes violent activities against things just as it does against persons. It is also clear that precisely this extension of the old state of affairs would be valuable to us; for until now, when in the mood for a pogrom during brawls heretics provoke the destruction of Jewish display windows and stores, they could hardly be touched by the criminal law, if it didn't come to violent actions.

B. Religious Insult

The law against religious insult was another weapon in the arsenal of the German justice system which was used against anti-Semitic attacks upon the Jewish religion and Jewish institutions. In many cases in which charges were laid and prosecutions pursued, convictions were obtained. One example is the case of Georg Quindel of Hanover, who, in 1924, published an article in his *voelkisch* newspaper, Der Sturm [The Storm], entitled "Der Judengott Jahwe" [The Jew-God Yahwe], in which he contended that there were two Yahwes — Yahwe being the unutterable name for the God of the ancient Hebrews — the second being a secret, devilish God worshipped in secret by the Jews. Rabbi Dr. Freund, who bore witness for the prosecution, was able to make short shrift of Quindel's theological aspirations. The court found Quindel guilty and sentenced him to a fine of 150 marks. Note was taken of the fact that Quindel had read many books, but, in the court's view, he lacked the mental capacity to digest them.[18]

There were a number of tricks used by anti-Semites to get around the provisions of this law, as well. Theodor Fritsch, perhaps the most prolific of the hate-mongers in both Imperial Germany and the Weimar

---

17 Picard is not completely accepting of the proposed revision here since it does not eliminate the possibility of levelling a mere fine in such a serious matter: see Dr. J. Picard (Koeln) *"Die Strafgesetzreform"* C.V.Z. (Juli 23, 1926), V Jg. Nr. 30 S. 393-95.

18 "Quindel wegen Gotteslaesterung bestraft: Mildernde Umstaende: geistige Unfaehigkeit" C.V.Z. (Oktober 12, 1924), III Jg. Nr. 41 S. 623.

Republic, and a man who did much to fertilize the ground for National Socialism, sought to convince the courts that his attacks on the God of the Jews concerned only the old deity of the ancient Hebrews, but bore no relation to the modern concept which had been influenced by the Prophets and, above all, by Christianity. He had some limited success in this regard.

Foerder pointed out the case of a charge under para. 166 laid against a newspaper which carried a report of a visit to a synagogue by a family of Russian Jews. The newspaper reported: "They offered thanks to their bloodthirsty and hate-filled God, for having given them the power to live without effort from the labour dripping with the sweat of the stupid, good-natured 'Goyims' (*sic*) [non-Jews]."[19] The court found the newspaper not guilty, arguing that the words "bloodthirsty" and "hate-filled" could not be construed as a "raw insult" given "the general ferment and nervousness of the present time." Furthermore, the court found no blasphemy in the article, suggesting that at most the Russian-Jewish family, perhaps Russian-Jewish families in general, were libelled by it. The prosecution appealed, and the Supreme Court overturned the verdict, arguing that, in portraying this Russian-Jewish family (and in not distinguishing it from other Jewish families) giving thanks to their God for advancing their unethical cause, the newspaper not only cast aspersions on the character of the family, but also upon their God. As far as the issue of the ferment and nervousness of the times was concerned, the Supreme Court suggested that this could not be the basis for determining whether or not an expression was libellous. The existing conditions can, at most, provide a basis for determining the extent of the penalty to be assessed.[20]

Two other possibilities of getting around the provisions of this law were used by defendants. The first of these was similar to the defence raised in connection with para. 130, concerning incitement to class hatred. It was asserted by many defence lawyers that the insult, which was not denied, was not directed against the Jewish religion, but against the Jewish race. This tact became important as the older Christian anti-Semitism yielded to the modern racist view. Foerder, for example, cited the case of a private tutor named Knobel who was charged under para. 166 for leading a group of 12- to 14-year-old *voelkisch* youths in spitting three times in front of a Jewish cemetery. Upon his apprehension, he claimed that he intended to show no disrespect to the Jewish dead, but rather, only contempt for the Jewish race. The Provincial Court of Glogau accepted this explanation without seeking to ascertain whether or not the accused had the intention of showing contempt for the

---

19   Foerder, *supra*, note 14 at 9.
20   *Ibid.*, at 10.

religious community of Jews, since a Jewish cemetery is a religious site within which religious ceremonies are conducted.

The other claim made by anti-Semites charged under this paragraph of the *Criminal Code* concerns the teachings of the Jewish religion, which, according to the wording of the law, were not protected. Attacks on the Christian doctrine of the trinity were prevented by defining such dogma as part of the religious institution or community, but the Jewish code of religious law was not offered the same protection.

One case, in which we see a state attorney accepting the *voelkisch* claims, concerns the publication of an anti-Semitic piece in the *voelkisch* paper, *Die Flamme*, which referred to:

> Jewish pigs, who, faithful to their religious law texts, the Talmud and Shulchan Aruch, defile non-Jewish women and girls.

> The rabbinical teaching makes these acts of these pig-priests into a *duty* and elevates them to a *religious law*, when it states: "The defilement of non-Jewish women is not a sin. Sanhedrin 52."

A complaint was lodged with the office of the state attorney in Bamberg. The response of the state attorney to the complaint is enlightening:[21]

> The article which is objected to in No. 23 of the "Flamme" advances the assertion "the rabbinical teaching makes the defilement of non-Jewish women and girls into a duty and into a religious law." Thus it contains an attack on the teaching of the Jewish religious community. Paragraph 166, however, according to its wording and origin, wishes to protect not the teaching of the religious communities, but only the society itself and its institutions against insulting attacks. According to the established administration of justice the teaching is not to be considered as an institution in the sense of this regulation. An attack against a doctrine is, therefore, not an infraction of paragraph 166 . . .

> Moreover, the article is not directed, as is shown in the wording, against the Jewish *religious community*, but rather "against the Jewish race"; an insult from this direction is not to be deemed a transgression against religion, but at most as libel. The prosecution of such can be pursued by means of a private action.

Thus, the prosecution on account of a transgression against a religion was terminated.

Difficulties in prosecuting these cases would have been lessened, in the view of the C.V., with the adoption of two new draft laws which would have replaced para. 166 in a revised *Criminal Code*. In draft para. 167 religious teachings also would have been covered. Furthermore,

---

21 "Gleicher Schutz allen Staatsbuergern" C.V.Z. (September 17, 1926), V Jg. Nr. 38 S. 499-500.

according to this draft, actual suffering would not have to be established, nor would the concept of God have to be involved in the action. Under this law, both Fritsch's and Knobel's attempts at avoiding a conviction would have been impossible.

The proposed para. 168 would have covered the disruption of religious services, no matter where they occurred. This would have been an improvement over existing legislation, according to which religious services must have been taking place in a recognized house of worship. Since Jews can pray anywhere, they were not accorded full protection under the law.

C. Insult, Libel, Slander

The Weimar Republic was notorious for the large number of libel cases which involved men of high office. Perhaps the most spectacular of these court cases was initiated by the first President of the Republic, Friedrich Ebert. Late in the War, Ebert joined a strike committee of munitions workers who had laid down their tools in spite of the difficult situation on the front. He was accused of treason by Rothardt, the editor of a Magdeburg newspaper. Ebert brought suit against him, and Rothardt was convicted and sentenced to three months in jail. Even though the court agreed that Ebert joined the strike committee *in order to bring the strike to a swift conclusion,* he was, nevertheless, guilty of treason in a legal sense. This is precisely the result that Rothardt had wanted to achieve. It was a tactic that was used time and again in the Weimar Republic to discredit public figures. The courts were thus used as forums for examining the lives of leading personalities in minute detail and casting aspersions upon their character at every turn.[22] Ebert was con-

---

22   This practice of maligning an opponent to the point that he brings suit in order to use the court proceedings to ask embarrassingly personal questions and raise doubts in the public mind as to his moral qualities was also used *against* anti-Semites. One of the most poignant examples of this concerns the libel suit by Pastor Muenchmeyer of the North Sea island of Borkum against several Jewish and non-Jewish authors, publishers and distributors of a pamphlet directed against him entitled "The False Priest, or the Chief of the Cannibals of the North Sea Islanders." Borkum had a national reputation for being a resort which did not welcome Jews. It had a sort of unofficial anti-Semitic anthem — the Borkum song — which was played by the band at a popular spa and sung regularly by the guests. The C.V. had a difficult time in getting the singing of the song and the playing of the music stopped. Muenchmeyer was one of the leaders of the anti-Semitic movement on the island. Forced to press charges at the circulation of the pamphlet, Muenchmeyer was discredited in court and put out of business, even though the defendants lost the case and paid a nominal fine. *Cf.* Alfred Hirschberg, "Muenchmeyer-Prozess auf Borkum" (May 14, 1926), C.V.Z. at 271-72; *ibid.,* "Disziplinverfahren gegen Muenchmeyer?" (May 21, 1926), C.V.Z. at 283; Bruno Weil, "Borkum" (May 28, 1926), C.V.Z. at 297-98; Niewyk, *supra,* note 10 at 111.

tinually haunted by such charges, leading some historians to suggest that his early death was hastened by the constant battles in the courts which he fought in order to clear his name.[23]

These trials often had a "Jewish" connection, even if the target of the libel or slander was not Jewish and had no connection to the Jewish community. Such was the case of Albert Grzesinski, President of the Berlin Police Department and Prussian Minister of the Interior (SPD). He was hounded continually by the Nazis in speech and in print, and took his tormentors to court 100 times, although, as Rasehorn points out, this represents only a fraction of the number of attacks which he suffered. He was described as a "Jew-bastard," the illegitimate progeny of a Jewish farmer named Cohn and a woman that worked for him. (In fact, both his mother and father came from respectable, middle class, non-Jewish, German families.) Grzesinski's personal life was also dragged through the mud. In spite of the fact that it was easy to prove that all these allegations were untrue, the Nazis seemed to put a great deal of effort into provoking Grzesinski to bring charges of libel against them.[24]

Rasehorn explains why they were so anxious to be taken to court:

> But the courts often didn't protect the person here, but rather harmed him. The administration of justice in the trials initiated by Ebert and the then Federal Chancellor Marx (Zentrum) was continued here. Marx, who was himself a judge for a long while, let it be known in a speech to the Reichstag on February 17, 1926 that he would no longer lay criminal charges for defamation and insult.

At times Grzesinski did not even have the satisfaction of winning the case against his defamers. In one trial, the judge found the allegation that someone was an illegitimate child with one Jewish parent not libellous, even if untrue.[25] Even when Grzesinski was successful in achieving a

---

23 Another famous example is that of Karl Helferich, former *Staatssekretaer*, who accused the first Minister of Finance, Matthias Erzberger (Zentrum) of being corrupt, and thus a liability to Germany, in a story in the *Kreuzzeitung* entitled "Fort mit Erzberger." Helferich, who became a leading figure in the DNVP, declared openly that he made his allegations in order to get Erzberger into court, where he could use the "truth defence" to pull Erzberger through the mud in public. Even though Helferich was fined 300 RM, Erzberger's career was ruined and he resigned. (Erzberger had raised the ire of the nationalist right with his peace resolution in the Reichstag in July 1917. On August 26, 1921 Erzberger was murdered by two former members of the Erhardt Brigade.) Petersen, *supra*, note 4 at 57.

24 Nazi member of the Prussian *Landtag*, Kube, wrote in a letter: "I have requested our *Gauleiter* for East Hanover, Mr. Telschow to employ the entire labour power of the local group of the National Socialist German Worker's Party for this politically altogether extraordinarily important trial." See Rasehorn, *supra*, note 4 at 208.

25 See "Calumniare audacter" (author anonymous), *Die Justiz*, Band VIII, 1932/33, at 106-121. *Cf.* Rasehorn, *supra*, note 4 at 173-74 and 209.

"victory" in court, the huge propaganda effect of such a trial was purchased for the small fine of 300-500 RM in each case.[26]

> Every simple propaganda film, every leaflet or every kind of other propaganda costs more and doesn't have nearly the lasting and impressive effect as this kind of agitation which appeals to the lowest instincts.

If non-Jews were occasionally subjected to this abuse, Jewish officials and public figures, *a fortiori*, had to reckon with this kind of hounding. The feisty nemesis of Goebbels, Vice President of the Berlin Police Department, Bernhard Weiss, went to court on a regular basis to contest the libel and slander directed at him by his enemies. Goebbels never referred to Weiss by name, but by the Jewish-sounding "Isidor." For this, Weiss dragged the Nazi propagandist to court again and again. And even though Weiss won his cases, Bering suggests that he was in fact the loser:[27]

> Weiss won all his trials, from the juridical point of view, but he was, nevertheless, always the loser. These supposedly harmless jokes and word games, which had as their object a change of name, were not at all harmless, because they always affected the identity of the person.

In light of this, Bering wonders "whether the police vice president would not have been better advised, in spite of everything, to simply allow the reproaches of the Nazis to reverberate in silence."[28]

There were many other such cases of libel throughout the course of the Weimar Republic. The famous libel trial of Theodor Fritsch, initiated by Max Warburg, went to five appeals and continued over several years.[29] There were also many, many instances of libel contested in the

---

26 "Calumniare audacter," *ibid.*, at 121; *cf.* Rasehorn, *ibid.*, at 210.

27 Dietz Bering, "Von der Notwendigkeit politischer Beleidigungsprozesse — Der Beginn der Auseinandersetzung zwischen Polizeipraesident Bernhard Weiss und der NSDAP," Walter Grab and Julius Schoeps (eds.), *Die Juden in der Weimarer Republic*, at 368.

28 *Ibid.*, at 321.

29 "Fritsch drei Monaten Gefaengnis verurteilt: Die endgueltige Erledigung einer Verleumdung" C.V.Z. (Dezember 19, 1924), III Jg. Nr. 51 S. 815; "Der Warburg-Fritsch-Prozess: Vor der Urteilsverkuendung in Hamburg" C.V.Z. (January 22, 1926), V Jg. Nr. 4 S. 41; "Der Ausgang des Warburg-Fritsch Prozesses: Fritsch zu 1000 Mark Geldstrafe verurteilt" C.V.Z. (January 29, 1926), V Jg. Nr. 5 S. 52; "Aufhebung eines Fehlurteils. Das Revisionsurteil in Sachen Warburg-Fritsch" C.V.Z. (April 23, 1926), V Jg. Nr. 17 S. 229-230; "Zur Neuauflage des Warburg-Fritsch-Prozesses" C.V.Z. (Oktober 22, 1926), V Jg. Nr. 43 S. 560; "Fritsch zu 4 Monaten Gefaengnis verurteilt" C.V.Z. (Oktober 29, 1926), V Jg. Nr. 44 S. 573; "Das Urteil im Prozess Warburg-Fritsch bestaetigt" C.V.Z. (April 1, 1927), VI Jg. Nr. 13 S. 164.

courts by less illustrious persons. Among these were cases of group libel brought by Jewish groups, notwithstanding the fact that the "crime" of group libel was not clearly defined in the *Criminal Code*, as we shall soon see. This absence of a clearly defined group libel remedy in the law was the subject of concern by the leaders of the C.V.,[30] who supported such a law in the new draft of the *Criminal Code*.[31] Historians of the *Abwehrtaetigkeit* in the Weimar Republic have also suggested that a law against group libel would have considerably strengthened the defensive arsenal of anti-racist forces.[32]

Although there were many paragraphs in the *Criminal Code* relating to the laws of insult, specifying who may bring charges and under which conditions, as Alfred Hirschberg points out in a study which was published by the C.V. in 1929, the juridical understanding of "insult" was something which was hotly contested.[33]

Here is an example reported by the C.V. Zeitung of a court case involving only two individuals: a physician sent a note to three neighbours who had called upon another doctor for their medical needs instead of the note sender. The overlooked practitioner inquired whether his nationalist activities — he was the local leader of a *voelkisch* group — was the reason for their not calling on him, or whether they simply preferred the services of a Jewish physician (the popular colleague in question was a Christian from a mixed marriage). The latter charged the former before an *Ehrengericht* (court of honour). The note sender was found not to be guilty, because the court saw no reason why the doctor should not inquire about the reasons why his neighbours were not using his services. This caused the C.V. to cynically write: "Geht es um die Kasse, benutzt man auch die Rasse! (If it's a question of money, race is used as well!)"[34]

Another case involved repeated insults of a German-Jewish landlord by a French tenant. The latter was in the habit of calling the former by the term "German pig." The Jewish landlord initiated proceedings against the tenant. The judge in the Berlin court ruled against the plaintiff with the following justification:[35]

---

30 Ludwig Hollaender, "Lehren Politischer Prozesse" C.V.Z. (Oktober 11, 1923), 11 Jg. Nr. 41 at 1.

31 "Kollektivbeleidigung" C.V.Z. (November 19, 1926), V Jg. Nr. 47 at 609.

32 See, *e.g.*, Arnold Paucker, *supra*, note 4 at 78.

33 Alfred Hirschberg, *Kollektiv-Ehre und Kollektiv-Beleidigung* (Berlin: Philo Verlag, 1929), at 9-34.

34 "Neugierige Fragen an einen Gutsbesitzer: eine Ehrengerichtliche Entscheidung" C.V.Z. (Juli 17, 1924), III Jg. Nr. 29 S. 431.

35 Erich Eyck, *supra*, note 12 at 23. A reference to the same case is found in "Offener Brief an Herrn Dr. Otto Liebmann, Herausgeber der Deutschen Juristen-Zeitung. Von Reichsjustizminister a.D. Dr. Gustav Radbruch, or-

> The plaintiff is not injured in his citizenship [and] according to his descent is not a person who is reckoned to the Germans in common parlance.

Eyck points out, in this connection, that the judge was incapable of feeling just how upsetting such insults were to members of the Jewish community.

There were many cases of insult which were levelled not at individual Jews, but at Jews as a group. As was stated above, no explicit law existed in the *Criminal Code* which offered the Jewish community protection from such collective attacks. Foerder suggested that the Jews would have had a better chance in the courts if charges were brought by an organization which represented all of Germany's Jews (the *Verband der Deutscher Juden*, which had been an umbrella organization representing most German Jews, had ceased to exist in 1922). In the absence of such an organization, charges would have to be brought by individuals or smaller organizations. This left an opening for anti-Semites to claim that the plaintiffs were not meant as the object of attack. According to a decision of the Supreme Court in 1881 (which actually concerned a case of collective defamation of Jews), it was necessary to prove that the defendant meant to insult certain persons and to specify which persons were meant to be insulted.[36] It was not so much the lack of an effective legal remedy that bothered Jewish jurists, but the inconsistency of the courts in applying the law differently according to which groups were being libelled. Foerder suggests that broader interpretations of the law were made, but not when it concerned the Jews. In 1880, for example, a journalist was charged with libel for writing an article in which he asserted that there were a large number of unprincipled careerists among Prussian judges. The Supreme Court found that an insult could be seen here against each individual member of this class, even though only an unidentified portion of this class was actually attacked. In fact, it was precisely on account of this indeterminateness that every member of the class had grounds for a libel action. Foerder points out that similar decisions were reached in relation to landed proprietors and Prussian officers.[37] Beer adds the following groups who received group protection in this fashion: the officer corps of a garrison, German non-commissioned officers, army trainers, German officers, the German troops that fought in Belgium, the conservative majority of an electoral meeting, the big landowners of a specific province, all clerics of the Christian religion, the Germans living among Poles in areas of mixed

---

dentl. Professor der Rechte an der Universitaet Kiel," in *Die Justiz*, Band I, 1925/26, Berlin, at 196. *Cf.* Rasehorn, *supra*, note 4 at 169.

36 Foerder, *supra*, note 14 at 43.

37 Foerder, *ibid.*, at 13.

composition, the members of a general synod, and detectives who were on duty at a specific place during a specific time. In fact, the only group which was excluded from this kind of protection was the Jews.[38]

Erich Eyck, writing in the C.V. Zeitung, reviewed the problem of group defamation from the point of view of Jewish interests. In the eyes of the law, only an individual could be libelled. A corporation or juridical person could not. However, a plurality of natural individuals who were conceptualized under a collective designation could be libelled, as in the case of officers of a garrison or judges of a certain district. This was true if the libel applied to every individual that fell under this specific collective designation. The libel did not have to refer to any particular individual(s); the libeller did not even have to know of the existence of the individual(s) in question. Eyck went on to say that there were a number of subjective elements at work here. Whether or not the general defamatory assertion could be seen to apply to the person bringing the charge was a matter which had not been consistently decided in juridical practice. Sometimes the law had drawn the definition of the group of offended persons narrowly, sometimes much more broadly. In the case involving the defamation of Germans by a Pole in an area of mixed ethnic composition, the court ruled:[39]

> The broad extent of the plurality of individuals who are affected by a collective defamation is not in itself in opposition to the fact that all those individual persons without exception can be conceived to be defamed if it can be assumed that this result is circumscribed by the intention of the defamer.

Eyck also called attention to a 1926 decision which promised the Jews similar legal redress. A leaflet of the *Voelkische Partei*, insulting to Jews, was distributed in Bretten (Baden) in relation to the elections on May 4, 1924. Five youths were fined 150 marks. They appealed the fine, arguing that the contents of the leaflet did not apply to the Jews in Bretten. The local judge agreed with them and they were acquitted. The *Amtsgericht* in Bretten justified the acquittal, on January 9, 1925, on the traditional grounds that "the defamations were not directed at a specific, limited circle of persons, since Jewry in its entirety is affected." On further appeal, however, the *Oberlandsgericht* at Karlsruhe ruled that "the defamation, with regard to its contents, is directed against every single member of the Israelites living in Bretten." The acquittal was overturned and the matter referred to a new hearing at the *Amtsgericht* in Pforzheim. This court found the defendants guilty and levelled fines

---

38 Beer, *supra*, note 11 at 233.
39 "Um die Frage der Kollektivbeleidigung: Eine juristische Untersuchung von Rechtsanwalt Dr. Erich Eyck" C.V.Z. (Februar 26, 1926), V Jg. Nr. 9 S. 101-102.

between 50 and 120 marks together with costs. As part of the sentence, the judgment had to be published within two months in the Sueddeutschen Volksblatt, the paper of the local DNVP, and the Brettener Zeitung.[40]

According to Eyck, this decision was important insofar as it broke with the argument laid down by the Supreme Court in 1881, according to which, libellous statements about Jews as a group could not be prosecuted. Nevertheless, this new ruling did not relate to defamations of Jews everywhere. The circle of Jews affected was limited to Jews of Bretten, speaking a peculiar dialect, on a certain day.

There were yet other problems facing complainants in cases of defamation. One of the protections of free expression which stood in the way of prosecuting libel or slander was the so-called "protection of legitimate interests" guaranteed in para. 193 of the *Criminal Code*. Foerder points out that, next to the excuse of extreme intoxication, the protection of legitimate interests was the most popular ground adopted by anti-Semites at their defamation trials. He also points out that this legitimate protection of free expression was often abused, in that it was sometimes successfully employed as a cover to unjustly accuse Jews of unethical or criminal behaviour. In one such case, the chairman of the Breslau section of the *voelkisch Deutscher Schutz — und Trutzbund* was taken to court by the C.V. for declaring, before an audience of 3,000, that the C.V. maintains a "murder central" in the Saxon town of Halle, which has offered a reward for the murder of a local *voelkisch* leader. The court found the defendant not guilty on the grounds that he had a justifiable interest in making the charge to the meeting, which was called by invitation only, to protect the *voelkisch* leadership from attacks by the C.V. On appeal, an Assessor Court overturned the verdict and found him guilty, but in a second appeal he was again found innocent.

In another case cited by Foerder and repeated by Beer, a *voelkisch* doctor was found innocent of defaming a Jewish colleague in a professional journal. He had accused him of having given false testimony in court for the benefit of a fellow Jewish physician in a dispute between that physician and a Christian patient. An Assessor Court had originally found the *voelkisch* doctor guilty of libel for insinuating that the alleged false testimony of the Jewish doctor stemmed from a supposed religious obligation to lie for a fellow Jew. But even though it had been ascertained that the Jewish doctor had in fact not testified falsely in support of his co-religionist colleague, the Appeal Court reversed the decision. The reasons given by the court are revealing. First, the court argued that the

---

40   "Um die Frage der Kollektivbeleidigung: Eine wichtige Gerichtsentscheidung" Dr. A. Kuntzemueller (Freiburg i. Br.) C.V.Z. (Februar 19, 1926), V Jg. Nr. 8 S. 88.

intention to libel could not be inferred from the form of publication of the charges against the Jewish doctor. Second, the court found that the accused believed that the Jewish doctor had lied to support his co-religionist. Furthermore, he included in his charge the explanation of why the Jewish doctor acted in the way he did. It was not for some selfish reason such as personal enrichment or career advancement, but rather out of a selfless religious duty. The accused believed that the Jewish religion demands that its followers lie for one another, if necessary, in relation to matters involving non-Jews. Whether or not such a religious obligation exists is irrelevant in the eyes of the court. The accused believed that it existed. The court also argued that a similar altruism could be seen in the willingness of the Jewish doctor to support a colleague, even by lying. Thus, no libel occurred since the accused demonstrated that the Jewish doctor acted out of religious duty and professional sympathy and not out of self-aggrandizing motives.[41] In other words, the court held that because the *voelkisch* doctor believed the Jewish colleague to have lied for his fellow Jew (even though this was shown to have been false) and because he had imputed a lofty motive for this alleged false witness, namely, love of a fellow Jew and sympathy for a fellow physician rather than hope for selfish gain, and because the *voelkisch* doctor believed that the Jewish religion demands immoral or illegal acts in support of fellow members (regardless of whether such religious demands exist or not), no libel had been committed.

Foerder goes on to suggest that the defamer may act to protect a legitimate interest when recourse to defamation is the only alternative left to the individual. In the case of anti-Semitic attacks it has often been the avenue of first choice.[42]

> In both of the above cases one cannot speak of the defamer being *forced* to give their Jew-hatred the free reign that they did. The leader of the meeting did in no way have to accuse the regional group of the *Central-Verein* in Halle of instigating murder, in order to cloak the supposed fearfulness of the German *Schutz-und Trutzbund* in Breslau. The doctor could have practiced the sharpest professional critique without at all touching upon the religious affiliation of his colleague.

Jewish complaints were not only directed at the failures of the system of justice to protect Jewish rights and interests, they were also voiced in regard to what was widely perceived as a double standard in applying the law. One area of deep concern involved the response of state attorneys to Jewish complaints. It was the prerogative of the state attorneys in cases of delicts concerning libel, coercion, threats and

---

41 See Foerder, *supra*, note 14 at 14-15; see also Beer, *supra*, note 11 at 235-36.
42 Foerder, *ibid.*, at 15-16.

bodily harm, to recognize a public interest in the prosecution. Very often, Jewish complainants were told that there was no public interest in the case, and hence they were advised either to pursue the charges by means of a private action or to simply drop the matter. Foerder describes the advantages in having a case prosecuted by the state attorney:[43]

> The practical consequences of these different treatments is shown above all in the fact that the aggrieved is a party in the private action [and] thus cannot be called as a witness, therefore under certain circumstances in relation to the denials of the accused and in the absence of other witnesses cannot offer any proof for the substance of his denunciation. In addition he must pay certain costs in advance. Moreover, when he must prosecute the case himself, he has no access to the state attorney, the organs of the police for, say, the necessary investigations. But beyond this an entirely different moral effect is, of course, worked upon the delinquent when he sees that the state attorney's office immediately takes the part of the aggrieved and helps him to achieve satisfaction.

Here are several examples of cases rejected by state attorneys for not being of public interest:[44]

> A Jewish woman was hit over the head with a walking stick by a leading anti-Semite without provocation and suffered severe nervous shock as a result.

> An old Jewish man was cursed in the crudest way and threatened with death by a young overseer at the Kurplatz in Salzbrunn.

> A young Jewish man was attacked and beaten up by five anti-Semitic rowdys on a public street at night.

> A Jewish salesman's display windows were smashed by a member of a respectable student organization. The student declared upon his being questioned by the police: "When I smash the windows of a Semite, that does no harm."

In contrast to these cases, the state attorneys seemed to have no problem in finding a public interest in the prosecution of cases brought by anti-Semites against Jews for forcibly removing their swastika pins. Sometimes these cases were treated as theft. Erich Eyck also criticized this double standard when he wrote: "that the same ideas which show themselves to be insufficient to count as libel of Jews, in another case go

---

43 Foerder, *ibid.*, at 16.
44 Foerder goes on to say that the rejections by the state attorneys in these cases were appealed, and in some cases all the way to the Ministry of Justice: *ibid.*

so far that it comes to criminal prosecution."[45] And Ludwig Hollaender, director of the C.V., pointed out on many occasions that the public outcry would be extremely intense should a Jewish author libel the Christian religion in ways which are done repeatedly by anti-Semites in relation to the Jewish religion.

IV. DISCUSSION IN LIEU OF A CONCLUSION

The above presentation covers only the most important areas of *criminal* law concerning racist provocation in the Weimar Republic. Excluded from consideration has been the important area of civil law, which afforded the Jewish minority certain protections, especially in the latter half of the republic with the largely successful campaign to stop the boycott movement against them. In addition, the civil courts were able to issue injunctions against the repetition of acts which had already been condemned by the criminal courts. This was particularly important in relation to libellous attacks on Jews in the Nazi press. Also excluded from consideration is the question of the use of laws *against* Jews. The range of items which could have been considered under this rubric would extend from the unjustified prosecution of a prominent Jew, Ludwig Haas, for murder in Magdeburg, to the attempts to outlaw the practice of ritual slaughter. Issues of Jewish civil rights were also left out of account.

At this point, I wish to consider several larger questions which have arisen in the course of my investigation and which deserve to be addressed directly. The first of these concerns the assessment of the record of the administration of justice in the Weimar Republic in relation to the legal prosecution of racists. Relevant here is the recent claim by Udo Beer, following the path cut by Niewyk, that the legal system did provide an instrument which generally offered the Jewish community effective protection and equal justice during the Weimar Republic.[46]

In considering this important issue, the first step must be to take into consideration the views expressed by the spokesmen of the Jewish community in the Weimar Republic. There can be no doubt that the great majority of C.V. leaders shared the following view, expressed by Alfred Wiener in relation to the conference of jurists organized by the C.V. in Berlin to consider the question of the justice system and the Jews:[47]

---

45 Eyck, *supra*, note 12 at 53.
46 See Niewyk, *supra*, note 10 at 113; Beer, *supra*, note 4 at 254, 268 and 303-305; Beer, *supra*, note 11 at 175-76.
47 "Die Juristentagung des C.V. Ueberblick — Ablauf — Ergebnis," Von Alfred Wiener, C.V.Z. (Juni 4, 1927), VI Jg. Nr. 25 S. 353-55.

Why this inner passion of the participants? Many may have been treading on new territory whose character captivated them. That here and there the basis of a verdict came, suspiciously, too close to the so-called science of race, did not escape them. They had also read in these pages highly unusual interpretations of paragraph 166 of the Reich's *Criminal Code*, which removed legal protection from the Jewish religion. But they were astounded, yes, they were shaken by the *great extent of such material*, of such low estimation of Jews and Jewry. And even if every reporter, every speechmaker is fearfully careful of even imagining in his wildest dreams a German judge capable of a conscious misjudgment — in relation to the thousands and thousands of justified verdicts in civil and criminal trials in which Jews were involved they all felt that the numerous reported cases of misjudgments, of actual errors of reasoning were not lapses of an individual, but rather often systematic consequences *of a frightening lack of knowledge, even misunderstandings of Jewish life and Jewish views of the world.*

. . . One may or may not wish to speak of a Jewish legal distress — the protection of Jews and Jewry through the laws is not sufficient, yes, it breaks down.

Frequent references by Foerder, Eyck, Hollaender, Reichmann, Weil and many others leave no doubt in the reader's mind that the generally accepted view of the leadership of the Central-Verein in relation to the administration of justice was a *critical* one. The rejection of this view by conservatives such as Kurt Alexander stand out as clear exceptions to the reader of the C.V. Zeitung. True, as both Niewyk and Beer point out, the situation in Prussia was far better than in Bavaria or East Prussia, and the practices of the civil courts were certainly more favourable than those of the criminal justice system.[48] The general picture which emerges, however, is of a Jewish community which has lost confidence in the administration of justice in general. Thus, Beer's claim that "(t)hose in charge of the C.V. Legal Defence Department, too, declared themselves satisfied by the judicial decisions of the German courts"[49] simply cannot be accepted.[50]

But if there was no condition of legal distress for Jews in the Weimar Republic, why did the *majority* of the C.V. legal experts continually refer to such a condition? I think that Beer correctly sensed the answer to this when he wrote that "the question of a specific Jewish state of distress in

---

48   See Niewyk, *supra*, note 10 at 101-102.

49   Beer, *supra*, note 11 at 175.

50   Beer himself admits that the record of the courts in cases of group libel was less than impressive: "Mit Ausnahme des Bereichs der Kollektivbeleidigung gelang es den Verletzten fast immer, in hoeheren Instanzen ihr Recht zu finden." *Supra*, note 4 at 254. But Niewyk points out that clearly half of the cases that he gathered concerned libel (individual and group) and this represented by far the largest category of cases before the courts. See Niewyk, *supra*, note 10 at 101.

respect of law and justice arose in connection with the wider debate on the 'crisis of confidence besetting justice', initiated by Erich Eyck, among others."[51] In fact, there was a large-scale and highly politicized debate about the crisis of the administration of justice during the Weimar Republic. The existence of a *Rechtskrise* or a *Vertrauenskrise der Justiz* was proclaimed largely by the liberal left (DDP) and the socialists (SPD), and it was denied largely by the Catholic party (Zentrum), the liberal right (DVP) and the German nationalists (DNVP). Almost all post-World War II historical research has supported the view of a condition of legal distress during the Weimar Republic.

A majority of German Jews supported the *Deutsche Demokratische Partei* (DDP).[52] Jewish support for the DDP was especially strong in Berlin. Ludwig Hollaender, the undisputed head of the C.V., was a member of the DDP. Most of the leadership of the C.V. were either members or sympathizers of the left-liberals. As such, they would have been close to the *Republikanischer Richterbund*, the Alliance of Republican Judges which carried the fight against the one-sided practice of justice in the Weimar Republic. It was these republican judges, socialists and liberals, who criticized Weimar courts for being "blind in the right eye," that is, treating the radical left more harshly than the radical right. It was they who exposed the monarchist and anti-democratic orientation of the majority of their colleagues and who showed how their interpretation of the law was not in consonance with the spirit of the Constitution.

Time and again the legal minds of the C.V. indicated that the Jewish concern for justice was part of a larger German concern. Alfred Wiener expressed this when he wrote: "*Impartial justice* — only this is Dr. Eyck's demand, not only for the sake of Jewish Germans, but indeed for the great German Fatherland."[53] No issue demonstrated the close identification between the liberal, democratic Weimar Republic and the Jews than the defamation of the republic as the *Judenrepublik* — the

---

51 Beer, *supra*, note 11 at 176. In fact, the first major treatment of the crisis of law was Foerder's pamphlet published by the Philo Verlag in 1924. Allusions to the crisis are found in the pages of the C.V.Z., and examples of miscarriages of justice appeared in *Im deutschen Reich*, the newspaper which preceded the C.V.Z. (which first appeared in 1922).

52 See Ernest Hamburger and Peter Pulzer, "Jews as Voters in the Weimar Republic," in XXX *Leo Baeck Yearbook* (London: Secker & Warburg, 1985), at 48; Arnold Paucker, "Jewish Self-Defence," in Arnold Paucker with Sylvia Gilchrist and Barbara Suchy (eds.), *Die Juden im Nationalsozialistischen Deutschland. The Jews in Nazi Germany 1933-1943*, Schriftenreihe wissenschaftlicher Abhandlungen des Leo Baeck Instituts, J.C.B. Mohr (Paul Siebeck) (1986), at 58.

53 Wiener, *supra*, note 47.

"Jew-Republic." In reporting a case in which a speaker to a *voelkisch* group of 60 to 70 members in the town of Gotha exclaimed: "We don't need the Jew-Republic, *fie* Jew-Republic!", the C.V. Zeitung expressed outrage at this united attack upon the republican democracy and upon the Jews. The fact that the Supreme Court did not see a clear insult here, increased the anger of the Jewish paper.[54]

Why Beer has not addressed the liberal character of the C.V. leadership, and linked their views on Jewish legal distress to it more forcefully, is not clear. A more straightforward approach would be to describe the views of the majority and then to discuss the dissenting opinions of men like Max Hachenburg and Kurt Alexander along political lines. Instead of denying the existence of a general crisis of law in the Weimar Republic through the back door, so to speak, Beer should have made his intention explicit. That there were *serious* problems and gaps in the administration of justice, especially in the criminal courts — regardless of what one chooses to call it — cannot be denied.

The second question which forces itself upon us, in reflecting on the experiences of the Weimar Republic, concerns the general effects of the trials of racists on the general population. Was the Jewish community well-served by having the trials? (I am referring only to those cases which followed upon complaints being laid by Jews or their agents.) That Jewish leaders themselves were cautious in this regard can be seen from the record. As early as 1919, Alfred Wiener suggested that the decision to press charges be carefully considered on a case-by-case basis and that only serious cases be pursued.[55] He wrote:[56]

---

54 The judgment of the court read in part as follows:
  "The expression 'Jew-Republic' can be used in many senses. It can designate the particular form of the democratic republic which is 'constitutionally established' by the Weimar National Congress; it can also include the entire form of the state which originated in Germany since the violent revolution in November 1918. It can also mean the *new legal and social order in Germany which was erected under the prominent participation of German and foreign Jews*. It can also signify the excessive power and the excessive influence which a small number of Jews, in relation to the total population, in fact exercise, in the opinion of large circles of the population in Germany."
  This called forth a comment from Emil Roth, who was the author of the piece:
  "In reading these reasons, the depressing knowledge cannot be suppressed that the aversion against Jewish fellow countrymen fed by prejudices of all kinds has found a place even in circles of the highest judges of the land; this must deeply distress every real friend of the Fatherland."
  See "Man darf Judenrepublik sagen!: ein merkwuerdiges Reichsgerichtsurteil" C.V.Z. (Maerz 19, 1926), V Jg. Nr. 12 S. 196.
55 Dr. Alfred Wiener, *"Die Pogromhetze" Im deutschen Reich*, XXV Jahrgang, Berlin, Juli/August 1919, Nr. 7/8 at 289-99.
56 *Ibid.*

We create martyrs for little money and the real wire-pullers of the movement remain untouched. And then it is not in the character of our times *expressis verbis* for one to hide behind the state attorney and policeman at every trifle. *Enlightenment*, that is the solution.

That the Nazis not only welcomed show trials, but actually tried to provoke them, is common knowledge. Julius Streicher, editor of the infamous Der Stuermer in Nuremberg, was particularly adept at redirecting the course of his trials. Instead of focusing on the libellous attacks he made on the Jewish religion, Streicher managed to turn the proceedings in such a way so as to place the Talmud on trial. He and other Nazis were able to harangue the court for hours and to have expert witnesses dismissed for being in the pay of Jewish interests. Between 1923 and 1933, Der Stuermer was either confiscated or taken to court 36 times. Bytwerk reports that, during a single 11-day period in 1928, five suits were pressed against members of the Stuermer staff.[57] The description, in the C.V. Zeitung, of the famous Talmud trial of November 1929 involving Streicher and his co-worker, Holz, is accurately rendered by Bytwerk:[58]

> The trial received national publicity, again adding to Streicher's reputation. The audience was once more strongly partisan. The C.V. Zeitung noted that Streicher and Holz addressed the court as if it were a mass meeting, which indeed is how they probably viewed it. The court room was a platform from which they could reach an enormous audience. The atmosphere in the court room is suggested by the audience's response to the State Attorney's call of eight months for Streicher and ten for Holz: the audience burst out in laughter. Streicher called upon the full reserves of showmanship. Expert witnesses were called, the Talmud in a multivolume Hebrew edition was produced, and spectacular tales of Jewish misdeeds were reported. Streicher, when questioned about the reliability of such stories, replied that they must have been true, otherwise they would not have been printed.

The benefits from Streicher's court room antics were reaped by Streicher and the Nazi party, and at times the fines that he was required to pay and the additional costs he incurred forced him to appeal for money. Yet, whatever the cost to Streicher and the party, they could not have purchased on the open market the publicity the trials received.[59]

> What were the rhetorical advantages of Streicher's trials? First, they gave him and the NSDAP large amounts of publicity, and to the

---

57 Randall Lee Bytwerk, *Julius Streicher: The Rhetoric of an Anti-Semite* (Northwestern University Ph.D., 1975), at 48.
58 Bytwerk, *ibid.*, at 53; see also C.V.Z. (November 1, 8 and 29, 1929).
59 Bytwerk, *supra*, note 57 at 54-56.

NSDAP the difference between fame and obscurity was more important than the difference between love and hate. Joseph Goebbels,
writing of his early struggles in Berlin, claimed that the most important
thing was to be known; only then could one win supporters. [*Signale
der neuen Zeit*, Munich, 1934, p. 48.] Streicher's trials certainly accomplished the goal of making the NSDAP known. The trials further
provided Streicher not only with the prominence that made of him a
sought after speaker, but also the material to speak upon. Audiences
were eager to hear Streicher's account of what happened at his most
recent trial. His convictions were used to support his case. "When one
visits a courtroom these days", he once told a meeting, "it is just like
walking into a synagogue." Naturally, an anti-Semite could not expect
a fair trial from a courtroom filled with Jews; his convictions were
entirely explainable. He told another meeting, "I doubt that there is
still a court in this nation or in this state that has the courage to
announce a German verdict." Guilt was therefore transformed into
innocence; convictions of anti-Semites were held to be un-German.
Trials also enabled Streicher to claim he was more important than he in
truth was. In 1928, for example, *Der Stuermer* claimed that each new
issue was studied in the offices of a hundred Jewish lawyers, in the hope
of finding something amiss. This claim was certainly untrue, but it was
also plausible to a Nuremberger who constantly read accounts of
Streicher's trials in the newspapers. Those trials that ended with jail
terms gave opportunity for Streicher to portray himself as a martyr in
truth's cause ... When Streicher began his jail terms, he was often
accompanied to prison by hundreds of his followers, making a celebration out of temporary defeat. While he was in jail, he sometimes wrote
articles for Der Stuermer. Protest meetings were often held, demanding
his release. His release became a cause for celebration. Six hundred
people came to meet him in 1926; several thousands, including Adolf
Hitler, in 1930. Streicher nearly always addressed a crowded public
meeting on the evening of his release. In short, a jail term was a fruitful
well of propaganda. Since his followers were convinced of his innocence, trials became evidence of his persecution. Ironically, the more
Streicher was brought to court, the more highly his followers thought of
him. They attended trials not to determine whether Streicher was
guilty, but to see a battle between truth and error, their selective
perception filtering out information damaging to Streicher. The courts
were an important element in Streicher's rhetorical campaign. Every
effort was made to secure extensive publicity. To the Jewish organizations, conviction was first seen as a victory; to the Nazis, the benefits of
a trial more than outweighed the costs. Paucker, for example, observes
that though the 1929 Talmud trial was hailed as a Jewish victory, it was
in truth a victory for the NSDAP.

Yet, the C.V. learned from such spectacles and avoided giving the Nazis
these kinds of platforms. As Paucker points out, the C.V. countered
propaganda by means of injunctions against newspapers and by hitting
the centres of distribution with threats of court action.[60]

    We have now come up against the limits of the law as a weapon

---

60 Paucker, *Der juedische Abwehrkampf, supra*, note 4 at 81-82.

against a mass racist political movement which is a major player in the political arena. At this point we may ask the question, what can *we* learn from the experiences of the Weimar Republic? The simple answer, of course, is not to repeat the history of Germany. Do not lose a war with your troops still beyond the borders of your country and with the army intact in the field; do not face high reparation payments to the victor nations; do not establish a republican democracy with a civil service which is monarchistic and authoritarian; do not go through a period of hyper-inflation; do not develop a mass *voelkisch* movement receptive to racist arguments; do not go through an economic depression with high unemployment; and the list could continue.

The Weimar Republic was a democracy, but it was only a tentative democracy. It was a democracy born of national disaster, which represented national betrayal to large segments of the population. Historians of the period refer to it as "the improvised democracy,"[61] as a "democracy without democrats."[62] Known also in extreme nationalist circles as the "Jew-Republic," the fate of the German Jews was the shared fate of the Weimar democracy. There was a legal system which offered Jews protection under laws as imperfect and as flawed as that system might have been. Had the administration of justice in the Weimar period functioned perfectly, and had all the draft amendments to the *Criminal Code* been enacted extending the legal protection further, it is hard to see what difference this would have made in a political culture which was, to a significant degree, anti-democratic. The defence of the Jews depended entirely upon the defence of the republic, and that depended primarily upon the political and economic, and not upon the legal, struggle.

If there is anything we can learn from the Weimar experience, I think it is this: The law can only be an effective instrument in containing, controlling and discouraging racist expression if it is founded upon a sound democratic political culture. This does not necessarily mean that we should abandon the law altogether as a regulator of racist expression. But it does mean that, whatever kind of regulation of expression we adopt, we must do so painstakingly, with a view to the fundamental requirements of human rights and democratic principles. Furthermore, the law should not be seen as a first, or even a prominent, line of defence. We should put our efforts into programs of education, political involvement in the community, funding for programs which lead to tolerance and understanding between groups and communities. We must also

---

61 Theodor Eschenburg, *Die improvisierte Demokratie* (Munich: R. Piper Verlag, 1963).
62 Paul Loebe, *Der weg war lang*, 3rd ed. (Berlin, 1954), at 95.

work to guarantee that our society will never leave large numbers of its members out in the cold. If we can achieve this, then, hopefully, the Weimar case of a democracy which was undermined and overrun by a racist political movement will be the first and last in human history.

HOW NOT TO FIGHT RACIAL HATRED

A. Alan Borovoy

After all the horrors of the 20th century, there is an understandable desire to suppress the racist invective to which we are periodically subjected. In this connection, it would be hard to imagine an obscenity more malevolent than the denial of the Nazi holocaust against the Jews of Europe. As a noted author so eloquently remarked, it was not enough for yesterday's Nazis to extinguish 6 million Jewish lives; their modern sympathizers seek to extinguish 6 million Jewish *deaths*. It is very understandable, therefore, that civilized people would wish to suppress such malevolence.

The problem, of course, is freedom of speech. Admittedly, freedom of speech is not, and cannot be, an absolute. Admittedly, there are circumstances in which it has to be fettered. Nevertheless, freedom of speech is the life-blood of the democratic system. For these purposes, it is the vehicle that enables the aggrieved of society to mobilize the support of others for the redress of their grievances. In this sense, it is what the American philosopher, Sidney Hook, called a strategic freedom: a freedom upon which other freedoms depend.[1] A wise old trade unionist once called free speech "the grievance procedure" of democratic society. As such, it is particularly important for the disadvantaged. Freedom of speech represents the one way that they can impress their interests on the body politic.

It is critical, therefore, that supporters of our anti-hate law face an issue that has too often been neglected: the virtual impossibility of formulating a prohibition so precise that it will nail the targeted hate propaganda without running a terrific risk of catching in the same net a lot of other speech which it would be clearly unconscionable for a democratic society to suppress. Canadian law now purports to prohibit the wilful promotion of "hatred" against people distinguished by race, religion and ethnicity.[2] There can be no reasonable objection to a law that prohibited the incitement of racial *violence* in situations of imminent peril. But "hatred" is a much more nebulous and, therefore, dangerous concept. What is the boundary line of hatred? We know that

---

1 See Sidney Hook, "Bread, Freedom, and Free Enterprise," in his *Political Power and Personal Freedom* (New York: Collier Books, 1962), 83 at 84.

2 Criminal Code, R.S.C. 1985, c. C-46, s. 319(2).

freedom of speech is often most important when it expresses strong disapproval. But where does strong disapproval leave off and hatred begin? Martin Luther King once described his own tactics as an exercise in constructive tension.[3] He knew that, if he was going to get anywhere, he had to upset people. But how does a blunt instrument like the law distinguish destructive hatred from constructive tension?

Even with the aid of a fine-tooth comb, we would be hard put to find a response to this issue in the judicial decisions on the constitutionality of our hate propaganda law. Those judgments discuss at great length how the aim of this law is to suppress unredeemed malevolent speech. But, apart from a fleeting reference in the Alberta Court of Appeal,[4] the judiciary has hardly mentioned the risk that this law is likely to catch the wrong people.

It is worth looking at some of the actual examples from Canada's 20-year history with this legislation. In considering these examples, we should bear in mind the fact that this country has been a relatively mild one as far as racial tensions are concerned.

In the mid-1970s, some young people were arrested for distributing literature at the Shriner's parade in Toronto. Their literature bore the words "Yankee go home." The charge was distributing hate propaganda. And, while the Crown attorney had the good sense subsequently to withdraw the charge, we should not be overly consoled. In the meantime, those young people suffered the suppression of their perfectly legitimate political protest and they spent a couple of days in jail.[5]

In the late 1970s, there was a dispute in Essex County over public support for French education. Two French Canadian nationalists, feeling frustrated over the apathy of the French community, composed and distributed anti-French material. Their goal was to arouse pro-French sympathy. Even if their conduct might appear somewhat bizarre, it is clear that these two activists were not involved in the kind of behaviour for which our anti-hate law had been designed. Nevertheless, they were charged with, and even convicted of, distributing hate propaganda. It was not until the Court of Appeal reviewed the case that the conviction was quashed and a new trial was ordered.[6] Fortunately, the Crown elected not to resume the matter.

---

3   See Martin Luther King, "Letter from Birmingham Jail," in J.M. Washington (ed.), *A Testament of Hope: The Essential Writings of Martin Luther King* (San Francisco: Harper & Row, 1986), 289 at 291.

4   *R. v. Keegstra*, [1988] 5 W.W.R. 211 at 239, reversed [1991] 2 W.W.R. 1 (S.C.C.). See the discussion in the postscript to this paper regarding the Supreme Court of Canada judgment in this case.

5   See "Hate Literature Charges Against 3 to be Dropped" (July 4, 1975), The Globe and Mail 1.

6   *R. v. Buzzanga* (1979), 49 C.C.C. (2d) 369 (Ont. C.A.).

In 1986, a film sympathetic to Nelson Mandela in South Africa was held up at the border for longer than a month because of allegations that it promoted "hatred" against white South Africans.[7] Consider the irony. Legislation designed to protect disadvantaged people like blacks winds up obstructing their ability to strike back at their segregationist enemies.

In 1989, there were two incidents. A Jewish leader became the target of a hate propaganda investigation.[8] He had expressed anger against the Austrians for having elected Kurt Waldheim as their president despite the reports of Waldheim's pro-Nazi activities during World War II. And Salman Rushdie's book, *The Satanic Verses*, was ordered detained at the Canadian border.[9]

Our democratic consciences should not be appeased by the fact that none of these cases led to a conviction. Freedom of speech is undermined not only by the convictions that are ultimately registered, but also by the prosecutions that are initially threatened. If we cannot engage in public discourse without the fear of facing a criminal charge, we are not enjoying freedom of speech. This is the phenomenon that certain American courts have so sensitively labelled "the chilling effect."[10] The risk of having our speech chilled increases with the vagueness of the laws that might apply. In order to avoid the possibility of prosecution, people might be impelled to ensure that their speech steered as far as possible from the prohibited zone. Very often, the likely casualty of such self-censorship would be perfectly legitimate speech.

The fact that those French Canadian nationalists ultimately avoided conviction does not tell us what an ordeal it was to go through a criminal trial. The fact that the Jewish leader was never charged does not tell us how potentially intimidating it would be for many people to be the target of a criminal investigation. The fact that charges were withdrawn against those anti-American activists does not tell us what it was like to be arrested and to spend a couple of days in jail.

Even if material is temporarily detained, rather than permanently seized, at the border, our democratic consciences should not be appeased. In the case of the Mandela film, we do not know the extent to which a one-month delay might have undermined the anti-apartheid activities that had been planned. In the case of the Rushdie book, we can imagine how a different political climate might have produced a more serious consequence than a 48-hour detention order.

---

7 See "Mandela Film is Scréened For Possible Hate Content" (December 24, 1986), The Globe and Mail A14.

8 See "Bronfman is Target of Complaint" (May 26, 1989), The Globe and Mail A11.

9 See "Canada Blocks the Satanic Verses" (February 18, 1989), The Globe and Mail A1.

10 See, *e.g.*, *Dombrowski v. Pfister*, 380 U.S. 479 at 487 (1965).

Moreover, there is good reason even to doubt how well the cause of racial dignity is served by the anti-hate law. In many ways, the requirements of a criminal prosecution are at variance with the canons of common sense. From the standpoint of common sense, the one thing you should not do is debate the merits of a malevolent obscenity. As Toronto Rabbi W. Gunther Plaut once observed, if someone calls your mother a whore, that is not a fit subject for debate.[11]

But, when you prosecute, you are often forced to debate the merits of the accused's position. Small wonder, therefore, that in the *Zundel* false news case, there was a discussion in court over the monstrous proposition that Auschwitz was not a Nazi death camp, but a Jewish country club.[12] And the prosecutor, not the defence, called a non-Jewish banker to the stand and asked him if he was being paid by an international Zionist Communist banker Jewish Freemason conspiracy.[13] The *question* was an obscenity. I am not necessarily blaming the prosecutor for this. He may well have felt that he had to cover all of the elements in the accused's defence. I am suggesting that the risk of farce is endemic to the very nature of the proceedings and it materialized in that case.

The question which emerges from all this is: why? Why should a sensible society incur all of these risks? Is it because the likes of Keegstra and Zundel are such commanding figures in our society? Is there any doubt that their respective constituencies could hardly fill a telephone booth?

The explanation for this legislation is found in the mid-1960s report of the government-appointed Cohen Committee which our superior courts have cited with approval. The following two sentences, taken from the *Cohen Report*, summarize the rationale behind the anti-hate law.[14]

> However small the actors may be in number, the individuals and groups promoting hate in Canada constitute a "clear and present danger" to the functioning of a democratic society. For in times of social stress such "hate" could mushroom into a real and monstrous threat to our way of life.

I would have thought that those two sentences could not co-exist.

---

11 "Prosecution in Zundel Trial Forced Long Odds" (March 1, 1985), The Globe and Mail 15.
12 *Ibid.*
13 "Banker Bemused at Examination in Zundel Trial" (January 30, 1985), The Globe and Mail M1.
14 Canada, House of Commons, *Report of the Special Committee on Hate Propaganda in Canada* (Ottawa: Queen's Printer, 1966) (Commissioner: M. Cohen), at 24.

How can something be called a "clear and present danger," not because of what is happening now or about to happen, but because of what *could* happen at some *other* time? How can that be called a clear and *present* danger? Oliver Wendell Holmes must be turning in his grave.

Is our society so bereft of ingenuity and resources that it cannot contain the influence of hatemongers without running the kinds of risks entailed in this legislation? In this connection, consider what happened in the case of James Keegstra, the mayor of Eckville, Alberta and the teacher who preached anti-Semitic doctrine in his classroom. As the news of his pedagogical activities began to emerge, he was removed from the classroom by the school board, decertified as a teacher by the professional association, and ousted as mayor by the Eckville voters.[15] All of this happened *before* criminal charges were ever laid against him. In short, he had been denuded of the components of clout before and without any criminal prosecution. My view is that he should have been allowed to wallow in the obscurity he so richly deserves.

Other hatemongers like Zundel *never* exercised any significant influence. As far as people like that are concerned, we should focus on creating an inhospitable climate for their propaganda. We should continue to improve our laws and actions against the really serious racial problems in this country — in jobs, housing and education. The fall-out from a stronger program against racist *deeds* is likely to weaken further the impact of racist *words*.

In my view, therefore, our anti-hate laws are too dangerous to freedom of speech, create too many problems for racial dignity, and are not needed to contain the influence of the hatemongers themselves. It is important, of course, that we continue the fight against race hatred. But it is also important that we choose the right means for doing so. In general, we should seek not to impose a legal muzzle but rather to inflict political censure. While such an approach cannot guarantee that we will find the right balance, alternative approaches *can* guarantee that we will find the wrong balance.

Postscript

Since this article was written, the Supreme Court of Canada finally addressed the risk that the anti-hate law could catch the wrong people.[16] In the course of reversing the Alberta Court of Appeal and upholding the

---

15   See D.J. Bercuson and D. Wertheimer, *A Trust Betrayed: The Keegstra Affair* (Toronto: Doubleday Canada, 1985).

16   *R. v. Keegstra, supra,* note 4. All of the following references to Dickson C.J.C.'s judgment can be found at p. 70.

constitutionality of the anti-hate law, Dickson C.J.C., for a 4-3 majority, acknowledged that he found this risk "worrying." But he contended nevertheless that any harassment suffered by those engaging in legitimate speech has been attributable not to "over-expansive breadth and vagueness in the law," but to misinterpretations of the law. The problem with this response is that it fails to acknowledge how the wording of the law inevitably confuses the authorities as to its narrow intent.

For these purposes, it is not enough to argue, as Dickson C.J.C. did, that the word "hatred" refers to "only the most intentionally extreme forms of expression." Nor is it enough to insist, as Dickson C.J.C. did, that, if the proper warnings are given in court, the danger of wrongful convictions will be minimized and freedom of expression will be "limited no more than is necessary." Judicial admonitions about the extreme nature of the word "hatred" cannot denude the word of its inherent subjectivity. Moreover, even if Dickson C.J.C. is right about the minimal risks of improper convictions, this does not adequately address the risks of improper prosecutions and investigations. Even if judges and properly instructed juries will not be likely to convict the wrong people, what does this tell us about the propensity of police officers to arrest the wrong people and customs officials to seize the wrong materials? No less important, what does it tell us about the inclination of people to muzzle their *own* legitimate speech because of the *fear* of being charged?

In a judgment that I find more compelling, McLachlin J., for the minority, also addressed the issue of nailing the wrong people. In her view, however, the subjective nature of the law creates an unacceptable threat to varieties of expression beyond those for which the law was designed.

RACIST INCITEMENT: GIVING FREE SPEECH A BAD NAME

Irwin Cotler

I. INTRODUCTION

As I begin this discussion of racist incitement and free speech, I am reminded of John Stuart Mill's classic essay, *On Liberty*,[1] which begins with an introduction that ends with an apology. As Mill approached his oft-quoted chapter on liberty of thought and discussion, he wrote:[2]

> Those to whom nothing which I am about to say will be new may therefore, I hope, excuse me if on a subject which for now three centuries has been so often discussed I venture on one discussion more.

If I venture on one discussion more, it is because I suspect that the alleged contradiction between freedom of expression and freedom *from* expression, as it pertains to the promotion of hatred, is more dialectical than real.

Simply put, my thesis is this: protecting visible, vulnerable minorities from being vilified and victimized by the promotion of hate propaganda may be the basis of freedom of expression and freedom to debate in both principle and reality. We know that speech can hurt. We have learned that words can maim. We have felt the pain. Indeed, we have been able to read the testimony of vilified members of identifiable groups describing, before parliamentary committees and as witnesses in

---

1   John Stuart Mill, *On Liberty*, edited, with an introduction by G. Himmelfarb (Great Britain: Penguin Books, 1974).
2   *Ibid.*, at 74.

court, the pain of what it means to be the victim of this kind of group vilification.[3]

Indeed, we have witnessed the dangers of racist incitement and the injury to its targets. We know that words can offend, injure reputation, fan prejudice and, regrettably, ignite the world.[4]

What is to be regarded as protected speech? Or more particularly, how do we distinguish protected from unprotected speech? Whether the wilful promotion of hatred is protected speech under the *Charter*[5] is no longer, if it ever was, just a matter of political theory or academic inquiry. It has become a major legal and jurisprudential question in this country.

II. THE STATE OF RACIST INCITEMENT LITIGATION

This discussion takes place in the aftermath of the Supreme Court of Canada hearing three important cases on racist incitement: the *Taylor*,[6] *Keegstra*[7] and *Andrews*[8] cases. It is no exaggeration to say that, in recent years, we have had in this country the most celebrated hearing on the issues of racist incitement and the law in the history of Canadian jurisprudence.

In the *Taylor* case, the Supreme Court heard an appeal from a decision of the Federal Court of Appeal, upholding the constitutionality of provisions in the *Canadian Human Rights Act*,[9] which make it a discriminatory practice to promote hatred of identifiable groups by using a telecommunication facility.

The two other cases heard by the Supreme Court involved the constitutionality of what is now s. 319(2) of the *Criminal Code*[10] — the prohibition against the wilful promotion of hatred. In the *Keegstra* case, the Supreme Court heard an appeal from a decision of the Court of

---

3 See M. Matsuda, "Public Responses to Racist Speech: Considering the Victim's Story" (1989), 87 Mich. L. Rev. 2320-81, where the author discusses the kind of pain and harm experienced by the victims of group vilification.

4 H.H. Wellington, "On Freedom of Expression" (1979), 88 Yale L.J. 1105-42.

5 *Canadian Charter of Rights and Freedoms*, Pt. I of the *Constitution Act, 1982*, being Sched. B of the *Canada Act 1982*, 1982 (Eng.), c. 11.

6 *Can. (Can. Human Rights Comm.) v. Taylor* (1987), 37 D.L.R. (4th) 577, affirmed S.C.C., No. 20462, 13th December 1990 (not yet reported) [Fed.].

7 *R. v. Keegstra*, [1988] 5 W.W.R. 211, reversed [1991] 2 W.W.R. 1 (S.C.C.).

8 *R. v. Andrews* (1988), 28 O.A.C. 161, affirmed 75 O.R. (2d) 481n (S.C.C.).

9 *Canadian Human Rights Act*, S.C. 1976-77, c. 33 [am. 1980-81-82-83, c. 143; 1985, c. 26].

10 *Criminal Code*, R.S.C. 1985, c. C-46, s. 319(2) [formerly R.S.C. 1970, c. C-34, s. 281.2(2)].

Appeal of Alberta, which held that s. 319(2) was an unjustifiable infringement of freedom of expression as guaranteed by s. 2(b) of the *Canadian Charter of Rights and Freedoms*. In the *Andrews* case, the court heard an appeal from a judgment of the Ontario Court of Appeal which had upheld s. 319(2) of the *Criminal Code.* The Ontario appeal court's finding that the prohibition against the wilful promotion of hatred was constitutionally valid was the reverse of the decision of its Alberta counterpart in the *Keegstra* case.

These three cases, however, do not represent all of the ongoing racist incitement litigation. In a fourth case, *R. v. Zundel*,[11] the Ontario Court of Appeal, in February 1990, upheld the constitutional validity of what is now s. 181 of the *Criminal Code* — knowingly spreading false news — as well as affirming the factual basis of Zundel's conviction. A fifth case involves Moncton school teacher Malcolm Ross. In this case, the New Brunswick Court of Appeal recently upheld the constitutionality of an inquiry, under the provincial human rights legislation, into Ross's dissemination of hate propaganda and Holocaust denial literature.[12]

An appreciation of this incredible array of litigation reveals a little known, but rather compelling, social and legal phenomenon: Canada has become a world centre for hate propaganda litigation in general and Holocaust denial litigation in particular. Moreover, the Canadian experience is now perhaps the most compelling legal precedent respecting the subject-matter of today's discussion.

III. DISTINGUISHING PROTECTED FROM UNPROTECTED SPEECH

A. The Scope of Section 319

I will set forth a set of principles which, taken together, may well allow us to distinguish between protected and unprotected speech. I acknowledge and support not only the significance, but the scope, of the principle of freedom of expression. I share the view, reflected in both the jurisprudence and academic writing, that freedom of expression is fundamental to a democracy. However, the rights and freedoms guaranteed in the *Charter*, including freedom of expression, are not absolute. As the Supreme Court of the United States noted in *Chaplinsky*,[13] there are

---

11   (1990), 53 C.C.C. (3d) 161.
12   *N.B. Sch. Dist. No. 15 v. N.B. (Human Rights Bd. of Inquiry)* (1989), 252 A.P.R. 181, reversing 238 A.P.R. 271 (C.A.). The inquiry was commenced under the *Human Rights Act* because the Attorney General of New Brunswick, Mr. James Lockyer, refused to initiate a prosecution under s. 319 of the *Criminal Code.*
13   *Chaplinsky v. New Hampshire*, 315 U.S. 568 (1942).

certain well-defined classes of speech whose punishment and preven-
tion have never been thought to raise any constitutional problem. In
other words, there is a certain genre of expression that lies outside the
scope of the *Charter*'s protection of freedom of expression. In my
opinion, the wilful promotion of hatred is expression which lies outside
the scope of *Charter* protection.

The question, however, remains: How do we distinguish destructive hatred from constructive tension? How do we ensure that we do not
catch unintended people in the net of criminal prosecution? It is my
contention that a set of criteria which distinguishes between the two
kinds of speech can be devised. The first question is: What are the
boundaries of hatred? How do we delineate where strong disapproval
breaks off and hatred begins?

The hate propaganda legislation in s. 319(2) of the *Criminal Code*
can serve as a useful case study as it underlies the propositions which
follow. As Justice Cory, then of the Ontario Court of Appeal, stated in
Andrews, s. 319(2) is not overly broad. Referring to s. 319(2), he noted:[14]

> It should not be struck down simply because one can imagine a rare and
> occasional application of its provisions that goes beyond constitutional
> bounds.

If one examines the law, it is not only narrowly drawn, but the
threshold of criminal conduct required is so high, and the section is
encrusted with so many defences, that the basic critique of this law is not
that it is unconstitutional, but, rather, that it is incapable of effective
enforcement. This may, in fact, explain why the Attorney General of
Ontario, Roy McMurtry, when petitioned by representatives of the
Holocaust Remembrance Association, refused to prosecute Ernst
Zundel under the hate propaganda legislation. Zundel was ultimately
prosecuted for knowingly disseminating false news pursuant to what is
now s. 181 of the *Criminal Code*. As noted above, James Lockyer, in
deciding not to prosecute Malcolm Ross under s. 319(2), cited the
difficulty of obtaining a conviction as his reason for not pursuing the
matter by criminal prosecution. I should note that the prohibition
against the publishing of false news is, in my opinion, overly broad and
should be amended, if not repealed. Nonetheless, the basic problem,
which led to use of this provision in the *Zundel* prosecution, was
concern that the requirements of s. 319(2) were too difficult to prove and
the chances of gaining conviction too low, and not that the provision
might be unconstitutional.

We should understand exactly what type of speech is criminalized

---

14   *Supra*, note 8 at 181.

by s. 319(2). The provision does not prohibit the dissemination of propaganda, or the dissemination of hatred, but rather the *promotion* of hatred; not just the promotion of hatred but the *wilful* promotion of hatred; and not against everybody, but only against certain identifiable groups;[15] and not just in any situation, but only in other than private conversations; and not pursuant to a complaint laid by just anyone, but only with the consent of the Attorney General. These qualifications make the section one of the most circumscribed provisions in the *Criminal Code*. The operation of the section, however, is further limited by the broad array of defences specifically available to someone charged under s. 319(2). A person charged under this provision must be acquitted if:[16]

(a) the accused establishes that the statements made were true;
(b) the accused, in good faith, expressed or attempted to establish by argument an opinion on a religious subject;
(c) if the statements made by the accused were relevant to any subject of public interest, wherein the discussion was for the benefit of the public, and if on reasonable grounds the accused believed them to be true; or
(d) if the accused in good faith intended to point out for the purpose of removal matters producing or tending to produce feelings of hatred towards an identifiable group in Canada.

Viewing this legislation prohibiting the wilful promotion of hatred against identifiable groups from this perspective, one can see that the statutory provision has extremely limited application. In fact, if one were to make an empirical and comparative assessment, the hate propaganda section has been applied less abusively than many other provisions of the *Criminal Code*, despite the fact that the criminal law, generally, may be abused in terms of the discretion in the laying of charges or in regard to catching individuals who were not intended to be included in the scope of a criminal sanction. Section 319(2) is one of the most narrowly drawn provisions in the *Criminal Code*.

B. Justifications for Prohibiting Racist Speech

What rationale supports the use of criminal sanctions to deter racist speech? A number of rationales support the constitutional validity of s. 319(2). First, hateful expression constitutes an assault on the very values and principles that underlie a free and democratic society, such as exists

---

15 That is, those groups "distinguished by colour, race, religion or ethnic origin": see *Criminal Code*, s. 318(4).
16 See *Criminal Code*, s. 319(3).

in Canada, one founded upon respect for the inherent dignity of the human person, and respect for cultural and group identity, and so forth. Racist speech is the very antithesis of the values and principles which underlie a free and democratic society.

More particularly, hate-mongering, of which incitement to racial hatred is perhaps the worst kind, constitutes an assault on the very values and interests sought to be protected by freedom of expression in any free and democratic society. In other words, the values and interests underlying freedom of expression — the purpose or rationale for protecting speech under the *Charter* — are inconsistent with the kind of hate-mongering that s. 319(2) prohibits and deters. Generally accepted rationales for the constitutional protection of freedom of speech include the following:

(a) freedom of expression is essential to intelligent and democratic self-government;
(b) freedom of expression protects an open exchange of views, thereby creating a competitive market-place of ideas which will enhance the search for truth; and
(c) expression is to be protected because it is essential to personal growth and self-realization.

While I do not take issue with the principles or rationales, or that these constitute the very basis for freedom of expression, I do contend that racist incitement is not only incompatible with any purposive reading of freedom of expression, but that it constitutes a veritable assault on each of these values and interests. More particularly:

(a) Racist incitement, at the outset, is not only antithetical to intelligent and democratic self-government, but also constitutes a *destructive assault* on the very notion of democratic self-government, particularly as it concerns the preservation and enhancement of a democratic, multicultural society.[17]
(b) Furthermore, racist incitement is not only incompatible with the competitive market-place of ideas which will enhance the search for truth, but, in fact, represents the very antithesis of that same search for truth. Hate propaganda seeks not to inform, but to incite; not to discuss, but to degrade; not to debate, but to defame; not to enlighten through an uninhibited, robust and open exchange of ideas — however unpopular, unpalatable, distasteful or offensive. Rather, it diminishes, if not denies through an incipiently violent expression, the search for any truth at all. Simply, such racist incitement constitutes a *per se* injury to the target group.

---

17   See s. 27 of the *Charter*.

(c) In terms of personal growth and self-realization, arguing that racial incitement is protected by freedom of expression is analogous to claiming that one is fulfilled by expressing oneself violently. Further, it is an assault on the self-realization of the target group whose loss of self-esteem and consequent self-abasement disclose the fallacy of the notion that hate propaganda is essential to personal growth and self-realization.

Second, a democracy like Canada has a moral and constitutional right, if not an obligation, to protect itself against movements and organizations which endanger its existence and which deny the basic tenets of a democratic society.[18] To paraphrase Justice Jackson, the Constitution is not a suicide pact.[19] There is a constitutional duty to protect victims of racist hate propaganda from the injurious effects of such speech.

Third, an understanding of freedom of expression in light of international human rights law — whether it be general principles of law recognized by the community of nations or international treaty law — requires that racist incitement be excluded from the protective ambit of freedom of expression. The content of Canada's international human rights obligations is an important indicium of how the rights and freedoms contained in the *Charter*[20] should be interpreted. In fact, if one looks to these basic obligations that Canada has undertaken, it is apparent that Canada has agreed to adopt immediate and positive measures designed to eradicate all incitement to, or acts of, discrimination. Further, in these international instruments, Canada has agreed to declare it an offence punishable by law to disseminate ideas based on racial superiority or hatred or incitement to racial discrimination.[21]

To conclude this point, therefore, I would submit that if Canada had not enacted legislation to prohibit racist incitement, as it has in ss. 318 to 320 of the *Criminal Code*, it would now be obliged to do so. Furthermore, it would find itself in default of its international obligations if these laws were set aside.

Fourth, it should be noted that within western Europe, 21 nation

---

18 *Ibid.*

19 *Terminiello v. Chicago*, 337 U.S. 1 at 37 (1949). Justice Jackson actually said: "There is danger that, if the Court does not temper its doctrinaire logic with a little practical wisdom, it will convert the constitutional Bill of Rights into a suicide pact."

20 *Slaight Communications v. Davidson*, [1989] 1 S.C.R. 1038. Dickson C.J.C. in *Keegstra, supra,* note 7, wrote that the prohibition of hate-promoting speech is an "obligatory aspect" of a signatory nation's guarantee of human rights.

21 *The International Convention on the Elimination of All Forms of Racial Discrimination* (1963), Yearbook of United Nations 330, 3 I.L.M. 164, 58 A.J.I.L. 1081, 660 U.N.T.S. 195.

states are party to the *European Convention for the Protection of Human Rights and Fundamental Freedoms*.[22] The Supreme Court of Canada has said that this Convention is of persuasive value in the interpretation of the scope of rights and freedoms under our *Charter*. When laws sanctioning racist speech have been challenged before the European court, that court has held that there are limits on freedom of expression which are designed to protect aggrieved minorities from the wilful promotion of hatred against them.[23] The European court has held that such limitations are constitutionally valid.

Fifth, I submit that the principle of freedom of expression must be interpreted in light of the fact that Canada is a multicultural western democracy. Section 27 of the *Charter* compels us to interpret the rights and freedoms contained in the *Charter* in accordance with the preservation and enhancement of Canada's multicultural heritage. Thus, the *Charter*'s guarantee of freedom of expression must be interpreted so as to protect identifiable groups in our multicultural society from publicly made statements which wilfully promote hatred against them. Such statements would risk the destruction of our multicultural society.[24]

Finally, we are invited by the courts to look at other free and democratic societies. Nineteen other free and democratic societies, in Europe and Latin America, have adopted legislation with objectives similar to s. 319 (2) of the *Criminal Code*. Courts in those countries have upheld these laws even though they are much broader in scope than the legislation existing in Canada.

Finally, as a principle of *Charter* interpretation, freedom of expression must be interpreted in light of other rights and freedoms protected by the Constitution. One of those other rights and freedoms is the principle of equality.[25] To look at this issue only in terms of freedom of expression and to ignore the issue of equality is to take a unidimensional view of something that the courts should view from a multidimensional perspective. What is involved here is not simply a freedom of speech issue, but an equality issue as well. The systematic dissemination of hate propaganda against minority groups will, over time, reduce the standing and respect of these groups in society and thereby create a

---

22 *The European Convention for the Protection of Human Rights and Fundamental Freedoms* (November 1950), 213 United Nations Treaty Senate 221; see also the *Covenant on Civil and Political Rights*, 6 International Legal Manuals 368, adopted by the General Assembly on December 16, 1966.

23 See s. 10 of the *European Convention, supra*, note 22. The Supreme Court of Canada in *Keegstra* came to a similar conclusion.

24 See Dale M. Gibson, "Section 27 of the *Charter*: More Than a 'Rhetorical Flourish' " (1990), 28 Alta. L. Rev. 589. See the Supreme Court of Canada in *Keegstra, supra*, note 7.

25 See *Charter*, s. 15. The Supreme Court of Canada in *Keegstra, supra*, note 7, saw the promotion of hatred, properly understood, as a practice of inequality.

state of discrimination and inequality. Finally, as evidence shows in modern times, racism has either led to, or facilitated, the commission of unspeakable crimes and caused untold suffering.[26] Thus, there exists a clear and present danger which could result from racist incitement.

IV. CONCLUSION

In conclusion, if one were to have regard to all the principles of *Charter* interpretation noted above, invoking any of these principles, or all of them, admits of no other interpretation than that the genre of speech which promotes racial hatred is not protected under the *Canadian Charter of Rights and Freedoms.*[27]

In other words, racist speech does not even come under the protection of s. 2(b) of the *Charter* to begin with. And if it does come under s. 2(b), then s. 319(2) would nonetheless be a reasonable limit prescribed by law which is demonstrably justified in a free and democratic society.

To allow racist incitement to be protected speech would give free speech a bad name.

---

26 David Kretzmer, "Freedom of Speech and Racism" (1987), 8 Cardoza L. Rev. 445. And see Cory J.A.'s passionate argument for the justifiability of s. 319(2) in *Andrews, supra*, note 8 at 174-75. He stated:

"When an expression does instill detestation it does incalculable damage to the Canadian community and lays the foundations for the mistreatment of members of the victimized group.

"I would have thought it sufficient to look back at the quintessence of evil manifested in the Third Reich and its hate propaganda to realize the destructive effects of the promotion of hatred. That dark history provides overwhelming evidence of the catastrophic results of expressions which promote hatred. The National Socialist Party was in the minority when it attained power. The repetition of the loathsome messages of Nazi propaganda led in cruel and rapid succession from the breaking of the shop windows of Jewish merchants to the dispossession of the Jews from their property and their professions, to the establishment of concentration camps and gas chambers. The genocidal horrors of the Holocaust were made possible by the deliberate incitement of hatred against the Jewish and other minority peoples.

"It would be a mistake to assume that Canada today is necessarily immune to the effects of Nazi and other hate literature."

27 Although, admittedly, the Supreme Court of Canada concluded that such speech was protected under s. 2(b), but justifiably limited by s. 319(2).

PART IV

DAMAGE TO REPUTATION: CIVIL DEFAMATION OR CIVIL LIBERTY?

The common law has long treated a person's reputation as a value requiring exacting protection. Consequently, the law of libel and slander developed with an overbearing eagerness to protect personal reputation rather than freedom of expression whenever they conflicted. The following papers put the present law of defamation into context with a view towards its reform, particularly in regard to expression about the conduct of public officials.

Lewis Klar discusses the common law causes of action, and the corresponding defences, which have been developed to further certain policy goals relating to the protection of reputation. He concludes that the common law rules favour the protection of reputation to an unacceptable degree. He discusses, particularly, a number of cases where politicians have been plaintiffs in suits where their competence was criticized by defendants. Even though the *Charter* may not apply to the law of libel and slander, it is asserted that the common law rules can either be applied differently or be amended by statute, so as to better balance between reputation and the competing value of freedom of expression.

Rodney Smolla discusses the historical roots of the law of defamation in the United States and the American constitutional solution to the conflict between the protection of reputation and the freedom of speech. It was with the landmark case of *New York Times v. Sullivan* that the United States Supreme Court reformed the law of defamation as it relates to the conduct of public officials in their official capacities. In order to succeed in an action, public officials would have to prove that the defamatory statement was made with actual malice. Smolla closes with a discussion of how the value of openness is essential to democratic societies.

Richard Dearden discusses the application of the *Charter* to the present law of defamation in Canada. He presents a forceful argument regarding the *prima facie* applicability of the *Charter*. It is then asserted that the present law would fail to withstand *Charter* scrutiny or, alternatively, would require the creation of a new category of qualified privilege in cases involving public officials. With particular reference to *Coates v. The Citizen*, he presents a case for the modernization of the law of libel in relation to allegedly defamatory remarks about public officials.

"IF YOU DON'T HAVE ANYTHING GOOD TO SAY ABOUT SOMEONE . . ."

Lewis Klar

I.   INTRODUCTION
II. THE DEFAMATION ACTION
III. *COATES v. THE CITIZEN*
IV. POLITICIANS AS PLAINTIFFS
V.   CONCLUSION

I. INTRODUCTION

It is the thesis of this paper that, in its efforts to balance a person's right to a "good reputation" with the right of all persons to express themselves freely without fear of liability, Canadian defamation law has not arrived at the correct balance. Canadian law has valued too significantly the protection of reputation at the expense of freedom of speech.

This imbalance is the result of two factors. Firstly, the substantive law of defamation, that is, the rules that are applied by the courts, are too heavily weighted in favour of protecting reputation. Secondly, even where the law is, at least theoretically, formulated in a way which promotes speech, it has been "whittled down by legal refinements" in its application by the courts.[1] This paper will present a brief summary of the substantive rules of defamation law which incline the law too favourably in the direction of protecting reputation.

It will be suggested that, although the *Canadian Charter of Rights and Freedoms*[2] certainly has the ability to impact upon Canadian defamation law and redress the imbalance, there are good reasons to fear that this will not happen. The scanty case law to date clearly shows that judges are not favourably disposed to altering the balance between reputation and speech by jettisoning existing common law defamation rules.[3] Furthermore, one must not think that the *Charter* has drawn the

---

1   In *Slim v. Daily Telegraph Ltd.*, [1968] 2 Q.B. 157, Lord Denning warned against doing this to the defence of "fair comment."
2   *Canadian Charter of Rights and Freedoms*, Pt. I of the *Constitution Act, 1982*, being Sched. B of the *Canada Act 1982*, 1982 (Eng.), c. 11.
3   The leading case so far is *Coates v. The Citizen* (1988), 44 C.C.L.T. 286 (N.S.T.D.), where this is clearly demonstrated.

common law's attention to the importance of "freedom of thought, belief, opinion and expression, including freedom of the press and other media of communication"[4] for the first time. The common law has long been aware of the importance of these values, and the critical role that the courts can play in their promotion or demotion. The courts have consistently held that values of free speech must be balanced by other equally important concerns, namely, the protection of reputation and privacy. There is, therefore, no reason to believe that courts which consciously have fashioned rules of defamation which provide what, in their best opinion, is the appropriate balance between speech and reputation, will now hold that the limitations which they themselves have imposed upon speech are not "reasonable limits prescribed by law as can be demonstrably justified in a free and democratic society."[5]

It will be suggested that the common law of defamation can, by applying its existing rules differently, better promote free speech, without the need for *Charter* intrusion, or other statutory reform. In some areas, however, new principles will need to be considered.

Finally, it will be submitted that, as a result of the common law's lenient approach to defamation law, the defamation action has too easily become a vehicle to restrain and restrict political dissent and criticism. Although politicians and other public figures are, not surprisingly, frequent litigants in defamation actions,[6] an analysis of the case law leads one to believe that it is too often criticism of their politics, and not real damage to reputation, which has given rise to litigation.

II. THE DEFAMATION ACTION

Although one normally thinks of the defamation action as being designed to protect a person's reputation from harm, to what extent do the rules of defamation law actually reflect this concern?

The plaintiff must establish three things to make out a *prima facie* case of defamation. First, the material must have been "defamatory." Second, it must have referred to the plaintiff. Third, it must have been published.

Although the definitions of "what is defamatory?" suggest that material is defamatory when it causes serious harm to a person's reputation,[7] the real rules of defamation law do not support this belief. The

---

4   *Charter*, s. 2(b).
5   *Ibid.*, s. 1.
6   Since people are interested in them, they are involved in controversial issues, and so forth.
7   Classic definitions state that material is defamatory when it "lowers a person in the estimation of right-thinking members of society generally"; when it holds the person named up to "contempt, hatred, scorn or ridicule"; when it causes a person to be "discredited," "detested," "shunned" or "avoided"; and so on.

issue of whether impugned material was defamatory is, in practice, not hotly contested between the litigants, or a difficult one for judges to resolve. It is very difficult to discover cases where a defamation action has floundered on this aspect of the action. The courts consider almost all "critical" material as constituting defamatory material. There are several reasons for this within defamation law itself.

First, in defamation law, damages are presumed.[8] Thus, in order to succeed a plaintiff need not show that there were any real monetary or other losses suffered as a result of the defamation.

Second, the test of whether material damaged a plaintiff's reputation is a hypothetical one. A court is not concerned with whether material actually did lower the plaintiff's reputation amongst those persons who were made aware of the material, but whether it would have had that effect on the "right-minded, reasonable" person. It does not matter whether the plaintiff's reputation was in fact affected by the material. It does not matter if those who heard the material did not believe it, knew it was false, or already had a low estimation of the plaintiff because they were aware of the material. It is not the meaning that is understood by the recipients of the material that is relevant to the determination of this issue, but the "ordinary and natural meaning" of the words given to them by the court.

Third, the truth or falsity of the material is not relevant to whether it is defamatory. If defamatory, the material is presumed to be false. A person is *prima facie* entitled to a good reputation, even if that person does not deserve one. It is up to the person who published the material to prove its truth, as a defence to the action.

Fourth, the publisher's intention to defame, its awareness that the material was defamatory and its reasonable care to ensure that it was not, are not relevant to the action, except insofar as these issues relate to the defences.

The low threshold requirement for defamatory material is illustrated in the recent case law. In *Russell v. Pawley*[9] for example, words stated within the context of a vigorous public debate, expressing surprise that the plaintiff, who was on sick leave from his job, could find so much time for his cause rather than going back to work, were held to be defamatory.[10] In *Moores v. Salter*,[11] a letter of reprimand by a superior

---

8   Except in those few jurisdictions which maintain separate rules for "slander," but even here, there are categories of slander which are actionable *per se.*

9   [1986] 4 W.W.R. 172, reversed 36 D.L.R. (4th) 625 (Man. C.A.).

10   There was a dissent in the Court of Appeal. Monnin C.J.A. stated that, in view of all of the "very unparliamentary, intemperate, derogatory and vituperative language" which was being used by all parties to the debate over French language rights in Manitoba, it was amazing to note that the plaintiff felt himself defamed by what was said in this instance. According to Monnin

stating that an argument between employees involved "violent displays of temper and the use of language not conducive to civilized human beings" was held to have been defamatory because it "would lead the general public to think less of the plaintiff."[12] In *Bennett v. Stupich*,[13] a political newsletter from an opposition member, suggesting that the Premier had Scotch with his dinner and thus was at times in no position to attend evening sittings of the Legislature, was held to be defamatory. This was so even though the plaintiff himself had commenced the debate by earlier stating that drinking at dinner time by various members of the Legislature was interfering with the evening sittings. In *Upton v. Better Business Bureau*,[14] a statement written in a bulletin of a "Better Business Bureau" to the effect that the bureau had received unanswered complaints concerning the plaintiff, and that other estimates ought to be obtained by customers contemplating work, was held to be defamatory, despite the acknowledgement by the court that the criticism was "mild."[15] In *Whitaker v. Hungtington*,[16] statements by a Member of Parliament, spoken in the context of a controversial debate, expressing the view that a radical group was running a union's affairs, and that, because of this, the union was undemocratic and not responsive to the wishes of its membership, were held to be defamatory. In *Hanly v. Pisces Productions*,[17] a frank letter written in response to a union's request for reasons explaining why the plaintiff was not hired by the defendant was held to be defamatory. The defendant explained that the plaintiff was not hired because of her lack of self-confidence, her failure to provide positive work references, and previously unsatisfactory work experiences. In *Vander Zalm v. Times Publishers*,[18] a political cartoon depicting the Minister of Human Resources plucking the wings off a fly, gleefully, was considered by the trial judge to have been defamatory. Although members of the Court of Appeal expressed doubts regarding

---

C.J.A.'s view, "democratic debate in a free and open civilized society, such as ours, has the necessary tolerance to accept such statements and it does not offend my sense of justice, fair play or democratic principles to say so": *ibid.*, at 626.

11 (1982), 37 Nfld. & P.E.I.R. 128 (Nfld. Dist.Ct.).
12 *Ibid.*, at 135. Note that the letter of reprimand was not made "public," but was published only to the employees involved and their superiors.
13 (1981), 125 D.L.R. (3d) 743 (B.C.S.C.).
14 (1980), 114 D.L.R. (3d) 750 (B.C.S.C.).
15 The court itself interpreted the words as meaning that the plaintiffs were "untrustworthy and are prone to overcharge," and then found these implications to be defamatory.
16 (1980), 15 C.C.L.T. 19 (B.C.S.C.).
17 [1981] 1 W.W.R. 369 (B.C.S.C.).
18 (1980), 109 D.L.R. (3d) 531, reversing 96 D.L.R. (3d) 172 (B.C.C.A.).

this finding,[19] this aspect of the decision was upheld. Finally, in *Holt v. Sun Publishing*,[20] an editorial which was critical of the manner in which two politicians were exercising their responsibilities was held to be defamatory. It is difficult to find a recently reported case where an action was dismissed because material was found not to be defamatory.[21]

The second aspect of a plaintiff's *prima facie* case is proof that the material published referred to the plaintiff. This, generally, is not difficult to establish. Where a person is expressly named or identified in the material, no further proof will be required. The fact that the person to whom the material was published was unaware of the plaintiff is of no relevance. Where a person is not named in material, the court must determine whether "reasonable persons" would think that the material referred to the plaintiff. It does not matter if the persons who heard the information thought that it did, or did not, refer to the plaintiff, if their views would not be those of the "average sensible reader." The intention, knowledge or reasonable care of the publisher of this material is not relevant to this issue. A court is not concerned with what a speaker meant to say, but with the meaning reasonable persons would take from what was said. Even if the speaker intended to refer to a fictitious person, if a real person was hit by the material, the case would be made out. The law's concern is clearly with the protection of reputation, and not with freedom of speech.

The third aspect of the plaintiff's *prima facie* case is proof of publication. The defamatory material must have been communicated to at least one person other than the person defamed. Each publication of defamatory material constitutes a new defamation. The law has relaxed its strict liability approach to defamation slightly with respect to the issue of publication. "Accidental" publication will not lead to liability. Only intentional or careless publication will.

It is in the defences to the plaintiff's *prima facie* case for defamation where one can determine the extent of the common law's interest in protecting speech. Do the defences actually encourage speech?

Truth or justification is a complete defence to a defamation action. This appears to be a strong endorsement of the value of speech. However, certain aspects of the defence weaken this view. First, it must be recalled that truth is a defence, and falsity is presumed. Truth must,

---

19 Only one Court of Appeal justice, Aikins J.A., was prepared to find that the trial judge should be reversed on this aspect of his judgment; the others, although expressing their doubts, did not feel able to say that the trial judge was wrong.

20 (1978), 83 D.L.R. (3d) 761, varied 100 D.L.R. (3d) 447 (B.C.C.A.).

21 Although it is true that, in some of these cases, the actions were dismissed based on a successful defence, the actions, as indicated above, were fought out at that level.

therefore, be proved by the defendant on the balance of probabilities. Second, it is the substance of the material which must be proved to have been true. The law does not permit the truthful republication of false material, except in limited circumstances. Third, the material must be substantially true, and no consideration is paid to the honesty or good intentions of the speaker. Fourth, the law treats the plea of truth as a republication of the defamation, and if the defence fails, the plaintiff's damages can be increased due to the fact that the defence was pleaded.

Absolute privilege is a complete defence to an action for defamation, but has little application to the ordinary person. It protects parliamentarians, high executive officers of government, judges, lawyers and others involved in judicial proceedings, and communications between spouses.

The two defences of "qualified privilege" and "fair comment" are the most important with respect to the issue of free speech. The basic notion underlying occasions of qualified privilege is that, in certain circumstances, a speaker may have a legal, moral, or social duty or interest to communicate information to persons, with a reciprocal duty or interest to hear that information. The defence, admittedly, has been successful in numerous cases. Here again, however, one must take account of its limitations. The first, and undoubtedly the most significant, limitation is that Canadian law refuses to recognize that newspapers or other forms of mass media have any special duty or interest in communicating information to the public. The leading cases of *Globe & Mail Ltd. v. Boland*[22] and *Banks v. Globe & Mail*[23] established this point in the early '60s, and it has remained solid law since then. It has been held that newspapers have the same right as everyone else to publish within the parameters of the law of defamation, but that there is no special "freedom of the press."[24] Thus, whatever disincentives apply to the public with respect to free speech apply equally to newspapers and broadcasters.

Unlike the defence of absolute privilege, a qualified privilege can be defeated by proof that the defendant either exceeded the privilege or was malicious. Excess privilege will exist where the publisher used words which were not relevant to the occasion, or communicated the material to persons who were not entitled to receive it. These are matters for the

---

22 [1960] S.C.R. 203.

23 [1961] S.C.R. 474.

24 There are certain advantages given to newspapers and broadcasters with respect to limiting damages by printing apologies and retractions. This does not go to issues of liability, however. As well, statutory protection is given to "fair and accurate" reports of certain types of proceedings. There are, however, several limiting conditions. In addition, these privileges are not in any sense directed to issues of free speech.

court to determine. A defendant cannot know beforehand what the scope of the privilege is, even if one exists. Furthermore, where material is published to the world at large through the media, it is generally considered to be an excess of privilege, even if the original communication was privileged with respect to a smaller group. Thus, politicians have lost their qualified privilege in certain cases where material communicated to a small group was picked up by the media and publicly disseminated. Any improper or indirect motive for publishing material will be considered evidence of malice, and will defeat a qualified privilege.

The defence of "fair comment," theoretically, is designed to protect comments or opinions on matters of public interest. How successfully does it accomplish this objective?

There are numerous hurdles over which defendants must jump in order to succeed on a defence of fair comment. First, the publisher must prove that the statement was truly a "comment" or "opinion," and not a statement of fact. It is well recognized that the distinction between a statement of fact and a statement of comment on fact is a very difficult one to make. It is very difficult for commentators to know in advance whether their statements will be considered to be opinion or fact. As well, comment must be based on fact. Further, the comment must be based on a matter of "public interest." Finally, it must be seen as a "fair" comment. In addition, malice will defeat the defence. All of these elements provide reasons for rejecting the defence. They also create considerable uncertainty as to the likelihood of successfully pleading fair comment. This, in itself, provides a disincentive to publishing material. The case law is indicative of the conservative attitude of courts towards the defence. That a newspaper was held liable for a comment published in a "letter to the editor" on the basis that the newspaper did not share the opinion of the letter writer,[25] and a cartoonist was held liable at trial for a political satire of a British Columbia Cabinet Minister,[26] indicates that technical refinements of the defence can rob it of its ability to act effectively to promote speech.

III. *COATES v. THE CITIZEN*

The first noteworthy *Charter* challenge to defamation law occurred in *Coates v. The Citizen*.[27] As noted above, the judgment lends little encouragement to those who believed that Canadian defamation law would alter its attitudes as a result of the *Charter*.

---

25 *Cherneskey v. Armadale Publishers Ltd.* (1978), 7 C.C.L.T. 69 (S.C.C.) [Sask.].
26 *Vander Zalm v. Times Publishers, supra,* note 18.
27 *Supra,* note 3.

In *Coates*, Richard J. held that the *Charter* applied to Nova Scotia's defamation law due to the enactment of the *Defamation Act*.[28] The Act provided "the connection necessary to allow application of the Charter to what otherwise is litigation between private parties." This allowed the *Charter* to apply not only to the statutory provisions which were under attack, but to the common law as well. The specific aspects of defamation law which were alleged to be unconstitutional were: (a) the presumption of falsity; (b) the presumption of malice; and (c) the presumption of damage.

In considering these arguments, Richard J. made several important points which lend support to the argument that the *Charter* will not alter the common law's traditional balance of speech and reputation. Richard J. rejected the contention that defamation laws have a "chilling effect" on speech. He noted that the common law "has been built up over centuries to respond to demonstrable needs." One of these is to provide the citizens with a defence "against the awesome power of the printed word." The existing law, according to Richard J., does not restrict the publication of news, does not prevent comment on perceived government ineptitude, does not stifle criticism of prominent political figures in the conduct of their duties, and recognizes the need for free and full public discussion. Richard J. agreed with Professor Brown's assessment that, unlike their American colleagues, Canadian judges have weighed more heavily the value of personal reputation over those of free speech and free press. Although "our judges cherish free speech and a free press no less than their American counterparts . . . they just happen to value personal reputation, particularly the reputation of public servants, more."[29] The conclusion was clear: The Defamation Act did not impinge upon the right of freedom of the press as set out in s. 2(b) of the *Charter*.

IV. POLITICIANS AS PLAINTIFFS

It is not surprising that politicians are frequently found as plaintiffs in defamation actions. They are public figures. They engage in public debate and engender controversy. Journalists want to write about them, and ordinary people want to read about them. Nevertheless, what does the case law reveal? What are the lawsuits about?

Recent reported case law indicates that several Provincial Pre-

---

28 R.S.N.S. 1967, c. 72.
29 R. Brown, *Law of Defamation in Canada* (Toronto: Carswell, 1987), at 5-6, quoted with approval by Richard J. in *Coates, supra*, note 3 at 313. This is where the reasoning breaks down. Can you cherish free speech as much as the Americans, while devising laws which clearly protect reputation more?

miers,[30] Federal and Provincial Cabinet Ministers,[31] Members of Parliament and of Legislative Assemblies,[32] municipal politicians,[33] the leader of the W.C.C.,[34] and a Senator,[35] have sued for defamation. Some of these lawsuits clearly involved allegations of serious offences against the plaintiffs, or delved into matters affecting their private, not public, persons.[36] Others, however, involved criticisms which I would describe as being political. They related to political issues: the competence of the politicians involved, their policies, and so on. It is with these cases that I have some concern.

A few cases can be used to illustrate this concern. In *Lougheed v. C.B.C.*, the Premier of Alberta sued for allegedly defamatory material concerning him which appeared in a television "docudrama." The essence of the program was a critical analysis of the manner in which the negotiations for a tar sands project had been conducted. The Premier alleged that he was portrayed as weak, irresolute, out of touch and incompetent.[37] In *Holt v. Sun Publishing*,[38] a Member of Parliament was criticized for the manner in which she was conducting an inquiry into Canadian prison conditions. The impugned editorial suggested that she should not have been wasting her time interviewing or carrying messages for Charles Manson and his groupies. The plaintiff, in fact, had interviewed one of his "groupies," but had not carried any messages. The trial judge found in favour of the plaintiff, and awarded $2,000. This was raised to $5,000 by the Court of Appeal. In *Christie v. Geiger*,[39] the head of a western separatist movement sued over an editorial which likened his movement to "an Alberta version of the Ku Klux Klan." This was held to have been defamatory and $30,000 damages were awarded.[40] In *Coates v. The Citizen*,[41] the Minister of National Defence

---

30 Namely, Premier Lougheed of Alberta, Premier Hatfield of New Brunswick, and Premier Bennett of British Columbia. Premier Getty of Alberta recently has instituted a defamation action against the Calgary Herald.

31 Namely, Federal Cabinet Ministers Munro and Coates, and Provincial Cabinet Ministers Vander Zalm (later Premier of British Columbia) and Thornhill.

32 Namely, Federal M.P. Simma Holt, Provincial M.L.A.s Farrell and Wells.

33 Langdon, Cherneskey and Boushy.

34 Christie, founder of the Western Canada Concept.

35 Lawson.

36 For example, accusations that a Federal Cabinet Minister made improper profits for himself, and wrongfully exercised his influence; accusations which reflected upon the plaintiff as a lawyer and not a politician; accusations which imputed criminal wrongdoing; allegations concerning private financial matters.

37 The case was settled out of court.

38 *Supra*, note 20.

39 (1984), 35 Alta. L.R. (2d) 316 (Q.B.).

40 Note that one Court of Appeal judge held that this was fair comment. The

sued for comments in a newspaper article suggesting that his visit to a West German bar may have posed a security risk. In *Bennett v. Stupich*,[42] the Premier of British Columbia sued for statements made by an opposition member. The controversy concerned night sittings of the Legislature and whether the Premier and others had Scotch with their dinner. Ten thousand dollars in damages was awarded. In *Vander Zalm v. Times Publishers*,[43] the Minister of Human Resources sued because of a cartoon suggesting that he was cruel and sadistic[44] in the way he was conducting his portfolio. The trial judge awarded damages; this was reversed on appeal. In *Lawson v. Chabot*,[45] a Canadian Senator embroiled in a labour dispute sued the Provincial Minister of Labour for remarks suggesting that he was unfit to be a Senator since he was counselling the union members to disobey labour laws. The court said that the remarks were published on an occasion of qualified privilege, but that this was exceeded when the remarks were publicized by newspapers. Four thousand dollars in damages was awarded.

It is suggested that political commentary should not be so vulnerable to defamation litigation. Although plaintiffs will always be free to sue, of course, even with more restrictive defamation laws, a judicial attitude which is less sympathetic to such suits will discourage litigation.

V. CONCLUSION

There are several ways in which Canadian law can redress the imbalance between the protection of reputation and protecting free speech.

The threshold for "what is defamatory" must be raised. The law must recognize that all critical comment is not defamatory, and that only where there is a real risk to reputation should material be considered to be defamatory.

A more radical change would be to require the proof of actual harm to reputation for a successful action. The persons who heard the material must have thought that it was defamatory, and that it referred to the plaintiff. The hypothetical question might be replaced by a requirement of actual evidence that the plaintiff's reputation was damaged.

There ought to be greater scope for the defence of "fair comment." The boundary between statements of fact and comment on fact can be

---

movement clearly did have some extreme right-wing elements.
41 *Supra*, note 3.
42 *Supra*, note 13.
43 *Supra*, note 18.
44 At least this is what the trial judge implied from the cartoon.
45 (1974), 48 D.L.R. (3d) 556 (B.C.S.C.).

moved. It is too difficult, at present, to distinguish between fact and comment, or to know where the courts will draw the line. The "public interest" requirement can be jettisoned. All opinions should be protected, as long as they do not allege false fact. Good faith and honesty ought to be presumed in all comment. Those alleging that comments were not honestly held, or were malicious, ought to be required to prove this. Political comment and criticism ought to be particularly cherished — not only in theory, but in practice.

Canadian courts can utilize existing defamation principles to better protect speech. If they do not do so, the *Charter* should be used to strike down some of the more restrictive elements of the existing law.

BALANCING FREEDOM OF EXPRESSION AND PROTECTION OF REPUTATION UNDER CANADA'S *CHARTER OF RIGHTS AND FREEDOMS*

Rodney A. Smolla

I. INTRODUCTION

Canada has entrenched freedom of expression as a constitutional guarantee in its *Charter of Rights and Freedoms*,[1] with its promise of "freedom of thought, belief, opinion and expression, including freedom of the press and other media of communication."[2]

Canada has also long followed the traditional common law rules for libel and slander in defamation actions brought to vindicate reputational injury.[3] Those rules are heavily weighted in favour of plaintiffs and the protection of their reputations.[4] Should the guarantees of free

---

1   *Canadian Charter of Rights and Freedoms*, Pt. I of the *Constitution Act, 1982*, being Sched. B of the *Canada Act 1982*, 1982 (Eng.), c. 11.
2   *Ibid.*, s. 2(b).
3   See generally, Richard G. Dearden, "Constitutional Protection for Defamatory Words Published About the Conduct of Public Officials"; Lewis Klar, " 'If You Don't Have Anything Good to Say About Someone . . .'," in this volume.
4   See Rodney A. Smolla, *Law of Defamation* (New York: Clark Boardman, 1986), sections 1.02-1.03.

expression in the *Charter* be interpreted to modify the common law rules governing defamation so as to provide breathing space for freedom of speech?

This article argues that how a society chooses to strike the balance between the protection of free expression and the protection of reputation says a great deal about the nature and character of that society's democracy, and its underlying culture. In the words of Justice Cory in *R. v. Kopyto*:[5]

> The very life-blood of democracy is the free exchange of ideas and opinions. If these exchanges are stifled, democratic government itself is threatened.

The *Charter* should be interpreted to modify the traditional common law rules in Canada governing reputation, bringing those rules into a balance more protective of free expression. The harsh one-sided rules of the common law are inconsistent with the values of an open and robust democracy, and they do not reflect the resilient and energetic spirit of modern Canadian culture.

II. THE CULTURAL UNDERPINNINGS OF THE ENGLISH COMMON LAW RULES

Common law nations inherited from Great Britain defamation rules that reflected the preoccupation with reputation and honour characteristic of English society.[6] Even English culture, however, had moments of self-doubt concerning its fetish for honour. In Shakespeare's *Othello*, for example, the character Iago utters lines that worship reputation:[7]

> Good name in man and woman, dear my lord,
> Is the immediate jewel of their souls.
> Who steals my purse steals trash — 'tis something, nothing;
> Twas mine, 'tis his, and has been slave to thousands;
> But he that filches from me my good name
> Robs me of that which not enriches him
> And makes me poor indeed.

But the same Iago in another scene in the same play speaks of reputation in far less reverential tones:[8]

---

5   (1987), 62 O.R. (2d) 449 at 462 (C.A.).
6   David Reisman, "Democracy and Defamation: Control of Group Libel" (1942), 42 Colum.L.Rev. 727 at 730; Smolla, "Let the Author Beware: The Rejuvenation of the American Law of Libel" (1983), 132 U.Pa.L.Rev. 1 at 14-17.
7   William Shakespeare, *Othello*, act III, scene iii, lines 158-64 in *The Complete Works of William Shakespeare*, The Cambridge Text (1980).
8   *Ibid.*, act II, scene iii, lines 261-66.

> As I am an honest man, I thought you had received some bodily wound. There is more sense in that than in reputation. Reputation is an idle and most false imposition; oft got without merit and lost without deserving. You have lost no reputation at all unless you repute yourself such a loser.

Shakespeare perceived a crack in English society's armour, if not its very psyche. Is the value of an individual wrapped up solely in appearances — in that "good name" that is the "immediate jewel" of the soul — or is the value of the individual more an *intrinsic measurement*, so that "[y]ou have lost no reputation at all, unless you repute yourself such a loser?" Is an individual's self-worth merely a product of what he or she appears to be to others, or is Iago's less famous speech closer to the mark? Should a stable, well-adjusted individual be content to measure his or her self-worth against the readings of an internal gyroscope of self-esteem?

III. THE REBELLIOUS AMERICAN MODIFICATIONS OF THE COMMON LAW

A. The Common Law's Lack of Balance

English culture and English law appeared to accept all of Iago's "[w]ho steals my purse steals trash" speech, and virtually none of his claim that "[r]eputation is an idle and most false imposition." It does not follow, however, that those nations that have inherited the common law need to strike the same balance. The United States, for example, has altered its legal structure to protect reputation less, and free speech more — a balance that is, at least in part, traceable to the American mythology of "rugged individualism" and "self-reliance," a mythology quite different from the pre-occupation with gentility, honour and appearances characteristic of upper-crust English society.[9]

It is important to understand, however, that the American alteration of the common law is *not* a crude, one-sided bargain in which free speech has been allowed to ride roughshod over all concerns for individual dignity and public civility. Indeed, the American experience teaches that there are a number of unexpected, counter-intuitive benefits that derive from a commitment to an open culture. Openness may, in the long run, actually foster cultural and political cohesiveness, and enhance the overall level of protection for individual human dignity.

---

9   See generally, Rodney A. Smolla, *Suing the Press, Libel, the Media, and Power* (N.Y.: Oxford University Press, 1986).

B. The American Constitutional Solution

No case better illustrates this irony than the landmark decision that began the alteration of American libel law, *New York Times Co. v. Sullivan,*[10] a case that demonstrated how the common law of libel, with its potent capacity to squelch free expression, could be used as a weapon to undermine human dignity, and divide a society. In the long term, the freedom of speech of the American civil rights movement that was given protection in the *New York Times* case has done more to heal American society than to divide it, and more to protect human dignity than to erode it.

New York Times Co. v. Sullivan is the starting point for all modern discussions concerning the American law of defamation. The case revolutionized the law of defamation by holding for the first time that the traditional defamation tort rules were subject to the overriding constraints of the First Amendment. The *New York Times* case arose out of the struggle for racial equality in the South. On February 29, 1960, Dr. Martin Luther King, Jr. was arrested on trumped-up charges involving two counts of perjury in connection with the filing of his Alabama state income tax return. On March 10, 1960, three weeks after King's arrest, the *New York Times* ran an editorial in support of King's efforts; the *Times* praised the efforts of blacks in the South to resist racism, and admonished Congress to "heed their rising voices, for they will be heard." That editorial phrase would later be picked up by a newly formed "Committee to Defend Martin Luther King" which, on March 29, 1960, published a full page advertisement entitled "Heed Their Rising Voices." At the bottom of the ad were the names of a number of prominent Americans comprising "The Committee to Defend Martin Luther King and the Struggle for Freedom in the South."[11]

The *New York Times* was paid a little over $4,800 for running the advertisement. The total circulation of the issue was about 650,000, but only 394 copies of the *Times* were sent to Alabama newsdealers, and only 35 copies found their way into Montgomery County, Alabama. The *Times* ad stirred up a whirlwind of bitter reaction in Alabama, and soon after its publication a number of Alabama politicians commenced libel suits, including separate suits by John Patterson, the Governor of Alabama, one former Montgomery city commissioner, and three incumbent Montgomery commissioners.[12]

A similar demand for a retraction was also made by one of the

---

10   376 U.S. 254 (1964).
11   R. Smolla, *Suing the Press, supra,* note 9 at 26-52.
12   *Ibid.*

incumbent Montgomery city commissioners, L.B. Sullivan, who, as Commissioner of Public Affairs, was supervisor of the Montgomery departments of scales, cemeteries, fire and police. The *Times* advertisement did not actually mention Sullivan by name, and much of the ad referred to events entirely outside Alabama. Some of the statements in the advertisement were false, but those errors were largely technical and insubstantial.[13]

After a trial that lasted only three days, the jury returned a verdict of $500,000 against the *Times* and four individual black ministers. The Supreme Court of Alabama affirmed the award. In affirming the judgment, the Supreme Court of Alabama held that "[w]here the words published tend to injure a person libelled by them in his reputation, profession, trade or business, or charge him with an indictable offense, or tend to bring the individual into public contempt," they are "libellous *per se*"; "the matter complained of is, under the above doctrine, libellous *per se*, if it was published of and concerning the plaintiff"; and that it was actionable without "proof of pecuniary injury . . . such injury being implied."[14]

Approving the trial court's ruling that the jury could find the statements to have been made "of and concerning" Commissioner Sullivan, the Alabama Supreme Court stated:[15]

> We think it common knowledge that the average person knows that municipal agents, such as police and firemen, and others, are under the control and direction of the city governing body, and more particularly under the direction and control of a single commissioner. In measuring the performance or deficiencies of such groups, praise or criticism is usually attached to the official in complete control of the body.

In sustaining the trial court's determination that the verdict was not excessive, the Alabama Supreme Court said that malice could be inferred from a number of factors: (1) the Times' "irresponsibility" in printing the advertisement while the Times had in its files articles already published which would have demonstrated the "falsity" of the allegations in the ad; (2) the Times' failure to retract with respect to Commissioner Sullivan, while retracting with respect to Governor Patterson, even though "the matter contained in the advertisement was equally false as to both parties"; and (3) the testimony of the Times secretary that, apart from the statement that the dining hall was padlocked, they thought the two impugned paragraphs were "substantially correct."[16]

---

13 *Ibid.*
14 *New York Times Co. v. Sullivan*, 144 So. 2d 25 (1962).
15 *Ibid.*, at 37.
16 *Ibid.*, at 50-51.

The Alabama Supreme Court summarily rejected the Times' constitutional objections with brief statements that "[T]he First Amendment of the U.S. Constitution does not protect libellous publications" and "the Fourteenth Amendment is directed against State action and not private action."[17]

The threat to the Times posed by the Alabama Supreme Court's affirmance went well beyond the $500,000 verdict in Sullivan's case. A string of other libel suits against the Times had arisen in Alabama in connection with its reporting on racial matters; in one of those suits another $500,000 verdict had already been returned, and the total potential liability from the various suits filed was $5,600,000. After some internal debate within the corporate hierarchy at the Times, the decision was made to pursue review in the United States Supreme Court.[18]

The opinion by Justice Brennan began by disposing of two preliminary contentions. First, the court stated that although the case was a civil tort suit between private litigants, the state rules of tort law applied by the Alabama court system imposed restrictions on the freedoms of speech and press, and that application of state power, even if it was effectuated through mere common law rules, was subject to the restrictions of the First Amendment.[19] This point is particularly relevant to the future evolution of Canadian jurisprudence, because of the holding in the *Dolphin Delivery* case that the *Charter* does not apply to private litigation completely divorced from any connection with government.[20] The court in *Dolphin Delivery* held that the *Charter* does apply, however, when the common law is the basis for some governmental action that is alleged to have infringed a *Charter* right or freedom. As explained more fully in the paragraphs below, the essence of the *New York Times* case is that, when the plaintiff is a public official using the common law of libel in a case arising from the discussion of the official's performance in or fitness for office, the common law *is* being used to effectuate governmental policy and to chill dissent. That central meaning of the American *New York Times* holding could thus survive the *Dolphin Delivery* standard. It would not be inconsistent with *Dolphin Delivery* for the Supreme Court of Canada to hold that when public officials bring a common law libel action arising from a story concerning their fitness for or performance in office, the *Charter*'s guarantee of free expression should be applied to modify traditional common law rules.

The United States Supreme Court held, in the *New York Times*

---

17 *Ibid.*, at 40.
18 R. Smolla, *Suing the Press, supra*, note 9 at 26-52.
19 *Supra*, note 10 at 265.
20 *R.W.D.S.U., Local 580 v. Dolphin Delivery Ltd.*, [1986] 2 S.C.R. 573 [B.C.].

case, that the First Amendment was not rendered inapplicable merely because the allegedly libellous statements were part of a paid "commercial" advertisement. The court stated that the *Times* ad was not a "commercial" advertisement in the sense that the court had previously defined "commercial speech." The ad communicated information, expressed opinions, recited grievances, protested claimed abuses, and "sought financial support on behalf of a movement whose existence and objectives are matters of the highest public interest and concern."[21]

The Supreme Court then summarized applicable Alabama law, which followed the common law rules typical across the United States at the time. Under Alabama libel law, a publication was "libellous *per se*" if the words tended to injure a person in reputation or to bring a person into "public contempt." The standard was met if the words were such as to "injure him in his public office, or impute misconduct to him in his office, or want of official integrity, or want of fidelity to a public trust." The words were required to be "of and concerning" the plaintiff, but where the plaintiff was a public official, the plaintiff's place in the government hierarchy was sufficient evidence to support a finding that the plaintiff's reputation had been affected by statements that reflected upon the agency of which the plaintiff was in charge. Once "libel *per se*" had been established, the defendant had no defence as to stated facts unless it could persuade the jury that those facts were true in all their particulars. This privilege of "fair comment" for expressions of opinion depended on the truth of the facts upon which the comment was based. Unless the defendant could discharge the burden of proving truth, general damages were presumed and could be awarded without proof of pecuniary injury. A showing of actual malice was a prerequisite to recovery of punitive damages, and the defendant could, in any event, forestall a punitive award by a retraction meeting certain statutory requirements. Good motives and belief in the truthfulness of the statements did not negate an inference of malice, but were relevant only in mitigation of punitive damages if the jury chose to accord them weight.[22]

The court then turned to the question of whether these Alabama rules were consistent with the First Amendment. In deciding the question, the court said that the analysis should not be linked to "mere labels," for the mere epithet "libel" did not render the speech unprotected.[23] The court then emphasized the "marketplace of ideas" theory of the First Amendment and the significance of the unfettered interchange of ideas:[24]

---

21 *Supra*, note 10 at 266, citing *N.A.A.C.P. v. Button*, 371 U.S. 415 (1963).
22 *Ibid.*, at 267.
23 *Ibid.*, at 269.
24 *Ibid.*, at 269, quoting *Stromberg v. California*, 283 U.S. 359 at 369 (1931).

The maintenance of the opportunity for free political discussion, to the end that government may be responsive to the will of the people and that changes may be obtained by lawful means, an opportunity essential to the security of the Republic, is a fundamental principle of our constitutional system.

And then, in the most famous line of Justice Brennan's opinion, he stated that the court thus considered the case:[25]

... against the background of a profound national commitment to the principle that debate on public issues should be uninhibited, robust, and wide-open, and that it may well include vehement, caustic, and sometimes unpleasantly sharp attacks on government and public officials.

Criticism of official conduct does not lose its constitutional protection, Justice Brennan argued, merely because it is effective criticism and hence diminishes the reputations of the officials involved. Justice Brennan then spoke of the lessons to be drawn from the great controversy over the *Sedition Act* of 1798, which first crystallized a national awareness of the "central meaning" of the First Amendment. That statute made it a crime, punishable by a $5,000 fine and five years in prison,[26]

... if any person shall write, print, utter or publish ... any false, scandalous and malicious writing or writings against the government of the United States, or either house of the Congress ... or the President ... with intent to defame ... or to bring them, or either of them, into contempt or disrepute; or to excite against them, or either or any of them, the hatred of the good people of the United States.

The Act, an Americanized "improvement" on the old English crime of seditious libel, required the jury to be judges both of law and of fact. Despite these qualifications, the Act was vigorously condemned as unconstitutional in an attack joined by both Thomas Jefferson and James Madison. Although no case challenging the validity of the *Sedition Act* ever reached the Supreme Court, Justice Brennan noted (as had Justice Holmes several decades earlier)[27] that "the attack upon its validity had carried the day in the court of history."[28]

Turning to the heart of his analysis, Justice Brennan then spoke of the necessity of fashioning libel rules that do not chill the free exercise of

---

25 *Ibid.*, at 270, citing *Terminiello v. Chicago*, 337 U.S. 1 at 4 (1949); *DeJonge v. Oregon*, 299 U.S. 353 at 365 (1937).
26 1 Stat. 596 (1798).
27 See *Abrams v. United States*, 250 U.S. 616 at 630 (1919) (Holmes J., dissenting).
28 *Supra*, note 10.

public criticism. The traditional common law tort rule that compels the critic of official conduct to guarantee the truth of all factual assertions — and to do so on pain of libel judgments virtually unlimited in amount — leads, Justice Brennan argued, to intolerable self-censorship. But why is the danger of self-censorship not alleviated by the common law defense of truth? The answer, Justice Brennan reasoned, is that the allowance of the defense of truth, with the burden of proving it on the defendant, does not mean that only false speech will be deterred. It is often too difficult to produce legal proofs that the alleged libel was true in all of its factual particulars. "Under such a rule, would-be critics of official conduct may be deterred from voicing their criticism, even though it is believed to be true and even though it is in fact true, because of doubt whether it can be proved in court or fear of the expense of having to do so."[29] This leads to an unhealthy timidity in which people tend to make statements steering wide of the danger zone. The traditional defamation rule "dampens the vigor and limits the variety of public debate."[30] Justice Brennan then stated the holding that would launch an entirely new era for the American law of libel:[31]

> The constitutional guarantees require, we think, a federal rule that prohibits a public official from recovering damages for a defamatory falsehood relating to his official conduct *unless he proves that the statement was made with actual malice — that is, with knowledge that it was false or with reckless disregard of whether it was false or not.* [emphasis added]

After announcing the new constitutional rule, the court, "in the interest of effective judicial administration," undertook a review of the record to determine whether it could constitutionally support a judgment for Sullivan. In undertaking that review, a series of important subsidiary principles emerged from the court's opinion, all of which would in later cases surface as important components of the constitutional picture. First, because the constitutional guarantees the court had fashioned would be inextricably bound up with questions of fact, the court engaged in "an independent examination of the whole record" to determine if the evidence would support a finding of actual malice.[32] Second, in undertaking the review of the evidence, the court stated that the proof of actual malice must be of "convincing clarity," a standard distinctly more rigorous than the preponderance of the evidence standard of proof that normally applied to civil actions.[33] Third, neither the

---

29 *Ibid.*, at 279.
30 *Ibid.*
31 *Ibid.*, at 279-80.
32 *Ibid.*, at 285.
33 *Ibid.*, at 285-86.

Times' failure to retract, nor its failure to check the facts in the ad against its own files, constituted "actual malice."[34] Finally, the statements in the ad were too far removed from a personalized attack on Commissioner Sullivan to constitutionally support a finding that the libellous material was "of and concerning" Sullivan.[35]

The *Times* decision profoundly changed the American law of defamation; it has proved to be a case of enduring vitality, a case that continues to foster intense debate, and continues to be drawn upon by American courts charged with the task of reconciling the strong societal interest in protecting reputation with the "central meaning" of the First Amendment.

IV. FASHIONING A BALANCE FOR CANADA UNDER THE *CHARTER*

A. Framing the Relevant Questions

It would be the height of presumption and arrogance to suppose that the modifications engrafted upon the common law of libel by the United States Supreme Court are necessarily appropriate for Canada under the *Charter*. Precisely because the balance between free expression and the protection of reputation is so symbolically important to a culture, outsiders from the United States have no business presuming to counsel Canada as to the balance appropriate for Canadian life. American free speech scholars can, however, share the American experience with Canada, in a spirit of collegial modesty, and at least be of assistance in helping Canadians frame the legal and cultural questions that must be addressed.

In contemporary Canadian society it is appropriate to ask whether healthy individuals dealing with one another in the complexities of modern social life should be encouraged to treat reputations as a serious and significant social value, but *not* as a value that dominates all others. Americans and Canadians share both the North American continent and a legal tradition drawn from England. And Canadians may find that they, like their American counterparts, have instincts about the relative roles of reputation and free expression very different from those of the English.

The common law of England was almost paternalistic in its protection of thin skins. The English common law grew out of a pre-democratic political society, a society divided into social classes and severely mindful of propriety and place. Canada's modern society, by contrast, is

---

34 *Ibid.*, at 288-91.
35 *Ibid.*

democratic and egalitarian. There is no social caste to be enforced in Canada. Canada may rightfully accept the wisdom of the common law that reputation deserves legal protection, but it should temper that wisdom with balanced rules that require a certain toughening of the mental hide as part of the price of an open society.

B. The Ingredients of a More Balanced Approach

At a bare minimum, Canada should consider whether the common law should be modified to make the plaintiff's burden in a defamation case more like that which a plaintiff bears in virtually all other causes of action known to modern tort law. The plaintiff should bear the burden of proving the basic elements of the defamation case. The plaintiff should bear the burden of demonstrating that the defamatory statement was false, that the defendant was guilty of fault in publishing the statement, and that the plaintiff suffered injury. Doctrines should be adopted that make it clear that only factual statements are actionable, and that expressions of opinion are absolutely protected.

C. The General Case for Openness as a Social Value

It might be objected that enhancing protection for freedom of speech at the expense of protection for individual reputation will actually have the perverse effect of degrading public discourse and diminishing participatory democracy. Able people, it might be argued, will be dissuaded from entering the public arena for fear that, in joining the political fray, they will forfeit some of the reputational protection they might otherwise have enjoyed. Similarly, it might be argued that the common law's solicitude for reputation was part of the communal glue that held the polity together, and that to countenance a relaxation of those common law rules would invite the sorts of *ad hominem* attacks on others that do not contribute to the sound resolution of public policy, attacks that undermine values of civility and cohesiveness.

These objections, however, are really nothing more than the bill of particulars in a much broader indictment of the whole notion of freedom of speech. A culture that chooses to genuinely embrace freedom of speech, freedom of the press, freedom of assembly and freedom of religion as part of the general matrix of guarantees of expression and conscience will inevitably be forced to make trade-offs. None of these rights comes for free. The irony, however, is that, in the long term, those societies that dare to take the brave step towards genuine openness tend to be more stable and better able to build a true sense of cohesive identity and community. That stability and cohesiveness comes, however, not through the forced fiat of law, but through the free trade of thought and feeling characteristic of a truly open democracy. While it is tempting to adopt the simple dichotomy between freedom of speech on the one hand and the protection of individual dignity and reputation on the other, in the long term a society that embraces free speech as a transcendent value will enhance, not diminish, individual human dignity.

A society that embraces openness will defend human expression and conscience in all its wonderful varieties, protecting freedom of speech, freedom of the press, freedom of religion, freedom of association, freedom of assembly and freedom of peaceful mass protest. These freedoms will be extended not only to political discourse, but to the infinite range of artistic, scientific and philosophical inquiries that capture and cajole the human imagination.

A society that wishes to adopt openness as a value of overarching significance will not merely allow citizens a wide range of individual expressive freedom, but will go one step farther, and actually open up the deliberative processes of government itself to the sunlight of public scrutiny. In a truly open culture the normal rule is that government does not conduct the business of the people behind closed doors. Legislative, administrative and judicial proceedings should, as a matter of routine, be open to the public.

Individual freedom of expression and openness in government are not, however, absolute. Speech may cause injury, including serious reputational harm, and in some cases it may be regulated or punished to prevent that injury. Some governmental deliberations must be confidential; no government could operate if every personnel decision or diplomatic initiative had to be made in full view of everyone. If openness is not an absolute value, it should be *nearly* absolute: for governments will always tend to exert too much control on individual speech and conscience, and will tend to be too jealous of their secrets and confidences. A society that wishes to take openness seriously as a value must devise rules that are deliberately tilted in favour of openness — tilted more than may at first seem reasonable — in order to counteract the inherent impulse of governments to engage in control, censorship and secrecy.

Ironically, democratic values and the value of openness are at times in conflict. While openness is an aid to democracy, the democratic process will on occasion produce decisions by the majority to squelch the speech of the minority. When democratic values and the value of openness come into conflict, a society will be both more stable and more free in the long run if the value of openness prevails. This is an extremely difficult principle to accept. Why should the concept of majority rule not always prevail in a democracy, even on questions of freedom of expression? How can protecting a minority viewpoint against the wishes of the majority actually be better for stability and order?

The justification for openness begins with the rationale that mankind's search for truth is best advanced by a free trade in ideas. In the words of the American jurist Oliver Wendell Holmes, "the best test of truth is the power of the thought to get itself accepted in the competition of the market."[36] The "marketplace of ideas" is perhaps the most powerful metaphor in the free speech tradition. In 1644, John Milton wrote in his *Areopagitica*:

> And though all the winds of doctrine were let loose to play upon the earth, so Truth be in the field, we do injuriously by licensing and prohibiting to misdoubt her strength. Let her and falsehood grapple; who ever knew Truth put to the worse, in a free and open encounter?

The marketplace theory justifies openness as a means to an end. However, an open society is also an end itself, an end intimately intertwined with human autonomy and dignity. Openness does not merely serve the needs of the polity, but also those of the human spirit — a spirit that demands to be heard. Openness is thus especially valuable for reasons that have nothing to do with the collective search for truth, the processes of self-government, or for any other conceptualization of the common good. It embraces a right to defiantly, robustly and irreverently speak one's mind just because it is one's mind. Even when the speaker has no realistic hope that the audience will be persuaded to his or her viewpoint, even when no plausible case can be made that the search for truth will be advanced, freedom to speak without restraint provides the speaker with an inner satisfaction and realization of self-identity essential to individual fulfilment.

It might be argued that this is an exceptionally selfish, almost hedonistic, justification for openness. If the majority is convinced that it is reasonable to stifle an individual's expression for the greater good of the whole society, why should the majority be prevented from imposing its view on the individual?

The answer is that the freedoms encompassed by the openness value, the freedoms of speech, press, religion, assembly and demonstration, are freedoms that define humanity itself. The fulfilment that comes from free expression is bonded to our capacity to think, imagine and create. Conscience and consciousness are the sacred precincts of mind and soul. The linkage of speech to thought, to our central capacity to reason and wonder, is what places it above other forms of fulfilment, and beyond the routine jurisdiction of the state.

Few in the modern world would defend the prerogative of the state to censor thought. Only by accepting that we are creatures of the state,

---

36 *Supra*, note 27 at 630.

and that even the intimate internal processes of mind that distinguish human existence are enjoyed at the state's sufferance, could such a monstrous and awesome intrusion be justified. To accept the proposition would be to accept the extinguishment of thousands of years of moral evolution, in which the world has come slowly and painfully to recognize that people possess certain entitlements to dignity and autonomy by sheer virtue of their humanity. Descartes' statement, "I think therefore I am," is an assertion about existence. If one adds, "I think, therefore I am somebody deserving of respect," one has an assertion about humanity.

Once the inviolable primacy of freedom of thought is accepted, the preferred position of openness as a societal value follows. This does *not* mean that the government has no more claim on regulation of speech than it does on thought — for unlike thought, speech involves other human beings, and thus can cause harm. However, it *does* mean that because speech is connected to thought in a manner that other forms of gratification are not, it is proper to place special burdens on the state when it ventures to regulate speech that would not exist when it regulates other aspects of human activity. It is no answer to insist that thinkers should keep their thoughts to themselves; for the human urge to think includes an urge to think out loud. Thought and speech are complimentary, reinforcing freedoms; freedoms that partake at once of the private and social aspects of personality. The human spirit is nourished by both thought and speech, as the body is nourished by both food and water.

This openness value both protects and provokes the expressive spirit. On its surface it is a negative restraint on government. However, beneath the surface lies a more vexing voice, one that affirmatively *encourages* citizens to speak, to take stands, to demand to be heard, to demand to *participate*. Freedoms of speech, press, association and assembly are means of participation: the vehicles through which individuals debate the issues of the day, cast their votes and actively join in the processes of decision-making that shape the polity.

This participatory value, it should be emphasized, is a value benefiting both the collective and the individual. Openness serves the state in several ways. If the best test of truth is the power of the thought to get itself accepted in the competition of the market, then the best test of intelligent political policy is its power to get itself accepted at the ballot box. A corollary is that openness facilitates majority rule. A society that has set out to govern itself democratically needs a large degree of openness to ensure that collective policy-making represents, to the greatest degree possible, the collective will.

Governments instinctively fear openness, often viewing it as promiscuous and dangerous, fostering a decline in order, efficiency and stability. However, when governments can be persuaded to err on the side of openness, they learn that quite the opposite is true: openness *improves* the resiliency and stability of government, and it often increases efficiency, by uncovering official iniquity or incompetence. While it may at times seem counter-intuitive, openness actually encourages social stability. In the words of the American Supreme Court Justice Louis Brandeis, the framers of the American Constitution had the insight to realize that:[37]

> ... order cannot be secured merely through fear of punishment for its infraction; that it is hazardous to discourage thought, hope and imagination; that fear breeds repression; that repression breeds hate; that hate menaces stable government; that the path of safety lies in the opportunity to discuss freely supposed grievances and proposed remedies; and that the fitting remedy for evil counsels is good ones.

If societies are not to explode from festering tensions, there must be valves through which the citizens may blow off steam. Openness fosters resiliency; peaceful protest displaces more violence than it triggers; free debate dissipates more hate than it stirs.

Most importantly, however, openness serves the interests, not of the government, but of the people. The participatory interest served by freedom of speech in a democracy grows out of the entitlements of citizens, not simply the needs of the state. Openness is the most powerful restraint mankind has yet devised on tyranny. It is through non-violent speech that the people may ferret out corruption and discourage tyrannical excesses, keeping government within the metes and bounds of the charter through which the people first brought it into existence. Openness vindicates the individual's right to join the political fray, to stand up and be counted, to be an active player in the democracy, not a passive spectator.

---

37   *Whitney v. Calif.*, 274 U.S. 357 at 375 (1927) (Brandeis J., concurring).

CONSTITUTIONAL PROTECTION FOR DEFAMATORY WORDS PUBLISHED ABOUT THE CONDUCT OF PUBLIC OFFICIALS

Richard G. Dearden

I. INTRODUCTION

Should libel defendants be given any constitutional protection for the publication of defamatory words about the conduct of public officials? This article proposes that libel defendants should be given constitutional protection in actions by public officials to truly guarantee freedom of the press pursuant to s. 2(b) of the *Canadian Charter of Rights and Freedoms*.[1]

---

1   *Canadian Charter of Rights and Freedoms*, Pt. I of the *Constitution Act, 1982*, being Sched. B of the *Canada Act 1982*, 1982 (Eng.), c. 11.

In *New York Times v. Sullivan*,[2] the United States Supreme Court was required for the first time to decide the extent to which the constitutional protections for speech and press limited a state's power to award damages in libel actions brought by public officials against critics of their official conduct.

Now that the *Charter* has constitutionally guaranteed freedom of the press, Canada's antiquated laws of libel as they apply to actions by public officials must be modernized, as was done in 1964 in *New York Times v. Sullivan*. Justice Brennan held that "debate on public issues should be uninhibited, robust, and wide open, and that it may well include vehement, caustic, and sometimes unpleasantly sharp attacks on government and public officials."[3] This statement is quite similar to the following remarks by Justice Cory in *Edmonton Journal v. Alta. (Attorney General)*:[4]

> It is difficult to imagine a guaranteed right more important to a democratic society than freedom of expression. *Indeed democracy cannot exist without that freedom to express new ideas and to put forward opinions about the functioning of public institutions.* The concept of free and uninhibited speech permeates all truly democratic societies and institutions. The vital importance of the concept cannot be over-emphasized. No doubt that was the reason why the framers of the *Charter* set forth s. 2(b) in absolute terms which distinguishes it, for example, from s. 8 of the *Charter* which guarantees the qualified right to be secure from unreasonable search and seizure. It seems that the rights enshrined in s. 2(b) should therefore only be restricted in the clearest of circumstances . . .
>
> That is to say as listeners and readers, *members of the public have a right to information pertaining to public institutions* and particularly the courts. Here the press plays a fundamentally important role . . . [emphasis added]

In *R. v. Kopyto*[5] Justice Cory held:

> The concept of free and uninhibited speech permeates all truly democratic societies. Caustic and biting debate is, for example, often the hallmark of election campaigns, parliamentary debates and campaigns for the establishment of new public institutions or the reform of existing practices and institutions. The exchange of ideas on important issues is often framed in colourful and vitriolic language. So long as comments made on matters of public interest are neither obscene nor contrary to the laws of criminal libel, citizens of a democratic state should not have to worry unduly about the framing of their expression

---

2 376 U.S. 254 (1964).
3 *Ibid.*, at 270.
4 [1989] 2 S.C.R. 1326 at 1336 and 1339.
5 (1987), 62 O.R. (2d) 449 at 462 (C.A.).

of ideas. The very life-blood of democracy is the free exchange of ideas and opinions. If these exchanges are stifled, democratic government itself is threatened.

To date, the Supreme Court of Canada has not had occasion to deal with a *New York Times v. Sullivan* argument pursuant to s. 2(b) of the *Charter*. However, the argument has been raised before a number of lower courts.

The *New York Times* argument was rejected by the Nova Scotia Trial Division in *Coates v. The Citizen.*[6]

The Manitoba Court of Appeal refused to consider the New York Times argument in *Pangilinan v. Chaves*:[7]

> In this court, the defendants' counsel argued that we should re-evaluate the law of defamation in light of the *Canadian Charter of Rights and Freedoms*. He said that the freedom of expression entitled the defendants to express a reasonably held belief: the onus should now be on the plaintiff to prove that the facts, which the defendants believed to be true, are untrue.
>
> In our opinion the *Charter* does not apply to an action, between private litigants, in which no public issue is raised: see *Retail, Wholesale and Department Store Union, Local 580 v. Dolphin Delivery Ltd.* (1986), 33 D.L.R. (4th) 174.

In *Getty v. Calgary Herald*[8] the defendants were denied an amendment to their statement of defence regarding s. 2(b) of the *Charter* which was described as "just an argument that everyone, including the press, has an unconstrained right or freedom to defame others. This proposed amendment has no merit in law." And in *Temple v. Toronto Sun Publishing Corporation*,[9] the master also held:

> The Charter cannot be set up as a defence to a common law action where the plaintiff does not have to rely on any "governmental" action as part of his case . . . The Charter cannot be raised as a "defence" to argue that the common law might be [applied and developed] . . . in a manner consistent with the fundamental values enshrined in the Constitution. That is a defence that the law of defamation should be

---

6 (1988), 85 N.S.R. (2d) 146, *per* Richard J. The findings of this case are discussed in detail, *infra*, in the text accompanying notes 56 to 62. For the record, it should be noted that the author was co-counsel with Gordon F. Henderson representing the defendants in *Coates v. The Ottawa Citizen*. Neither the plaintiff nor the Attorney General of Nova Scotia nor the Attorney General of Canada participated in the argument of this pretrial motion.

7 Man. C.A., No. 205/88, 8th November 1988 (not yet reported).

8 (1990), 104 A.R. 308 at 318 (M.C.), *per* Master Funduk.

9 Alta. Q.B., Master Funduk, 4th April 1990 (not yet reported), at 1-2.

different than what it is. A defence that the law should be "reformulated" is not a defence.

The defendants in *Christie v. Geiger and Edmonton Sun*[10] also raised a *New York Times* argument. Both the trial judge and the Court of Appeal held that the *Charter* had no application because the defamatory words were published prior to the proclamation of the *Charter*.[11]

> ... the safe anchorage of *New York Times v. Sullivan* is not available to these appellants [defendants] simply because of the date of the publication ... Whether the standards of proof in *New York Times v. Sullivan* take support from the Canadian Charter of Rights and Freedoms will be decided in a timely case. For the purposes of this case we simply reject the argument, pressed in *New York Times v. Sullivan*, that defamation is inherent in media discussion of public affairs and personages.

The defendants in *Hill v. Church of Scientology*[12] brought a pretrial motion for dismissal of a libel action arguing that public officials could not sue for defamatory statements relating to their official conduct unless they proved that the statements were made with knowledge of falsehood or at least reckless disregard as to the veracity of the statements. The motion was dismissed because such an issue was not meant for a decision upon a motion but had to be determined by the trial judge after evidence was adduced at trial.[13]

> If in fact the defendants can show a Charter infringement of their s. 2(b) rights, how, on an application in Weekly Court where matters are decided on affidavits and transcripts, could justice ever be done to the opposite party who must be given an opportunity to convince the court that the impugned law is an exception under s. 1 of the Charter of Rights and Freedoms?

It is to be noted that the *New York Times v. Sullivan* argument pursuant to s. 2(b) of the *Charter* was dealt with in a pretrial motion before Justice Richard in *Coates v. The Citizen*.[14]

Snider v. Calgary Herald[15] held that it was unnecessary to decide

---

10   35 Alta. L.R. (2d) 316, *per* Foisy J., affirmed [1987] 1 W.W.R. 357 at 362, *per* McClung J.A. (C.A.).

11   *Ibid.*, at 362-63.

12   (1985), 35 C.C.L.T. 72 (Ont. H.C.).

13   *Ibid.*, at 79, *per* O'Driscoll J.

14   *Supra*, note 6. A *New York Times v. Sullivan* argument should be dealt with prior to trial so that the plaintiff and defendant know before the trial starts who has the burden of proof and what they must prove to make their case.

15   (1985), 34 C.C.L.T. 27 at 57 (Alta. Q.B.), *per* Miller J.

whether the defendants could rely upon a *New York Times v. Sullivan* argument, requiring a public official plaintiff to prove actual malice, because one of the defendants had, in fact, acted maliciously.

This article examines how the present-day laws of libel in Canada infringe s. 2(b) of the *Charter* and are not saved by s. 1 of the *Charter* unless libel defendants are given the constitutional protections set out in *New York Times v. Sullivan* in libel actions commenced by public officials. The applicability of s. 32 of the *Charter* as interpreted by *Retail, Wholesale and Department Store Union, Local 580 v. Dolphin Delivery Ltd.*[16] is also briefly reviewed. In the event that s. 32 of the *Charter* prevents libel defendants from claiming constitutional protections equivalent to those recognized in *New York Times v. Sullivan*, it is proposed that s. 2(b) of the *Charter* can be used as the basis for the creation of a new category of qualified privilege in libel actions brought by public officials.

II. *NEW YORK TIMES v. SULLIVAN*

The New York Times published an "editorial" advertisement communicating information, expressing opinion, reciting grievances, protesting claimed abuses, and seeking financial support on behalf of the black right-to-vote movement and the black student movement. An elected commissioner of the City of Montgomery, Alabama (Sullivan) brought a libel action against the publisher of the New York Times and against black and Alabama clergymen whose names appeared in the advertisement. The Circuit Court, Montgomery County, Alabama, entered a judgment on a verdict awarding $500,000 to the plaintiff.

The United States Supreme Court held that the law applied by the Alabama courts was constitutionally deficient because of its failure to provide the safeguards for freedom of speech and of the press that are required by the First and Fourteenth Amendments in a libel action brought by a public official against critics of his official conduct.

The question before the United States Supreme Court was whether the common law presumptions that existed in libel actions in Alabama, as applied to a libel action brought by a public official against critics of his official conduct, abridged the freedom of speech and of the press guaranteed by the First and Fourteenth Amendments to the Constitution of the United States of America. The plaintiff relied heavily, as did the Alabama courts, on the proposition that the Constitution did not protect libellous publications. Justice Brennan rejected this proposition and held that:

---

16   *R.W.D.S.U., Local 580 v. Dolphin Delivery Ltd.*, [1986] 2 S.C.R. 573 [B.C.].

(1) libel must be measured by standards that satisfy freedom of the press;[17]
(2) erroneous statement is inevitable in free debate and must be protected if freedom of the press is to have the "breathing space" it needs to survive;[18]
(3) the fear of damage awards (general damages being presumed at common law without proof of pecuniary injury) may be markedly more inhibiting than the fear of criminal prosecution;[19]
(4) the pall of fear and timidity imposed upon those who would give voice to public criticism is an atmosphere in which freedom of the press cannot survive.[20]

Justice Brennan held that the common law presumptions in libel actions lead to self-censorship:[21]

> A rule compelling the critic of official conduct to guarantee the truth of all his factual assertions — and to do so on pain of libel judgments virtually unlimited in amount — leads to a comparable "self-censorship". Allowance of the defense of truth, with the burden of proving it on the defendant, does not mean that only false speech will be deterred. Even courts accepting this defence as an adequate safeguard have recognized the difficulties of adducing legal proofs that the alleged libel was true in all its factual particulars ... Under such a rule, *would-be critics of official conduct may be deterred from voicing their criticism, even though it is believed to be true and even though it is in fact true, because of doubt whether it can be proved in court or fear of the expense of having to do so. They tend to make only statements which "steer far wider of the unlawful zone"* ... The rule thus dampens the vigor and limits the variety of public debate. It is inconsistent with the First and Fourteenth Amendments.
>
> *The constitutional guarantees require, we think, a federal rule that prohibits a public official from recovering damages for a defamatory falsehood relating to his official conduct unless he proves that the statement was made with "actual malice"* — that is, with knowledge that it was false or with reckless disregard of whether it was false or not. [emphasis added]

It is to be noted that Justices Black, Douglas and Goldberg in *New York Times v. Sullivan* held that the New York Times had an *absolute*, unconditional right to publish their criticisms of the Montgomery, Alabama agencies and public officials despite the harm which may flow from media excesses and abuses.

---

17 *New York Times v. Sullivan, supra,* note 2 at 268-69.
18 *Ibid.,* at 271-72.
19 *Ibid.,* at 277.
20 *Ibid.,* at 278.
21 *Ibid.,* at 279-80.

III. INFRINGEMENT OF SECTION 2(b) OF THE *CHARTER*

A. The Common Law Presumptions

Defamation is a strict liability tort.[22] The present-day laws of libel operate so as to, in effect, create a reverse onus on a libel defendant. A plaintiff establishes a *prima facie* cause of action as soon as it is proven that the words complained of:

(1) are reasonably capable of a defamatory meaning;
(2) refer to the plaintiff; and
(3) have been published.

A plaintiff does not have to prove that the words complained of are in fact defamatory. The plaintiff need only prove that the words are "reasonably capable" of a defamatory meaning. A defamatory meaning is one that would be understood by reference to an ordinary, reasonable and right-thinking person. It is not necessary for the persons to whom the words were published to understand them in a defamatory sense if a reasonable person would do so. Words will be considered to be defamatory where their publication tends to lower the plaintiff's reputation in the estimation of "right-thinking" members of society.[23]

Once a plaintiff proves the publication of allegedly libellous words, there is no need to prove that damages have in fact been suffered by the plaintiff. It is presumed, without proof, that "some damage will flow in the ordinary course of things from the mere invasion of [the plaintiff's] absolute right to reputation."[24]

Secondly, a plaintiff is not required to prove malice on the part of the defendant — there is a presumption of malice.[25] The presumption of "legal malice" has the strength of a "finding" of malice. It is not a mere evidentiary presumption that may be rebutted by a defendant, in the absence of a qualified privilege.[26]

Thirdly, a plaintiff need not prove that the defamatory words were false. This is presumed in the plaintiff's favour. A defendant bears the onus of proving that the precise statements complained of are true, with the exception of those that do not materially injure the plaintiff's reputa-

---

22 *Christie v. Geiger, supra,* note 10.
23 R.E. Brown, *The Law of Defamation in Canada* (Toronto: Carswell, 1987), at 40.
24 *Ratcliffe v. Evans,* [1892] 2 Q.B. 524 at 528.
25 *Snider v. Calgary Herald, supra,* note 15 at 52, *per* Miller J.
26 *Gatley on Libel and Slander,* 8th ed. (Toronto: Sweet and Maxwell, 1981), at 328.

tion, having regard to the truth of the remaining charges. A defendant's belief in the truth of the statements published is insufficient.[27]

B. The "Chilling Effect" of the Presumptions

The United States Supreme Court found in *New York Times v. Sullivan* that the common law presumptions of falsity, malice and damages infringe the First Amendment. The court found that they created a fear of damage awards and deterred the press from voicing their criticism of public officials, even though the criticism is believed to be true and even though it is in fact true, because of doubt whether it can be proved in court or fear of the expense of having to do so (that is, they created a "libel chill").[28]

The argument that the laws of libel infringe s. 2(b) of the *Charter* is based on the assertion that the common law presumptions made in favour of a public official plaintiff in a libel action have a "chilling effect" on the dissemination of truth. The heavy burden placed upon a defendant to a libel action has the effect of suppressing not only the expression of falsehood, but also the expression of truth. The "chilling effect" of the laws of libel in defamation actions is of particular constitutional consequence when it is political speech that is deterred. "A free press stands as one of the great interpreters between the government and the people. To allow it to be fettered is to fetter ourselves."[29] A free press not only fosters individual self-expression but also affords the public access to discussion, debate and the dissemination of information and ideas vital to a free and democratic society.[30]

In *Coates v. The Citizen*,[31] the defendants filed 11 affidavits to prove a "chill." Affidavits were filed before Justice Richard by Murdoch Davis (Assistant Managing Editor of The Citizen), Peter Desbarats (Dean of the Graduate School of Journalism, University of Western Ontario), Walter Stewart (the Max-Bell Visiting Professor at the School of Journalism and Communications, University of Regina), Geoffrey Stevens (Managing Editor of The Globe & Mail), Tom Kent (former Chairman of the Royal Commission on Newspapers), Linden McIntyre (host of CBC Radio's Sunday Morning), James MacNeill (Editor and Publisher of a community newspaper, The Eastern Graphic), Parker Barss-Donham (freelance journalist), and David Cadogan (publisher of five com-

---

27 *Halls v. Mitchell*, [1928] S.C.R. 125 at 134 [Ont.].
28 *Supra*, note 2 at 277-79, *per* Brennan J.
29 *Grosjean v. American Press Co.*, 297 U.S. 233 at 250 (1936); see also *Klein v. Law Soc. (Upper Can.)* (1985), 50 O.R. (2d) 118 at 170 (Div.Ct.).
30 *Can. Newspapers Co. v. Can. (A.G.)* (1986), 55 O.R. (2d) 737 at 748 (H.C.).
31 *Supra*, note 6. The case is discussed in the text accompanying notes 56 to 62.

munity newspapers in New Brunswick). In addition, two affidavits were filed by U.S. media law experts, Rodney A. Smolla (James Gould Cutler Professor of Constitutional Law and Director, Institute of Bill of Rights Law, College of William and Mary) and Bruce W. Sanford (Baker & Hostetler, Washington).

Justice Richard held that "The affidavits support The [Ottawa] Citizen's position that present defamation laws have a "chilling" influence on journalists and media executives."[32] However, Justice Richard took objection to the form of some of the affidavits "because they contained all sorts of opinions, hearsay, speculation and editorial comment."[33]

"Chill" can occur as a result of two concerns — money and proof. The media can be chilled by fear of large damage awards and high legal costs. In *Snyder v. Montreal Gazette*,[34] Justice Lamer expressed concern about the chill that could be created if large damage awards were made against the media in libel actions:

> Though it is a secondary consideration, there is one other factor that must be taken into account in defamation cases. These often involve newspapers, press agencies and radio or television stations. In coming to the rescue of a defamation victim, the courts must not overlook the fact that the written and spoken press is indispensable and is an essential component of a free and democratic society. Moreover, both the Quebec and Canadian Charters recognize the importance of the press (s. 3 of the *Charter of Human Rights and Freedoms* and s. 2 of the *Canadian Charter of Rights and Freedoms*). *If information agencies are ordered to pay large amounts as the result of a defamation the danger is that their operations will be paralyzed* or indeed, in some cases, that their very existence may be endangered. Although society undoubtedly places a great value on the reputation of its members that value, as it is subjective, cannot be so high as to threaten the functioning or the very existence of the press agencies which are essential to preserve a right guaranteed by the Charters. [emphasis added]

Small community newspapers are particularly vulnerable to this "chill" because they cannot afford libel insurance or legal costs in defending an action and therefore steer far clear of contentious stories about public officials. In addition, stories about public officials may not be published by large and small media simply because the story is not worth the risk of defending a libel action.

"Chill" can also occur as a result of the operation of the common law presumptions of falsity, damages and malice which, in effect, im-

---

32 *Ibid.*, at 150.
33 *Ibid.*, at 151.
34 [1988] 1 S.C.R. 494 at 510, *per* Lamer J. (as he then was), dissenting in part.

pose a reverse onus on libel defendants. The nine Canadian deponents in *Coates v. The Citizen* gave examples of credible and reliable stories about public officials that were withheld from publication because their contents (or innuendos) could not be proven in a court of law. The courts have stricter rules of proof than newsrooms. For example, a journalist would rely on a photocopy of a document as proof of an allegation whereas a court may only admit the original document as proof of the allegation. In addition, a story may be 100 per cent accurate at the time of publication but cannot be proven to be true several years later at a libel trial because:

(1) a witness refuses to testify or becomes adverse in interest for fear of repercussions should that witness be identified in open court;
(2) the sources of the story cannot be located and the journalist's tape recording of the interview of the source is ruled inadmissible because of the hearsay rule of evidence; or
(3) the government of the day obstructs the libel defendants from obtaining the evidence they need to make their defence by invoking Crown immunity from discovery, Crown privilege or issuing a *Canada Evidence Act* certificate.[35]

Those who argue that the threat of libel actions by public officials does not "chill" robust expression must ask themselves why parliamentarians enjoy an absolute privilege to express their views on the floor of the House of Commons or a Legislature? The reason for the absolute privilege is very simple — to prevent those parliamentarians being "chilled" from expressing their views on a matter of public interest. Why should a Member of Parliament's right to speak about matters of public interest with absolute immunity from a libel action be higher than the ability of members of the public or the press to speak about the conduct of that very same public official?

IV. SECTION 1 OF THE *CHARTER*

In the event that the common law presumptions of falsity, damages and malice are found to infringe s. 2(b) of the *Charter*, can these laws be saved by s. 1 of the *Charter* which states:

The *Canadian Charter of Rights and Freedoms* guarantees the rights and freedoms set out in it subject only to such reasonable limits prescribed by law as can be demonstrably justified in a free and democratic society.

---

35 The use by governments of Crown immunity from discovery, Crown privilege and *Canada Evidence Act* certificates (R.S.C. 1985, c. C-5) is discussed, *infra*, in the text accompanying note 55.

To be demonstrably justified in a free and democratic society, the person seeking to uphold a law that infringes the *Charter* (in this case the public official plaintiff), must prove that the law meets two central criteria.[36] First, its objective, which the measures responsible for a limit on a *Charter* right or freedom are designed to serve, must be important enough to warrant overriding a constitutionally protected freedom. At a minimum, an objective must relate to concerns which are "pressing and substantial" in a free and democratic society.

Second, once a sufficiently significant objective is recognized, the means chosen to implement the objective must be reasonable and demonstrably justified. There are three components to this proportionality test:[37]

(a) the measures adopted must be carefully designed to achieve the objective in question. They must not be arbitrary, unfair or based on irrational considerations. They must be rationally connected to the objective;

(b) the means, even if rationally connected to the objective, should impair as little as possible the right or freedom in question;

(c) the effects of the measures must not be disproportionate to the objective which has been identified as being of sufficient importance. The more severe the deleterious effects of a measure, the more important the objective must be if the measures are to be reasonable and demonstrably justified in a free and democratic society.

The historical roots of the common law presumptions of falsity, damages and malice serve as an important background against which the *Oakes*[38] test must be applied.

A. Historical Roots of the Law of Libel

The common law presumptions of falsity, malice and damages that arise in a libel action were never designed to meet the exigencies of contemporary society. The law of libel is tied to historical roots of libel law that are today anachronistic.[39]

The origins of the modern tort of defamation can be found in ancient human history, when criticism of a society's leadership was a serious offence ("thou shalt not revile the Gods, nor curse the rules of thy people" — *Exodus* 22:28). Those parts of our law of libel that are

---

36 *R. v. Oakes*, [1986] 1 S.C.R 103 at 138; *R. v. Edwards Books & Art Ltd.*, [1986] 2 S.C.R. 713 at 768.

37 *R. v. Oakes, ibid.*, at 139-40; *Edwards Books, ibid.*, at 768.

38 *Ibid.*

39 This history is briefly outlined in *Coates v. The Citizen, supra*, note 6 at 151-52.

based on the common law are founded largely on the laws of ancient Rome.[40] Under the Anglo-Saxon *Lex Talionis*, it was decreed that if a man should be found guilty of slander his tongue should be removed or redeemed by the price of his head.

Prohibitions against criticism of public figures were broadened in England in 1275 with the enactment of *De Scandalum Magnatum*, or scandal of magnates. During the reign of Richard II, the legislative objective of *De Scandalum Magnatum* was further buttressed by the *Statute of Gloucester*,[41] which provided for the imprisonment of "every deviser of false news, of horrible and false lies, of prelates, dukcs, carls, barons and other nobles and great men of the realm."

In 1476, the printing press was introduced to England.[42] Duelling soon became a popular means of seeking redress, while the printing press permitted rapid and widespread expression of political dissent. Alarmed, the great men of the realm enacted *Pro Camera Stellatum*,[43] which created the Court of the Star Chamber, a tribunal of the King's advisers charged with eliminating offences by which the "policy and good rule of this realm is almost subdued." The Star Chamber assumed strict control over the press. After the abolition of the Star Chamber by the Long Parliament in 1641, jurisdiction over all forms of defamation was assumed by the King's common law courts. These courts continued to "perpetrate . . . the more repressive doctrines of the Star Chamber" with respect to political speech and the press. In addition, the common law judges, in order to fill the gap that had been created in 1641, did not hesitate to adopt and incorporate into the common law the law which had been created and developed in the Star Chamber. Their efforts in this direction consolidated the basis of the law of defamation as we know it today.[44]

Much of our present law of libel comes indirectly from the jurisprudence of the notorious and repressive Star Chamber, a body of law which owes much of its development to a rash of duelling in the Middle Ages and a desire to eliminate critical political speech. As a result, the existing law of libel, with its presumptions of falsity, malice and damages, reflects no compromise between the competing interests of

---

40 Peter Carter-Ruck, *Carter-Ruck on Libel and Slander*, 3rd ed. (London: Butterworths, 1985), at 17; Law Reform Commission of Canada, *Crimes Against The State*, Working Paper 49 (Ottawa: L.R.C., 1986), at 3.

41 1378 (2 Ric. 2, c. 5).

42 Carter-Ruck, *supra*, note 40 at 20; Law Reform Commission of Canada, *Defamatory Libel*, Working Paper 35 (Ottawa: L.R.C., 1984), at 3.

43 1487 (3 Hen. 7, c. 1).

44 O.S. Hickson and P.F. Carter-Ruck, *The Law of Libel and Slander* (London: Faber & Faber, 1953), at 17; R.E. Brown, *supra*, note 23 at 21; *Jones v. Jones*, [1916] 2 A.C. 481 at 489-90 (H.L.).

freedom of expression about the conduct of public officials and the protection of reputation. The public interest in the free expression of political speech is unqualifiedly subjugated to the interests of a public official in his or her reputation.

The total absence of balance between the public interest in the free expression of political speech and the protection of reputation is exemplified in the arbitrariness of the present elements of the cause of action of libel and the requirements of proof. These are not provisions that have been carefully designed by a lawmaker to minimize the deleterious effects that flow from the impairment of the constitutionally entrenched freedom of the press.

B. Presumption of Damage

The existing law of libel relies upon a finding that words published by a defendant will have the tendency of harming a plaintiff's reputation, without requiring any proof that they, in fact, have such an effect. Furthermore, the law then allows for recovery of purportedly compensatory damages without evidence of actual loss or harm. The existence of injury is presumed from the fact of publication.

In *R. v. Kopyto*,[45] Justice Cory dealt with an analogous presumption. In a discussion of the offence of contempt of court (scandalizing the court), Justice Cory held that the offence did not satisfy the proportionality test:[46]

> Without requiring any proof of the matter, the offence *assumes* that the words which are the subject-matter of the charge will bring the court into contempt or lower its authority. This I take to be an unwarranted and questionable assumption, and leads me to conclude that the offence has not been "carefully designed to achieve the objective in question". By undertaking the proceedings the prosecution must be taken as alleging that the words spoken by the accused which were "calculated to bring the administration of justice into disrepute" will in fact have such an effect. If this is not the basis of the charge then the measure adopted is arbitrary, unfair or based upon irrational considerations. If the essence of the charge is, as it must be, that the words spoken do bring the court into contempt, then *it would not be unreasonable to require the prosecution to prove that this is in fact the effect of those words.* [emphasis added in last sentence only]

Justice Cory held further that real and substantial danger of prejudice or clear and present danger to the administration of justice should also be an essential condition of the offence of scandalizing the court, as it

45 *Supra*, note 5.
46 *Ibid.*, at 475.

would go some distance towards ensuring that the offence "impairs" as little as possible the right or freedom in question:[47]

> In the absence of such a requirement the limitation imposed by the offence cannot meet the proportionality test as it is both arbitrary and irrational, *based as it is on the unproved assumption that the comment will lower the authority of the court.* [emphasis added]

C. Presumption of Malice

The arbitrary, unfair and irrational nature of the common law presumptions of falsity, damages and malice is further evidenced by the absence of a requirement of any element of fault on the part of the libel defendant. In *R. v. Kopyto*, Goodman J.A. stated:[48]

> In my opinion the application of the Charter to the common law now places a limitation on freedom of expression and opinion as they relate to the administration of justice from utterances or statements which consist of assertions of facts which are false *and are known to be false* by the person making the assertion *or are recklessly made* by such person. It also places such limitation on those freedoms where the utterances consist of an expression of an opinion which is not honestly and sincerely held. That limitation and consequently the offence of contempt is constitutionally valid, however, only where the utterance or statement is found to result in a clear, significant and imminent or present danger to the fair and effective administration of justice. [emphasis added]

The minimum threshold of constitutional proportionality in all cases of defamation requires that some element of fault on the part of the defendant must be present for liability to ensue.[49]

Where the plaintiff is a public official and the alleged defamation relates to the plaintiff's official conduct, society's interest in the protection of political speech requires, under the Constitution of the United States, that, for liability to ensue, the plaintiff must show with convincing clarity that the statement was made with knowledge that it was false,

---

47 *Ibid.*, at 476.
48 *Ibid.*, at 500-501.
49 It is to be noted that art. 1053 of the *Civil Code of Québec* requires fault to be proven in a defamation action:
> "Every person capable of discerning right from wrong is responsible for the damage caused by his fault to another, whether by positive act, imprudence, neglect or want of skill."

See also *Philadelphia Newspapers Inc. v. Hepps*, 12 Media L. Rep. 1977 at 1981 (1986); *Gertz v. Robert Welch Inc.*, 418 U.S. 323 at 348, 350 (1974); *Defamation Act, 1974* (No. 18 of 1974) New South Wales, s. 22(1); *Austin v. Mirror Newspapers Ltd.*, [1986] 1 A.C. 299 at 313 (P.C.).

or with reckless disregard as to whether it was false or not.[50] Reckless conduct is not measured by whether a reasonably prudent person would have published, or would have investigated before publishing. There must be sufficient evidence to permit the conclusion that the defendant in fact entertained serious doubts as to the truth of the publication.[51]

D. Presumption of Falsity

Under the existing law of libel, a plaintiff does not have to prove that the allegedly defamatory statements are false. This is anomalous in that it is well established that a plaintiff only has the right to the protection of a reputation which the plaintiff, in fact, actually enjoys:[52]

> ... the law will not permit a man to recover damages in respect of an injury to a character which he either does not, or ought not, to possess.

This is why the truth of allegedly defamatory statements constitutes a complete defence in an action for defamation, even in cases where the defendant was malicious in publishing the defamatory, but truthful, words.

A defendant should not bear the onus of proving that a public official plaintiff does not have a right to the reputation claimed. If a public official's cause of action depends upon the existence or integrity of the official's reputation, proof of falsity by the plaintiff should be a precondition to that cause of action. It is the defendant who risks that the truth of the statement cannot be proven conclusively in a court of law. Thus, in some cases, the law protects the plaintiff's reputation undeservedly.

Where the speech at issue is political speech, the burden of inconclusiveness should not be borne by the defendant. The onus should be on the public official plaintiff to prove the falsity of the statement. In *Philadelphia Newspapers Inc. v. Hepps*,[53] Justice O'Connor held:[54]

> [In those] instances when the fact-finding process will be unable to resolve conclusively whether the speech is true or false ... the burden of proof is dispositive ...
>
> [W]here the scales are in such an uncertain balance, we believe that the Constitution requires us to tip them in favour of protecting true speech. To ensure that true speech on matters of public concern is not deterred,

---

50 *New York Times v. Sullivan, supra,* note 2 at 279, 285.
51 *St. Amant v. Thompson,* 390 U.S. 727 at 731 (1968).
52 *Watkin v. Hall* (1868), L.R. 3 Q.B. 396 at 400.
53 *Supra,* note 49.
54 *Ibid.,* at 1981.

we hold that the common-law presumption that defamatory speech is false cannot stand when a plaintiff seeks damages against a media defendant for speech of public concern.

The unfairness of requiring a defendant to prove the truth of political speech about a public official is highlighted by the existence in Canada of the prerogatives of Crown immunity from discovery, Crown privilege, and certificates issued pursuant to s. 39 of the *Canada Evidence Act*.[55] The Crown can use these prerogatives and certificates to block access by a defendant to evidence necessary to prove the truth of the statements in question about the public official plaintiff. This obstruction can, and does, occur even when the press has used government officials as sources for the allegedly libellous story. It is unreasonable for the law to place the burden of proof on one party to a dispute while protecting the other side through rules that suppress evidence required to meet that onus.

There is no better illustration of this statement than the evidentiary obstructions faced by the defendants in the *Coates v. The Citizen* action.[56] In brief, the facts in *Coates v. The Citizen* are as follows:

(1) the plaintiff, while Minister of National Defence, was on a four-country NATO tour which he described as "a very serious in some ways sensitive and delicate mission" relating to national defence;

(2) the plaintiff had dinner at Canada's military base in Lahr, Germany and at approximately midnight went to a nightclub called "Tiffany" for a nightcap with his acting chief of staff and press secretary;

(3) the nightclub, also known as a "B-girl bar," featured, *inter alia*, strippers and non-stop porn movies and had backrooms available for patrons to have private discussions with the B-girls;

(4) as soon as Major General David Wightman (Commander - European Forces) learned of the Defence Minister's whereabouts at Tiffany, he immediately dispatched a plainclothes military policeman to Tiffany to make sure no harm came to Mr. Coates;

(5) a member of Mr. Coates' Ottawa staff reported his visit to Tiffany to the Clerk of the Privy Council. The Clerk of the Privy Council reported the visit to the Prime Minister who immediately ordered a security investigation;

(6) The Citizen reported that "Prime Minister Mulroney's office had been advised that Defence Minister Robert Coates and two of his

---

55 R.S.C. 1985, c. C-5.

56 See *Mulroney v. Coates* (1986), 54 O.R. (2d) 353 at 365-67 (Catzman J.), affirmed Ont. C.A., 23rd April 1987 (unreported); *Southam Inc. v. Theriault* (1987), 61 O.R. (2d) 758 (H.C.) (Smith J.); *Coates v. The Citizen* (1987), 85 N.S.R. (2d) 23 (T.D.), at 3-6 of the original judgment, *per* Richard J.

chief aides paid an early morning visit to a West German night club in an incident that may have posed a security risk." Mr. Coates pleaded that this statement was libellous;

(7) a number of meetings took place between officials of the Prime Minister's Office and Mr. Coates the day of the publication of The Citizen article. Mr. Coates announced his resignation that day in the House of Commons and also stated that he had commenced a libel action against The Citizen;

(8) the Prime Minister subsequently spoke about the circumstances of Mr. Coates' resignation on a number of occasions in the House of Commons, as did his Press Secretary outside the House of Commons.

In *Mulroney v. Coates*,[57] the defendants obtained letters of request from the Nova Scotia Trial Division to the Ontario Supreme Court for the examination for discovery of 13 witnesses who were necessary and proper witnesses with information pertaining to the libel action. The witnesses were Prime Minister Brian Mulroney, Deputy Prime Minister Erik Nielsen, the Clerk of the Privy Council, five officials working in the Prime Minister's Office, and five Department of National Defence employees. Justice Catzman ruled that the questions proposed to be asked of the Prime Minister, the Deputy Prime Minister and the Clerk of the Privy Council "will inevitably trespass upon ground covered by the suggested prerogative or immunity" from discovery and, therefore, did not order the enforcement of the letters of request for these proposed deponents.[58] However, the other ten deponents were ordered to attend examinations for discovery. During those examinations, counsel for the Crown made *over 100 objections* to questions asked by counsel for the defendants on the basis of Crown immunity from discovery.

It is to be noted that Mr. Coates was examined for discovery for six days, without objection from the Crown, about matters dealing with his role as Minister of National Defence and the events that were reported in the allegedly defamatory article. Several years after this legal battle in the Ontario courts regarding issues of Crown immunity from discovery, Erik Nielsen wrote his autobiography *The House Is Not A Home*,[59] recounting his recollection of the circumstances leading up to the resignation of Mr. Coates and his understanding of the events that were reported in the allegedly defamatory article. Mr. Nielsen stated, "so, who fired Bob Coates? The Prime Minister made the decision, naturally, but I was the messenger."[60] This is an example of one of the critical

---

57   *Ibid.*
58   *Ibid.*, at 366.
59   (Toronto: MacMillan, 1989).
60   *Ibid.*, at 250.

pieces of evidence that the defendants sought to obtain in order to defend themselves, but were unable to obtain because the government of the day legally obstructed the defendants from obtaining the required evidence.

Justice Richard described the defendants as being in a "Catch 22 situation."[61] "Catch 22" indeed, but the fact remained that the defendants were prevented from exercising normal rights of discovery because of a claim of Crown immunity from discovery. Had this action not been dropped by Mr. Coates, the defendants also expected to face claims of Crown privilege and certificates issued under s. 39 of the *Canada Evidence Act* — both devices preventing the defendants from proving their case in a court of law.[62]

E. A Reasonable Balance

The reverse onus in effect created by the common law presumptions of falsity, malice and damages is unreasonable where the opposing interest is free access by the public to the expression of political speech. Because a free press affords the public access to discussion, debate, and the dissemination of information and ideas vital to a free and democratic society, the existing law not only has an effect upon the media that is disproportionate to the legislative objective of protecting private reputations, but it also severely affects the interest of the public in the free communication of information and ideas concerning political issues. This is an interest that is itself enhanced by the democratic rights entrenched in s. 3 of the *Charter*. Where public interest in political speech is concerned, the severity of the deleterious effects of the existing law is entirely disproportionate to the objective of protecting the interest of a public official's reputation. Indeed, the existing law exhibits no concern whatsoever for balancing the opposing interests at stake.

In order to qualify as a reasonable limitation on "freedom of thought, belief, opinion and expression, including freedom of the press and other media of communication," which is guaranteed by s. 2(b) of the *Charter*, the law of libel must require, at a minimum, that a public official libel plaintiff meet the burdens as to falsity, malice and damages adopted by the Supreme Court of the United States in *New York Times v. Sullivan*[63] — the plaintiff must prove that the defendant published

---

61 *Coates v. The Citizen, supra*, note 6 at 157.
62 It is to be noted that the Ontario Law Reform Commission in its *Report on the Liability of The Crown* (Toronto: Ministry of the Attorney General, 1989), found the common law rule of Crown privilege, as established in *Carey v. Ont.*, [1986] 2 S.C.R. 637, is generally satisfactory and need not be altered.
63 *Supra*, note 2.

false statements with knowledge that they were false or with reckless disregard of whether they were false or not, and must require the plaintiff to prove actual damage to reputation.

V. *DOLPHIN DELIVERY* — DOES SECTION 32 OF THE *CHARTER* APPLY?

In *Retail, Wholesale and Department Store Union, Local 580 v. Dolphin Delivery Ltd.*,[64] it was held that the *Charter* applies to the common law but does not apply to private litigation completely divorced from any connection with government. The *Charter* applies to the common law where the common law is the basis for some governmental action which is alleged to have infringed a guaranteed right or freedom.

The Manitoba Court of Appeal in *Pangilinan v. Chaves*,[65] relying on *Dolphin Delivery*, held that the *Charter* did not apply to a libel action between two private litigants in which no public issue is raised. Justice Richard dealt with the applicability of the *Charter* in *Coates v. The Citizen*:[66]

> The *Defamation Act*, as has been said, is partly a codification of the common law and partly statute law . . .
>
> Allowing that the instant action is one in the category of disputes between private parties, can the *Charter* be invoked to assist the Citizen in this application. This question was answered in the *Dolphin* case by requiring that a degree of government involvement or connection be present . . . In this action we have the contention that the *Defamation Act*, a provincial statute, is contrary to the *Charter* in that it militates against freedom of the press. The [Ottawa] Citizen contends that it must be struck down as being of "no force and effect". I find that the *Defamation Act*, being a provincial statute does provide that connection necessary to allow application of the *Charter* to what otherwise is litigation between private parties. It is the *Act*, and the common law which impose upon the [Ottawa] Citizen the several "reverse onuses" complained of . . .
>
> Both the *Act* and the common law are amenable to *Charter* supervision. I think it matters not that some of the common law principles are subsumed into the *Act*. If I am wrong in this, and Coates relies on the common law rules of defamation, then, the *Charter* has no application due to the absence of the requisite governmental nexus.

The *Charter* applies to otherwise private lawsuits if there is a

---

64   *Supra*, note 16.
65   *Supra*, note 7.
66   *Supra*, note 6 at 154-56.

sufficient governmental connection or intervention.[67] The Supreme Court of Canada also noted in *R.W.D.S.U. v. Dolphin Delivery* that "[t]he element of governmental intervention necessary to make the *Charter* applicable in an otherwise private action is difficult to define."[68]

In *Coates v. The Citizen*, the defendants argued that there was a substantial and clear government connection through the operation of the *Defamation Act*[69] of Nova Scotia. The defendants argued that certain provisions of the *Defamation Act* dealt with issues of damages, malice and falsity, and, as a result, this provided the necessary "governmental connection hook" into the common law presumptions to engage s. 2(b) of the *Charter*.

Through the *Defamation Act*, the Legislature of Nova Scotia has specifically allowed and regulated actions for defamation against the proprietors or publishers of newspapers and their employees. Sections 17 to 22 specifically provide for such actions upon terms provided in the statute. Through these provisions, the Legislature has "authorize[d] action"[70] which, therefore, must comply with the *Charter*. The existence of a previous cause of action against newspapers at common law does not detract from the current statutory basis of such libel actions. Many statutes codify common law causes of action or rules in whole or in part, but, once they take statutory form, they are amenable to *Charter* review. This is also true of a statutory authorization to bring the action and to apply the common law rules.

The legislative application of the law of libel to newspapers incorporates elements of that cause of action as known at common law. Section 17 of the Nova Scotia *Defamation Act* refers to actions for defamation, which is defined in s. 2(b) as meaning libel or slander, which therefore refers to the common law elements of those causes of action. In addition, the reference to "causes of action" in s. 24 is a statutory reference to common law. The *Defamation Act* of Nova Scotia also constitutes clear statutory adoption, modification or preservation of the common law relating to libel as the law for the province of Nova Scotia. The legislative action as evidenced in the *Defamation Act* has both implicit and explicit dimensions.

Implicit advertence to, and acceptance of, the common law in the Nova Scotia *Defamation Act* is present in ss. 2(b), 3, 4, 5, 6, 8, 13 and 14. Explicit legislative adoption or preservation of specific common law rules in the Nova Scotia *Defamation Act* is present in the following provisions:

---

67 *Dolphin Delivery, supra,* note 16 at 599.
68 *Ibid.*
69 R.S.N.S. 1967, c. 72 (now R.S.N.S. 1989, c. 122).
70 P. Hogg, *Constitutional Law of Canada,* 2nd ed. (Toronto: Carswell, 1985), at 671.

(a) s. 9 constitutes legislative approval of the presumption of falsity, placing the onus of proving truth on the defendant. It contains a limited modification of the presumption of falsity;

(b) the same is true with respect to s. 10. By providing that a defence of fair comment will not fail "only" on the basis set out therein, the provision constitutes legislative approval of the failure of a defence of fair comment on the remaining common law basis;

(c) s. 13(7) constitutes express legislative preservation of common law privileges. Not only has the Legislature consciously decided not to limit existing privileges, but it has also decided not to "abridge" existing privileges so as to provide extended safeguards or alter the balance of interest with respect to the media;

(d) viewed against the background of the common law distinction between legal or constructive malice and actual or express malice, s. 21(1) constitutes an express legislative assumption and approval of the irrebuttable presumption of legal malice. In this provision, the Legislature consciously preserved the presumption with respect to proof of liability while allowing modification of the rule only with respect to mitigation of damages;

(e) viewed against the background of the common law, s. 22(1) constitutes legislative approval of the common law presumption of general damages. In excluding general damages in the limited circumstances in s. 22(1), the Legislature adopts and approves the recovery of general damages in all other circumstances applicable at common law. In the context of libel, general damages means the damages which are presumed and need not be proved.[71]

These statutory provisions illustrate that the Nova Scotia Legislature considered and, through the *Defamation Act*, adopted, modified or preserved each aspect of the common law presumptions claimed to be unconstitutional:

(a) the presumption of falsity (ss. 9 and 10);
(b) the presumption of malice (s. 21);
(c) the presumption of damage (s. 22).

Furthermore, the Nova Scotia Legislature has authorized defamation actions against newspapers and broadcasters and their employees.

A libel action by a public official differs from the fact situation in *Dolphin Delivery* wherein no statute was relevant to the action. In *Dolphin Delivery*, the plaintiff was suing regarding a tort that had no statutory basis. In libel actions, the plaintiff is suing regarding a tort with a statutory reference and basis authorized by a Legislature.[72] Therefore,

---

71 *Gatley, supra*, note 26 at 451.
72 *Dolphin Delivery, supra*, note 16 at 603.

in libel actions by public officials the "connection to government" required by *Dolphin Delivery* exists and, thus, s. 32 of the *Charter* is not an obstacle to libel defendants seeking *New York Times v. Sullivan* constitutional protections.

The following words of Justice Brennan in *New York Times v. Sullivan* are apt in that the United States Supreme Court rejected the *Dolphin Delivery* obstacle raised by the public official libel plaintiff in that case:[73]

> We may dispose at the outset of two grounds asserted to insulate the judgment of the Alabama courts from constitutional scrutiny. The first is the proposition relied on by the State Supreme Court — that "The Fourteenth Amendment is directed against State action and not private action". That proposition has no application to this case. *Although this is a civil lawsuit between private parties, the Alabama courts have applied a state rule of law* which petitioners claim to impose invalid restrictions on their constitutional freedoms of speech and press. *It matters not that that law has been applied in a civil action and that it is common law only, though supplemented by statute.* The test is not the form in which state power has been applied, but, whatever the form, whether such power has in fact been exercised. [emphasis added]

This finding in *New York Times v. Sullivan* is a complete answer to any *Dolphin Delivery*/ s. 32 *Charter* obstacle that may be raised by a public official libel plaintiff.

VI. A NEW CATEGORY OF QUALIFIED PRIVILEGE?

This article also proposes an alternative to the *New York Times v. Sullivan* constitutional protections — the use of s. 2(b) of the *Charter* to create a new category of qualified privilege in libel actions involving the conduct of public officials.

It is clear that the common law of libel must be developed and applied in accordance with the dictates of the *Charter*. Coupling this principle with the fact that the categories of qualified privilege are never closed, a strong case can be advanced that s. 2(b) of the *Charter* can be used to create a new category of qualified privilege with respect to defamatory words published about the conduct of public officials.[74]

---

73 *New York Times v. Sullivan, supra,* note 2 at 265.
74 See Michael R. Doody, "Freedom of the Press, the Canadian Charter of Rights and Freedoms, And A New Category of Qualified Privilege" (1983), 61 Can. Bar Rev. 124; Clare Beckton, "Freedom of the Press in Canada: Prior Restraints," in P. Anisman and A. Linden (eds.), *The Media, The Courts and The Charter* (Toronto: Carswell, 1986), at 119.

This alternative argument was made in *Coates v. The Citizen*, but Justice Richard held that it would be premature to make the determination:[75]

> As a "fall back" position, the Citizen asks that an order issue that it is entitled to a defence of qualified privilege respecting the statements published. Although I have doubts that such a defence is available in these circumstances I am of the view that such a determination would be premature. Such a determination could only be fairly made when more of the evidence is before this court.

Common law rules are subject to the *Charter*. In *Dolphin Delivery*, Justice McIntyre stated: "Does the *Charter* Apply to the Common Law? In my view, there can be no doubt that it does apply."[76] The courts must, on a case by case basis, apply and develop the common law consistently with the *Charter*.[77]

> Where ... private party "A" sues private party "B" relying on the common law and where no act of government is relied upon to support the action, the *Charter* will not apply. I should make it clear, however, that *this is a distinct issue from the question whether the judiciary ought to apply and develop the principles of the common law in a manner consistent with the fundamental values enshrined in the Constitution. The answer to this question must be in the affirmative.* In this sense, then, the *Charter* is far from irrelevant to private litigants whose disputes fall to be decided at common law. But this is different from the proposition that one private party owes a constitutional duty to another, which proposition underlies the purported assertion of *Charter* causes of action or *Charter* defences between individuals. [emphasis added]

The qualified privilege argument is not that the plaintiff owes, or has breached, any constitutional duty to the defendants, but rather that the law upon which the public official libel plaintiff relies is based upon principles and values that are seriously discordant with those entrenched in s. 2(b) of the *Charter*. The law must be developed in such a way as to foster those values identified as fundamental in the *Charter*.[78] Section 2(b) of the *Charter* affects the interpretation of the defence of qualified privilege, with the effect that libel defendants should now be ensured the benefit of a defence of qualified privilege when publishing political speech.

---

75 *Supra*, note 6 at 162.
76 *Supra*, note 16 at 592.
77 *Ibid.*, at 603.
78 *Ibid.*

A. The Defence at Common Law

The common law has recognized, over the years, that it is in the interest of society to protect certain types of occasions upon which persons should be allowed to speak freely, where the degree of public inconvenience that would result from a restriction on freedom of speech would outweigh that arising from a violation of a private interest in reputation. This was achieved, in part, by the development of a defence of qualified privilege.

For a defence of qualified privilege to apply, a number of requirements must be met. The first is that a statement must be made on a privileged occasion. This exists where a statement is made by a person in the discharge of some public or private duty, or for the purpose of pursuing or protecting some private interest, provided it is made to a person who has a corresponding interest in or duty to receive it.[79]

There are three tests used to determine the existence of a privileged occasion:

(i) the recipient must have a material and legitimate interest in receiving, or duty to receive, the subject-matter of the communication. The subject-matter of the communication must be one which the courts will protect, and not one which springs from gossip or curiosity. It must be a matter of substance, apart from its mere quality of news;[80]

(ii) the communicant must have either a private interest, or an interest that is mutual or common with that of the recipient, in communicating the statement to the recipient; or

(iii) alternatively, the communicant must have a social, legal or moral duty to communicate the statement to the recipient.

In general, certain types of relationships have been perceived to be socially valuable. Where such a relationship exists between the communicant and the recipient, the existence of the relationship may itself justify an interest or duty in communicating the information in such a way as to create a privileged occasion. The subject-matter of the communication, although relevant, is not necessarily determinative, unless trivial or unrelated to the privileged occasion claimed. Courts have recognized a social utility in protecting communications made within the context of relationships that have been identified as socially valuable or legitimate.

Even in the absence of such a relationship, a communication may be such that it raises a duty in the communicant to communicate a

---

79   *Gatley, supra,* note 26 at 187.
80   *Sapiro v. Leader Pub. Co.,* [1926] 2 W.W.R. 268 at 275 (Sask. C.A.).

statement to the recipient in the public interest or in the interest of a third party, or in the private interest of the communicant. It is the subject-matter of the information communicated that is of utmost importance in this respect, so as to create a privileged occasion.

Even where a privileged occasion is found to exist, the defence may be lost if the publication is made to an audience, a portion of which has no legitimate interest in the information, or the remark is in excess of, or unrelated to, the privileged occasion, or is made for a purpose unrelated to the occasion.[81] Furthermore, a defence of qualified privilege may be defeated if the plaintiff in a defamation action can show that the publisher of the statement made on a privileged occasion was motivated by common law actual or express malice, that is, the publisher "abused the occasion by using it for an improper purpose, personal spite or ill will, or by excessive or irrelevant publication, or by a lack of belief in the truth of what was written."[82]

B. Does the *Charter* Create a New Category of Qualified Privilege?

Before the enactment of the *Charter*, courts resisted giving the media the benefit of a defence of qualified privilege on the following grounds:

(i) the media was held not to have a duty to provide information even where the public had a legitimate and compelling interest in receiving such information; therefore, no privileged occasion was held to arise;[83]

(ii) the publication by the media was held to be publication "to the world." Thus, it was assumed that publication was made to an audience, a portion of which had no legitimate interest in the information. Therefore, even if a privileged occasion had been found to exist, it was held to be lost.[84]

The publication of commentary on the conduct of a public official relating to public office is a communication conveyed in circumstances

---

81 *Jones v. Bennett*, [1969] S.C.R. 277 at 297 [B.C.]; *Brown, supra,* note 23 at 589-92.

82 *Camporese v. Parton* (1983), 150 D.L.R. (3d) 208 at 226 (B.C.S.C.).

83 *Globe & Mail Ltd. v. Boland*, [1960] S.C.R. 203 at 207; *Banks v. Globe & Mail Ltd.* (1961), 28 D.L.R. (2d) 343 at 349 (S.C.C.); *England v. C.B.C.*, [1979] 3 W.W.R. 193 at 220 (N.W.T.S.C.).

84 *Sapiro v. Leader Pub. Co., supra,* note 80 at 275; *England v. C.B.C., ibid.,* at 220; *Douglas v. Tucker*, [1952] 1 D.L.R. 657 at 665-66 (S.C.C.) [Sask.]; *Lawson v. Chabot*, [1974] 3 W.W.R. 711 at 720-21 (B.C.S.C.); *Jones v. Bennett, supra,* note 81 at 297; *Paul v. Van Hull* (1962), 36 D.L.R. (2d) 639 at 657 (Man. Q.B.).

that warrant the protection of a defence of qualified privilege, having particular regard to the entrenchment of "freedom of thought, belief, opinion and expression, including freedom of the press and other media of communication" in s. 2(b) of the *Charter*. It is well established that the categories of qualified privilege are not closed:

(i) ... the circumstances that constitute a privileged occasion can ... never be catalogued and rendered exact;[85]

(ii) the rule being founded upon the general welfare of society, new occasions for its application will necessarily arise with continually changing conditions.[86]

All of the elements required to create a privileged occasion are present in the case of words published about the conduct of public officials. The public has a material, legitimate, and vital interest in political speech and in the proper organization and functioning of government.[87]

Even before the enactment of the *Charter*, the media was recognized judicially as the "representative" or "agent" of the public.[88] The media, therefore, has a common or mutual interest in the dissemination of information in which the public has a legitimate and mutual interest. Alternatively, this could be characterized as a social or moral duty to gather and disseminate information.[89]

Furthermore, the role of the media in Canada has been given constitutional status in s. 2(b) of the *Charter*. Express recognition has been given to "freedom of the *press* and *other media* of communication." This has been done in absolute terms.[90]

The words of s. 2(b) of the *Charter*, at a minimum, recognize the reliance of the public on the news media, and signify an assurance that improper impediments will not be erected to frustrate that reliance interest. While s. 2(b) of the *Charter* cannot be said to impose a duty on the media, it does protect the expectation of citizens that the public duty assumed by the press can be freely performed.

The First Amendment to the United States Constitution has been

---

85 *London Association for Protection of Trade v. Greenlands Ltd.*, [1916] 2 A.C. 15 at 22 (H.L.).

86 *Howe v. Lees* (1910), 11 C.L.R. 361 at 369 (Aus. H.C.).

87 *London Artists Ltd. v. Littler*, [1968] 1 All. E.R. 1075 at 1086 (Q.B.); *Stopforth v. Goyer* (1979), 23 O.R. (2d) 696 at 699-700 (C.A.); *Parlett v. Robinson* (1986), 37 C.C.L.T. 281 at 291 (B.C.C.A.); *Loos v. Robbins*, [1987] 4 W.W.R. 469 at 473 (Sask. C.A.).

88 Law Reform Commission of Canada, *Public And Media Access To The Criminal Process*, Working Paper 56 (Ottawa: L.R.C., 1987), at 9-14.

89 *Stopforth v. Goyer, supra*, note 87 at 699; *Parlett v. Robinson, supra*, note 87 at 294.

90 *Edmonton Journal, supra*, note 4 at 1336, *per* Cory J.

interpreted to reflect not only the reliance of the public on the media, but also the vital interest that society has in protecting the media's special role.[91] This view of the First Amendment has been summarized by Powell J. in his dissenting judgment in *Saxbe v. Washington Post Co.*:[92]

> An informed public depends on accurate and effective reporting by the news media. No individual can obtain for himself the information needed for the intelligent discharge of his political responsibilities. For most citizens the prospect of personal familiarity with newsworthy events is hopelessly unrealistic. On seeking out the news the press therefore acts as an agent of the public at large. It is the means by which the public will see that free flow of information and ideas essential to intelligent self-government. By enabling the public to assert meaningful control over the political process, the press performs a crucial function in effecting the societal purpose of the First Amendment.

The press assumes a special position in relation to the public, exercising responsibilities that have been recognized and reinforced through the constitutional protection offered by s. 2(b) of the *Charter*. Entrenchment recognizes a mutuality of interest between the press and the public, and recognizes the public duty with which the press has been entrusted and which it assumes in informing the public about matters of national interest. This interest or duty on the part of the media, combined with the vital interest of the public in receiving political speech, is sufficient to create a privileged occasion. The view of the media's role and the public good taken by the Supreme Court of Canada in *Globe & Mail Ltd. v. Boland*,[93] having been formulated in the absence of an express constitutional right of the public to receive political speech through a free press, should be regarded as superseded.

VII. SUMMARY

This article proposes that libel defendants should be given constitutional protection for defamatory words published about the conduct of public officials. The ancient common law presumptions of falsity, malice and damages which pre-date the Star Chamber should not survive *Charter* scrutiny today. Now that Canada has constitutionally entrenched freedom of the press, protections must be given to libel defendants in actions by public officials as was done by the United States

---

91 See *Grosjean v. American Press Co., supra*, note 29 at 250; *Time Inc. v. Hill*, 385 U.S. 374 at 389 (1967); *Red Lion Broadcasting Co. v. F.C.C.*, 395 U.S. 367 at 390 (1969); *First National Bank of Boston v. Bellotti*, 435 U.S. 765 at 782 (1978).
92 *Saxbe v. Washington Post Co.*, 417 U.S. 843 at 863 (1974).
93 *Supra*, note 83.

Supreme Court in 1964 in *New York Times v. Sullivan* through the First Amendment to the Constitution of the United States of America.

The common law presumptions "chill" expression, which infringes s. 2(b) of the *Charter*. The laws of libel have the effect of suppressing the free expression of political speech by libel defendants. To the extent that the presumptions operate as a reverse onus or impose strict liability, they are inconsistent with s. 2(b) of the *Charter*.

Further, the current law of defamation cannot be justified under s. 1 of the *Charter*. The law of defamation was never designed to meet the exigencies of contemporary society. It is tied to historical roots that are anachronistic in today's world. As a result, the existing law, with its presumptions of falsity, malice, and damage reflects no compromise between the competing interests of freedom of expression and the protection of reputation. As is evident, the present elements of the cause of action for libel have not been carefully designed to minimize the deleterious effects that flow from the impairment of the entrenched right of freedom of the press.

Justice Richard was very concerned about the power of the media today ("The awesome power of the printed word"; ". . . trite to say that the published press . . . has great impact on society"; ". . . devastating impact of the written word is well known").[94] Perhaps Justice Richard viewed the defendants' *New York Times v. Sullivan* argument as an extension of that "awesome power."

Justice Richard also held that the law of libel (1) did not restrict the publication of the news; (2) did not prevent comment on perceived government ineptitude; and (3) did not stifle criticism of prominent political figures in the conduct of their duties.[95] With respect, these findings contradict the evidence adduced before His Lordship in *Coates v. The Citizen*. In addition, these findings ignore the concerns about the operation of the common law presumptions of falsity, damages and malice expressed by the United States Supreme Court in *New York Times v. Sullivan*, especially the three justices who would have given the media an absolute privilege regarding words published about the conduct of public officials.

In essence, Justice Richard adopted certain passages from Professor Brown's text, *The Law of Defamation*, wherein the American and Canadian approaches to reputation were compared. Justice Richard then relied upon these passages to hold that Canadian courts have valued reputation over freedom of the press.[96] However, it must be stressed that these passages from Professor Brown's text refer to the attitudes of

---

94 *Coates v. The Citizen, supra*, note 6 at 161.
95 *Ibid.*
96 *Ibid.*, at 161-62.

Canadian courts *prior to* the adoption of the *Charter.* Nor does Professor Brown suggest that the pre-*Charter* Canadian approach to reputation should continue now that the *Charter* constitutes part of the supreme law of Canada.

Freedom of the press was not constitutionally entrenched at the time when libel defendants tried to assert a special protection for the media.[97] It is submitted that the answer to a *New York Times v. Sullivan* argument pursuant to s. 2(b) of the *Charter* cannot be arrived at by simply comparing the Canadian approach to reputation to the American approach. A proper *Charter* analysis requires a determination as to whether the common law presumptions of falsity, malice and damages operate in such a way (*viz.* strict liability and reverse onus) that they infringe or deny s. 2(b) of the *Charter* ("chill"). Justice Richard "allowed for the moment that the laws of defamation in Nova Scotia do impose a serious limitation on freedom of expression of the media."[98] Once a libel defendant proves infringement, the onus is on the proponent of the limitation to prove it is saved by s. 1 of the *Charter* in accordance with the test set out in *Oakes.*[99] Because this analysis was not conducted in *Coates v. The Citizen,* it is respectfully suggested that this decision should not be followed.

It is argued in this article that the interpretation of s. 32 of the *Charter* (application of the *Charter*) by the Supreme Court of Canada in *Dolphin Delivery,*[100] does not prevent libel defendants from invoking a *Charter* defence such as that afforded libel defendants in the United States by *New York Times v. Sullivan.* In addition, s. 2(b) of the *Charter* can assist in providing libel defendants with an alternative defence by creating a new category of qualified privilege with respect to defamatory words published about the conduct of public officials. The common law has recognized, over the years, that it is in the interest of society to protect certain types of occasions upon which a person should be allowed to speak freely, where the degree of public inconvenience that would result from a restriction on freedom of speech would outweigh that arising from a violation of a private interest in reputation. This was achieved, in part, by the development of the defence of qualified privilege.

It is well established in common law that the categories of qualified privilege are not closed. All of the elements required to create a privileged occasion are present in a case involving public officials. The public has a material, legitimate and vital interest in political speech and

---

97   *Globe & Mail v. Boland, supra,* note 83.
98   *Supra,* note 6 at 160.
99   *Supra,* note 36.
100 *Supra,* note 16.

in the proper organization and functioning of government. Even before the enactment of the *Charter,* the media had been recognized judicially as the "representative" or "agent" of the public. The media, therefore, has a common or mutual interest in the dissemination of information in which the public has a legitimate and mutual interest. Alternatively, this could be characterized as a social or moral duty to gather and disseminate information.

Should libel defendants be given constitutional protection similar to that set out in *New York Times v. Sullivan* or, alternatively, a qualified privilege governing the publication of defamatory words about the conduct of public officials? Categorically, yes!

PART V

COMMERCIAL SPEECH: FREE EXPRESSION AND FREE ENTERPRISE

As a result of the fact that commercial enterprises have been the most active challengers of legal prohibitions on speech since the enactment of the *Charter*'s guarantee of freedom of expression, the Supreme Court of Canada has been called upon to define the scope of constitutionally protected commercial expression on a number of occasions. In a series of landmark cases, beginning with *Ford*, the court has unequivocally endorsed the idea that commercial speech is a category of constitutionally protected expression. The authors in this part debate the merits of that inclusion.

Ronald Rotunda explains that, tied to the notion of constitutionally guaranteed speech in the United States, there exists a belief that the people are fit to rule themselves both in their public and private lives and that, as reasoning beings, they are entitled to information about the economic choices which they face. Rotunda contrasts the Platonic view, that the multitude are unfit for self-government, with the Aristotelian view, which sees the multitude as reasoning beings, fit to make decisions for themselves. Consistent with the Aristotelian view, and the rationale based on self-government, Rotunda argues that truthful information regarding lawful consumer choices must not be suppressed. If government wishes to sway consumer choices, it must do so by education or counter-speech.

In contrast, Lorraine Weinrib believes that the Supreme Court of Canada has moved too far in the direction advocated by Rotunda. Rather than approaching commercial expression with a distinctively Canadian approach, the court has adopted American constitutional constructs without regard to Canada's differing social, political and legal culture. Weinrib justifies the protection of the language of choice in commercial communications as an aspect of individual autonomy, a rationale that fits within the *Charter*'s scheme of rights protection. The court, however, is alleged to have gone further than is necessary by giving commercial expression a constitutionally significant role, thereby creating a basis for conceptual confusion in subsequent cases. In doing so, the court has endured justified criticism, constitutionalizing, not only the marketplace of ideas, but the idea of the marketplace itself.

COMMERCIAL SPEECH AND THE PLATONIC IDEAL: LIBRE EXPRESSION ET LIBRE ENTREPRISE

Ronald D. Rotunda

I. INTRODUCTION

In 1928, in his famous dissent in *Olmstead v. United States*,[1] Justice Brandeis wrote that the United States Constitution "conferred, as against the government, the right to be let alone — the most comprehensive of rights and the right most valued by civilized men."[2] When Justice Brandeis focused on this need for privacy, over 20 years before George Orwell published his vision of the future in *1984*, he was building on the philosophical debates between Aristotle and Socrates.[3] The present dispute over whether a government should restrict advertising that may affect an individual's right to decide for himself or herself whether to use legally available products or services — such as cigarettes, food high in fat, or drinks that contain a lot of sugar — reflects an age-old controversy that goes back at least as far as these philosophical disputes.

We must assume, of course, that the speech in question — for example, a television commercial, a newspaper advertisement — is truthful and non-misleading. Just as the state may prohibit fraud, it may prohibit truly misleading advertising.[4] In addition, the commercial

---

1 277 U.S. 438 (1928).
2 *Ibid.*, at 478, *per* Justice Brandeis, dissenting.
3 Orwell's *1984* was published in 1949. On privacy, see the often-cited work by Warren and Brandeis, "The Right to Privacy" (1890), 4 Harv. L. Rev. 193.
4 In fact, the government's interest in protecting the public from false or genuinely misleading advertising is so great that the U.S. Supreme Court has held

activity that is the subject of the speech must be lawful. Promotion of an illegal activity — such as advertising for "men only" jobs in violation of sex discrimination laws, when gender is not a *bona fide* occupational qualification[5] — is not protected speech. Given the fact that the government has made the activity illegal, it certainly should be able to prohibit solicitations to commit an illegal act. Otherwise, contract murderers would be able to advertise their services freely.

Should the government be able to dampen interest in a lawful product or service by making it a crime to truthfully advertise the product or service? Do such restrictions on so-called "commercial speech" violate any basic principles of freedom of expression and imply a lack of faith in the ability of individuals to reason, to make choices and to accept their consequences?

Socrates would have had no trouble answering these questions, for he rejected democracy, which he treated with condescension and scorn. His philosophy was based on the assumption that the people are not fit to rule themselves. For Socrates, the ruler is the "shepherd" and the people are the herd of sheep that the shepherd makes sure are "safe and fed." It is, in this view, "the business of the ruler to give orders and of the ruled to obey." The governed are the multitude, the "herd"; government

---

that the government, when it prohibits false or misleading commercial speech, will not be subjected to overbreadth analysis and will not be required to demonstrate that its law is no more extensive than necessary to achieve the legitimate goal: *Ohralik v. Ohio State Bar Assn.*, 436 U.S. 447 at 462-65 (1978). As the text explains, advertising prohibited as misleading must be *truly* misleading. Compare *Re J.(R.M.)*, 455 U.S. 191 (1982), where a lawyer's advertisement claiming that he was a member of the United States Supreme Court bar was technically true, but "could be misleading to the general public unfamiliar with the requirements of admission to the Bar of this Court" (at 205-206). But the state of Missouri's absolute prohibition of this advertisement violated the First Amendment because there was no finding in the record specifically identifying this information as misleading. Moreover, restrictions short of an absolute prohibition — *e.g.*, requiring a statement explaining the nature of the Supreme Court bar — may have sufficed to cure any possible deception. The government regulation on speech must not be more extensive than necessary to serve the asserted governmental interest.

Contrast *Irwin Toy Ltd. v. Que. (A.G.)* (1989), 58 D.L.R. (4th) 577 at 622 (S.C.C.): "The report [of the Federal Trade Commission of the United States] thus provides a sound basis on which to conclude that television advertising directed at children is *per se* manipulative. Such advertising aims to promote products by convincing those who will always believe." If these young people are so easy to convince and manipulate, should not the court equally presume that they will believe their parents (the real purchasers of the advertised toys), when their parents tell them that the toys are too expensive, not appropriate for their age, and so forth?

5   *E.g., Pittsburgh Press Co. v. Pittsburgh Comm. on Human Rights*, 413 U.S. 376 (1973).

exists, not by the consent of the governed but by the submission of the governed. In the ideal world of Socrates, subjects would be ruled by an expert, the "one who knows." Just as patients should obey the orders of their doctor (who is the expert), and athletes should obey their coach (who is the expert), similarly, the multitude should obey "those who know how to rule."[6]

Though he spoke approximately a century later, Aristotle's rebuttal of Socrates was directly on point. And, oddly enough, his book on *Politics*, written over 2,300 years ago, is full of contemporary insights. Aristotle begins by telling us that man is a "political animal." Our word "political" comes from the ancient Greek word for "city," which is "*polis*."[7] The ancient Greek city was not merely an urban area; it was a sovereign city state and a community. When Aristotle said that man is a political animal, he meant that humans, unlike other animals, are endowed with *logos*, the ability to speak, to reason, to make decisions, to distinguish right from wrong. We are "political" animals because we have the ability to reason, not because we are obsessed with the next election.

II. FREE SPEECH AND ITS ROLE IN SELF-GOVERNMENT

The basic assumption of Aristotle, in contrast to Socrates, was that the people should have the ability to obtain information and the ability to exercise free speech; thereafter, they could use this information and speech to reason with each other and make decisions by majority rule. The people, he believed, are fit to rule themselves, to decide for themselves. Aristotle, in a very real sense, was the harbinger of the famous footnote 4 of *Carolene Products*, where Chief Justice Stone explained that laws restricting speech should be subject to "more exacting judicial scrutiny" because such legislation "restricts those political processes which can ordinarily be expected to bring about repeal of undesirable legislation."[8]

6 See, *e.g., Xenophon*, 7 vols. (Loeb Classical Library, 1918-1925), 4.6.12 (4:343-45); 3.9.11-13 (4:229-31); *ibid.*, 3.2.1; 3.8.10-11 (4:229); Plato, 8 vols. (Loeb Classical Library, 1925-1931). These issues and the philosophical battles are discussed with care in I.F. Stone's recent book, *The Trial of Socrates* (Boston: Little, Brown & Co., 1988). "In the *Timaeus* and its sequel, the *Critias*, Plato pictured the Golden Age of man as a time when gods tended their human herds as men later tended their cattle." *Ibid.*, at 15.

7 On the importance of language and the origin of words, see generally, R. Rotunda, *The Politics of Language* (Iowa City: Iowa University Press, 1986).

8 *U.S. v. Carolene Prod. Co.*, 304 U.S. 144 at 152-53, n. 4 (1938). See generally, 2 R. Rotunda, J. Nowak & J. Young, *Treatise on Constitutional Law: Substance and Procedure*, §§ 15.4, 15.7 and 18.3, and 3 R. Rotunda, J. Nowak & J. Young, §§ 20.7(a) and 23.5 (St. Paul, Minn.: West Pub. Co., 1986).

In the Platonic dialogue, *Gorgias*, Socrates attacked the practices of oratory and rhetoric as mere flattery of the common mob. I.F. Stone's recent book on *The Trial of Socrates* explains that the "unspoken premise of the Socratic assault on oratory was disdain for the common people of Athens."[9] Socrates did not believe that the rulers could reason with "the herd." In contrast, Aristotle's *Rhetoric* began by affirming:[10]

> ... that mankind generally had sufficient intelligence to be reached by reasoned argument. Such a faith lies at the very foundation of democracy; free government has no future where men can be treated as a mindless herd. Thus from the very opening lines of the *Rhetoric*, we are in a different universe from that of the Socratic and the Platonic, and breathe a different air.

Antiphon was another critic of Socrates and of Plato, who was to Socrates what Boswell was to Johnson. Antiphon spoke of the equality of man and the importance that man-made laws be arrived at by the consent of the governed.[11] This intellectual ancestor of Jefferson anticipated the *Declaration of Independence* by over 2,000 years.[12]

The framers of the American Constitution knew of the debate between the followers of Plato and Socrates, who believed that the common people were "the multitude" or the "herd," who were not fit to decide for themselves and who had to be governed by "one who knows," and the followers of Aristotle, who believed that people were reasoning beings, who should not be deprived of information and free speech, and who were fit to decide for themselves. In *The Federalist Papers*, James Madison tells us that government is based on the assumption that man has the ability to reason, and that a democracy is a better form of government because it relies on the reasoning of all the people, not, as Plato or Socrates would have it, on the reasoning of one person, the "one who knows." Specifically, Madison, the prime author of the Constitution,[13] tells us:[14]

---

9   I.F. Stone, *supra*, note 6 at 92.
10   *Ibid.*
11   Kathleen Freeman, *Ancilla and the Pre-Socratic Philosophers* (Cambridge: Harvard University Press, 1970), at 147-48, Fragment 14 Ox. Pap. translated, cited in I.F. Stone, *supra*, note 6 at 43-44.
12   I.F. Stone, *supra*, note 6 at 43-44.
13   Rotunda, "Bicentennial Lessons from the Constitutional Convention of 1787" (1987), 21 Suffolk L. Rev. 589 at 604-10.
14   *The Federalist Papers*, No. 49, ¶7 (February 5, 1788). The authorship of the various *Federalist Papers* is somewhat in dispute. See, Adair, *The Authorship of the Disputed Federalist Papers*, William & Mary Quarterly (3d Series), vol. 1, at 97-122 (April 1944), and at 234-64 (July 1944). *Cf. Stanford v. Kentucky*, 109 S.Ct. 2969 at 2980 (1989) (opinion of Scalia J., joined by Rehnquist C.J. and White and Kennedy JJ., stating that for the court to roam, rudderless, outside

The reason of man, like man himself, is timid and cautious when left alone, and acquires firmness and confidence in proportion to the number with which it is associated . . . In a nation of philosophers, this consideration ought to be disregarded. A reverence for the laws would be sufficiently inculcated by the voice of an enlightened reason. But a nation of philosophers is as little to be expected as the philosophical race of kings wished for by Plato.

In the oft-cited civil liberties decision, *Meyer v. Nebraska*,[15] the United States Supreme Court similarly acknowledged that life would be different in America if government was like Plato's ideal commonwealth or the city-state of Sparta (a place that Plato and Socrates admired). In both places, *Meyer* noted, the government sought "to submerge the individual and develop ideal citizens." But the court observed that such "ideas touching the relation between individual and state were wholly different from those upon which our institutions rest."[16]

In general, America's legislative efforts have accepted this basic belief in the worth of the common man and woman. If a matter that is subject to federal legislative jurisdiction is of the type where the people sought to be protected have the ability to make their own judgments and choices, then Congress has rejected a paternalistic approach. Of course, when the subjects of protection are not able to make reasoned choices, it is appropriate for the government to step in and make the choices for them.

Laws protecting children fall into this category, because children do not have the same reasoning abilities as do adults. Thus, if it is illegal to sell a product (such as "adult" magazines) to children,[17] it should be constitutional to enact a narrowly tailored statute designed to prohibit advertising specifically directed at encouraging children to buy the product that is illegal for them to purchase.

The state, however, may not overreact. For example, the state, in the guise of protecting children, may not constitutionally forbid the general public from reading or having access to materials on the grounds

---

the constitutional and statutory text "is to replace judges of the law with a committee of philosopher kings").

15   262 U.S. 390 (1923). *Meyer* invalidated a Nebraska law that prohibited the teaching of any subject in any language other than the English language to pupils who have not passed the eighth grade. The law applied to every "private, denominational, parochial or public school."

16   *Ibid.*, at 402.

17   *E.g., Ginsberg v. N.Y.*, 390 U.S. 629 (1968), upholding a statute that defined illegal "obscenity" in terms of an appeal to the prurient interest of *minors*. The court emphasized that the statute cannot be overbroad; that is, it may not seek to prevent the general public from reading or having access to materials on the grounds that the materials would be objectionable if read or seen by children. In addition, the statute must not be vague.

that the materials would be objectionable if read by children.[18] Similarly, although the state may forbid cigarette advertisements that urge 12-year-olds to smoke, it may not forbid all cigarette advertisements simply because 12-year-olds will also see them.[19] In other words, the state may not "burn the house to roast the pig."[20] The state law should be narrowly tailored and serve compelling governmental interests.

When the factors going into a decision are very complex, we also properly rely on the government for protection. Thus, it is proper for the United States Food and Drug Administration to regulate the safety and effectiveness of new drugs, because factors going into that decision are complex, requiring extensive experimentation and scientific expertise. The ability to evaluate such drugs is outside the ken of the ordinary lay person. Though the F.D.A. may not regulate this area as efficiently and effectively as some would like, the general principle that some federal

---

18 *Butler v. Mich.*, 352 U.S. 380 (1957). See *Sable Communications of Calif., Inc. v. F.C.C.*, 109 S.Ct. 2829 (1989), where the court held that §223(b) of the *Communications Act* of 1934, as amended in 1988, can constitutionally impose an outright ban on "obscene" interstate, pre-recorded, commercial telephone messages ("dial-a-porn"), because the protection of the First Amendment does not extend to obscene speech. However, the court invalidated the portion of the statute that imposed an outright ban, regardless of age, on "indecent," that is, "adult" dial-a-porn messages. The government could ban such messages as to children, but not as to adults. The means used in the statute were improper because they were a total legislative ban, not narrowly tailored to serve the purported purpose of protecting children. Using access codes, scrambling rules and credit card regulations would constitute a more carefully tailored way of keeping indecent dial-a-porn out of the reach of minors without having a total ban. See also, *supra*, note 17.

19 It is interesting to note that several countries — Portugal, most of the Scandinavian countries, Italy, Singapore, Kuwait and Thailand — have enacted virtual total bans of cigarette advertising in both the television and print media. Such a ban is now proposed in France, and the European Community is considering similar advertising restrictions as well. Canada enacted such a ban in the summer of 1989. Lipman, "France Heartens Anti-Tobacco Advocates" (March 30, 1990), Wall Street Journal (Midwest ed.) at B6, cols. 1-3.

Yet, the smoking of cigarettes does not seem to have diminished in such countries. Smoking is much more popular in Asia and Europe than it is in the United States, which has no total ban. The ban on advertising should, however, make it more difficult for newer brands, with lower tar and nicotine levels, to inform consumers of their existence; the advertising bans, in other words, will raise barriers to the entry of competing brands to the market, even if the lack of advertising does not reduce overall consumption. Indeed, the advertising bans may increase consumption by giving cigarettes the image of "forbidden fruit."

20 *Butler v. Mich.*, 352 U.S. 380 at 383 (1957). Even in the case of children, it is one thing for the state to ban advertising aimed at children that is genuinely misleading; it is quite another to ban advertising because of purportedly generalized concerns about children and their reasoning ability. See Beetz J., joined by McIntyre J., dissenting, in *Irwin Toy Ltd. v. Que. (A.G.), supra*, note 4.

regulation may be appropriate to prevent the marketing of unsafe drugs, or the marketing of drugs in a misleading manner, is not contrary to the democratic tradition.

In contrast, the F.D.A. does not make the paternalistic decision to deprive consumers of the ability to choose to buy foods high in fat, cholesterol or sugar. The law does require that food labels truthfully list the ingredients so that consumers then have the information necessary to make reasoned decisions. Various organizations and individuals can educate consumers about the dangers involved with these foods, but there is no paternalistic banning of them. More importantly, given that these products are legal, there is no effort to ban non-deceptive advertising about them,[21] even though many people say that they cannot stop eating potato chips, or that seeing commercials about ice cream makes their bodies crave fatty foods. As a result, some of these people will suffer the ill effects of heart disease, high blood pressure, obesity and so forth.

The government should seek to protect people from themselves by education, not by a law restricting free speech in an effort to dampen people's consumptive choices. It is certainly proper for parents to require their children to exercise, have enough sleep and so on. But adults are not children, and the federal government is neither our parent nor our big brother.[22] As the United States Supreme Court has noted: "The purpose of the Constitution and Bill of Rights, unlike more recent models promoting a welfare state, was to take the government off the backs of people."[23]

The federal securities laws of the United States offer another example where government has chosen to follow the democratic model, rather than the model of Socrates or the model of the Platonic guardian/

---

21   In the United States, Congressmen Luken and Synar, for example, have sponsored Bills that would, in substance, bar tobacco advertisements that use colours or pictures, thus permitting text-only advertisements: Lipman, *supra*, note 19. However, the Supreme Court has held that the state may not prohibit non-deceptive advertisements that use illustrations. *Zauderer v. Office of Disciplinary Counsel*, 471 U.S. 626 at 647 (1985): "The use of illustrations or pictures in advertisements serves important communicative functions: it attracts the attention of the audience to the advertiser's message, and it may also serve to impart information directly. Accordingly, commercial illustrations are entitled to First Amendment protections afforded verbal commercial speech."

22   *Cf.* Justice Douglas, dissenting to a denial of *certiorari*, in *Olff v. East Side Union High Sch.*, 404 U.S. 1042 at 1044 (1972): "One's hair style, like one's taste for food, or one's liking for certain kinds of music, art, reading, recreation, is certainly fundamental in our constitutional scheme — *a scheme designed to keep government off the back of people.* That is not to say that the police power of the state is powerless to deal with known evils. An epidemic of lice might conceivably authorize a shearing of locks. Other like crises might be imagined." [emphasis added]

23   *Schneider v. Smith*, 390 U.S. 17 at 25 (1968).

dictator. The federal system mandates full disclosure of all material information so that the investor can make an informed judgment of whether or not to buy the offered investment. In order to assure a level playing field, the federal laws also ban trading on inside information. It is certainly appropriate for the government to require the disclosure of risks, to assure that information is true and complete, and to prohibit deceptive advertising; then, investors using the free market-place can decide for themselves whether to purchase stock.

The United States government does not engage in "merit" review of the investments; like most of the rest of the world,[24] it does not determine that the proposed offering of stock presents "excessive investment risk,"[25] or is based "upon unsound business principles."[26] Some of the individual states in the union do engage in merit review of stock offerings, but it has come under academic criticism as an ineffective and paternalistic method of protecting investors.[27] In general, it is better to require more disclosure, more speech, rather than imposing merit review which attempts to weed out seemingly unsound investments.

Nonetheless, in some cases, the United States has chosen the Platonic, rather than the Aristotelian, approach. Probably the most infamous example of the United States rejecting its strong tradition and belief in the democratic process is prohibition, our "Noble Experiment" of the 1920s. The purposes of prohibition were certainly noble — to create a healthy, alert, sober citizenry. The means to achieve this end —

---

24 L. Loss and E. Cowett, *Blue Sky Law* (Boston: Little, Brown & Co., 1958), at 18: "Only in the United States and Canada, at the state and provincial level, are there rigorous substantive standards governing the sale of securities." See also, *ibid.*, at 17: "This kind of paternalistic attitude toward the investor is peculiar to the United States and Canada."

25 "Report on State Merit Regulation of Securities Offerings" (1986), 41 The Business Lawyer 785 at 787.

26 Quoted in W. Cary, *Cases and Materials on Corporations*, 4th ed. unabridged (Mineola, N.Y.: Foundation Press, 1969), at 1480.

27 *E.g.*, Mofsky and Tollison, "Demerit in Merit Regulation" (1977), 60 Marquette L. Rev. 367 at 378 (an empirical study of merit regulation compared securities denied registration in a state based on merit regulation but allowed in other states without merit regulation; these securities were compared with securities allowed registration in a state with merit regulation; "on balance, returns on securities denied registration were as high as those for securities registered"). See also, *Blueprint for Reform: The Report of the Task Group on Regulation of Financial Services* (1984), at 42: Merit regulation has "often resulted in unnecessary economic barriers to the capital formation process." (October 7, 1983), 15 Sec. Reg. & L. Rep. at 1882, quoting Jack Bailey, executive director of the Iowa Development Commission: "We have lost jobs in Iowa and now we need risk capital to get the state going again. Merit review has flagged those efforts because some companies don't want to put up with it." "Blue Sky Red Tape" (June 1957), Fortune Magazine 122.

forced abstinence — were fatally flawed, based on a paternalistic assumption, the model of the Platonic guardian/dictator. The experiment was a massive failure because the government tried to treat adults as if they were children.

With the end of prohibition there was fear that the people would turn, in massive numbers, to "demon rum." In fact, despite the legalization of liquor and the resulting explosion in liquor advertisements, the number of drinkers increased by only 10 per cent.[28] The mammoth enforcement efforts behind prohibition hardly made a dent in the number of drinkers,[29] but it did serve to make criminals out of ordinary citizens and to increase the power of organized crime. Indeed, the main legacy of this "Noble Experiment" was the emergence of organized crime as a major force in American life. Over a half century later, we still are left with this unintended bequest.

No one, of course, should drink excessively. And those who suffer from alcoholism should not drink at all. Prohibition and the banning of liquor advertisements, however, were not the way to reduce alcoholism. Alcoholics Anonymous (A.A.) has proved to be a very successful method to treat alcoholism. A.A. does not blame alcoholism on the manufacturers, vendors or advertisers of liquor, that is, those who urge us to buy it. A.A. tells its members that they are adults, personally responsible for their own choices. Any effort to blame third parties, A.A. says, is an improper exercise in denial.[30]

Society has now chosen to deal with the issue of alcohol by educating people about its dangers — for example, publishing research showing a statistically significant relationship between drinking even a very small amount of alcohol and breast cancer[31] — so that individuals can decide for themselves whether the risks (the possibility of cancer) are worth the benefits (we also know that moderate consumption of alcohol during the meal may aid digestion).[32] Today we seek to educate pregnant

---

28 Kupfer, "What to Do About Drugs" (June 20, 1988), Fortune Magazine at 39-40.

29 Interestingly, in recent years the public in the United States has voluntarily turned away from hard liquor — not because of *less* speech (a ban on liquor advertisements) but because of *more* speech (greater publication about the health dangers of excessive alcohol).

30 See, *e.g.*, Chickering, "Denial Hardens the Drug Crisis" (July 25, 1988), Wall Street Journal (Midwest ed.) at 12, col. 6.

31 (May 7, 1987), New York Times at I-1, col. 1 (referring to findings published in the New England Journal of Medicine that show that women have a higher risk of breast cancer if they take as few as three alcoholic drinks per week).

32 The State of California has recently implemented a multi-million dollar anti-smoking advertising campaign, in line with the principle that the best remedy for the speech with which we disagree is more speech, not less: see Mydans, "California Opens All-Out War on Tobacco and Its Marketing" (April 11, 1990), New York Times at A1, col. 1, and A12, col. 1.

women about the dangers of drinking while pregnant, but the government does not ban liquor advertisements even if seen by pregnant women.[33]

This basic presumption against unnecessary governmental interference extends beyond the Constitution and the belief in federalism. It is a basic policy belief, as well, that government should not unnecessarily intrude on one's private life. These beliefs are reflected in the constitutional restrictions on the government's power to restrict advertising of birth control pills.[34] Similarly, as the United States Surgeon General and others have urged, we do not quarantine AIDS victims, we educate them, and others, on the risks of contracting AIDS and the methods available (for example, condoms) to reduce the risk.

III. COMMERCIAL SPEECH AND THE DEMOCRATIC IDEAL

It is not grandiose to suggest that the efforts to discourage and dampen the use of a lawfully available product or service by forbidding or restricting an individual or corporation[35] from engaging in truthful advertising related to that product or service is simply another illustration of the age-old battle between privacy, the right to make private choices, on the one hand, and government intrusion on the other; between self-determination and personal freedom, on the one hand, and George Orwell's Big Brother on the other; between embracing the basic assumption of democracy that people are fit to rule themselves, on the one hand, and embracing the model of the Platonic guardian/dictator on the other.[36]

---

33 Indeed, some suggest that to make it a crime for a pregnant woman to drink may raise questions about a woman's constitutional privacy rights: see, *e.g.*, *Roe v. Wade*, 410 U.S. 113 (1973).

34 *Griswold v. Connecticut*, 381 U.S. 479 (1965) (use); *Carey v. Population Services Int.*, 431 U.S. 678 (1977) (advertising).

35 In the United States a corporation is an incorporeal "person" for purposes of the Fourteenth Amendment: *Santa Clara County v. Southern Pac. Ry.*, 118 U.S. 394 (1886). Thus, it is unconstitutional for a state to enact a criminal statute that forbids corporations from spending money for the purpose of influencing the vote on referendum proposals: *First Nat. Bank of Boston v. Bellotti*, 435 U.S. 765 (1978). Corporations, like other persons, have the right of free speech. A newspaper, for example, loses no rights under the United States Constitution simply because its owners decide to incorporate. But *cf., Irwin Toy Ltd. v. Que. (A.G.), supra*, note 4.

36 It is because of this basic philosophical battle that groups like, for example, the American Civil Liberties Union have joined the tobacco industry in the United States in opposing various proposed federal laws designed to restrict the free speech and constitutional rights of tobacco manufacturers and those who choose to use tobacco.

The purpose of restrictions on truthful, non-misleading, non-coercive commercial speech is typically to dampen demand for a lawfully available product or service by forbidding speech about the product or service. The government seeks to paternalistically protect people from themselves by keeping them in ignorance. A belief in the democratic ideal rejects this view that the people are the Platonic "herd" who must be manipulated. The United States Supreme Court has rejected these rationales, and has held that commercial speech is protected by the First Amendment. As Justice Douglas said a quarter of a century ago, "the State may not, consistently with the spirit of the First Amendment, contract the spectrum of available knowledge."[37] The people have the capacity for self-government, even if they decide to make choices that some of us may view as unwise.[38]

Restrictions on commercial speech are not only inconsistent with the Aristotelian premises that form the basis for a democratic state, they also embrace the Socratic belief that the government should manipulate the "herd" by depriving the people of information. Moreover, government regulation of commercial speech imposes hidden costs in addition to the asserted benefits that attend governmental control of commercial activity.

The majority of people (the "herd") might reject a ban on advertising if they knew of the disguised economic burdens such regulation creates.[39] If the legislature did not hide the costs and benefits of a policy decision, but fully revealed this information, the people likely would develop faith in the legislature's rational weighing of interests. If a state, for example, decided to favour a particular business by granting it a monopoly, the people, who speak through their representatives, gener-

---

37 *Griswold v. Connecticut*, 381 U.S. 479 at 482 (1965). See also, Rand J., in *Switzman v. Elbling* (1957), 7 D.L.R. (2d) 337 at 358 (S.C.C.) [Que.], recognizing that freedom of expression is "little less vital to man's mind and spirit than breathing is to his physical existence."

38 People engage in risky behaviour all the time, such as drinking alcohol, diving off the high board, and riding motorcycles. For people to engage in such activities does not necessarily mean that they are irrational and that the activity should be banned. It may simply mean that some people are more risk adverse than others; while some people may be unduly cautious, others are not.

It was many years ago that the U.S. Surgeon General first announced the statistical link between smoking and cancer and other health risks. Yet some people still choose to smoke, notwithstanding the warning labels. Some people may find a benefit in smoking; see, *e.g.*, Time Magazine (May 30, 1988), at 56, col. 3: ". . . smokers become more alert and may actually even think faster. In addition, nicotine may produce a calming effect by triggering the release of natural opiates called beta-endorphins. Thus a smoker literally commands two states of mind — alertness and relaxation."

39 See, *e.g.*, Lipman, "Foes Claim Ad Bans Are Bad Business" (February 27, 1990), *Wall Street Journal* (Midwest ed.), at B1, col. 3, and B7, cols. 1-3.

ally are considered sufficiently competent to weigh the advantages of such a decision as against the disadvantages. The legislature has wide discretion with which it may decide not only to create the monopoly, and establish a regulatory body to monitor it, but also to tax the people to subsidize it, and otherwise to control its distribution. The costs, as well as the benefits, are relatively apparent to the people. Thus they accept the process and the means by which their representatives reached this decision, even though the people may not agree completely with the ultimate judgment.

In contrast, the public's insight into legislative decision-making suffers when legislators regulate truthful speech. Because of the hidden burdens inherent in any regulation of speech, even the regulators, at best, may not perceive the full consequences of its regulation.[40] At worst, the legislature, by disguising its true objectives, may implement a policy that the majority of people would oppose if they had received adequate information about the true costs of the proposal. The legislature, in short, might impose regulations that a majority of the people would have rejected if they were fully cognizant of the regulation's true burdens. Restrictions on advertising reflect an anti-democratic means of implementing other policy judgments.

A simple example illustrates the point. The majority may wish to assist small, less efficient pharmacies in their efforts to compete effectively with chain store druggists. Moreover, the majority may wish to discourage the legal use of legitimate drugs. The legislature may achieve these goals through several means. To discourage the use of drugs, the state could place a special tax on drugs and thus raise their cost and lower the incidence of their use. To aid the small druggist, the state could grant tax advantages or outright subsidies to pharmacists who have no affiliation with chain stores and have gross sales below a fixed amount. The combined effect of a tax on all drugs and a subsidy to the small druggist would discourage drug use and aid the small pharmacist. To decide whether the advantages of discouraging legitimate drug use and aiding small business outweigh the disadvantages, the public need only com-

---

40 After the 1965 ban in the United States of cigarette advertisements on television, it became more difficult for producers of new low tar and low nicotine cigarette brands to introduce their products. The television ban also virtually eliminated the anti-cigarette advertisements. "Changing Fashions in Free Speech" (May 18, 1976), Wall Street Journal (Midwest ed.), at 18, col. 2.
The ban on cigarette advertising also helped all of the tobacco companies to eliminate a substantial cost to them, thus making the cigarette companies more profitable. See, (1990), 12 American Association of Individual Investors 28. If all the cigarette companies had got together and agreed to eliminate television advertisements, that would be an antitrust violation. The government ban accomplished the same result without worry about antitrust problems.

pare the perceived benefits of these goals with their costs. The public can measure the costs of this legislative judgment in terms of higher taxes and costs for consumers. The legislature would arrive at its decision openly and, therefore, presumably in a rational manner.

Alternatively, the state could effect its two goals by prohibiting the truthful advertising of drug prices. A prohibition on advertising discourages the workings of a competitive market system and imposes transaction costs on the efficient transfer of information, which should result in price increases.[41] Advertising that informs the consumer of the availability of less expensive alternatives of fungible products generally should lower prices. Indeed, lower prices should result even assuming that all of the costs of advertising are added to the price of the product and passed on to the consumer, because increased demand should create economies of scale.[42]

Empirical studies of drug prices where no commercial advertising is allowed indicate that there is less competition and, thus, significantly higher drug prices. An American Medical Association survey in Chicago showed that the price of the same amount of the same drug varied up to 1,200 per cent.[43] Price disparities of this magnitude would not exist in a market that permitted price advertisements, because advertising would facilitate both comparison shopping by consumers and competition by druggists.[44] The ban on advertisements, therefore, increases drug prices

---

41 Benham, "The Effect of Advertising on the Price of Eyeglasses" (1972), 15 J. Law & Econ. 337; *Staff Report to the Federal Trade Commission*, "Prescription Drug Price Disclosures" (1975), §III at 1-4.
Cf. Buchanan, "Advertising Expenditures: A Suggested Treatment" (1942), Journal of Political Economy 537; P. Samuelson, *Economics*, 9th ed. (N.Y.: McGraw-Hill, 1973), at 48 ("In the idealized model of an efficiently acting competitive market mechanism, consumers are supposed to be well informed.").

42 How much of the advertising is added to the cost of the product and thus passed on to the consumer is a function of the elasticity of demand. If a product has a very elastic demand (*e.g.*, bread: if wheat prices drop a lot, people do not suddenly eat a lot more bread; if wheat prices are raised substantially, many people will simply shift to other comparable commodities such as potatoes), it is difficult for the retailer to pass on much of the costs of advertising. In such cases, the retailer will have to absorb much of the cost, resulting in lower profit margins rather than higher retail prices. Even if demand is inelastic, there still should be a reduction in prices because the cost of information is less. See, *supra*, note 40 and accompanying text.

43 *Virginia State Bd. of Pharmacy v. Virginia Citizens Consumer Council Inc.*, 96 S.Ct. 1817 at 1827, n. 17 (1976).

44 A Federal Trade Commission staff study concluded that allowing the advertising of drug prices would save consumers millions of dollars: *Staff Report to the Federal Trade Commission*, "Prescription Drug Price Disclosures" (1975), at 119.

and concomitantly discourages legitimate drug purchases. The absence of easily obtainable information about drug prices insulates the less efficient druggists from price competition.

The results of a restriction on truthful commercial speech are the same as the results of a tax on all drugs and a tax advantage for a given class of druggists. However, the impact of the method used to achieve this result is decidedly different. The costs of the restriction on speech are not measured easily, and if the true costs were known, the majority might prefer lower drug prices. Restrictions on commercial speech obstruct the decision-making process, for the public can much more easily weigh the costs of subsidies or tax advantages than it can weigh the costs of limitations on the exercise of First Amendment rights. Nevertheless, the immediate economic results are the same: higher drug prices.

A broader scope of judicial review should exist in these instances of legislative judgment based on hidden costs than exists when the costs of the legislative decision are obvious. A court decision that requires a legislative body to reveal the true expense of a legislative decision does not infringe on the majority's substantive right to give aid to small pharmacies. Such a judicial mandate is not anti-majoritarian, for it encourages an open decision-making process: this process facilitates more rational legislative decisions because it reflects the Aristotelian belief in the worth of the common person. In contrast, the Platonic dictator/guardian would have no qualms about manipulating the "herd."

In *Virginia State Board of Pharmacy v. Virginia Citizens Consumer Counsel Inc.*[45] the Supreme Court held unconstitutional, as a violation of free speech, a state statute prohibiting pharmacists from advertising prescription drug prices. This decision represents an important contribution to the democratic quality of judicial review. The decision permits a state to implement any legitimate substantive state policy it believes necessary, but, at the same time, it requires that state to implement its policy within a framework that is conducive to a democratic decision-making process. As a result of *Virginia Pharmacy*, legislatures may achieve the policy objectives of commercial regulation only within a framework that exposes the ultimate costs of that regulation.

As the court in *Virginia Pharmacy* recognized:[46]

> So long as we preserve a predominately free enterprise economy, the allocation of our resources in large measure will be made through

---

45 425 U.S. 748 (1976). *Cf. Ford v. Qué. (P.G.)* (1988), 54 D.L.R.(4th) 577 at 609-13 (S.C.C.).

46 *Ibid.*, at 765.

numerous private economic decisions. It is a matter of public interest that those decisions, in the aggregate, be intelligent and well informed. To this end, the free flow of commercial information is indispensable. [I]t is also indispensable to the formation of intelligent opinions as to how that system ought to be regulated or altered.

Thus, said the court, protection for commercial speech serves the important First Amendment goal of "enlighten[ed] public decision-making in a democracy."[47] It is the alternative to a "highly paternalistic approach" where the "State's protectiveness of its citizens rests in large measure on the advantages of their being kept in ignorance."[48]

Similarly, in *Central Hudson Gas & Electric Corp. v. Public Service Commission*,[49] the court invalidated a state regulation which completely banned promotional advertising by electric utilities. The purpose of this regulation was to promote conservation by dampening demand. The purpose was laudable, but the means were unconstitutional. Even though the state could have banned the wasteful use of electricity directly, it did not have the constitutional power to ban advertising which promoted electrical use.[50]

IV. CONCLUSION

In *Virginia Pharmacy* the court concluded that the choice "between the dangers of suppressing information, and the dangers of its misuse if it is freely available" is the choice "that the First Amendment makes for us."[51] To advocate the complete suppression of advertising relating to lawfully available products or services in an attempt to dampen interest in such products or services, is to reject this basic Aristotelian premise of

---

47   *Ibid.*
48   *Ibid.*, at 769-70.
49   447 U.S. 557 (1980). See also, Blackmun J., joined by Brennan J., concurring in the judgment, at 575, citing Rotunda, "The Commercial Speech Doctrine in the Supreme Court" (1976), U. Ill. L. Forum 1080 at 1080-83.
50   See also, *Lakewood (City) v. Plain Dealer Publishing Co.*, 108 S.Ct. 2138 at 2147 (1988): "[The] 'greater-includes-lesser' syllogism ... is blind to the radically different constitutional harms inherent in the 'greater' and 'lesser' restrictions. Presumably in the case of an ordinance that completely prohibits a particular manner of expression, the law on its face is both content and viewpoint neutral. In analyzing such a hypothetical ordinance, the court would apply the well-settled time, place, and manner test. The danger giving rise to the First Amendment inquiry is that the government is silencing a channel of speech ... Therefore, even if the government may constitutionally impose content-neutral prohibitions on a particular manner of speech, it may not *condition* that speech on obtaining a license or permit from a government official in that official's boundless discretion." [emphasis in original]
51   *Supra*, note 45 at 770.

democratic society, that people have a right to more information, not less, so that they can make well-informed decisions, not ignorant ones.[52]

No longer does speech shed its First Amendment protections because of its commercial nature. Although the state and federal governments still may impose reasonable regulations on the time, place and manner of speech, and although the regulations may seek to discourage or prohibit false or misleading advertising, or advertising of illegal products or services, a legislature should be loath to suppress the dissemination of concededly truthful information about entirely lawful activities. Allowing such speech, rather than restricting it, serves to encourage more rational majority decision-making. A state should not hide behind the commercial speech doctrine.

If a state wants to make an activity or product more expensive, or if it wants to aid a particular class of people or certain economic interests, the state may implement these policy goals directly and forthrightly,

---

52 *Posadas de Puerto Rico Assoc. v. Tourism Co.*, 478 U.S. 328 (1986), offers authority for the proposition that the state may ban tobacco advertising directed towards children (or any other group for whom the purchase of tobacco is illegal); such a ban already exists.

Posadas does not offer, outside the confines of the peculiar facts of that case, authority to ban all cigarette advertising. This point is discussed in R. Rotunda, *et al., supra*, note 8, §20.31 (Pocket Part, 1989). During oral argument in *Posadas*, the counsel for Puerto Rico said that a casino *advertising in a Spanish language daily with 99 per cent local circulation* would be permitted to advertise casino gambling, so long as the advertising "is addressed to tourists and not to residents" (transcript of oral argument, at 26, quoted in Rotunda, "The Constitutional Future of the Bill of Rights: A Closer Look at Commercial Speech and State Aid to Religiously Affiliated Schools" (1987), 65 No. Carolina L. Rev. 917 at 926 and n. 51). Puerto Rican law already prohibited casinos from admitting persons under 18 or from offering their facilities to the public of Puerto Rico. If the law in fact prohibited Puerto Ricans from engaging in casino gambling, we should not be too surprised that the court upheld a ban on advertising that invited Puerto Rican residents to enter the casino in order to gamble.

It is noteworthy that the majority in *Posadas* frequently cited *Central Hudson* with approval. The *Posadas* court gave no hint that it was in any way undermining *Central Hudson*, a precedent only six years old. Justice Powell, who authored *Central Hudson*, joined the majority opinion in *Posadas*: Rotunda, *ibid.*, at 921-29. Even the Puerto Rican courts agreed that a total ban on advertising of casino gambling was "capricious" and "arbitrary": 478 U.S. at 334-35.

Even the majority in *Posadas* agreed that if one has a constitutional right to do something or to buy something, then it would be unconstitutional to forbid advertising encouraging that purchase. Thus, if it is lawful to speak English, if one has a constitutional right to speak English, it should be unconstitutional to forbid an individual from advertising in English: see *Ford v. Qué. (P.G.), supra*, note 45.

either by taxes, by subsidies, by statutorily authorized price-fixing,[53] or by other similar devices. The state should not seek to accomplish these results by forbidding the discussion or the advertising of factual information, or by restricting advertisers from publishing advertisements designed to be easily understood.[54] The state, in short, should not seek to prevent people "from being convinced by what they hear."[55]

---

53 Price-fixing by the state is exempted from the federal antitrust laws: *Parker v. Brown*, 317 U.S. 341 (1943). *Cf. Goldfarb v. Virginia State Bar*, 421 U.S. 773 (1975).

54 Some American Congressmen have proposed banning the use of colours or pictures in tobacco advertisements. Such a law would allow only so-called "tombstone" or all text advertisements. Lipman, *supra*, note 19. However, in *Zauderer v. Office of Disciplinary Counsel*, 471 U.S. 626 (1985), the court, *per* Justice White, prohibited a state from disciplining an attorney who solicited legal business by running newspaper advertisements containing non-deceptive illustrations. The advertisement offered to represent women who had suffered from the Dalkon Shield Intrauterine Device. The advertisement included a drawing of the Shield. See generally, R. Rotunda *et al., supra,* note 8, §20.31 at 148-49.

55 *Capital Broadcasting Co. v. Mitchell*, 333 F. Supp. 582 at 594 (D.D.C., 1971) (Wright J., dissenting).

DOES MONEY TALK?
COMMERCIAL EXPRESSION IN
THE CANADIAN
CONSTITUTIONAL CONTEXT

Lorraine E. Weinrib

> ... television advertising directed at young children is *per se* manip-
> ulative. Such advertising aims to promote products by convincing
> those who will always believe.[1]

Both geographically and culturally, Canadians live in the shadow of
the United States. Some would say this proximity defines us and works
to obscure the distinctive qualities of things Canadian. It can even
distort a decidedly Canadian creation — the Canadian Constitution.

Unlike routine legal prescriptions, rules about land-holding, tax
liability or consumer protection, for instance, constitutions do not cross
national borders easily. Constitutions express a country's self-under-
standing of its past and its present, and perhaps most importantly, its
hopes for the future.[2] Many nations may share the vocabulary that
expresses these aspirations: sovereignty, democracy, freedom, equality
and fairness. Yet these words are not simply fungible universals. On the
contrary, their meaning is at least partly shaped by history and nourished by a specific set of institutions.[3] To ignore the context of constitutional norms is to risk misunderstanding their content.

This paper applies these reflections to the question of constitutional
protection for commercial expression. Its theme is that the issue in
Canada should have its own distinctive — and by that I mean, at least in
part, distinctively Canadian — cast. My comments are an extended
caveat against the facile assumption — evidenced in the Supreme

---

1   *Irwin Toy Ltd. v. Que. (A.G.)* (1988), 58 D.L.R. (4th) 577 at 622 (S.C.C.).
2   Montesquieu, *The Spirit of the Laws* (Cambridge: Cambridge University Press,
    1989), B.I, cc. 3, 9, 11-14.
3   Constitutions are not only particular and contextualized, however. They also
    capture the development of these abstract concepts in the international arena as
    well as in the world of ideas. In addition to reacting to events of national
    moment, constitutions also react to events on the world stage. It is important,
    as argued later, to understand the *Charter* as a post-Second World War
    instrument.

Court's judgments on commercial expression — that the constitutional doctrines of the United States are readily transferable to Canada.

In the American system, commercial expression arises as a subcategory of the general prohibition against the governmental abridgment of free speech.[4] Initially, the Supreme Court of the United States resisted the call to extend the protection afforded to speech of a political nature to expression in the commercial market-place.[5] In its view, such expression merely manifested the speaker's desire for "gainful occupation," but did not engage the values underlying the protection of free speech: political self-government, the emergence of truth in a market-place of ideas, and respect for the autonomy of the individual. These values, in combination, supported an almost absolute proscription on governmental interference in the content of speech. An analytically elusive definitional exercise branded disfavoured categories of expression — pornography, incitement to violence and defamation, for example — as "not speech," with the result that they attracted not lesser or limited protection, but no protection at all.

More recently the Supreme Court of the United States has retreated from this categorical denial of constitutional protection to commercial speech. Instead, it developed a lower level of review for restrictions on marketplace expression. Commercial speech is now "speech," albeit of a qualified kind. The court has distinguished between the stringent protection afforded to "core speech" (that is, the political speech and expressive conduct traditionally protected by the First Amendment in this century) and the more relaxed protection of speech in the furtherance of business transactions. Commercial speech is considered both more durable and verifiable than core speech;[6] it has less, or

---

4   U.S. Const., First Amendment: "Congress shall make no law . . . abridging the freedom of speech . . . ." The prohibition applied to the federal government generally and was held by the U.S. Supreme Court to apply to the states as embraced by the liberty guarantee in the Fourteenth Amendment in *Stromberg v. California*, 283 U.S. 359 (1931), and *Near v. Minnesota*, 283 U.S. 697 (1931). See Nimmer, *Freedom of Speech* (New York: Mathew Bender, 1984), at ss. 4.01 [A-B], and D.A. Anderson, "The Origins of the Press Clause" (1983), 30 U.C.L.A. L. Rev. 455 at 483.

5   *Valentine v. Chrestensen*, 316 U.S. 52 (1942). For a detailed history of the development of American doctrine in this area and the argument that the commercial speech cases have been anomalous because they rest on an erroneous as well as elusive ascription of motive, see McGowan, "A Critical Analysis of Commercial Speech" (1990), 78 Calif. L. Rev. 359. McGowan argues against what he sees as the United States Supreme Court's progressive retreat to its initial position, affording less and less protection to speech it deems commercially motivated.

6   The commercial speaker can be called to a higher standard of accuracy so that laws can prohibit false and misleading speech. There is no possible chilling effect because the speaker is unlikely to be discouraged in response to regula-

minimal, redeeming social and political worth because it relates to property rather than individual liberty; it is often expressive of the corporate, rather than the individual, persona; it is profit-oriented and, accordingly, less expressive of individual personality; it engages the "rights" of the listener, rather than the speaker, and thus reflects the process of information dissemination itself; the recipient of such speech is considered, in some respects, more vulnerable to ignorance and harm, and thus in need of at least some protection.[7]

The notions of self-government, truth in the marketplace of ideas, and individual autonomy have figured prominently in the American controversy about commercial speech. Those who advocate stronger protection for commercial speech claim that commercial speech evinces the same values as core speech. They sometimes argue that the two kinds of speech are indistinguishable or, in the extreme, that commercial speech merits *more* protection![8] Moreover, they claim that protection for commercial speech, and the free and informed decisions to which it leads, is essential for the proper functioning of the free enterprise economy.[9]

Those who regret the United States Supreme Court's new protection of commercial discourse deny the commonality of commercial and core speech, and express fear that the relaxed protection of commercial speech bodes ill for the continued strict protection of core speech. They are apprehensive about identifying constitutional rights and liberties with economic (and ultimately corporate), rather than with dignitary (and inherently individual), interests.[10] Critics also point out that the political arena is the appropriate forum for working out a society's commitment to the use and exploitation of its resources. They contend that courts should not pre-empt debate on the appropriate degree of

---

tion, because of the profit motive. Accordingly, the presumption against prior restraints and the overbreadth doctrine may not apply. See Watson, "Regulating Commercial Speech: A Conceptual Framework for Analysis" (1980), 32 Baylor L.Rev. 235 at 236-37. For a critique of this position on both empirical and theoretical grounds, see McGowan, *supra*, note 5.

7   The American case law permits extensive regulation of false and misleading commercial speech on this basis.

8   Coase, "The Market for Goods and the Market for Ideas" (1974), 64 Amer. Eco. Rev. 384 at 389, and "Advertising and Free Speech" (1977), 6 Journal of Legal Studies 1.

9   See Fiss, "Free Speech and Social Structure" (1986), 71 Iowa L.Rev. 1405, for the view that the United States Supreme Court's decision in striking down attempts to structure public debate through regulation of the media has favoured capitalism at the expense of democratic self-determination, which requires state support of a rich public debate.

10   "The Corporation and the Constitution: Economic Due Process and Corporate Speech" (1981), 90 Yale L.J. 1833.

persuasive advocacy regarding life-style, health care, substance abuse and stereotyping.

This is not the place to assess the merits of these competing arguments. Rather, my concern is with the appropriateness of transplanting the American jurisprudence, without much reflection, to the Canadian constitutional context.[11]

As noted earlier, there are three conceptual strands to the jurisprudence on speech rights in American case law: the self-government rationale, the market place of ideas metaphor, and the autonomy principle. The first two, in my view, are too closely tied to American history and politics to be imported into Canada. The third is different. It builds on ideas common to the American and Canadian constitutional systems. It also resonates with the international understanding of rights protection developed in the last 50 years, an understanding embodied both in the *Charter*'s[12] text and its interpretation.

The self-government rationale is firmly embedded in the grand experiment of American republicanism.[13] It is a prescription for government by a sovereign people and derives from the establishment of a new *grundnorm* after the American Revolution. Ultimate power is vested in and exercised by the people and for the people, regardless of the values espoused.[14] Speech rights are jealously protected because public debate is essential to the achievements, and even the survival, of the polity. This rationale aims not primarily at producing true utterances,[15] but at

---

11 My argument is not that Canadian courts or commentators should ignore American constitutional theory. The rich legacy of analysis and case law provide a wonderful resource for *Charter* analysis. We ignore it at our peril. See, *e.g.*, Gibson, "Constitutional Law — Freedom of Commercial Expression Under The Charter — Legislative Jurisdiction Over Advertising — A Representative Ruling: *Attorney-General of Quebec v. Irwin Toy Limited*" (1990), 69 Can. Bar Rev. 339. I simply urge more caution in importing ideas about rights that are infused with the particularity, both historical and institutional, of American constitutionalism.

12 *Canadian Charter of Rights and Freedoms*, Pt. I of the *Constitution Act, 1982*, being Sched. B of the *Canada Act 1982*, 1982 (Eng.), c. 11.

13 Articulated in the work of Meiklejohn. See "The First Amendment Is an Absolute" (1961), Sup. Ct. Rev. 245, and *Political Freedom: The Constitutional Powers of the People* (New York: Harper & Brothers, 1965). See also Powe, "Scholarship and Markets" (1987), 56 George Washington L.Rev. 172 at 182 *ff*.

14 The relationship of these ideas to the revolution is express:
    "We, the People, acting together, either directly or through our representatives, make and administer law. We the People, acting in groups or separately, are subject to the law. If we could make that double agreement effective, we would have accomplished the American Revolution."
    Political Freedom, supra, note 13 at 15.

15 Meiklejohn, *Political Freedom, ibid.*, at 75:
    "The First Amendment is not, primarily, a device for the winning of new

fostering the best type of citizen. The assumption is that enriching the opportunities for intellectual and artistic development will make the political will express the best of human possibilities. The paradigm for such speech is direct democracy, not parliamentary democracy.[16]

The second strand, the market place of ideas formulation, understands speech to be a means to truth. It assumes that existing knowledge and opinion expands or improves through the testing and competition of the "marketplace."[17] The remedy for speech that may be erroneous, ill-advised, hateful or untrue is more speech. To suppress speech that has these undesirable characteristics is wholly unacceptable because only the marketplace, not those who hold the power to suppress, can be the arbiter of truth.

The truth-seeking idea has roots in the amazing flowering of speech that animated and justified the American Revolution. Indeed, the metaphor serves to sustain the centrality of that formative moment in American constitutionalism.[18] This process-oriented model presupposes the perfectibility of humanity and, by extension, of society.[19]

Implicit in the economic metaphor, bolstered by this historical resonance, is the understanding that an unregulated marketplace works well in ascribing value and worth through informed decision-making. It is a rational place. This image is particularly interesting in the context of

---

truth, though that is very important. It is a device for the sharing of whatever truth has been won. Its purpose is to give to every voting member of the body politic the fullest possible participation in the understanding of those problems with which the citizen of a self-governing society must deal."

16 Meiklejohn, *Political Freedom, ibid.*, at 16: "If the government, as an institution, has broken down, if the basic agreement has collapsed, then both the right and the duty of rebellion are thrust upon the individual citizens." See also Schauer, *Free Speech: a philosophical enquiry* (Cambridge: Cambridge University Press, 1982), at 37-39: "The difficulties of the paradox of freedom as applied to speech may perhaps be lessened if we now examine the procedure of the traditional American town meeting. That institution is commonly, and rightly, regarded as a model by which free political procedures may be measured. It is self-government in its simplest, most obvious form." A town meeting employs a moderator, for organization and order, and, by vote of all the people, chooses debates and settles issues of communal interest. Government is the servant to this institution.

17 A detailed criticism of the assumptions underlying the market-place of ideas approach is set out in Baker, *Human Liberty and Freedom of Speech* (New York: Oxford University Press, 1989), at 12 *ff.*

18 See, *e.g.*, Cohen, "Creating a Usable Future: The Revolutionary Historians," in Greene (ed.), *The American Revolution: Its Character and Limits* (New York: New York University Press, 1987); Bailyn, *The Ideological Origins of the American Revolution* (Cambridge: Harvard University Press, 1967); Wood, *The Creation of the American Republic* (New York: Norton & Co., 1969).

19 Schauer, *supra*, note 16, c. 2.

a discussion of commercial expression. Like a snake swallowing its tail, the reality of market relationships is validated through its own metaphorical image. The metaphor invites us first to understand the role of expression through certain presuppositions about the market and then to apply that understanding to the market itself. The weakness of this procedure is that those presuppositions about the market are no longer unquestioned.[20]

These two approaches, so clearly informed by the Revolution, that took America down a different path from our own, do not adapt well to contemporary Canadian constitutionalism. The self-government rationale presupposes that the sovereign people can make of government what they will. In Canada, in contrast, the sovereignty of the Crown in a parliamentary system, committed to the irreducible dignity of the individual, precludes such a presupposition. The hypothesis of a marketplace in which ideas battle and truth ultimately prevails has been falsified by the triumph of Nazism in Weimar Germany. The *Charter*, in its substantive commitments to fundamental freedoms, justice and equality, recognizes — as do other post-war constitutions and international systems of rights protection — that the price exacted by such a commitment to process over substance is unacceptable.

In addition, the relationship of politics and economics has had a different history in Canada than in the United States. Confederation was premised on ideas of collective economic endeavour because of its vast territorial expanse and its regional make-up. It is arguable that political values have ruled the economic world rather than *vice versa*.

The third strand, commitment to the autonomy of the individual, is the least dependent on the particular history and political culture of the United States. Although consistent with the classical liberalism that motivated the American political experiment and that continued to hold some sway as American constitutionalism developed, it has also animated much of the thinking about rights since the Second World War.

In the autonomy model, rights are not instrumental to other agendas. The value of freedom of speech or expression does not lie in its contribution to truth or to a certain kind of political arrangement. Rather, a constitutional guarantee of free speech reflects the understanding that language and other forms of meaningful expression actualize the

---

20 Fiss, *supra*, note 9 at 1413, n. 25 discusses the metaphor's origins. For a more detailed literary-legal history and analysis of the metaphor, see Cole, "*Agon at Agora: Creative Misreadings in the First Amendment Tradition*" (1986), 95 Yale L.J. 857. For a critique of commensurability in free speech adjudication, see Wright, "Does Free Speech Jurisprudence Rest on a Mistake?: Implications of the Commensurability Debate" (1990), 23 Loyola of Los Angeles L.Rev. 764.

capacity for human self-realization.[21] The focus is, thus, on the meaningful expression of the thinking faculty, rather than on the system of communication itself or the correlative activity of receiving and responding to what has been communicated.

Canadians can easily recognize individual autonomy as a central feature of our new structure of rights protection.[22] The rights enumerated in the *Charter* cover the range of political, legal and egalitarian interests that have crystallized in the last half of the 20th century as essential to individual dignity. Judicial interpretation has affirmed the orientation towards the autonomy and dignity of the individual rightholder. Under the Supreme Court's "purposive" mode of interpretation, the judiciary evolves the content of the right from the body of values for which rights protection is established.[23] This interpretation is

---

21 Emerson, *The System of Freedom of Expression* (New York: Random House, 1970), at 6, articulates the autonomy principle, as one of four main premises underlying freedom of expression in a democratic society, as follows:
   "First, freedom of expression is essential as a means of assuring individual self-fulfilment. The proper end of man is the realization of his character and potentialities as a human being. For the achievement of this self-realization the mind must be free. Hence suppression of belief, opinion, or other expression is an affront to the dignity of man, a negation of man's essential nature. Moreover, man in his capacity as a member of society has a right to share in the common decisions that affect him. To cut off his search for truth, or his expression of it, is to elevate society and the state to a despotic command over him and to place him under the arbitrary control of others."
   The other three premises for freedom of expression espoused by Emerson are:
   (1) as an "essential process for advancing knowledge and discovering truth" (at 6-7);
   (2) to provide participation in decision-making by all members of society (for the legitimacy of government is the consent of the governed) and in the building of culture generally (at 7);
   (3) a method of achieving a more adaptable as well as a more stable community by substituting rational discussion for force (at 7).
   Emerson states that while the validity of these premises is unproved, American society nevertheless is "based upon the faith that they hold true" (at 8).
22 I am not suggesting that American and Canadian ideas of autonomy are the same — indeed, given my view of the importance of national experience and values to constitutionalism, they could not be. See the discussion of Justice Wilson's treatment of equality, which starts off with an American "invisible fence around the individual" approach and ends with the individual situated and contextualized in a free and democratic society: L.E. Weinrib, "Abortion Policy on Demand: Constitutional Rights, Statutory Purposes and Institutional Design," forthcoming in U.T.L.J. See also MacKay, "Freedom of Expression: Is It All Just Talk?" (1989), 68 Can. Bar Rev. 713.
23 *Hunter v. Southam*, [1984] 2 S.C.R. 145 at 157: ". . . it is first necessary to specify the purpose underlying [the right]; in other words, to delineate the nature of the interests it is meant to protect." In *R. v. Big M Drug Mart Ltd.*, [1985] 1 S.C.R.

to be "large and liberal," not to include an ever greater number of interests, but more perfectly to realize individual dignity. In addition, the grounds on which the enumerated rights may be limited are restricted to the very values implicit in the enumerated rights themselves.[24] When rights or freedoms collide with the strongly held views of those who hold a majority in a legislative body, a temporary departure from constitutional norms is permitted, but only when expressly undertaken.[25]

Against this background one can evaluate the analysis in the Canadian Supreme Court on the question whether the *Charter* offers constitutional protection to commercial expression. I focus on three cases: *Ford v. Québec (P.G.)*,[26] *Irwin Toy Ltd. v. Quebec (A.G.)*,[27] and *Rocket v. Royal College of Dental Surgeons*.[28] I shall argue that the court followed the line of analysis which I have advocated in *Ford*, but fell into analytic confusion in *Irwin Toy* and in *Rocket*, largely because it failed to isolate, analyze and reject those strands of American thinking which do not fit the conceptual framework of rights protection under the *Charter*.

In *Ford*, the Supreme Court invalidated Quebec's law mandating the use of French only in public signs, posters and commercial advertis-

---

295 at 344:

"... the purpose of the right or freedom in question is to be sought by reference to the character and the larger objects of the *Charter* itself, to the language chosen to articulate the specific right or freedom, to the historical origins of the concepts enshrined, and where applicable, to the meaning and purpose of the other specific rights and freedoms with which it is associated within the text of the *Charter*. The interpretation should be ... a generous rather than a legalistic one, aimed at fulfilling the purpose of the guarantee and securing for individuals the full benefit of the *Charter*'s protection."

24 Section 1 reads:

"The *Canadian Charter of Rights and Freedoms* guarantees the rights and freedoms set out in it subject only to such reasonable limits prescribed by law as can be demonstrably justified in a free and democratic society."

The Supreme Court has correctly identified the concept of a "free and democratic society" as the "genesis" of the rights and freedoms guaranteed: see *R. v. Oakes*, [1986] 1 S.C.R. 103 at 135-36 [Ont.]. For the view that s. 1 amplifies these ideas, see L.E. Weinrib, "The Supreme Court of Canada and Section One of the *Charter*" (1988), 10 Sup. Ct. L.Rev. 469.

25 L.E. Weinrib, "Learning to Live With the Override" (1990), 35 McGill L.J. 541.

26 (1988), 54 D.L.R. (4th) 577 (S.C.C.).

27 *Supra*, note 1.

28 (1990), 71 D.L.R. (4th) 68 (S.C.C.) [Ont.]. Discussion of the s. 2(b) issue in *Ref. re Criminal Code*, ss. 193 & 195.1(1)(c) (1990), 56 C.C.C. (3d) 65 (S.C.C.) [Man.], a case decided in May 1990, is beyond the scope of this paper because it raises a different aspect of expression doctrine. The challenge to the criminal offence of soliciting in a public place relates to the expressive features of negotiating for the purchase or sale of sexual activity.

ing. The issue was whether choice of language in commercial communications was protected by s. 2(b) of the *Charter*.[29] In analyzing the "choice of language" issue, apart from the commercial context to which the law applied, the court quoted from a previous judgment in which its focus was clearly on individual autonomy and expression as one of its essential features:[30]

> The importance of language rights is grounded in the essential role that language plays in human existence, development and dignity. It is through language that we are able to form concepts; to structure and order the world around us. Language bridges the gap between isolation and community, allowing humans to delineate the rights and duties they hold in respect of one another, and thus to live in society.

Applying that general approach to the legislation challenged, the court continued:[31]

> Language is so intimately related to the form and content of expression that there cannot be true freedom of expression by means of language if one is prohibited from using the language of one's choice. Language is not merely a means or medium of expression; it colours the content and meaning of expression. It is . . . a means by which a people may express its cultural identity. It is also the means by which the individual expresses his or her personal identity and sense of individuality.

The court rejected the narrow view that s. 2(b) protects content only — and thus not language of choice — because the protection of expression is tied to freedom of thought, belief and opinion, all of which are coloured by one's particular language. In addition, the court acknowledged the political dimension of choice of language, especially in respect of a legislative measure prohibiting the use of specific languages, by referring to the expression of an individual's identity and sense of individuality as well as a people's cultural identity through language. It quoted, in this context, from the work of an authority on language:[32]

> . . . language is not merely a *means* of interpersonal communication

---

29 Section 2(b) reads as follows:
  "Everyone has the following fundamental freedoms . . .
    (b) freedom of thought, belief, opinion and expression, including freedom of the press and other media of communication."

30 *Ref. re Language Rights under S. 23 of Manitoba Act, 1870 and S. 133 of Constitution Act, 1867* (1985), 19 D.L.R. (4th) 1 at 19 (S.C.C.), quoted in *Ford, supra,* note 26 at 604.

31 *Ford, ibid.,* at 604.

32 J. Fishman, *The Sociology of Language* (Rowley, Mass: Newbury House Publishers, 1972), at 4, in *Ford, supra,* note 26 at 605-606.

and influence. It is not merely a *carrier* of content, whether latent or manifest. Language itself *is* content, a reference for loyalties and animosities, an indicator of social statuses and personal relationships, a marker of situations and topics as well as of the societal goals and the large-scale value-laden arenas of interaction that typify every speech community. [emphasis in original]

The court thus made clear its understanding that choice of language is prerequisite to expression of individual autonomy and, by extension, to the individual's connection to, and identification with, a larger social context. It then turned to consider the significance of the commercial context to which the legislative prohibition applied. Initially, the court took the position that "commercial expression" does not have "any particular meaning or significance in Canadian constitutional law" in contrast to the special category of commercial speech under the First Amendment to the United States Constitution.[33] The court concluded that the question under the *Charter* was whether the guarantee of freedom of expression should *not* extend to expression in the commercial context, rather than the "difficult definitional" problem of whether commercial expression was included within s. 2(b).[34]

After surveying the American approach to commercial speech, the court noted, correctly in my view, that its American counterpart had begun to extend its constitutional concern, under the rubric of commercial speech, to the individual as consumer, and thus to the calibre of information flow in the economic arena on which economic decisions are made. Autonomy, as read by the U.S. Supreme Court, included one's perception of one's best interests in the marketplace based on channels of communication open to truthful and non-misleading advertising. In the result, under the banner of freedom of speech, that court re-established the bond between rights and the market economy.[35]

This connection between speech and economics should have alerted the Supreme Court of Canada to the dangers of free trade in constitutional ideas. Even without it, the submissions of the Attorney General of Quebec, contrasting the intermesh of political and economic rights under the American *Bill of Rights* with the *Charter*'s deliberate omission of the economic interests, should have sufficed. The court preferred not to heed these structural stop signs. Instead, it went beyond what lay before it for decision in *Ford* and indicated its acceptance of the view that commercial expression:[36]

---

33   *Ford, ibid.*, at 610.
34   *Ibid.*
35   *Ibid.*, at 611-12. See *Powe, supra*, note 13 and the discussion of the *Posadas* case referred to, *infra*, note 64.
36   *Ford, supra*, note 26 at 618.

... protects listeners as well as speakers [and] plays a significant role in enabling individuals to make informed economic choices, an important aspect of individual self-fulfillment and personal autonomy. The court accordingly rejects the view that commercial expression serves no individual or societal value in a free and democratic society and for this reason is undeserving of any constitutional protection.

In my view, the court reached the right decision in *Ford*, but, in absorbing more American doctrine than appropriate, laid the groundwork for subsequent confusion.

The "purposive" understanding of the content of the rights and freedoms guaranteed by the *Charter* is concededly expansive, but only in the name of the values the *Charter* prescribes. Because the *Charter* text focuses on expression as the medium of thought that manifests both the individuality and common humanity of right-holders, economic benefit to the recipient of expression or of media output has no constitutional significance. What is constitutionally protected is free expression as a right. It does not fall to the courts to monitor the reception and use of information in the particular economic matrix in which we now find ourselves. The court must identify and protect the *Charter* values of autonomy, whether they arise in the context of commercial expression or not. The category is thus unhelpful and, as we shall see, misleading.

This foray into the American categories of speech protection was of little consequence in *Ford*. It did not affect the court's conclusion that the impugned legislation infringed the expression rights of those who used English in signs and advertising.[37] The commercial context was irrelevant and the court so determined. *Irwin Toy*, however, is different. Here, the court considered the constitutionality of Quebec's prohibition of television advertising directed at children under 13 years of age.[38]

---

37 In *Irwin Toy, supra*, note 1 at 608, the court explains its decision in *Ford*:
    "... [in *Ford*] the centrality of choice of language to freedom of expression transcends any significance that the context in which the expression is intended to be used might have. It was therefore unnecessary in that case to inquire further whether the restriction of commercial expression limited freedom of expression."

38 The impugned legislation prohibited advertising directed at children under 13 years of age, to be determined according to the goods advertised, the manner as well as the time and place of presentation. The regulations exempted magazine ads and made specific prohibition against a number of misleading or disreputable practices unsuitable for an impressionable audience. The problem before the court, however, was not really the extent of constitutional protection for advertising or even advertising directed at young children. The real issue was the claim to constitutional protection for expression that effected undue exploitation of a captive and wholly credulous audience. See Charren, "Children's Advertising: Whose Hand Rocks the Cradle?" (1988), 56 Cincinnati L.Rev. 1251 at 1252, for the view that "advertising to young children is inherently deceptive, that children cannot understand the machinations of the market-

Because the court in *Ford* had deviated from a purposive interpretation of *Charter* rights, and succumbed to the allure of the American category of commercial speech, its analysis in *Irwin Toy* was both internally inconsistent and unduly hospitable to American conceptions.

The court's analysis starts with the proposition that only some activity falls within the guarantee of freedom of expression, namely expressive activity that attempts to convey meaning.[39] The guarantee is to "ensure that everyone can manifest their thoughts opinions, beliefs," indeed "all expressions of the heart and mind" and the "mind and spirit,"[40] even when such expression is "unpopular, distasteful or contrary to the mainstream."[41] This freedom is fundamental to a "free, pluralistic and democratic society" because of the inherent value of diversity in "ideas and opinions" to both the individual and to the community.[42]

This discussion is well within the autonomy model of expression, because it ties the protection of expression to the individual personality.[43] However, in this context the court invokes a statement by Justice

---

place, and they have difficulty figuring out the difference between editorial and commercial speech." The author also decries the recent development of commercial programming for children, namely "program length commercials," financed by toy manufacturers to promote and market their wares. In result, the programming itself is a commercial sales pitch rather than "entertainment." She concludes by arguing that the Federal Trade Commission's mandate to protect the public interest is ignored to the extent it leaves the "unique" child audience to the market-place. For the history of toy advertising and the argument that there is no distinction between the "program length commercials" and other programming, see Steiner, "Double Standards in the Regulation of Toy Advertising" (1988), 56 Cincinnati L.Rev. 1259 at 1261 *ff.* and 1269 *ff.*

39　*Irwin Toy, supra,* note 1 at 606.

40　*Per* Rand J. in *Switzman v. Elbling* (1957), 7 D.L.R. (2d) 337 at 358 (S.C.C.) [Que.]. *Irwin Toy, supra,* note 1 at 606.

41　*Irwin Toy, ibid.*

42　*Supra,* note 1 at 606.

43　The court later quotes from T. Emerson, a leading proponent of the autonomy model of free speech analysis, in "Toward A General Theory of the First Amendment" (1963), 72 Yale L.J. 877 at 886, a passage that indicates the primacy of individual autonomy in a scheme of social community rather than the market place of ideas evolving a truth paradigm:

". . . the theory of freedom of expression involves more than a technique for arriving at better social judgments through democratic procedures. It comprehends a vision of society, a faith and a whole way of life. The theory grew out of an age that was awakened and invigorated by the idea of a new society in which man's mind was free, his fate determined by his own powers of reason, and his prospects of creating a rational and enlightened civilization virtually unlimited. It is put forward as a prescription for attaining a creative, progressive, exciting and intellectually robust community. It contemplates a mode of life that, through encouraging toleration, skepticism, reason and initiative, will allow man to realize his full potentialities. It

Cardozo of the United States Supreme Court to the effect that free speech is the "indispensable condition of nearly every other form of freedom."[44] This reference to expression as the prime right, now an established idea in the American system of constitutionalism, is the first suggestion of conceptual confusion. The passage in which this quotation occurs reaffirms the court's earlier acceptance of the freedom of conscience and religion, set out in s. 2(a) of the *Charter*, as quintessential, as is evident from the idea that expression serves freedom of thought, opinion and belief.[45] The suggestion that expression conditions these other rights, however, reverses this ranking and signals, as I shall now set out, a quite different mode of rights protection to that which was enunciated earlier by our Supreme Court.

The court makes clear that human activity that is wordless can have meaning and, for that reason, can attract protection under s. 2(b) of the *Charter*.[46] It does not recognize, however, that activity that takes the form of expression can nonetheless be devoid of meaning in the constitutional sense if it does not work to realize human autonomy. The court, by way of illustration, notes that violence (or threats thereof), although expressive, is not protected under s. 2(b) but neglects to articulate the reason why: namely, that such expression does not reflect the distinctively human quality of expression. Moreover, the court does not appear to recognize that, in considering the constitutional *vires* of television advertising aimed at children, it confronts another instance of form without intention to deliver meaning.[47]

Without analysis, and without reference to its previous account of the protection of free expression as having as its purpose the protection of expression of the "heart and mind" of the individual, the court asserts that advertising aimed at children conveys meaning and thus protected expressive content.[48] The court does not appear to consider relevant the nature of advertising as the language of invitation to commercial trans-

---

spurns the alternative of a society that is tyrannical, conformist, irrational and stagnant."
Irwin Toy, supra, note 1 at 608.

44 *Palko v. Connecticut*, 302 U.S. 319 at 327 (1937), quoted in *Irwin Toy, supra*, note 1 at 606.

45 In *Big M Drug Mart, supra*, note 23 at 347, Dickson J. (as he then was), writing for the majority, took the position that freedom of conscience and religion is the "prototypical and paradigmatic right." For a brief account of how the American system came to understand itself as subscribing to expression as its deepest value, despite the text of the First Amendment, see L.E. Weinrib, "The Religion Clauses: Reading the Lesson" (1986), 8 Sup. Ct. L.Rev. 506.

46 *Irwin Toy, supra*, note 1 at 607, and note 38.

47 *Ibid.*

48 *Ford, supra*, note 26 at 608.

actions or the corporate arrangements through which it is most commonly expressed.[49]

Such considerations might have given the court pause. The "heart and mind" of no one is engaged in the advertising of toys to young children by institutions such as Irwin Toy. Moreover, the court's focus upon the recipient audience and its right to receive information is somewhat problematic when advertising is aimed at young children who, the evidence discloses, until about age 6 cannot differentiate fact from fiction, and only then slowly begin to develop the capacity to recognize and evaluate a sales pitch.[50]

Having determined that commercial expression, as a category, falls within s. 2(b), and that Quebec's regulation of advertising aimed at children infringed Irwin Toy's freedom of expression, the court turned to consider, under s. 1 of the *Charter*, whether the infringement was a reasonable limit demonstrably justifiable in a free and democratic society.[51] On this question, the court split three to two in finding the burden of justification satisfied. The majority analysis followed the format of the now established sequence of argumentation originally set down in *R. v. Oakes*,[52] but, due to the flaws in the discussion leading to the recognition of the right and the finding of infringement in the earlier part of the judgment, emphasized the empirical dimension of the case at the expense of the conceptual analysis that had earlier informed its *Charter* analysis.[53]

The majority found Quebec's purpose to be the "pressing and substantial objective" that the *Oakes* test requires. The "protection of a group which is particularly vulnerable to the techniques of seduction

---

49 See Baker, *supra*, note 17.

50 Evidence to this effect and the finding that such advertising is "*per se* manipulative" is set out at *Irwin Toy, supra*, note 1 at 620-23 in the context of the court's discussion of justification of the recognized right. The court, at 611-12, appears to adopt the distinction it ascribes to T. Scanlon, "A Theory of Freedom of Expression," in Dworkin (ed.), *The Philosophy of Law* (London: Oxford University Press, 1977), at 161, between a government purpose to control attempts to convey meaning (by restricting content or form tied to content), on the one hand, and to control behaviour without the "intervening element of thought, opinion, belief, or a particular meaning," on the other hand. Here again there appears to be a gap between the theoretical or doctrinal discussion and the actual regulatory scheme under review.

51 *Irwin Toy, supra*, note 1 at 614-30.

52 [1986] 1 S.C.R. 103 at 135-40 [Ont.].

53 The court states as the central question "whether the evidence submitted by the government establishes that children under 13 are unable to make choices and distinctions respecting products advertised and whether this in turn justifies the restriction on advertising put into place." See *Irwin Toy, supra*, note 1 at 619.

and manipulation abundant in advertising," the court found, addresses questions of equality.[54] So far, the values of rights protection are evident. However, the majority also made reference to other considerations. For example, this passage of the judgment noted the presumed economic imbalance between producers and consumers, as well as the general concern in Western societies about the pervasive power of the media and the resultant interference with the family and parental authority. When the court came to consider the line drawn by the legislature in setting the age categories embodied in the legislation, it deferred to legislative judgment. The values that inform these considerations, while perhaps not obviously connected to the marketplace of ideas and self-government rationales for constitutional protection of free expression, are closer to them than to the autonomy model. Oddly, the court refers to, but does not recognize as falling within this latter type of value structure, the special rules developed in contract law reflecting the pre-autonomous status of children.[55]

The proportionality analysis displays a mix of these rationales as well. Under the test for minimal impairment, the majority posits a distinction between legislative policies that pit the individual against the state, for example, asserting claims to protection of legal rights arising under ss. 7 to 14 of the *Charter*, and policies that mediate "between the claims of competing groups."[56] For the former type of claim the judiciary can assess whether the measure is minimally intrusive; for the latter, the expectation is only to strike a balance based on an assessment of conflicting evidence and opinion, as well as limited resources. A self-government rationale is evoked: "Democratic institutions are meant to let us all share in the responsibility for these difficult choices." The legislature can rank its priorities according to its view of urgency and need.[57] One can only ask how effective children under 12

---

54   This aspect of the analysis, in *Irwin Toy, supra*, note 1 at 620-23, reflects the values found in s. 15 of the *Charter* in two ways. First, it evokes the protection of those who may be disadvantaged because of age and also the idea that equality must reflect the different position of persons in society rather than offering a standardized and formal equality to those to whom nature and social arrangements have not dealt an even hand. See *Big M, supra*, note 23 at 336 and *Andrews v. Law Soc. of B.C.* (1986), 27 D.L.R. (4th) 600 (B.C.C.A.).

55   *Irwin Toy, supra*, note 1 at 623.

56   *Ibid.*, at 625.

57   Here the court refers to *R. v. Edwards Books & Art Ltd.*, [1986] 2 S.C.R. 713 [Ont.], a case where rights to freedom of religion under s. 2(a) of the *Charter* were subordinated to government protection against economic disadvantage of employees. See *Irwin Toy, ibid.*, at 625. The Supreme Court of Canada recognized employees as a disadvantaged group whose interests may be forwarded under a s. 1 analysis in *Slaight Communications Inc. v. Davidson*, [1989] 1 S.C.R. 1038.

are in making their needs known, their priorities felt.

The final component of analysis under the s. 1 justification, the evaluation of the deleterious effects as against the government's pressing and substantial objective, swings the majority back to considerations of autonomy. The impugned legislation does not press too heavily on the right-holder because all that is at stake is revenue. Here in the last stage of *Charter* analysis we find the point that should have been first: if advertisers under the legislation want to convey meaningful incentives to purchase their wares, they are free to advertise to parents and other adults — the actual purchasers of children's products, albeit a more difficult target audience. Or they can engage in permitted types of advertising, for example, educational advertising.

When we read the various parts of the *Irwin Toy* judgment, and compare it to the earlier discussions of rights protection generally, and focus on the reasons for protecting expression in a free and democratic society, we can only wonder whether the richness of the American theoretical and legal literature in the area and the complexity of the sequential stages of *Charter* analysis have inhibited the court from connecting the discussion of facts, legislative policies and their effects to *Charter* values. In the gaps we find an unreflective absorption of American concepts, categories and controversies. The mode of analysis in *Irwin Toy* impoverishes our understanding of Canadian rights protection by proliferating the interests that qualify as rights and then filtering the resulting excess through an exercise in political judgment under the cover of a s. 1 justification.

Subsequent case law, I shall argue, has perpetuated this confusion. In particular, the protection of the recipients of expression as economic actors has developed into a free-standing value unconnected to, at times in tension with, the values of individual autonomy that inform the Canadian system of rights protection. By importing the United States Supreme Court's market-place of ideas metaphor without examining its presuppositions, the Supreme Court of Canada could not resist following that court into its protection of the real marketplace. Informed by the view that the recipient audience is vulnerable at large, and that the judiciary is its champion, our Supreme Court has rendered constitutional litigation an occasion to undo legislative schemes that forward the quintessential values for which constitutional guarantees stand.

In *Rocket v. Royal College of Dental Surgeons*,[58] Justice McLachlin, writing for a seven-member panel of the Supreme Court of Canada, struck down a "professional misconduct" code promulgated by the College of Dental Surgeons under the *Health Disciplines Act* of Ontario which, *inter alia*, restricted advertising by dentists. The code restricted

---

58 *Supra*, note 28.

public advertising by dentists to professional cards, announcements of new practices, modest public signs, and telephone directory listings of prescribed content. Permissible communication to patients included only appointment cards and reminder notices. In particular, the code precluded information as to qualifications, procedures or equipment, while permitting information identifying the dentist and describing the location and, usually, hours of practice.

The offending magazine and newspaper advertisement, headed "New Faces of the Canadian Establishment," displayed photographs of two dentists and praised their industry and entrepreneurial prowess for having established North America's largest store-front dentistry operation. It went on to endorse their success as "business people" responding to the need for "change." The advertisement appeared to be placed by Holiday Inn to tout itself as the hotel of choice for the business travel of those who share a commitment to "changing needs." The restriction of this advertisement, in the determination of the court, infringed freedom of expression and was not justified under s. 1.

Oddly, no analysis of the advertisement itself was offered. It might have been valuable for the court to examine, for example, whose rights to expression were in issue. The professional code applied to the dentists, *qua* dentists, not to Holiday Inn. The advertisement focused on the two individuals, not as dentists and not in their individual capacity, but as successfully progressive entrepreneurs and frequent — and presumably enlightened — consumers of hotel services.[59] By association, the advertisement promoted the idea of store-front dental facilities as being progressive and responsive to the public's need.[60] Cases involving freedom of expression engage such difficult analytic questions, that some deliberation on the nature of the advertisement would have enriched the reasoning in the judgment.

Also intriguing is the court's failure to focus upon the intended audience for the advertisement. It emphasized the importance of informed consumer decisions in choosing one's dentist, the judicial role in

59 The advertisement does not suggest that the two dentists were good dentists or even that they carried on dental practices. The information provided is that they work long hours and travel a lot on business. There is no promotion of their professional services. The advertisement does not suggest that Holiday Inn is their choice of hotel for personal, as distinguished from business, travel. It may, to some readers, suggest otherwise. The text of the advertisement is set out in the judgment, *ibid.*, at 70.

60 The advertisement makes an association between the progressive character of the entrepreneurial approach shared by the dentists and Holiday Inn, on the one hand, and store-front dental facilities, on the other. This innovation makes delivery of dental services more "convenient and accessible for the public." The public's response is described as "overwhelming" as evidenced by the rapid expansion and entry into the American market. *Ibid.*

protecting vulnerable groups, and the public's need for detailed information about the availability of dental services in special circumstances, but did not bring the discussion home to the advertisement in issue.[61]

The judgment describes the main outlines of the American approach to commercial expression, concluding that the *Charter*'s explicit limitation provision dictates a different course of analysis. McLachlin J. notes the United States Supreme Court's distinction between categories of commercial speech, in particular, its differentiation between advertising that provides verifiable information about standard products and advertising that contains subjective claims as to the quality of professional services, the former warranting more constitutional protection from state regulation than the latter.[62] She takes the view that the *Charter* precludes such categorization. In its place, the *Charter* protects all commercial speech under s. 2(b), and then calls for a weighing of competing values, in the context of the specific litigation, under s. 1.[63]

The judgment makes only brief reference to the values underlying the extension of constitutional protection to advertising. The case poses, we are told, a conflict between "the need to regulate the scope of professional advertising" and the "value of free expression."[64] Advertising involves more than "economics." It has intrinsic value as expression for advertisers, and enables its audience to make "informed economic choices" that promote individual fulfilment and autonomy.[65] In answering the "first question" posed by the case — whether commercial speech is protected under s. 2(b) of the *Charter* — in the affirmative, McLachlin J. gives no indication that rights crystallize certain pre-

---

61 The court notes that potential dental patients should be able to obtain information as to the languages spoken by a dentist and office hours. (The code imposes some restrictions on providing information about office hours.) See, *ibid.*, at 81-82.

62 *Ibid.*, at 75-76.

63 *Ibid.*, at 75.

64 *Ibid.*, at 74. In *Posadas de Puerto Rico Assoc. v. Tourism Co. of Puerto Rico*, 478 U.S. 328 (1986), the United States Supreme Court upheld a state statute that prohibited advertising by gambling casinos, which were legal in Puerto Rico. The prohibition applied to ads directed to Puerto Ricans. It did not prohibit advertising the casinos outside the state. Thus, the listener interests of the local population were not sufficient to protect advertisements for a legal activity. This case is not mentioned in the Supreme Court of Canada's apparently approving references to the recognition of listeners' interests in the U.S. case law. For a discussion see Strauss, "Constitutional Protection for Commercial Speech: Some Lessons from the American Experience" (1990), 17 Can. Bus. L.J. 45 at 46-48. After concluding that *Posadas* denies the proposition that listeners have a protected interest in decision-making in commercial matters, Strauss questions what protection the First Amendment affords to commercial speech.

65 *Supra*, note 28 at 74.

eminent values in the Canadian legal order and, for that reason, stand prior to other interests.

The professional code restricting dentists from most types of advertising infringed s. 2(b) because it interfered with permissible forms of expression, that is, all radio and television advertising as well as regular newspaper advertisements, and it restricted meaning by limiting the type of information to be offered to the public. Regrettably, the court does not tell us what kinds of meaning are at stake. Is it truthful, verifiable information about standardized products? Or is it subjective, abstractly descriptive claims about professional services that are of an infinite variety and nature and particularly important to the individual because the services in question touch upon very important concerns, such as health or legal rights? Since the judgment has just drawn this very distinction from the American case law, indeed quoted from that case law, it is somewhat surprising that the benefit of the American experience is not carried home to the case at bar.

Since this basic distinction about the kinds of meaning contained in professional advertising is not developed, it is not surprising that the court does not attempt to illuminate the more exotic kind of advertising in issue here. Thus, McLachlin J. does not discuss the nature of the interests that dentists or other professionals may have in endorsing their consumer choices, here the hotel operations they patronize on business trips. Nor does the court take into account the explicit association of store-front dentistry with highly successful entrepreneurial behaviour, progressive life-style, and public popularity. It appears that when the United States Supreme Court opened the door to constitutional protection to commercial speech under the First Amendment, it created an irresistible threshold.

Having found a right and an infringement, McLachlin J. turns to consider the limitation under s. 1. Speaking generally, she identifies the issue at stake as "primarily economic" and concludes that justification is more forthcoming than if opportunity to participate in the political process or the market place of ideas were in issue.[66] Similarly, justification is easier when the impugned legislative scheme works to protect the special concerns of children or the disadvantaged, or to resolve competition between groups, rather than confrontation between the state and an individual.[67]

Applying these views in the context of this case, she determines that the limitation discussion must acknowledge the interests of consumers of dental services. The balancing process must take into account the "important public interest" in one's ability to choose a dentist on the

66   *Ibid.*, at 79.
67   *Ibid.*

basis of "necessary or relevant" information.[68] Here, reference is made to the vulnerability of consumers to advertising of dental services because claims would be "inherently incapable of verification."[69]

McLachlin J. accepts the purpose of the impugned regulations, to maintain a high standard of professionalism, as differentiated from commercialism, and to protect the public from irresponsible and misleading advertising. She finds the regulations rationally related to these purposes. Turning to the question of minimal restriction, she notes that "it is conceded that dentists should be able to advertise their hours of operation and the languages they speak" because such information is verifiable, unlike claims to professional prowess.[70]

Unfortunately, that does not appear to be the issue that the case raises, although it does derive from the American case law reviewed at the beginning of the judgment. It would be interesting to know whether McLachlin J. reads this advertisement as informational, for example, as to store-front dental services, or not, given her emphasis of this distinction at this stage of the analysis. The issue that is raised by the case, which seems to have eluded the court, is whether dentists come free from the bonds of professional constraint when they engage in the promotion of business structures that provide professional services in the shopping mall mode.

Having found the prohibitions too broad, the discussion proceeds to the last part of the test, proportionality. It is not satisfied because the code prohibits much more than is necessary to realize the aims of professionalism and an informed marketplace for dental services.

What interests me here is how removed the judgment is, not only from the values of individual dignity adumbrated in the early *Charter* jurisprudence, both in the considerations of rights content and limitation, but also from the developmental discussion of commercial expression in *Ford*[71] and *Irwin Toy*.[72] The clash of Holiday Inn's advertisement with the professional code for dentists did not become an occasion to deliberate upon freedom of expression in a modern democracy, or the friction between one's relatively free personal and relatively constrained professional persona, or even the freedom of professionals to lend their aura of expertise and authority to their own and to someone else's commercial ventures. Instead, *Charter* review presented an opportunity to invalidate an established code of professional regulation that, somewhat ironically, appeared to forward the values identified as *Charter* protected by proscribing, *inter alia*, glitzy promotion that does nothing

---

68　*Ibid.*
69　*Ibid.*, at 79-80.
70　*Ibid.*, at 81.
71　See, *supra*, text accompanying notes 28 to 35.
72　See text accompanying notes 36 to 57.

to forward informed consumer choices. Whether on the ground of definition, as in the American approach, or on the *Charter*'s own sequenced value structure of rights and limits, one would not have expected constitutional protection to attach to this type of non-verifiable hype.[73]

The result of the case is, thus, dismaying. It seems clear that this kind of advertisement would be proscribed under a valid regime of regulation of dentist's professional advertising because the assertion for protection is based on exclusively commercial grounds and the restriction does not forward the interests of those who seek dental services to information that is truthful, verifiable and helpful in making important decisions on matters of health. Yet, the court struck down the code of professional conduct in its entirety.

This result follows, in my view, from too superficial an understanding of the American jurisprudence on freedom of speech and too casual an importation of the concepts developed in that jurisprudence. In the *Rocket* judgment we see the values that inform Canadian rights protection only vaguely, filtered through American constitutional constructs, informed by a very different history, as well as a different social, political and legal culture. Before our eyes, the idea of democracy disappeared, the marketplace of ideas became the marketplace, and notions of irreducible humanity were blurred.

The Holiday Inn advertisement championed those who keep up with the times. In deliberating upon the constitutional validity of the regulations that restricted advertising by dentists, the court manifested its ability to be progressive by using the *Charter* to open up channels of communication between dentists and the Canadian population as consumers of dental services. It styled itself the champion of the disadvantaged. In so doing, the court also opened the door to the kind of advertising that makes the marketplace for professional services a jungle for the would-be consumer, especially those whose resources, energy and acumen are in short supply.

The critics of the *Charter*, both before and since entrenchment,

---

73 The court could have sustained the prohibition to the extent that it forwarded values of professionalism and an open marketplace of information in dental services, fairly broad values for freedom of expression to embrace, and frowned upon restrictions that were inconsistent with those values. In terms of the coherence of *Charter* litigation, one must question the advisability of rewarding such a side-swipe at a regulatory structure. One possible explanation is that the Canadian Supreme Court here followed its American counterpart, perhaps unwittingly, in using speech protection ostensibly to preclude deception, but actually to undermine professional anti-competitive self-regulation. See Strauss, *supra*, note 64. He notes two dangers in this judicial proclivity: a retreat into substantive due process and the possibility of trivializing protection of speech rights outside this narrow area.

have decried the vesting of political power in the hands of unelected and unaccountable judges. The development of doctrine in these cases merits this critique. If the large and liberal vision of rights comes to include values foreign to the Canadian conception of rights, and if s. 1 justifications become a judicial recapitulation of the wide range of considerations open to legislatures, then the critics of the *Charter* have won through current interpretation what they lost through entrenchment and early interpretation. And Canada's mode of rights protection will have lost its distinctively Canadian accommodation of freedom and democracy.

PART VI

DEMONSTRATIONS AND PICKETING: ASSEMBLY, EXPRESSION AND THE CHARTER

The right to assemble, demonstrate and picket is central to the concept of a democratic polity. It is not only an opportunity to express oneself, but a chance to be seen and heard. Assemblies have been, traditionally, occasions for intervention by public and private authorities. While the tactics used in the 1919 Winnipeg general strike have fallen out of vogue, lawful and peaceful assemblies can still be prohibited, despite the enactment of the *Charter*.

Moe Litman discusses how private property historically has accommodated important societal values, including the free flow of information. By tracing the common law roots of private property, he debunks the notion of property interests as being absolute and argues that private property should be seen as an interest which must yield, in some instances, to freedom of expression. Litman pays particular attention to the way in which shopping mall owners should accommodate demands of access to their malls for expressive purposes.

While *R.W.D.S.U. v. Dolphin Delivery* ushered in the recognition of picketing as a constitutionally protected activity, the Supreme Court of Canada in that case also held that the *Charter* did not apply to the courts which issue injunctions restraining picketing in private labour disputes. Peter Gall reviews the proceedings in the *Dolphin Delivery* case leading up to the Supreme Court's ruling. Gall is of the view that the court should not have ruled on the issue of the applicability of the *Charter*, as it had not been dealt with in the courts below and was not properly argued before the court itself. He foresees the court reconsidering its ruling in *Dolphin* on the issue of applicability, as well as on the issue of whether secondary picketing is a constitutionally protected activity.

David Kretzmer discusses how states must allocate resources to protect the right to demonstrate, particularly in urban settings where demonstrators may face a hostile audience. In order to balance the right to demonstrate with public safety, the police too often have been delegated the responsibility of issuing permits for demonstrations, with wide degrees of discretion as to when and whether to allow public assemblies. Kretzmer discusses how the courts in Israel have intervened to override police ordinances which have required demonstration permits. He discusses how a balance is being struck between the citizens' right to assemble and the interests of the state in adequately allocating police resources in order to prevent violence at demonstrations while not sacrificing public security elsewhere.

FREEDOM OF SPEECH AND PRIVATE PROPERTY: THE CASE OF THE MALL OWNER

M.M. Litman*

I. INTRODUCTION

Freedom of speech and property are inextricably intertwined. Speech occurs on, in, through and with the aid of, property. The relationship between these two interests is both symbiotic and adversarial. Professor Iakovlev, in his recent Martland lecture,[1] noted that the institution of property played an important role in preserving those fundamental values which have given the Soviet people *glasnost, perestroika* and, more generally, the vitalization of democracy. It was in the privacy of the family home that these values were passed on, and thereby preserved. Privacy is, of course, one of the most important functions which the institution of property serves.[2]

---

* I would like to express my appreciation to my colleagues June Ross and David Schneiderman at the University of Alberta, and Lakshman Guruswamy at the University of Arizona, for their incisive comments on earlier drafts of this paper.

1 The Fifth Annual Martland Lecture, Faculty of Law, University of Alberta (February 6, 1990) (unpublished).

2 See Laskin C.J.C.'s judgment in *Harrison v. Carswell* (1975), 62 D.L.R. (3d) 68 at 73 (S.C.C.) [Man.]. See also the *Task Force on the Law Concerning Trespass to Publicly-Used Property as it Affects Youth and Minorities* (Ontario: 1987), at 10 (Chairman: Raj Anand).

Property is not only an incentive to free speech, but is also capable of impeding speech. For commercial, political, practical and other considerations, the proprietary right of exclusion may be exercised by property owners so as to prevent the transmission of information. There is little doubt that owners of residential property can, and should be able to, exclude members of the public from speaking freely on their property. The privacy function of property not only ensures freedom of speech to owners and their licensees, but also ensures freedom from the speech of others.

Prior to the advent of the *Charter*,[3] clashes between the value of free speech and the forces of property ordinarily resulted in the latter prevailing. This result obtained whether the property owner was the state, a private person or a corporation.[4] Moreover, this result obtained irrespective of the type of property that was involved. It made little difference whether the property in question was committed to commercial,[5] recreational,[6] transportation or communication purposes.[7] Although free speech was judicially enshrined as a fundamental, even cherished, value of Canadian society, it could not be exercised on or with the property of another without that other's consent. This attitude has survived the enactment of the *Charter*, even, perhaps surprisingly, in relation to state-owned properties. In *N.B. Broadcasting Co. v. Can. (C.R.T.C. Comm.)*[8] this attitude formed the core of the Federal Court of Appeal's repudiation of the claim by the New Brunswick Broadcasting Corporation to a right of access to broadcast frequencies for the purpose of exercising its *Charter* right of speech or press. The relevance of property to this claim is that broadcast frequencies are deemed by the

---

3   *Canadian Charter of Rights and Freedoms*, Pt. I of the *Constitution Act, 1982*, being Sched. B of the *Canada Act 1982*, 1982 (Eng.), c. 11.

4   See Roman Stoykewych, "Street Legal: Constitutional Protection of Public Demonstration in Canada" (1985), 43 U. of T.F.L.R. 43 at 50-54. See also A.L. Goodhart, "Public Meetings and Processions" (1937), VI Cambridge L.J. 161, and, in particular, *Ex parte Lewis* (1888), 21 Q.B.D. 191.

5   *Harrison v. Carswell, supra*, note 2.

6   See *Adrian Messenger Services & Ent. Ltd. v. Jockey Club Ltd.* (1972), 25 D.L.R. (3d) 529 (Ont. H.C.). In that case the plaintiffs failed to gain access to a racetrack for the purpose of placing bets as agent for others. In the course of his judgment Fraser J. stated:

> "It is not in dispute that the courses where the meets are held and bets taken are the private property of the defendants. Their operations are closely supervised but their property is still private.
>
> "In my opinion the plaintiffs have not established any right by common law, by statute, by contract, or by licence to go on the lands of the defendants. Their action, therefore, fails."

7   See Stoykewych, *supra*, note 4.

8   (1984), 13 D.L.R. (4th) 77 (Fed. C.A.).

Broadcasting Act of Canada to be public property.[9] Thurlow C.J.F.C., who delivered the judgment of the court, responded to the corporation's claim as follows:[10]

> The freedom guaranteed by the Charter is a freedom to express and communicate ideas without restraint, whether orally or in print or by other means of communication. It is not a freedom to use someone else's property to do so. It gives no right to anyone to use someone else's land or platform to make a speech, or someone else's printing press to publish his ideas. It gives no right to anyone to enter and use a public building for such purposes.

The same view was articulated, and somewhat amplified, by Pratte J. in *Committee for the Commonwealth of Canada v. Can.*[11] In that case the plaintiffs sought to disseminate their political ideas by distributing pamphlets and carrying placards in the public areas of the Dorval airport. After the airport authorities put a stop to these activities, the plaintiffs sought a declaration that their free speech rights had been violated. Pratte J., in dissent, held that the plaintiffs' rights did not authorize them to use the airport's property for expressive purposes.[12] He then elaborated as follows:[13]

> The government has the same rights as any owner with respect to its property. Its ownership right, therefore, is exclusive like that of any individual. The only qualification to this rule arises from the fact that the property owned by the government is frequently intended for use by the public, which then has a right to use it for the purposes for which the government intends it.

In sum, Pratte J. viewed property as being antithetical to the right of free speech because it inherently involves an exclusive or monopolistic right of control or exclusion. Moreover, this control exists whether the ownership of the property is private or public. On this latter point, the majority of the court, in separate judgments, disagreed with Pratte J. Both Hugessen and MacGuigan JJ. concluded that the scope and nature of the control of the government owner is considerably different from that of the private owner. Unlike the private owner, the government

---

9   *Broadcasting Act*, R.S.C. 1970, c. B-11, s. 3(a).
10   *Supra*, note 8 at 89.
11   (1987), 36 D.L.R. (4th) 501, affirmed 77 D.L.R. (4th) 385, application for re-hearing refused S.C.C. No. 20334, 8th May 1991.
12   *Ibid.*, at 506-507, where he states that "[f]reedom of expression authorizes each individual to express himself by using the property he owns or is entitled to use; it does not authorize him to use things he does not own to express himself."
13   *Ibid.*, at 507.

"cannot make its ownership right a justification for action the only purpose and effect of which is to impede the exercise of a fundamental freedom."[14] The clear implication of both of the majority judgments in the *Committee for the Commonwealth* case is that Pratte J.'s views accurately describe the law regarding private, as opposed to public, ownership.

This paper will assess the assumption that private ownership is absolute and, therefore, unyielding to other interests. Though this assumption has obvious importance to virtually all types of privately held property, particular attention will be paid to the shopping centre cases in which picketers and demonstrators have attempted to engage in expressive activities. It will be asserted that, in a general sense, property is capable of accommodating the interest of free speech, and that the time is ripe, even in the context of a purely private dispute that does not engage the *Charter of Rights*, for a reconsideration of the decision in *Harrison v. Carswell.*[15] In that case, the Supreme Court of Canada ruled that the owner of a shopping mall could succeed in statutory trespass proceedings against a person engaged in a lawful strike, notwithstanding that she was peacefully picketing her employer's premises. The situs of the picketing was one of the common areas of the mall. The majority of the court did not consider it to be material that the public had been invited to the mall without restriction.

II. PROPERTY AND THE "ABSOLUTE" RIGHT OF EXCLUSION

Pratte J.'s thesis of property involves two basic assumptions. First, property always entails a right of exclusion, and second, the right of exclusion is "absolute or unqualified."[16] Implicit in this second attribute of property is the notion that the right of exclusion will prevail over all countervailing interests.

The first assumption is reasonably well founded. It is well accepted that property is comprised of various standard incidents, including rights of disposition, use, possession, enjoyment, destruction and exclusion.[17] Property exists even if all of these incidents are not present.[18] In

---

14   *Ibid.*, at 510, *per* Hugessen J.
15   *Supra*, note 2.
16   This will be elaborated on, *infra.*
17   R. Cunningham, W. Soebuck & D. Whitman, *The Law Of Property* (1984), ss. 1.2 at 7.
18   For American authority for this proposition, see Cunningham, *et al.*, *ibid.*, and *First Victoria Nat. Bank v. U.S.*, 620 F. 2d 1096 at 1104 (5th Circ., 1980). Scottish law would also seem to support this proposition. In *McCaig v. Glasgow Univ.*, [1907] S.C. 231, a direction to convert property into cash and throw it into the

particular, property may exist even though there is no right of destruction,[19] or even absent the very important right of disposition.[20] Can property exist if there is no right of exclusion? Blackstone's definition of property would seem to preclude such a possibility. In his view, "property is that sole and despotic dominion which one man claims and exercises over the external things of the world, in total exclusion of the right of any other individual in the universe."[21] Modern, and perhaps more progressive, theorists also view the right of exclusion as an essential aspect of property.[22] Felix Cohen in his classic analysis of private property stated emphatically that:[23]

> ... [p]rivate property may or may not involve a right to use something oneself. It may or may not involve a right to sell, but whatever else it involves, it must at least involve a right to exclude others from doing something.

It seems uncontroverted that the right of exclusion is not merely a standard incident of property, but an essential and intrinsic part of its substantive content.

---

sea was invalidated. Despite the absence of the right of destruction it is clear that the money would be viewed as a form of property which could be bequeathed on death. Moreover, in Canada some courts have held that professional licences are property for the purpose of matrimonial property division, notwithstanding the inalienability of such licences. See *Corless v. Corless* (1987), 34 D.L.R. (4th) 594 (Ont. U.F.C.) and *Caratun v. Caratun* (1987), 9 R.F.L. (3d) 337 (Ont. H.C.); *cf. Linton v. Linton* (1988), 11 R.F.L. (3d) 444 (Ont. H.C.). Whether or not *Corless* and *Caratun* are properly decided on the merits, and there is doubt that they are, clearly they imply that in the absence of the right of disposition property can still exist. Finally, see Professor Donovan Water's article, "Voting Trust Agreements and the Zeidler Case" (1988), 50 Est. & Tr.Q. 51 at 63, where he states that "[t]he fact that a right is made non-assignable by the law or by parties does not prevent it being property, if it otherwise would be . . . It is simply the case that one characteristic of property is thereby taken from the right."

19   See *McCaig v. Glasgow Univ., ibid.*, at 242, and to the same effect, see *Brown v. Burdett* (1882), 21 Ch. D. 667.

20   *Supra*, note 18. Posner postulates that the right of disposition is an essential aspect of an efficient system of property rights. See R. Posner, *Economic Analysis of Law* (Boston: Little, Brown, 1972), at 12. It is interesting to note that the newly promulgated property laws of the Soviet Union permit land ownership, but not the right of disposition except to heirs: see the Edmonton Journal (March 1, 1990), at 1.

21   W. Blackstone, *Commentaries 2* (1765).

22   F.S. Cohen, "Dialogue on Private Property" (1954), 9 Rutgers L.Rev. 357. See also J. Cribbet *et al., Cases and Materials on Property*, 3rd ed. (Mineola, N.Y.: Foundation Press, 1972), at 4, who adopt Cohen's definition of property, including its emphasis on the right of exclusion.

23   *Ibid.*, at 371.

What makes a right of exclusion proprietary or absolute is its reach. It is a right which can be exercised by its owner against all other persons. In other words, it is a right which may be enforced against the world at large. Such a right may be contrasted with a purely contractual right which may only be enforced against a specific individual or individuals. Blackstone's definition ("sole and despotic . . . [right of] exclusion . . . of any other individual in the universe") contemplates precisely this limitless form of right. The same is true of Cohen's summary of the concept of property. He states that property is anything to which the following label can be attached:[24]

> To the world: Keep off unless you have my permission, which I may grant or withhold. Signed: Private citizen. Endorsed: The state.

A rigid and literal application of this definition would preclude all things from being property. Even the landowner cannot meet the standard of a right of absolute exclusion. Social policy dictates, and always has, that the state and its agents, that is, peace officers, health inspectors and others, have the right in defined circumstances to occasionally enter private lands.[25] Moreover, and this point is particularly significant for the thesis of this paper, the landowner's right of exclusion has never been absolute even in respect of private persons.

In Anglo-Canadian common law there are at least three different circumstances in which the interests of private persons have been recognized to prevail over the proprietary right of exclusion.[26] The first is somewhat exceptional and is demonstrated by the 1947 Alberta case of *Dwyer v. Staunton*.[27] In that case, the plaintiff, a farmer, sued a neighbouring rancher for trespass to land. The defendant had been travelling

---

24 *Ibid.*, at 374.
25 The *Ontario Task Force on the Law Concerning Trespass to Publicly-Used Property as it Affects Youth and Minorities* attributes to Blackstone the view that the "law prevented the smallest infringement of property rights, even for the good of the entire community": *supra*, note 2 at 12, citing J. Vandevelde, "The New Property of the Nineteenth Century: The Development of the Modern Concept of Property" (1980), 29 Buff. L.Rev. 325 at 328-32. Whether or not Blackstone was of this view, surely it was an exaggeration.
26 See the text following this footnote for a discussion of these circumstances. The finders cases, arguably, provide an example of a fourth situation. Where an object is found on a portion of private land to which the public is invited there is authority, albeit controversial authority, for the proposition that the landowner's right to the lost item is somewhat diminished and perhaps subservient to that of the finder. See *Bridges v. Hawkesworth*, [1843-60] All E.R. 122; *Hannah v. Peel*, [1945] 2 All E.R. 288; *Parker v. Br. Airways Bd.*, [1982] 2 W.L.R. 503 (C.A.). See also footnote 28 for a discussion of easements of necessity which may be viewed as a fifth situation in which the right of exclusion is limited in favour of private persons.
27 [1947] 4 D.L.R. 393 (Alta. Dist. Ct.).

on a public highway which was blocked by a snow-drift. As a result, and notwithstanding the plaintiff's protestations, the defendant chose to drive over the plaintiff's land. An action was brought and failed. Sissons D.C.J. concluded that under the circumstances the defendant was legally entitled to interfere with the plaintiff's possession of his lands.[28]

The second and third situations in which the right of exclusion is circumscribed in favour of private persons bear some important similarities to the shopping mall cases. Like shopping centres, both innkeepers and common carriers solicit, and are engaged in the business of serving, the public at large. However, neither can refuse to service a particular customer on the basis of the so-called absolute right of exclusion that is entailed in the private ownership of an inn or carriage.[29] For proprietors of these common callings exclusion can only be legally justified if it is based on good reason. If, for example, the inn or carriage is full, or if the customer or the item sought to be carried is dangerous or annoying, the decision to exclude is supportable in law.[30] The mere assertion of bare title by the innkeeper or common carrier was, and is, an insufficient legal basis for an exclusion. It is interesting to note that, in both the United States and Australia, cases which have qualified the right of private landowners to exclude members of the public have made explicit reference to the common calling cases.[31] That innkeepers and

---

28   In a similar vein, the readiness of property law to imply an easement of necessity may be another qualification of the absolute right of exclusion. Once such an easement is implied, the owner of the servient tenement cannot sue the dominant tenant for trespass if the dominant tenant has properly utilized his or her right of way. Such an easement will be implied for the purpose of providing access to land retained by a grantor if the grantor has granted a plot of land and in so doing has isolated him or herself. Similarly, if the grantor has granted a plot of land, and in so doing has isolated the grantee, an easement of necessity will be implied: see E. Burn, *Cheshire's Modern Law of Real Property*, 11th ed. (London: Butterworths, 1972), at 519. The law relating to easements of necessity seems to have been put in place by the medieval period: see A. Simpson, *An Introduction To The History Of The Land Law* (London: Oxford University Press, 1973), at 100-101, 107, 244-47. For the English view of the current status of such easements, see *Nickerson v. Barraclough*, [1981] 2 All E.R. 369 (C.A.). This case places easements of necessity on the footing of implied grants or reservations and not as something arising from public policy. If indeed this is the case, such easements cannot properly be viewed as examples of property law limiting the exclusionary powers of owners. Rather, the owners have limited their own exclusionary powers by granting or reserving the easements.

29   Jurgen Basedow, "Common Carriers: Continuity and Disintegration in U.S. Transportation Law" (1983), 13-14 Transportation Law Journal 1; Crossley Vaines, *Personal Property*, 5th ed. (London: Butterworths, 1976), at 120, 134.

30   Basedow, *ibid.*, at 11-12.

31   *Forbes v. N.S.W. Trotting Club* (1979), 25 A.L.R. 1 (H.C.); *Uston v. Resorts Int. Hotel Inc.*, 445 A. 2d 370 (N.J.S.C., 1982). In these cases it was held that the exclusion of successful gamblers, respectively, from privately owned race

common carriers do not have an absolute right of exclusion could not have been in the mind of the Ontario Court of Appeal when it decided *R. v. Peters*. This is apparent from the following view expressed by that court:[32]

> [A]n owner who has granted a right of entry to a particular class of the public has not thereby relinquished his or its right to withdraw its invitation to the general public or any particular members thereof, and that if a member of the public whose invitation to enter has been withdrawn refuses to leave, he thereby becomes a trespasser and may be prosecuted under the *Petty Trespass Act*.

R. v. Peters is an important case because it was considered by the majority of the Supreme Court in *Harrison v. Carswell* to be of controlling authority. The *Peters* case itself was appealed to the Supreme Court, but that court neither expressly adopted nor rejected the reasoning of the Ontario Court of Appeal.[33]

In American law there are at least two additional circumstances in which courts have limited the proprietary right of exclusion in favour of

---

tracks and from a casino, without just cause, was illegal. In *Forbes*, Murphy J., at 28, stated:

"A householder exercising his property rights of exclusion is not in the same position as persons with licences to conduct public halls, restaurants, theatres or racecourses. From early times, the common law has declined to regard those who conduct public utilities, such as inns, as entitled to exclude persons arbitrarily (see *White's* case (1558), 73 ER 342 (KB))."

In *Uston*, Pashman J., at 375, referring to the case of *State v. Schmid*, 84 N.J. 535 at 562 (1980), stated:

"[That case] recognizes implicitly that when property owners open their premises to the general public in the pursuit of their own property interests, they have no right to exclude people unreasonably. On the contrary, they have a duty not to act in an arbitrary or discriminatory manner toward persons who come on their premises. That duty applies not only to common carriers . . . innkeepers, owners of gasoline service stations . . . or to private hospitals . . . but to all property owners who open their premises to the public. Property owners have no legitimate interest in unreasonably excluding particular members of the public when they open their premises for public use."

32 (1970), 16 D.L.R. (3d) 143 at 146, affirmed 17 D.L.R. (3d) 128n (S.C.C.). A similar proposition submitted by counsel for the mall owner in the *Harrison v. Carswell* case, *supra*, note 2 at 70, was characterized as "extravagant" by Laskin C.J.C. in his dissent.

33 The Supreme Court did not hear the appeal at large. Rather, it was asked two questions of law, the first related to the constitutional validity of the Ontario *Petty Trespass Act*, and the second inquired into the legal ability of the owner of a shopping plaza to sue for trespass under the Act. The court concluded that the Act was constitutional and that the owner did, indeed, have the ability to sue under it. In the result, the Supreme Court agreed with the determination of the case by the Ontario Court of Appeal. The judgment was cursory to an extreme.

private interests. One instance was considered and defined in the remarkable case of *International News Service v. Associated Press.*[34] In that case, a majority of the U.S. Supreme Court held that Associated Press, as a result of its efforts and expenditures in gathering news, had acquired sufficient proprietary rights in that news so as to be able to exclude commercial competitors from news reports and summaries prepared by it until such time as the news had lost its commercial value. International News Service, a competing wire service, had been copying news reports from bulletin boards, and from early editions of newspapers affiliated with Associated Press, and had been selling the reports to International News customers in either original or rewritten form. That the proprietary right of exclusion enjoyed by Associated Press could not be exercised against the world at large was specifically acknowledged. Indeed, because this proprietary right could only be exercised against competitors it was characterized as "quasi-property." As against non-competitors, that is, the public, it was regarded as "common property" in respect of which there were no rights of exclusion.

The second American case in which the proprietary right of exclusion was limited in favour of private interests is the instructive and pertinent case of *State v. Shack.*[35] In that case Tejeras and Shack, two employees of government funded non-profit corporations, entered a farm owned by Tedesco for the purpose of providing medical and legal services to migrant farm workers. The mandate of the non-profit corporations included the provision of health services and legal advice and representation to migrant farm workers. Tejeras sought to assist a migrant worker who needed sutures removed. Shack wished to consult a particular migrant worker with respect to a legal problem. Shack was also present to contend with the legal difficulties that were anticipated would arise as a result of the attempted entry onto the farm. Shortly after entry Tejeras and Shack were confronted by Tedesco. After some discussion, Tedesco offered to locate the migrant workers in question, but insisted that the workers be attended to in his presence. When this offer was declined on grounds of privacy Tedesco summoned the authorities, who reluctantly charged Shack and Tejeras with violation of New Jersey's trespass statute. The defendants were convicted at first instance,[36] but successfully appealed. Their acquittals were based purely on private law principles.[37] Weintraub C.J., delivering the opinion of the

---

34   248 U.S. 215 (1918) (U.S.S.C.).
35   277 A. 2d 369 (N.J.S.C., 1971).
36   Convictions were entered by both a municipal court and, on appeal by trial *de novo*, a county court.
37   See, *supra*, note 35 at 371-72, where the court states that it was unnecessary to explore the defendants' constitutional claims because it is "satisfied that under . . . State law the ownership of real property does not include the right to bar

New Jersey Supreme Court, held that the conduct of the defendants was not trespatory because the possessory right of the farm owner had not been invaded. More specifically, he held that there was legal justification for the interference of Tedesco's possessory interest.[38]

It should be clear from the foregoing that, though the right of exclusion is an essential attribute of property ownership, the scope of this right may, and does, vary. In most instances, the right is absolute in the sense that it may be exercised against all private persons, but in other circumstances, both exceptional and routine, the right of exclusion may be compromised slightly or even significantly. That the right of exclusion may be limited seems to have been lost on many of the courts who have deliberated on the issue. Even commentators who have criticized the judgment in *Harrison v. Carswell* have assumed that the early common law conception of property was, indeed, absolute.[39] The foci of their energies have been (quite properly) to criticize the courts for adopting a rigid and ancient view of property, developed in a static agrarian society in which competing uses of land and, more generally, other competing interests, were absent or minimal.[40] In *Harrison v. Carswell* itself, Laskin C.J.C., in his dissent, questioned the "aptness" of "old doctrine developed upon a completely different social foundation."[41] It may well be that our idcas of property were developed in a mediaeval society, but, transcending generalities, it is undeniable that even then property was not absolute. To the mediaeval lawyer the notion that an innkeeper or common carrier did not have an absolute right of exclusion would have been anything but surprising.

---

access to governmental services available to migrant workers and hence there was no trespass within the meaning of the penal statute."

38   See the text accompanying notes 58-61, *infra*, for a review of these justifications.

39   See, *e.g.*, John Ulmer, "Picketing In Shopping Centres: The Case of *Harrison v. Carswell*" (1975), 13 O.H.L.J. 879 at 883, where he states that the absolute notion of property is "an unchallengeable tenet of property law a few centuries ago."

40   See Ulmer, *ibid.*, at 881, where he writes: "[T]he history of trespass to land is bound up with the need of an agricultural society to establish continuous and exclusive rights to the ownership of land." See also Morton J. Horwitz, "The Transformation in the Conception of Property in American Law, 1780-1860" (1972-73), 40 U. of Chic. L.R. 248, where it is stated that "the prevailing ideals of absolute property rights arose in a society in which a low level of economic activity made conflicts over land use extremely rare." Finally, see R. Stoykewych, *supra*, note 4 at 54.

41   *Supra*, note 2 at 75.

III. PUBLIC POLICY AND THE QUALIFIED RIGHT OF EXCLUSION

What has been the legal basis for diluting the absolute right of exclusion? The answer, of course, is public policy. The same forces which have shaped the substantive content of property — its standard incidents and the ever-present right of exclusion — have tempered the right of exclusion. Like all legal institutions, property is instrumental or purposive in character. It promotes diverse, and frequently competing, interests including psychological, moral, economic, sociological and pragmatic interests.[42] Some of these interests are of profound importance and greatly affect the quality of our human existence. This is particularly true of the privacy and security functions which property serves. Moreover, some of the interests promoted by property are instrumental themselves. For example, privacy promotes the interests of intimate association and, as noted above, free speech. Even economic well-being, which is a vital, if not paramount, goal of the law of property,[43] promotes individual freedom, provides individuals with a sense of security and independence, and contributes substantially to pluralism in the community.[44] It is because property is not an end in itself[45] that it has been referred to, without exaggeration, as a "human right."[46] That property promotes, and indeed is merely an expression of, human values has vital significance to the issue of whether property should

---

42 See J. Cribbet, "Concepts In Transition: The Search For A New Definition Of Property" (1986), U. of Ill. L.R. 1 at 39, where the author states "Many disciplines — history, philosophy, economics, sociology, law — shape our concept of property." See also Cohen, *supra*, note 22 at 368-69.

43 See Morton J. Horwitz, *supra*, note 40.

44 Horwitz, *ibid.*, at 290, has argued that it was the growing accommodation of economic interests that transformed property from an "absolute notion, an end in itself, to the notion of a productive asset which was instrumental in its character . . . justified not for its own sake but for its contribution to increased national wealth."

45 Cribbet, *supra*, note 42 at 41 quotes the renowned European jurist, Professor von Jhering, as stating that "[t]here is no absolute property, i.e., property that is freed from taking into consideration the interest of the community, and history has taken care to inculcate this truth into all people." See R. von Jhering, *Der Geist Des Romischen Rechts Auf Den Verschiedenen Stuffen Seiner Entwicklung* 7, 4th ed. (1878).

46 For an elaboration of this theme, see Leonard W. Levy, "Property as a Human Right" (1988), 5 Constitutional Commentary 169. For judicial support of this proposition, see *Lynch v. Household Fin. Corp.*, 405 U.S. 538 at 552 (1972) (U.S.S.C.), where Stewart J. remarked "[t]hat rights in property are basic civil rights has long been recognized." See also *State v. Shack*, supra, note 35 at 372 where Weintraub C.J. stated that "[p]roperty rights serve human values. They are recognized to that end, and are limited by it."

accommodate the interest of free speech by moderating the normal right of exclusion associated with ownership.

Even in the absence of historical experience it would be rather surprising if the proper balance of the various underlying goals, values and policies which shape, and give substance to, property invariably gave rise to an absolute right of exclusion. The myriad of underlying interests, the different contexts in which these interests would have to be balanced, the changes over time to these interests and their priorities in relation to one another, and changes to the contexts in which property issues arise, make it inconceivable that justice could always best be served by either the unqualified right of exclusion or the complete absence of this right. Surely, the middle ground between property and no property, that is, the qualified right of exclusion, will be the best solution to some problems.[47] That the curtailment of absolute property is possible, even necessary, for both social policy and contextual reasons, is adverted to in the following extract from *State v. Shack*:[48]

> The subject is not static. As pointed out in 5 Powell, Real Property (Rohan 1970, § 745, pp. 493-494), while society will protect the owner in his permissible interests in land, yet . . . "[S]uch an owner must expect to find the absoluteness of his property rights curtailed by the organs of society, for the promotion of the best interests of others for whom these organs also operate as protective agencies. The necessity for such curtailments is greater in a modern industrialized and urbanized society than it was in the relatively simple American society of fifty, 100, or 200 years ago. The current balance between individualism and dominance of the social interest depends not only upon political and social ideologies, but also upon the physical and social facts of the time and place under discussion."

The case law described earlier in this paper pertaining to common carriers and innkeepers suggests that owners' rights have been diminished for public policy reasons since at least mediaeval times.[49] Though the precise reasons underlying the obligation of inns to receive guests is somewhat debatable, it seems clear that, at a minimum, the law was attempting to promote security of the person or, more generally, public

---

47 See Laskin C.J.C.'s dissent in *Harrison v. Carswell, supra,* note 2 at 75, where he observes that courts in the United States appreciate that competing interests cannot properly be reconciled by a "flat all or nothing approach." In other contexts, property law, in both its common law and statutory form, has recognized the wisdom of rejecting the "all or nothing" approach. See, *e.g., Festing v. Allen* (1843), 12 M. & W. 279, *Andrews v. Partington* (1790), 3 Bro. C.C. 60, 401, and the Alberta *Perpetuities Act,* R.S.A. 1980, c. P-4, s. 7.

48 *Supra,* note 35 at 372-73.

49 At least since *White's* case, *supra,* note 31, decided in 1558.

safety.[50] There is also considerable credibility to the theory that the duty to provide hospitality for guests furthered the interests of commerce.[51] The rationale for the obligation of common carriers to haul the goods of all who demand their services is even more debatable. It has been argued that the obligation has economic or commercial roots.[52] Others have argued that the origin of this obligation is political.[53] It is suggested, however, that the political rationale, if closely read, can also be viewed in commercial or economic terms.[54] In any event, the only credible

---

50 In *R. v. Rymer* (1877), 2 Q.B. 136 at 140-41, Denman J. stated that "the object of the law upon the subject of an innkeeper's liability is merely to secure that travellers shall not, while upon their journeys, be deprived of necessary food and lodging." A more informative and colourful explanation was provided by the Supreme Court of New York in *Crapo v. Rockwell*, 94 N.Y.S. 1122 (1905). In its discussion of the innkeeper's strict liability for loss of its guest's goods the court stated, at 1123:

> "[T]his rigorous rule had its origin in the feudal conditions which were the outgrowth of the Middle Ages. In those days there was little safety outside of castles and fortified towns for the wayfaring traveller, who, exposed on his journey to the depredations of bandits and brigands, had little protection when he sought at night temporary refuge at the wayside inns, established and conducted for his entertainment and convenience. Exposed as he was to robbery and violence, he was compelled to repose confidence, when stopping on his pilgrimages overnight, in landlords who were not exempt from temptation; and hence there grew up the salutary principles that a host owed to his guest the duty, not only of hospitality, but also of protection. With the march of civilization and the progress of commercial development, the conditions in which the common-law liability of the innkeeper to his guest originated have passed away; but other conditions exist, which render it wise and expedient that the modern hotelkeeper should respond for the loss of his guest's property."

51 In an early 19th century commentary on the state of the law pertaining to innkeepers it was said:

> "[R]igorous as this law may seem, and hard as it actually may be in one or two particular instances, it is founded on the great principle of public utility to which all private considerations ought to yield; for travellers who must be numerous in a rich commercial country, are obliged to rely almost implicitly on the good faith of inn-holders."

See W. Jones, "An Essay on the Law of Bailments," in Lord Teignmouth (ed.), *The Works of Sir William Jones 8* (1807), at 426.

52 Basedow, *supra*, note 29 at 5-9.

53 *Ibid.*, at 8-9. Basedow, also suggests at pp. 7-8, that there may be a purely legal rationale for the rule. However, he rejects this explanation as the least persuasive of the various theories.

54 *Ibid.* This is apparent from the following extract where Basedow develops the political rationale as follows:

> "The English feudal society, during the 17th and 18th centuries, spent only a part of the year on the land from which it derived its income. For much of the year the nobility lived in towns supported by income from the surround-

contemporary justification for the rule requiring common carriers to accept the goods of all persons is the furtherance of commerce. In sum, the qualification of the property rights of innkeepers and common carriers is based upon the public policies of supporting both productive economic activity and the safety of the public.

The mobility and safety of the public appear to have been the reasons for qualifying the rights of exclusion of the plaintiff farmer in *Dwyer v. Staunton*.[55] Sissons D.C.J. specifically addressed the balance between property rights and these interests, and concluded as follows:[56]

> I have considerable sympathy with the plaintiff in his insistence on his private property rights. Those rights should be respected, but I must hold that there are higher rights — the rights of the public.

In principle, if the social imperatives of security of the person, public mobility and economic development are capable of moderating property rights, then the same should be true of other pressing social values, including freedom of expression. Both the *International News Service* case and *State v. Shack* support this hypothesis. In the former case it was the public interest in the free flow of information, including information about current events, that circumscribed the limited pro-

---

ing estates. Hence, the aristocracy depended heavily upon both the availability and the safety of carriage for passengers and goods. The movement of commodities could not be entrusted to the arbitrary, profit-oriented decisions of those engaged in the industry. The liability of the carrier had to be tightened to forestall collusion with thieves. Although the same danger existed with respect to other bailees, they were less important to the nobility. The professions which survived as common callings into the 19th century can be easily linked to the infrastructure of transportation. This is obvious for common carriers of all kinds, such as ferrymen, bargemen, wharfingers, lightermen, innkeepers, as well as farriers and smiths, who were indispensable links in the preindustrial transportation chain . . .

"In a sector of the economy where both monopoly and competition coexisted, the dependency of the upper classes on public transportation is the better explanation for the particular burden which the common law imposed indiscriminately on all common carriers. In economic terms, transportation generated positive external effects of a political, social and economic nature which extended beyond the individual transport operation and were not sufficiently rewarded by the carrier's charges . . ."

55 *Supra*, note 27 at 395 where *Morey v. Fitzgerald*, 56 Vt. 487 at 489 (1884), is relied on for the proposition that private property may be interfered with for reasons of "public safety or convenience." Moreover, *Broom's Legal Maxims*, 10th ed. (1939), at 2 is quoted in support of the defendant's right to enter to the plaintiff's private lands in view of "the public good that there should be, at all times, free passage along thoroughfares for subjects of the realm."

56 *Ibid.*, at 397.

prietary right in news awarded to the Associated Press.[57] In *State v. Shack* several reasons were offered as justifications for moderating the standard proprietary right of exclusion. Protection of the migrant workers' privacy and their opportunity "to live with dignity and to enjoy associations customary among . . . [American] citizenry" were considered vital interests which should override the property owner's interests, including commercial interest, in controlling access to his or her property.[58] An additional reason relied upon by the court for curbing the customary proprietary right of physical control was the importance attached to protecting free speech, not as an end in itself but as a means of ensuring the viability of important social policy to which government was committed.[59] Indeed, Weintraub C.J. framed the central issue in the case as "whether the camp operator's rights in his lands may stand between the [underprivileged and powerless] migrant workers and those who would aid them."[60] The conclusion that property would not be permitted to be a barrier to such aid was supported by Weintraub C.J.'s observation that "the key" to protecting migrant farm workers was "communication."[61] It seems beyond debate, as both *International News Service* and *State v. Shack* clearly demonstrate, that in American law free speech as an instrumental value[62] is capable of trumping rights

---

57 See the early part of Brandeis J.'s dissenting judgment, though, admittedly, he is not absolutely explicit about this: *supra*, note 34 at 234-35. For reasons of public policy, it is undoubted that ideas and information do not ordinarily generate exclusive rights in their originators or those engaged in the gathering and dissemination of the same. Most, and certainly the most important, exceptions to the non-proprietary status of information are statute-based (*e.g.*, patents, copyright and trademarks). Associated Press' proprietary right in the news in the *Int. News Service* case was awarded against the backdrop of the common law's commitment to an open society in which ideas freely circulate. It is interesting to observe that one of the express reasons why Associated Press was considered to have quasi-property in the news was to promote the policy of gathering and disseminating news by creating an incentive for such activity: *supra*, note 34 at 235, *per* Pitney J.). Accordingly, the policy of promoting the uninhibited circulation of information and ideas in society was instrumental in both the award of property to Associated Press and the limitation of this right.

58 *Supra*, note 35 at 372.

59 The policy was to provide assistance, including medical and legal assistance, to migrant farm-workers. Not only was this policy explicitly articulated by Congress as a legislative goal (see Title III-B of the *Economic Opportunity Act* of 1964, 42 U.S.C.A. ss. 2701 *et seq.*), but its implementation was also funded by a government agency, the Office of Economic Opportunity, created by the same legislation.

60 *Supra*, note 35 at 372.

61 *Ibid.*

62 Though free speech may be a virtuous end in itself, its instrumental utility has long been recognized by scholars, law reformers and the judiciary. It is certainly

of property owners.

IV. THE STATUS OF FREE SPEECH IN ANGLO-CANADIAN PRIVATE LAW

There is no doubt whatever that the Canadian private law system is committed to the value of information flowing freely in the community. Canadian courts have actively asserted the value and importance of free speech in various contexts. Prior to the *Charter*, they did so primarily through an implied Bill of Rights theory. In several cases it was maintained that free speech is the cornerstone of Canadian political liberty and democracy.[63] Though the theory was rejected more recently by a majority of the Supreme Court,[64] the language of the cases which en-

---

the primary mechanism through which information and ideas are circulated in the community at large. It promotes and advances the discovery and dissemination of truth and knowledge, the development of intelligent democratic self-government, the enhancement of the faculties of the citizenry and their polity, self-actualization and realization of individuals through the development of personal morality and rational thought, and, even the development of friendships. See Laurence H. Tribe, *American Constitutional Law* (Mineola, N.Y.: The Foundation Press, 1978), at 576-79, and R. Moon, "The Scope of Freedom of Expression" (1985), 23 O.H.L.J. 331. The values advanced by the law's commitment to the free flow of information are adverted to in the *Report on Trade Secrets* prepared by the Institute of Law Research and Reform of Alberta, Report No. 46 (July 1986). The report, at 123, notes that:

". . . as the importance of information has come to be better appreciated in contemporary societies, a great deal of theoretical and empirical work has been undertaken in disciplines of sociology, economics, communications science, and political science. All of those studies emphasize the interactive character of information and knowledge and its importance, not just to technological progress, but for individual human development as well."

Of course, "human development" is a concept of considerable scope. It is suggested that it covers much of the same ground as the human interests promoted by free speech. The empirical studies referred to in the report are discussed in *Background Paper on Improper Interference with Computers and the Misappropriation of Commercial Information* (Edmonton: Institute of Law Research and Reform, 1983). In addition, Dickson J. (as he then was), in *Cherneskey v. Armadale Publishers Ltd.* (1979), 90 D.L.R. (3d) 321 at 344 (S.C.C.), has suggested that the free flow of new and different ideas is one of the few means for getting unorthodox and controversial ideas before the public. In his view:

". . . [c]itizens, as decision-makers, cannot be expected to exercise wise and informed judgment unless they are exposed to the widest variety of ideas, from diverse and antagonistic sources. Full disclosure exposes and protects against false doctrine."

63 For a collection and discussion of these cases, see C. Beckton, "Freedom of Expression," in Tarnopolsky and Beaudoin (eds.), *Canadian Charter of Rights and Freedoms* (Toronto: Carswell, 1982), at 75-120.

64 See *A.G. Can. v. Montreal* (1978), 84 D.L.R. (3d) 420 (S.C.C.).

dorsed the theory was so effusive and forceful in stressing the importance of free speech that it is difficult to escape the conclusion that free speech is one of the fundamental values which nurtures the common law and circumscribes the rights conferred by it. By way of example, one can point to the classic simile developed by Justice Rand in the case of *Switzman v. Elbling* when he stated that free speech "is little less vital to man's mind and spirit than breathing is to his physical existence."[65] Similarly, Canadian writers have argued that the free flow and exchange of ideas and opinions is of profound importance, and even essential, in a democratic state.[66] Surely there is a credible basis for inferring that those values which form the life-blood of Canadian society provide substance to the public policy of the Canadian legal system, even in its private law manifestations.

The evidence that free speech is an influential factor in the development of private law is irrefutable. As noted above, the policy favouring the uninhibited circulation of ideas and information has long been advanced by the common law, and it is for this reason that our courts have been very hesitant to recognize information or ideas as being the subject-matter of property.[67] The law of defamation also gives expression to the interest of free speech. The United Kingdom's Faulks Committee Report on the law of defamation observed that the torts of libel and slander have two conflicting purposes: to enable individuals to protect their reputation and to protect their right of free speech.[68] In the view of the committee, the challenge to the law of defamation is to "preserve a proper balance between them."[69] In Canada, Dickson J. (as he then was) expressed precisely the same views and added that the various defences to a defamation action, including the defence of fair comment, "give substance to the principle of freedom of speech."[70] He then expanded as follows:[71]

> It is not only the right but the duty of the press, in pursuit of its legitimate objectives, to act as a sounding board for the free flow of new and different ideas. It is one of the few means of getting the heterodox and controversial before the public. . . . The public interest is incidentally served by providing a safety valve for people [through the defence of fair comment].

It is perhaps not surprising, therefore, that the defence of fair

---

65 (1957), 7 D.L.R. (2d) 337 at 358 (S.C.C.) [Que.].
66 Beckton, *supra*, note 63 at 75.
67 See note 57, *supra*.
68 *Report of the Committee on Defamation* (U.K., 1975), Cmmd. Paper 5909 at 4.
69 *Ibid.*
70 *Cherneskey, supra*, note 62 at 342, 343.
71 *Ibid.*, at 344.

comment has been portrayed as "one of the essential elements which go to make up our freedom of speech."[72] The law of defamation, therefore, clearly demonstrates that a "private" interest of considerable consequence, the reputation of an individual, can yield, at least somewhat, to the goal of furthering the free flow of information and ideas.

Personal reputation is not the only portentous interest which has been modified by this goal. The goal of national security also has been said to be subject to the balancing process when it conflicts with the right of free speech. In *Attorney General v. Guardian Newspapers Ltd. (No. 2)*,[73] the British Attorney General sought to utilize private law to enjoin various newspapers from publishing extracts from, and information contained in, the celebrated book *Spycatcher*. In addition, two other remedies were sought: an accounting for profits earned in respect of the serialization of the book, and a general injunction restraining future publications of all material derived from the book's author Peter A. Wright, and all other members of the security service. The duty of secrecy or confidentiality upon which the Attorney General's claim was based was founded in private law. The source of the duty was the employment of Mr. Wright and others with the British security service MI5. This private law duty was transmitted to the various defendant newspapers pursuant to the rule that third parties who come into confidential information, with knowledge of its sensitivity, are bound by the duty of confidence.[74] At first instance, it was argued by the Attorney General that the national security interest, dependent as it was on a strict duty of confidence or secrecy, was a paramount interest that would, as a matter of course, override the interest of freedom of expression. The defendant newspapers, on the other hand, asserted that the prior restraints which were being sought by the plaintiff, even in furtherance of the interest of national security, were anathema to, and an improper fetter of, free speech. Scott J. responded as follows:[75]

> In my opinion, neither view is acceptable. Society must pay a price both for freedom of the press and for national security. The price to be paid for an efficient and secure security service will be some loss in the freedom of the press to publish what it chooses. The price to be paid for free speech and a free press in a democratic society will be the loss of

---

72 *Slim v. Daily Telegraph*, [1968] 2 Q.B. 157 at 170, *per* Denning M.R.
73 [1988] 3 All E.R. 545 (Ch. D., C.A., H.L.).
74 See Scott J.'s and Lord Griffiths' discussions of this point, *ibid.*, at 579-84 and 651-52, respectively.
75 *Ibid.*, at 570. That the interest of free speech and national security have to be balanced against one another was also a central theme of the decision of the Court of Appeal. See, *e.g.*, pp. 611, 623, 629. At the House of Lords level, two of the five judges expressly adopted the balancing approach, Lord Griffiths at 652 and Lord Goff at 659. The remaining Law Lords did not reject the balancing approach.

some degree of secrecy about the affairs of government, including the security service. A balance must be struck between the two competing public interests. Each side, the government on the one hand and the press on the other, is entitled to assert its view of the relative values of these particular interests and of the extent to which one must give way to the other. . . The United States Congress has done so in the form of the First Amendment. Parliament has not. And so it is for the courts to strike the balance.

Even the cases which have considered the conflict between the mall owners' rights of property and the rights of others to engage in expressive activity in malls, seem to leave little doubt that free speech is an interest which private law can accommodate. In *Harrison v. Carswell* the majority of the Manitoba Court of Appeal characterized free speech as both a form of public policy and a "common law right."[76] Though the majority of the Supreme Court of Canada overturned the Manitoba court's dismissal of the trespass conviction, it is noteworthy that they did not reject this characterization by the Court of Appeal.

Whatever doubt may have existed about whether free speech is a head of public policy capable of informing private law should have been eliminated by the enactment of the *Charter*. McIntyre J. made this point in general terms in the *Dolphin Delivery* case when he wrote that:[77]

[the issue of whether the *Charter* applies to private litigation between private litigants] is a distinct issue from the question whether the judiciary ought to apply and develop the principles of the common law in a manner consistent with the fundamental values enshrined in the Constitution. The answer to this question must be in the affirmative. In this sense, then, the *Charter* is far from irrelevant to private litigants whose disputes fall to be decided at common law.

That the judiciary ought to infuse private law with the values set out in the *Charter*, or more generally the Constitution, is not a new idea. In 1983, La Forest J., in an extra-judicial article written for the Canadian Bar Review, stated boldly that "the Charter surely constitutes an authoritative statement of Canadian public policy."[78] Several earlier cases,[79] including the important property case of *Re Wren*,[80] had adopted the

---

76 (1974), 48 D.L.R. (3d) 137 at 141, *per* Freedman C.J.M.
77 *R.W.D.S.U., Loc. 580 v. Dolphin Delivery Ltd.*, [1986] 2 S.C.R. 573 at 603 [B.C.].
78 "The Canadian Charter of Rights and Freedoms: An Overview" (1983), 61 Can. Bar Rev. 19 at 28.
79 See, *e.g.*, *Walkerville Brewing Co. v. Mayrand*, [1929] 2 D.L.R. 945 (Ont. C.A.), and the cases cited therein; see also *Seneca College of Applied Arts & Technology (Bd. of Gov.) v. Bhadauria* (1981), 124 D.L.R. (3d) 193 (S.C.C.) [Ont.].
80 [1945] 4 D.L.R. 674 (Ont. H.C.). The case is somewhat controversial and was

view that both legislation and public law were touchstones of public policy capable of overriding private rights associated with contract and property. Undoubtedly, insofar as either barometer is concerned, the Constitution of Canada is the most reliable gauge of public policy in Canada.[81] In at least one case decided since the enactment of the *Charter*, the public policy embraced by the Constitution did affect the content of private law. In *Native Communications Society of B.C. v. M.N.R.*,[82] the Federal Court of Appeal held that an Indian non-profit corporation had the status of being a common law charity, and was therefore entitled to be registered as a charitable organization under the *Income Tax Act*. The corporation, pursuant to the terms of its certificate of incorporation, was committed to training native people in communications technology, and was also engaged in the publication of a newspaper containing news and information of interest to native people. Its charitable status was based upon its fit into the residual category of charitable purposes, namely, a trust for a purpose beneficial to the community. In assessing whether the society came within this residual category, Stone J. used contemporary bench-marks of social values, namely the *Indian Act* and s. 35 of the *Constitution Act, 1982*.[83] From these, he reasoned that Canada was fundamentally committed to the "welfare of the Indian people," and, since the corporation's purposes and activities contributed to this goal, it satisfied the requirements of a trust of general public utility.[84]

The foregoing leaves no doubt that, in principle, public policy, including the policy in favour of free speech, may, and in some cases should, diminish rights normally associated with private interests, including property. A view to the contrary might be considered to have emanated from *R. v. Stewart*.[85] In that case, the court refused to characterize confidential information as property for the purpose of the theft provisions of the *Criminal Code*. Lamer J. (as he then was), who

---

described as "wrong in law" by Henderson J.A. of the Ontario Court of Appeal in *Noble v. Alley*, [1949] 4 D.L.R. 375 at 390, reversed on other grounds (uncertainty and restraint on alienation) [1951] 1 D.L.R. 321 (S.C.C.) [Ont.]. However, it is crucial to note that the approach utilized to ascertain public policy by MacKay J. in *Re Wren* — as opposed to the conclusion reached by the learned judge — was endorsed by Laskin C.J.C. in *Seneca College of Applied Arts & Technology (Bd. of Gov.) v. Bhadauria, ibid.*, at 202. Laskin C.J.C.'s specific words were that he has no "quarrel with the *approach* taken" by MacKay J. [emphasis added].

81 This, of course, is not to say that the Canadian Constitution is a comprehensive code of public policy.

82 (1986), 23 E.T.R. 210 (Fed. C.A.).

83 *Ibid.*, at 221, 223.

84 *Ibid.*, at 223.

85 (1988), 50 D.L.R. (4th) 1 (S.C.C.) [Ont.].

delivered the judgment of the court, provided several reasons for the court's refusal, including that "society's best advantage may well be to favour the free flow of information and greater accessibility by all [to the information of the alleged owner]."[86] This statement is, of course, consistent with the thesis of this paper that the interest of free speech may override interests which ordinarily give rise to proprietary exclusivity. However, Lamer J.'s judgment can be read as suggesting that the policy in favour of the free flow of information is only relevant in the public law context, and cannot be considered in private litigation. In his reasons for judgment, Lamer J. took pains to make clear that the issue being resolved before the court was one of criminal law, rather than civil law. Moreover, he observed that even if confidential information was property for civil law purposes, this conclusion was not determinative for the criminal law. He then made the following comments:[87]

> It is understandable that one who possesses valuable information would want to protect it from unauthorized use and reproduction. In civil litigation, this protection can be afforded by the courts because they simply have to balance the interests of the parties involved. However, criminal law is designed to prevent wrongs against society as a whole. From a social point of view, whether confidential information should be protected requires a weighing of interests much broader than those of the parties involved. As opposed to the alleged owner of the information, society's best advantage may well be to favour the free flow of information and greater accessibility by all. Would society be willing to prosecute the person who discloses to the public a cure for cancer, although its discoverer wants to keep it confidential?

If this passage is meant to suggest that broad issues of public policy do not affect private litigation, it is out of accord with the realities of private law, including property law. Lamer J. should only have been suggesting that the policy favouring the free flow of information was germane to the property issue in the criminal context, and not that it was immaterial in the civil context.

V. FREE SPEECH AND THE MALL CASES

It is clear that public policy, including free speech, can have, and has had, varying effects on private rights, including property. No doubt, each of the instances discussed above in which property rights have been diminished for reasons of public policy can be distinguished in a myriad

---

86   *Ibid.*, at 12. Lamer J. at the same page also expressed apprehension that the recognition of information as property would have adverse consequences for the mobility of the labour force.

87   *Ibid.*, at 11-12.

of ways from one another and from the focus of this paper, the mall cases. The policies generating the subordination of property rights are variable, as is the precise form that this subordination takes. The innkeeper and common carrier cases can be distinguished from the mall cases on the basis that the limitation of the proprietary right of exclusion in the former cases merely prevented property owners from excluding customers who were seeking to use and pay for the proprietors' services. In the mall cases, the restriction sought would go further, and would prevent property owners from excluding people who not only do not wish to conduct business, but in some cases are at the mall for the very purpose of disrupting the business enterprise. These differences should not be ignored, but should also not be viewed as *per se* justifications for judicial refusal to dilute the property rights of mall owners. Different contexts in which property interests clash with other interests bring to bear different considerations, and in some cases justify different solutions. What is required is a pragmatic approach, without misconceptions about the nature of property, and close analysis of the best possible accommodation of the competing interests. In the mall context, the cases which have considered whether property rights must yield to expressive activity have been very divided. Even the "final word" on this issue, the Supreme Court decision in *Harrison v. Carswell*, emerged from a sharply divided court.[88]

In those cases which have upheld the rights of mall owners to exclude persons engaged in picketing or demonstrations, the courts generally have not engaged in any policy analysis. On the contrary, they have rationalized their conclusions by clinging to the stereotypical view that private property, by definition, equips its owners with the right to exclude invitees from their lands. In *R. v. Page*,[89] a case involving trespass proceedings brought against a loiterer, and not a person wishing to engage in expressive activity, Haines J. noted that property is either private or public, that there is "no such thing in our law as quasi-public premises," and that private owners (such as mall owners) have "all of the rights and duties" of owners "at common law, including the right to invoke the provisions of the Petty Trespass Act."[90] The Ontario Court of Appeal in *R. v. Peters* adopted virtually the same approach.[91] Even in

---

88 The majority comprised six judges and the minority three judges. Their differences related to fundamental legal process issues, including their respective visions of the proper role of the Supreme Court of Canada. The language utilized was immoderate and provocative: *supra*, note 2, particularly at 69-70 and 83.

89 [1965] 3 C.C.C. 293 (Ont. H.C.).

90 *Ibid.*, at 296.

91 *Supra*, note 32 and associated text. As noted in the text, no reasons were given by the Supreme Court in the *Peters* case for affirming the view of the Court of Appeal that the mall owner had sufficient possession of the mall sidewalk so as

Harrison v. Carswell, where various policy issues were addressed, the "bottom line" of the majority judgment was that, if a property owner's right of exclusion is going to be altered, such alteration ought to be effectuated by the legislature.[92]

The cases which have endorsed the legality of expressive activity on mall property have tended to focus on the "public character" of mall lands.[93] This unique character of privately held lands arises from the invitation to and the use by the public of the lands. In *Harrison v. Carswell*, Freedman C.J.M. of the Manitoba Court of Appeal stated that the public's access to malls means that the proprietary interest of their owners is "private property with a difference": that is, "private property that may have to be treated as qualified, depending on the particular situation that has arisen."[94] On appeal, Laskin C.J.C., in dissent, described as "extravagant" the submission that an owner of a shopping centre which is "freely accessible to the public" could whimsically revoke the licence of a member of the public to be on mall lands.[95]

Why should the public character of private lands have the effect of modifying the proprietary right of exclusion? After all, the public's presence in malls is based on the exercise of property rights by mall owners. These owners have conferred on the public a gratuitous right of entry.[96] From a property owner's perspective it could be argued that it would be wrong and ironic if the act of exercising property rights had the effect of diminishing those rights. Certainly, there does not seem to be any reasonable basis in estoppel for suggesting that the mall owner has lost the right of exclusion: it can persuasively be maintained that the invitation to the public impliedly is limited to "shopping for commercial purposes."

In private law there is precedent for diminishing the property rights of owners of land to which the public has been invited. This is the case with respect to innkeepers, and is also the case with respect to lost items found on the "public part" of private lands.[97] Common carriers who

---

to be able to avail itself of the remedy for trespass under the applicable legislation.

92 *Supra*, note 2 at 83.

93 See *Zeller's (Western) Ltd. v. Retail Food etc. Union, Loc. 1518* (1963), 42 D.L.R. (2d) 582 at 585-86 (B.C.C.A.), and *Grosvenor Park Shopping Centre Ltd. v. Waloshin* (1964), 46 D.L.R. (2d) 750 at 755 (Sask. C.A.).

94 *Supra*, note 76 at 138.

95 *Supra*, note 2 at 69-70. Laskin C.J.C., at 73, also stresses the public character of malls.

96 See Cohen, *supra*, note 22 at 373, where he says that "[p]rivate property is a relationship among human beings such that the so-called owner can exclude others from certain activities or *permit others to engage in those activities*" [emphasis added].

97 See text associated with note 29 *ff. supra*, which discusses the position of

have invited the public to utilize their carriage chattels have also been regarded as having qualified rights in their property. With respect to innkeepers and common carriers, as we have seen, there are specific policy reasons justifying this result. In the "finding" cases the rationale is at best debatable and perhaps non-existent.[98] What then is the rationale in the mall context for the reduction of the property rights of the mall owner? The case law has been less than explicit on this point. In some cases, no rationale has been explored.[99] In other cases, the rationale has been based on a vague analogy which often assumes the very point at issue. Typical of this latter approach is the following statement by Laskin C.J.C. in *Harrison v. Carswell*:[100]

> Recognition of the need for balancing the interests of the shopping centre owner with competing interests of members of the public when in or on the public areas of the shopping centre, engaged Courts in the United States a little earlier than it did the Courts in this country. Making every allowance for any constitutional basis upon which Courts there grappled with this problem, their analyses are helpful because they arise out of the same economic and social setting in which the problem arises here. Thus, there is emphasis on unrestricted access to shopping centres from public streets, and on the fact that access by the public is the very reason for the existence of shopping centres; there is the comparison drawn between the public markets of long ago and the shopping centre as a modern market place; there is the appreciation that in the light of the interests involved there can be no solution to their reconciliation by positing a flat all or nothing approach.

Another approach is based on the assertion that the mall is a functional substitute for "main street."[101] Because it operates as a community gathering place, property law regulating the mall should be moderated to account for the public purpose served by the mall.[102] Whether it is legitimate to characterize malls in this manner, and whether it follows from this that a moderated regime of property law should be imposed upon the mall owner, there is a very specific justification for diminishing the property rights of such an owner in the interest

---

    innkeepers and common carriers. See also, *supra*, note 26 for a brief outline of the finders point and the citations to the leading cases.

98 The proposition that lost items found on the "public part" of private land belongs to the finder rather than the landowner may be based upon nothing more than a misreading of precedent. See a discussion of this point in *Hannah v. Peel, supra*, note 26 at 290-91. Of course, the owner of the lost item has a superior right over both.

99 See the cases cited, *supra*, note 93.

100 *Supra*, note 2 at 75.

101 See Kowinski, *The Malling of America: an Inside Look at the Great Consumer Paradise* (N.Y.:William Morrow, 1985), at 65.

102 See the Ontario Task Force, *supra*, note 2, particularly c. 4 at 48.

of accommodating free speech. The development of malls has interfered with speech in both a *de facto* and *de jure* sense and, therefore, the mall owner should be required to compensate the public for that which the mall has taken away. Historically, as it is true today, public highways and streets were forums for effective assembly and expressive activity aimed at particular businesses or endeavours. So long as the activities were peaceful, did not obstruct passage, and were not otherwise illegal, speech and assembly were permitted. In these circumstances there was no nuisance.[103] Trespass was not an issue as their was no invasion of the possessory space of the private owner. The state, the proprietary owner of the streets and highways, had no legitimate interest in, and often no motivation for interfering with, expressive activity occurring in this manner. In this traditional setting, where speech aimed at private interests could effectively be exercised on public property, there was no reason to diminish, or even challenge, the rights of exclusion of private owners. But in the recent past this context has been altered: retail goods are being sold, and services delivered, in malls, in some cases mega-malls. As a result, demonstrations and picketing in the traditional public forums often would be exercises in futility.[104] If property rights were permitted to insulate lessees of land from the influence of speech, an important, if not essential, check and balance will have been lost.[105] With the proliferation of the "malling of America,"[106] the scope of this

---

103 *Williams v. Aristocratic Restaurants (1947) Ltd.*, [1951] 3 D.L.R. 769 at 785-87 (S.C.C.) [B.C.].

104 This point was recognized in the recent case of *Cadillac Fairview Corp. v. R.W.D.S.U.* (1987), 62 O.R. (2d) 337, affirmed 71 O.R. (2d) 206 (C.A.). In this case a mall owner failed in its attempt to exclude union organizers from the common areas of the mall. At pp. 218-19 of the appellate judgment, Robins J.A., delivering the judgment of the court, stated that "[i]f employees entered from the public streets, those streets obviously could be used by the union and its supporters to distribute literature and solicit employees. As it is, organizing activity on the public streets is impracticable." For a discussion of this case see the text associated with note 168 *ff., infra.*

105 In the *Cadillac Fairview* case, *ibid.*, an analogous point was accepted by the Court of Appeal. At p. 216 the argument that the Labour Relations Board had no jurisdiction to abrogate or interfere with Cadillac's private property rights was rejected on the basis that the *Labour Relations Act* required the board to determine whether, in the circumstances of the case, the assertion of property rights amounted to unfair interference with the rights of the employees to information and to benefit from organizational activity. In the course of his judgment, Robins J.A. stated, at p. 219, that "[i]f private property rights are indeed absolute . . . the shopping centre itself creates a buffer of private property between employees and the union which precludes the exercise of . . . organizational rights at the entrance to the work place where the activity can most effectively be conducted."

106 See Ontario Task Force, *supra*, note 2 at 54-59 for a description of the increasing incidence and importance of shopping malls.

problem would not be insignificant. Merchants involved in the sale of controversial materials, perhaps racist in nature, would be less vulnerable to protest if they were capable of paying the steeper rents demanded by mall owners. Their "poorer" competitors (perhaps rightfully) would continue to be susceptible to the pressures created by expressive activity.

In sum, if the law conferred on mall owners the absolute right of exclusion, it would be rendering property into a socially irresponsible institution, a virtual fortress impenetrable to even compelling social policy. Property law must be alert to seemingly innocuous changes in society which subtly affect the civil rights of the public. The theory that innovation of the physical setting in which goods and services are delivered to consumers can affect property law is hinted at in *State v. Shack*. Referring to the balance in property of private and public interests, Weintraub C.J. adopted Professor Powell's statement that:[107]

> The current balance between individualism and dominance of the social interest depends not only upon political and social ideology, but also upon the *physical and social* facts of the time and place under discussion. [emphasis added]

Undoubtedly, the claim that the proprietary rights of mall owners should be tempered in the interest of salvaging civil rights formerly enjoyed on public property will be criticized as a misrepresentation. After all, at common law, Crown ownership of public lands, including streets and highways, was virtually equivalent to private ownership.[108] Therefore, the Crown's right of exclusion, except for the purposes to which the lands were dedicated, was in effect absolute.[109] That free speech and assembly took place on public lands was not evidence of the existence of civil rights but of the tolerance and fair-mindedness of the Crown — these liberties were enjoyed at the sufferance of the Crown. This point was made by Wills J. in *Ex parte Lewis*, where he said of speech and assembly on public lands that:[110]

> Things are done every day, in every part of the kingdom, without let or hindrance, which there is not and cannot be a legal right to do, and not unfrequently are submitted to with a good grace because they are in their nature incapable, by whatever amount of user, of growing into a right.

If speech and assembly exercised on public lands were never civil

---

107 *Supra*, note 35 at 373.
108 Stoykewych, *supra*, note 4 at 50.
109 *Ibid.*, at 51-54.
110 *Supra*, note 4 at 197.

rights, there would seem to be little substance to the notion that mall owners "should give back what they have taken away." Setting aside the fact that, through their developments, mall owners have interfered with these rights in a *de facto* sense, the advent of the *Charter* has given free speech and assembly on public land the new status of *de jure* rights. In the post-*Charter* era, the Crown cannot, on its own initiative, interfere with assembly or speech on its lands without compelling justification.[111] Whatever may have been the status of free speech and assembly on public lands, and the effect these interests had on mall developments prior to the enactment of the *Charter*, under the *Charter* they are real rights which should not be circumvented by private property developments. As a matter of private law, property has not been, and should not be, a refuge for the accountability of its owners or lessees, especially, I would suggest, in relation to activities engaged in by these owners on their lands. Even owners of residential premises, because their properties almost always adjoin public highways and streets, are exposed to the risk of public criticism.

Are significant interests of mall owners compromised by accommodating speech on mall property? The answer to this question forms the core of Laskin C.J.C.'s judgment in *Harrison v. Carswell*. His answer was no. Laskin C.J.C. observed that in a residential context the absolute right of exclusion is a justifiable mechanism for the protection of the privacy interest.[112] But in the mall context there is no parallel interest that can justify the mall owner having the same degree of control. He stated:[113]

> What does a shopping centre owner protect, for what invaded interest of his does he seek vindication in ousting members of the public from sidewalks and roadways and parking areas in the shopping centre?

---

111 See *Ctee. for Commonwealth of Can. v. Can., supra*, note 11. See also *Can. Newspaper Co. c. Directeur des services de la voie publique et de la circulation routière de Québec (Ville)* (1986), 36 D.L.R. (4th) 641 at 658-62 (C.S. Qué.), where Bernier J. appears to accept the proposition that expressive conduct on streets and public ways (in that case the distribution of newspapers) is now constitutionally protected. In *Can. Newspaper Co. v. Victoria (City)*, [1988] 2 W.W.R. 221 at 242, affirmed 46 C.R.R. 271 (B.C.C.A.), Murray J. expresses disagreement with Bernier J.'s "reasons for judgement" and "the reasoning contained in the American authorities quoted by him." However, the thrust of the disagreement seems to be based on the notion that the refusal to permit newspaper vending boxes to be placed on city streets, parks and other public land could be justified under s. 1 of the *Charter* as a prohibition designed to preserve the unique aesthetic appearance of the city of Victoria. There was no indication in the *Victoria* case that Murray J. disagreed with the broad proposition that speech activities on public lands are constitutionally safeguarded.

112 *Supra*, note 2 at 73.

113 *Ibid.*, at 73-74.

There is no challenge to his title and none to his possession nor to his privacy when members of the public use those amenities.

This purposive approach to defining the scope of proprietary rights is the only aspect of either the majority or dissenting judgments which directly and cogently responds to the merits of the issue before the court. The better parts of both judgments are preoccupied with collateral, though not unimportant, issues. Because of the continuing importance of *Harrison v. Carswell*, even in the post-*Charter* era,[114] the next section of this paper will identify, analyze and evaluate these issues.

Dickson J.'s judgment provides five reasons for refusing to dilute the property rights of the mall owner. Four can be characterized as legal process justifications. The first is that any accommodation of free speech would countermand the controlling authority of the *Peters* case,[115] decided only four years earlier by the court. This was a much debated point in the judgment itself.[116] Academicians have also been attentive to this issue. The overwhelming scholastic opinion supports Laskin C.J.C.'s firm view that *Peters* had not decided conclusively the issue which arose in *Harrison v. Carswell*.[117] Not only does *Peters*, on its own terms, purport only to answer the narrow and, arguably, abstract question of whether an owner of a shopping centre has a sufficient possessory interest so as to bring an action in trespass, but, far more importantly, it answers the question without reasons. It does not address (let alone resolve), in any manner, the issue of whether the competing social interests of picketers might be considered a legal justification for an alleged trespass. It does not address why other competing social interests, for example, those which underlie the privileges of hotel guests and customers of common carriers, are such legal justifications, and how the interests of picketers might be distinguished from these social

---

114 See *281856 B.C. Ltd. v. Kamloops Revelstoke Okanagan Bldg. Trades Union* (1986), 37 C.C.L.T. 262 at 269 (B.C.C.A.), *per* Anderson J.A., in which he held that even if the *Charter* was applicable to scrutinize exclusions from malls of individuals engaged in expressive activity, until overruled by the Supreme Court itself, *Harrison v. Carswell* still represents the law of Canada. That the injunction sought in the *Kamloops* case was interlocutory, according to Anderson J.A. at 267, made it "inappropriate" to in effect overrule *Harrison*.

115 *Supra*, note 32.

116 Indeed, in quantitative terms, approximately half of each of the majority and dissenting judgments addresses this issue.

117 See, *e.g.*, J. Ulmer, *supra*, note 39; J. Colangelo, "Labour Law: *Harrison v. Carswell*" (1976), 34 U.T.L.R. 236; and S. Coval and J.C. Smith, "The Supreme Court And A New Jurisprudence For Canada — *Harrison v. Carswell*" (1975), 53 Can. Bar Rev. 819. The reasons for supporting Laskin C.J.C.'s view of the authority of *Peters* are diverse and numerous. Most of these are not explored in this paper.

interests. At best, therefore, *Peters* is an unreasoned pronouncement by the Supreme Court. Surely, as Laskin C.J.C. stated in his dissent, before a case can be said to be controlling it should have "addressed itself to the difficult issues that reside in the competing contentions" of the parties.[118] John Ulmer has made this point neatly and poignantly by stating that "[i]n the Supreme Court at least, precedent ought to be the servant of judicial reasoning, not its master."[119] Resolving the competing interests at stake in *Harrison v. Carswell* on the authority of the *Peters* case truly amounts to "mechanical deference" to the doctrine of *stare decisis*.[120] For the reasons explained above, this is all the more true in the era of the *Charter*, because the legal context in which the issue presents itself also has changed. Therefore, whether or not *Peters* should have been viewed as conclusive authority in 1975 when *Harrison v. Carswell* was decided, it should not be determinative today.

The second and third reasons posited by Dickson J. for refusing to moderate the mall owner's property rights are interrelated. He was concerned that tampering with standard notions of property for the purpose of supporting expressive activity would introduce an unacceptable level of subjectivity into the process of developing law, and, further, that if such subjectivity were engaged in by the courts, the judiciary would be guilty of usurping the legislative function. Dickson J. articulates his concern about subjectivity as follows:[121]

> The submission that this Court should weigh and determine the respective values to society of the right to property and the right to picket raises important and difficult political and socio-economic issues, the resolution of which must, by their very nature, be arbitrary and embody personal economic and social beliefs.

This is a curious and, in the context of *Harrison v. Carswell*, an incorrect assertion. Judicial recognition of rights always advances certain interests and constrains others. Even the least controversial of rights, such as the right of residential owners of property to exclude trespassers from their lands, interferes with the interest of the public in unrestrained mobility. It follows that the right of exclusive possession of a landowner, and, in a larger sense, the entirety of the property concept itself, is inherently a product of balancing interests.[122]

---

118 *Supra*, note 2 at 72.
119 *Supra*, note 39 at 885.
120 See, *supra*, note 2 at 69, where Laskin C.J.C. poses the question of whether the Supreme Court must "pay mechanical deference" to the doctrine of *stare decisis*.
121 *Supra*, note 2 at 82.
122 The significance of this is that the dichotomy between the interest in free speech and the right of property is a false one. A proper balance would involve the "standard" interests underlying property and the interest in free speech.

Balancing necessarily entails weighing and determining the respective values of competing interests. To suggest that the balancing process by its very nature turns on either the personal beliefs of judges or is arbitrary, tends towards exaggeration, perhaps even substantial exaggeration. No doubt these dangers exist, but they are not inescapable. The responsibility of the judiciary with respect to any given problem is to identify and weigh the competing interests that will be affected by the resolution of a particular problem and to balance these interests in a manner that best promotes the public interest. Only if this is done openly can the balancing process be accurately tracked and reviewed for its soundness. In identifying and ordering interests, the judiciary is not called upon to provide its personal opinion, but to assess the status and stature of these interests within the legal system.[123] Undoubtedly, there are vagaries in this process which raise the spectre of personal bias, but, at least in many cases, this spectre can be discounted. Free speech is a consecrated value of compelling importance to the legal system, and not merely an idiosyncratic preference of Laskin C.J.C. In this regard, it is interesting to note that the *Report on Trade Secrets* of the Alberta Institute of Law Research and Reform has characterized the free flow of information as a "compelling" interest.[124] It also suggests that "legal impediments to the free flow of information should require distinct justification, and that each exception to the general norm should be granted only in sufficient, but no more than sufficient terms."[125] Accordingly, taking into account free speech and treating it with due deference when it conflicts with other established interests is neither arbitrary, nor a product of personal belief.

Even the most orthodox of property notions can be tested on the basis of the proposed "analytical model" of first identifying, second, attaching weight to, and finally balancing, the competing interests. For example, as noted above, public mobility is diminished by the standard right of exclusion enjoyed by the owner of residential property. However, the interest of privacy which is promoted by this right is so compelling, particularly since public thoroughfares allow for effective public mobility, that the primacy of the privacy interest is clearly justified. In the context of *Harrison v. Carswell*, surely Dickson J. did not believe that preferring the right of property over the right to picket can avoid the necessity of judicial judgment in the balancing of these

---

123 See S. Coval and J. Smith, *supra*, note 117 at 828, where they state that how various interests are weighed is not a matter of discretion, but rather entails an assessment of "how the law itself has ordered such goals." It is acknowledged, however, that much of this ordering has been done previously by judges exercising their common law function.

124 *Supra*, note 62 at 124.

125 *Ibid.*, at 123.

interests. Where property prevails over speech, an interest which our courts have described as being of profound importance is disregarded. If speech were to prevail over property the same would be true. If a compromise is struck, and the two interests accommodated, is that necessarily a product of arbitrary or subjective decision-making? Undoubtedly, the balancing which Dickson J. refused to carry out in *Harrison v. Carswell* is qualitatively the same type as that engaged in by the courts in the innkeeper and common carrier cases,[126] *Dwyer v. Staunton*,[127] the *International News Service* case,[128] *State v. Shack*,[129] *R. v. Stewart*,[130] and the defamation cases discussed earlier in this paper. The resolution of the balancing process varies with the context and the precise interests which are in competition. In cases involving residential ownership, compelling interests have been thought to be advanced best by the standard proprietary right of exclusion. In other cases, such as *Stewart*, the courts recognized that dominant interests, including both employment mobility and the free flow of information, would be retarded by conferring property rights on individuals.[131] In yet other cases, as has been seen, a compromise between competing interests was reached. The proprietary right of exclusion was qualified.

The challenge in *Harrison v. Carswell* was to assess whether the compromise solution best advanced the public interest. In jumping to the conclusion that "property is property" and courts should not be involved in balancing interests, Dickson J. merely camouflaged the particular balance which his decision effectuated. It is his decision, and not that of the dissenting court, which should be viewed with suspicion or scepticism. After all, what legitimate interest of the property owner is advanced by the majority decision? Laskin C.J.C. was unable to identify such an interest, and for this reason was prepared to modify the usual scope of the property owner's right of exclusion. Beyond stating that the right to property is a societal value, Dickson J. did not identify the property owner's competing interest. Though it is undoubtedly true that society reveres property, that is beside the point. Such an assertion does not address the issue of what is the proper balance between society's commitment to property and its commitment to free speech, another cherished but competing value. Moreover, the argument that society values property suffers from a false notion of what property really is. Property is a conclusory construct designed to further the public interest. It is a label attached to an interest which the legal system believes is

126 See text associated with note 29 *ff.* and 49 *ff., supra.*
127 See text associated with note 27 *ff.* and 55, *supra.*
128 See text associated with note 34, *supra.*
129 See text associated with note 35 *ff.* and 58 *ff., supra.*
130 See text associated with note 85 *ff., supra.*
131 See text associated with notes 85 and 86, *supra.*

best protected by conferring on a person exclusive rights. The legal system should not value property *per se*. Rather, it ought to value the interests which underlie the property concept. Property does not and should not have an existence independent of such interests. As Professor Walter Hamilton has written, "[i]t is incorrect to say that the judiciary protected property; rather they called that property to which they accorded protection."[132] Without identifying the interest being protected under the guise of property, Dickson J.'s preference for property over speech, subject to the cogency of his other reasons,[133] can only be arbitrary, or a product of unstated preferences or mistaken analysis.

Dickson J.'s third concern, that the court not legislate a solution to the *Harrison v. Carswell* problem, is also unfounded. While recognizing the ability of the court to "act creatively," he suggested that the limit of the judicial function is to reason from "principled decision and established concepts."[134] He added, quoting the celebrated American jurists, Holmes and Cardozo, that advances in the law brought about by judges should only be "interstitial" and should only emanate from "consecrated principles."[135] I would suggest, however, that these proposed limitations on the proper role of courts were respected more in Laskin C.J.C.'s dissenting judgment. The driving force behind Laskin C.J.C.'s dissent was the sacrosanct principle of free speech. What Laskin C.J.C. was attempting to do was give it expression in a new setting by moderating an essential incident of property. He did so without sacrificing substantially any identifiable underlying interest advanced by property. That this is both an incremental and interstitial development is attested to by the innkeeper and common carrier cases, as well as the other cases in which the absolute right of exclusion has been modified by common law judges. These cases have been narrowly confined to their unique circumstances, and even in their cumulative effect have not had a major impact on the role of property in the legal system.

A fourth, and even less persuasive, concern expressed by Dickson J. was that the Supreme Court of Canada not usurp the function of the legislature of Manitoba who enacted the *Petty Trespass Act*. In his view, changes to this legislation should be made by the "enacting institution ... which is representative of the people ... and not by this Court."[136] This would be a powerful point if the legislation in question defined the substantive content of trespass and, in particular, formulated the de-

---

132 Hamilton and Till, "Property" 12 *Ency. Doc. Sci. 536* (1933).
133 These are discussed, *infra*, in the text immediately following note 134 and also in the text immediately preceding and accompanying notes 163 and 164.
134 *Supra*, note 2 at 81.
135 *Ibid.*
136 *Ibid.*, at 82.

fence of privileged entry.[137] Instead, the Act and other provincial trespass to land statutes merely incorporate the common law pertaining to trespass. Thus, there is no legislative notion of trespass or privileged entry for a common law court to change. It follows that there is no basis whatsoever for the concern that, by deliberating whether entry into a mall for the purpose of engaging in expressive activity is a privileged entry, a court is usurping the function of the legislature.

Dickson J.'s final objection to the prospect of subordinating property rights to rights of speech was that it would create substantial uncertainty. He cited two U.S. cases which, he warned, illustrate "the uncertainties and very real difficulties which emerge when a court essays to legislate as to what is and what is not permissible activity within a shopping centre."[138] Professors Coval and Smith have summarized this concern as an apprehension about "indeterminacy which is so important to the law and to the public who must know what [the law] is before it can be relied upon."[139] There is no doubt that any accommodation of property and speech will give rise to a degree of uncertainty which would not exist if standard notions of property simply prevailed. The same, of course, is true of the accommodation of any interest which has the effect of subtracting from the absolute right of exclusion of the property owner. In the innkeeper and common carrier cases, limiting the property owner's right of exclusion did not create intractable problems of indeterminacy. Guests and carriage items, it will be recalled, could be refused if inclusion were not practicable, for example, if the hotel or the carriage was full or if inclusion would interfere with the legitimate commercial interests of the proprietors. Consequently, if guests were annoying or goods were dangerous, the right of exclusion could be exercised with legal justification. Lines had to be drawn, and litigation determined, on

---

137 At common law, trespass occurs when there is an unlawful or unjustified interference with the possessory interest that a person has in land. Privileged interference does not give rise to liability. What is privileged depends on the social imperatives of a society. See Prosser, *Handbook of the Law of Torts*, 4th ed. (St.Paul: West Publishing Co., 1971), at 98-99, which is quoted by Laskin C.J.C., *supra*, note 2 at 76. These imperatives are not static. Privilege, therefore, mirrors the changing values and circumstances of changing societies. The early law of trespass was not developed with the unique circumstances of malls in mind. Thus, whether entry into a mall for the purpose of engaging in expressive activity is a privileged entry is an issue which should have been viewed by Dickson J. as unresolved at common law and, in light of the provisions of the Manitoba *Petty Trespass Act*, untouched by statute.

138 *Supra*, note 2 at 81-82. The cases cited are *Amalgamated Food Employees' Union, Loc. 590 v. Logan Valley Plaza Inc.*, 391 U.S. 308 (1968), and *Lloyd Corp. v. Tanner*, 407 U.S. 551 (1972).

139 *Supra*, note 117 at 820.

a case-by-case basis, whether any given exclusion was justified. Exclusion was justified if based on the uncleanliness of the guest, but not, apparently, if based on the illness of the guest.[140]

In balancing competing interests, certainty can be facilitated by the development of guiding principles. Subject to overriding public policy, innkeepers and common carriers could exercise their rights of exclusion to protect the commercial integrity of their enterprises. In *Harrison v. Carswell*, Laskin C.J.C. also viewed the commercial interests of mall owners, tenants and mall users as the touchstone for the proper exercise of the right of exclusion. He stated:[141]

> ... members of the public are privileged visitors [of shopping malls] whose privilege is revocable only upon misbehaviour (and I need not spell out here what this embraces) or by reason of unlawful activity. Such a view reconciles both the interests of the shopping centre owner and of the members of the public, doing violence to neither and recognizing the mutual or reciprocal commercial interests of shopping centre owner, business tenants and members of the public upon which the shopping centre is based.

It is suggested that, in Laskin C.J.C.'s view, misbehaviour occurs when the conduct of a visitor in itself interferes with the commercial activity of a mall. Are the guidelines provided by Laskin C.J.C. a sufficient protection of the commercial interests of mall owners and business tenants? Could it not be said that picketing and demonstrations, *per se*, threaten these commercial interests? After all, in many cases, business interests are the very targets of the expressive activities of protestors. In answering this question it is crucial to distinguish between expressive activity and its effect. Speech, if conducted peacefully and in a manner which does not intimidate and which otherwise accords with legal requirements, should not, in itself, affect the business viability of a mall or its tenants. Though lacking statistical evidence, I feel safe in observing that on some occasions peaceful and lawful protests have little or no effect on the level of commerce, while on other occasions the effect has varied between mild and severe. What explains this diversity of impact? The answer, I would suggest, is the influence that speech has on the recipients of the information. Sometimes the public is swayed and other times it is not. To preclude speech on the ground that its effect may impair commerce, when it is conducted in a manner which does not in itself impede commercial activity, seems highly suspect. Doing so on the basis of property would assign a censorship function to property. Property would then be relegated to the mischievous role of interfering with

---

140 See Crossley Vaines, *supra*, note 29 at 134.
141 *Supra*, note 2 at 74.

one of the essential functions of free speech, that is, its role as a public check and balance against immoral and improper conduct. Property should not, in these circumstances, foil "rational appeal to persuasion."[142]

No doubt, if Laskin C.J.C.'s opinions ultimately prevail, the legitimate commercial interests of mall owners and tenants will require courts to ascertain times of, locations for, and the permissible number of persons who may be involved in, the exercise of expressive activity. Laskin C.J.C. openly recognized that judicial attention would have to be paid to these matters. He stated:[143]

> ... it does not follow that because unrestricted access is given to members of the public to certain areas of the shopping centre during business hours, those areas are available at all times during those hours and in all circumstances to any kind of peaceful activity by members of the public, regardless of the interest being prompted by that activity and regardless of the numbers of members of the public who are involved. The Court will draw lines here as it does in other branches of the law as may be appropriate in the light of the legal principle and particular facts ...

The drawing of lines would have to be done on a case-by-case basis. Factors such as the size and the layout of the mall, the particular location of the target business and the normal operating hours of the mall will all impact on the reasonableness of a particular expressive activity. No doubt, there is some uncertainty inherent in this process, but no more than is involved in judicial regulation of street-based demonstrations. Over time a body of law will emerge to provide guidance to the various interested parties.

Laskin C.J.C.'s judgment seems to suggest that a mall is a public place open to expressive activity, but those engaging in such activity may not unduly interfere with the conduct of mall business. If this is the case, expressive activity can be engaged in or on mall property even if unrelated to the mall or any of its businesses, or even if it can be more effectively conducted elsewhere. A close reading of the previously quoted passage suggests that it is not at all clear that the dissenting judges in *Harrison v. Carswell* are in fact committed to this open-door policy. There is sufficient flexibility in this passage to permit a court to conclude that areas of a shopping mall may not be available at all to persons wishing to engage in expressive activity, depending on the interest being

---

142 See *Halifax Antiques Ltd. v. Hildebrand* (1985), 22 D.L.R. (4th) 289 at 296 (N.S.T.D.), quoting T. Emerson, *The System of Freedom of Expression* (New York: Random House Inc., 1970), at 444-45.

143 *Supra*, note 2 at 77.

promoted by the activity and other circumstances. In concluding that Sophie Carswell was entitled to engage in picketing in the complainant's mall, Laskin C.J.C. considered it important that she was "an employee involved in a labour dispute with a tenant of the shopping centre, and hence having an interest, sanctioned by the law, in pursuing legitimate claims against her employer."[144] Where else, other than the mall, could effective picketing be done by Ms. Carswell?

The issue of whether malls are open to all expressive activities, subject only to the behavioral impropriety of those involved, is, of course, far from settled. Without deeply engaging the issue, there are at least two reasons why courts might endorse a limited access policy over that of an open-door policy, notwithstanding that the latter would contribute to certainty in the law. First, an open-door policy might be viewed as imposing an unfair burden on the mall owner who would have to shoulder the increased costs of maintenance, clean-up, and the provision of security. Why should a private commercial enterprise bear such additional costs where the expressive activity relates to a public interest issue, such as the right to life, and when the issue bears no relevance to activities and endeavours at the mall? Second, courts may want to be circumspect about what will stubbornly be viewed by many as a deprivation of the ancient right of exclusion. Though Laskin C.J.C. was unable to identify the "invaded interest" for which the complainant in *Harrison v. Carswell* sought the right to oust at will members of the public, there may be an economic rationale for maximizing the proprietary right of exclusion. Posner has suggested that "the more exclusive the property right, the greater the incentive to invest the right amount of resources in the development of the property."[145] This rationale, on its face, admits to degrees of exclusivity. Presumably, the appropriate degree depends on countervailing policy. If speech can be exercised effectively or more appropriately elsewhere it may be that the mall owner should be able to preclude such speech from taking place in the mall.

Indisputably, the proper balance between the legitimate interests of the mall owner in controlling exclusively the activities of visitors and the interest of others to engage in speech activities is considerably more complicated than the balance which courts have had to strike between the interests of innkeepers and common carriers and the public who utilize their services. Accordingly, if Laskin C.J.C.'s views are adopted, there will be substantially more doctrinal uncertainty clouding the relative property rights of the mall owner and the civil rights of persons wishing to use the mall for speech purposes than was generated by the

---

144 *Ibid.*, at 74.
145 *Supra*, note 20 at 12.

law of innkeepers and common carriers. However, there is no reason to believe that the magnitude of the indeterminacy will be so great and so prolonged that the public interest would not be advanced by accommodating these competing interests. Laskin C.J.C., in his dissent, notes that courts "draw lines," indeed, "habitually draw lines" in other branches of the law.[146] In the formative stages of resolving legal problems, naturally, there will be some uncertainty about the precise location of those lines. But, over time, it seems hardly plausible that the proper balance between the interests which underlie property and the interest in free speech is so elusive that workable guidelines will never be developed. In discussing the uncertainty that would arise in the private law sphere if the *Charter* were to apply to purely private litigation, Professors Elliot and Grant make the following point:[147]

> Certainty and predictability are, of course, important goals in any legal system and there is no doubt that our ability to achieve them would suffer if the courts were to engage in the kind of examination of heretofore well-established common law rules and principles the *Charter* calls for. But any lack of certainty and predictability would, it can safely be said, be shortlived, and is something with which we would be prepared to live. For us the real concern is about the ability of the courts to fashion a better legal regime for the private sphere by engaging in the kind of inquiry required by the *Charter*.

Comprehensive legislative regulation may be a preferable solution to the problem.[148] But that is not a legitimate reason for courts to protect property at the expense of speech, any more than it would be a legitimate reason for the courts to protect speech at the expense of property.

VI. *HARRISON v. CARSWELL* AFTER THE *CHARTER OF RIGHTS*

The guarantee of free speech in the *Charter* has obvious and direct implications for the *Harrison v. Carswell* controversy. If the *Charter* is applicable to this controversy, then the rules governing its resolution, at least in a presumptive sense, will be more favourable to those wishing to engage in expressive activity than was the case at common law. This is because under the *Charter* there is a presumption in favour of the protection of the various specified rights and freedoms. The early in-

---

146 *Supra*, note 2 at 72, 77.
147 Robin Elliot and Robert Grant, "The Charter's Application In Private Litigation" (1989), 23 U.B.C. L.Rev. 459 at 493-94.
148 *E.g.*, see Bill 149, *An Act to Amend The Trespass to Property Act*, 2nd Sess., 34th Leg. Ont. 1989, which went no further than 2nd reading (February 14, 1989).

dications about the *Charter*'s applicability to the *Harrison v. Carswell* scenario are mixed. In *Russo v. Ontario Jockey Club*, the exclusion of a successful bettor from race-tracks operated by the defendant was challenged.[149] Ms. Russo had been served with written notice, pursuant to ss. 3 and 5 of the Ontario *Trespass to Property Act*, requesting her to leave the premises and notifying her that any subsequent attendance at any of the tracks owned by the Jockey Club would result in her arrest and prosecution. No reasons were given for the club's action. It was apparent that the plaintiff's "misconduct" consisted of the economic damage she visited on the defendant as a result of her betting skills. In a pre-trial motion on a question of law, Boland J. held that, both under the common law and the *Trespass to Property Act*, property owners have the exclusive right to determine who may enter and remain on their property.[150] Moreover, he held that the *Charter* had no application to this action because it was a private action between individuals.[151] No consideration was given to the issue of whether the defendant's use of trespass legislation triggered the application of the *Charter*. Having concluded that landowners, including the defendant, can exclude whomever they wish from their lands and that the *Charter* does not apply to alter this situation, Boland J. stated that this right of exclusion "seems to apply equally to the owner of a home as to the owner of a 'public area,' such as an exhibition, a shopping mall or a race track."[152]

On the other hand, in *R. v. Layton*[153] the *Charter* was applied to limit the effect of the *Trespass to Property Act*. In that case, the accused was attempting to organize employees of a department store situated in a mall by distributing leaflets in the common area of the mall. Scott J. invalidated the effect of the legislation on the basis that it infringed the *Charter* guarantees of freedom of expression and association.[154]

It is not entirely clear why the *Charter* was applied, but it appears to have been based upon the fact that Mr. Layton was being prosecuted under the *Trespass to Property Act*.[155] In principle, this seems to be

---

149 (1987), 62 O.R. (2d) 731 (H.C.).
150 *Ibid.*, at 733, 736.
151 Boland J. concluded that it made no difference that the defendant was closely regulated by government: *ibid.*, at 736.
152 *Ibid.*, at 736.
153 (1986), 38 C.C.C. (3d) 550 (Ont. Prov.Ct.).
154 *Ibid.*, at 572, 574.
155 *Ibid.*, at 562, where Scott J. states that he "see[s] [the *Charter*] as opening the door to a new assessment of statutes such as the *Trespass to Property Act*." He also states, at 563, that the issue in the case is "whether or not the appellant's freedom of expression has been infringed by the action taken pursuant to s. 2(1)" of the Act. Finally, he notes at 563 that "[t]he question, in the present case, [is] whether or not the appellant's freedom of expression has been infringed by the action taken pursuant to s. 2(1) of the *Trespass to Property Act*."

correct. Surely, a prosecution under a statute is a sufficient form of state action to warrant the application of the *Charter*.[156] That the dispute underlying a prosecution is a private one is beside the point. Private disputes often form the backdrop for criminal acts and subsequent criminal proceedings. Moreover, that the prosecution in *Layton* was based upon a provincial statute that incorporates the common law makes no difference.[157]

Assuming that the *Charter* applies to trespass proceedings brought under trespass legislation, what is the current status of *Harrison v. Carswell*? In the *Kamloops Trades Union* case,[158] the British Columbia Court of Appeal adopted the view that *Harrison v. Carswell* is still good law in Canada, at least insofar as the lower courts are concerned. The court did not consider in any detail whether the concerns expressed by Dickson J. had continuing validity in the era of the *Charter*. Rather, the court founded its opinion on the general observation that in *Harrison v. Carswell* the Supreme Court could have altered the law of trespass and that "[t]his is not a case where the law prescribed by the Charter is so different from pre-existing law that we can approach the issues in this case from an entirely new perspective."[159] Consequently, the Court of Appeal concluded that though the Supreme Court may, as a result of the *Charter*, reach a different conclusion than it did in *Harrison*, this determination should only be made by that court and not "by this Court [especially] on an interlocutory appeal."[160] On the other hand, in the *Layton* case, Scott J. concluded that *Harrison v. Carswell* is not only no

---

156 See *R. v. Lerke* (1986), 25 D.L.R. (4th) 403 (Alta. C.A.); *Blainey v. Ont. Hockey Assn.* (1985), 52 O.R. (2d) 225 (C.A.); and *R. v. Big M Drug Mart Ltd.*, [1985] 1 S.C.R. 295 [Alta.].

157 See *Coates v. The Citizen* (1988), 216 A.P.R. 146 at 155-56 (N.S.T.D.) where, in respect to a defamation action in which the plaintiff was relying on certain reverse onus provisions of the Nova Scotia *Defamation Act*, it was said:
"I find that the *Defamation Act* being a provincial statute does provide that connection necessary to allow application of the *Charter* to what otherwise is litigation between private parties. It is the *Act* and the common law which impose upon the Citizen the several "reverse onuses" complained of. . . . Both the *Act* and the common law are amenable to *Charter* supervision. I think it matters not that some of the common law principles are subsumed into the *Act*."

158 *Supra*, note 114.

159 *Ibid.*, at 269.

160 *Ibid.*, at 269, 267. With respect to the court's emphasis on the interlocutory nature of the proceedings, see *Man. (A.G.) v. Metro. Stores Ltd.*, [1987] 3 W.W.R. 1 (S.C.C.), where it was argued that proceedings before the Manitoba Labour Board based upon the provisions of the *Labour Relations Act* should be stayed on an interlocutory basis because the provisions of the Act contravened the *Charter*. The stay was denied.

longer binding but that the issue is "completely open."[161] He reasoned as follows:[162]

> What must be remembered . . . is that those members of the public who in the past could be excluded from property controlled by the occupier, or whose invitation to enter could be revoked by the occupier, were persons whose rights and freedoms were not guaranteed by the Charter . . .
>
> In the present case the occupier has invited the general public to enter upon the "common area" of the mall for one overriding purpose, and probably for the sole purpose, of giving them access to the tenants in order that business may be carried on for the mutual benefit of the public and the tenants, which in turn results in commercial benefit to the mall owners. In my view, the occupier cannot set a condition on its invitation whereby the invitees enter the mall with money in hand but must leave their Charter rights and freedoms outside the mall property. These invitees are different persons from those pre-Charter persons who appear in *R. v. Peters* and in *Harrison v. Carswell* . . . If the occupier wishes to create and maintain private property having an essential public character as part of a commercial venture, it cannot in my view escape the responsibility or the expense of preserving at least a bare minimum of its invitees' freedom of expression guaranteed by the Charter. Anything less would not, in my view, be regarded as reasonable by fair-minded people in our democratic society.

What is conspicuously absent from this extract, though not entirely from the judgment, is a consideration of Dickson J.'s policy reasons in *Harrison v. Carswell* for refusing to moderate the absolute nature of the right of exclusion. The continued vitality of *Harrison* depends on the cogency of these reasons in the post-*Charter* era.

There is little doubt that the concerns which inhibited Dickson J. from engaging in a substantive analysis of the competing interests in *Harrison v. Carswell*, whatever their merits may be in a common law controversy, are considerably less compelling in a *Charter* context. This is so for several reasons. First, as Scott J. observed, *Peters* can no longer be regarded as being a "decisive" authority. Second, the degree of latitude for "judicial law-making," though not unlimited, clearly would be significantly greater. Such law-making would not only be a judicial right, but a constitutionally mandated responsibility. Third, the balancing process which Dickson J. refused to engage in, in the context of the court's common law role, is also "mandated" by the *Charter*. The *Charter* requires balancing of its protected rights and freedoms with other competing interests valued in a free and democratic society. These latter two reasons for viewing the current law as free from the shackles of

---

161 *Supra*, note 153 at 569-70.
162 *Ibid.*, at 568-69.

the majority decision in *Harrison v. Carswell* were endorsed by Scott J. in the *Layton* case.[163] Fourth, Dickson J.'s concern for the primacy of legislation (the *Petty Trespass Act*) would be of no moment. Invalidating legislation on the basis of a *Charter* infringement is one of the primary responsibilities of the courts. Moreover, his final concern relating to indeterminacy, though clearly worthy of consideration, would not justify the absolute triumph of property over speech. At least temporarily, some degree of uncertainty is inherent in the process of balancing interests. Therefore, the expectation of uncertainty in law as a result of the application of the *Charter* should not, in itself, warrant a refusal to balance. If it did, many, if not most, applications of the *Charter* would be thwarted. This is implicit in the following response of Scott J. to the argument that permitting expressive activities in malls will render trespass law uncertain. He stated:[164]

> There are, and will continue to be, many statutes whose post-Charter limits, and indeed very existence, must now be tested if necessary by repeated court challenges. No diligent search is required to find abundant statutes to which the Charter has brought "an air of uncertainty." The *Trespass to Property Act* is entitled to no special consideration and no exemption from this process.

Finally, as noted earlier in this paper, there is no reason to believe that the uncertainty that would be created by a rational balancing of property and speech interests in the mall context would be so severe and so prolonged that balancing should be avoided at the cost of effective free speech.

If the effect of the *Charter* is to reverse *Harrison v. Carswell*, a likely strategic response would be for mall owners to avoid the use of trespass legislation. The purpose in doing so would be to dodge the *Charter*. By enforcing property rights through the use of common law injunctions,[165] or through the exercise of self-help (with the assistance of security

---

163 *Ibid.*, at 569, where Scott J. makes these points as follows:
"Finally, the respondent submits that the balancing of rights as among employees, employers and third party property owners in situations such as those which obtain on mall property is best left to provincial and municipal government. The appellant argues that in this submission the respondent completely disregards the existence of the Charter. It is under the Charter, appellant contends, that his fundamental freedoms are to be weighed against the property rights of the mall owner. I agree."

164 *Ibid.*

165 In *281856 B.C. Ltd v. Kamloops Revelstoke Okanagan Trades Union, supra,* note 114 at 264, the British Columbia Court of Appeal expressly left open the issue of whether an injunction with respect to purely private rights in which government is neither directly nor indirectly involved can be subjected to *Charter* scrutiny.

personnel),[166] the dispute might well be rendered into a purely private matter involving private persons and, therefore, beyond the reach of the *Charter*. It may well be, therefore, that the common law will continue to be the major battleground between mall owners and those wishing to utilize mall property to engage in speech.

The recent cases which have considered the common law status of *Harrison v. Carswell* have not enthusiastically embraced its views. In *Russo v. Ontario Jockey Club*, Boland J. deferred to the authority of *Harrison*, not because he was persuaded by it, but rather because he considered his hands to be tied. He stated:[167]

> It is clear from a review of the trespass case-law in Canada, the United States and Australia, that *only Canada has not yet recognized that the broad right of landowners to exclude persons is inappropriate when the land is open to all the public.* Chief Justice Dickson in *Harrison v. Carswell* ... has effectively precluded the possibility of judicial development in this area by stating that only the legislature should make changes in the law of trespass ... [emphasis added]

Yet a stronger sentiment was expressed in *R. v. M. (E.B.).*[168] In that case, a transit authority initiated trespass to property proceedings against two teenagers who had been asked to leave a subway station because of their misconduct. The teenagers left, but subsequently returned. Naismith J., after reviewing Boland J.'s reasons for judgment in the *Russo* case and, in particular, the above extract, stated that the case law "begins to take on the appearance of an apology."[169] He then proceeded to distinguish *Harrison v. Carswell* on the footing that, in the case before him, it had not been established beyond a reasonable doubt that the notice required by the *Trespass to Property Act* had been given, and also on the basis that the highly public nature of the Transit Authority[170] "resurrects the spectre of s. 15 of the Charter and probably

---

166 For the right of a property owner to physically eject trespassers, see *Ball v. Manthorpe* (1970), 15 D.L.R. (3d) 99 (B.C. Co.Ct.); *Jordan House Ltd. v. Menow* (1973), 38 D.L.R. (3d) 105 (S.C.C.) [Ont.]; and *O'Tierney v. Concord Tavern Ltd.*, [1960] O.W.N. 533 (C.A.). The right to eject is unquestionable. Most of the cases have been concerned with placing limits on this right to ensure that only reasonable force is utilized in any ejectment, that the ejectment is conducted reasonably and does not leave the ejectee subject to a risk of injury after being ejected.

167 *Supra*, note 149 at 735.

168 Ont. Fam. Ct., Nasmith J., Nos. A354097-2, A354098-3, 5th April 1988 (not yet reported).

169 *Ibid.*, at 8.

170 *Ibid.*, at 12, where Naismith J. states that the public nature of the transit authority business is even more extensive than the public aspects of shopping in malls or betting at race-tracks.

makes it applicable."[171] In the course of drawing these distinctions, Naismith J. observed that, though he was bound by the majority judgment in *Harrison v. Carswell*, he was nevertheless "loath to extend [*Harrison*] beyond the situation where the land is a shopping mall or the Ontario Jockey Club to the situation where the land is a public transportation system."[172]

Even in the mall context, *Harrison v. Carswell* has recently been distinguished by the important decision of the Ontario Court of Appeal in *Cadillac Fairview Corp. v. Retail, Wholesale & Department Store Union*.[173] In that case, both at the Divisional and Appellate Court levels, an application for judicial review of an order of the Labour Relations Board was dismissed. The board found various parties, including Cadillac Fairview Corp., the mall owner, guilty of unfair labour practices in excluding union representatives from the mall. The representatives were attempting to organize the employees of Eaton's, one of Cadillac Fairview's prime tenants. It was argued that the order of the board infringed on the proprietary right of the mall owner to demand removal of the organizers under both the common law and the Ontario *Trespass to Property Act*. This argument was rejected by Robins J.A., who delivered the judgment of the court. In his view, the board acted within the ambit of its jurisdiction in balancing, on the one hand, the employees' statutory right of access to union communications issued for the purpose of organizing the employees and, on the other hand, the property rights of the mall owner.[174] The employees' statutory right was founded on s. 3 of the Ontario *Labour Relations Act*, which provides that "[e]very person is free to join a trade union of his own choice and participate in its lawful activities."[175] In Robins J.A.'s view, this provision necessarily implies the right to receive information from unions pertaining to the issue of organizing employees. He stated:[176]

> ... it is manifest that employees must have access to union communications and opportunities for organizational activity. Having given employees the right to decide for themselves whether or not to join a union, the legislature can be assumed to have intended that they be permitted to make a free and reasoned choice. Such a choice necessarily implies that employees have access to union information free from

---

171 *Ibid.* Naismith J. did not comment on whether *Harrison v. Carswell*, if litigated today, would attract the scrutiny of the *Charter* on the basis that the applicability of the *Trespass to Property Act* is a sufficient form of government involvement or action.

172 *Ibid.*, at 11.

173 *Supra*, note 104.

174 *Ibid.*, at 220.

175 R.S.O. 1980, c. 228.

176 *Supra*, note 104 at 217-18.

restrictions that unduly interfere with the flow of information or their freedom of choice. The legislature can also be assumed to have recognized that the organizational rights guaranteed by s. 3 may come into conflict with traditional property and commercial rights in a variety of situations.

The authority of the Labour Relations Board to remove restrictions which interfere with the flow of union information appeared to be based on the prohibition in the Act against unfair labour practices. Section 64 prohibits employers and others acting on behalf of employers from "participating in or interfer[ing] with the formation selection or administration of a trade union."[177] The conclusion that Cadillac Fairview was guilty of an unfair labour practice was premised on the employees' right to benefit from organizational activity, and the duty of employers and their "agents" to refrain from interfering with this activity. However, it is not in all cases that the exclusion of union organizers from a mall is properly viewed as an unfair trade practice. According to Robins J.A., two factors tipped the balance in favour of the view that Cadillac Fairview had conducted itself illegally. First, the union, in its attempts to disseminate information to the employees, had conducted itself in a manner which did not interfere with the business interests of the mall owner or its lessees and, second, there was no other effective forum for the dissemination of the information other than in the mall itself.[178] Having found the mall owner guilty of an unfair labour practice, the Labour Relations Board ordered Cadillac Fairview to permit the union to engage in limited organizational activities on the mall premises.

How could such an order be reconciled with *R. v. Peters* and *Harrison v. Carswell*? The answer is that, in those cases, the issue of the mall owner's right of exclusion did not arise in the context of a "labour relations statute and . . . [was] not judged in that framework."[179] In both of the Supreme Court cases the trespassers sought, albeit unsuccessfully,

---

177 *Supra*, note 175.
178 For an extensive discussion of the absence of an effective forum for communication, see Robins J.A.'s reasons for judgment, *supra*, note 104 at 218-19. At p. 220, Robins J.A. summarizes the balancing process engaged in by the Labour Relations Board in the following terms:
  "It examined Cadillac Fairview's commercial interest in its no-solicitation policy in light of the lack of means of communication with employees available to the union off the shopping centre premises. To the extent that there was no commercial interest that required protection, the Board found a violation of the Act and abrogated the no-solicitation rule. Once Cadillac Fairview was found to have no valid business purpose that would justify its interference with the protected union activity, its property rights were required to yield, at least to the limited extent ordered by the Board, to the employees' s. 3 organizational rights."
179 *Ibid.*, at 220.

to justify their trespass on common law grounds, whereas in *Cadillac Fairview* there was a statutory basis for the planned future incursions on the possessory interest of the mall owner. As Robins J.A. stated, referring to *Peters* and *Harrison*, "these precedents cannot be read so as to give shopping centre owners the unfettered right to control the use of their premises without regard to the provisions of the *Labour Relations Act*."[180]

If *Cadillac Fairview* has been correctly decided by the Ontario Court of Appeal, and I suggest it has, the decision has considerable significance for unions attempting to organize employees of mall businesses. The underlying reasoning in the case is applicable to virtually all provinces who have provisions equivalent to ss. 3 and 64 of the Ontario *Labour Relations Act*.[181] Undoubtedly, the biggest impediment to the portability of the *Cadillac Fairview* decision to other cases involving attempts to organize employees of mall businesses is that an unfair labour practice generally can only be committed by an "employer or employers' organization" or "a person acting on behalf of the employer or employers' organization."[182] In *Cadillac Fairview*, some of the reasons for concluding that the mall owner acted on behalf of the employer, Eaton's, were idiosyncratic to the facts of that case. However, most were not.[183] On the other hand, it must be emphasized that *Cadillac Fairview* cannot be viewed as a breakthrough which has reversed, in general terms, the dogma that mall owners have an absolute right of exclusion. It is an exception to that rule, albeit an important exception. Though its scope is not entirely clear, we know it has no application outside the labour relations field. Hence, it does nothing to improve accessibility to malls for persons who wish to engage in expressive activities relating to non-labour issues. To pursue the example given earlier in this paper, there is no board with authority to provide entry into malls to persons who wish to demonstrate against the sale in malls of racially divisive material. Moreover, even in a labour context, *Cadillac Fairview* has limited application. Many of the issues, activities and goals which are likely to mobilize labour organizations to engage in expressive activities are not protected, directly or indirectly, by labour relations legislation. There is no reason to believe, for example, that *Cadillac Fairview* has any implications for a union which wishes to protest against the use of non-unionized labour in the renovation of a mall or, more generally, to

---

180 *Ibid.*
181 See, *e.g.*, ss. 19 and 146(1)(a) of the Alberta *Labour Relations Act*, S.A. 1988, c. L-12.
182 See s. 64 of the Ontario *Labour Relations Act, supra,* note 175.
183 These reasons are listed in the decision of the Divisional Court. See *supra*, note 104 at 343-44. Robins J.A. adopts the reasoning of Gray J. of the Divisional Court in this regard: *supra*, note 104 at 222.

engage in secondary picketing. Whether *Cadillac Fairview* can be extended to a primary picketing situation, such as that involved in *Harrison v. Carswell* itself, is unclear and remains to be seen.[184]

Cadillac Fairview and the other few cases which have recently distinguished themselves from, or voiced discomfort with, *Harrison v. Carswell* are significant, for they exhibit judicial willingness to reconsider the aptness of applying absolute notions of property in the mall context.

VII. CONCLUSION

For reasons discussed earlier in this paper, both the *Charter* and labour relations legislation are likely to have a limited impact on the mall owner's right to exclude persons engaged in expressive activity. In the case of labour statutes this is not surprising, as they are not intended, *per se*, to promote free speech. In these statutes, freedom of expression is an implicit and necessary mechanism through which a specified, but limited, number of other goals, such as the desire to provide the labour pool with a meaningful opportunity to organize, are achieved. In the case of the *Charter*, despite its commitment to safeguarding expressive activity, in practice it is likely to be of only limited effect. Even if the displacement of *Harrison v. Carswell* by the application of the *Charter* is a foregone conclusion, which it is not,[185] it appears that the *Charter* can be bypassed through the simple expediency of avoiding the use of trespass to property legislation and relying instead on the private right of exclusion afforded by the common law. This, of course, is the unfortunate legacy of what *Dolphin Delivery* failed to deliver.[186] It appears, therefore, that in the mall context it is largely up to private law to champion or suppress free speech. As frightening and depressing as this thought may be to civil libertarians, such a reaction may be premature

---

184 Primary picketing is a statutory right, but interference with this right is not prohibited, at least explicitly, by the unfair labour practices provisions of the various labour relations statutes. Whether such a prohibition may be read into these provisions is not clear. It is suggested that, based on *Cadillac Fairview*, an order of a Labour Relations Board which provides a union or a group of employees with access to a mall owner's property can only be properly founded on the infringement of a statutory prohibition by the mall owner. If such an order could be founded on mere interference with the right to picket, then *Cadillac Fairview* has enormous implications.

185 See the discussion in the text associated with note 159 *ff.*, *supra*.

186 This turn of phrase is borrowed from Professor Gibson's article entitled "What Did *Dolphin Deliver?*" in G.A. Beaudoin (ed.), *Your Clients and the Charter — Liberty and Equality* (Montreal: Yvon Blais, 1988), at 75.

and unduly pessimistic.[187] Property law is as much a creature of the public interest as any other field of law. It has been shaped, and will continue to be contoured, by the same courts utilizing the same raw materials as have moulded the very significant commitment of the common law to the free flow of information.

This paper has attempted to demonstrate that there are several reasons for being optimistic that *Harrison v. Carswell* will be reconsidered and reversed. The majority view in that case seems to have been based on the supposition that property is inherently absolute and that the dramatic step of depriving its owner, even to a limited extent, of its unbridled power is a matter for legislative policy. This supposition, I have suggested, as a matter of historical record, is not entirely accurate. Proprietary rights of exclusion, like other private rights, have been modified or subordinated to accommodate a variety of interests since the early days of the common law, and continue today to yield to such interests. The policy in favour of the free flow of information or free speech has had a significant influence on critically important private rights, such as the right to maintain one's reputation and the right to protect the privacy of confidential and potentially very valuable information. It has even been said, in the *Guardian Newspaper* case, to be an interest which should be balanced against the public interest in national security.[188] There is no reason in principle why free speech should not be part of the constellation of considerations which affect the determination of whether property rights exist and, if so, whether those rights are tempered by the public interest.

Another reason for believing that *Harrison v. Carswell* may have reached its time is that the dissenting approach of Laskin C.J.C. accords with, and stands up to the scrutiny of, a purposive analysis. Modern decision-making, in both public and private law, is imbued with the purposive approach. It is commonplace for rules to be scrutinized in terms of underlying policy, and this is so even with respect to the most "technical" of property law issues.[189] Such an approach is attractive because it is a check against the development and application of both overbroad and under-inclusive doctrine. In *Harrison v. Carswell*, the

---

187 In *State v. Shack, supra*, note 35 at 372, Weintraub C.J. stated that, on the facts of that case, private law would serve the interests of migrant workers "more expansively" than constitutional law. Presumably this is because private law is not limited by the artifice of the state action requirement.

188 See the text associated with note 73 *ff., supra*.

189 See *Can. Export Gas & Oil Ltd. v. Flegal* (1977), 80 D.L.R. (3d) 679 (Alta. T.D.), where Stevenson J. (as he then was) engages in this form of analysis to determine whether an exception to the operation of the rule against perpetuities should be extended to an option to perpetually renew a *profit à prendre*.

dissenting judgment concluded that neither the essential business purpose of the mall, nor any other identifiable interest, was jeopardized by the expressive activity of Sophie Carswell. Similarly, in *Cadillac Fairview* the Court of Appeal held that once the mall owner "was found to have no valid business purpose that would justify its interference with the protected union activity, its property rights were required to yield . . . to the employees' . . . organizational rights."[190]

Yet another reason for being optimistic that *Harrison v. Carswell* will be overturned is based on direct analogy to the *Cadillac Fairview* decision. In that case, the Ontario Court of Appeal recognized the severe difficulties faced by unions in their attempts to communicate with unorganized employees of mall businesses outside the physical confines of the mall.[191] Indeed, on the facts of that case it was clear any such attempt would be ineffectual. The court stated:[192]

> In the case of Eaton's, its large work-force of full and part-time employees is employed in a store wholly located within the Eaton Centre. None of the employee entrances to the store premises abut public property; they are all within private property under the control of Cadillac Fairview. If employees entered from the public streets, those streets obviously could be used by the union and its supporters to distribute literature and solicit employees. As it is, organizing activity on the public streets is impracticable. Employees using the subway need not use the public streets and those using the public streets are indistinguishable from others entering the Eaton Centre.

Since, in *Cadillac Fairview*, the statutory right of employees to organizational information depended on access by the union to the mall, the court upheld the order of the Labour Relations Board that such access be provided. Any other approach would have permitted private property to override this fundamental statutory right. On this point, Robins J.A. stated:[193]

> If private property rights are indeed absolute, the result is that, while the areas of the shopping centre necessarily used by employees to gain entrance to their work place are functionally equivalent to the public streets, the shopping centre itself creates a buffer of private property between employees and the union which precludes the exercise of . . . organizational rights at the entrance to the work place where the activity can most effectively be conducted.

Similarly, if title to mall property can be the basis for excluding

---

190 *Supra*, note 104 at 220.
191 *Ibid.*, at 218-19.
192 *Ibid.*
193 *Ibid.*, at 219.

speech which can only be meaningfully conducted on mall premises, then the right to free speech, and with it the potential utility of the speech, will have been undermined. Surely, in some cases it is legitimate for courts to insist that forums which make speech effective be made available to those who wish to engage in expressive activity. Since mall owners have, through their developments, deprived the public of an effective forum for the exercise of speech which is targeted at particular businesses and business practices, it is entirely reasonable that the common areas of malls be substituted for these forums. It would be regrettable, indeed, if mall developments sterilized the presumptive constitutional right to influence by persuasion members of the public on the streets of our land.

The degree of commitment by our courts to free speech as an instrumental value will be tested in part by their willingness to ensure that conditions which make free speech effective are not negated by private property developments. The scale and incidence of mall developments suggest that their effect on free speech is significant and, undoubtedly, of growing importance. In adjudicating the competition between free speech and property it is to be hoped that courts will not be victimized by the metaphor that property is a bundle of rights. Property is both more and less than that. Built into its very fabric are numerous limitations and responsibilities. These reduce the rights of property owners, but increase the stature of property as a socially responsible construct. Like all other legal institutions, property is evolutionary. It responds to changes in society itself. Accordingly, the bundle of rights and responsibilities which constitute property is no longer the same as it once was, and differs today from what it will be in the future. Professor Cribbet, in analyzing the evolution of American property law, has stated that "[p]roperty does include state-protected individual rights, but the balance between individual and social rights and responsibilities is in transition."[194] He goes on to remark that the developing trend is "an increase in the social responsibilities of the land owner and a corresponding decrease in the owner's rights."[195] In the case of malls, the social responsibilities of their owners must be responsive to what the public has lost as a result of their development. Though the evidence is sparse, there are some indications that the courts are becoming increasingly supportive of this point of view. In envisioning property in the 21st century, Professor Cribbet foresaw:[196]

... a property law more nearly fashioned to serve the needs of a

---

194 *Supra*, note 42 at 6.
195 *Ibid.*
196 See "Property in the Twenty-First Century" (1978), 39 Ohio St. L.J. 671.

relatively free people, with less reification of the "thing" (land or chattel) and more emphasis on the rights of society as a whole. The winds of doctrine are not all blowing in that direction, but enough of the signs are emerging so that I, for one, do not despair.

It is hoped that these winds of doctrine sweep north of the 49th parallel.

DOLPHIN DELIVERY AND THE PROCESS OF CONSTITUTIONAL DECISION-MAKING — SOME LESSONS TO BE LEARNED

Peter A. Gall*

I. INTRODUCTION — WHAT YOU DO NOT KNOW ABOUT THE *DOLPHIN DELIVERY* CASE AND WHY IT IS IMPORTANT
II. THE HISTORY OF THE *DOLPHIN DELIVERY* CASE — WHY THE ISSUES RAISED IN THE CASE WERE NOT READY FOR ADJUDICATION BY THE COURT
III. CONCLUSION — WHAT THE *DOLPHIN DELIVERY* CASE TEACHES US ABOUT THE PROCESS OF CONSTITUTIONAL DECISION-MAKING AND WHY IT MIGHT BE RECONSIDERED BY THE COURT

I. INTRODUCTION — WHAT YOU DO NOT KNOW ABOUT THE *DOLPHIN DELIVERY* CASE AND WHY IT IS IMPORTANT

In my address today, I am going to talk about the *Dolphin Delivery* case,[1] a case in which I had first-hand involvement as counsel for Dolphin Delivery. I am sure that most of you know that *Dolphin Delivery* was the first decision of the Supreme Court of Canada dealing with the applicability of the *Charter*[2] and with freedom of expression under the *Charter*. Most of you are also probably aware that the court's treatment of the applicability issue has generated a considerable amount of criticism from the academic community.[3] In the view of the academic

---

*   This paper was prepared for oral presentation. Brief footnotes were added later.
1   *R.W.D.S.U., Loc. 580 v. Dolphin Delivery Ltd.*, [1986] 2 S.C.R. 573 [B.C.].
2   *Canadian Charter of Rights and Freedoms*, Pt. I of the *Constitution Act, 1982*, being Sched. B of the *Canada Act 1982*, 1982 (Eng.), c. 11.
3   See, *e.g.*, B. Slattery, "The *Charter*'s Relevance to Private Litigation; Does Dolphin Deliver?" (1986-87), 32 McGill L.J. 905; D. Beatty, "Constitutional Conceits: The Coercive Authority of the Courts" (1987), 37 U.T.L.J. 183; Petter and Monahan, "Developments in Constitutional Law: The 1986-87 Term"

commentators, the court's decision that the *Charter* does not directly apply to the common law is, at best, very muddled and, at worst, plainly and obviously wrong.[4] The court's handling of the freedom of expression issue has been better received. The academic community has generally applauded the court's decision to include secondary picketing within the ambit of s. 2(b) of the *Charter*, although some concern has been raised about the relative ease with which the common law restrictions on secondary picketing were found to be a reasonable limit under s. 1 of the *Charter*.

What most of you probably are not aware of, though, is the history of the *Dolphin Delivery* case — that is, how these issues arose and were argued by counsel and how they were handled administratively by the three courts that heard the case, including the Supreme Court of Canada. And that is what I am going to talk about today — not just because it makes for an interesting story about what has become a "famous" *Charter* case, but because I believe that a knowledge of the background history of the *Dolphin Delivery* case assists us in better understanding the process of constitutional decision-making.

Specifically, I think that once you come to know the history of the *Dolphin Delivery* case, you will realize, as I now do, that the court never should have granted leave in this case, not because the issues it raised were not of national importance, but because these issues, at least in the context of this case, were not ready for adjudication by the court.[5] As you will see, the issues in the *Dolphin Delivery* case were not fully developed or dealt with in the courts below, or even before the Supreme Court itself, and, as well, it was probably too soon in terms of the development of our jurisprudence under the *Charter* for the court to even be dealing with whether the *Charter* applied to the common law and whether secondary labour picketing came within the ambit of freedom of expression under the *Charter*. The court's treatment of these issues could, no doubt, have benefited from it first having dealt with the more basic applicability and freedom of expression issues.

(1988), 10 Supreme Court L.Rev. 61 at 130-31; Hutchinson and Petter, "Private Rights and Public Wrongs: The Liberal Lie of the *Charter*" (1988), 38 U.T.L.J. 278; D. Gibson, "What Did Dolphin Deliver?" in G.A. Beaudoin (ed.), *Your Clients and the Charter — Liberty and Equality* (Cowansville: Les Éditions Yvon Blais, 1987), at 75. For an excellent discussion of the *Dolphin Delivery* decision and the applicability issue generally, see Elliot and Grant, "The *Charter*'s Application in Private Litigation" (1989), 23 U.B.C.L.Rev. 459.

4   Professors Elliot and Grant describe the court's decision in *Dolphin Delivery* as "almost at war with itself; the evident desire for logical coherence pitched against the equally powerful desire to avoid the *Charter*'s application to the private sector": *ibid.*, at 481.

5   For a general discussion of this point, see Alexander Bickel, *The Least Dangerous Branch*, 2nd ed. (New Haven: Yale University Press, 1986), at 113-99.

Given the history of the *Dolphin Delivery* case, and in light of the criticism the court's decision in that case has provoked and the court's subsequent decisions in the labour law trilogy[6] and in the *Professional Institute*[7] case, I also believe there is a very good chance that the court will at some future time rethink its decision in *Dolphin Delivery* — at least on the applicability of the *Charter* to the common law, and possibly even on whether secondary picketing is a form of protected expression under s. 2(b) of the *Charter*.

II. THE HISTORY OF THE *DOLPHIN DELIVERY* CASE — WHY THE ISSUES RAISED IN THE CASE WERE NOT READY FOR ADJUDICATION BY THE COURT

As the court noted in its decision, the *Dolphin Delivery* case did not involve any actual secondary picketing. All that existed was a threat to engage in secondary picketing. The Retail Wholesale Union (RWU) was on strike against Purolator Courier in B.C. According to the RWU, Purolator was continuing its operations in B.C. during the strike through a related company named Supercourier. Prior to the strike, Dolphin Delivery had performed delivery services for Purolator, and after the strike began, Dolphin Delivery began performing the same delivery services for Supercourier. The RWU, wanting to stop Purolator's operations in B.C., threatened to picket, and thereby shut down, Dolphin Delivery's operations, if Dolphin Delivery continued to perform delivery services for Supercourier while the strike was ongoing.

As Dolphin Delivery's own employees were members of another union (the CBRT), Dolphin Delivery believed that if the RWU carried out with its threat to picket, it would have the intended effect of shutting down the company's operations. By the same token, Dolphin Delivery wanted to continue its relationship with Supercourier. So, Dolphin Delivery went to court to seek an injunction preventing the RWU from carrying out its threat to picket the company's operations. The chambers judge granted the injunction primarily because, in his opinion, the RWU had failed to establish that Purolator and Supercourier were in fact one and the same operation. Once the injunction was granted, the union was prevented from picketing Dolphin Delivery. Therefore, no actual secondary picketing ever took place.

---

6 The labour law trilogy are *Ref. re Pub. Service Employee Rel. Act (Alta.)*, [1987] 1 S.C.R. 313; *P.S.A.C. v. Can.*, [1987] 1 S.C.R. 424; and *R.W.D.S.U., Locs. 544, 496, 635, 955 v. Sask.*, [1987] 1 S.C.R. 460.

7 *Pro. Inst. of Pub. Service of Can. v. N.W.T.R. Commr.* (1990), 72 D.L.R. (4th) 1 (S.C.C.).

This turned out to be significant later on, after the constitutional issue was raised on appeal, because it meant that there was no evidence about the consequences or effects of the secondary picketing. We only had Dolphin Delivery's belief that the picketing would shut down its operations, as threatened by the RWU. The lack of actual evidence on this point proved troublesome to the court when it came to analyze the freedom of expression issue under s. 1 of the *Charter*.

What is even more significant, though, about the fact that no actual picketing took place, is that this meant that the freedom of expression issue — whether picketing is a form of protected expression under s. 2(b) of the *Charter* — never actually arose in the case. There was only a threat to shut down Dolphin Delivery's operations through the use of a picket line if Dolphin Delivery continued to perform services for Supercourier. Therefore, this was not the textbook case of picketing to communicate information about a company's involvement in a labour dispute — it was really a case of a threat to inflict economic harm, which we argued was not deserving of constitutional protection regardless of whether picketing came within the scope of s. 2(b) of the *Charter*.

The other important point to note about the proceedings before the chambers judge is that the constitutional issue was not even raised. The case was presented and argued entirely under the common law — and while there was argument over how the common law principles or rules should be applied to the facts of the case, there was no suggestion that these common law rules or principles should be modified to accord with the *Charter*.

Therefore, not only was there no evidentiary base laid before the chambers judge for the development or exploration of a *Charter* challenge to the common law rules governing secondary picketing, the chambers judge did not even deal with the constitutional issue. That issue only arose on appeal.

It now seems obvious that the British Columbia Court of Appeal should have been very reluctant to take on the constitutional issue for the first time on appeal, particularly given the paucity of evidence before the chambers judge. But we never thought to raise this concern before the Court of Appeal, and the Court of Appeal itself did not indicate that it saw this as a problem. That may seem very strange given all that we have learned subsequently about *Charter* litigation, but you have to remember that this was one of the first non-criminal *Charter* cases in B.C., and all of us, both lawyers and judges, were at the very beginning of our "learning curves" about the *Charter*.

In its factum before the British Columbia Court of Appeal, the RWU argued, first, that the chambers judge had misapplied the common law and, in the alternative, that the common law restrictions on secondary picketing were inconsistent with the constitutional guarantees of freedom of expression and freedom of association in ss. 2(b) and

2(d) of the *Charter*. We argued in our reply factum that the chambers judge had not misapplied the common law, and, in response to the constitutional arguments, that the *Charter* did not apply to the common law, but in the alternative, if it did, that the right to picket did not come within the scope of either s. 2(b) or s. 2(d) of the *Charter*, and that in any event, the common law restrictions on secondary picketing were a reasonable limitation under s. 1 of the *Charter*. As you can see, all the possible issues in this case were covered in the parties' factums before the British Columbia Court of Appeal.

It is important to note that the Attorney General for B.C. did not intervene at the Court of Appeal level, even though he was notified of the constitutional challenge. Therefore, the arguing of the *Charter* issues was left at this stage solely to the immediate parties, Dolphin Delivery and the RWU.

Prior to the actual hearing of the appeal before the Court of Appeal, a pre-hearing conference was held with one of the justices sitting on the case, Esson J.A. (now Chief Justice of the British Columbia Supreme Court). Esson J.A. asked the parties if there was any possibility of narrowing the issues raised in the factums that had been filed. Specifically, he wondered whether the union really wanted to advance its argument on the merits of the case — that is, that the chambers judge had misapplied the common law — and whether we really wanted to argue that the *Charter* did not apply to the common law.

As a result of Esson J.A.'s comments, an agreement was reached by counsel whereby the union abandoned its argument on the merits and we abandoned our argument that the *Charter* did not apply to the common law. As counsel for Dolphin Delivery, we thought this agreement helped us considerably. We had been very troubled by the potential problem we faced in justifying, on the one hand, the chambers judge's application of the common law to the facts of this case — which, in our view, required a very restrictive interpretation of the common law — and then, on the other hand, if picketing came within s. 2 of the *Charter*, in having to prove under s. 1 of the *Charter* that the common law adequately balanced the competing interests involved. By not having to face an appeal on the merits, we could "paint" the common law restrictions on picketing in the most favourable light, confident that it would not come back to haunt us on the facts of our particular case. This obviously made our case under the *Charter* that much easier.

At the same time, we did not have much confidence in our applicability argument — not only because of Esson J.A.'s comments, but also because it seemed to us both as a matter of principle, and based on the authorities and commentary in the United States,[8] and what little

---

8   *New York Times v. Sullivan*, 376 U.S. 254 (1963); see also Tribe, *American Constitutional Law* (Mineola: Foundation Press, 1978), at 1166, where Pro-

there was at that time in the way of authorities and commentary in Canada,[9] that the *Charter* had to apply to the common law. Surely, or so we thought, the *Charter*, which is the "supreme law," should apply both to statute law as well as judge-made law, particularly since it is the courts that have been given the principal responsibility of enforcing the *Charter*.

I am sure that the union also saw this agreement as being to its advantage. The RWU, no doubt, had a very jaundiced view of the common law restrictions on picketing and believed that it was an appropriate time to test these restrictions under the *Charter*. By getting rid of the applicability issue, the *Charter* challenge would have to be dealt with squarely by the B.C. Court of Appeal.

Again, it is important to remember the period in which this case arose. After the *Charter* was introduced, there was a lot of excitement, and indeed great expectations, about the changes that the *Charter* would bring to our legal system. In the labour relations field, there was a belief on the part of both management and labour that the *Charter* could be used to substantially alter our collective bargaining system. Both sides leaped into the fray to attack those laws that were seen as being inimical to their interests. Management challenged, among other things, the restrictions on so-called "employer free speech" during union organizing campaigns[10] as well as laws permitting union security clauses in collective agreements,[11] and unions challenged the restrictions on collective bargaining and the right to strike,[12] and in the *Dolphin Delivery* case, the right to engage in secondary picketing. The *Dolphin Delivery* case, therefore, was really a by-product of the heady early days of the *Charter*, when many lawyers, as well as other groups and individuals in the country, thought that the *Charter* could be used to alter significantly the legal framework governing various areas of our society including, in the labour relations area, the laws governing our collective bargaining system.

---

fessor Tribe states "[t]he general proposition that common law is state action is hardly controversial."

9   *Operation Dismantle Inc. v. R.* (1985), 18 D.L.R. (4th) 481 at 494 (S.C.C.), *per* Dickson C.J.C.; P. Hogg, *Constitutional Law of Canada*, 2nd ed. (Toronto: Carswell, 1985), at 677-78; D. Gibson, *The Law of The Charter: General Principles* (Toronto: Carswell, 1985), at 98-99.

10 *Bank Employees Union (Ont.), Loc. 2104 v. Bank of Montreal* (1985), 10 C.L.R.B.R. (N.S.) 129 (Can.), and *Placer Dev. Ltd. v. C.A.I.M.A.W., Loc. 17* (1985), 11 C.L.R.B.R. (N.S.) 195 (B.C.).

11 *Arlington Crane v. Ont. (Min. of Labour)* (1988), 56 D.L.R. (4th) 209 (Ont. H.C.).

12 The labour law trilogy, *supra*, note 6.

Fuelled by this enthusiasm about the *Charter*, and as a result of the agreement reached by counsel pursuant to the pre-hearing conference held by the Court of Appeal, the *Dolphin Delivery* case proceeded solely on the constitutional issues, but without the applicability issue being addressed. After the hearing of the appeal on this basis, a majority of the Court of Appeal found that picketing did not come within either s. 2(b) or 2(d) of the *Charter*, and all three justices ruled that, in any event, the common law restrictions on secondary picketing, at least in the circumstances of this case, were a reasonable limit under s. 1 of the *Charter*. The union then appealed the decision of the Court of Appeal to the Supreme Court of Canada.

In its appeal to the Supreme Court of Canada, the RWU abandoned its argument under s. 2(d) of the *Charter*. As I understand it, this was not because the RWU and the trade union movement did not think that the right to picket was an important element of their freedom to associate, but because it was thought that it was better to leave the freedom of association argument to the other labour law cases that were proceeding in the courts which involved challenges to statutory provisions restricting the right to strike and the right to engage in collective bargaining.[13] In the view of the trade union movement, these other cases raised more squarely the freedom of association issue and, therefore, were better cases than *Dolphin Delivery* to advance this issue.

At that time, this appeared to be a sensible decision. Picketing is more readily seen as a form of expression than as a necessary ingredient of the right to associate. Therefore, it seemed preferable to leave the freedom of association issue to those cases involving the right to strike and the right to engage in collective bargaining, where the freedom of association interests of trade unions seemed to be much more directly implicated.

However, with the benefit of hindsight, particularly after the court's decisions in the *Dolphin Delivery* case and the labour law trilogy, it is now apparent that it was a mistake to separate the right to picket from the right to strike and the right to engage in collective bargaining. Picketing, at least in the labour relations context, is simply a tool that is used to prosecute a strike. The right to picket and the right to strike really go hand in glove. Therefore, if the right to strike and the right to engage in collective bargaining lie at the heart of the union's associational interests, so must the right to picket.

By the same token, if the right to picket is a form of expression under s. 2(b) of the *Charter*, then, necessarily, so must be the right to strike, because they both are used to communicate the fact of a labour dispute. The right to engage in collective bargaining must also be seen as

---

13 *Ibid.*

a form of expression, because the right to picket and the right to strike are simply incidents of the broader right to engage in collective bargaining, which has as its very purpose to enable workers to exercise a collective "voice" in the workplace over matters pertaining to their terms and conditions of employment.

Therefore, the right to picket cannot really be separated from the right to strike and the right to engage in collective bargaining in the way they were in the *Dolphin Delivery* case and the "right to strike" cases — with picketing being argued under s. 2(b) and the right to strike and the right to engage in collective bargaining being argued under s. 2(d). These activities should have been considered as a package and dealt with as such under both ss. 2(b) and 2(d) of the *Charter*.

Of course, that was not possible, as happened, if the *Dolphin Delivery* case was heard before the labour law trilogy. In order to deal with all of these matters as a package, it would have been necessary to hear the *Dolphin Delivery* case along with the labour law trilogy. In that way, the court could have been presented at one time with a more complete picture of how our legal system dealt with the rights of unions in our collective bargaining system, and could have then seen the connections between picketing and the right to strike and the right to engage in collective bargaining. As it was, though, because the *Dolphin Delivery* case was heard first, the court was only exposed in that case to the picketing issue — and therefore did not see at that time the connections between the *Dolphin Delivery* case and the labour law trilogy, and how the right to picket, and the right to strike, and the right to engage in collective bargaining, all fit together.

The next important development in the history of the *Dolphin Delivery* case was the hearing of the leave application before the court. The leave application was argued in the usual way, with the union contending that the issue of whether picketing was protected under the *Charter* was of national importance and with us arguing that it was not. No mention was made of the applicability issue — because, as far as the parties were concerned, there was no applicability issue, and the court itself apparently had not yet seen any applicability issue raised on the facts of the *Dolphin Delivery* case. It would appear that the court, at least at the time of the leave application, saw the case as only involving the freedom of expression issue — and it was very difficult for us, as counsel for *Dolphin Delivery*, to deny that this issue was of national importance. In fact, the panel of the court hearing the leave application did not even call on the appellant to argue the point, and simply out of courtesy gave us an opportunity to argue otherwise, which we tried to do, but to no avail.

It never occurred to us that what we really should have been arguing was that the court should not take on the case, not because the issues raised in it were not of national importance, but because these issues were not ready for adjudication. Of course, the reason why it never occurred to us was that it appeared at that time that these issues were ready for adjudication. What more was required? There was no applicability issue as far as the parties were concerned, and we never gave any thought to the process of constitutional decision-making, that is, to whether it made any sense to deal with the picketing issue at that time under only s. 2(b) of the *Charter*, when there were other cases coming along which raised the broader issues of the right to strike and the right to engage in collective bargaining under s. 2(d) of the *Charter*.

Again, none of this is surprising, because at that stage of our collective thinking about the *Charter*, little thought was being given by anyone to the proper development of the court's jurisprudence under the *Charter*. Therefore, leave was granted in the *Dolphin Delivery* case without the applicability issue even being raised or any consideration being given to whether the issues in the *Dolphin Delivery* case should be adjudicated by the court at that time.

The factums filed with the court by the RWU and the company made no mention of the applicability issue. Again, as far as the parties were concerned, there was no applicability issue. However, some of the intervenor's factums raised the possibility of an applicability issue, but these factums were not filed until just prior to the hearing of the appeal. The court itself never indicated before the hearing date that it wanted to hear argument on the applicability issue. Accordingly, the parties arrived at the hearing of the appeal prepared only to deal with the issue of whether the common law restrictions on secondary picketing contravened the constitutional guarantee of freedom of expression enshrined in the *Charter*.

Imagine our surprise then when the court announced, soon into the union's oral argument, that it wanted to hear submissions from the parties on the applicability of the *Charter* to the common law. Counsel for the union pointed out to the court that an agreement had been reached by the parties, with the concurrence of the B.C. Court of Appeal, not to raise the applicability issue, but Dickson C.J.C. quickly told us that no such agreement was binding on the court, and that the justices of the court wanted to hear argument on this issue.

It seems obvious now that the hearing of the appeal should have been adjourned to allow the parties to prepare properly their submissions on the applicability issue. However, the hearing was not adjourned, and the parties only had the evening before the second day of the hearing of the appeal to consider the applicability issue. With all due respect to the court, that was hardly adequate given the complexity and importance of this issue, particularly since the issue had never been argued before, or dealt with by, the courts below in this case.

As counsel for *Dolphin Delivery*, we were faced with the additional dilemma of not knowing what position we should take on the applicability issue. On the one hand, despite what Dickson C.J.C. said, we felt bound by our agreement with the RWU, particularly since we had reaped the benefit of that agreement by the RWU abandoning its appeal on the merits. As well, as mentioned above, we thought that as a matter of both logic and principle the *Charter* should apply to the common law. On the other hand, we had a client to represent, and it was in the client's best interests to win the case on any ground we could.

In the final analysis, we decided to support the RWU in its argument that the *Charter* applied to the common law. So did the Attorney General for B.C., as well as all of the other intervenors except the Attorney General for Canada. Therefore, both of the immediate parties in the *Dolphin Delivery* case, namely the union and the company, as well as the Attorney General for B.C., argued in favour of the *Charter* applying to the common law.

That, in a nutshell, is the history of the *Dolphin Delivery* case. What this history shows us is that the applicability issue was not dealt with at all in the courts below and was not fully or even properly dealt with before the Supreme Court itself, and that the court's treatment of the freedom of expression issue could have benefited not only from a better evidentiary record, but also from consideration being given to the interrelationships between the right to picket and the right to strike and engage in collective bargaining.

III. CONCLUSION — WHAT THE *DOLPHIN DELIVERY* CASE TEACHES US ABOUT THE PROCESS OF CONSTITUTIONAL DECISION-MAKING AND WHY IT MIGHT BE RECONSIDERED BY THE COURT

As you know, the court held that the *Charter* did not apply to private litigation based on the common law, although it also said that the courts have a responsibility to develop the common law in accordance with the *Charter*. I still to this day do not understand the difference, but it is obvious from its decision that the court thought that if the *Charter* applied to private litigation based on the common law, it would mean necessarily that the *Charter* applied to all private activity. I do not think that is so — as we argued before the court. A distinction can be drawn between using the *Charter* to create new common law causes of action — which would mean that the *Charter* would govern all private activity — and using the *Charter* to modify existing common law causes of action — which would not involve the *Charter* applying to all private activity, but only to those existing common law rules governing that activity. It would mean that our existing common law rules governing private activity would be brought into conformity with the *Charter* in the same way as statutory laws governing private activity.

The court also concluded that picketing was a form of expression protected under s. 2(b) of the *Charter*, but, even though there was an absence of any actual evidence supporting the common law restrictions on secondary picketing, the court went on to find that the common law restrictions on secondary picketing were reasonable limits under s. 1 of the *Charter*. Strictly speaking, it was unnecessary for the court to even get into the freedom of expression issue once it held that the *Charter* did not apply to the common law restrictions on secondary picketing. And the fact that the court did deal with the freedom of expression issue, counted with the way that the decision on the applicability issue is written, leads me to conclude that the court changed its mind on the applicability issue after the part of the decision dealing with the freedom of expression issue had already been written, and that the court then decided to leave this part of the decision in, even though it had now decided that the *Charter* did not apply in this case.

That, of course, is simply speculation on my part. However, despite the fact that the court's decision on the freedom of expression issue has been better received by the academic community, I still question whether the court should have dealt with this issue at all. Having now dealt with it, I believe there is a good chance that the court will change its mind on this issue in the future. The reason I say that is because the court's decision in the *Dolphin Delivery* case, that picketing is constitutionally protected under s. 2(b) of the *Charter*, is inconsistent with its subsequent decisions in the labour law trilogy[14] and in the *Professional Institute*[15] case. In those later cases, the court ruled that the right to strike and the right to engage in collective bargaining should not be accorded even *prima facie* constitutional protection under the *Charter*. If that is so, the right to picket, which after all is simply an incident of the right to strike, should also not be given *prima facie* constitutional protection.

That conclusion seems to follow both as a matter of logic and principle. If picketing is a form of expression, should the right to strike and the right to engage in collective bargaining not also be considered forms of expression protected under s. 2(b) of the *Charter*? Of course, the labour law trilogy and the *Professional Institute* case were not argued under s. 2(b) of the *Charter*, but that was only because of the tactical decisions that were made by the trade union movement and not because, as a matter of logic or principle, the right to strike and the right to

14 *Supra*, note 6.
15 *Supra*, note 7.

engage in collective bargaining should not be considered forms of protected expression under the *Charter*, particularly if picketing is treated in this way.

Having said that, though, the outcomes in the labour law trilogy cases and the *Professional Institute* case undoubtedly would have been the same regardless of whether they had been argued under s. 2(b) of the *Charter* as well as s. 2(d). The reason is that, after some more experience with the *Charter* and some more thought about applying the *Charter* to the laws governing the structure of our collective bargaining system, the court has come to the conclusion that the *Charter* has no useful role to play in this sphere. I agree with that conclusion, as I think most of the labour relations community now does.

After the initial burst of enthusiasm about the changes the *Charter* might bring to our system of labour relations, I think most people in the labour relations field now believe that changes to our labour laws should be brought about through the legislative process, and not through the courts, particularly given the access that both labour and management have to the political process. And, given the court's conclusion that it is preferable not to use the *Charter* to change the rules governing our collective bargaining system, it now seems apparent, at least to me, that the court should rethink its decision in the *Dolphin Delivery* case to accord *prima facie* constitutional protection to picketing — which, as I have stressed, is only a part of and, therefore, of lesser importance in our system of collective bargaining than the right to strike and the right to engage in collective bargaining.

It also seems to me that by the time the court decided the labour law trilogy, it had also recognized the jurisprudential problem it faced if it gave a very broad scope to the fundamental freedoms so as to encompass the right to strike and the right to engage in collective bargaining, and then had to engage in a free-wheeling balancing of interests under s. 1 of the *Charter* to determine whether restrictions on these fundamental freedoms were justified. I think that the court is of the view that it is preferable, at least in the labour relations context, not to give a broad definition to the fundamental freedoms in order to avoid having to decide these labour relations cases in a seemingly less principled way under s. 1 of the *Charter*.

In any event, this is all part of the learning process about the *Charter*. And the message that I want to leave with you is that, because of the history of the *Dolphin Delivery* case, including the timing of the case, I think it would have been preferable, in terms of the development of our jurisprudence under the *Charter*, for the court not to have granted leave to appeal in the *Dolphin Delivery* case. This is because the issues raised in the case were simply not ready for adjudication by the court.

I think you can see there are hints in the court's decision, particularly in its comments about the fact that no actual picketing took place in the *Dolphin Delivery* case, that the court itself came to this view as it struggled to write its decision. However, again, that is only speculation on my part. But, it cannot be denied that the history of the *Dolphin Delivery* case teaches us an important lesson about the process of constitutional decision-making — something which I am sure the court fully appreciates and has taken into account on subsequent leave applications — and that is that, just because a case may raise issues of national importance, it does not mean the court should hear the case. It may be that, as in *Dolphin Delivery*, the issues raised in such a case, even though they are of national importance, are not ready for adjudication and should await another dispute at another time before they are decided by the court.

ALLOCATING RESOURCES TO PROTECT DEMONSTRATIONS: THE ISRAELI APPROACH

David Kretzmer

I. INTRODUCTION

A number of legal systems which have a principled commitment to freedom of speech shared an initial reluctance to recognize the right to demonstrate in public places as part of that freedom. Doctrines of property, public or private, and the consideration of public order were accorded precedence over the desire of citizens to express their views on public issues in the streets and parks.

At the end of the last century, legislation was passed in the United States restricting the right to speak on Boston Common. The legislation was upheld by the Supreme Court, which quoted with approval the following statement made by Oliver Wendell Holmes, then a justice of the Massachusetts Supreme Court:[1]

> For the legislature absolutely or conditionally to forbid public speaking in a highway or public park is no more an infringement of the rights of a member of the public than for the owner of a private house to forbid it in his house.

The Supreme Court of Canada adopted a similar approach much more recently. In *A.G. Can. v. Montreal*,[2] the issue was the validity of a Montreal by-law that gave the Executive Committee of the city the

---

1   *Davis v. Mass.*, 167 U.S. 43 (1897).
2   (1978), 84 D.L.R. (3d) 420.

power to prohibit all assemblies, parades or gatherings. The court stated:[3]

> Freedoms of speech, of assembly and association, of the press and of religion are distinct and independent of the faculty of holding assemblies, parades, gatherings, demonstrations or processions on the public domain of a city . . . Demonstrations are not a form of speech but of collective action. They are of the nature of a display of force rather than of that of an appeal to reason; their inarticulateness prevents them from becoming part of language and from reaching the level of discourse.

In Israel, the Supreme Court was reluctant for a long time to interfere with the police's discretion to deny a permit for demonstrations requiring one. The court's attitude was that the police were best equipped to judge matters of public order and that there was no place for judicial intervention.

Attitudes in all three systems have since changed radically. Strong support now exists for protection of a right to demonstrate as part of the right to freedom of expression. In the U.S., in *Hague v. C.I.O.*,[4] Roberts J. declared:[5]

> Wherever the title of streets and parks may rest, they have immemorially been held in trust for the use of the public and, time out of mind, have been used for purposes of assembly, communicating thoughts between citizens, and discussing public questions. Such use of the streets and public places has, from ancient times, been part of the privileges, immunities, rights, and liberties of citizens.

Similarly, in the leading Israeli case of *Sa'ar v. Minister of Interior and Police*,[6] Justice Barak included freedom of assembly and processions among the basic freedoms of man recognized by the Israeli legal system, and added:[7]

> The highways and streets were meant for walking and driving, but this is not their only purpose. They were also meant for processions, parades, funerals and such events.

In Canada, since the adoption of the *Charter*,[8] the courts seem to have abandoned the *Montreal* approach according to which the right to

---

3   *Ibid.*, at 439.
4   307 U.S. 496 (1939).
5   *Ibid.*, at 515.
6   (1980), 34 P.D. (2) 169.
7   *Ibid.*, at 178.
8   *Canadian Charter of Rights and Freedoms*, Pt. I of the *Constitution Act, 1982*, being Sched. B of the *Canada Act 1982*, 1982 (Eng.), c. 11.

demonstrate in the streets has nothing to do with freedom of expression. The majority opinion of the Federal Court of Appeal in *Committee for the Commonwealth of Canada v. Canada*[9] views the right to use public places for expressive purposes as covered by the freedom of expression clause in the *Charter*.

The reluctance to recognize the right to demonstrate in public places as part of the right to freedom of expression reflects a very real concern with a central characteristic of demonstrations that is absent in other forms of expression. A demonstration may be described as "the use of public places for expressive purposes."[10] As such, it may imply not merely the use of a public place, but the appropriation of that place for the expressive use of the demonstrators. This appropriation may involve denying the public's right to use the said place for alternative purposes, subjecting those who are using the place and surrounding places to inconvenience and annoyance, and making passers-by a captive audience to views and ideas to which they do not choose to be exposed. To the extent that demonstrations involve a captive audience, they may in fact imply an incursion on freedom of expression. If freedom of expression includes, as it must, the right to hear the opinions of others, it surely must also include the right not to hear opinions which we choose not to hear.

Demonstrations in urban areas require policing, which may be extremely costly, especially when the demonstrators present highly controversial views that are anathema to a large section of the public. The result may well be that a small minority forces the majority to foot the bill incurred from the minority's exercise of the right to express views that the majority finds abhorrent. Thus, for example, in the case of the notorious attempt of the American Nazi Party to demonstrate in Skokie: though it would be inconceivable to ask Holocaust survivors to pay the expenses of distributing a Nazi pamphlet or newspaper or making a Nazi broadcast, these same survivors may be required to bear the expense involved in protecting the "expressive use" of a public place by the Nazis who call for their extermination. It is, of course, true that the object of protecting a particular demonstration is not to protect the substantive views of the demonstrators, but to protect the very freedom to demonstrate. However, by using a form of expression that may impose considerable costs on society, the demonstrators force us to foot the bill for the expression of certain views.

It should be clear from the outset that, by presenting the problems

9 (1987), 36 D.L.R. (4th) 501, affirmed 77 D.L.R. (4th) 385, application for re-hearing refused S.C.C. No. 20334, 8th May 1991.

10 See Barnum, "The Constitutional Status of Public Protest Activity in Britain and the U.S." (1977), Public Law 310, who talks of expressive use of public places.

of protecting demonstrations, I do not wish to suggest that the right to demonstrate is not worthy of protection. To the contrary, in the next section I shall try to show why this right must be recognized as part and parcel of the right to freedom of expression. However, recognition of the right does not address the question of its proper boundaries. The real question, when analyzing the right to demonstrate, is the cost to be paid in terms of other values in order to protect this right. This is the question that now faces legal systems that have come to terms with the principled recognition of the right. The focus of the present paper is the way the Israeli legal system has handled that question.

II. THE BASIS FOR THE RIGHT DEMONSTRATE

As seen above, the right to demonstrate was not initially perceived as part of the right to freedom of expression. The present discussion begins, therefore, by showing why this right should definitely be included in the basket of rights called freedom of expression.

For the purposes of the present discussion, I have adopted the definition of a demonstration as the "use of a public place for expressive purposes." As such, the demonstration has some communicative advantages over other types of expression.[11] It is a form of expression open to persons and sections of society who are unable to communicate their views in other ways, either because they do not express themselves in a way that is acceptable in the established media or because they are denied access to the media. It allows group expression, which can emphasize not only the substantive view of the demonstrators, but the intensity with which the view is held, and can also provide some indication of the degree of public support for a view. Being a form of collective action, as well as a form of expression, the demonstration may help to create solidarity among like-minded people and strengthen their resolve to advance their views. The demonstration also allows for spontaneity of expression. Finally, in a society in which we have a plethora of communication media, a view which is presented in the conventional fashion may be lost. Media coverage of a demonstration may give more exposure to the view than would otherwise be the case.

The common feature of the above communicative advantages of the demonstration is the emphasis on the chance of being heard, rather than on the chance of speaking. It is this feature of the demonstration that makes it central to any concept of freedom of speech as an integral part of democratic government. For the fundamental test of democracy

---

11 I have presented these communicative advantages before in somewhat more detail: see D. Kretzmer, "Demonstrations and the Law" (1984), 19 Israel L.Rev. 47.

is that the government is for the people, by the people, and of the people. As the representative of the people, government must hear what the people have to say. The people themselves must have every chance not only of exposing the government to their views, but of communicating views to each other. The major proponent of free speech as an essential of democratic government, Alexander Meiklejohn, put the matter as follows:[12]

> We listen, not because critics of the American form of government desire to speak, but because we need to hear. If there are arguments against our theory of government, our policies in war or in peace, we the citizens, the rulers, must hear and consider them for ourselves. That is the way of public safety. It is the program of self-government.

Democratic theory is certainly not the only argument for the protection of free speech. It is, however, an important argument for the special status which is in fact accorded to free speech in democratic societies. The premise of this paper will be that in a democratic regime the right to demonstrate has to be recognized as an integral component of free speech.

III. DEMONSTRATIONS AND THE ALLOCATION OF PUBLIC RESOURCES

Balancing freedom of expression against other values has occupied the courts and academic writers alike. Having established that the right to demonstrate must be regarded as part and parcel of the right to freedom of expression, does it not follow that the same principles and policies that have been analyzed thoroughly in the general context of speech should apply when the right to demonstrate clashes with other values or interests? The answer is only partially in the affirmative. Protecting the right to demonstrate can have significant consequences on resource allocation and it is this factor that requires us to consider the question of balancing in cases of demonstrations separately from the question in other speech contexts.

The resource allocation implications of protecting the right to demonstrate may be illustrated from the following cases that concerned the Israeli public in recent years:

---

12 See A. Meiklejohn, *Free Speech and its Relation to Self-Government* (New York: 1948), at 66.

1. According to a political agreement struck between religious and secular parties in the Jewish community before Israel was established as an independent state, cinemas were closed on the sabbath in towns with a Jewish majority. Municipal by-laws were passed making that closing mandatory. In recent years, the secular majority in some towns has revolted against this decision and cinemas have been allowed to open on Friday evenings. Sections of the organized orthodox religious community called for mass protests against the opening of the cinemas and Friday evening demonstrations by several thousand people became a regular occurrence. Given the large numbers involved, and the depth of passions aroused between the ultra-orthodox demonstrators and the secular cinema-goers, the police were required to provide a significant force to keep order. This meant mobilizing off-duty policemen and bringing in reinforcements from other areas, diverting police from other duties. The demonstrations went on every Friday night for months.

2. In 1983, the Commission of Enquiry on the massacres at Sabra and Shatila published its report. A huge procession and demonstration took place calling for the resignation of the Minister of Defence. Towards the end of the demonstration a hand-grenade was thrown at the demonstrators and one demonstrator was killed. Exactly one month later, a political group (not the same group that had organized the original demonstration) applied for a permit to hold a procession along the route that had been taken in the first demonstration. The police refused to grant the permit. They argued that, in the general atmosphere following the fatal end to the previous demonstration, the threat to public order was too great to allow the demonstration. The applicants petitioned the Supreme Court which refused to accept the view of the police.[13] It ordered the police to grant the permit for the procession. The procession took place, but only after 400 policemen had been assigned to keep the peace.

   In both of the above cases the public expenditure involved in policing a demonstration was by no means insignificant. The two cases differed in that the demonstration in the second case was a one-time event. The cost of policing the demonstration was largely a function of the fear that opponents of the demonstrators would employ violence against them. It was thus a classic example of the well-known hostile

---

13 See *Levi v. Dist. Police Commander* (1983), 38 P.D. (2) 398. An English translation of this decision appears in *Selected Judgments of the Supreme Court of Israel*, vol. VII, 1983–87 (Jerusalem: Ministry of Justice, 1988), at 109.

audience question.[14] In the cinema case the demonstration was repeated week after week. Furthermore, part of the threat was the fear that the demonstrators themselves would attempt to use force in order to prevent people from attending the cinema.

In spite of the differences, both instances illustrate the resource allocation problem that arises over demonstrations. By deciding to make expressive use of a public place, a group can compel society to allocate public resources in a certain way. The demonstrators outside the cinema every Friday night necessitated the diversion of police resources from other uses. By standing on their right to demonstrate when the police could do no less than provide significant protection, the demonstrators in the second case imposed a cost on society that was diverted from some alternative use. It may well be that the use to which those resources were put was in some sense preferable to its alternative use. But who is to decide? The legitimate channel for public resource allocation decisions is the political process. If political minorities can unilaterally change those decisions, do they not thereby pervert the political process?

It is, of course, tempting to see the resource allocation problem presented by demonstrations as a non-issue. Democracy has a cost and the price of demonstrations is part of that cost. The problem with this type of argument is that it avoids the issue. Of course democracy has a price and, once we have accepted that the right to demonstrate must be accepted as part of the democratic conception of free speech, it is obvious that protecting that right must be part of the cost of democracy. However, the question is not whether we should be prepared to pay in order to protect the right to demonstrate, but whether there should be limits to this right, based on considerations of cost. Could it possibly be argued that the protestors against the opening of cinemas on the sabbath had exhausted their right to demonstrate after one, two or three weeks and that thereafter the public could refuse to absorb the costs? The implication would be that they would be warned that a demonstration would not be allowed (or a permit denied for the demonstration if one was required). Could the police have justified their refusal to allow the demonstration in the second case, by pointing to the alternative use of the force required to police the demonstration? Could they have diverted the demonstration to an alternative site in which the cost of policing

---

14 This question has been thoroughly canvassed in the law journals. See, *e.g.*, Note, "Freedom of Speech and Assembly: The Problem of the Hostile Audience" (1940), 49 Col. L.R. 1118; Carson, "Freedom of Assembly and the Hostile Audience: A Comparative Examination of the British and American Doctrines" (1960), 15 N.Y.L. Forum 798; Blasi, "Prior Restraint on Demonstrations" (1970), 68 Mich. L.R. 1481; Barnum, "Freedom of Assembly and Hostile Audience in Anglo-American Law" (1981), 29 Am.J.Comp.L. 59.

would have been reduced? How does one decide between policing a demonstration and policing a high-crime urban area, not to mention providing security in a society threatened by terrorist acts? The answer, "provide more police for all these tasks," is not a satisfactory one. First, more police means less of some other public good, such as health services or education, or more public spending, which may have significant economic implications. Second, increasing the size of a police force has civil liberties implications of its own. From a civil rights perspective, it is not necessarily something one would want to encourage.

IV. THE ISRAELI APPROACH

A. Background

Israel is a parliamentary democracy that, like Britain, has neither a formal constitution nor a Bill of Rights. Nevertheless, the Supreme Court of Israel has over the years developed a "judicial bill of rights." It has accorded those liberties and basic rights recognized in liberal democracies the status of principles that are an inherent part of the legal system. These principles are what I have elsewhere termed "soft legal principles," in that they are subject to the whim of parliamentary legislation.[15] The courts may not strike down primary legislation on the strength of the argument that it is inconsistent with one of the recognized freedoms, such as freedom of expression. However, these principles must guide the authorities and the courts in the interpretation of legislation, they may not be abridged by administrative action or subordinate legislation unless such abridgment is based on express statutory authority, and all administrative authorities must ascribe adequate weight to those principles in the use of their statutory powers.

The right to hold processions and outdoor assemblies in public places is regulated in Israel by the Police Ordinance, enacted during the period of the British Mandate over Palestine and still in force today. This ordinance provides that persons wishing to hold processions or open-air meetings must obtain a permit from the district police commander.[16] It states that the commander has the power to grant the permit, refuse it or grant it subject to conditions.

The criminal law, based as it is on English common law, also contains a number of offences that are highly relevant in "demonstra-

---

15 See, *supra*, note 11 at 64.
16 A "procession" is defined as "fifty or more persons proceeding together or assembling with the object of proceeding together from one place to another"; a "meeting" is 50 or more people who meet in open air "for the purpose of hearing any speech or address upon any topic of political interest, or for the purpose of any discussion upon any such topic."

tion situations." The main offence is "unlawful assembly." On many occasions the police have used these offences as a pretext for dispersing demonstrations that do not require permits. Evidence of this police practice led the Attorney General to publish directives that make clear the limits of the police power to disperse demonstrations that do not require permits. These directives seem to have had their effect on police practice.

The concern of the present paper is with the permit system, which has been the focus of the main Supreme Court decisions.

B. Development of Jurisprudence

As stated above, the initial attitude of the Supreme Court of Israel was to ignore the freedom of expression elements in demonstrations and to place emphasis on considerations of public order. Attempts to persuade the court to interfere with the refusal of the police to grant a permit met with the reply that the discretion had been given to the police and that the court would not interfere with this discretion.

The turning point came in the case of *Sa'ar v. Minister of Interior and Police*.[17] A group of citizens wished to hold a procession through main streets in Jerusalem to protest against the shortage of housing for young couples. The police turned down the request for the permit, adding that they would allow an assembly outside the prime minister's office (which was the planned final destination of the procession). Among the reasons given for refusing the permit was the inconvenience that would be caused to the Jerusalem public "including car owners and users of public transport." The disappointed applicants petitioned the Supreme Court in its capacity as a High Court of Justice.

Justice Barak declared that the right to demonstrate is one of the fundamental rights which, while not inscribed in any formal constitutional document, is one of the recognized rights in the Israeli legal system. When exercising his statutory power to grant or refuse demonstration permits, the police commander is not doing the applicant a favour. The citizen has a basic right to demonstrate and the police commander may not use his statutory power to restrict that right unless weighty considerations demand it. The commander is obliged to find a balance between the right to demonstrate and legitimate conflicting interests, such as public order and public convenience. As Justice Barak put it:[18]

In exercising the "traffic" consideration, a balance must always be

---

17   *Supra*, note 6.
18   *Ibid.*, at 171.

struck between the interests of citizens who wish to hold an assembly or procession and the interests of citizens whose right of passage is affected by that assembly or procession. Just as my right to demonstrate in the street of a city is restricted by the right of my fellow to free passage in that same street, his right of passage in the street of a city is restricted by my right to hold an assembly or procession.

Justice Barak did not provide the commander with a general balancing test. He did, however, rule that the commander had to follow a "minimal restriction" approach — a permit was not to be denied because of interference with traffic if the disruption to traffic could be minimized by restrictions on time and place. Applying this approach, Justice Barak ordered the police to grant the permit, as the inconvenience to the public could be reduced significantly by restricting the procession to one side of the highway.

In the *Sa'ar* case the cost to the public was a direct function of the demonstrators' decision to use the highway for expressive purposes. Two later decisions addressed the hostile audience question in which the cost is a function of the expected opposition of others to the demonstration and their use of force to express that opposition.

Fear of a hostile audience obviously poses a challenge to the legal system. The right to demonstrate is meaningless unless it is protected against those who wish to use violence to destroy it. On the other hand, it would seem unreasonable to demand that the police protect demonstrators at any cost while denying them the right to place some restrictions on demonstrations so as to avoid predictable violence.[19]

The facts in *Levi v. Dist. Police Commander*[20] were presented above. The police fears of a hostile audience threat were based on the experience at a demonstration one month previously in which a demonstrator had been killed by a hand-grenade. At the time of the application for a permit for the second demonstration, the perpetrator had not yet been apprehended. Nevertheless, the court was unimpressed with the police's fear of danger to public order. It held that the police could deny a permit in such circumstances only if two conditions were met:

1. that it could show that it had allocated police to protect the demonstrators; and
2. that notwithstanding this allocation of resources there still remained a "probable danger" of a serious breach to public order.

The court accepted that the demands on police resources could be taken into account in judging the adequacy of police protection. Justice

---

19 See V. Blasi, "Prior Restraints on Demonstrations" (1970), 68 Mich.L.R. 1481 at 1510.
20 *Supra*, note 13 and accompanying text.

Barak stated explicitly that the reasonableness of the police measures taken to protect the demonstration will depend on available forces, their skill and equipment, the expected size of the demonstration and the number of onlookers. Furthermore, other duties of the police must be taken into account. The police have to allocate their forces in such a way as to ensure the reasonable discharge of all of their duties.

Police are reluctant to admit that they cannot effectively police a demonstration. However, they may argue that doing so would force them to abandon other missions. If they can prove this, the court has to decide whether the police decision to refrain from allocating their resources in order to protect the right to demonstrate was reasonable.

The second point regarding the "probable danger" requires some explanation. The landmark Israeli case establishing freedom of expression and other basic rights as protected legal principles is the decision of Justice Agranat in *Kol Ha'am v. Minister of Interior*.[21] The Press Ordinance enacted during the British Mandate gives the Minister of Interior the power to order suspension of a newspaper if material published therein is, in his opinion, likely to endanger the public peace. The minister had exercised this power to suspend publication of two communist papers for 10 and 15 days.[22] In his historic judgment, Justice Agranat ruled that the statutory provision defining the power of suspension had to be interpreted in accordance with the free speech principle. This meant that it could not be exercised unless the danger to public order met the test of "high probability."[23] As there was no high probability of harm to the public peace by the items published, the minister had exceeded his statutory authority.

The high probability test was originally adopted in the specific context of the Press Ordinance. Justice Agranat decided that the word "likely" in the relevant statutory provision should be interpreted to mean "probable" rather than possible. However, in later decisions the court decided that the basis for adopting this test was wider than the restricted context of the Press Ordinance, and that it could be used in other contexts in which the need arose to balance freedom of speech and public order. Since then, this test has become the dominant, though not

---

21 (1953), 7 P.D. 871.
22 The background to the closure was a report in a daily newspaper (subsequently denied) that the government would be prepared to send 200,000 troops to fight alongside the Americans in Korea. The Communist papers published harsh attacks on the government in which they intimated that people may be called on to refuse army service.
23 This test is in theory similar, though not identical, to the American "clear and present danger test," though this latter test was rejected by Justice Agranat in the *Kol Ha'am* case.

exclusive, balancing test in free speech cases in Israel. In the *Levi* case, Justice Barak extended the test to the hostile audience situation.

In applying the above tests in the *Levi* case, Justice Barak held that the danger to public order was based on speculation and not on hard facts. On reasonable evaluation, with prudent foresight, the facts could not be said to establish any substantial likelihood of danger. The fear of danger to public order was mere conjecture and could not sustain the decision to deny the demonstration permit.

The *Levi* case was followed by another important hostile audience case, this time from the opposite side of the political spectrum.[24] Nationalistic Jews, angered by the government's refusal to allow group prayers by Jews on the Temple Mount, intended to hold a mass public prayer meeting *cum* demonstration near one of the gates leading to the Temple Mount on Jerusalem Day, which marks the unification of Jerusalem under Israeli control in 1967. While their meeting did not require a permit, they approached the police in advance to ensure that they would not disperse the meeting on the grounds of a threat to public order. Previous experience had shown that the fear that Muslims might react violently to what they perceived as an attempt to take over the Temple Mount would prompt the police to avoid trouble by dispersing the gathering. Indeed, the police informed the organizers of their objections to the place and time of the planned meeting and would not allow it. The organizers petitioned the Supreme Court.

The court was not sure whether the issue was one of freedom of worship or the right to demonstrate. It decided, however, that whichever way one looked at it the danger to public order did not meet the high probability test and could, therefore, not justify prior restraint. The police could not decide in advance that the demonstration would not be allowed, though they retained the power to disperse the gathering if, at the time, a danger to public order were to arise that could not otherwise be contained.

As can be seen from the above cases, the Supreme Court of Israel has addressed the resource allocation question in the restricted context of denying a permit for a demonstration on public order grounds. In this context, the resource question is taken into account in assessing the adequacy of the force available to ensure public order. The courts have not had to address the question posed above in the example of the cinema demonstrations.[25] The police had shown week after week that

---

24 See *Temple Faithful v. Min. of Police* (1983), 33 P.D. (2) 449.

25 In the cinema case the police never made the argument and so the matter did not reach the courts. However, the dilemma was presented to the writer by the officer who had been in charge of the police at the demonstrations.

they were capable of maintaining order if they allocated a large force to do so. What would have been the attitude of the court if at some stage the police had stated that "enough is enough"? Would the fact that the demonstrators had exercised their right to demonstrate for a number of weeks have been relevant in deciding that the necessary force would not be allocated to protect public order and that the demonstration would therefore not be allowed?[26]

V. CONCLUDING REMARKS

The resource allocation problem that I presented in the introduction is far broader than the limited context in which it has been discussed in Israeli decisions. Nevertheless, the significance of the Israeli decisions is that they have articulated the question. Furthermore, while they have recognized that arguments based on the allocation of police resources might be used in order to justify a police refusal to allow a demonstration, in actual fact they have never found that a given demonstration legitimately was denied a permit on these grounds.

The Israeli legal system has come a long way in providing protection for the right to demonstrate. Initial attitudes of preference for other values and the refusal to realize the importance of this form of expression in the democratic framework have long been abandoned. In practice, the demonstration has become an extremely common form of political expression that illustrates all the communicative features mentioned above. An interesting question is the relationship between the prevalence of this form of expression and the attitudes of the Supreme Court. In changing its approach to demonstrations, was the court reacting partly to the reality of demonstrations as a central form of expression? Or is the prevalence of this form of expression a function of the liberal attitude of the court?

---

26 It should be pointed out that this question will only arise in those cases in which the demonstration requires a permit. Many of the weekly demonstrations now held in Israel by various political groups are stationary protest vigils that do not require a permit. The police may only disperse such vigils if a reasonable fear arises of a threat to public order by the protestors, or if they are unable to contain the threat to public order presented by hostile bystanders.

PART VII

GOVERNMENT OF THE PEOPLE: FREEDOM OF EXPRESSION AND THE INSTITUTIONS OF GOVERNMENT

The exercise of governmental authority in the form of the police power, national security agencies, government secrecy, and regulation of electoral campaigns all potentially have a great impact on the practice of free expression. Has the *Charter* influenced the development of government institutions to enhance the democratic process and foster democratic accountability? The papers collected here explore a variety of governmental processes which affect free expression.

Peter Desbarats considers how the administration of justice generally can have a negative effect on freedom of the press. The attitude of Canadian law enforcement agencies is discussed, with the reference to incidents such as the prosecution of journalist Doug Small for being in possession of a leaked budget. The attitude of courts and parliamentarians, with reference to television camera access to their proceedings, is also reviewed. Desbarats sees all of the foregoing as being exemplary of the Canadian penchant for secrecy, and sees much work to be done in the pursuit of free press and access to information.

Jean Jacques Blais, on the other hand, sees the Canadian record in this regard as encouraging. He reviews the measures for balancing public accountability with the need for secrecy developed in regard to the Canadian Security Intelligence Service and its civilian oversight body, the Security Intelligence Review Committee. He also reviews the need for Cabinet secrecy in regard to budget preparation, but argues for a greater degree of openness in regard to documents classified as Cabinet documents.

Desmond Morton reviews the history of limiting electoral expression by means of caps on campaign expenditures by third parties.

This regulation of the electoral process has been seen as a limit on free expression when it is most counted: in the exercise of democratic politics. Morton presents the rationale for such limits on expression as a means to equalize opportunity for electoral success. The *Charter*'s impact in this area has served to strike down our electoral expense law and to free up private sources of funding during election campaigns.

FREE SPEECH, THE PRESS AND THE ADMINISTRATION OF JUSTICE

Peter Desbarats

A journalist should be able to provide the kind of sweeping endorsement of freedom of expression that lawyers can analyze, qualify and whittle away at. When a journalist does this, he or she is often accused of acting out of self-interest. Journalists work for an industry that is, or should be, based on freedom of expression. In this case, principle and profit would appear to coincide neatly. I suggest that this is a superficial reading of the journalist's role, a reading that serves neither journalism nor society well. For the journalist, freedom of expression is not a "licence to kill," but a responsibility that carries heavy obligations with it. For society, freedom of expression is not a luxury or a nuisance, but a necessity.

Freedom of expression is not the exclusive property of the news media, of course, but the condition of freedom within a society can usually be judged by the degree of freedom possessed by its journalists. It is not accidental that an increase in the freedom of the Soviet press was one of the first signs of the structural changes that have radically altered the Soviet political and economic systems in the past few years. Nor was it coincidental that demands for freedom of the press reached a peak in China just before the events in Tiananmen Square. It is axiomatic that you cannot have democratic government, and all the institutions of democracy, without a free press; among those institutions, the courts are particularly sensitive to freedom of the press. A free press is an essential component of an independent judiciary helping to protect it from political interference. In this respect, everyone involved in the administration of justice — judges, lawyers and police officers — should be among the leading defenders of freedom of the press and what I would call, in general terms, an "open society."

This is not always the case. These natural allies are often at odds with one another. The police provide the most extreme example. In the past year, several events have demonstrated a police attitude towards the media that is shocking in its negativism and frightening in its consequences. A minor instance was an appearance of Royal Canadian

Mounted Police (R.C.M.P.) Commissioner Norman Inkster last year at the annual conference of the Centre for Investigative Journalism,[1] Canada's national association of journalists. Commissioner Inkster began the session with a riddle: "What is black and brown and looks great on a reporter?" The answer: "A doberman pinscher." This just might have been funny if it had not reflected a deep-seated fear and loathing of the press at the highest levels of the R.C.M.P.

We received a glimpse of this in early testimony at the trial of Doug Small, the Global reporter accused of receiving a stolen budget document. According to one R.C.M.P. officer, some senior members of the force undertook this assignment in the spirit of a lynch mob. They were quoted, in court testimony, as relishing this opportunity to finally "get" a journalist. Staff Sergeant Richard Jordan told the court that R.C.M.P. Deputy Commissioner Henry Jensen, the second highest ranking officer in the force, "showed facial expressions and body language that denoted anger and aggression . . . toward journalists in general and Doug Small in particular."[2]

In the politically motivated, dangerous and ultimately ridiculous pursuit of Doug Small, the Cabinet found willing accomplices at the very top of our national police force. It is truly frightening to think what they might be capable of in a more serious situation, although we had a glimpse of that during the so-called "October Crisis" of 1970. I will never forget the day when the R.C.M.P., operating under the *War Measures Act*,[3] arrested one of my colleagues in the middle of an editorial meeting at the C.B.C. in Montreal and held him without trial or bail for weeks, until he was finally released, no charge ever having been laid against him. He went on to become a member of Montreal's city council and, ironically, a leading newspaper columnist of extremely conservative views.

The R.C.M.P. attitude revealed in the Doug Small case did not surprise me. Police officers and the press usually encounter one another in stressful situations where their objectives may be in conflict. The bitter suicide note left by a Winnipeg constable in 1989, in the middle of an investigation into the shooting of a native leader, blamed the media for hounding him to death.[4] Understandable as that reaction might have been under the circumstances, it reinforced the image of the press as an

---

1   P. Kuitenbrouwer, "RCMP: A change in style?" (1989), 39 Bulletin - Centre for Investigative Journalism 33.
2   "Budget Leak — Mountie tells court of push to charge" (November 8, 1989), London Free Press, at A5.
3   R.S.C. 1970, c. W-2 [repealed by the *Emergencies Act*, S.C. 1988, c. 29].
4   " 'Probe of Harper shooting screwed up', officer says in suicide note to friend" (November 1, 1989), The Globe and Mail, at A1.

institution guided primarily by self-interest and careless about the consequences of its own actions.

I have no intention of making a blanket defence of the press, any more than I would want to condemn the attitudes of all police officers towards journalists. Journalists are often guilty of excessive zeal, to put it kindly, in the pursuit of truth. Corrupt, venal and even vicious characters are found in the ranks of journalists as they are among police officers. But I would suggest that instances of deliberately destructive reporting are relatively rare in Canada, and certainly not frequent or outrageous enough to justify the kind of attitude that was revealed in the Doug Small case. After all, we do not have a sensational press in this country compared with the tabloid press of Britain, Australia or the United States. The journalistic tradition in Canada has been one of responsibility, even timidity, in the face of authority. And while it is true that news media have been less than responsive to public concerns about their conduct than they should have been, the past decade has seen a rapid growth in voluntary systems of accountability. Press councils now cover print media in virtually every region of the country, five major daily newspapers and the French- and English-language services of the C.B.C. have full-time ombudsmen, and regional Broadcast Standards Councils will soon provide a voluntary system of public accountability for commercial broadcasters. Taken together, these mechanisms hardly indicate an industry that believes in riding roughshod over the rights of individuals. One probably could say that the response of journalists and media owners to these new structures has been more positive, on the whole, than the attitude of some police forces to citizen review boards.

It is my belief that the negative or defensive stance of the police towards the press in Canada arises, in the main, not from concrete examples of misconduct by the media, but from a strong streak of authoritarianism in the Canadian character. This is not an original observation, but it remains an unpopular and neglected one in Canada, where we like to think of ourselves as belonging to a relatively open and free society. Certainly, we do enjoy a high degree of individual freedom, thanks in large part to our British heritage and to our good luck in inhabiting a large and productive piece of global real estate alongside a relatively congenial neighbour that also happens to be the richest society in the world. Like the British people of our own day, however, we often assume that the structures of democracy guarantee democratic practices. In fact, the Britain of today is generally acknowledged to have one of the most secretive governments in the Western world, arising from a long tradition of elite rule and deference to authority. In this respect, we are often closer to our British traditions than to the more open and aggressive populism of American politics.

In some respects, this tradition has served us badly. Not long ago, for example, I attended a conference in Ottawa that was examining barriers to the effective communication of environmental information in Canada. Part of the problem was a lack of expertise and editorial resources in the Canadian news media; the other side of the coin, however, was an attitude, common to Canadian bureaucracies, that jealously guarded information from the prying eyes of the public, the media, and even from politicians. If anything, this has become more pronounced in our own era, often called "the information age," when official information is regarded by government as a strategic resource. An example of this attitude is contained in a relatively new R.C.M.P. directive on handling media inquiries. The very first paragraph of the policy reads: "Ensure that any information released to the news media does not interfere with an investigation or arrest or result in embarrassment, injury or injustice to anyone either innocent or accused." This emphasis on the importance of not releasing information, rather than the necessity of providing for the freest possible information flow in a democratic society, is typical of information policies generally in Canadian bureaucracies. My own experience in the Ottawa press gallery of the 1980s taught me that the Canadian instinct is always to release as little information as possible to the press, and to try to discourage uncontrolled leakage of information from lower levels of the bureaucracy, referring all requests for information to senior levels where they are invariably handled slowly and cautiously. This contrasts with the American attitude in Washington, according to colleagues who have reported from both capitals. In the United States, public officials are still influenced by the policy of the public's right to know and this affects the attitude of bureaucrats who recognize the role of the media as a surrogate for the public in its quest for information.

Americans have a much greater propensity than we have to question restrictions on freedom of information. American news media, for instance, have recently been taking a close look at restrictions against publishing the names of rape victims in the media. At first glance this would seem to be a restriction that everyone should accept on humanitarian grounds. Last November, however, it was questioned by the female editor of an Iowa newspaper who tried to look behind the humanitarian rationale. "A tenet of journalism holds that we ought to come as close as possible to printing the facts as we know them," wrote Geneva Overholser in the Des Moines (Iowa) Register. "Going against this rule in the case of rape victims feels to me very much like participating in the onus, the stigma, that I find so unjust."[5] In other words, were editors (usually male) who refused to print names of rape victims motivated fundamentally by a belief that being raped stigmatized a woman either because it threw doubts on her moral character or because it made her less desirable or marriageable according to the male-oriented standards of society?

"Editors do not hesitate to name the victim of a murder attempt," Ms. Overholser continued. "Does not our very delicacy in dealing with rape victims subscribe to the idea that rape is a crime of sex rather than the crime of brutal violence that it really is?" Ms. Overholser did not feel profoundly enough about this to start publishing the names of rape victims, but her editorial persuaded one victim to come forward. The result was a controversial series in her newspaper detailing the ordeal of Nancy Ziegenmeyer, the wife of a mechanic in Grinnell, Iowa. The series attracted national attention, including a front-page story in the Sunday edition of the New York Times in which Ms. Overholser stated that "as long as rape is deemed unspeakable — and is therefore not fully and honestly spoken of — the public outrage will be muted as well."[6]

I cite this case not to suggest that newspapers should start publishing the names of rape victims tomorrow, but to point out that restrictions on the flow of information from official bodies to the public, even if they appear to be based on rational or humanitarian grounds, often have social origins and social effects which have to be constantly re-examined.

Experience has shown that the benefits of opening the doors to our governing institutions have far outweighed the disadvantages. In the 19th century, it was feared that the presence of scribblers in the public galleries would hinder debate and throw the British Parliament into disrepute. In my own time, the scribblers in the press gallery had become so conscious of their dignity that they, and not the parliamentarians, resisted granting membership in the gallery to a television journalist. For many years, Members of Parliament objected to allowing television cameras in the House of Commons, although they stood in line in a basement room beneath the House for the opportunity to be interviewed by television reporters and to appear on the nightly television news.

Television coverage is now as routine as the printed *Hansard* in the

---

5 G. Overholser, "We should not have to keep hiding rape" (November 1989), ASNE Bulletin 32.

6 "A Name, a Face and a Rape: Iowa Victim Tells Her Story" (March 25, 1990), The New York Times, at 1,15.

House of Commons in Ottawa and many provincial legislatures, although as recently as May 1990 the Supreme Court of Nova Scotia resolved a dispute over television access between the Nova Scotia government and several television networks.[7] Even in this bastion of conservatism, however, the argument was not about the principle of television coverage, which the Nova Scotia government accepted, but about methodology: whether the cameras would be part of an official "electronic *Hansard*," as they are in Ottawa, or owned by the networks. In a recent appearance before the House of Commons committee in Ottawa studying proposals to modify television coverage of the House, I was surprised to find that my approach to television in the House had become more conservative than that of the Members. They were in favour of allowing television wider latitude in showing the House at work — and their report ultimately recommended this[8] — while I voiced concerns about the difficulty of maintaining editorial neutrality if a television director were allowed to select "shots" for their story-telling or dramatic value.[9]

Today we see our courts wrestling with the same problem, and the result, I feel safe in predicting, will be the same. In this case, it is the Americans who have led the way. According to statistics cited recently by Judge Barbara Crabb in District Court in Madison, Wisconsin, 43 states now permit television coverage of the courts.[10] Judge Crabb was hearing a request by Wisconsin broadcasters to allow television coverage of a hearing on the treaty rights of Chippewa Indians to hunt and fish and cut timber on public land in northern Wisconsin. The case illustrated how restrictions on television coverage are becoming less plausible in the United States. Judge Crabb agreed that televising the proceedings "would promote greater understanding of the complex and divisive issues" involved, and petitioned the Ad Hoc Committee on Cameras in the court room of the Judicial Conference to suspend its usual prohibition. Despite the fact that all parties involved in the case supported television coverage, the Ad Hoc Committee denied her request. "I consider that, however strongly I may disagree with the Judicial Conference's position on this question, I am not free to disregard it," Judge Crabb stated.

---

7   *N.B. Broadcasting Co. v. Donahoe* (1990), 71 D.L.R. (4th) 23, affirmed N.S.C.A., No. 02295, 21st March 1991, leave to appeal to S.C.C. granted No. 22457, 16th May 1991 (not yet reported).

8   Canada, House of Commons, *Minutes of Proceedings and Evidence of the Standing Committee on Elections, Privileges, Procedure and Private Member's Business*, "Watching the house at work" (December 7, 1989), No. 18.

9   *Ibid.*, No. 11 (November 1, 1989), 11:7.

10   "Judge rules out cameras in Wisconsin court" (February 26, 1990), 118:9 Broadcasting 40.

When even judges in the United States are uncomfortable with the prohibition against cameras in federal court and a few remaining states, these last barriers seem destined to fall in the near future. In Canada, the decision of the Commons to permit televising of its committees, the common practice of permitting television coverage of provincial inquiries, and the proposal to expand the C.B.C.'s parliamentary channel into a 24-hour public affairs channel, similar to C-SPAN in the United States, will increase the pressure to open the doors of our courts to television.

When this decision is made, as it will be inevitably, I hope that our judges will take advantage of the opportunity to use it as an occasion to reaffirm their belief in an open society guided by the common sense of an informed citizenry.

FREEDOM OF EXPRESSION AND PUBLIC ADMINISTRATION

Jean Jacques Blais

I. INTRODUCTION

The purpose of this paper is to review how government secrecy interfaces with the "freedom of expression" guaranteed by the *Canadian Charter of Rights and Freedoms*.[1] The right to vote acknowledged by s. 3 of the *Charter* is, in a liberal democracy, an essential means of expression. Section 2(b) of the *Charter*, recognizing the "freedom of thought, belief, opinion and expression, including freedom of the press and other media of communication," can best be exercised, in Canada, through the electoral process. One can conclude that, in the context of public administration, "freedom of expression" is synonymous with the ability to choose how, and by whom, one is governed. The two provisions, ss. 2(b) and 3 of the *Charter* are, therefore, intimately related.

There can be no true democracy without a free, informed vote. There cannot be such a vote without open, unrestrained and frank public expression of views and opinions. Information is both the catalyst and the fuel of intelligent debate, needed both to call the governors to account and to permit the selection of those to be charged with the administration of the public good.

Secrecy is the absence of information, the deprivation of intelligence, and is antithetical to the notion of public knowledge. Yet, it is also essential to the proper functioning of a democratic society. It is

---

1   *The Canadian Charter of Rights and Freedoms*, Pt. I of the *Constitution Act, 1982*, being Sched. B of the *Canada Act 1982*, 1982 (Eng.), c. 11.

necessary to protect the security of the state, to identify and control elements that would threaten public order, both internal and external. It is also essential to our executive system of government. Without secrecy, the central administrative concept of Cabinet solidarity, without which the "Whitehall system" could not function, would be inoperative.

The decision-making process requires secrecy, as it requires information. Accountability of the governors to the governed, without which democracy would be a sham, needs information to be meaningful, but must be respectful of the need for secrecy for purposes recognized by principles of public administration. The co-existence of both the need for information and the need for secrecy has, in recent times, provoked calls for the revision of structures and institutions to ensure effective administration while promoting respect for the rights of individuals and groups.

As the Globe and Mail[2] put it in an editorial commenting on the Ontario Law Reform Commission's recent report on Crown liability:[3]

> Perhaps the growth of governments has made people more conscious of their presence and anxious about their powers; perhaps one bill of rights breeds others. Whatever the reason, legislatures and governments across Canada have accepted increasing restraints on their capacity to act without being effectively challenged by individual citizens and groups. The Ontario commission's report follows in this healthy spirit of calling the democracy to account.

II. EASTERN EUROPE AND SECRECY

We have all been following the events in Eastern Europe and the U.S.S.R. with awe. We have appreciated the irony of Westerners being better informed of events in that region over the last 40 years than Eastern Europeans, who were systematically deprived of information or provided wrong information. In a recent Public Broadcasting Service production in the United States, the well-known newsman, Ted Koppell, described how the people in Poland, in the period immediately prior to the accession of Solidarity to power, had to smuggle news of Lech Walesa's reception in the western countries, including Canada, through video cassettes, which were then copied and viewed on communal video cassette recorders. That activity was made necessary by the Polish news media, directed by the Jaruzelski government, engaging in a process known as "disinformation": providing information which the provider knows to be untrue for the purpose of causing the listener to react to the lie in an anticipated manner.

---

2 April 5, 1989.
3 Ontario Law Reform Commission, *Report on the Liability of the Crown* (Toronto: O.L.R.C., 1989).

The seemingly compulsive secrecy, or the suppression of information that characterized the communist regimes, hid from their population the maladministration in which they engaged and the privileges that the rulers had secured for themselves. The chief purpose was to eliminate the need for the rulers to account to the public they were meant to serve for their acts and omissions. Eventually, through the influence of television, the video cassette recorder and other effective and irrepressible means of communications, the shroud was lifted.

No greater argument in favour of minimizing administrative secrecy can be made than the unfolding phenomenon east of the rusted remains of the Iron Curtain. It would be of interest to review Marxist-Leninist experience to draw a list of all the reasons advanced to justify the maintenance of secrecy. It would make for an interesting experiment in human inventiveness. A recent edition of C.B.C.'s "The National," describing the high level of pollution in East Germany, graphically described how a local population was unknowingly being poisoned by industrial waste. The pollution readings, which, in Canada, are made available to populations daily, were deemed in East Germany to be "state secrets."

The conclusion, drawn by the shocked nationals at the public revelations of the personal conduct and style of living of their leaders, was that the stubborn resistance to change by their leaders was motivated more by a determination to stay in power than by a loyalty to Marxist-Leninist precepts. The dogged resistance to change by all the leaders in place, the major efforts at controlling events through the manipulation of information, the activities of the Secret Services and the tightening of secrecy were to ensure that the errors of more than a generation of doctrinaire Marxist rule would not be made public and the government would not be overturned. The wave of Gorbachev-style *glasnost*, or openness, proved irresistible. Once the U.S.S.R. removed its approval of the repressive measures employed by the so-called satellites, the lid came off. Power was essential to preserve secrecy, and secrecy essential to the preservation of power.

III. THE CANADIAN SYSTEM

I would not be so bold as to suggest that, in Canada, the relationship between power and secrecy is so intimate. However, power is power wherever it is exercised, and it is not easily surrendered, whether in Canada or abroad. The hard-fought contest for the Liberal Party leadership in 1990, including the odd delegate selection process and the periodic accusations of unsavoury tactics, is evidence that, even in the Canadian context, power has its attraction. The efforts made to secure a party's nomination in any election, the elbowing within any Cabinet to lock onto a more advantageous portfolio, indeed any contest whose prize is greater access to power, reveals how seriously the acquisition of power is taken by those who would rule. Once achieved, the leaving is difficult, as shown more recently by the behaviour of the British Columbia Premier, Mr. Van der Zalm, in retaining his leadership in the face of substantial opposition. Similar cases are legion.

In liberal democracies the people are given the ultimate choice as to whom power will be given. That reality makes both the politician and the bureaucrat sensitive to the need to account to the electorate, who hold the ultimate power. Information is central to this public accounting. It will permit the elected members of Parliament to test the performance of their government and its officials, as well as provide to the Canadian public the findings upon which they may form their judgment.

To facilitate the process of accountability, we have devised an adversarial, partisan mechanism which provides for systematic opposition to what the executive proposes. The "loyal" opposition seeks to test what is being advanced for weakness, allegedly for the greater good. The prize for being an effective opposition is the chance to exercise power and to control the destiny of the nation.

The opposition is often perceived as being imbued with scepticism, not to say mistrust, for those governing. Their activities, at times, appear overly aggressive, not to say destructive, which may affect their credibility. Those in government, in the face of opponents who would wrest from them their ability to govern at the first opportunity, are perceived as succumbing to the instinct to hide that which renders them vulnerable and to engage in self-serving hyperbole to highlight that which may ensure their hold on the right to rule. The very nature of this process gives rise to the view that the electors are not getting all that is needed to make their judgment.

In the face of that perception, efforts have been made to ensure that the public is getting a true picture of the government's behaviour, and that whatever information is not available is being justifiably withheld. The concern was best expressed by Professor J.R. Mallory:[4]

> Government in a modern democracy is largely in the hands of a bureaucracy, using the term in a neutral sense as meaning a body of professionally competent, hierarchically organized administrators. The major problem in modern constitutional government is to retain an effective control, by public opinion and by legal restraints, of the apparatus of the state which constantly expands with the increased public demand for more social welfare services and with the growing

---

4   J.R. Mallory, *The Structure of Canadian Government* (Toronto: MacMillan, 1971), at 116.

burden of national defence in a world that can be nourished only by the full and effective functioning of the political and legal restraints on abuse of power.

The recommendations of the McGrath report[5] address the need for greater power to be exercised by the House of Commons over the Executive. It advocates an altered standing committee system structured to mirror government departments and enabled to examine the operations and administration of those departments. Officials could be called to testify, with the cooperation of their ministers, on the discharge of their administrative responsibilities. The effect of the recommendations is to provide more information to Members of Parliament as to the workings of government departments in order to facilitate accountability.

IV. SECRECY AND THE OMBUDSMAN

The passage in July 1983 of the federal *Access to Information Act*[6] and the *Privacy Act*[7] and, subsequently in June 1984, the *Canadian Security Intelligence Service Act*,[8] has furthered the process of accountability through access to information while respecting certain human rights and security imperatives. Canada has eschewed the introduction of a general ombudsman, and has opted instead for more specialized middle persons charged with securing accountability from government. While the public is not given access to the classified information, its surrogate gets to see the information and, once having done so, advises the public whether the information is properly kept secret or whether there is an ulterior motive on the part of the information custodian in maintaining the secrecy. The Information Commissioner is such a middle person, as is the Privacy Commissioner.

A third body operates under the same principle. It is the Security Intelligence Review Committee (SIRC), and, being familiar with its operation, I will describe it with a view to persuading the reader that the accountability essential to our system of government can be promoted even while secrets are kept.

SIRC is an instrument of government accountability that is mandated to protect state secrets while ensuring that those coming within its purview, and operating in secret, exercise the power that has been provided to them within the limits imposed by our democratic institutions.

---

5   *Report of the Special Committee on Reform of the House of Commons* (Ottawa: Supply and Services, 1985) (Chairman: James A. McGrath).
6   R.S.C. 1985, c. A-1.
7   R.S.C. 1985, c. P-21.
8   R.S.C. 1985, c. C-23.

As we have seen in the unfolding events of Eastern Europe, the administrative principle most susceptible to abuse is that of national security. It is a nebulous concept, difficult to define, and has been used to conceal a multitude of sins. Nevertheless, it is a legitimate notion, essential to the protection of the state. Canada, emulating the British in its invocation of the Royal Prerogative, created a security establishment largely by executive order and, until 1984, avoided the normal processes of parliamentary accountability in relation to its operations. With the adoption of the *Canadian Security Intelligence Service Act*,[9] in the dying days of the Trudeau administration, the Canadian Security Intelligence Service (CSIS) was created, provided with a mandate, and subjected to legislative and judicial controls. One of those mechanisms of control is SIRC, of which I have been a member since 1984.

The secrecy-accountability issue, as it relates to the activities of CSIS, was resolved by providing for two agencies of control to assist and complement the convention of ministerial responsibility to Parliament. The first is the office of the Inspector General, charged with reviewing the activities of the service, monitoring compliance by the service with its operational policies, and reporting to the Solicitor General on its findings.[10] The second is SIRC. It has the responsibility of reviewing the performance of the service, as well as the reports emanating from the other review processes, and the directions issued to the service by the minister. A second major responsibility is the investigation of complaints made against the service arising from its activities, including recommendations relating to security clearances.[11]

As Professor Mallory argued in the quotation above, the major preoccupation in public administration is the concentration of power in an increasingly powerful public service, and the consequent potential for abuse. One instrument of control is information on how, and for what purpose, the power is exercised. The adversarial nature of our democratic institutions, permitting the opposition parties to closely examine the government of the day in the country's legislatures and committees, was intended to secure the necessary information and call the administration to account. However, the growing complexity of government and the little time available to elected officials to pursue, in detail, all the questions that come within their responsibilities, have made it essential that other means be provided to assist in the controlling function.

I have had the privilege of being Solicitor General, and thus the minister responsible for the CSIS predecessor, the Security Service of

---

9   *Ibid.*
10 *Ibid.*, ss. 30-33.
11 *Ibid.*, ss. 34-55.

the Royal Canadian Mounted Police (R.C.M.P.). I now have had the pleasure of sitting on a committee that deals with CSIS behaviour. I can assure you that, even though on a part-time schedule with SIRC, averaging five days per month, my ability to know what is happening, and to be comfortable with that knowledge, far surpasses anything that I could ever have achieved under the former arrangements. The precision of a legislated mandate, the structured reporting process and the identified expectations of all interested parties, have established competent accountability and have improved efficiency and effectiveness.

Our committee is composed of politically experienced Privy Councillors, representing the three parties in the House of Commons. It reports to Parliament, and was given the right of access to all the information under the control of the Security Service. Such an arrangement was deemed preferable to a parliamentary committee, whose adversarial nature might jeopardize sensitive information. A leak, provoked by partisan considerations, would make it difficult for the service to obtain foreign intelligence from its international network, which the Canadian community, not having an offensive intelligence gathering capacity, depends on.

We now have filed six annual reports. The system works. The proof of the recognition that it works may well be found in the nature of the changes proposed by the parliamentary committee charged with the review of the legislation, pursuant to its provisions, after the first five years of operation.[12] While it would be unwise to speculate on what the changes may be, I would be ready to predict that the main principles of the existing regime will not be changed.

However, the past five years have not been uneventful. There have been significant changes in the way that CSIS operates. The changes have been, without exception, improvements of the *status quo ante.* The most important event was the issuance of a report by a task force headed by Gordon Osbaldeston, a former secretary to the Cabinet of both Prime Minister Trudeau and his successor.[13] His recommendations were well-researched, reasonable, and are being implemented at a rapid rate.

I have reviewed the task force report, in light of the SIRC annual reports, to ascertain to what extent the activities of the committee might have had an impact on the work of the Osbaldeston group. Elements of each of the 34 recommendations made by the task force are to be found

12 *Ibid.,* s. 56. The committee's recommendations can now be found in Canada, Report of the House of Commons Special Committee on the Review of the CSIS Act and the Security Offences Act, *In Flux, But Not In Crisis* (Ottawa: Queen's Printer, 1990) (Chairman: Blaine Thacker).
13 Canada, Report to the Solicitor General by the Independent Advisory Team on CSIS, *People and Process in Transition* (Ottawa: Solicitor General of Canada, 1987).

in the SIRC reports that preceded them. As an example, the first recommendation speaks of the appointment of a Deputy Director responsible "for all Personnel Services, Training and Development and Official Languages." Our report (86/87) recommends the appointment of a Deputy Director to oversee a special official language plan and better staff relations. Other examples include: the issue of personnel mobility between CSIS and the Public Service — first raised by SIRC in its 85/86 report; the discontinuance of counter-subversion targeting and the integration of the section into the counter-intelligence and counter-terrorism sections, as raised in our 86/87 report; and the concept of the devil's advocate recommended in our 86/87 publication and partially accepted by Osbaldeston.

The Osbaldeston recommendations, and their successful implementation, would not have occurred had it not been for the work of the Security Intelligence Review Committee, and that of the Inspector General. While it is not an unpleasant assertion for one involved in the process to make, my purpose in raising the issue is to show how administrative reforms to improve efficiency and responsiveness were brought about. What is more significant to this group is that the changes took place discreetly and effectively in an area of high sensitivity, as a result of a surrogate to Parliament having a statutory right to secret information. What made our scrutiny possible was CSIS's confidence that its innermost secrets would be protected.

At the time of the implementation of the *CSIS Act*, the view was that our efforts would be oriented primarily towards ensuring that the activities of CSIS were conducted within the legislated mandate. That proved not to be a major difficulty. The service was conscious of its mandate, and carried forward from the Security Service of the R.C.M.P. a code of ethics that made compliance comfortable and anticipated.

As our reviewing activities advanced, the committee recognized that its observations, and consequent comments, related more and more to the operational efficiency of the service. As an example, our first major study dealt with the bilingual nature of the service. Our report, *Closing the Gaps*,[14] on the need to improve the official language practices of CSIS, had little to do with protecting the rights of Canadians from the intrusive powers of the service; our concerns were the operational limitations occasioned by the inability of the service to function effectively in the French language as well as a concern about compliance with the *Official Languages Act*.[15]

Our complaints investigations, where we reviewed CSIS files re-

14 SIRC, *Closing the Gaps: Official Languages and Staff Relations in the Canadian Security Intelligence Service* (Ottawa: Supply and Services Canada, 1987).
15 R.S.C. 1985, c. O-3.

lated to individuals who brought to our attention cases where they had been refused security clearances in relation to their becoming landed immigrants, citizens or upwardly mobile civil servants, provided us with an unexpected window into the service's day-to-day operations. We also reviewed complaints from individuals related to alleged improprieties by CSIS, which again permitted the committee to probe into CSIS operations, not only to ensure compliance with the Act, but to analyze and evaluate their *modus operandi.*

The formal public report to Parliament provides a vehicle for both the dissemination of the information we could publish and the recommendations we could disclose and an enforcement mechanism in areas where the suggested reforms were not readily acceptable.

V. THE COMMUNICATIONS MEDIA AND SECRECY

Apart from the democratic institutions themselves, and the players structurally identified as participants, powerful agents have inserted themselves in the process of controlling the abuse of power: the communications media. Their stock-in-trade is information with which they seek to influence public opinion. They blow the whistle on any activity that they deem worthy of public attention, while advocating such policy positions as they or their owners may prefer.

While their role has been appreciated as essential to the preservation and improvement of democratic institutions, it has excited a substantial amount of controversy and is bound, in the Canadian context, to provoke a great deal more.

As Albert Abel wrote in 1968:[16]

> The journalists argue that they act as public monitors of administrative behaviour, standing guard to discover and reveal official skulduggery and fumbling, and that as such they are an essential agent in the democratic process. They claim on that account free access to virtually all offices, files and gatherings. The claim strikes me as mildly hypocritical and wildly exaggerated.
>
> As to hypocrisy, I venture to submit that what the media mainly want is a free supply of raw material to be processed for profit into a marketable commodity, to wit, news, with motives very much like those of lumber or mining operators who wish to exploit Crown lands on their own terms . . .
>
> The extent to which the press does or even can provide an effective safeguard against maladministration has been exaggerated. It often

---

16 "Administrative Secrecy" (1968), 11 Canadian Public Administration 440 at 440-41.

does less than it could with the materials already at its disposal. A classic example is the discreet pussyfooting of the provincial press and notably the English language press during the Duplessis regime and Canadian history from Family Compact times on, teaches that the press of the other provinces cannot take a holier-than-thou attitude. With honourable exceptions, they have done less than they could have. It is not clear that limitations on availability of information have been as great a cause of muffling as have self-imposed limitations arising from political alignments or business prudence.

Given the ever-increasing concentration of ownership of the media, both print and electronic, Mr. Abel's criticism is still most timely and, while perhaps provocative, is an essential part of the debate around administrative secrecy. The question is: whose interests are being served by the communications media? That of the Canadian voter whose sole lever is a single vote in the ballot box, because of circumstances of language, origin, race, financial or social status, or that of the privileged and powerful elites who control the media, and whose reality the media are able to reflect and protect?

The media base their argument for access on s. 2(b) of the *Charter*. Freedom of the press is certainly one aspect of freedom of expression, the ability to make one's views known, and to protect and promote one's interests. One would assume that the drafters of that section perceived that the media, in exercising their right of expression, would be a reflection of the national reality. Is that the case? What impact does the concentration of ownership have on the media's ability to reflect the Canadian mosaic? Are all elements of the mosaic being well served by the existing communications media? If not, is there a role to play on the part of the Canadian government to ensure a better reflection of the Canadian reality in the media, as part of ensuring the respect for the freedoms enumerated and recognized in s. 2(b)?

In their interpretation of the *Charter*, the courts have taken a more *laissez-faire* attitude towards freedoms as they relate to government action, not insisting that affirmative action be taken to ensure their exercise, where they might have insisted on government intervention to protect a right. However, I support the view expressed by Wayne McKay[17] where he states:

> In doing a purposive analysis of the *Charter* judges must also be mindful of the real effects of a particular interpretation. In many instances positive government action and not merely restraint is required to make a fundamental freedom meaningful.

In any event, freedom of expression is, in the present context,

---

17   A. Wayne McKay, "Freedom of Expression: Is it all Just Talk?" (1989), 68 Can. Bar Rev. 713 at 726.

recognized as essential to the exercise of a fundamental right which the government surely has an obligation to enforce: the right to vote as provided by s. 3 of the *Charter*. In that light, does the government not have an obligation to address the issue of the concentration of press ownership? Could the government of the day not be called on by the courts to deal with the issue?

VI. SECRECY AND THE BUDGET

A great deal has been said as to the propriety of budget secrecy, mostly negative. It poses a major dilemma in our system of government. Cabinet needs secrecy to operate. The reason is simply that, Cabinet, being a deliberative body dealing with issues that directly affect the public good, must have the freedom to debate the merits of any position openly and frankly. Having reached a decision, preferably, but not always, through consensus, solidarity amongst the Cabinet members is needed to ensure the effective implementation of decisions. To secure that solidarity, any dissenting minister, whose opposition may have contributed to the quality of the debate, must be assured that his position will not be made public. Otherwise, solidarity would quickly disintegrate.

If the government is to meet the increasing demands for services made by Canadians in an increasingly complex and sophisticated society, it needs money. If the means of meeting its financial requirements were arrived at through the normal Cabinet deliberative process, with full participation of all ministers, the danger of leaks would be dramatically increased. Many players in the marketplace would not hesitate to attempt to obtain pre-budget information for private gain. Cultivating sources close to the decision-makers has, as we all know, become a profession in the nation's capital, and the necessity of reducing the number of potential sources is self-evident.

I recognize that there is a threat to the principle of accountability in the practice that has developed. The debating time available in the House on the budget is limited to six days. While some measures may require supporting legislation, the approval of the budget may well constitute approval of the principle of the legislation for all intents and purposes. The ability of the process for accountability to take hold is seriously limited, a fact recognized by both the elected and non-elected officials.

The Executive, under our system, is in a position to introduce major policy initiatives through the budgetary process, thus avoiding debate. Budget preparation involves the Minister of Finance, the Prime Minister, and few others. Secrecy surrounds the deliberations, so that most Cabinet ministers are ignorant of what the fiscal policy of the government contains. I recall the introduction of the National Energy Program, a most controversial initiative, through a budget in 1980. Even though I supported the programme, I was given little chance to voice my views in Cabinet, since it was given little time on the agenda. There was no need for debate, except to gauge the level of support that the Minister of Energy could expect from his colleagues after he and the Minister of Finance sneaked it in on budget night.

Is there a solution? Suggestions have been made that we should follow the American process where the administration submits its budget to Congress and then proceeds to negotiate with the legislators the ultimate package to be implemented. Our Parliament is not strong enough, and perhaps too partisan, for such a system to work. While the Commons Finance Committee has taken on a higher profile, even a maverick such as Don Blenkarn feels the partisan claw pull him back to the party line from time to time.

VII. SECRECY AND CONFIDENCES OF THE QUEEN'S PRIVY COUNCIL

The last subject I wish to address is that related to Cabinet secrets, other than in the budget preparation context.

While there are ongoing differences of view as between the parties subject to the provisions of the *CSIS Act*, one area of dispute should be discussed. It is the question of access to Cabinet documents. Under the Act,[18] "No information . . . other than a confidence of the Queen's Privy Council for Canada . . . may be withheld from the Committee on any grounds." The question did not arise in the early years of our mandate. In fact, as a former Cabinet Minister who had to address the issue of Cabinet documents with the McDonald Commission, I felt that the exception, as formulated, was acceptable.

However, during the fifth year of our term, having requested from CSIS certain planning documents, SIRC was told that since they were prepared for Cabinet consideration, they could not be produced. Eventually, the problem was resolved by the material information, extracted from the Cabinet-bound format, being made available.

However, the issue of access to Cabinet confidences did not go away. In our proposals to the Special Committee of the House dealing with the five-year review (recommendation 12), we proposed the repeal of s. 39(3) of the *CSIS Act*, so that the committee would "have access to all information under the control of the service, regardless of its source."

As I indicated previously in dealing with budget secrecy, there is a

---

18 S. 39(3).

need for confidentiality if the Cabinet form of government, with its collective decision-making mechanisms, is to be effective. But that confidentiality must be maintained, as well, *vis-à-vis* officials whom the minister may not wish to have informed of his position, no matter what papers are prepared for his consideration. If the minister does not want his officials to know, then he will keep the confidence. If he does, then it ceases to be as sensitive to the deliberative process, since others than those directly involved are informed. If others are informed, then why not members of SIRC who are subject to the same oaths of secrecy?

The Information Commissioner, facing similar provisions in her Act, has negotiated a memorandum of understanding with the Clerk of the Privy Council providing for the responsible minister, or the clerk himself, to certify that he has looked at the record and that it constitutes a "confidence of the Queen's Privy Council." As a result, she can claim to have obtained the assurances from the highest government levels. However, such an understanding does not address the underlying difficulty, namely that the statutory definition of "Cabinet confidence" was drafted before the creation of the middle persons that I have described and, consequently, the definition needs to be changed. Given the importance of the Cabinet solidarity principle to effective executive decision-making, there is a need for "Cabinet confidence." The minutes of Cabinet meetings are kept so secret that only those participating in the deliberations can review them or gain access to them. Those are the real secrets, and rightly protected. The other documents and records listed in s. 39(2) of the *Canada Evidence Act*,[19] except for para. (d) dealing with inter-ministerial communications, may not need to be protected. Other "confidences," while properly kept secret, are not sufficiently sensitive so as to be kept from bodies such as ours, charged, as the public's surrogate, with ensuring proper accountability while maintaining such secrecy as is essential to public administration. Is our function any less important than that of CSIS? If not, then why should documents available to them not be reviewable by SIRC?

As an example, Murray Rankin, in his paper on Cabinet confidences prepared for SIRC, reminds us that:

> Short of formal Orders-in-Council, the Cabinet also acts simply through decisions reported in the proceedings of cabinet meetings. Termed "R.D.s" or "C.D.s", these decisions are given distinctive identifying numbers [and] are transmitted to the Ministers and Deputy Ministers concerned. An excellent example was the Cabinet directive that initially established the Security Service of the RCMP, the forerunner of CSIS. Another such C.D. was the previous authority for the government's system for the classification of documents.

While those executive measures were kept secret, it surely had

---

19   R.S.C. 1985, c. C-5, s. 39(2).

nothing to do with the principle of Cabinet solidarity. Is there any question that, in today's world, those documents, essentially dealing with matters affecting "national security," should be kept from SIRC, and that Parliament would accept that state of affairs?

VIII. CONCLUSION

Public administration, as has been pointed out time and again, in a society becoming ever more complex, needs to be under constant scrutiny. On reflection, even in the light of the criticisms that are justifiably advanced, the Canadian experience has not been bad. Our democratic institutions are highly rated by the international community. Perhaps we have been able to reach, at least in part, a just society, where the public good is being competently sought out, even if our aim may be off from time to time. We still have a way to go, and I suspect always will. At least I would hope that our collective destiny is for the long haul.

For the governors to have the ability to govern, under our system, they need the consent of the governed. In the exercise of power, the governors must render account if their decisions are to be consented to. The use of secrecy is itself such a decision, for which the governors are accountable, and ways and means need to be found for the governed to be satisfied with the justification proffered.

SHOULD ELECTIONS BE FAIR OR JUST FREE?

Desmond Morton

In this paper I propose to address a specific aspect of Canada's attempt to reconcile free speech, democratic institutions and equality, with particular reference to financing political parties by individuals and corporations. I do so with some trepidation, being neither a lawyer nor an accountant. My chief contact with the federal *Election Expenses Act*[1] has been to watch my wife struggle through the duties of a candidate's agent and occasionally, no doubt, complicate her work with my advice.

I accept, with some hesitation, the historian's duty to set the issue of election financing and free speech in an historical context. Without unreasonable regression, I would begin analyzing election finance with the adoption of the secret ballot. Until then, according to Jean and Marcel Hamelin in *Les moeurs électorales*, open elections were best influenced by mob violence.[2] While hiring, feeding and watering a useful mob could be costly, both sides could normally count on partisan spirit to provide much of the fuel. Open voting may have been the ultimate in free speech, but it was a right, like others, best exercised with trepidation or on the side of the big battalions.

Ballots civilized elections, claim the Hamelins, by substituting bribery for battery. The reform added enormously to the cost, and may well have undermined morality. So pleaded W.B. Vail after losing the very first by-election conducted under the new rules. Sir Charles Tupper, he moaned, had subverted an entire congregation of Baptists to the Tories by dropping a 20-dollar gold piece in the collection plate. Other citizens had betrayed their manhood by being untrue to the bribes they had accepted.[3]

---

1 S.C. 1973-74, c. 51; now the *Canada Elections Act*, R.S.C. 1985, c. E-2.
2 Jean and Marcel Hamelin, *Les moeurs électorales dans le Québec de 1791 à nos jours* (Montréal: Les Editions du Jour, 1962), R. III.
3 "The law is calculated to make people deceitful in every thing, it has a demoralizing tendency and elections in future will be lotteries": Vail to Mackenzie, January 24, 1878, National Archives of Canada, Mackenzie Papers, M-199, at 1847-1848.

Since both of our great historic parties shared the problem, both required vast quantities of the "needful" and both were cautious about publicizing or reforming their practices. If Sir John A. MacDonald met with businesses in Toronto's notorious "Red Chamber" at the Walker House to discuss tariffs and party prospects, provincial Liberals under the "Christian Statesman," Oliver Mowat, demonstrated the lucrative possibilities of regulating the liquor traffic. The astonishing feature of election finance is not how often scandals burst on the scene, but how seldom. The McGreevy affair of 1891 produced a requirement for candidates' agents; Beauharnois in the 1930s required no more than a brief journey for Mackenzie King into "the Valley of Humiliation" and led to prosecutions.[4]

Serious reform, like so much that affected Canada in the 1960s, began in Québec. The determination of post-Duplessis Québec to remove such symptoms of *le grand noirceur* as *"pots-aux-vins"* pushed the government of Jean Lesage into legislation that broke the cake of custom. Perhaps it was easier for *Québecois* to ignore the British parliamentary fiction that parties did not exist. Québec legislation provided for the regulation of political parties, control of electoral expenses and state subventions. That, and the melancholy scandals that enveloped the Pearson government after 1963, helped launch the Barbeau Commission of 1964 on which the late Professor Paltiel exercised such an influence. If its official recommendations in October 1966 fell short of Québec practice, the advent of Pierre Elliott Trudeau in 1968 and, even more, the influence of the NDP on the post-1972 Liberal minority helped give Canada Bill C-203, the *Election Expenses Act* of 1974.[5]

However debatable any of its specific terms, the principles of the 1974 law are worth recalling. Sixteen years later they are relevant and, one might hope, uncontroversial. The Act established that political parties, as well as their candidates, are actors in the democratic process and subject to account. The Act proclaimed that contributing to a political party or candidate is a public act, to be encouraged, with specially strong incentives for smaller donors. Publicity was important not merely to discourage corrupt practices, but to alleviate public suspicion of improper influence. The Act recognized that elections cost serious money but that, to equalize opportunity, the most costly electoral activity, mass media advertising, should be restricted to a set period of 28 days. Moreover, the state should subsidize the costs of serious parties and candidates, defined for the former as winning 12

---

4   Khayyam Z. Paltiel, *Political Financing in Canada* (Toronto:McGraw-Hill, 1970), at 112-14.

5   Alphonse Barbeau et al., *Report of the Committee on Election Expenses* (Ottawa: Queen's Printer, 1966); Khayyam Z. Paltiel (ed.), *Studies in Canadian Party Finance* (Ottawa: Queen's Printer, 1966); *supra*, note 1.

seats and for the latter as winning 15 per cent of the votes in a constituency.[6]

Since 1974, there have been significant amendments to the *Election Expenses Act* in 1977[7] and 1983.[8] The latter series substituted a 22.5 per cent rebate on party electoral expenses for an excessively complex system of subsidizing radio and television advertising. Parliament also attempted, with the enthusiastic support of all three of the main political parties, to tighten the restriction on third party intervention[9] in election campaigns, a bid challenged in Alberta by the National Citizens' Coalition and overturned in 1984 as an unreasonable restriction on the *Charter*-guaranteed right of free expression.[10]

There is a Scottish version of a fairly cross-cultural proverb: "God save us from having our wishes fulfilled." How far has the wish for fair and free elections been fulfilled by the 1974 law and its successors? Despite its complexities, the *Election Expenses Act* has generally been observed and respected by parties, candidates and armies of untrained volunteers. The number of political donors, small and large, has increased considerably, as framers of the Act had intended. Publicizing those who contribute over $100 has led to remarkably little publicity beyond a one-day rash of newspaper articles when the reports appear. If the goal has been to equalize party opportunities, preliminary statements from the 1988 campaign show Progressive Conservatives, Liberals and New Democrats well within a million dollars of each other, continuing a trend towards equalization conspicuous since 1979 when the Act was first applied.[11]

Complacency may be unjustified. So are appearances. While the three major parties seem to be equal in their campaign coffers, aggressive management and a much wealthier individual and corporate clientele have given the Conservatives, through their PC Canada Fund, a two-to-one advantage over both the Liberals and the NDP in dollars

---

6   Khayyam Z. Paltiel, "The Election Expenses Act of 1974" Paper to the CPSA (Edmonton: June 3, 1975).
7   S.C. 1977-78, c. 3.
8   S.C. 1980-81-82-83, cc. 96, 164.
9   S.C. 1980-81-82-83, c. 164, s. 15. The term creates confusion with so-called "third parties" such as the Progressives, Social Credit or the CCF, but it has an acceptable clarity in law and seems preferable to other, more value-laden expressions.
10 *Nat. Citizens' Coalition v. Can. (A.G.)* (1984), 11 D.L.R. (4th) 481 (Alta. Q.B.), and K.Z. Paltiel, "The 1984 Federal General Election and Developments in Canada Party Finances," in Howard Penniman (ed.), *Canada at the Polls 1984: A Study of the Federal General Elections* (Durham, N.C.: Duke University Press, 1988), at 140-45.
11 Paltiel, *supra*, note 10 at 145-55, and Charlotte Gray, "Fundraising Power" (March 1989), Saturday Night.

collected. Loopholes in the *Election Expenses Act* allow parties to decide whether the costs of research, polling, pre-election preparation and staff will count as election expenses or not. In 1984 and 1988, the Tories admit they spent twice as much before the election as they did in the campaign. That left Conservative managers free to respond to the very volatile 1988 electorate while their impoverished rivals could not. In contrast, the NDP counts everything it can in order to collect as much of the 22.5 per cent federal subsidy as possible. Admittedly, Liberals, and even the NDP, are free to emulate the efficiency of the PC Canada Fund, and to a degree they have done so, with direct mail appeals and efforts at centralization. The point is that equality may be more apparent than real and the *Election Expenses Act* regulations need to be tightened.

The provisions of the Act have not ended criticism of political fundraising and contributions by corporations and unions, nor of the large tax expenditures entailed in granting relief to political contributors. The *Lavigne* case in Ontario, currently before the Supreme Court of Canada,[12] was promoted by the National Citizens' Coalition as a *Charter* challenge to political contributions by unions. It invites the observation that shareholders have much less influence than union members about corporate donations to their favourite political parties.

Another feature of the *Election Expenses Act*, the attempt to exclude "third party" intervenors from pouring money into election campaigns, provoked the sole significant *Charter* challenge to the Act.[13] The shocking possibility that Canadians might be gagged during an election when they should above all be free, was shrewdly exploited by the National Citizens' Committee in its 1984 and 1988 national ads. Surely, there is a contrary argument that freedom requires a measure of fairness and equality. Canadian law has faced the reality that free speech in an election costs money and that fair elections require some equality of resources. Whether this is best accomplished by restricting income, as in Ontario's election expenses legislation,[14] or by controlling expenditures, as in federal law, may be a matter of empirical appraisal, it is surely reasonable to insist that fairness should not be subverted by "third parties."

In elections from 1979 to 1984, third party intervenors, on issues ranging from baby seals to abortion, added to the general clamour and may have influenced a few local campaigns, but that was not true in 1988 when the campaign resolved itself into a free trade referendum. By Charlotte Gray's estimate, $10 million was spent by contending parties

---

12 *Lavigne v. O.P.S.E.U.* (1989), 56 D.L.R. (4th) 474, reversing 29 D.L.R. (4th) 321 and 41 D.L.R. (4th) 86, leave to appeal to S.C.C. granted 56 D.L.R. (4th) 474.
13 *Supra*, note 10.
14 *Election Finances Reform Act*, R.S.O. 1980, c. 134.

— more precisely, $9.25 million by supporters such as the NCC and the Canadian Coal Association. The Canadian Alliance for Trade and Job Opportunities claimed to spend $5.2 million for free trade advertising on behalf of 196 members. Alcan, Noranda, Shell and the Royal Bank admitted to providing the Alliance with $1 million each. The Toronto Star, strongly opposed to the deal, earned $550,000 from ads in support. Opponents, such as the Pro-Canada Network, spent $750,000.[15]

Whether or not all the money was spent wisely is anyone's guess — compare the Pro-Canada comic book, produced for $500,000, with the turgid four pages of prose carried by virtually every major newspaper on behalf of the pro-free trade Canadian Alliance for Trade and Job Opportunities at a cost of $2 million. In any case, opinion polls showed a remarkable pro-free trade swing in public opinion in the final days of the campaign — favouring the side that was free to spend much more than the $8 million to which any one political party was restricted. Jean-Marc Hamel, the Chief Electoral Officer, had no illusion about the fairness of the proceedings: "It's as if two boxers get into the ring under the same rules, in the same weight category, with the same gloves and, all of a sudden, a spectator jumps in and starts hitting one of them with a hammer."[16]

Elections, some will claim, are not sporting competitions. The federal government itself worked with some ingenuity to support the "No" side in the Québec referendum of 1980 with, for example, temperance advertising that featured a conspicuous "non" to excess. Firms that stood to gain or lose billions on the outcome of the 1988 election felt no obligation to play by the Marquis of Queensbury rules or the *Election Expenses Act*. Some also argued, from powerful American precedents, that *political* free speech must be more than normally unfettered. Canadians might answer with some pride that their elections were more free because they are more fair. Freedom needs fairness if it is not to be subverted.

Is it unreasonable that a right exercised for years and months before an election might be restrained during the weeks of a campaign, and utterly eliminated in the final 48 hours before voting, when monstrous lies may be circulated without hope of rebuttal? The evil tone of some recent American federal and state elections underlines the point. I confess to the prejudices of someone with more respect for politicians and parties than for those who pressure them from the safety of the sidelines. People who endure the heat of active politics, and who struggle with the painful compromises of public life, have more of my sympathy than those armed with the blinding simplicity of a single issue or who

---

15 *Supra*, note 11.
16 *Ibid.*

possess a substantial private financial stake in the outcome of an electoral contest. The 1983 amendments excluding "third parties" from engaging financially in an election campaign may have gone too far, but inclusion in the process should involve submission to rules enforcing the public nature of such a role. Groups and individuals eager to influence electoral outcomes should have to accept the rules. Otherwise, we risk the rule of plutocracy and, ultimately, the return of mobs more menacing than those which once justified the secret ballot.[17]

The *Election Expenses Act* has earned other criticisms. From the outset, it has been the creation of the three major political parties and, to no one's astonishment, it has tended to serve their interests. Indeed, the mystery is revealed by the existence of the Ad Hoc Committee, used, if not created, by the Chief Electoral Officer to advise him, and filled by nominees from the Progressive Conservatives, Liberals and New Democratic Party. The committee has doubtless been convenient, practical and a source of much electoral expertise. It also seems a little exclusive. It may now suit Canadians to have only three parties — much as Liberals and Conservatives used to insist that God and good sense intended us to have only two. Nor is there obvious discrimination against new parties. After all, 12 parties contested the 1988 election. The barriers to registration are low, and all who qualified can issue the all-important tax receipts to contributors. However, one wonders whether an Ad Hoc Committee with Reform, the Bloc Québecois, and especially the Confederation of Regions Party included would find 15 per cent a reasonable minimum to collect a candidate's deposit and election expenses, or spending 10 per cent of the party's national limit as a basis for the 22.5 per cent rebate. The Ad Hoc Committee may be a fine institution, but its composition is objectionable.[18]

Another defect, increasingly apparent, is the absence of controls on spending for intra-party competitions for leadership and nominations. Those who live in areas of one-party dominance, such as Alberta, Trudeau's Québec, or Ontario's urban ethnic ridings, know that the M.P. usually has been chosen as soon as the dominant party's nomination process has concluded. Yet, there are no effective controls on pre-nomination spending or the corrupt influences inherent when individuals must solicit large sums of money for personal advancement. The recent Liberal leadership campaign apparently had too high an entry fee for Lloyd Axworthy because, he insists, his political views were unacceptable to wealthy backers, and it caused problems for Sheila

---

17 F. Leslie Seidle, "Controlling Federal Election Finances," in John C. Courtney (ed.), *The Canadian House of Commons Essays in Honour of Norman Ward* (Calgary, University of Calgary Press: 1985).

18 On the Ad Hoc Committee, see Paltiel, *supra*, note 10 at 140-41.

Copps. Those competing seriously in the contest have presumably satisfied the views of their affluent backers. This should cause concern to more than Liberals. Mr. Mulroney's rise to the Conservative leadership was allegedly paved by large sums of money which, if you believe his critics, have been richly repaid since 1984. The NDP's leadership contest might have been a lot less frugal if imminent power had hung on the outcome. Very reluctantly, and with some uncertainty about mechanisms, I have been forced to the conclusion that the principle of fairness in political spending should apply to individuals seeking access to major party office as well as in party-backed contests.

Will these problems be addressed? Since, almost without exception, the defects in the *Election Expenses Act* favour the party in power, it is hard to see why a government with many pressures on its legislative agenda and with little appetite for reform would seek to reform the *Election Expenses Act*. Provided it retains the primary allegiance of the business community and the wealthy, Conservatives can count on the financial advantages they found in the 1974 Act. The Senate, said Sir John A. Macdonald, exists to protect minorities and "the rich are always fewer in number than the poor."[19] Opposition parties, now far less affluent than the Tories, might welcome reform, but they too have something to lose. All three major parties gain from "a closed shop," and all three benefit from the looseness about central party expenses before and during a campaign.

However, I recall my inbred prejudices about the courts and their capacity to render wise and disinterested political judgments. For all their sins, elected politicians and the governments they support have given us the rights and freedoms Canadians now possess, including the *Charter* that embodies so many of them. It may be proverbially difficult for Canadians to admit that their laws and institutions are better than their neighbours', but we should sometimes make the effort. Accepting that elections must be fair as well as free, Canadians have been well served by the principles of the *Election Expenses Act*. If the practices need revision, it should be done with an oil can and a screwdriver, not a sledgehammer.

---

19   Cited in Sir Joseph Pope (ed.), *Confederation* (Toronto: Carswell, 1895), at 58.

CONTRIBUTORS

Jean Jacques Blais is a partner with Lette, McTaggart, Blais, Martin in Ottawa. He is a member of the Canadian Security Intelligence Review Committee which reports to the Canadian Parliament on security matters. He sat in the House of Commons from 1972 to 1984 and held numerous portfolios with the government including Postmaster General, Solicitor General, Minister of Supply and Receiver General, and Minister of National Defence.

A. Alan Borovoy is General Counsel of the Canadian Civil Liberties Association, a post he has held for over 20 years. He is the author of numerous articles on civil liberties in Canada and the book *When Freedoms Collide: The Case for Our Civil Liberties* (1988).

Stanley A. Cohen is Coordinator, Criminal Procedure Project and Special Counsel, Charter of Rights, Law Reform Commission of Canada. Currently he is an adjunct professor of law (common law section) at the University of Ottawa and formerly was an associate professor of law, McGill University. A member of the Manitoba bar, he is the author of *Due Process of Law: The Canadian System of Criminal Justice* (1977), and *Invasion of Privacy: Police and Electronic Surveillance in Canada* (1982), as well as numerous articles.

Irwin Cotler is professor of law at McGill University and director of its Human Rights Program. He has served as legal counsel to political prisoners in South Africa, Latin America, the Middle East, China and the Soviet Union. He has appeared as counsel in numerous constitutional and *Charter* cases, including the *Operation Dismantle* and *Keegstra* cases.

Richard G. Dearden is a partner with Gowling, Strathy & Henderson in Ottawa. He acts as counsel regarding freedom of the press and libel issues for various media including The Ottawa Citizen, Southam News, The Montreal Gazette and the Canadian Association of Journalists. He is vice chairman of the International Bar Association's Defamation and Media Law Committee.

Peter Desbarats is Dean of the Graduate School of Journalism, University of Western Ontario. He has published widely on Canadian media and is himself a renowned journalist and editor. His latest book is *Guide to Canadian News Media* (1990).

Peter A. Gall is a partner with Heenan, Blaikie in Vancouver. He has acted as counsel in leading *Charter* cases including *Dolphin Delivery* and

Stoffman v. V.G.H. He has authored numerous papers including "Freedom of Association and Trade Unions: A Double Edged Constitutional Sword" (1984), and "The Mandatory Retirement Cases: What They Tell Us About the Charter" (1989). He was formerly assistant professor, and since 1981 has been adjunct professor with the Faculty of Law, University of British Columbia.

Lewis Klar is professor of law, University of Alberta and specializes in the law of torts. He is the co-author of *Canadian Tort Law: Cases, Notes and Materials*, 9th ed. and is the author of *Tort Law* (1991).

David Kretzmer holds the Louis Marshall Chair of Environmental Law at the Hebrew University of Jerusalem. He has written extensively on civil rights issues. His most recent book is *The Legal Status of the Arabs in Israel* (1990).

M. David Lepofsky is counsel to the Ontario Attorney General, Constitutional Law and Policy Division. In this capacity, he has acted as counsel in many freedom of expression cases, including *Canadian Newspapers* and *Squires.* He is author of *Open Justice: The Constitutional Right to Attend and Speak About Criminal Proceedings* (1985), and numerous articles including "Towards a Purposive Approach to Freedom of Expression and Its Limitation" (Cambridge Lectures 1989). He is a part-time member of the Faculty of Law, University of Toronto, teaching a course on freedom of expression.

Cyril Levitt is professor of sociology at McMaster University. Dr. Levitt was a Humboldt Fellow and Visiting Professor at the Free University of Berlin in 1985 and Visiting Professor in Canadian Studies at Hebrew University of Jerusalem in 1988-89. He is the author of several books including *The Children of Privilege* (1984), and the co-author of *The Riot at Christie Pitts* (1987).

Harold J. Levy is a member of the Toronto Star Editorial Board. As a criminal lawyer, he practised in the Ontario courts for ten years before becoming Special Projects Coordinator for the Law Society of Upper Canada, and special advisor to the Law Reform Commission of Canada. He is the author of *A Reporter's Guide to Canada's Criminal Justice System* (1988).

M.M. Litman is professor of law, University of Alberta. He is the author of numerous articles in the areas of property, succession and trusts, and restitution. He is the founding editor of Estates and Trusts Reports and is Visiting Professor and Scholar-in-residence at the University of Arizona 1990-91.

Kathleen Mahoney is associate professor of law at University of Calgary. She is a founding member and legal committee member of the

Women's Legal Education and Action Fund (LEAF). She is the author of numerous articles and is editor of *Women, the Law and the Economy* (1985), and the co-editor of *Equality and Judicial Neutrality* (1988).

Thelma McCormack is professor of sociology at York University where she teaches courses in political sociology and feminist theory and public policy. She has written extensively on feminist issues, communications, gender and politics and has recently completed the monographs *Politics and the Hidden Injuries of Gender* and *Abortion and the Ethics of Motherhood*.

John P. McLaren is Lansdowne Professor of Law at the University of Victoria. He was a member of the Special Committee on Pornography and Prostitution in 1983-85. His research interests in the field of legal history have led to the publication of numerous articles, including "Chasing the Social Evil: Moral Fervour and the Evolution of Canada's Prostitution Laws" (1986), and "Maternal Feminism in Action — Emily Murphy, Police Magistrate" (1988).

Desmond Morton is professor of history and principal, Erindale College, University of Toronto. He specializes in Canadian political, military and industrial relations history. He is the author of many books including *A Military History of Canada*, revised ed. (1990), and *Working People*, 3rd ed. (1990).

Ronald D. Rotunda is professor of law at the University of Illinois. He is a former visiting professor at the European University Institute, Florence, Italy and a former Fulbright Professor in Caracas, Venezuela. He has authored over 85 articles and 19 books on constitutional law and legal ethics, including *Treatise on Constitutional Law: Substance and Procedure* (1986), co-authored with John Nowak.

David Schneiderman is executive director of the Centre for Constitutional Studies, University of Alberta. He was formerly research director for the Canadian Civil Liberties Association. His publications include, as co-author, "An Appeal To Justice: The Right to Publicly Funded Appeals and *R. v. Robinson; R. v. Dolejs*" (1991), and, as editor, *Language and the State: The Law and Politics of Identity* (1991).

Rodney A. Smolla is James Gould Cutler Professor of Constitutional Law, and Director of the Institute of Bill of Rights Law, at the College of William and Mary, Marshall-Wythe School of Law. He has authored numerous articles and three books including *Suing the Press: Libel, the Media & Power* (1986), and *Jerry Falwell v. Larry Flynt: The First Amendment on Trial* (1988).

Lorraine E. Weinrib is associate professor, Faculty of Law and Department of Political Science, University of Toronto. Previously, she was

Deputy Director of Constitutional Law and Policy, Ministry of the Attorney General of Ontario. Her articles, advocating institutional coherence of the *Charter*, include "The Supreme Court of Canada and Section One of the Charter" (1988), and "Learning to Live With The Override" (1990).

INDEX